Preromanticism

Preromanticism

Marshall Brown

Stanford University Press   1991
Stanford, California

Stanford University Press, Stanford, California
© 1991 by the Board of Trustees of the Leland Stanford Junior University
Printed in the United States of America

CIP data appear at the end of the book

TO MY PARENTS

Long may their presence
and their works

of duty
civility
and love

abide in future memory

Acknowledgments

A new approach to the later eighteenth century has been facilitated by new directions in the study of literature. While specifically acknowledging only more limited, local insights, I have drawn broadly on various recent French thinkers—particularly Derrida, Foucault, and Serres—as well as on formalist and structuralist critics. Generally the authors who have helped me most began or established themselves as students of the later seventeenth or the eighteenth century, and their approaches apply in less startling ways to this period than to the romantic poets, on whom they have most often been brought to bear by American critics. The marxist criticism of Bloch, Jameson, Kristeva, Said, and Williams has helped me to address problems of literary history (though not in ways that they would necessarily embrace), as have Emil Staiger's books *Stilwandel* and *Spätzeit*. My principal inspirations, however, have come from writers of a century ago—Burckhardt, Taine, Wölfflin—profound minds whose wisdom is nearly lost because they worked in modes different from our own. From that great flowering I have, in my conclusion, culled Matthew Arnold for my purposes, a bad critic, but all the greater a visionary for persistently reiterating a message when he did not know how to apply it. Of many superb books on various aspects of the period, mostly cited in the notes, none has been more illuminating than Charles Rosen's *The Classical Style*.

My real introduction to the period was in an unforgettable class on Collins's "Ode to Evening" taught by Geoffrey Hartman, his first on his return to Yale. His example has been a constant inspiration, though a distant goal. I wish I had kept a list of all the friends, mentors, and chance acquaintances who helped with advice, encouragement, and correction. I haven't, and I won't make the doomed attempt to reconstitute it. Displaying their names would not in any event repay the gratitude I feel. I will make an exception only for James Turner, my harshest critic, who might otherwise still not believe me thankful for the comments that made me thoroughly rewrite the Sheridan chapter, probably not yet to his satisfaction. For errors of fact that remain, I ask indulgence; for errors of thought and reasoning, just correction.

Not an exception, but a special obligation goes to the Press readers, especially Cliff Siskin; to the Press editors, Helen Tartar and Ellen Smith; to my magnificent copy editor, Nancy Atkinson; and to Stanford University Press, for its faith in so large and slow a book. Boston University, the University of North Carolina, and the University of Virginia all generously allowed me to teach courses on the period, often at an advanced level, at times when I was not a regular and continuing member of their faculties. In retrospect I realize how much my students—at the three schools just named, at the University of Colorado during my nine years there, and now at the University of Washington—have meant to me and have taught me, above all the inimitable Steve Dillon. Stephen Swords and Graham Shutt drudged cheerfully checking quotations and references. Marje Urban faithfully typed, retyped, and corrected draft after draft, year after year; Sandy Spahn shared with me the joy of translating the whole manuscript out of one word-processing program into another. I cannot imagine a better proofreader than Dorrit Brown, the only fourteen-year-old who will ever read this book. The index was prepared by Barbara Roos, with the assistance of a grant from the University of Washington. The libraries of the above institutions and the University of California at Irvine offered constant, and different, pleasures; of others where I made raids or put in cameo appearances I cannot forbear mentioning the Boston Athenaeum for admitting a nonmember to read a volume from George Washington's library, Stanford for good-natured struggles to operate the compact stacks in the Medical School Library in search of a useless essay on Beaumarchais that wasn't there, and the University of Southern California's Hoose Library of Philosophy, one of the nation's unhonored treasures, where Ross Scimica helped me find the essay and so much else.

The University of Colorado gave me a year's fellowship and a semester's leave without pay, during which much of the book was written; even more, it gave me a place to work, and students, and colleagues. A subsequent leave from the University of Washington has given me the leisure to polish the text and update the notes to the limit of my imperfect ability. The editors of *ELH* and *Studies in Romanticism* gave permission to reprint the essays that form the basis of Chapters 1 and 3. Jane gave me everything; without her, this book would not have been written. Without Dorrit and Benedict it would have been written faster, but far less agreeably. Without my parents it would not have been possible, and not just for biological reasons.

Contents

A Note on Citations

Citations are given in the form judged most helpful to readers. Wherever possible, works in prose are identified by part and chapter, act and scene, or other standard divisions, as well as by page number in the source text. Works in verse are cited either by title only or by title and line number, with rare exceptions. The following conventions are observed.

COWPER: The *Olney Hymns*, the couplet satires, and "The Poet, the Oyster, and the Sensitive Plant" are cited from *Poems*, ed. Baird and Ryskamp. *The Task* and "Yardley Oak," which are not yet included in that edition, are cited from *Poetical Works*, ed. Milford.

GOLDSMITH: The principal source text is *Collected Works*, ed. Friedman. A very few passages not included there and cited from *Works*, ed. Cunningham, are so designated.

KANT: The pagination is given from the first (A) or second (B) edition, as is conventional.

SHERIDAN: The plays are cited from *Dramatic Works*, ed. Price. Since the pagination of the two volumes is consecutive, no volume number is included in citations. The poems are cited from *Plays and Poems*, ed. Rhodes.

STERNE: No volume numbers are included in citations of *Tristram Shandy*, since the volumes of the Florida text are paginated consecutively.

WORDSWORTH: I have used the available volumes of the Cornell edition, as entered in Works Cited. However, since *The Prelude* has as yet been only partially edited in that series, I cite it from de Selincourt's edition, in the 1850 text where not specially noted. The remaining works are cited from *Poetical Works*, ed. de Selincourt and Darbishire.

Preromanticism

Introduction

Preromanticism has a bad name. Rightly so. It began as the province of positivists—originally in France and later in England and America as well—who traced the origins of the phrase "green night" or of the motif of underground passageways and thereby dissolved history into incoherent minutiae.[1] So we may read in Paul van Tieghem's classic work, *Le Sentiment de la nature dans le préromantisme européen*, "Collins's 'Ode to Evening' contains quite accurate details [*des détails assez justes*] rather than a unified impression [*une impression d'ensemble*]; the author tried to take note of too many different aspects."[2] Such a judgment is really a portrait of its author: in view of his later assertion (223) that Collins was perhaps the first to blend solitude, evening, and silence, it is clear that the blindness to coherence—as well as to so obvious a predecessor as Pope's *Eloisa to Abelard*—is van Tieghem's own. So flimsy are the evidences of what Georges Gusdorf continues regularly to call "le romantisme avant la lettre."[3]

But while I concur with many critics who have attacked or renounced the term in its old form, I do not concur with their alternatives.[4] The prevailing tradition in English literary studies of the later eighteenth century is to seek out an imperious unity. Whether we characterize the period with the term of process, as in Northrop Frye's widely cited definition, with that of insubstantiality, as in Fredric Bogel's rewarding recent study, or in other ways, we risk turning history into a substance or pattern of which literary works are mere accidents or ramifications. These consolidated period definitions are by no means wrong, and they do rescue us from sinking in the positivist mire of facts, but they draw attention away from the discoveries and innovations of the masterpieces of the age. The reader of this book will encounter a wealth of problems—each one articulated by a literary masterpiece in a way that leads toward a possible solution—but not a compact characterization of the unity of the period. Throughout this book the prefix in "preromanticism" is to be understood—in contrast to all previous scholarship known to me—in its differentiating sense. It does not designate a preliminary state of romanticism or a predisposition, such as others have found in later eighteenth-century fragments of dream, sentiment, or love of nature. Rather, "preromanticism" is meant to resemble terms like "preclassic" or "Pre-Raphaelite," or perhaps "premature," said of a baby in the sense that it is not ready to be born. I call the period preromantic precisely because it was *not yet* romantic.[5]

Traditional accounts of preromanticism were motivated by the inescapable fact that a crisis of expression, above all in Britain, lasted through the second half of the century. Masterpieces are few, and no major author of the period produced with anything like the ease of a Pope or a Wordsworth. Wordsworth and Coleridge understood what they were after in their major works and wrote at length about it, and so in their way had Dryden and Pope. But most of the preromantics left the task of writing about literature to unimaginative professors of rhetoric and belles lettres. Even Johnson was astonishingly reticent about his own output, and Goldsmith, Sheridan, and Sterne left virtually no indications that they knew why they wrote as they did. Biographical factors will explain each case individually, but they will not explain why these cases dominate the period. Collins, Smart, and Cowper went mad; Gray and Johnson were melancholic; Boswell was a self-proclaimed hypochondriac. Goldsmith, while perhaps not so flighty as Boswell portrays him in the *Life of Johnson*, could not conclude his major poems, and Sheridan, after bursting on the scene in his twenties, relapsed into business, politics, and drink and failed to execute countless subsequent dramatic projects. Only Chatterton, the romantics' own favorite preromantic, writing in a fraudulent language, matched the voluminous frenzy of nineteenth-century madmen like Hölderlin and Clare. Any period that counts a thousand pages of table talk masquerading as a biography (see Greene, "'Tis a Pretty Book") or forty volumes of epistolary gossip by a wealthy dilettante among its lasting monuments has talked too much around the main point. Whether they plunged into drudge work or out of life, evasion was the order of the day for all the greatest talents of the period.

Yet positivist criticism did not know how to ask the question that this book raises. It is: what hindered the greatest authors of the period from writing? Minor writers freely uttered their incoherent feelings or rehashed clichés from the first half of the century; with them in view we can portray the period as an age of sensibility, or as the decadence of enlightenment. But the greatest authors in their greatest moments engaged in rigorously controlled struggles toward new modes of expression. The typical masterpiece of the period is startlingly brief; the major exception to this rule is *Tristram Shandy*, but even that novel was issued in short parts composed of very short chapters and achieves its crowning triumph, I argue, in its last two pages. And then, when new resources were found—and it happened with astonishing suddenness for Wordsworth, for Kant, and for those who underwent the impact of the new philosophy—the floodgates opened.

In treating the later eighteenth century as a period of flux, I respect the authors' own sense of their age. The illustration—the frontispiece and title page from a period edition of Edward Young—tells the story. In my first chapter I argue that there is less of the preromantic graveyard in Young's text than his readers thought a few decades later. But by 1777 he had clearly caught the public imagination as a transitional poet, divided between the rational cemetery on the left and the grisly deathbed on the right. The authors who followed him felt the uncertainties that these illustrations communicate. As I argue in my third chapter, an age of sensibility was inevitably an age of dissatisfaction. In their writings as in their lives the figures studied in this book appear restless and impatient. They wanted change.

The term "preromanticism" has always been attacked for its teleology, but that is the very reason I welcome it. The great authors were striving ahead for something new, and when they failed to identify a goal, they were left powerless. The real problem with earlier studies of preromanticism is that they are not teleological enough. The notion of a "romantisme avant la lettre" is self-contradictory. Eighteenth-century writers either are romantics or they are not; distinctions can be made and nuances described, but they cannot be both of their age and of a later one. If "preromanticism" implies that romanticism was already present in 1750, even in scattered form, then there is no looking ahead and no historical dynamic. That kind

Say pensive muse, whom dismal scenes delight?
Frequent at tombs and in the realms of night
This truth how certain.—when this life is o'er,—
Man dies to live, and lives—to die no more!

Frontispiece and title page of 1777 edition of Edward Young's Night
Thoughts.

NIGHT THOUGHTS

ON

LIFE DEATH and IMMORTALITY

by the late Dr. YOUNG

to which are added

The Life of the Author with a

Compleat INDEX and GLOSSARY

by G. Wright Esq.

Wait the great teacher Death.

London.

Printed for J. & F. Rivington, W. Johnston, T. Longman,
E. & C. Dilly, J. Dodsley, T. Cadell & W. Otridge.

MDCCLXXVII.

of study reads history backwards, not forwards. A telos is a goal in the distance; it is not yet there when a teleological process is under way.[6]

I originally intended this book as a general critical survey of the acknowledged masterpieces of the half century between Pope and Wordsworth, but in the event Johnson and Smollett have been treated only in passing, and my account of the gothic novel, though integrally related to this project, has grown too large and will appear as a separate book; only a few allusions to that ghost of a future volume have been retained. What remains in the present work still cuts a broader path across the period than other interpretive studies. Having written in different genres and tones and from different political, social, and cultural perspectives, Gray and Collins, Goldsmith and Sheridan, Sterne and Cowper are rarely brought together, for they share little besides their unfulfilled ambitions, that is, their preromanticism.

The bulk of the book consists of close readings of individual works, often in conjunction with the surrounding literary context. To establish a starting point I have begun with a synthetic discussion of poetic style at midcentury. To my mind, Thomson and most of Gray and Collins have more in common with their contemporaries and recent predecessors than with a poet like Cowper, who wrote decades later. This is not the traditional view, but it has gained ground since Chapter 2 was first published.[7] Goldsmith gets more space than other writers not only because his works have been insufficiently analyzed but also because he left us more masterpieces (four) of more different kinds (three) than any of his contemporaries, and each deserves its due. I have allowed myself only one relatively brief chapter on a Continental figure. Like Goldsmith and Sheridan, Beaumarchais remains extremely popular yet little analyzed; he comes out of a tradition that intermingles with the British dramatic tradition of the period; and—above all—his work makes explicit tendencies that are latent in the farces of Goldsmith and Sheridan. Overlapping principles govern the arrangement of my chapters: works in the same genre are grouped together, and the discussions of Goldsmith's works are also kept together, since a common thread links them. Consequently, I had to postpone the analysis of *Tristram Shandy*, which is in any case generally regarded as the most advanced work of the period. The interpretive chapters can, however, be read selectively, or in a different order.

This overlapping of the materials is intrinsic to history. It can be masked, as often happens in monographs restricted to a single theme or genre, but it cannot be overcome. The dispersion of tendencies found in the masterpieces of preromanticism is typical of any period when seen from within, though it is not always so strongly felt. Even high romanticism is no freer of turbulence than any other period, as the most recent criticism has at last begun to show.[8] It takes a backward look to fuse the diverse tendencies of a period into a distinctive new totality. Consequently, I find the unity of preromanticism in romanticism, not in itself.[9] My last chapter portrays that unity in its Wordsworthian form. Even that chapter, perhaps the least conventional in the book, is not free from history: it analyzes Wordsworth's hopeful struggle toward a new style, and then, passing quickly over the Great Decade and saving *Michael* for the Conclusion, it describes that style as it was consolidated in a late sonnet. A settled overview requires a twilight retrospect.[10]

Each of my interpretations undertakes to describe the language and form aimed at by a particular work. While language remains a fashionable topic these days, form is, in many critical circles, unfashionable. It is too regularly dismissed as the mere shell of expression, the body in which literary energies are imprisoned. Even so sophisticated a critic as Jonathan Arac speaks of the "formalist annihilation of time" (75). Yet formalism ought not to be the dead horse to which New Criticism and, even more, structuralism, often reduced it.[11] The surge of interest in the body as the locus of passionate life should be carried over to the bodies of literary works. It is worth remembering what Lessing well knew two centuries ago: that literary form is in its essence gestural, music and painting together, time informed with meaning.

Through its individual style—its language and its form—each work becomes the vessel for ideas that are adapted to its capacity to carry them. The most disconcerting feature of my book for those accustomed to a more traditional intellectual history may well be the way that ideas appear in a secondary role and flicker in and out of focus. I am firmly convinced that an author can only express ideas upon learning how to express them, and that new ideas can only develop in consequence of new styles of expression. In many cases, the preromantics fashioned empty vessels that only their successors were able to fill. The Wordsworthian retrospect helps to clarify which ideas mattered, and it may be useful if I enumerate some of these leading themes here, in my own anticipatory review.

One theme is self-consciousness. Young's *Night Thoughts* gestures incompletely toward romantic self-consciousness in reaction against Thomson's sociable world-consciousness. The discovery of the pure form of romantic self-consciousness was one of the great intellectual events of the period: I describe it in Cowper's reveries and, briefly, in the more familiar contemporaneous versions of Kant and Rousseau. That discussion of texts of the 1780s comes early in the book as a kind of foreshadowing. Then, as part of the long clearing of the ground, I describe various entanglements of the pre-romantic consciousness. In the fashion of Johnson's refutation of Berkeley, it finds that the world is a stone that won't go away: its entanglements include the seated traveler's denial of his own predicament, the blushing attempts of good nature—above all of the Vicar of Wakefield—to purify its experience, Sheridan's angst, the uncertain paternities of Schiller, Beaumarchais, and Sterne, and Tristram Shandy's problems of interpretation. These constitute so many stumbling blocks preceding the late Wordsworth's absorption in the stony matter surrounding him.

My second great theme is time, which Kant binds up with consciousness. It first appears in the pure and empty form of Collins's "Ode to Evening." The emptiness of time becomes loss in Goldsmith's poems but is redeemed as pure sequence in *The Vicar of Wakefield*, articulated by Sterne's cock-and-bull story, and reinvested with driving emotion by Sheridan. Before turning to Wordsworth, my last chapter reviews the topic of hope in three poets from late in the eighteenth century, for mastery of time as the structure of human consciousness enables the romantics to orient their experience toward the future.[12] "And so I dare to hope," as Wordsworth says at a key point in "Tintern Abbey" (line 65): by combining pure reverie with an overview of his past (in the ensuing lines) and with intense feeling he evokes a general sense of future potential so powerful that there is no need to specify the content of the hope.[13]

In accord with Kant's priorities, space is secondary in my readings. Yet my reader can trace a similar development of the sense of space, even though it is rarely focal. The "Elegy Written in a Country Churchyard" unveils space in its purest and emptiest form. Diderot's *Rêve de d'Alembert* (like Kant's refutation of Berkeley in the second edition of the *Critique of Pure Reason*) reveals how intimately the consciousness of space, even when it is empty, is tied to the existence of a world of objects; the vast spaces of *Die Räuber*, of Blake, and of *The Borderers* then press the issue upon us. Goldsmith's traveler measures out a geography to which he is actually blind, while the narrator of *The Deserted Village* sees a space that is incommensurable with present experience. So, through a series of failures, we accumulate an awareness of what it means to encounter an objective world; at last Figaro learns how to control his environment through action as he stage-manages the darkened labyrinth of Almaviva's garden. In Britain the little worlds of the vicar and of Uncle Toby are also controlled, known spaces, but they remain constantly threatened by the great world outside. Only in the transformations of Wordsworth's stone do subject and object, center and horizon, time and space finally come into perfectly articulated alignment.

Articulation as such is the focus in Chapter 5, "The Economy of Sensibility." Totality was the prize that sensibility tried to purchase too cheaply. Totality turns out to be a dialectical concept composed of antithetical elements, which I call partitioning and wholeness, or disposition and simplicity. *The Vicar of Wakefield* achieves the latter while sacrificing the former; the conclusion of *Tristram Shandy*, published a year later, achieves just the reverse. The two faces of totality appear conjointly but in opposition in *She Stoops to Conquer*, serving to define but not yet quite to perfect what romanticism was to know as organic form.

I thus close the circle of this summary by returning to the question of form. The aphorism at the end of Gray's Eton College ode associates the neatness of perfected form with a denial of worldly knowledge. To conclude, one might point out, you have to stop. Many preromantic writers did not know how to stop, and that problem becomes Goldsmith's besetting infirmity. Yet closure turns out, like time and space, to have purifying attributes that accompany its negative ones. Out of the exclusion of reality grow the imagination and its conception of the ideal realm of the aesthetic. Goldsmith's greatest accomplishment, in *The Vicar of Wakefield* and again in *The Deserted Village*, was the construction of an aesthetic realm that liberated literary form from its bondage to ideas and to ethics. Goethe and George Eliot praised him for that liberation, and I hope to have shown why an author who seems to matter so little today (however delightful we may find him) mattered so much to them. Goldsmith's imagination, however, like the nineteenth-century images of him, looked nostalgically backward. It needed the power of hope to turn it around and marry it to an active and productive time sense. That is where my Wordsworth chapter begins because in that productive and self-conscious perfection of a form that embraces inner and outer senses alike romanticism begins.

CHAPTER ONE

On Textual Production

I presume that the author of an important work of literature normally means in some way to do something new. No author, we are
often told, wants to be a follower; the anxiety of belatedness is the
poet's occupational disease. Critics have not been kind to the numerous major romantic and postromantic figures—from Scott and
Wordsworth down to Zola and Conrad—who, as common consensus
has it, outlived their inspiration and grew old repeating themselves.
Far worse was the plight of writers in the later eighteenth century,
who often seemed to have so little substance that they could only
imitate their forebears. In poetry, the modes of Pope and Thomson prevailed almost without exception; in the theater, sanitized
and formulaic versions of seventeenth-century comedy and tragedy.
Yet within the heroic couplet format, for instance, Pope himself
had experimented with pastoral, didactic, confessional, panegyric,
narrative, and satiric subjects, setting a standard of virtuosity for
the century to follow. Subsequent authors—Richardson, Fielding,
Johnson, Goldsmith, Smollett, and Sheridan—typically succeeded
better in their second (rarely their third) try in a given form than
in their first, but were not otherwise happy repeating their successes. Young and Cowper both achieved more lasting fame for a
single major piece in blank verse than for the groups of moral satires
with which they earlier acquired popular favor. Gray's completed
poems typically come two or three to a type, but he never tried to
copy the "Elegy Written in a Country Churchyard," and Collins's
Odes Descriptive and Allegorical is notable, among other things,

for the variety of its meters. Nowhere from 1740 until at least 1790 do we see the normal phenomenon of the romantic period, when authors—Wordsworth, Coleridge, Austen, and the later Crabbe—freely repeated and not infrequently recaptured earlier successes. In the later eighteenth century, when genius has nothing to add, it falls silent.

Innovation has three components: the project, the context of reference, and the work in which expression is embodied. This introduction will discuss each element separately. First, however, I want to consider their interrelationship. For within the formula I have proposed, the three form a compound that exhibits distinctive characteristics. Context and project are juxtaposed as past to future, with the work as a presence that intervenes to link the two. There is, then, a complete temporal system. It is not, however, a uniform temporality. Innovation always has the character of a project directed toward a virtuality: the future remains on the work's horizon. Even a work like *Tom Jones* that confidently announces at the outset a plan that it successfully carries out cannot ensure the durability of its innovations. A project without this element of risk or uncertainty is a firmly rooted presence, which is to say that it has the character of a subsisting past. What can be done safely and easily or what is known with assurance constitutes the background rather than the foreground, inheritance rather than innovation. To be sure, a background is as essential as a project. An innovation may break with the past, but you cannot break with the past unless you have a past. The work itself, finally, is the link between past and future. It is the realm of presence. Yet, in such a case presence is not neutral, since it frays the path from past to future. The work carries out the intentions of the writing or conveys its meaning; the metaphors in both verbs are revealing. Work is performed by the work of art—a simple but indispensable fact.

Past, present, and future, in this sense, are textual modalities. There are other threesomes that might be invoked as well, particularly to the extent that the context can be equated with the culture and the expectations of the audience. We could speak of the work as a message emitted by the author to the public, or as an object, an "it," mediating between an I and a you. Or we could adopt Raymond Williams's terminology of residual, dominant, and emergent features (*Marxism and Literature*, chap. 8). All such formulations, however, risk externalizing the three components from one another and leaving the work in a subaltern role. The work is not distinct from the project it performs, not even as distinct as a message is from its contents. And it does not confront its cultural contexts so much as enter them whenever it succeeds in transforming them. The aim of the author's uncertain project is precisely to give to the work the stability that we associate with the cultural tradition. A work of literature is fundamentally homogeneous, or absorptive, in contradistinction to a sign.

The three components, then, are aspects of temporality *within the work*, not separate points on a time line outside of and prior to their existence. The past appears in the work as subsistence, the present as action, the future as incipience. The critical analyses in this book aim at characterizing the temporal aspects and thus the historical action of the works they discuss. It is not only unnecessary but potentially even misleading to speak separately about author and audience—not because they do not exist, but because the work does not do its job unless they meet within it.[1] A piece of writing may well be a mere instrument communicating a message, and the message may be new, but then the novelty is located outside the message in the audience that hears it for the first time, and it grows old as the audience changes. Such a piece of writing is not a work; it does not do anything new. *The ambition to innovate that I have presupposed is tantamount to a desire to incorporate the three modes of time within the bounds of the work.* Let this characterization serve as my definition of the work of art.[2]

The project is the horizon of the new. In one sense it is the most familiar of the three components, in another the most problematic. We speak about meanings and intentions with a colloquial readiness that can easily betray us. Novelty is not something superadded; the author who wishes to make the work new needs to objectify these ambitions by incorporating them into its working. "Death is the mother of beauty," as Stevens wrote, and behind all the talk in recent decades about the death of the author lies the necessary repression of subjectivity. From the author's perspective this may or may not generate enormous anxiety; from the work's perspective, however, the question of subjectivity cannot even be allowed to arise. The moment intentionality is psychologized and attributed to a motive in a mind, the future is removed from the work into the surrounding world and tied to the limited context of a fixed historical moment. There is nothing fallacious about external intentions, but they relate to the work like any other externality, that is, as facts. If they enter the work, they do so like other facts, as part of the conditioning context. But it is a fallacy to identify the author's intentions with the work's project. What the author wants to say is one thing; what the work does with the author's desires is something else.

The texture of a project will necessarily appear uneven. Intentionality implies a kind of transcendence: an act of the mind directed beyond the contents of the mind. Creating a new object or a new possession would be a relapse; it is necessary, instead, to create a new possibility. As a horizon of futurity, the project is not contained in a self-sufficient work, but exists for something beyond. As possibility, the project exceeds the conditions under which it came into being and even its own actualization. At stake in the interpretations that follow are things as varied as a new language for the self, a new opening for endings, a new use for soliloquy. But in whatever form, they disrupt the placid surface of controlled achievement.

I look, then, within the work for moments or aspects of transcendence. The transcendence that makes a work significant beyond itself exists in counterpoint to the more familiar values of closure and self-limitation. At its heart, New Criticism recognized that closure is never enough by qualifying it with irony and paradox, but the meaning of that qualification was too readily ignored. Closure entails restriction, boundary, limitation—in aiming at something new, the work must pass beyond boundaries and break through limitations. Many of the works I study here concretize the threshold in images that evoke the iconography of creativity—doorways and windows, surfaces and depths, enclosures and the pathways leading through or beyond them. In various works the threshold may function dialectically as a contradiction to be solved, dialogically as a question that elicits a response, or alluringly as an invitation to be pursued. In whichever form, the gesture of halting to confront a situation and then moving ahead again seems to me an essential given of creativity. Our buried metaphors take the nature of literary projects seriously: a denouement unravels what the complication has knotted up, a resolution redisperses what a problem has thrown together. It remains tempting to assimilate literary achievement to philosophic or didactic utterances whose achievement is to take a stand, but my interpretations try to do justice to the virtues of openness in literary masterpieces.

Infinitely many things said or done precede and surround the writing of any given work. These constitute the writer's world. But they are not, as such, the internally constituted context. For a context is a sorted and inventoried depository, not a soup. Expectations and models, norms and forms confront the writer as conceptually articulated possibilities to be drawn upon. Unless there be writers capable of rejecting the past wholesale, the context is not the enemy but the starting point of expression. It is the stable past from which future movement comes, the reality that feeds developing possibility. Recognition precedes discovery; perhaps this is the reason why in primitive cultures without a sufficient preexisting archive authors create their own by means of formulaic utterance. The works studied in this book are composed of labeled or labelable elements. Heroes and villains, settings and incidents, images and motifs, genres and meters: nothing is written that does not belong to a category. Categories are the vehicles of thought; in this connection the work's project of creating new possibilities may be reformulated as that of transforming the categories of thought. In identifying transcendence with transformation we can see the genesis of Nietzsche's notion of transvaluation.

In the past few years the pendulum of studies in literary history has swung toward privileging historical contexts. "A book is made by its public," we read in Marilyn Butler's *Romantics, Rebels and Revolutionaries*, a distinguished yet extreme example of the type. A brief discussion of Butler's study will illustrate not just why I have chosen a different path, but how the historicist project itself gravitates back from contexts toward texts.

"Literature, like all art, like language"—so Butler articulates her premises—"is a collective activity, powerfully conditioned by social forces, what needs to be and what may be said in a particular community at a given time. . . . Authors are not the solitaries of the Romantic myth, but citizens. Within any community tastes, opinions, values, the shaping stuff of art, are socially generated. Though writers are gifted with tongues to articulate the Spirit of the Age, they are also moulded by the age" (9–10). Where history makes literature in this fashion, it seems safe to say, literature does not make history. The same "corporate author" that engendered Blake's works (43) also, it would seem, begot Thelwall's, and so radically historicist an approach leaves no principle for discriminating between the two. Indeed in the later Blake, who "turn[ed] away from the material world of political action and the senses five," this approach can only find a betrayal to be interpreted *cancrizans* as "the shadow of a collective frustration and postponed, if not lost, hope" (54), a kind of communal solitude. The gain of this style of reading lies in the clarification of social issues. That is an invaluable accomplishment, beautifully performed by Butler. But there is a counterbalancing loss in elucidating the mission of the writer. Radical historicism implicitly, and sometimes explicitly, presupposes the impotence of art: writers are distinguished by the force of their disillusionment. Romantic rebels find their allotted place divisively crying in the wilderness, romantic reactionaries in self-division, expressing "doubts about the stability of the present social synthesis, and . . . growing anxieties about the future" (151, about the later Scott). It is not surprising, then, that as the book gathers momentum and develops greater sympathy (the later Blake and Wordsworth are bad rebel and reactionary, respectively, whereas Shelley and Scott are good rebel and reactionary) the repressed returns—as text. At first an impoverished view results when German romanticism is considered to have been "born from social experience, out of unemployment, frustration and rejection of the outside world" or when Coleridge is regarded as "the product of a social experience so far more common perhaps in Germany than in England" (74). But as the picture builds up, Keats, for instance, is seen in relation to Milton and Coleridge, Hazlitt, Byron, and Shelley, not to Peterloo and Ricardo. He and Shelley are "conscious of having moved beyond didacticism"; they "made a literary movement which represented revolution, but one could not call it revolutionary literature" for the reason that "when abstract concepts are taken up in literature, in good literature at least, they undergo the transformations that the single subjective consciousness imposes" (154). The historicist confronts choices between seeing history as the moving force and seeing literature in that role, between taking historical realities and taking literary realities as the stuff of literature. And the momentum of the subject matter, a literary "movement," impels even a historian like Butler in the latter direction.[3]

Properly speaking, a context cannot be of a different nature from the texts it accompanies. The one is naturally assimilated to the other: historical events are the contexts of other events, texts (including, of course, events rendered in texts) of other texts. The first passage quoted in the previous paragraph uses the phrase "shaping stuff," as if history could be form and matter or accident and substance all at once. The spirit instinctively resists this imperialism. History is many things—and historical study consequently yields many legitimate kinds of insight—but to the spirit it necessarily appears congealed and inert. To the extent that literature produces meaning, its material will be the static, panoramic, and articulated text of the past. That is the stuff that it shapes, the only stuff that it can shape.

The work carries out its project by elaborating its material. An author who merely takes a position is outmoded the next day, whereas a work never entirely gets left behind so long as it remains in motion. The perspective of textual production leads me to ask what changes within the work and, more specifically in most cases, how the end differs from the beginning. To the extent that there are innovations in method in this book, they lie here. Taking temporality as the constitutive category of literary creation, I read all structural features of the work as reflections upon it. Reiterated images and consistent ideas belong to the all-too-fixed past. Instead, attention here will be directed precisely toward the order that may be discovered in modifications and variations. One element that is always in motion in any narrative or dramatic work is plot. It is, however, easy to overlook the cultural investment in the plot. Either the presence or the absence of a narrator can function to partition plot from author, while character-centered accounts of plot encourage limiting the author's involvement to psychological considerations. I believe, in contrast (as I have argued in "Plan Vs. Plot"), that plot almost always embraces more than either narration or character. It is neither impersonal nor merely personal, but rather transpersonal. Consequently it is possible to see plots as allegorical enactments of the author's situation. In the plot, if anywhere, we can see the work's projection of how change takes place. Plots enact the movement of history.

The framework for conceptual innovation, motivic transformations, and plot emergence is generic organization. While generic types are neither rigidly limited in number nor inflexible in definition, they appear, especially in eighteenth-century works, to impart an externally based stability to the flux of literary expression. Yet even genre comes alive in many of the works studied here. In projecting new possibilities of expression the authors often develop new forms. Novelty is just as much related to prior conditions in this area as in others, and just as dynamic. New forms as such are not the concern; indeed, only in retrospect can a new form be seen to have been established. Rather, the readings will concentrate on the movement of forms. One of the most powerful motors of innovation in the eighteenth century seems to be the interrelating of existing genres, such as ode and satire at the end of *The Deserted Village, comédie larmoyante* and farce in *She Stoops to Conquer*, picaresque and neoclassic comedy in *The Marriage of Figaro*, picaresque and epistolary novel in *Humphry Clinker*, or novel and drama in *The Castle of Otranto*. With respect to ideas, images, plot, and genre alike, the work elaborates its premises in order to open new directions.

Some problems of interpretation are eased or even dispelled as soon as we take movement rather than coherence to be the constitutive impulse of literary structures. Decades of modern critical study have fruitlessly sought a pattern in Collins's *Odes*; the perspective is greatly simplified if we look instead for an itinerary that the collection follows. The individual poems are not building blocks but passageways, as indeed Collins's imagery unambiguously suggests. Likewise, it becomes possible to relate the rejection of inherited forms in *Tristram Shandy* to a search for a new form, conducted through a meditation on Sterne's major predecessors (I focus on Fielding and Boccaccio). Curiously, the accepted New Critical notion of form secretly regards conclusion and discovery as incompatible. Only if the end confirms what was premised at the start does it recognize closure. This is to take a narrow view of where a deduction may lead and, ultimately, to opt for conclusions in which nothing is concluded. Well-wrought urns are not the happiest resting places for life.

It follows, then, that perfection must take second prize. That is not a paradox that need concern the student of preromanticism very much. Those interested in perfect works of art do not flock toward the later eighteenth century and will certainly not draw their paradigms from that period. Yet the mixed reputation of *The Vicar of Wakefield* should provoke thought in this connection. Its idyllic surface and peerless construction have consigned it to the rank of an exquisite period piece. To rescue it from its glorious ignominy I find it necessary to seek out ways in which its perfection is available. The problem is that its self-containment has often been judged instinctive, thoughtless, and therefore without consequence. The work only becomes historical at the moment when it becomes a lamp rather than a mirror. Reflection turns outward, changing from mere pattern and sparkle to consciousness. Consciousness is a central topic of this book because it is the link between work as product and work as effectivity.

Every work that does something new, that frays a passage, must therefore have a moment of what Harold Bloom calls breaking. We may compare a work of art to an organic entelechy, but not if we regard an entelechy as a self-balanced world or a lamp that shines inwardly.[4] An organism is inwardly propelled toward development, as the seed toward the plant and the plant back toward the seed; it constantly absorbs nutriments and releases its products, and dies when it comes to rest.[5] We capture the work's life, then, in its moments of opening or rupture. Each work reaches a limit where its thrust shows most clearly, though that limit be so minute as an ambiguous pronoun in Gray's "Elegy," so diffuse as Goldsmith's foolish narrator, or so unmarked as the ambiguity of voice in Sterne's cock-

and-bull story. At the moment of disorder purposive discovery nears: the point of breakthrough is also that of breakdown. "A man of genius," says Stephen Dedalus, "makes no mistakes. His errors are volitional and are the portals of discovery" (Joyce, *Ulysses* 190). Without negation there is no self-consciousness, and without self-consciousness no impact.

Such, in the abstract, are the recurrent motifs of the interpretations that follow. No rigid formula controls them, but there is a regular interest in the elements of literary form that I have been describing: a stock-taking of the context of articulated, stable, inherited components; a tracing of the path of transformations elaborated by the work; and an identification of the troubled or confused moment when consciousness breaks free of its determinants and becomes purposive, projecting new potentialities toward the future. Ideologically, my method risks the most at the moments, already signaled, when I translate from the formal elements of the work to the external temporality of past, present, and future. I can only say that materialist readings that base their external temporality on an objectively identifiable past, present, and future seem to me grandly inhuman, and I have wagered the attempt of countering them with a history written to human scale. There is no intent to deny the great events of the past—the French Revolution foremost among those within the span of this book—but there are worse ways to understand these than in terms of the powerful thoughts and forms of thought from which their momentum derives.[6]

The temporality of events seems more uniform than the stratified temporality of texts. Past, present, future—what could be simpler and more regular? But that is a delusion. To the historian of events his subject's future is already known, as a foregone conclusion, and its past must always be selectively represented as an antecedent condition. Between them the subject itself assumes the guise of an unpredictable suspension amid divergent necessities—a real or an apparent suspension, depending on the historian's orientation. Predisposition, contingency, and fatality are the three heterogeneous modes of historical narration. The aftermath of the Glorious Revolution, the Age of Walpole or of Johnson, the cradle of the American and French revolutions—the future as result, the present as experience, the past as preparation—these converge in name and date only. But the elements of a text, however unevenly foregrounded, remain homogeneous because they share a common substance. The heterogeneity of events is signaled by the absurdity of saying that the future enters the past when it becomes present; the homogeneity of texts is signaled by the inevitability with which works enter the cultural context in elaborating their projects.

The substance shared by context, elaboration, and project is language in its active form as expression, or style. Style will thus be the fundamental material (or static) category of this entire study, as movement is its fundamental formal (or dynamic) category. I treat style in the broadly etymological sense in which it includes all traces of the author's pen. Deconstructive approaches regard these traces as marks of division from a transcendental figment. But the dream of pure presence that the text fails to attain is itself projected by that text. If there is division, the style engenders it; if there is belatedness, the text first sets the terms of its own inadequacy. It remains the first thing in fact, however haunted it may sometimes be by imaginary things-in-themselves to which it wishes to cede priority.

Nietzsche's gay science never entirely forgot that division presupposes unity, and he reminds us not to confuse our transcendental metaphors for style with psychological literalisms. "Culture," he writes in the first of the *Untimely Meditations*, "is above all the unity of artistic style in all expressions of the life of the people"; but epigonality, or belatedness, is a pretext for the quietist Philistinism of historicists, whereas "everything genuinely productive is offensive."[7] Unifying and divisive at once, rooted and productive, style is both the most immediate of phenomena—an absolute, preconscious constraint on expression—and also the most nebulous, verging on the ineffable "spirit of the age."[8] The style is never more than partially actualized in the textual surface; the dispersed traits that identify it are only epiphenomena, traces, indices. Hence stylistic innovations steal upon the consciousness even of those who later hold themselves or are held responsible for them. Yet as the ground or "truth" of its varying manifestations, the style is a unified reality, and its arrival may be considered a distinct event, even though not localizable in a single text or author.

Style is my *prima materia*, and I am better at describing than at defining it. The intersection of the common and the personal, it is as much a tone or an attitude as it is a form of expression. I like the phrase "manner of proceeding," which Geoffrey Tillotson uses in his *Augustan Studies*, one of the two fundamental works on eighteenth-century poetic style (the other being Donald Davie's *Purity of Diction in English Verse*). Every age, every writer, every work has its own ways of combining words and thoughts, and these are at once its reserve, its actuality, and its potential. I begin, then, with an account of style at midcentury, and from that *Lebensäußerung des Volkes* comes all the rest. I confess that I remain fonder of the page that discusses Goldsmith's vowel harmony than of anything else in the present study, for no better reason than that I was unable to enjoy reading his poetry until I chanced to imagine that I could now hear his voice. Jacques Derrida has recently given us the otobiography, or life history of the ear, and Geoffrey Hartman's troubling studies of words and wounds have established the study of otopathy. But the track that leads from the voice to the ear, from the soul's voice to the heart's ear, remains, I am convinced, as intact and mysterious as ever.

CHAPTER TWO

The Urbane Sublime

Ein Geist, heißt es, ist ein Wesen,
welches Vernunft hat. So ist es denn also
keine Wundergabe, Geister zu sehen; denn wer
Menschen sieht, der sieht Wesen, die Vernunft
haben.

Kant, *Träume eines Geistersehers* A 8

Even the best sublime poetry of the eighteenth century often seems intolerably naive. The style is self-consciously inflated, the formal sense is deficient, and the poets display a fatal attraction to spirits, ghosts, and Muses. As a result, an uncomprehending reader is apt to discount these poems as the effluvia of an epidemic of bad taste. Yet the eighteenth century attached far more importance to matters of taste than the twentieth does, and in its day the poetry gave enjoyment—and not just enjoyment, but often delight, amazement, transport—to countless readers, including many of great knowledge and discernment. Clearly the sensibility of these readers was different from our own. If we wish, then, to explain the success and the historical destiny of the sublime style, we must patiently reconstruct the criteria according to which the poets wrote.

George Eliot's notorious attack in her essay "Worldliness and Other-Worldliness: The Poet Young" (*Leaves* 9–62) is a case in point. By inquiry into Young's sincerity, Eliot arrives directly at the dismissive conclusion that he was (to borrow Hume's phrase) a liar by profession.[1] And to be sure, the widespread use of first-person forms in Young, as in other poets of the age, is liable to strike a psychologically sophisticated modern reader as hollow and insincere. But this impression is misleading. It may be accurate to call the poets liars, but it is anachronistic to condemn them on that account. Bishop Hurd, for one, quotes Hume's catchphrase with approval in order to defend poetic license. Poets should and do lie, he argues, though they have no intention to deceive and are "not so unreason-able" as to "expect to have their lyes believed."[2] Instead of condem-nation, Eliot's brilliant dissection of Young ought thus properly to have led to the insight that all the poetry of the period, even includ-ing apparently confessional outpourings, is deliberately and con-sciously artificial.

From this perspective the sublime poets are seen to have more in common with the satirists than is generally acknowledged. It has been the prevailing though not universal practice to divide the poets into two opposing camps: the comic and the serious, the clever and the pompous, the critically detached and the uncritically self-involved, or, more simply, the good and the bad. Thus in a well-known essay, included in a volume entitled *Hateful Contraries*, William Wimsatt wrote that "Augustan poetry at its best . . . was the last stand of a classic mode of laughter against forces that were working for a sublime inflation of ideas and a luxury of sorry feel-ing."[3] Subsequently, a provocative essay by Peter Hughes treated us to the spectacle of a conflict waged between, on the one hand, the rational forces of Counter-Reformation and Enlightenment, who speak with the tongues of men, and, on the other, the barbarian en-thusiasts, who speak with the tongues of heroes or of gods.[4] Such "dualistic" accounts, however important their differences in detail, ultimately all stress the "dissociation" between two poetic modes as well as the "discontinuities" inherent within the sublime mode.[5]

In contrast to this widespread view, I wish to suggest that the satiric and the sublime poets wrote on the basis of common stylistic presuppositions. They employed similar kinds of verbal artifice, en-tertained similar conceptions of formal organization, and envisioned similar purposes with respect to much the same audience. There is a continuity between the satiric and sublime modes, as well as be-tween the sublime mode and ordinary experience. Important conse-quences follow from these observations. They allow us to see the earlier eighteenth century as a unity with its own integrity, rather than as the battleground for competing styles representing incom-patible intellectual syntheses. More important, they also allow us to see what the unity of the period consists in. It was a period able to encompass within a single stylistic framework a remarkable and re-markably shifting range of tone and subject matter. Its thought pro-cesses are characterized by their continuity, their fluidity, and their reluctance to be polarized, in short, by what might fancifully be called a benevolent latitudinarianism of the understanding. My ultimate purpose in showing the unity within diversity of early eighteenth century verse is thus to make a statement not just about poetic style, but about the eighteenth-century mind.

For reasons that will become increasingly clear, I choose to call the dominant style of the period the urbane sublime.[6] I will only present the more difficult half of the case here, showing the urbanity within leading examples of sublime verse. I indicate in passing some salient points of contact with Pope, trusting that the elevated seriousness that informs much Tory satire is by now generally recognized.[7] This chapter, then, offers a tripartite analysis of the style of eighteenth-century sublime poetry with the aim of bringing to light the principles governing its composition. The opening section deals with the most obviously troublesome aspect of the style, its artificial and inflated rhetoric, taking as an example one of the century's most palpable and most artful poetic lies, Thomas Gray's "Ode on a Distant Prospect of Eton College." The second section turns to Thomson's *The Seasons* and to Collins's *Odes* in order to examine the period's formal sense, and the third to Young's *Night Thoughts*, in order to describe the purpose of the style and to account for its fascination with the supernatural.

The Language of the Eton College Ode

Decorum is a notable problem with much eighteenth-century poetry. The style often appears ill assorted to the subject matter. As a result, it becomes difficult to gauge the intended stylistic effect or to evaluate the role played by the poetic and rhetorical artifices in achieving the poetic aims. I have chosen to begin with the Eton College ode because its unusual tonal richness and precision make a determination of the stylistic level relatively easy and therefore render the ode more readily accessible than the other poems I will discuss. As the most finished example of its type, it offers the best initial test of a thesis about eighteenth-century style.

How ought we to respond to the ode? We are told that Gray disliked sports and suffered through school on that account. Hence there is no biographical justification for treating the poem as the result of a sudden fit of sentimentality or as the spontaneous overflow of powerful feelings. Rather, the tone is set by the closing lines, "where ignorance is bliss, / 'Tis folly to be wise." This is a neatly turned, pointed epigram, which should be attributed neither to the naive spontaneity of the children nor to the deep meditation of the seer; instead, it is a clever reversal that intervenes to ward off the dangers of too much prophecy. In assessing the tone of Gray's "praise of Folly," we can hardly forget that this is an erudite poem, written by a poet notoriously intolerant of readers less learned than he was, and that it is prefixed by a cynical motto, in the original Greek, derived from the comic poet Menander. The poem is a little excursion through time toward a pastoral retreat, but at the end Gray has neither become a child nor forgotten the difficulties of the road; instead he has been enabled to contemplate both his childhood and the perils of life with learned equanimity and ironic detachment. And since the place *where* ignorance is bliss is the abode of "grateful science," Eton College, the ignorance that Gray praises cannot be that of an unlettered "village Hampden," but must rather be the simplicity of a self-sufficient mind unconcerned about past or future and uncontaminated by base and worldly engagements.[8]

The closing lines thus arrive at a mood of disciplined coolness in which we, as readers of the epigram, have already begun. It has been generally overlooked that this tone runs throughout the poem and constitutes Gray's answer to the temptations of time-bound worldliness. The first half describes the ritualized games of the children, unchanged for centuries, in an even more ritualized, distanced rhetoric. The hint of condescension results from a restricted and imitative diction (descending even to echo effects such as "less pleasing—thoughtless—regardless"), from a deceptive and confusing syntax ("While some on earnest business bent / Their murm'ring labours ply / 'Gainst graver hours, that bring constraint / To sweeten liberty"), and from a punning vocabulary (such as "bent" and "ply," which describe the "earnest business" in terms drawn from the world of ball games and boat races). In the second half the "sprightly race" gives way to a race of spirits, yet a certain lightness remains. The poem slides into a different perspective and a larger temporal framework, but it is a carefully prepared, Marvellian shift: quasi-personifications such as "lively cheer of vigour born" smooth the transition to the only slightly more vivid personifications of the second half.[9] Unlike the similar but more realistic Latin fragment describing an eruption of the Glaurus, which Gray had written shortly before, the second half of the ode offers constant reminders that this is but a mock kingdom, inhabited by would-be poets who snatch inspiration "in every wind," set in a landscape that apes the brow of its royal founder, and threatened only by an even more shadowy mock court. The pathos of distance in the first stanza suggests a potentially

unbridgeable gap between the sophisticated poet and the hieratic setting, and the poem's self-conscious distancing is merely intensified
when this cast of theatrical demons erupts out of the "vitals" of the
earth to taunt and chase the life out of imaginary victims. The rhetorical antitheses in the closing aphorism continue to hint at inevitable separations. To be sure, the pathos does increase as the
poem progresses, but this is counteracted by increasingly impersonal grammar, so that as danger closes in on the figures, they in
effect progressively retreat from its grasp. The changes of mood are
thus more apparent than real, while the subdued wit, the continuities of imagery, and the even tenor of the poetic diction serve to
stabilize the tone and to protect against the imminent terrors of
experience.

I do not wish to exaggerate the ode's good nature to the exclusion of all else. The poem lends itself to more than one interpretation, for poetic diction is by nature imprecise and therefore generously open to various readings. Moral pathos and psychological
conflict are as much a part of the ode as is urbane irony. Yet there is
more than just the wit of the closing lines to suggest that Gray's
final purpose was to tame his fear of the spirits, to restore simplicity
of mind, and to inculcate a stance of urbane detachment. The motto
serves as an additional guide, not to the exclusive meaning, but at
least to the prevailing attitude of the ode:

> Ἄνθρωπος· ἱκανὴ πρόφασις εἰς τὸ δυστυχεῖν.

Just as Gray's "No more," echoes Menander's ἱκανή, so it is tempting to link the Greek πρόφασις to the gloomy predictions of the visionary, as if the phrase meant, "The children are men, and that is
sufficient to prophesy their doom." Any reader who makes this link,
however, is the unwitting butt of yet another urbane witticism, for
πρόφασις means "reason" or "pretext," not "prophecy." The spirit of
the Menander adage and the tone that governs the poem are not
those of the sublime visionary, but rather those of the venerable and
evasive Father Thames, who remains silent, and of the urbane poet,
who decides at the end, using a word etymologically related to πρόφασις, not to tell the children their "fate." In the modern world, as
Collins's "Ode on the Poetical Character" tells us, the "inspiring
Bow'rs" have been "o'erturned" or at least "curtain'd close." There
should be reasons, but no prophecies.

A chief virtue of the urbane sublime, then, is its discretion. It
speaks in generalities and with indirection; it does not descend to
particulars. The silence of Father Thames when asked to name the

children conforms in this respect to the tenets of the man who, more than any other, set the tone of the age, Joseph Addison: "If I attack the Vicious, I shall only set upon them in a Body; and will not be provoked by the worst Usage I can receive from others, to make an Example of any particular Criminal. . . . It is not *Lais* or *Silenus*, but the Harlot and the Drunkard, whom I shall endeavour to expose; and shall consider the Crime as it appears in a Species, not as it is circumstanced in an Individual" (*Spectator*, no. 16; 1: 72).

The urbane stylist refuses either to be teased out of his detachment or, as Addison goes on to say, to be coerced into partisanship. For if the urbane style is discreet, it is also tolerant; it is couched in generalities and therefore leaves the reader great discretionary latitude in his interpretation. The urbane sublime is a liberal style, conducive to ease and familiarity. It reflects an artful effort to domesticate the supernatural and irrational and to deprive them of their terrors. Again the Spectator, that most ubiquitous and genial of all eighteenth-century ghosts, defines the stylistic ambition:

> For my own Part, I am apt to join in Opinion with those who believe that all the Regions of Nature swarm with Spirits; and that we have Multitudes of Spectators on all our Actions, when we think our selves most alone. But instead of terrifying my self with such a Notion, I am wonderfully pleased to think that I am always engaged with such an innumerable Society in searching out the Wonders of the Creation, and joining in the same Consort of Praise and Adoration. (*Spectator*, no. 12; 1: 54)

In passages like these, "Mr. Specter" (as some of the imaginary correspondents call him) points the way toward a comprehensive style of writing, capable of encompassing an unusually great range of high and low subjects, and even (though much more distantly) toward the conversation poems of Coleridge and Wordsworth and the integrated romantic landscape, with its marriage of the sublime and the beautiful, the spiritual and the natural.[10] Yet in one important respect the poets of midcentury went beyond Addison's example. Like many successful allegorical modes, Gray's poetic diction has what Angus Fletcher has called a cosmic dimension.[11] That is, it is both decorative and inflationary. Common nouns tend to sound like capitalized personifications, dead metaphors revive, and the generalizing diction is apt to treat any action as the icon of a higher truth. In spite of its detachment, in other words, the style calls attention to the importance of its subject. In Gray's ode, for instance, both the ornate landscape and the elaborate rhetoric have a specifically national function: the hillside school by the Thames near Windsor becomes an image of the ancient aristocratic order of England. Within the "little reign" lie dignity, virtue, and moderation; without lie trespass and extremity, or (in the parallel terms of the "Elegy") "the paths of glory" and ultimately "the grave." Behind the urbane wit of Gray's style, then, there does lie a noble message: human passions are irrational demons that can be contained by preserving the native English purity and simplicity of manners. Let there be no more Cromwells, even if there will also be no more Miltons; better the muteness of Father Thames—or the reticence of Gray himself.[12]

Gray strikes a difficult balance here. The hillside at Windsor encompasses the middle ground between precepts emanating from the "stately brow" of the school on the heights and the prophetic visions rising from the river below. In his cento of the poem Walter Pater clearly intuited its tendency to burst its frame.[13] For in fact Gray holds back more than we are inclined to realize. He labors to mute color: grove, lawn, mead, turf, and shade all precede the monosyllabic flowers, an arrangement that emblematizes a significant restraint imposed on his style, underneath the elaborate rhetoric.

In this style, in particular, the texture of allusion becomes at least as much a vehicle for exclusion as for incorporation. Father Thames ought to bring a political message like his ancestor, "the Father of the *Roman* flood" in the *Aeneid*,[14] and perhaps he does not answer because Gray's questions are beneath his dignity. The poem is a discreet allegory, steering a middle course between the hollow idealizations of Thomas Tickell's *Oxford* or (satirically) of Thomson's *Castle of Indolence*, on the one hand, and the somber oracles addressed to Virgil in Horace's *Odes* 1.3 and in Thomson's *Liberty*.[15] Gray's psychology, based on prognostications sudden and drastic enough for King Lear, is hardly credible. But the language works if we take its intention to be that of masking politics. Behind the "Ministers of human fate" and the "Queen" of "The painful family of Death" lie concerns about ministers and queens, as we see from the excluded resonances of civil strife in phrases like "inly gnaws the secret heart" and "Those in the deeper vitals rage."[16] Gray's sublimity is a patina, insubstantial in itself, but serving to cover up harder and gaudier metal underneath, "whence *this grey Scene*, a Mine / Of more than Gold becomes and orient Gems, / Where *Egypt, Greece*, and *Rome* united glow" (*Liberty* 4.128–30). The Eton College ode is a greater poem than *Liberty* precisely because the poetic style of the day helps Gray to look around and beyond his fears. At its highest reaches the urbane sublime is hypnotic in effect and succeeds as an antidote to the evils of the day.

Formal Balance in Thomson and Collins

Because of its inherent discretion the urbane sublime is able to tolerate many apparent paradoxes. It is both high and light, sophisticated and primitive, liberal and aristocratic, elevated and capable of describing the most mundane phenomena, innovative and doggedly conventional.[17] It is perhaps the presence of these contradictory impulses, rather than its unnatural inflation, that often makes modern readers ill at ease with eighteenth-century poetry, and it is certainly the persistence of contradictory impulses that makes the history of eighteenth-century poetry so baffling to write. Having used the Eton College ode to illustrate the style, I should like to turn to Thomson's *Seasons* in order to demonstrate the intellectual coherence underneath the superficial inconsistencies and seemingly ill-defined ideology of this poetry.

The issue is the way form constrains style. Poetic diction, in particular, has generally been studied in historical perspective, at the expense of its contextual function.[18] Often, in serious as in satiric verse, a principle of compensation applies. Thus the Eton College ode spends its most rotund Latinity on the children's games and falls back on monosyllabic Anglo-Saxon adjectives for its more sublime and visionary moments. The passage on birds' nests in Thomson's "Spring," lines 631–86, offers an even more obvious example of this reverse decorum. On the one hand, there is a clear vertical hierarchy, with "humble" nests on the ground and the various other types sorted by altitude; the sense of propriety is strengthened by the repetition "kind Concealment," "kind Duty," "kindly Care," where "kind" has the connotation "appropriate to the species." Yet on the other hand, the tree birds build simple "Nests"; the somewhat less dignified, thievish swallow erects a somewhat more pretentious "Habitation," while the ground-nesting species are granted the noblest oratory: "humble Texture," "artful Fabrick," and even, surprisingly, "Domes" (Latin *domus*). Similarly, while the idle male bird, who "takes his Stand / High," is described in generally simple diction, his menial better half "assiduous sits," a bad etymological pun that elevates even as it ridicules.[19]

One of Thomson's hesitations illuminates the impulse behind this reverse decorum. The first version of "Winter" describes how cattle, when they return at evening, "ask, with meaning Low, their wonted Stalls" (line 124).[20] The revision, made a few months later, reveals the concealed lexical and grammatical ambiguities so typical of the urbane sublime: it changes the capitalization to "with Meaning low," thus inverting the hierarchy of adjective and noun. By means of this metamorphosis the animal noise is shown to be a meaningful speech act. The transformation is paradigmatic of the style as a whole. The urbane sublime cannot condescend to an object without elevating it. Yet neither can it express sympathy without taking cognizance of difference: the Low may have a meaning, but it is a "Meaning *low*." No matter how egalitarian the gestures, the sense of hierarchy is inescapable. Indeed, both leveling and gradation are implicit in the adjective-noun structure that forms the backbone of the style. Whether the adjective and noun are related as species to genus, abstract to concrete, or figurative to literal, the pairing of words almost always implies a divided perspective and yet also works to moderate the rigid stratifications of "classical" decorum.[21]

The pacing and structure of *The Seasons* exhibit a comparable differentiated moderation, or "art of discrimination" as Ralph Cohen has called it.[22] The poem was most carefully composed and the contribution of each word duly weighed. Yet as methodically as Thomson went to work, the constant effect is one of wandering and of choices still to be made; the tone remains deliberative rather than decisive. The poet sustains his slow progress through the year by nourishing a permanent sense of anticipation, and he typically resists temptations toward culmination.

Just as the rejection of prophecy characterizes Gray's poetry from the early "Latin Verses at Eton" ("Fata obstant; metam Parcae posuere sciendi," line 79) to the late "Descent of Odin" (where the prophetess herself commands in lines 88–89, "That never shall enquirer come / To break my iron sleep again"), so too *The Seasons* regularly retreats from transcendence. Thus after finding himself "in airy Vision rapt," Thomson's "every Sense / Wakes from the Charm of Thought: swift-shrinking back, / I check my Steps" ("Summer," lines 585–89; this version has been toned down from the earlier, "I stand aghast"). After a passing enthusiasm for "visionary Vales," he draws back with the line, "Or is this Gloom too much?" ("Autumn," lines 1030–37). After hymning nature's stunning impact on his "ravish'd Eye," he concedes, "But if to that unequal" (lines 1365, 1367). Most notably, the end of the whole poem subsides from present epiphany ("Winter," lines 1041–43: "And see! / 'Tis come, the glorious Morn! the second Birth / Of Heaven, and Earth") to merely predicted epiphany (1068–69: "The Storms of WINTRY TIME will quickly pass, / And one unbounded SPRING encircle All"). To the eighteenth-century rhymester, even "ecstasies" arrive "by degrees." [23] We are faced with a great intensity of verbal energy at every point, but with a diffuse and enervating whole.

Concomitantly, the forms preferred by the age are the georgic, the progress, and the loco-descriptive poem. Each of these combines steady movement with an affectionate dwelling on particulars, and in consequence a rhetoric develops in which the compactness of the classical period is compromised by excessive itemization. The many diffuse catalogues in *The Seasons* are obviously deficient in rhetorical unity and focus, but even in the Eton College ode the strict triadic cadences of the opening stanzas succumb as the excitement grows:

> *This* racks the joints, *this* fires the veins,
> *That* every labouring sinew strains,
> *Those* in the deeper vitals rage:
> Lo, *Poverty* to fill the band,
> That numbs the soul with icy hand,
> And slow-consuming *Age*.[24]

In *The Seasons* this technique of discrimination by means of superfluous enumeration is related to an emphasis on gradual, deliberate order, presided over by a host of mild, intermediate divinities, each with its own realm, and with no universal controlling power in evidence. In lieu of the fixed, sculptural "stationing" that Keats praised in Milton, there is a flexible positioning; the mind tries to assign each spirit "to his Rank," but the perceptions are indistinct and changing, "ever rising with the rising Mind" ("Summer," lines 1793, 1805). Evening, that mild spirit that so entranced men's minds later in the century (see Hartman, "Evening Star"), best represents Thomson's moderation as well:

> CONFESS'D from yonder slow-extinguish'd Clouds,
> All Ether softening, sober *Evening* takes
> Her wonted Station in the middle Air;
> A thousand *Shadows* at her Beck. First *This*
> She sends on Earth; then *That* of deeper Dye
> Steals soft behind; and then a *Deeper* still,
> In Circle following Circle, gathers round,

> To close the Face of Things. A fresher Gale
> Begins to wave the Wood, and stir the Stream,
> Sweeping with shadowy Gust the Fields of Corn;
> While the Quail clamours for his running Mate.
> Wide o'er the thistly Lawn, as swells the Breeze,
> A whitening Shower of vegetable Down
> Amusive floats. The kind impartial Care
> Of Nature nought disdains: thoughtful to feed
> Her lowest Sons, and clothe the coming Year,
> From Field to Field the feather'd Seeds she wings.
>   ("Summer," lines 1647–63)

In so gentle a matriarchy as that of nature, how could life help but be pleasant? Little in Thomson's world is firm and earthbound or surging and fiery; instead, when summer's heat is not simply "Exuberant Spring," then it is almost always a liquid, "dazling Deluge" that (punningly?) "reigns" ("Summer," lines 697, 435). Indeed, Thomson is fascinated, as in the lines on Evening, with air and water, the ambient elements that allow suspended substances to move easily up and down through the many levels of existence. Above all, as the multiple puns of the lines on the mock snowfall show, air and water are "amusive," intrinsically poetical because they imitate the "musing," deliberate course of thought itself. Thomson's early Preface to "Winter" harps on this theme as it describes the temperate pleasures of his poem's "calm, wide, Survey" of nature. Poetry, he says, is associated with "the most charming Power of Imagination, the most exalting Force of Thought, the most affecting Touch of Sentiment"; it displays "a finer, and more amusing, Scene of Things"; it can "amuse the Fancy, enlighten the Head, and warm the Heart."[25]

What passes for artifice and inconsistency is thus more adequately understood, at least in the better poetry of the century, as the easy, "musing" acceptance of shifting orders and fluid hierarchies.[26] This applies to politics as well as to poetic forms. Thomson, like Gray, Akenside, and the Wartons, can startle the present-day reader by simultaneously praising modern liberty and ancient privilege without any sense of strain:

> Oh, QUEEN of Men!
> Beneath whose Sceptre in essential Rights
> Equal they live, tho' plac'd for common Good,
> Various, or in Subjection or Command;
> And that by common choice.
>   (Thomson, *Liberty* 3.328–32)

Yet there is no inconsistency to such a political vision; its viability is demonstrated equally by the examples of ancient Rome and of modern Britain with her "BOUNDED KINGS" (4.1146).[27] Nor is there any greater inconsistency to the century's flexible conception of formal structure and poetic style. These, like the politics, reflect the poets' view of the nature of society. For if we ask what determines both the tone and the organizational sense of the urbane sublime, the answer is its social basis.

"Social" is the word that resolves the apparent paradoxes of the urbane sublime: "I believe there was never so reserved a solitary, but felt some degree of pleasure at the first glimpse of an human figure. The soul, however, unconscious of its social bias in a crowd, will in solitude feel some attraction towards the first person that we meet" (Shenstone, *Men and Manners*, entry 75, p. 150). The Muse, as Thomson says, is "most delighted, when she social sees / The whole mix'd Animal-Creation round / Alive, and happy" ("Autumn," lines 381–83). In the best of all possible worlds even the vegetable kingdom would be social: "Great Spring, before, / Green'd all the Year; and Fruits and Blossoms blush'd, / In social Sweetness, on the self-same Bough" ("Spring," lines 320–22). In these lines the very alliterations are sociably sorted, as often in Thomson, into neighboring pairs.[28] The word's range—from the nobly societal to the collegially sociable—reflects the range of the style itself, yet all the variations are reducible to a single concept, the continuous give-and-take of social intercourse.

Even the poetry of William Collins, the most inward and difficult poet of the century, retains the easy sociality of the urbane sublime.[29] The *Odes on Several Descriptive and Allegorical Subjects* begin, it is true, with an attempt to summon the cognate tragic emotions of pity and fear. However, Collins then turns away from these passions of art and toward the "genuine Thought" and "temp'rate Vale" of Simplicity. His "Tale," to which the last line of the "Ode to Simplicity" refers, becomes the subject of the following "Ode on the Poetical Character," which relates a "Fairy Legend" about the origin of poetry. This ode has often been misread as a sublime allegory on the solitary genius, but Earl Wasserman, in his essay on the poem, has demonstrated that its intent was actually to differentiate Collins's more humble aspirations from those of the truly inspired Milton. Nor is the legend so elevated as the Pindaric form and intricate syntax would lead one to expect: the prevailing meter is that of "L'Allegro" and "Il Penseroso" (from which the description of

Milton in lines 63–64 derives), and urbane lightening is provided by an epistle-like opening and by a creation myth that portrays god rather as a divine couturier than as a divine artificer. The remaining "musings"—the word occurs five times, beginning in the "Ode to Simplicity"—are all devoted to social virtues. Only in the "Ode to Evening" does the solitary sublime again become a temptation, and then only for a passing instant: whereas in the "Ode on the Poetical Character" Collins's "trembling Feet . . . pursue" the Miltonic bowers, the peremptory violence of nature in "Evening" "Forbid[s] my willing Feet," thereby repressing the urge to wander alone on high. Collins's refuge "beneath the Sylvan Shed" and his invocation to *"Fancy, Friendship, Science,* rose-lip'd *Health"* are often regarded as a break in tone and a betrayal of the poem's romanticism; in fact they fulfill one of the fundamental impulses of his poetry. The intricate daily minutiae of individual observation, which is always liable to be distracted by some passing bat or beetle, are properly absorbed into the more long-ranged and "simple" perspective of seasonal and social regularities. The final diptych of social odes, "The Manners" and "The Passions," crowns the volume with a palinode to the opening poems. "The Manners" replaces the "Buskin'd Muse" of the "Ode to Pity" with humor's "comic Sock." "The Passions" passes the tragic emotions in review only in order to let each refute itself: thus, Fear recoils in fear, Anger is too impatient to remain, Despair "beguil[es]" itself, and so forth. The ode concludes by praising the sociability and "native simple Heart" of Music.[30]

The Direction of Young's Thoughts

Nowhere is the musing character of eighteenth-century consciousness more apparent than in Young's *Night Thoughts.* Young gives us, consequently, the best occasion for considering the direction and purpose of an apparently aimless meander. Though few today would dare to call this poem "captivating," as Percival Stockdale did early in the nineteenth century (*Lectures* 1: 587), and though Young's writing is relatively free from conventional poetic diction, it would be a mistake to overlook his urbanity. The poem is not a silent meditation, but rather a long monologue addressed to a reprobate named Lorenzo, and Young is careful to vary the pacing, to lighten the tone with ironic sallies, and to intersperse frequent parenthetical asides and self-references, all so as to preserve a conversational feeling. While the poem's theme is the correction of the individual, its standards are social, and its very discursiveness is seen as the best weapon against false pride:

> In *Contemplation* is his proud Resource?
> 'Tis poor, as proud, by *Converse* unsustain'd;
> Rude Thought runs wild in *Contemplation*'s Field;
> *Converse*, the Menage, breaks it to the Bit
> Of due Restraint; and *Emulation*'s Spur
> Gives graceful Energy, by Rivals aw'd
> 'Tis Converse qualifies for Solitude.
>
> (2.488–94)

The rhetoric is informal and completely nonperiodic; the current of thought never stops, but only ebbs and flows as each sentence funnels into a successor of greater or lesser intensity. The view of life is Heraclitean—"Life glides away, *Lorenzo*! Like a Brook; / For ever changing, unperceiv'd the Change" (5.401–2)—and the poem's utter formlessness mirrors this view of life. Wherever it is opened—and some early editions are indexed to facilitate browsing—the reader enters into the middle of an elevated, consoling conversation.

This very formlessness, so hard to appreciate today, was one source of the poem's charm in its own day. The great enemy, the great divide, as Young often says, was death, and by avoiding any divisions or articulations the final reckoning could be postponed indefinitely. It is fitting that the longest night by far is called "The Consolation," for length, expansiveness, and infinite repetition constitute the best anodyne against the fear of death:

> Dost ask *Lorenzo*, why so warmly prest,
> By Repetition hammer'd on thine Ear,
> The Thought of Death? . . .
> . . . That Thought ply'd Home,
> Will soon reduce the ghastly *Precipice*
> O'er hanging Hell, will soften the Descent,
> And gently slope our Passage to the Grave.
>
> (5.682–89)

Everything described in the poem turns out to be gentle, nothing abrupt; everything is intermediate, nothing absolute; everything is in flux, nothing fixed. "The World's no Neuter," says Young (8.376), and he means that there is no impartial, unchanging standard of reference. All things are value-laden, and all values are relative and variable. The poem's theodicy is based not on rational persuasion, but rather on making the reader conscious of the eternal variability of life. Young's most common strategy is easy to paraphrase: things may look bad, but they might be worse, and worse, and worse, and so they come to seem, by contrast, better, and better, and better. The only absolute is that the value of things must be determined by our consciousness of them:

> WORTH, conscious Worth! should *absolutely* reign;
> And other Joys ask Leave for their Approach;
> Nor, unexamin'd, ever Leave obtain.
>
> (8.978–80)

The aim of *Night Thoughts* is to examine our feelings and to make us conscious of the variability and relativity of values. But to the eighteenth-century mind this is a tautology: all consciousness is consciousness of relative value. Thus Young writes, "So grieve, as conscious, Grief may rise to Joy; / So joy, as conscious, Joy to Grief may fall" (8.763–64). One might therefore just as well say the aim of *Night Thoughts* is, simply and absolutely, to make us conscious. This is what I meant when I said that the urbane sublime imitated the musing course of thought. In its deliberate ebb and flow, in its indeterminacy, in its hierarchic tendency, in its heightening of experience, the urbane sublime expresses the very form of eighteenth-century consciousness.[31]

In his *Augustan Poetic Diction*, Geoffrey Tillotson points out that the word "conscious" was never ethically neutral in eighteenth-century usage, but always positively or negatively charged (77). One spoke of "conscious pride," "conscious shame," "conscious sin," "conscious virtue." Thus Steele writes, "every Thought is attended with Consciousness and Representativeness; the Mind has nothing presented to it, but what is immediately followed by a Reflection or Conscience, which tells you whether that which was so presented is graceful or unbecoming" (*Spectator*, no. 38; 1: 160). For Steele, it must be added, there is also the possibility of excess self-consciousness, which he terms "Affectation." For the sublime poets, on the other hand, consciousness is all: "Is *Conscience*, then, / No Part of Nature? Is she not *Supreme*?" (*Night Thoughts* 8.841–42). The urbane sublime style is intended to interest and affect the reader, to heighten his moral sensibilities, in sum, to correct and educate his "brute unconscious gaze" (Thomson, "A Hymn on the Seasons," line 28).

In the eighteenth century consciousness is hardly to be distinguished from intuition, knowledge from faith; even Hume, though he exposed this state of affairs to view, despaired of changing it. We do not find the grand oppositions of romantic dialectic—spirit against matter, general against particular, eternal against temporal—

and the poetry can only seem incoherent if we look for them. Instead there is nuanced gradation, slow accumulation, and constant flux. At times, *Night Thoughts* can seem almost Wordsworthian (it is even quoted in "Tintern Abbey"), but it lacks Wordsworth's stoppings and reversals, his overflowings, submergings of consciousness and restorations, in short the dialectical intensity of the Wordsworthian sublime. Indeed, Young's poem, though less discreet and therefore less intriguing than Gray's Eton College ode, is a particularly valuable witness because it so clearly reveals the presuppositions of the age. Death, for instance, is not the annihilation of life, but its culminating stage: "Our Birth is nothing but our Death begun" (5.719). Immortality is not the opposite of mortal life, nor even simply its perpetuation; it is an intensification, "the Crown of Life" (3.526): "It is but Life / In stronger Thread of brighter Colour spun, / And spun for ever" (6.77–79). Death does not terminate our consciousness but elevates it:

> In Life embark'd, we smoothly down the Tide
> Of *Time* descend, but not on *Time* intent;
> Amus'd, unconscious of the gliding Wave;
> Till on a sudden we perceive a Shock;
> We start, awake, look out; what see we there?
> Our brittle Bark is burst on *Charon's* Shore.
>
> (5.411–16)

This last quotation, to be sure, forces a distinction, but it is a distinction that the poem has already clarified. Death is a shock. But it is only a shock to the "brute unconscious gaze" of the natural savage. It is not a shock to those who have been educated in their lifetime to a conscious, rational faith:

> *Faith* builds a Bridge across the Gulph of Death,
> To break the Shock blind *Nature* cannot shun,
> And lands Thought smoothly on the farther Shore.
>
> (4.721–23)[32]

Though Young does give in cursory fashion the customary proofs of religion, he does not view reason primarily as dialectics, but rather as the ground of belief:

> My Heart became the Convert of my Head;
> And made that Choice, which once was but my Fate.
> "On Argument alone my Faith is built:"
> *Reason* pursu'd is *Faith*; and unpursu'd
> Where Proof invites, 'tis Reason, then, no more.
>
> (4.740–44)

This last theme is sounded again and again: the head and the heart are allied; thought consciously prolonged is feeling:[33]

> Think you my Song, too turbulent? too warm?
> Are *Passions*, then, the Pagans of the Soul?
> *Reason* alone baptiz'd? alone *ordain'd*
> To touch Things sacred? Oh for warmer still!
> . . .
> Passion is Reason, Transport Temper *here*.
>
> (4.628–31, 640)

The cool and the warm, reason and passion, urbanity and sublimity are mutually self-sustaining.[34] The apparent inconsistencies of eighteenth-century poetry are not contingent facts of an unsuccessful style, but constitutive structures of a particular form of experience. Where consciousness is understood as the elevation of sensation, all things become manifest, not in themselves and not by contrast with their opposites, but by comparison with higher or lower degrees on a scale of intensities. "Nothing is great or little otherwise than by Comparison," says Swift's Gulliver (2.1; p. 87); "all judgment is comparative," says Johnson's Imlac (*Rasselas*, chap. 30, p. 80). The serious exists only in relation to the more comic, elevation of style only with reference to its potential degradation, the liberal or new only as a relaxed modality of the aristocratic or old; order and formal perfection are inseparable from freedom and formal flexibility; nature and organism are hardly distinguishable from art and mechanism; poetry and prose differ only in degree of intensity. Indeed, even dissolute scheming and divine wisdom are related "as the waining, and the waxing Moon" (*Night Thoughts* 5.352). The very lines most ridiculed by George Eliot—"More generous Sorrow while it sinks, exalts, / And conscious Virtue mitigates the Pang" (1.300–301)—find their explanation as yet another expression of this creed. Constant rising and sinking are a part of man's middle state, and consciousnessness is the force that both recognizes our instability and reconciles us to it.[35]

From this point of view even the fascination with ghosts and Muses becomes comprehensible. They are figures of conscious, that is, of heightened, perception. Young says as much, using an image that, however much it may seem to anticipate the "Ode to the West Wind," speaks for a vastly different sensibility:

> *Truth* bids me look on Men, as *Autumn* Leaves,
> And all they bleed for, as the Summer's Dust,
> Driv'n by the Whirlwind, lighted by her Beams,

I widen my Horizon, gain new Powers,
See Things invisible, feel Things remote,
Am present with Futurities.

(5.336—41)

Young, like Shelley, speaks of being haunted, but it is a happy haunting that emphasizes the copresence of the spirits and declines to be "the trumpet of a prophecy":

Pale *worldly Wisdom* loses all her Charms;
In pompous Promise from her Schemes profound,
If future Fate she plans, 'tis all in Leaves
Like *Sibyl*, unsubstantial, fleeting Bliss!
At the first Blast it vanishes in Air.

(5.345—49)

The personified "Things invisible" that abound in the poetry of the century thus body forth the expanded horizon and broader perspective of the enlightened mind, as opposed to the "heedless," earthbound superstitions of Collins's hermit.[36] The spirits are the reminders of the social bond, the universal intercourse, and the comparability of all things.

CHAPTER THREE

Transcendental Aesthetics

It was Kant, late in the century, who formulated the conditions under which a generalized consciousness might operate. Finally becoming conscious of consciousness would mean taking self-consciousness rather than a Cartesian world-consciousness as the ground of experience. It would entail a degree of introspection alien to the genial sociability of the urbane sublime. The marks of that change in Kant and other writers of the 1780s are the topic of the next chapter.

As the time lag hints, a complex development prepared the way. Philosophically, the process can be followed in Kant's early essays, with results that are then systematized in the opening chapter of the *Critique of Pure Reason*, the "Transcendental Aesthetic." Kant's solitary rethinking of premises, however, was overshadowed by a change in the sensibility of the time. Although Kant's lifelong admiration for English poetry is well known, it is not my purpose here or elsewhere to document influences of poetry on philosophy. Rather, I want to illustrate new ways of feeling—or new languages of feeling—in relation to which alone the new doctrines can be understood.

The "Transcendental Aesthetic" concerns space and time. Kant calls these the pure forms of sensible intuition.[1] By that phrase he means that they are the general conditions under which perception can occur. Space and time envelop our conscious perceptions. Consequently, we do not perceive space and time themselves, we cannot measure them, and they cannot be subdivided into parts—distinct spaces or times. They are not objects that can be known, as they were for Newton, since they determine the manner in which cognition occurs. Nothing can be predicated of them; indeed, as a later section of the *Critique of Pure Reason* shows, there is no way to determine even whether they are finite or infinite. What, then, are these pure forms? What does it mean to imagine entities, components of experience, that can be neither known nor thought? Another term Kant uses for them is *Sinn*—sense, or feeling. Space is the outer sense, time is the inner sense. But again, what is the nature of a sense that is not a sensation or a sense organ? Descartes had defined man as a thinking being: *Ego cogito, ergo sum.* The notion of a feeling or a sense beyond reason was inconceivable. Outside of thought lay not the forms in which thought might take place, but only madness. For Kantian idealism to replace Cartesian rationalism, then, man had to be reimagined as a feeling rather than a thinking being. That entailed rethinking the relationship of reason to sanity—a complex, largely post-Kantian development that I plan to analyze in a future book on the gothic novel. And it also entailed developing a new sense of being-in-the-world, of the envelope of space and time in which our perceptions and thoughts are embedded. The development of that new sense is the subject of the present chapter.

Consider the polarizing tendencies of the urbane sublime. It is not easy to reconcile intensity with expansiveness. In most poetry of midcentury, conscious heightening chimes imperfectly with relaxed sociability. The grander flights of georgic and descriptive poetry fall prey to self-assertion: Mallet's *Excursion* gives us a strenuously humorless Thomson, heedlessly noisy, while Somerville's *Chase* replaces Virgilian mastery with the spectacle of victory, implicitly vindicating the special status of the poetic imagination by vindictively equating warriors with dogs, reason with instinct, and courtliness with a sentimentalized version of courtesy. Many of the poems in this vein are admirably contrived testimonials to the diverse stylistic and conceptual forces at play, but poets uncertain whether they are writing "learned converse, or ingenuous song"[2] make too many compromises for effective balance. And the moral poetry of the satirists and song writers focuses its injunctions too exclusively on individual defect and merit.[3] The moralist's voice, like the satirist's, is disjunctive; he sees and knows more than the rest of mankind, and he speaks to, not for, the public. It is hard to keep to the middle; even the "No more" of the Eton College ode has an audience of one that is uneasily compounded of low and high, the enfeebled poet and the enthusiastic prophet. The task of becoming conscious seems to entail amplifying either the public or the private voice and therefore to put at risk the ideal of a voice that might speak for all.

Two poems at midcentury do find that universal voice, and in so doing they generate purified senses of space and of time that were to be fundamental for the philosophical anthropology of the romantic period. They are the two poems most often singled out as the greatest nonsatiric poems of the period, Gray's "Elegy Written in a Country Churchyard" and Collins's "Ode to Evening." The spreading night of both poems is not a tragic failure of vision, as it threatens to be in the "Ode on the Poetical Character" and later in Keats's "Ode to a Nightingale." Rather, it is associated with a substitution of the epitaphic for the epiphanic that saves them from the preachiness of most graveyard literature.[4] Both reverse the odic "I see and sing" (the formula explicitly adopted in Keats's "Ode to Psyche"), most notably when the speaker of the "Elegy," in his only self-reference, inherits the world in darkness ("And leaves the world to darkness and to me"). The speakers are absorbed into a spreading echo.

Johnson was absolutely precise in his remark on the commonplaceness of the "Elegy." In the "Elegy" the long delay between the death of light in the first stanza and the Epitaph at the end leaves room for much reflection, but also for increasing doubt as to who points the moral or adorns the tale.[5] The death of light in Collins's "Ode" is less distinctly funereal, yet more benumbed, as the "last cool Gleam" leads to thoughts of "chill . . . Winds." Consciousness dissolves while Evening is universalized: the hut takes over the observer's role, and perception subsides from "Views" to "hears" to "marks o'er all." Gray-fingered dusk draws the veil: an antidawn and an antirevelation even more boldly conceived than Gray's. Both poems seek out the voice of nature not in the heat of day, but in the embers of life ("Elegy," lines 91–92). They pursue consciousness in its most general and hence most unassertive forms. My argument, then, will be that these two poems parcel out between them, beneath the threshold of awareness, the emergent language of what Kant came to call the pure forms of sensible intuition: space, the province of the "Elegy," and time, the province of the "Ode."

Gray's Churchyard Space

Space has always been recognized as a problem in Gray's "Elegy." The speculation concerning the location of Gray's churchyard is as idle as that concerning Goldsmith's Aurora, yet also as natural. For it reflects the tension that runs through the poem between particu-

lar place and universal space. In the early stanzas the repeated possessives drive toward local dominions, and so indeed do the definite
articles.[6] At twilight the private consciousness faces dormancy unless it is rescued by positioned singularities ("Save where," "Save
that from yonder ivy-mantled tow'r"). Dominion is ubiquitous: in
the owl's "solitary reign," the children's envied sire, the war to subdue nature to cultivation. It is not by chance that the three model
figures named in the fifteenth stanza were all politically involved in
bloody tyranny, nor that the body politic provides the standard for
judging the village's emulation or privation. In the "precincts of
the . . . day" presence always commands, however limited its terrain, and funeral monuments compete to prolong the paternal domination of the forefathers. If they cannot demand homage, they can at
least implore "the passing tribute of a sigh." If nothing else survives,
the heaving turf of line 14 remains a literally posthumous assertion
of territoriality. In country and city alike, action stratifies mankind
into levels of domination, and, discomfortingly, identity remains
conceived as place in the scale of being. Hence the promptings from
the poem itself toward finding the churchyard. It has no power if it
has no location, and no reality or truth if it has no power.

On so imperious a mentality Gray casts a light too cool to be
called irony. Its ideal is a repose that the noises of the place disturb.
Thus, the erotically charged gem and flower retain their purity only
so long as their unnatural locations protect them. ("Ray serene" is
properly a sky phrase—"serene" means "of evening"—doubly displaced, in a cave and under water.) Though Ambition errs in mocking "useful toil," Gray's own tone becomes condescending when
he reaches "homely joys, and destiny obscure"; though Grandeur
shouldn't smile at annals so "short and simple" that they are heard
rather than read, Gray himself seems to discredit the poor when he
calls them "noiseless," not audible at all. This is, one notes, a poem
of the day, not of the year: properly speaking, these poor can have no
annals, but only an "artless tale."[7] Gray hovers constantly, as in this
phrase, on the brink of oxymoron (fires living in ashes, "mindful of
th' unhonour'd"), which it is easy to interpret as rejection, as if for
Gray "*any* mode of 'life' is finally unacceptable."[8] No doubt about
it, the poem expresses reservations about rich Cromwells and poor,
mute Miltons alike.

Still, reserve is to be carefully distinguished from criticism.[9]
Gray had previously appeared in public representing three versions
of minimalism: the insects of the "Ode on the Spring," the children's games of the Eton College ode, and the bath-os of the "Ode on

the Death of a Favourite Cat." The "Elegy" keeps a more even tenor than any of these, striving for a sublimity of the subliminal variety that Gianni Scalia has called "the sublime of depth." [10] It wants to take a stand without asserting any pride of place. Its fundamental principle is a return to the ground: a combination of regression and leveling most clearly seen in the seventh stanza, which retreats from harvest through plowing to setting out, and then concludes, in less conflictual language, with the hewing of wood. Negations are as plentiful as possessives, yet they are typically oblique or postponed so as not to cancel out the strong diction and heroic images. The poem works as hard to compare rich and poor as to contrast them. They share life as well as illusions. Death destroys the illusions: "The boast of heraldry, the pomp of pow'r, / And all that beauty, all that wealth e'er gave." But it does not put out the flame of life, which survives, perhaps only in epitaphs and in "trembling hope," but which is assuredly there: "Ev'n from the tomb the voice of Nature cries, / Ev'n in our Ashes live their wonted Fires."

The animals, the muttering poet, the lisping children, and the "still small Accents whisp'ring from the Ground" (Eton College manuscript, line 83) are all forms of the voice of nature that is forever speaking. For as heartlessly as the poem criticizes social existence— all forms of social existence—even as firmly is it attached to natural life. It is not a poem written in blackness like the "Ode on the Spring" ("Thy sun is set," line 49) or confirming blackness like the Eton College ode, where the speaker faces "shade" (the rhyme word in line 4 and again in line 11), only imagines the children whom Father Thames is supposed actually to "ha[ve] seen," and eventually views "black Misfortune's baleful train" and "The painful family of Death." Rather the "Elegy" is situated at twilight and with its eye on "the warm precincts of the chearful day." Death is mute and deaf (lines 43–44); the Epitaph is the text of life.

But it is life in its most general form, reinterpreted so as to speak to mankind generally. Where all men are comparable, consciousness seeks a universal voice. The poem's one "me" (line 4) adjoins its one "now" (line 5), but immediately gives way under the impulse of Gray's conception to "all" (line 6, changed from "now" in the Eton College manuscript). As there is no place, no individual who is the subject of the Epitaph, and no year, so there is also no day in the poem, but rather an eternal, timeless moment. Gray's resignation purges the dross of anxiousness out of our pleasing being, leaving the intimacy of a heavenly "friend" and the passivity of a "trembling hope." It is a successful quietism that transmutes the restless, heaving turf of the beginning into the concluding "lap of Earth." At evening, as contours dissolve, the universal eye looks beyond individual destinies—why should we know their fate?—toward the enveloping space of earth and heaven. Man leaves the turbulence of (urban) society and (rural) family in order to reenter his general home in the friendship of spirits and the protection of Mother Nature and Father God. In itself death is privation, but for Gray relationship persists and enlarges at the end of life.[11]

In diction, imagery, and argument, then, Gray presses in this poem toward a universal consciousness.[12] Beginning in a compound of obscurity and contradiction, the poem veers stanza by stanza from silence to noise, high to low, dark evening to bright morn, field to home, peace to conflict, poor to rich. These are gestures toward comprehensiveness in a world whose totality is composed of parts. The poetical youth is an outsider to this entire psychosocial economy. "His wayward fancies" (line 106) are constitutionally placeless, and the antique language that describes him belongs nowhere. A youth in a world of hoary-headed swains and aged thorns, a figure of morning (and noon) in a poem for which morning exists "No more" (line 20), a being born, it seems, only to die,[13] he negates all the earlier contradictions and classifications: "nor yet beside the rill [nature], / Nor up the lawn [gentry], nor at the wood [laboring peasantry]." In pointing out the lines summarizing the youth's "fate," the "hoary-headed Swain" takes a step beyond the silent, "hoary Thames" at Windsor, yet without achieving prophetic authority, since he is illiterate, enjoys a merely conjectured existence, and discerns only part of the youth's fate. Perplexity better describes the tone of the swain's speech, with its grave puns ("pore," "lay"); in it the youth escapes capture, a figure alien yet ubiquitous. The Epitaph shifts abruptly yet again; after the vivid personifications in the body of the elegy and the exotic Spenserianism of the swain's speech, the poem ends in grayly looming abstractions. It has the pallor of a language for which differences no longer exist.

After so many appeals to voice and so many failures of merely metaphorical reading (Knowledge's "ample page" ne'er unrolled, history not "read . . . in a nation's eyes," the babbling brook listlessly pored over), after the bookish language of the swain's speech and his curious designation of the Epitaph itself as a "lay," this arrival at a plain-style written text functions as a release. The reader's muted voice neither can nor needs to say much, but his brevity is accompanied by a settled clarity, completion (a large bounty as largely recompensed), and universality ("all") that subsume all the foregoing partitions and contradictions. For once the eighteenth century gives us the image of something known fully and in itself, rather than partially and relationally. The knowledge is purchased with the loss of power and position: the contents are impoverished, the knower undefined. One could hardly say, finally, who the youth is, since neither his merits nor his frailty are disclosed. Only metaphysicals remain definite here ("the lap of Earth," "the Bosom of his Father and his God"), and the four indefinite articles stand in striking contrast to all the abstract definite articles of the main text. Thus, it is not that someone comes in the end to know someone or something. Yet the poem still evokes the possibility of a language and a consciousness beyond station, beyond definition, and beyond identity.[14]

It is far from obvious to take the "Elegy" as a poem about the mind.[15] One's primary impression is, perhaps, that it is a remarkably physical poem. Movement is everywhere, in the plowman's way, the paths of glory, the genial current of the soul, the noiseless tenor of the villagers' way, the passing tribute of a sigh, the parting soul, the roving youth. For so traditional a society, it is a remarkably restless existence. The villagers' ardor is more than tinged with sexuality— "Some heart once pregnant with celestial fire"—and so is that of city dwellers:

> But Knowledge to their eyes her ample page
> Rich with the spoils of time did ne'er unroll;
> Chill Penury repress'd their noble rage,
> And froze the genial current of the soul.

This stanza, which praises the city indirectly by describing how impoverished rural life is, proves on reflection to be obliquely sarcastic about urban culture as well. For it is followed immediately by the famous gem and flower stanza. With its "spoils of time," we may infer in retrospect, the city ravages the sweetness of desert flowers, and its warm "current," while "genial," may not protect the serene purity of pearls so well as the "unfathom'd caves of ocean." Passions lurk in both environments, and they are distinctly not those of the mind alone.

Yet they act on the mind. What George Wright calls the poem's Berkeleyanism lies in the fact that passions seek less an object than a receptor, whether it be the owl's moon, the politician's listening senates, or the sigh that responds to the frail memorial. The poem may recognize a sexual dynamism to knowledge—despoiling time, unrolling her ample page—but its vector is antiphysical. Owl and moon preside over the churchyard in an alliance of wisdom and chastity aiming to protect a bower from molestation. While the verbs are active, inversions and syntactic ambiguities damp their noble rage. Of the three exemplary villagers, it is the mute, inglorious Milton who is specifically said to "rest" (as Hutchings points out, "Syntax of Death" 505), allying him with another poet, the youth of the artless lines. At the end, death mysteriously consumes passion: one day the youth is lovelorn, the next he has vanished. Gray clear-sightedly concedes the omnipresence of bodily impulses, yet his message is that the only fruition and repose are of the mind.

Critics have written of the instability of Gray's poetry, its constant self-criticism and inability to ground the self.[16] This is true to a point, but it is to condemn Gray to the "narrow cell" of the forefathers and to deny him the "large . . . bounty" of the poetic youth. In the main body of the "Elegy," to be sure, the quasi-sexual violence of fathers and forefathers is omnipresent—molesting owls, felling trees, ogling the spoils of Knowledge, secreting "The struggling pangs of conscious truth," and quenching "the blushes of ingenuous shame"—yet the Epitaph imagines as a surrogate a family romance of purest ray serene. Merits and frailties rest hand in hand in the androgynous lap-bosom of Nature-God, in a utopia purged of sexual desire (since the youth wished only "a friend") and of the turbulence of "fame and fortune." "*Fair Science*" retains the merest tinge of a purified eroticism, as does the single tear, while the youth as unknown knower becomes a figure of objectless, apathic cognition. The "Elegy" gives a voice that can be perceived without being uttered and an abode that needs neither a local habitation nor a name. "Common place" is the perfect term for the churchyard in whose grave lines all may rest.[17]

For a poem often thought to be a paean to rural laborers, the "Elegy" has a startlingly impoverished notion of work. Rather than conceiving it as a cooperative and constructive process—of which Adam Smith was to give so powerful an account in *The Wealth of Nations*—Gray's partitive consciousness divides work into periods ("evening care," line 22), repetitive events ("Oft," line 25), impersonal encounters ("Their furrow oft the stubborn glebe has broke," line 26), and synecdochic reductions ("How bow'd the woods beneath their sturdy stroke!" line 28). None of the associated adjectives—"busy," "jocund," "sturdy"—implies comprehension, and "toil" (line 29) is, precisely, thoughtless, primitive effort. Gray eliminated in revision a stanza containing the phrase "our Labours done," for rural labor knows no finality. Urban life, by contrast, is imaged as finality without effort: "the pomp of pow'r" without the struggle, "The paths of glory" without the conquest, "the rod of empire" that sways without earning the right, "the spoils of time" without the battle, "Th' applause of list'ning senates" without the victory, distribution ("To scatter plenty o'er a smiling land") without production. The widely separated smiles of disdainful grandeur (line 31) and of the people (line 63) suggest the city's detachment from the producing substratum, while the competition among the farmer's children for "the envied kiss" (line 24) signals that the rural struggle has no end. Such partitioning of the spheres of life both ironizes and idealizes: ironizes because all spheres are incomplete segments of a whole present only in the mind of the poet, idealizes because each element is absolutized as a changeless essence. What is systematically excluded is the order of appropriation—work that, by making something, makes it one's own.[18]

That is how Gray manages to convey a spatial imagination— with a full complement of divisions, locations, and affinities—that nevertheless remains universal. It is a world of possession without property. Possessives designate actions ("plods his weary way," "wheels his droning flight," "ply her evening care," "their sturdy stroke"), commonalities ("Their furrow," "their team"), parts of living beings ("their eyes," "Their name," "its old fantastic roots"), usurpation ("her secret bow'r," "The little Tyrant of his fields"), death's domain ("his narrow cell," "their lowly bed"). Only once— before the Epitaph, where all the conditions are changed—does the poem single out an object of possession, and then only in an affective relationship: "his fav'rite tree" (line 110). Nothing is owned, and hence nothing concrete can be imparted: "And all that beauty, all that wealth e'er gave," "He gave to Mis'ry all he had, a tear." Everything and nothing is shared with all and none in a world that is everywhere and nowhere. Life is emptied of its contents in order to make of the universe one vast container.

Critics often write as if the "Elegy" stays put and meditates on a particular, though unidentifiable, place. We do it more justice if we assume that the poem—like every work of art, I believe—acts to transform its initial conditions. The indefinite articles of the Epitaph should teach us at last how precise is the indefinite article of the title. We must learn not to seek knowledge of a particular place, as if to possess it mentally, but instead to accept a settled consciousness without a founding gesture or explicit starting "point." Rather than defining a social ideal, the poem turns away from social aspirations in order to evoke the transcendental basis of all experience.

Collins's Evening Time

As Gray's "Elegy" evokes the form of space, so Collins's "Ode to Evening" evokes that of time. And in the "Ode" as in the "Elegy" the evocation is not given from the start, but rather engendered through the poem's work. The "Elegy" begins with deficient modes of space—particular spaces, statuses, and stations—that it succeeds in purging. Likewise, the "Ode" begins with deficient modes of time. Impure and unstable movement obscures the purified inner sense that the poem allows us finally to glimpse. No more than in the "Elegy" can the pure form of sensible intuition be attributed to an empirical consciousness, for it is precisely the discovery of what lies beyond empirical consciousness that is at issue. The "Elegy" progresses by means of a diffusion of consciousness, so that the concluding stanzas can speak for space in general in a voice that is beyond localization. That broadening may be inappropriate to the purification of the inner sense; in any case, it is not the method followed by the "Ode." Collins's speaker remains present, and baffled, throughout. The new sensibility emerges not at the end but, more mysteriously, from within the text of the poem. That makes the "Ode" a more difficult poem than the "Elegy" and perhaps explains the latter's markedly greater popularity, in its own day and since. The itinerary of the interpretation, however, will be very similar: an examination of the speaker's troubled temporality, followed eventually by a description of the poem's resolving breakthrough.

In many respects the "Ode to Evening" is opposed to the "Elegy." It is conventional in form and bold in diction. It approaches a natural universality in the middle, but then both of its versions retreat, in one text to a protected social position ("regardful of thy quiet Rule"), in the other to a protected location ("sure-found beneath the Sylvan Shed"). Collins protests too much that his goddess is cloistered, and he draws the veil, ever so gently, over the glimmering intuitions of roughness. Sexuality is denied and therefore neither comprehended nor controlled. In the imaginary progress of the seasons it is hard to say whether Spring courts or tends Eve, whether or not Summer's dalliance ("loves to sport") addresses her, whether "sallow *Autumn*" woos, protects, or denies her by covering her up with leaves. With Winter the repressed violence breaks out, turning Eve from the ground of being into an object. ("Robes," whose etymological association with robbery and rape is highlighted here, is the only one of Eve's attributes too specific to be associated with a diffused feature of the landscape.) Following these charged scenes the escape in the last stanza seems evasive and poetically awkward. A single bad pun present only in the final version is all that remains to remind us of the pacified sexuality of Gray's Epitaph: "and hymn [him] thy fav'rite Name!" Divinity is even less responsive here than in the Eton College ode and far less responsive than in the "Elegy." The speaker's conjectural refuge under the sylvan shed should not mislead us into believing that his anxieties have been quelled.

The "Elegy" manages to maintain an equilibrium between two orientations of desire: the social or artificial desire for power and the physical or natural desire for love. The natural noises of the swallow are poised against the gentry noises of cock and horn, housewifely labor against filial spontaneity, cultivation (harvest and furrow) against collection, ambition against grandeur, wealth against beauty, gem against flower, and so forth. Finally it reaches the null point where differences are abolished, a point "to Fortune and to Fame unknown," where it is impossible to say whether fortune means money and fame natural recognition, or fortune natural accomplishment and fame social repute. The "Ode to Evening," by contrast, virtually excludes reference to social passions, creating an unbalance in which it rests uneasily. The speaker begins enfolded by evening, and where there is no distance, it is hard to understand what motivates the hesitant intensity of his appeal, or why he should need to discommode himself to follow a goddess who is everywhere. His feet are a little too eager and hint at a restless dissatisfaction that the text does little to explain. Only when the last stanza is so oddly imposed on the poem can we intuit why the transcendental or natural satisfactions of evening—"religious Gleams" or "last cool gleam," in the two versions of line 32—are so avidly sought and yet not enough. "Oaten Stop, or Pastoral Song" faintly evokes a tension in need of reconciliation (as if the reed were nature, the song culture), but tips the scales toward nature, as does the "Sylvan Shed," which confirms the unexpressed deficiency of civilized values. Even by Collins's usual standards the goddess is too powerfully mythic, the speaker too subconscious (he muses, but only his feet *will*). In this deprived state, what the poem enacts is a frustrated, lost, and inarticulate desire for stabilizing companionship.

It is essential to recognize how greatly the two versions of the final stanza diverge. The first version, "regardful of thy quiet Rule," emphatically moves into the social mode. "*Fancy, Friendship, Science, smiling Peace*" are an ascending series of qualities rising from the internal through the personal to the public and the communal. The revision, "sure-found beneath the Sylvan Shed," shies back into primitivism. Only one item is changed in the ensuing list, but that changes everything: "*Fancy, Friendship, Science*, rose-lip'd *Health*" now descends from the freedom of imagination and the generosity of friendship to the privacy of knowledge and the merely physical condition of the body. In the first version Fancy is irresponsible, Science productive, and "smiling" the sign of an attitude that encourages participation by all; in the second Fancy is liberating, Science is a private study (the "fair Science" of Gray's Epitaph), and "rose-lip'd" an unshared corporeal attribute, the object of admiration or even envy. The first series is too social for the poem, the second not social enough for the lonesome speaker. Both versions begin, "So long," with an awkward duration entirely disproportionate to the evanescence of evening. The last stanza, then, can be defended, if at all, only as a symptom of still unrequited placation. We need not believe the speaker's hypothetical "sure-found"; he persists in appealing to Evening because he does not possess her.

The speaker petitions Evening with the formula "*Maid* compos'd." It is difficult to know whether the adjective is descriptive, desiderative, or propitiatory (an antiphrasis like "Eumenides"). Like almost everything else in the poem, composure is an issue rather than a possession. The formula calls the identity of Evening into question. She is a fleeting goddess who cannot be captured without surrendering her identity. In the "Elegy" the speaker's "me. / Now" evaporates into a universal perspective; in the "Ode to Evening" the loss of control functions similarly as an intuition of a reality beyond particularity. In what sense does Evening respond to the speaker's need for an Other? What kind of being is she, and where is she to be found?

Opposing Evening's real or desired composure is the speaker's distraction. His intricate syntax has difficulty keeping to the point. Consciousness for him is expansive and centrifugal: from folding star to circlet to attendants at the lamp to wreaths to the shedding of dew. Or it is diffusive, as in the gradually expanding phrases of lines 34–40, issuing in the all-encompassing veil. "Gradual dusky Veil" is itself a distracted phrase in its wandering from time to space via the double meaning of "dusky." It is curious that so muted a speaker asks to be taught "some softened strain"; evidently, there is a concealed strain on him that surfaces chiefly in his excessive sensitivity to the disturbing noises of the shrill bat and the sullen beetle and in his prickly reaction to the "heedless" hum. "Genial lov'd" suggests a desired if somewhat unequal reciprocity of affection. Beneath the petition to the "Maid compos'd" lies the desire to be made composed.[19]

In a poem that begins with song and ends with hymn, it is difficult to keep music out of the picture. As we shall see, this means
ultimately that the Other who brings the promise of repose must be
found as an inner voicing, not as an external, let alone a social, object of sight. The speaker wants to stay in step with Evening, to
march to her tune: "Then lead, calm *Vot'ress.*" In this poem progress has the effect of subordinating visual impression to the rhythms
of the day and the year. Even a "cool Gleam" can be too striking for
the eye. The sublime epiphany of the first version ("Whose Walls
more awful nod / By thy religious Gleams") gives pause for thought
("Or if . . ."); the natural epiphany of the revision provokes a softened, yet still anxious, temporal musing ("But when chill blustring
Winds . . ."). At the end of the "Ode to Simplicity" Collins rejects
the "divine Excess" of a "cold Work" that "may charm our Eye" in
favor of "thy temp'rate Vale: / Where oft my Reed might sound . . . /
And all thy Sons, O *Nature,* learn my Tale." "Evening" struggles
more laboriously back from eye to ear: from what the hut views to
the "simple Bell" that it hears, from the light of Summer and "sallow *Autumn*" to Winter's noise.

Collins, in general, is unwillingly a pictorial poet.[20] "The shad'wy
Tribes of *Mind*" ("Poetical Character," line 47) keep rising up in visions that never successfully materialize. They only "appear, / To
hail the blooming Guest" ("To a Lady on the Death of Colonel
Ross," lines 29–30); and if they really come "And gaze with fix'd
Delight" ("Ross," line 33), they provoke an abrupt turn of thought to
"deep Despair" and "joyless Eyes" ("Ross," lines 37–42). Collins is
savage about the temptation to visionary excess, calling it "Rapture
blind" ("Poetical Character," line 53). No rational consideration
prompts the "But when" of "Evening" or the "But lo" of "Ross";
they can only be explained, I think, as a constitutional inability to
be fulfilled by the satiety of the eye. Hence it is, perhaps, that Collins's personifications remain parts and attributes rather than whole
bodies. The eye is too singular in its perspective and in its framing of
a scene; concord comes only from an ear that hears what all hear.
Therefore even a "last cool Gleam" cannot calm Collins, whereas
even Winter's yell can pave the way toward intimations of harmony.
The curious movement to social virtues at the end of "Evening" and
several other odes is one part of a complex of unprepared transitions
that are motivated by a deep yearning for continuities such as only
music can provide.

Natura non facit saltus is a maxim that the ode generically questions. With its "leaps" and "bounds" (Herder), its whooping and vaulting (Bloom), its form is predicated on discontinuities.[21] Music may sustain the ode's flow from underneath—the "melodies unheard" of the "Grecian Urn," the continuous but often unattended warbling of the nightingale, the twitterings of autumn's music—but the passion of sudden vision is its defining characteristic. In willingly moving from stop (especially in the stuttering phrase "If aught of oaten stop") toward song, the "Ode to Evening" is thus written consciously against the grain. Nevertheless, the poem cannot so easily escape its own destiny. However slowly Evening comes on, the pace picks up as it approaches the psychic plunge into Winter. At first the speaker steals after Eve, but the goddess who approaches almost unperceived departs first in the pomp of a royal procession and eventually, it seems, in fear and disarray. This is (perhaps following Thomson's 1726 *Winter*, lines 40–63) an ode of leave-taking that begins with the parousia of a repeated "now" and then strives throughout to delay a departure. Since the star of line 21 is already the evening star, the car that is then prepared must be destined not to bring Evening on the scene, but to carry her away. The natural background here is the light that flickers rapidly across the hills as the sun sets. This is, then, an increasingly if unsteadily animated pursuit poem. The eye leaps in a moment from star to flower or from lake to heath to upland fallows, following Evening's abrupt appearances.[22]

An acolyte of the hymnic ear who nevertheless foolishly entrusts his fate to the odic eye, the speaker loses the race for Evening.[23] He must always lose it because it is in Evening's nature never to abide her suitors. She is by nature "chaste"—another of the poem's conceptual puns that ruffle its wavy surface for those who read with the ear—because she is forever chased, never caught. "Shrinking Train" assures us that she will elude Winter too, whatever violence he may do to her regalia. In terms of the speaker's perceptions the poem ends in incoherence, with unfounded superlatives ("gentlest," "fav'rite") that single out undefined particulars of what should be a universal phenomenon (does she also have ungentle influences?) and thus miss the sought-after composure of the elusive goddess.

But in this ode the speaker is not the central figure, and his failure is the poem's success. As he loses his bearings, Evening grows on the poet. At first "reserved," hidden away in the dark corners of the landscape beneath the skirts of the setting sun and accompanied by minute, terrestrial phenomena, she gradually rises up through the landscape and into the sky. Eye and ear find her close up at the start, but spreading out into the distance later on. Attended at first by Hours but later by seasons, she begins small enough to be served by tiny elves and ends large enough for the leafy earth to be her lap. She begins subordinated to "the bright-hair'd Sun"; by the end her "Tresses" have replaced his, bathing in the atmosphere (spring's "Show'rs") while the sun's hair is bathed lower down, in the ocean. The speaker remains attached to fleeting earthly lights, whereas the celestial realities of the slowly setting sun and rising stars are larger and more continuous. The dusky veil covers the earth but opens the sky to view. Thus it is important that we take literally what is said of Winter, who attacks only the attributes of Evening. Her train shrinks; her robes are rent, too, but she has grown out from under them.[24] From this perspective—the poet's, as opposed to the speaker's— there is nothing abrupt about the ending or about the poem's other turns: the emergence and growth of Evening continue unabated.

Personification is here liberated from the constraints of visualization. Parousia fades away into a kind of manifestation that does not need to appear, or a personification without presence. Visual pallor (paly circlet, shadowy car, and the rest), allied with affective pallor (chaste, meekest, gentlest, together with *"Fancy, Friendship, Science,* rose-lip'd *Health"*) conjure up a notion of a substratum behind observable phenomena. To the speaker it verges on tragedy that Evening cannot be grasped, and he projects his frustrations onto a nature that breaks into violence in response to her retirement. But it is precisely in leaving that Evening shows forth her essence. The speaker anticipates an embodiment such as is characteristic of eighteenth-century personification (see Wasserman, "Inherent Values"); the poet finds instead a personification *in itself* that refuses to become a personification *for us.* Evening becomes herself by outgrowing her fictive body. The corporeal form for which the speaker yearns is her spectral emanation, and it does indeed pass daily across the face of the earth. But the passage *beyond* is what makes her Evening. The speaker both fails and succeeds in his desire to join Evening by suiting his numbers to her stillness, a double outcome expressed by the otherwise baffling switch from violent Winter to rose-lipped Health. He fails because Evening has no body, no place, no home, and therefore cannot be found. But he succeeds because Evening is precisely what is always slipping away: hence, what steals through her vale may really suit it. To lose her as a phenomenon is to find her in thought.[25]

In its manifestations time is unsteady, sometimes abrupt, disruptive, or fragmented. Such it is when it calls us to conscious action:

> When Time his Northern Sons of Spoil awoke,
> And all the blended Work of Strength and Grace,
> With many a rude repeated Stroke
> And many a barb'rous Yell, to thousand Fragments broke.
> ("Ode to Liberty," lines 22–25)

But Evening is the steady, musical pulse beneath the manifestations of life. The various oedipal readings of the "Ode to Evening" are true to its surface, that is, to the tense imaginings of the speaker, but they miss the dark, unstated background that underwrites its poetic accomplishment. In continuation of my thesis that what matters most in this poem is what it keeps in the shadows, I suggest that its true name for Evening is the one that is never spoken, namely, Even-ing.[26]

The desire for desire is a common issue in this enfeebled period.[27] By the second version of the "Ode to Evening" the speaker manages to ask of Evening a slender boon: "Then lead . . . my willing Feet," replacing the first version's "Then let me rove." This falls far short of the "Teach me to feel" that, in one form or another, concludes most of the preceding odes in Collins's volume. Nor is his unstated longing for intensity of feeling requited. Instead, by joining with Evening, desire is transmuted. The "meeting Soul"—the phrase comes from the "Ode to Simplicity," which forecasts "Evening" in many respects—finds no Other, but instead the generative inwardness of self. The quietism of the last lines sheds a new gleam on the moment of meeting. Epiphany and turn in one, "Thy genial lov'd Return" now suggests not so much reciprocity as reflexivity—return upon herself, rotation, not return to the speaker. It is in Evening's nature to produce nothing beyond glinting reflections, yet always to be coming around again, and her flow of spirits mingles with a flow of emotions. If Evening is a regent, her kingdom is a state of mind. She is not a supernatural being confronting us, but more like a supernature in which we find our Being, transcendental yet, in her humility, not in the least transcendent. By the time it reaches its safe and gentle—and by no means inappropriate—conclusion, the poem has drawn us into a movement that knows no outside. Desire is not re-aimed (to use Bloom's term), but refined away: it is no longer necessary where no impotent stasis threatens.

The poem calls into question the whole notion of the individual as an intentional being. As a cult form, the ode had always tended to submerge the one into the many (as in Keats's line "So let me be thy choir"), and to that extent there is no surprise when Collins's speakers lose themselves at the end in social virtues. But cult forms are primitive and chthonic, whereas the belatedness of "Evening" dissolves their earthy originality into atmospherics.[28] Roger Lonsdale's notes (Lonsdale, ed., *Poems*) inform us that "Springs," early in the first version, does not mean fountains or sources, but is rather a metalepsis for brooks—middles, rather than beginnings. The revision, "solemn Springs," avoids the solecism of "brawling Springs," but continues to question originality. The next line encourages a desynonymization: "Thy Springs, and dying Gales" urges "Springs" back toward living origins. The poem edges repeatedly in this way toward origins: in the pun on "born[e]," in the "Star *arising*," in the "*fresh'ning* Dew," in the preparation of the car. But as termination is tentative in the ode—a temporary refuge under a shed—so initiation is even more so. "While . . . while . . . while . . . or . . . so long": time marches on, with no beginning. Some things go to bed at night, others (bats, beetles, and stars) arise. In the eternal circulation of waters, of feelings, of meanings, a relative renewal is possible, but no real initiation. Absolutes steal on us gradually—"last," "meekest," "gentlest"—as Evening is revealed to be, not the primitive, but the inside of being. Selfhood is not an oedipal confrontation with the Other, but a being-with-others in a progress without beginning or end, originality or imitation, desire or repletion.

These two poems, Gray's "Elegy" and Collins's "Ode," took the urbane sublime style as far as it could go. Comparative thinking was always flexible, but also always entailed an element of competition in value or status. These two poems mute evaluation, eliminating the scale and universalizing relationship. The one comparative in Collins's ode is a mystery: if the "*Pleasures* sweet" are "lovelier still" than either the "fragrant *Hours*," the flowery elves, or the dewy nymphs, it can only be because they are more thoughtful— "pensive" and (at least by syntactic proximity) "shadowy." Pure mind takes over, effacing in the "Elegy" distinctions of higher and lower, leader and follower, or elder and younger, in the "Ode" distinctions of near and far, soft and loud, fast and slow. Hence we get in the former poem pure space without precedency, in the latter pure sequence without domination. (This is a difficult argument about the "Ode." I remind the reader that it is predicated upon taking the storm in lines 33–34 and the later outburst of Winter as figments of the speaker's imagination that do not interrupt the real progress of Evening from "last cool Gleam" through "gradual dusky Veil" to the complete absorption of the "shrinking Train" into vast night.) The poems leave behind the urgent animism that calls forth spirits in all other significant poems of the period, such as I have illustrated from *Night Thoughts*.[29] Mind is left to its own devices, "musing slow," and finding its way to universals that are beyond time in the former poem, beyond space in the latter.

To go further was to provoke a crisis. For thought, however unpressured, is not spontaneous in either poem. It continues to depend on perceptions to trigger it. The thought is always about something, however vague or general. The Youth—any youth—Evening—any evening—space—time: these are still promptings from outside the mind. Though generalized and not evaluative, thought in these poems remains relational, and therefore also social. To rest thought in pure time and pure space together would mean eliminating any externality and, with it, any conventional measure of truth. Thought then becomes an auto-affection. Kant eventually learned how to give a philosophical content to this intersection of a transcendental ego with a thing in itself, an abstract subjectivity and a featureless objectivity, and various imaginative writers of the 1780s and beyond learned how to give it an empirical meaning. But for the moment that could only appear as the emptying out of all reality. The "Elegy" and the "Ode" thus stand conjointly on the brink of solipsism, which proceeded to become the biographical curse of so many poets of the next decades.[30] As poets, Gray and Collins could only retreat into Manners and Passions, or into primitivism. The end of "The Bard" directly conjures up the abyss of liberation, but via suicide, and dark shadows light in the mesode of the "Ode on the Poetical Character" (particularly in the figure of the tercel, who is blindfolded except when he hunts), but not to comforting effect. My next chapter leaps ahead to the moment when darkness becomes truly generative and not just (as in the Wartons) a pretext for privileged communion with the goddess Natura.

CHAPTER FOUR

The Discovery of Consciousness

My definition of the urbane sublime style comprised three elements: the fluid and generalizing language, the "social" principle that organizes comparative thinking, and the finality of consciousness (the natural completion of perception as death was taken to be the natural completion of life). As yet this is only a static description of the style. Ultimately the purposiveness of a project transforms its founding conditions. The recursion that makes of style a goal as well as a source is one of the major topics of Edward Said's early work; as he has written, "style is *not* the *origin* of a text, but that which the *beginning* of a text intends" (*Beginnings* 254). Here, then, I wish to examine the history of the urbane sublime, the transformation and demise of a form of thought and of writing. For a new style was engendered by the urbane sublime in its very movement toward actualization of its system of norms.

Superficially complex, the change was propelled by a shift in a single value, just as (to borrow Saussure's comparison) a single move alters the relationship of all the pieces on a chessboard. We have seen how in Gray and Collins consciousness begins to be separated from experience. When the separation is completed by the joining of the pure forms of space and of time, consciousness becomes generalized into an abstracted reverie, disembodied and out of touch with the world of sensation. Where the new conception prevails—and I believe that it emerges in a remarkably punctual way—a romantic sensibility can be said to have replaced an empiricist one. This remains to be shown in detail, through a comparative study of the leading writers of the transition. But in anticipation it may be observed that the urbane sublime style was characterized by moderation and restraint and that a complete and unrestrained expression of the style comes perilously close to a violation of its spirit. Even though the prevailing style in Goldsmith's day was still unquestionably that of a generation or two earlier, its basic sociality often seems to have decayed into "some mechanical forms of good breeding" (*The Vicar of Wakefield*, chap. 4, in *Collected Works* 4: 33). The sentimental preromanticism of the last decades of the century is a style in need of a new foundation, and it tends to look increasingly to the individual for a plenitude no longer perceived in the social experience: "Still to ourselves in every place consign'd, / Our own felicity we make or find" (lines 431–32, supplied by Johnson to Goldsmith's *The Traveller, or A Prospect of Society*). The following pages are devoted to analyzing a stylistic impasse and its consequences in William Cowper, the poetical successor of Thomson, and in Kant and Rousseau, respectively the philosophical successor and the personal antagonist of Hume.

The Task 1: The Ground

William Cowper's repeated bouts of insanity haunt his major work without ever being acknowledged within it. In *The Task* consciousness confronts its own dissolution in perhaps the only way it can, subliminally. For how can consciousness know what it has no share in? Surprisingly, it can, but only when dissolution is reconfigured as generalization or as abstraction. That is what happens in *The Task*, perhaps without Cowper's full awareness.

It is striking that Cowper did not lay claim to the inspiration that is conventionally said to be the compensation for a poet's madness. His writing is that of a problem-ridden, moody latecomer.[1] Several of the poem's many self-consciously emblematic self-portraits depict "a poet, or . . . one like me" (6.751) not as a divine Pindaric infant kissed by the bees, but as a derivative collector and mellifluous purveyor of honeys and fruits:

> He travels and expatiates, as the bee
> From flow'r to flow'r, so he from land to land;
> The manners, customs, policy of all
> Pay contribution to the store he gleans;
> He sucks intelligence in ev'ry clime,
> And spreads the honey of his deep research
> At his return—a rich repast for me.
> He travels, and I too.
>
> (4.107–14)[2]

Like the daily newspaper, which is the subject of this passage, *The Task* is indiscriminate in both subject matter and style.[3] Ranging from the palace to the alehouse, veering without transition from satire to meditative description to self-pity, jostling obscure Latinisms against colloquial familiarity ("slumb'ring oscitancy . . . / The nurse no doubt," 2.774−75), the poem is constant in nothing, not even in its praise of inconsistency. Not surprisingly, Cowper's expressed preference is for an undemarcated world, "some boundless contiguity of shade" (2.2), and his favorite season is winter, when a protective mantle of snow falls, "o'erwhelming all distinction" (5.97). This negativity is not without its cost. Far more than Wordsworth in *The Prelude*, Cowper stresses the aimlessness of his "devious course uncertain" (3.3), and at one point asks himself, "Roving as I rove, / Where shall I find an end, or how proceed?" (4.232−33). This poet is no prophet, except in the punning sense authorized by the epigram to the Eton College ode: "I am a man: sufficient excuse for unhappiness."

The poem is congenitally restless. Although book 1, "The Sofa," is devoted in large measure to searches for repose and comfort, and although Cowper continues to the last to cast about for a stable definition of his "task," the demands of universality prove irresistible. Cowper seems to want to draw the ultimate consequences from the relational tendencies of the urbane sublime by demonstrating that absolutely *all* things are related, without exception. This explains the poem's refusal to rest content with any determinate level of style and its repeated indignation at the confidence of word-merchants who sell "accent, tone, / And emphasis in score" (2.359−60). One of Cowper's most characteristic and piquant stylistic devices is the juxtaposition of a learned term with a humbler synonym: "dooms and devotes," "a syncope and solemn pause," "diligence was choice," "slumb'ring oscitancy," "th'agglomerated pile," "he burns with most intense and flagrant zeal," and so forth. The technique derives from Thomson's compensatory reverse decorum, and yet the effect (apart from the burlesque opening of book 1) is much less pointed and urbanely witty. The same can be said of the rare and unobtrusive puns, such as the *contradictio in adjecto* "With all this thrift they thrive not" (4.399). The impression that the poem leaves is not of balanced flux, but of the programmatic juxtaposition of discordant elements.

The Task, in sum, is formless by intent, not by default. It is a farrago or *satura*, whose very randomness, to which Cowper so often calls attention, is calculated to reflect both the homelessness and the universal fellowship of man:

I see that all are wand'rers gone astray
. . .
How then should I and any man that lives
Be strangers to each other?

(3.124, 200–201)

We have no fixed abode or seat, for, as Cowper elsewhere says, "Truth is not local" (*Retirement*, line 119). Our external relations do give us roots that must be cultivated, and Cowper, like his predecessors, terms these relations "social." But he uses the word with a different nuance, reserving it for chance and merely personal connections, and specifically excluding superior ties—of the sort that Gray celebrates—based on nationality, interest, or kinship:

Man in society is like a flow'r
Blown in its native bed; 'tis there alone
His faculties, expanded in full bloom,
Shine out; there only reach their proper use.
But man, associated and leagu'd with man
By regal warrant, or self-join'd by bond
For int'rest sake, or swarming into clans
Beneath one head for purposes of war,
Like flow'rs selected from the rest, and bound
And bundled close to fill some crowded vase,
Fades rapidly, and, by compression marr'd,
Contracts defilement not to be endur'd.

(4.659–70)

Cowper seems to envision man as a displaced vegetable, perpetually ill at ease, for "all hate the rank society of weeds" (3.670), and in search of the perfect paradise garden where all can grow undisturbed and yet in mutual support, free from evil tempters (3.680–81 alludes to Milton's Satan) or false magicians (like "Capability" Brown, 3.766).

The hotbed cucumber, which is the subject of a large set piece in book 3, is an apt emblem of the *satura* (or poetic banquet) and represents the urbane sublime becoming conscious of its own artificiality. Faintly ridiculous in appearance, the "prickly and green-coated gourd" (3.446), hard to the eye and yet soft to the touch, lush in growth and cool to the palate, impatient to spread but only to be propagated with "discreet delay" (3.504), is alternately the most exquisite and the humblest of vegetables: "when rare / So coveted, else base and disesteem'd— / Food for the vulgar merely" (3.447–49). It may seem fanciful to describe the products of the urbane sublime as literary cucumbers, yet this was the very image chosen by Dr. Johnson, the century's greatest apostle of individual integrity, to expose the unnaturalness of the style: "Talking of Gray's Odes, he said, 'They are forced plants, raised in a hot-bed; and they are poor plants; they are but cucumbers after all.'"⁴ Goldsmith, too, who serves Boswell in the biography as the chief foil to Johnson, is described at his introduction as another poor plant, delightfully social, but of no natural substance: "His mind resembled a fertile, but thin soil. There was a quick, but not a strong vegetation, of whatever chanced to be thrown upon it. No deep root could be struck. The oak of the forest did not grow there; but the elegant shrubbery and the fragrant parterre appeared in gay succession" (*Life of Johnson* 1: 412).

In exaggerating the formlessness of the urbane sublime and in testing the limits of its decorums, Cowper thus confronts the reader with a split between nature and culture, which dilemma his predecessors, with their more restricted range, managed to avoid. His anxieties relate directly to the difficulty of integrating a personality under any cultivation too wild or too refined and in any environment more natural or more artificial than the "enclos'd demesne" (1.331) of dignified gentility; that is, they focus, as a letter tells us, on the problem of raising cucumbers.⁵

In its hesitations and its inconsistencies—its preference now for solitude, now for society, now for constancy, now for variety, now for humility, now for greatness, now for the heart, now for the head— *The Task* thus deconstructs and disarticulates the conversational ebb and flow of the urbane sublime.

I have adopted Derridean terminology here because it is exact. Unlike that of his predecessors, Cowper's world is riven by one "fatal diff'rence" (*Hope*, line 282), that between nature and culture, or weed and plant. And, furthermore, no area seems exempt, for the split, repeatedly displaced, seems to traverse the whole of Cowper's experience. It divides bad societies from good:

> 'Tis liberty alone that gives the flow'r
> Of fleeting life its lustre and perfume;
> And we are weeds without it.
> (*Task* 5.446–48)

It divides bad men from good: "But grace abus'd brings forth the foulest deeds, / As richest soil the most luxuriant weeds" (*Expostulation*, lines 213–14). It divides the hand of nature from the hand of man:

> Though nature weigh our talents, and dispense
> To ev'ry man his modicum of sense,

Yet much depends, as in the tiller's toil,
On culture, and the sowing of the soil.
        (*Conversation*, lines 1–6)

But the division between nature and culture, wilderness and garden, or weed and plant, penetrates to the heart of nature itself, so that no realm seems primitive or untouched:

What parts the kindred tribes of weeds and flow'rs?
    . . .
Thus hopes of every sort, . . .
    . . .
If wild in nature, and not duly found,
Gethsemane, in thy dear hallow'd ground,
That cannot bear the blaze of scripture light,
Nor cheer the spirit, nor refresh the sight,
Nor animate the soul to Christian deeds,
(Oh cast them from thee!) are weeds, arrant weeds.
        (*Hope*, lines 289–301)

It is not surprising that "Cowper's favoured oppositions show a repeated tendency to turn on him" (Dawson, "Cowper's Equivocations" 30), for the fatal difference is inscribed by the blaze of scripture at the very center and origin of Christian experience.[6]

Yet despite the ubiquity in his writing of difference and *différance* ("discreet delay"), Cowper departs from the Derridean model. For Derrida meaning is disseminated, that is, imbued with sexuality and propagated by fragmentation and dispersion. Yet Cowper, a bachelor in an age of poetic sterility, is the reverse of a disseminator; content to sit home and peruse the papers, he would not participate in the active dissemination of news, unless it were the one kind of news that always remains pure and unfragmented, the Good News of the Gospels. Meaning for Derrida is always metaphorical; it is a heliotrope following an incandescent sun, the transcendent, imaginary literal meaning that is constantly turning and never approachable. Yet the core of *The Task* is a genuine and literal passion for a plant, the cucumber, which is doubly heliophobic, both by nature (because it flowers in the shade of its own leaves) and by culture (because the greenhouse protects it from the spring sun as well as from the winter frost). Thus, in horticulture the original difference is effaced: "Assistant art / Then acts in nature's office" (3.541–42).

The force of Cowper's style, then, is reconstructive as well as deconstructive. If it undermines the urbane sublime, it does so in order to establish a new synthesis. Cowper's poetry is engaged in a search for a unified origin and stable foundation for experience. The

1781 satires, from which some of my quotations have been drawn, envision a transcendent origin, the God who is the gardener of Gethsemane and who, in His purity, caused the flowers to spring up separately from the weeds. Human experience has, of course, no access to such a purity of origin. But *The Task* goes further; it displaces the divine origin out of its transcendence and into the human realm, as an immanent "god in us." This translation of origins, which took place in the 1780s and grounded what we know as the romantic style of the following decade, served to reestablish the possibility of human experience on a newly stabilized foundation. The intentionality of Cowper's style was directed toward this new, romantic synthesis, and the success of the enterprise of which *The Task* forms a part can be measured by a late utterance by the greatest figure of the transition, Immanuel Kant: "Here now is what Archimedes needed but did not find: a firm point to which reason can affix her lever, without attaching it either to the present or to a future world, but only to her inner idea of freedom" ("Von einem neuerdings erhobenen vornehmen Ton in der Philosophie" A 420).

I do not mean that we should share the arrogant (and actually rather defensive) confidence of the late Kant, as if the romantic style had in fact established an ultimate and unshakable foundation. But if we are to understand the shifting constellations presented by history, we need to acknowledge that there are works and periods of relatively greater coherence and others intervening of relatively greater instability, periods dominated by resolutions and others by problems, periods whose internal divisions are latent and others whose are manifest. Too probing and unsettling an analysis can conceal as much as it reveals. Let us ask, then, with the naive confidence of the historian, what labor Cowper's style performs. What is the intention of the poem? What is the task of *The Task*?

The Task 2: Consciousness

We have seen that the formal disorganization of the poem is a mimetic representation of the problems of mental coherence and personal identity.[7] Cowper is embarked on a search for himself. Consequently the poem's metaphors for intellectual activity are the best indicator of its ambiguous position as continuation and dissolution of the urbane sublime.

In his chapter on "Personal Identity" in the *Treatise of Human Nature* Hume had described the mind as a social fluid, both "a kind of theatre, where several perceptions successively make their appearance; pass, re-pass, glide away, and mingle in an infinite variety of postures and situations" (253), and also "a republic or commonwealth, in which the several members are united by the reciprocal ties of government and subordination, and give rise to other persons, who propagate the same republic in the incessant changes of its parts" (261). Hume is delighted with the variety and the "easy transition of ideas" and derives personal identity "entirely from the smooth and uninterrupted progress of the thought along a train of connected ideas" (260). Cowper echoes these conceptions, but with greater psychological intensity and with a programmatic sense of the fragility of the mind and the uniqueness of its achievement. Only great creators, he says, manage such an integration, and then only at the cost of painful effort; the multitude in the audience remain foolish and dissipated:

> There is a pleasure in poetic pains
> Which only poets know. The shifts and turns,
> Th'expedients and inventions, multiform,
> To which the *mind* resorts, in chase of terms
> Though apt, yet coy, and difficult to win—
> T'arrest the fleeting images that fill
> The mirror of the *mind*, and hold them fast,
> And force them sit till he has pencil'd off
> A faithful likeness of the forms he views;
> Then to dispose his copies with such art,
> That each may find its most propitious light,
> And shine by situation, hardly less
> Than by the labour and the skill it cost;
> Are occupations of the poet's *mind*
> So pleasing, and that steal away the thought
> With such address from themes of sad import,
> That, lost in his own musings, happy man!
> He feels th'anxieties of life, denied
> Their wonted entertainment, all retire.
> Such joys has he that sings. But ah! not such,
> Or seldom such, the hearers of his song.
> (2.285–305, my emphasis)

These lines set a rigorous standard for the governance of the commonwealth of the mind. They continue empiricist views such as those of Hume, but in a way that stretches them to the breaking point. Hume's synthesis of ease and discipline can still be achieved, but whereas it can be achieved easily for Hume, Cowper sees it as a difficult synthesis, requiring its own arduous discipline and costing much anxiety. Nor does Cowper's own poem measure up to the demands of these lines, for no one would claim that *The Task* achieves its most conspicuous success through the confident and orderly arrangement of parts. On the contrary, the composition of the poem seems to accord more nearly with an alternative view, also expounded within it and equally derived from the empiricist tradition. Whereas the lines quoted above see personal identity from the point of view of the unifying mind and emphasize the mind's control over perception, its opposition to the world, and its isolation, the alternative view emphasizes the sociability of the heart, its freedom, spontaneity, and variety. Thus, after beginning the poem's first digression, Cowper says, in a programmatic defense of his inconsistency:

> Thou know'st my praise of nature most sincere,
> And that my raptures are not conjur'd up
> To serve occasions of poetic pomp,
> But genuine, and art partner of them all.
>
> (1.150–53)

Far from advocating artful disposition, Cowper here prides himself precisely on the natural disarrangement of his praise of nature, that is, in Hume's phrases, "the incessant changes of its parts" and not "the reciprocal ties of government and subordination."

When pushed to the limits, the urbane sublime thus decomposes into strictly contradictory principles of identity and coherence. Of Cowper's two versions of empiricism, it is the latter—the spontaneous empiricism of the natural heart—that seems the more true to Hume's easy and cheerful spirit. But it is the former—the disciplined empiricism of the mind—that more accurately continues Hume's ideas. For the urbane sublime neither recognizes a split between head and heart or nature and culture nor sees a need to defend its integrity and sincerity.[8]

Thus Cowper's poem unravels the urbane sublime in the very act of unfolding its implications. Yet the poem remains a search for identity; or perhaps we should say that it becomes a search for identity through the very gestures that make identity problematic. In any case, *The Task* is full of attempts to give definition and structure to the fluid principles of the urbane sublime; Cowper wants his *satura* to clarify the intention of the style.

We have seen that these attempts often contradict one another. But it is yet more remarkable that even taken singly the gestures at definition remain urbanely fluid and imprecise. Society, for instance, is an individual's chance relations with the surrounding world, provided that these relations are not based on prior affinity; in sum, it is an individual's sympathy with his environment, and barely distinguishable from the benevolent sympathy that the solitary individual feels toward animals (6.295–347). "The shifts and turns / Th'expedients and inventions" of art are painful labors that "arrest the fleeting images" and lead to "musings" and "pleasing" self-forgetfulness, but such artifice differs little from its apparent opposite, the sincerity of "raptures . . . not conjur'd up," for these latter, purportedly spontaneous effusions turn out to result from what to others would seem "long toil" (1.128) and from a contemplative posture that dwells on carefully selected, pleasing scenes. The more carefully the terms are examined, the more they seem to vanish and melt into one another. Although Cowper appears to demarcate his poem into distinct paragraph-long scenes and his experience into emblematically distinct mental states, in fact the paragraphs ramble into one another with accumulative (rather than contrastive) links, and the mental states constantly shift and fuse.

An even more portentous example of Cowper's shiftiness is his version of the theme of Thomson's *Liberty*, bounded freedom:

> We love
> The king who loves the law, respects his bounds,
> And reigns content within them: him we serve
> Freely and with delight, who leaves us free:
> But recollecting still that he is man,
> We trust him not too far.
>
> (5.331–36)

Despite superficial similarities, this is quite different from Thomson's respect for proper place and ancient authority. Cowper's true king is a puppet of the law. His job is to enforce one-sided boundaries: to restrict interference with individuals while not restricting their freedoms. Yet his own status is different, for his actions are bounded and not free. Insofar as he is a man, he is to be distrusted; he should not aspire to the conspicuous eminence of "paltry pageant" (5.348). Ideally, he should be something less than a man, a mere servant, perhaps a mere ornament to the nation: "He is our's, / T'administer, to guard, t'adorn the state" (5.341–42). It is evident that the very best king would be nothing more than the law itself, an invisible, imperceptible boundary line around each individual. Such a king, in fact, we have inside us, if we will only acknowledge it; it is the "moral sense," that "STILL SMALL VOICE" that commands obe-

dience from a man in order that it may "set him free" (5.670–87).
The name that Cowper gives the best king, at this point, is "conscience" (5.666).

The notion of an invisible boundary immediately clarifies the
function of all those nebulous demarcations—emblematic figures as
well as psychological categories—that haunt Cowper's poem (rather
as personified abstractions haunt the poetry of his predecessors): the
aim is to define but not to delimit the self. While he wants to be
fenced off from vice (3.75–76, 679–83), Cowper resents all other
rigid barriers, such as mountains and brick walls (2.17–19; 4.770–
73), and he is enamored of borders that can be crossed with ease: the
low stile, the unbarred gate, the unguarded door (1.136, 330–33;
4.559). Another such invisible boundary and silent discipline is the
blank verse of the poem, a much more demanding meter than the
"artful" and sociable "chime" of the couplet (6.1020–22; cf. *Retirement*, lines 567–68) because, as the preface to Cowper's blank verse
translation of Homer tells us, it requires of its practitioner much
greater variety and freedom of handling. Of a different order entirely,
though its custodian has much in common with both the artist and
the king, is the greatest of all the invisible boundaries, the one belonging to that triune God called nature, time, or causality:

> He sets the bright procession on its way,
> And marshals all the order of the year;
> He marks the bounds which winter may not pass,
> And blunts his pointed fury; in its case,
> Russet and rude, folds up the tender germ,
> Uninjur'd, with inimitable art;
> And, ere one flow'ry season fades and dies,
> Designs the blooming wonders of the next.
> . . .
> Nature is but a name for an effect,
> Whose cause is God.
>
> (6.190–97, 223–24)

Cowper's fundamental, though unexpressed, "silent, task" (3.378) is
the restless pursuit of an impalpable form of self-cultivation that
will differ from the social conventions of his day in not constraining
the "root sincere" ("Yardley Oak," line 116) of his natural existence.

There is yet one more term for this impalpable form of selfhood,
a term of special interest to the historian concerned with the intentionality of ideas because the conception to which it refers was embryonic in Cowper's day. In one of his most romantic passages, the
source for Coleridge's "Frost at Midnight," Cowper writes:

> I am conscious, and confess,
> Fearless, a soul that does not always think
> . . .
> I gaz'd, myself creating what I saw.
>   (4.284–85, 290)[9]

It is consciousness that the romantics will make into the invisible boundary of the self, the intangible dividing line between being and nonbeing, the form of all that is and also the ground of freedom. Cowper's epochal innovation in these lines does not lie in the recognition that the mind helps to create what it perceives, but rather in the divorce of consciousness from attention. Cowper's grammar is indefinite—in itself an indication of the exploratory character of the lines—but the most natural reading would attribute to them perhaps the earliest absolute use of "conscious" as an unmodified predicate in the English language.[10] For the first time in English, so far as I can discern, consciousness becomes autonomous, independent of the world in which the conscious being lives.[11] Even if we read the lines, less plausibly, as containing a bold, elliptical zeugma—"I am conscious [of], and confess [to possessing], / . . . a soul that does not always think"—they still express the conception that consciousness is a minimal state of intellectual existence, a "waking dream," "indolent vacuity of thought" (4.287, 297).[12]

The whole poem, in fact, is such a waking dream, a long string of loosely connected, flickering images, fancy's "brittle toys" (4.307). It is Cowper's projection not of the rational mind, aware and in control of the forms it is creating, but of the subrational, "thoughtful or unthinking mind, / The mind contemplative, with some new theme / Pregnant, or indispos'd alike to all" (4.279–81). In its entirety the poem is "an emblem of myself" (1.213), composed of many small emblems.[13] Each such emblem reflects Cowper's desire to objectify the self by discovering the very structure of consciousness, that invisible portal through which one enters into the possibility of knowledge and of free actions.[14]

This desire remains unexecuted in *The Task*. Because he preceded the Kantian revolution (or because he lacked Kant's genius), Cowper's poem only sets forth, though with impressive consistency, the preconditions for the dialectical theory of consciousness and for the romantic-meditative style. For this reason, *The Task* appears rather as the continuation and fulfillment of an old tradition than as the foundation of a new one. Or, better still, it appears as the parodistic disintegration of a moderate style pushed to extremes. The startling juxtapositions, the sudden transitions and surprising transformations, the rhythmic flexibility, the formal diffuseness of the urbane sublime are all present, but without the continuities of imagery and theme that unify earlier works. What Cowper lacks, and what he prays for, in a notable imitation of Collins's "Ode to Evening" (as if he were praying to his predecessor in madness rather than to nature) is "composure" (4.260).[15] In various passages the key concepts of the urbane sublime appear and then "go out in fume" (3.172): society, authority, and even consciousness itself. Divested of contingent factors, consciousness is no longer the awareness of relative and comparative difference, but rather the exemplary intuition of absolute difference, and in particular the intuition of the self in its radical difference from the world. Consciousness was destined to be the name for that conception of personal identity, that pure self-presence, which the urbane sublime exhausted itself in discovering. If we can say that the didactic purpose of the style was to make us conscious, then we can say with equal justice that its hidden, historical intention was to ground personal identity through becoming conscious of consciousness itself.

Kant with Rousseau

It was Kant who performed the philosophical reckoning with the urbane sublime.[16] His early essay *Träume eines Geistersehers* (Dreams of a Ghost-Seer) opens with two chapters that summarize the main ideas associated with the style: the spiritual (or intellectual) world and the material world live in uninterrupted communion with one another; the spiritual world is a universal society, with no fixed boundaries; it is an intermediate realm, higher than the material world but lower than the universal spirit (or God); death is not a rupture but a "natural continuation" (A 46) of our spiritual life and an unveiling of our moral essence; poets use symbols and personifications in order to make us conscious of the spiritual and moral world, and furthermore some specifically gifted individuals can perhaps see spirits directly. Near the end of the second chapter, however, the perspective shifts abruptly, and the seemingly sympathetic synopsis gives place to criticism. There is no way, we are now told, to distinguish true spirits from imaginary phantasms; daydreamers at least know that their daydreams do not have external existence in the material world, whereas ghost-seers attribute external reality to their visions. But spirits are by definition incapable of assuming an external, material existence; therefore we can have no knowledge of them: "The philosophical doctrine of spiritual beings . . . determines with certainty the limits of our insight, and persuades us that the various appearances of *life* in nature and their laws are all that it is granted to us to know, but that the principle of this life, that is, spiritual nature, which we do not know but presume, can never be positively conceived" (A 79–80).[17] Kant thus draws the same fundamental consequence from the urbane sublime as Cowper: he reinterprets the spirits as an invisible boundary of existence.

From the insight of this essay, that the intellectual world is the negative limit of awareness about which nothing can be known positively, Kant was to develop the concept of a "regulative ideal," which plays a leading role in his three critiques. And to this invisible boundary the *Critique of Pure Reason*—the masterpiece that both completes (purifies) and overturns (criticizes) the Age of Reason— adds a second intangible, the invisible threshold called consciousness. Since raw sense data are confused, Kant looks to consciousness to provide an involuntary organization—logically prior to attention and to the will—and thus to guarantee, with no loss of freedom, the transcendental unity of apperception. The greatness of the first edition of the *Critique of Pure Reason*—what makes Kant and not Cowper the initiator of a new era—was that it dared to analyze the mechanisms of liminal consciousness and thereby opened whole new possibilities of form and of expression.

Yet Kant's own form and expression remain strangely, almost grotesquely, rooted in the eighteenth century. While the major works of his immediate successors, Fichte, Schelling, and Hegel, are dramatic voyages of discovery, full of peripeties and sudden recognitions, Kant chose the sober and stately form of the treatise. Indeed he exaggerated the sobriety of the form with his insistence on rigid architectonic symmetry. There is nothing intrinsically remarkable in this, but it becomes remarkable when combined with Kant's willful neglect of form, clarity, and even grammar in the construction of his sentences. In the critiques the organizational paradoxes of eighteenth-century poetry return, but in reverse; the three critiques have great intensity as a whole, but are verbally diffuse and enervating at every point.

Most of what can be said about Kant's obstinate neglect of stylistic grace has been brilliantly set forth by Jean-Luc Nancy and need not be repeated here.[18] But Nancy does not discuss the one specifically documentable choice that Kant troubled himself to make, the choice to clothe his revolutionary ideas "in a dead and learned language."[19] The logic behind this preference for obscure, obsolete, or newly coined Latinisms is doubtful: a note in the *Critique of Judg-*

ment defends learned languages on account of their invariability, whereas the *Critique of Pure Reason* defends them, in spite of their variability, because they can be so economically adapted to the requirements of special contexts. But whatever the logic, there is no difficulty in identifying the stylistic affinities of his precept: Kant revives dead language for essentially the same reason that Thomson and Gray revive dead metaphors. One need only observe the terminological welter—with its "idea" and "ideal," its "transcendent" and "transcendental," its "axioms," "anticipations," "analogies," and "postulates," its "syntheses" of "apperception," "reproduction," and "recognition" (none of these is an ordinary German word), its "amphibole," "paralogisms," and "antinomies," not to speak of its "dialele" or "dialexis" (the text is uncertain), its "subreption of hypostasized consciousness," and its "euthanasia of pure reason"—one need only pass these terms in review to recognize an eighteenth-century trait gone mad. Such extravagances differ from the personified abstractions of the urbane sublime in that they reify states of consciousness rather than emotions and moral sentiments, but their function is comparable: on the one hand they make a hearty public appeal to a coherent social group bound together by a common schooling, while on the other hand they are meant to elicit a high-level, consciously reflective response.[20] In the *Critique of Pure Reason* Kant explains his extraordinary linguistic revivals as the only alternative to the "arrogance of legislating in languages," which is "a desperate measure" that "rarely succeeds." As a stylist, Kant is at worst an aristocrat, whereas the innovative individualist would be a dangerous autocrat.

Yet as a philosopher Kant *is* an autocrat, not an aristocrat. The often confessed slovenliness and viciousness of the style contrast peculiarly with the heavy emphasis that the moral philosophy places on individual responsibility. And the refusal to allow the individual to legislate in language must always seem idiosyncratic in the philosopher who discovered that experience is only possible if the individual is the legislator of his world: "The understanding . . . is itself the legislation for nature, i.e., without understanding there would nowhere be nature" (*Critique of Pure Reason* A 126–27). But were these contradictions not historically motivated? For I have argued that the intention of eighteenth-century style was to become conscious of consciousness (or to invent man, if I may be allowed to borrow Foucault's terminology without accepting his philosophy of history in toto). But the exploration of consciousness was only possible after the abolition of a style with a social rather than an individual basis. Poised as ever between epochs, Kant represents an intermediate stage, when the intention had been fulfilled and the task of investigating consciousness finally articulated, but before the investigation was brought to the point where the individual was emancipated to legislate his own style. At this stage, in the work of Cowper as well as that of Kant, the social, or urbane sublime style still prevails, but as a parody of itself, self-baffled and in quest of a renovation from outside.[21]

Rousseau is the other great writer of the transition. Kant's verbal style, with its abolition of social constraint and emancipation of the individual, can be described in terms that seem to be drawn directly from Rousseau's politics. And indeed the structure of Rousseau's *volonté générale* corresponds closely to that of the generalized consciousness which Kant posited without ever addressing the problem of other minds: an unexplained uniformity among men becomes the basis for a radical individualism in which, however, the individual's actions remain bound by laws to which he has always already subscribed, either freely (Rousseau) or spontaneously (Kant). Rousseau serves as a linking figure between Cowper, with his insecurities, and Kant, with his posture of inflexible moralism, and telling similarities can be traced in detail as well as in the general situation.[22] I do not wish to undertake a full-scale analysis here, particularly since the picture is further complicated by the multiple meanings of the French word "conscience." Only a few observations will be necessary to complement my previous discussions.

As early as the "Profession de foi du vicaire savoyard" in book 4 of *Emile* (1762), Rousseau aligns "conscience" with feeling ("sentiment") and situates it prior to the reasoning powers. This correction of the traditional priority is comparable to that which we have seen in the later texts of Cowper and Kant. The passage is often quoted, but is worth reconsideration:

> We feel before we know [*avant de conoitre*], and since we do not learn to wish our good and flee our ill, but hold this desire from nature, so the love of good and hatred of bad are as natural as the love of ourselves. The acts of *conscience* are not judgments, but feelings; although all our ideas come to us from outside, the feelings that appreciate them are within us, and it is by them alone that we know [*connoissons*] the appropriateness or lack thereof that exists between us and the things we should seek or flee. (*Oeuvres* 4: 599)

As the editors say, in an unhelpful note, "the interplay of our ideas and our feelings is complex" (4: 1559). It is clear, at any rate, that

Rousseau's *conscience* encompasses more than just moral sentiments; it engenders knowledge as well as feeling. Its acts give us,
to be sure, a knowledge prior to knowledge, but also a sentiment
prior to "ideas from outside," that is, prior to sensation. And it evidently produces both emotional certainties and utilitarian intellectual discriminations. It would not be outrageous to suggest that *conscience* here prefigures the pure undifferentiated sense of self of the
romantics.

Yet the passage is perplexed. And the difficulties are compounded
by another, rarely quoted, from the end of book 3, which directly
contradicts the Vicar's opinions: "The *conscience* of each sensation
is a proposition, a judgment. Therefore so soon as you compare one
sensation to another you are reasoning. The art of judgment and the
art of reasoning are exactly the same" (4: 486). Careful reading of the
context shows that precisely the same kind of *conscience* is at issue
here as in the "Profession de foi": it involves "virtue," that is, moral
as well as intellectual truths (4: 500), and it precedes the influx of
"ideas" from outside (4: 499). The contradiction—one passage asserting, the other denying that *conscience* is a judgment—should
not be interpreted as a sign that one text speaks for Rousseau while
the other does not. Rather it shows the genuinely problematic status
of consciousness at this stage in history, while by their mutual ex-
clusions these passages hint at the nature of that consciousness
which was to be discovered, neither judgment nor sentiment, neither knowledge nor feeling.

Rousseau himself did not describe this pure state of consciousness until the famous passages in the *Confessions* and the *Rêveries
du promeneur solitaire*, late works first published in the pivotal decade, the 1780s. Since these passages do not speak of *conscience de
soi*, but rather, insistently, of a blissful "feeling," they have generally
been misinterpreted.[23] But the divergence among Rousseau's critics,
like the contradictions in *Emile*, can direct us toward the proper
synthesis. The dominant view treats Rousseau's self-consciousness
as an emotionalized version of the Cartesian cogito: "It is the consciousness of something other than thought, and this consciousness,
immediate and evident, is itself an affective and not an intellectual
act, that of *feeling one's existence, one's self*" (Baczko, *Rousseau*
214). It is easy, following in this line, to overlook the transcendental
activity of feeling and to treat it as posterior awareness of a preexisting selfhood. Thus Rousseau's contemporary, Marmontel, writes,
"Memory has distractions, empty intervals. The inward sense [*le
sens intime*] has none. When we forget the past, we are, as it were,

detached from the present, whereas the continuity of the feeling of existence *testifies* at each instant to the individuality and the successive identity of the sensible, thinking being."[24] Yet Pierre Burgelin, again beginning from Descartes, has argued forcefully that the subjective emotion attached to self-consciousness in Rousseau is only his pleasure at witnessing the result, while the work actually performed is of an objective and cognitive nature, in which "présence à soi" is joined by "présence au monde."[25] In this view *conscience* and its concomitant bliss are the form not of selfhood but of being-in-the-world. In actuality, the tendency of Rousseau's ontology was more radical than either of these views, more revolutionary perhaps than could be adequately expressed in the French of his day. It led, as Marcel Raymond has well written with respect to the revery on Lake Bienne, to the discovery of a state "beyond not only all thought . . . , but almost beyond all affectivity."[26] Like Cowper's "indolent vacuity of thought" (*The Task* 4.297), it is not only pre-cognitive, but pre-emotive as well. It is a kind of pure, uncathected libido.

Romantic self-consciousness gives rise to thoughts and feeling, jointly and coevally.[27] Thus it is that the identical ontological structure can appear as a moral universal (*volonté générale*) in Rousseau and as an epistemological universal (*allgemeines Bewußtsein*) in Kant. And thus it is, more generally, that the texts of Kant and Rousseau shed light on one another and on their common historical enterprise. The architectonic assurance of Kant shows us the success and stability—a relative, not an absolute, stability—of the discovery toward which Rousseau and Cowper were anxiously groping. And conversely, the anxieties of these authors reveal a rift hidden in the substructure of Kant's system that opened a space for further historical movement and renewal. In the last analysis, his Archimedean "last of the last" is an illicit, metaphysical auto-affection; with a backward glance at the hated *Confessions*, Herder maliciously called it "the onanism of pure-impure reason," a brilliant jibe whose force lives on in the neo-Freudian metacritiques of Adorno and Derrida.[28] The marriage of Kant and Rousseau, it might be said, is a happy one for Rousseau, but an unhappy one for Kant.

The Task 3: Revolution

The convergence of Cowper and of Rousseau with the rudiments of Kantianism illustrates the need to subsume both the history of ideas and the history of poetry under a general history of consciousness.

Treated in isolation, even in the distinguished work of Josephine Miles, the history of poetry threatens to subside into a mere register of shifting feeling states and modes of ornamentation. And the history of philosophy is liable to succumb to the weak teleological temptation that sees each thinker as falling into a hole from which his successor rescues him as thought moves ever closer to the plenitude of truth. This is the style of historiography that writes as follows (I quote here an evident lapse in a sensitive and discriminating book): "The deepest root of Hume's scepticism, I have argued, lies in his want of a theory of the person, and similarly, the heart of Kant's answer to him lies, not so much in the specific arguments on cause, as in his demonstration that the existence of mind as agent is presupposed in the very analysis of experience itself" (Grene, *Knower* 141).

The progress of ideas and theories alone cannot account for historical movements. Kant did not in fact correct or refute Hume in any definitive sense, any more than Cowper corrected or refuted Thomson (his principal "source") or Rousseau Montaigne, or else we should no longer read Hume and should prefer Cowper to Thomson and likewise Thomson to Milton. Rather, Kant and Cowper differed from their predecessors in the more fundamental way that I have interchangeably called an alteration in their style or in their basic presuppositions: a new importance attributed to identity, formal unity, and sincerity, a greater earnestness of spirit, and, what appears to be basic, a changed view of the nature and role of consciousness. Hume and Kant are valuable not because of ideas whose "truth" and conceptions whose "validity" can never ultimately be established, but rather because their works offer a rational codification and, so to speak, a discursive reenactment of the spirit of the age. To be sure, avenues of thought were open to Kant to which Hume was blind. But conversely, Hume's thought follows roads equally inaccessible to Kant. The difference between the earlier and the later writer is not that between negative and positive, absence and presence, but rather that between one positivity and another. "The deepest root of [Hume's] sceptical system"—here I quote the same historian on a different page—was not that Hume lacked what Kant later found, but rather that Hume possessed a quality for which Kant later substituted others: "this benignity of his forms the deepest root of his sceptical system" (Grene, *Knower* 105).

But if intellectual developments must be understood in terms of stylistic change, how is stylistic change to be explained? Little would be gained in explanatory power if the historian merely replaced the description of a fairly evident change in visible facts with the description of a concealed change in buried presuppositions. Yet I have in effect taken the characteristic development from Thomson to Cowper and from Hume to Kant for granted as one part of my definition of the urbane sublime. To assert, as I have done, that the historical intention of the style was to become conscious of consciousness does not clarify why this was so. Might not some other intention have been equally compatible with the midcentury urbane sublime? Can any mechanism account for the evolution of the style?

In order to suggest an answer to these questions, it is necessary to return to the texts. What must remain striking, in spite of my attempt to discriminate between the two, is the overlap between the author's intention and the work's project, between making the reader conscious and discovering consciousness. This overlap is not coincidental. As a goal, consciousness became an object of concern. But then it could no longer be an unreflected, self-evident quality. In the course of time the urbane sublime thematized consciousness and thereby turned it into a problem. Thus, a central issue in Cowper's *Olney Hymns* (written in the early 1770s) is not becoming conscious, but becoming conscious enough:

> I hear, but seem to hear in vain,
>   Insensible as steel;
> If ought is felt, 'tis only pain,
>   To find I cannot feel.
>
>   (9.5−8)

Feeling (or consciousness) has a paradoxical quality here; it seeks to achieve intensity through overcoming resistance, and it creates the necessary resistance by turning against itself. Hence in these poems the heightening of attention, with the relativistic gradualism that this implies in the eighteenth century, appears to be the result of hesitation, opposition, and violent conversion:

> My best desires are faint and few,
>   I fain would strive for more;
>   . . .
> Oh make this heart rejoice, or ache;
>   Decide this doubt for me;
> And if it be not broken, break,
>   And heal it, if it be.
>
>   (9.13−14, 21−24)

And then, suddenly, with the "discovery of consciousness," in *The Task* as in the *Rêveries*, the feeling of not feeling is found to be not a pathological state but an unveiling of selfhood.

Through such means didactic intention comes to determine historical project. The assertion of intention leads to "doubt" about the present situation (to use the term of the hymn just quoted) and consequently to exploration. Yet the distance between intention and project must again be stressed, for it is only their separation that opens a space for historical forces to operate and that accounts for the chronological spread. Intention posits a quality as a self-evident goal, an objective to be aimed at; project treats the quality as a subject of meditation and as a problematic starting point. More simply, historical projects take ends and strive to convert them into beginnings. The conversions portrayed in the *Olney Hymns* are not just personal and psychological experience, but also emblems of the historical process. In the same fashion, the discontinuities of stylistic change are also reflected in the contradictions to which I have previously pointed—the equivalence of personal identity and chaotic disorganization in *The Task* and the combination of discipline and arbitrary willfulness in Kant's style.

However much authorial intention and textual project may resemble one another, they remain antithetical; the one deals with ends taken as self-evident and natural, while the other reflects on troubled beginnings. There can no more be a smooth transition from the "natural" to the reflective or "cultural" view of consciousness than from nature to culture in any other respect; rather there must be an appearance of sudden reversal and radical infidelity. After all, it is not only South American Indians who attribute the power to bridge the gap between nature and culture to a deceiving, trickster god (see note 4 in this chapter); the Western tradition too has its Mercury, patron of thieves, who, as Horace tells us, gave man language and thereby cured his "wildness."[29] In the *Dreams of a Ghost-Seer* Kant adopts the role of Mercury, psychagogue and hermeneut, so as to carry out a similar, educative intent: "I deceived my reader in order to benefit him" (see n. 17 in this chapter). And it is worth remembering that Rousseau's *Confessions*, though it opens with a ringing denunciation of the artifices of past ages and an appeal for a new standard of truth and sincerity, nevertheless remains one of the most devious books ever written, not only repeatedly pitting the author against himself in bitter self-accusation, but also misleading the readers in order to guide them toward a new order of experience. As Jean Starobinski says, "in deforming his image he reveals a more essential reality, which is the look he casts on himself, the impossibility he is in of grasping himself in any other way than through deforming himself."[30]

What of Cowper? Does *The Task* also reflect the infidelity and deceit of the historical process? It does so, I think, by presenting an objectified, "alienated," third-person description as the most revealing self-portrait in the poem. The alienation that divides the author who initiates the description from the cucumber that he describes as the end product of his labor corresponds to the divorce between consciousness as beginning and as end, or between project and intention. It is true that Cowper insists on the close correspondence between the gardener and the hothouse garden that is "the creature of a polish'd mind" and "attest[s] his bright design" (3.640, 654). But even if garden and gardener are luminous reflections of one another, and even if another passage (3.596–605) makes the garden an actor in the theater of the gardener's mind—or is it the gardener who, as Roscius and Garrick, acts in the theater of the garden's mind?—even so, the dialectic of correspondence and reflections is too intricate for any easy historical or epistemological model to apply. Simple causality in the botanical realm does not yield significant reflections, but only meaningless disorder, "the rank society of weeds" (3.670). But the process by which a producer produces a product that resembles him is not straightforward or natural; it requires a "magic summons of th' Orphean lyre" (3.587).

The hothouse has its Spectre, or antithetical complement, in the magnificent ice garden of book 5, which resumes the play of reflections—as well as all the other imagery in the earlier passage concerning nature and culture, wet and dry, and so forth—and reaffirms the deceitfulness of temporality.[31] This too is a magic garden with "shrubs of fairy land" (5.113), and one that is more clearly fraudulent than the hothouse:

> 'Twas transient in its nature, as in show
> 'Twas durable: as worthless, as it seem'd
> Intrinsically precious; to the foot
> Treach'rous and false; it smil'd, and it was cold.
> (5.173–76)

Even in the company of Kant and Rousseau the whole passage would repay careful study for the commentary it offers on causality, correspondence, and process, but I will pause to consider only one strand. The ice garden, Cowper suggests, is the product of a divine craftsman:

> Thus nature works as if to mock at art,
> . . .
> Performing such inimitable feats
> As she with all her rules can never reach.
> (5.122–26)

But the art with which nature here strives, building grottoes and ruined turrets overgrown with "trees / And shrubs" (5.112–13) is that of the English gardener. Both mockup and mockery, the ice garden is thus an ambivalent reflection of an activity whose "rival pow'rs" (5.123) in their turn imitate those of nature. (This mutual imitation contrasts with the "less worthy," more highly artificial Russian ice palace of lines 127–70.) And yet the nature which the English gardener imitates is not wild and weedy nature, but tame "nature in her cultivated trim" (3.357), a nature, that is, which imitates art.

Wer ist der Jäger, wer das Wild? Nature imitates art imitates nature imitates art. Infinite and ineluctable are the reflections of this self-contradictory, troubled and difficult period: "Mirror needed none / Where all was vitreous" (5.160–61). In this mockery of process, there is nothing genuinely firm, no fixed starting-point; "The same lubricity was found in all" (5.165). Let us concede that all of human experience is marked by textuality, difference, displacement, and the like. Nevertheless, this conditioning is more apparent and more troublesome at certain periods than at others. The 1780s, a decade of revolution in literature and philosophy as in politics, was such a troubled era, a time of graphic disturbance, lodged between what should be recognized as relatively confident periods, comparatively articulate and vocal. Or, in Harold Bloom's cabbalistic terms, we may call it a period of breaking, characterized by "too strong a force of *writing*," when "an original pattern yielded to a more chaotic one that nevertheless remained pattern" (*Kabbalah* 40–41), lying between the ironic style of the eighteenth century (a style of limitation) and the restitution of representation (or self-presence) in the early romantics.

Throughout this chapter I have drawn on terms from recently prominent thinkers like Derrida, Foucault, and Bloom. They are invaluable models because of the originality and precision of their methods of analysis. Yet the respect for historical specificity of the first and the respect for the dynamic logic of history shared, I think, by the latter two reflect long-established values in our culture. Part of my purpose in this book is to update traditional critical procedures; part, equally, is to work toward a reconciliation of new methods with the intellectual traditions from which they have sprung. In the spirit of such a reconciliation I shall conclude this chapter by quoting the century-old judgment of Cowper by one of the greatest and most unjustly maligned historians of our literature:

New theories could not arise in this society armed against new theories. Yet the revolution made its entrance; it entered disguised, and through a by-way, so as not to be recognized. It was not social ideas, as in France, that were transformed, nor philosophical ideas, as in Germany, but literary ideas; the great rising tide of the modern mind, which elsewhere overturned the whole edifice of human conditions and speculations, succeeded here at first only in changing style and taste. It was a slight change, at least apparently, but on the whole of equal value with the others; for this renovation in the manner of writing is a renovation in the manner of thinking: the one led to all the rest, as the movement of a central pivot constrains the movement of all the indented wheels. (Taine, *History* 2: 307–8)

CHAPTER FIVE

The Economy of Sensibility

> O, Julie, que c'est un fatal présent du ciel qu'une âme sensible! . . . Il m'en
> a trop coûté d'être sensible.
>
> Rousseau, *Julie, ou La Nouvelle Héloïse*, letter 26

Sensibility and Farce

We sometimes call the second half of the eighteenth century the Age
of Sensibility. Sensibility is commonly understood as the cult of
feeling, whose tradition of sentimental morality can be traced back
at least to Shaftesbury and ahead to the romantics.[1] In the most characteristic works of the 1760s and 1770s feeling is not productive but
reactive in character; sentiment compensates for the deficiencies of
sensation. It is less often the reasons of the heart than the heart's
evanescent impulses—the systole of irritability and the diastole of
sympathy—when reason has been silenced. Yet this age when feelings were paramount was also a time when their expression became
increasingly problematic. Intense feelings for nature and humanity
were accompanied by the intense anxieties about the integrity of the
self that can be discerned in the madness or near madness or concern
with madness or in the feelings of incapacity and sterility that beset
so many of the leading authors in England and on the Continent.
What is the link between sensibility and the stylistic rupture that
has been illustrated from *The Task*?

"We are astonished by thought; but sensation [*sentiment*] is just
as marvelous," writes Voltaire in his *Dictionnaire philosophique*
(s.v. "Sensation," *Oeuvres* 58: 150). Already in Locke the place of
sensation is exceptionally problematic. It is an internal operation of
the mind that is already functioning while the mind is still a blank
sheet with nothing in it. Operations of the mind are one of the two

"Fountains of Knowledge," yet unlike the other, objects, they remain unknown for part or all of our lives: "Like floating Visions, they make not deep Impressions enough, to leave in the Mind clear distinct lasting *Ideas*" (*Essay* 2.1.2, 8; pp. 104, 107). In Locke this paradox of mental operations is part of an extended and complicated dialectic of feeling and thought, primariness and secondariness, qualities and abstractions, authority and free will, time and space, propriety and property. By the latter half of the eighteenth century, however, many thinkers singled out sensibility as the original and chief issue. "We always perceive despite ourselves, and never because we wish it," writes Voltaire; "it is impossible for us not to have the sensation that nature destines for us, when the object strikes us" (*Oeuvres* 58: 150). And this means we are inundated by a sea of perceptions, adrift in an infinitely large and hence sublime and terrible world. If everything in my mind comes from outside, then what, if anything, am I? What is the extent, what are the limits of my being?

The drastic character of most of the best writing of these decades is, I believe, an expression not of power but of debility. Sensibility almost seems to entail a kind of inverse solipsism, a belief that everything is real except oneself. Johnson's Herculean efforts to restore the integrity of Shakespeare's texts and of the English language emblematize the perils of sensibility: universal sympathy threatens the meaningful coherence of experience, yet the only possible remedy seems to be further atomization of feeling and meaning, into annotations or lexical entries. Hence the endless labors of distraction in which Johnson discomposed himself for the benefit of his readers' composure. The melancholy expressed in his prefaces is diagnosed in advance by an earlier encyclopedic spirit, Robert Burton's Democritus Junior: "When you see a fellow careful about his words, and neat in his speech, know this for a certainty, that man's mind is busied about toys, there's no solidity in him" (*Anatomy* 1: 32). As in Burton, so throughout these decades excess of matter (both spiritual and physical) points to a "void in the heart."[2] Johnson's very appearance—overstuffed and immobile—indeed also seems emblematic. By etymological association it evokes what can well come to seem the prevailing cast of this frantic yet sterile period—not melancholy nor tragedy, but farce. Once we see this connection—also anticipated by Burton—between the emptiness of melancholy or sentimental melodrama and the emptiness of farce, we can begin to understand why farces are so prominent among the enduring literary publications of these turbulent decades, including the theatrical works of Goldsmith, Sheridan, and Beaumarchais, such farcelike novels as *Humphry Clinker* and *Tristram Shandy*, the frivolous *Castle of Otranto*, the frivolous historical spectacle of *The Decline and Fall of the Roman Empire*, and then, in the 1780s, Cowper's "satirical banquet," *The Task*.[3]

Farce is by definition both full and empty: stuffed with matter and devoid of meaning, all composition and no communication.[4] It is striking how many works of this period that are not comic by design have nevertheless come to seem unintentionally comic, stumbling over their own ponderousness. Almost inevitably, the windy rhetoric of *Ossian* sounds like flatulence: "Oozy daughter of streams, that now art reared on high, speak to the feeble, O stone! after Selma's race have failed! Prone, from the stormy night, the traveller shall lay him, by thy side: thy whistling moss shall sound in his dreams. . . . He shall burst, with morning, from dreams" ("Colna-Dona," in Macpherson, *The Poems of Ossian* 1: 289). Northrop Frye, to be sure, has interpreted such overblown writing in a more benign fashion, yet even from a near-contemporary we can document the more farcical, scatological reaction:

> Klopstock felt the intripled turn
> And all his bowels began to churn
> And his bowels turned round three times three
> And lockd in his soul with a ninefold key
> That from his body it neer could be parted
> Till to the last trumpet it was farted.[5]

Diderot and Stolberg

Perhaps the most drastic—and hence most revealing—essay on sensibility was Diderot's dialogue *Le Rêve de d'Alembert*, written in the late 1760s, though not published until 1830. Diderot's premise is the empiricist theory of personal identity, which he satirizes by literalizing it. From the moment that Locke had defined personal identity as a function of consciousness rather than as a substance in its own right, the limits of the person had become a matter for doubt.[6] And the doubt deepened as the philosophy of the succeeding century resolved consciousness into its source in sensation. Locke had said that the identity of persons consists in the unity of their memory, and therefore that Socrates might be a different person when asleep and when awake. Diderot responds by presenting in the main portion of his "dream" a sleep-talking d'Alembert who spouts Pyrrhonist doctrines such as "There is nothing precise in nature" (*Oeuvres philosophiques* 311), which are diametrically opposed to the scien-

tific materialism defended by the waking d'Alembert in the introduction ("Entretien entre d'Alembert et Diderot"). Likewise, Diderot
satirizes the Great Chain of Being by literalizing it as a continuum.
If, as the old precept goes, there are no gaps in nature (*natura non
facit saltus*), then ultimately all distinctions are leveled. In particular, as d'Alembert says to Diderot in the very first speech of the
work, suppose you reject the notion of a soul (which is admittedly a
"contradictory" one); in that case, if "this sensibility that you substitute for it . . . is a general and essential quality of matter, then a
stone must think" (257–58). And Diderot assents to d'Alembert's
proposition that there is little difference "between a man and a
statue, between marble and flesh" (259).[7] Thus Diderot forces the
question of sensibility by driving Enlightenment doctrines to their
limit. The ensuing dialogue makes a merry farce, replete with scatological aposiopesis that anticipates *Tristram Shandy* and *Jacques le
fataliste*, but also a serious one that infuriated d'Alembert himself.
It shows the self to be permeable; spatial limits dissolve, and temporal experience is fragmented.

Yet something even less tangible than feeling remains in reserve
to manifest an irresistible power in this Protean self of sensibility.
The result is to explode the sensible self from within. For what is it
that feels and thinks? Is it for instance some particular organ within
us such as Descartes's pineal gland? If so, the dialogue argues, then
this *sensorium commune* or (in traditional jargon) this soul may be
compared to a spider in the middle of its web. Without such a unifying center of our experience, we should be nothing but a reticulation
of nerves and bones, a conglomerate of animalcules. But positing a
point at the center does little to alleviate the problem; it merely
shifts the question from one of unity to one of limits. Just as we have
no way to tell precisely when an ingested substance becomes part of
us or when an engendered being becomes separate, just as our body
itself can grow or shrink, just as sleep and dreams show us that consciousness comes and goes by degrees with no clear boundaries, so
above all the power and weakness of the senses seem to make the
self expand and contract until the notions of inside and outside lose
all definition. The world that I feel stops at the ends of my fingers,
and yet I feel the heat of the sun the minute I step out of the shadows; the world that I smell enters my body blown by the breezes
sometimes from distant meadows; the world that I see stretches to
the ends of the universe, and yet I cannot reliably feel my flesh, and I
can never see my own eyes. Thus it is that the self has an inner limit
that is just as mysterious and indeterminate as its outer limit.
Bordeu, one of Diderot's speakers, says that the network "has at its

origin no sense that is proper to it: does not see, does not hear, does not suffer. It is produced, nourished; it emanates from a soft, insensible, inert substance that serves as its pillow, and on which it sits, listens, judges, and pronounces" (330–31).[8] The body that is open to influxes from without must be radically porous: the world flows into it, and it flows into the world. Hence at times "I exist as if in a point; I almost cease being matter, I perceive only my thought," whereas at other times one's "ideal dilation can be without limits" (333). And the fourth, temporal dimension of unity becomes equally problematic. Bordeu derives personal identity from the "common origin that constitutes the unity of the animal" (330), but the re-awakened d'Alembert denies any scientific validity to the viewpoint: "Athwart all the vicissitudes that I endure in the course of my existence, perhaps not having at present a single one of the molecules I brought at birth, how have I remained myself for the others and for me?" (341). In the ravings of his dream d'Alembert merely draws the ultimate consequences of such skepticism by drawing dogmatic assertions out of its negations: "All is in a perpetual flux," he says (311). "All changes, all passes, only the all remains" (299–300). "There is only a single great individual, the all" (312).[9]

The sensible self is an unfathomable mystery. It is local, yet not localizable either in space, for instance in some particular organ, or in time, in the originating moment of conception or the seed from which it grew: hence (to give Sterne's book an allegorical reading) Tristram Shandy's difficulty getting himself born. There is no rationale of the self. It is what it is; nothing more can be said: "Because it is I who act thus, he who can act differently is not I; and to assert that in the moment when I do or say a thing, I can say or do otherwise, that is to assert that I am I and that I am another" (*Oeuvres philosophiques* 364). Already in Pope, who prefigures later developments in so many ways, the integral self is infected by Protean fragmentation, and this not just in *The Dunciad*, whose Dulness so often functions as a precise, nightmarish anticipation of the sensibility that was to come, but with varying intensity throughout his career, for instance again in the *Epistle to Cobham*:

> See the same man, in vigour, and in gout;
> Alone, in company; in place, or out;
> Early at Bus'ness, and at Hazard late;
> Mad at a Fox-chace, wise at a Debate;
> Drunk at a Borough, civil at a Ball,
> Friendly at Hackney, faithless at Whitehall.
>   (lines 130–35)

And fifty years later, fifteen years after the composition of *Le Rêve de d'Alembert*, we find the identical fragmentation of identity and self-questioning and the subsequent turning to inarticulate sentimentality in the famous monologue from a play that its author titled *La Folle Journée* (The Mad Day), but that we know by its subtitle, *Le Mariage de Figaro*:

> Oh what a bizarre series of events. How has this happened to me? Why these things and not others? Who set them upon my head? Forced to travel the road I entered unwittingly, and shall leave unwillingly, I have strewn as many flowers around it as my gaiety let me; I still say my gaiety, without knowing if it is mine any more than the rest, nor even what this *Me* is about which I concern myself: a formless assemblage of unknown parts, then a mean and empty-headed being, a lusty little animal, a young man ardent for pleasure, enjoying all delights, living off all trades; master here, valet there, according to the whims of fortune! ambitious from vanity, hardworking by necessity, but lazy . . . with rapture! an orator in danger, a poet for relaxation, a musician on occasion, a lover by mad gusts, I have seen all, done all, exhausted all [*tout usé*]. Then the illusion was destroyed, and, too disabused . . . Disabused! . . . Suzon, Suzon, Suzon! what torments dost thou give me! (5.3, in *Oeuvres* 471, Beaumarchais's suspension points)

Only in delirium or in a clandestine work can such ideas be pushed to their limits. Waking, enlightened thought cannot face its own consequences. If the end of the work is to deny unity, then the work can allow itself no end. Therefore Diderot's works are characteristically *entretiens*, unfinished conversations that have neither beginning nor ending, but instead "hold the middle." Here is how the formal problem is raised in *Le Rêve de d'Alembert*:

> *Mad de L'Espinasse*: Let us get to your consequences.
> *Bordeu*: That would never end.
> *Mad de L'Espinasse*: So much the better. Speak on. [*Dites toujours*, literally, talk forever.]
> *Bordeu*: I don't have the courage.
> *Mad de L'Espinasse*: And why?
> *Bordeu*: It is that in the way we are going you brush against everything and deepen nothing.
> *Mad de L'Espinasse*: What of it? We are not composing, we are chatting.
>
> (*Oeuvres philosophique* 349)

"Nous ne composons pas, nous causons": the pun on the last verb, subliminal though it may be to a French ear, is relevant here. We cause, we initiate many things, but we lack the courage to conclude, to produce finished compositions. Much earlier in the century Pope had already argued, in the *Epistle to Cobham*, that the unity of the self, the ruling passion, is reliably revealed only at the end of life. To compose is to come to rest; to conclude is to die. Thus arises the problem of literary closure, the troubling commutative relationship that exists between the unity of the person and the unity of the work. Sensibility must be loosely structured in order to remain open to the outside. "The keystone is a relative and evolving truth, never determined once and for all" (Suzuki, "Chaîne des idées" 334). The very gesture that establishes unity and limits also destroys the organism.

We can now see why the writing of this period is typically open-ended. Process as form (to use Frye's categories) does not represent a striving for the infinite as do the fragmentary forms of early German romanticism—nor, I add, as do the visionary leaps of Blake—but rather a fear of the end. Where all of life is "one ebb and flow of follies" or a "long Disease," the poets are already implicitly foretelling the final darkness; the only difference between Pope, from whom these phrases come (*Imitations of Horace*, Epistle 1.1, line 168; *Epistle to Dr. Arbuthnot*, line 132), and Sterne, to whom they so well apply, is that Pope continues to imagine an ideal Other—Arbuthnot, the physician of the body; St. John, the physician of the soul; Pope's mother, the perfected origin, and so forth—who represents the integrated personality that the poet lacks. For Blake the swiftness of time is "the mercy of Eternity" (*Milton* 1.24.72–73) because the transforming power of time conquers the rigid fixation of objects. For the man of sensibility the swiftness of time is a race away from and toward death, as in book 7 of *Tristram Shandy*; he expects mercy rather from the slowness of time that delays the inevitable. Again Pope is by inclination a precursor, though Pope ever struggles against the current of sensibility or feminine passivity within himself:

> So slow th' unprofitable Moments roll,
> That lock up all the Functions of my soul;
> That keep me from Myself; and still delay
> Life's instant business to a future day.
> (*Imitations of Horace*, Epistle 1.1, lines
> 39–42)

Indolence is, etymologically, the absence of suffering. If so many authors from Hume and Pope through Coleridge berated themselves constantly for their indolence—including Johnson, surely one of the least indolent men who ever lived—this can be seen as a psychic strategy for keeping the self in reserve, safe from the onslaughts of sensation and the ravages of time. "Men unfeeling and unsusceptible," writes Henry Mackenzie (*Mirror*, no. 14, March 13, 1779; 2: 89–90) "commonly beat the beaten track with activity and resolution; . . . but persons endowed with that nice perception of pleasure and pain which is annexed to sensibility, feel so much indescribable uneasiness in their pursuits, and frequently so little satisfaction in their attainments, that they are often induced to sit still, without attempting the one or desiring the other."

What happens to morality in the indolent domain of sensibility? "But, doctor," asks Mme de l'Espinasse in *Le Rêve de d'Alembert*, "vice and virtue? Virtue, this word so holy in all languages, this idea so sacred among all nations!" (364). Dr. Bordeu is ready with the answer: the concept of virtue "must be transformed into that of beneficence, and its opposite into maleficence" (364). Here it must be noted that Bordeu does not say "benevolence" and "malevolence": since there is no essential self, only what it does matters, not what lies within it.[10] Taken to its logical conclusion, sensibility does not lead to a doctrine of moral feeling such as is implied by Pope's lines "Not always Actions show the man: we find / Who does a kindness, is not therefore kind" (*Epistle to Cobham*, lines 61–62). Pope predicts that some essence of character will be manifested in the end, but for Bordeu feelings are responses devoid of responsibility and therefore can never coalesce into a guiding, shaping spirit: "A man is happily or unhappily born; he is insensibly led by the general torrent which conducts one man to glory, the other to ignominy" (364). Eventually the influence of Rousseau and Kant was to restore a notion of moral feeling to currency, now understood as a negation—the resistance offered by the private self to the seductions of worldliness. But here at the height of sensibility, feeling can be conceived in no other way than as a paradox of paradoxes, an insensible, unfeeling, and unfelt torrent. Sensibility's indolence coexists with a power of transformation so overwhelming that it sweeps even accepted notions of morality away with it.

Sensibility wears its paradoxical heart on its sleeve in "Über die Fülle des Herzens" (On the Fullness of the Heart), a widely disseminated short essay published in 1777 by a minor poet of the Sturm und Drang, Friedrich Leopold Graf zu Stolberg (reprinted in *Sturm und Drang: Kritische Schriften* 791–800). The title phrase was widespread in the period as a designation for feelings rich in sympathy and enthusiasm. Such feelings are, of course, never self-contained; they are prone to overflow at any moment in a bath of tears or a tide of generous activity. Stolberg's essay in particular was composed to praise the power of fullness. Stolberg writes "that fullness of the heart is more than a mere passive irritability, that every slackening of nature is disgraceful, and that a yielding sensibility, which teaches youths to whimper and to smile, extinguishes the divine spark within them" (791–92). On the contrary, the divine spark that fills the heart is power, and those whose hearts fill up with strong emotions and do not leak out through the eyes are "the strong-feelers" ("die Starkempfindenden," 794).

Now we may well wonder what a strong feeling is. Colloquially we still use the expression for a feeling that bears in strongly upon us, and indeed, Stolberg's "strong-feeler" must be particularly receptive to the sublimity of the sea, of the immeasurable future, of the heavens "beyond the stars of midnight" (797). Yet the strong-feeler is also strong in himself, a deep and productive well of feelings and not just a vessel. He will thrill with powerful sentiment in circumstances that fail to touch the weakling: "From the strong-feeler feelings often flow that are alien to the other; the divining rod will oft quiver, without finding gold" (794). It is a commonplace of Klopstock and his followers, including Stolberg, that a mote of dust is just as sublime as the whole universe, and Stolberg makes it clear that a strong-feeler is one who feels everything. He itemizes: nature, the sciences, history, poetry, religion. And he subdivides and itemizes further: "Thou didst rock me in thine arms when I was yet a feeble boy, thou didst show me blissful joy in the shadow of the woods, by the murmur of brooks, in fields and meadows, hast led me drunkenly toward the rising, heaven-reddening morn and hast sent gentler pleasures down upon me with the evening dew, when the sun set and in the east rose the moon accompanied by the evening star" (794–95). In such effusions parataxis seems on the verge of breaking under its own weight. The feeling heart is part and parcel of the universe, but it seems to traffic more in parcels than in functional parts of a genuine totality. The rhetoric soars, yet the essay ends by evoking the dust on the feet of the pilgrim through life. The strong-feeler feels everything, yet it turns out that the goal of all this sentiment, and the most difficult feeling to attain amid the bombardment of sensations, is the lowest grade of self-consciousness, the feeling of self. Sometimes, only sometimes, on calm moonlit eves the spark of Prometheus comes within reach: "At such moments the whole soul, the true better self feels itself again in all its strengths and immortalities; for the mask that we drag around with us in the tumult of the world, with the bells of folly tinkling round about, yawning and yawned at, oh, who would not spit upon it with hatred in hours of self-feeling!" (796). The greatest strength of all, together with the most favorable and unthreatening of circumstances, is required for the heroic labor of reassembling the parts of the self into a whole.

"Über die Fülle des Herzens" is of value because it so openly displays how contradictory feeling is at the core. Stolberg inveighs against rationalists—"To you nothing is true, everything contradiction; to the wise man nothing is contradiction, much true, some things dark" (792)—but what he means by this is that sensibility is indiscriminate and suffers infinite contradictions to coexist. The full heart expands to the universe or shrinks to a point of light; in moments of ecstasy it can perhaps feel itself, but nothing in Stolberg's feckless effusion suggests that the self has a shape or a definition. Feeling leads to more feeling, not to action or to knowledge.[11]

The Good-Natur'd Man

Who or what is the man of feeling? The question is posed most directly by Goldsmith's first play, *The Good-Natur'd Man*. Its answer takes the form of an unarticulated pun: the man of feeling is a prodigal son. Goldsmith's central character, the fatherless Honeywood, has gained the affections of Miss Richland, apparently by virtue of his unstinting generosity with his fortune. But near the end of the play he nearly loses her affections again on account of the unstinting generosity of his feelings, as he pleads the cause of his rival, the foolish and hypocritical Lofty. The alliance of Honeywood and Lofty comes as no surprise, for Goldsmith has begun in the very first scene to delineate the plight of the good-natured man, namely, that his selflessness leaves his identity just as unstable as the hypocrite's. In his "neglect of himself" (act 1; 5: 20), knowing no limits, open to all influences, he lacks all definition. "How can I be proud of a place," complains his uncle, Sir William, "in a heart where every sharper and coxcomb find an easy entrance," and a few lines later he adds that his follies "are as boundless as his dissipation" (act 1; 5: 19–20). His surface is infinitely vulnerable to the superficially infinite good nature of the hypocrite.

The play is a world defined by contrasts—Mr. Croaker's misanthropy versus his wife's effervescence (act 1; 5: 24–25); Miss Richland's prudence versus her guardian's cunning (act 1; 5: 33); Honeywood's susceptibility balanced against his friend Leontine's steadiness (act 1; 5: 29); Honeywood's open versus Miss Richland's concealed generosity; her generosity versus the frugality of Leontine and his secret fiancée, Olivia; the concealed identities of Sir William and Olivia versus the known identities of the rest. Within this world Honeywood and Lofty are allied in recognizing no separation from their surroundings: for the man of universal benevolence the whole universe is *me*, while the hypocrite exists in the world as a universal *not-me*. Because they lack the contrast of self against world, they lack definition: "There are some faults so nearly allied to excellence," as Sir William acknowledges, "that we can scarce weed out the vice without eradicating the virtue" (act 1; 5: 20). The hypocrite recognizes in the good-natured man a mirror image of his own emptiness: "The man, to be sure, was immensely good natur'd. But then I could never find that he had any thing in him" (act 2; 5: 40). The line between the two grows ever more difficult to draw as the play proceeds, until the point arrives at which Olivia explicitly accuses Honeywood of harboring the wasp's nest of hypocrisy: "What a base insincere man was your master, to serve us in this manner. Is this his good nature?" (act 4; 5: 61).

To some extent the action of the play provokes identity crises for all the central characters, but this is above all true of the man of feeling and the man without feelings. "Who am I, I say, who am I!" (act 5; 5: 79), Lofty cries out as he is about to be unmasked by Sir William (who himself has been masked up to this very point). The play is a farce, of course, and Lofty's identity crisis sounds shallow and stagy, even though the next time he speaks he is genuinely a reformed man. Honeywood's identity crisis comes from without rather than within—so to speak, for this distinction has little meaning for Honeywood. Specifically, it comes from Leontine. Earlier, at the end of act 2, Leontine expressed unshakable faith in his friend: "I know so much of his honest heart, that if he can't relieve our uneasinesses, he will at least share them" (act 2; 5: 44). Yet by the last act Leontine's faith is utterly destroyed. "I know you. Sir, I know you," he exclaims. "All the seeming sincerity of your professions I now find were only allurements to betray; and all your seeming regret for their consequences, only calculated to cover the cowardice of your heart. Draw, villain!" (act 5; 5: 73). A crisis, to be sure, though here too it is hard to know how seriously to take this lapse into stilted tragic diction in the midst of a farce.

Who then is the man of feeling? How can we know or define the man who refuses to define himself? Sensibility begins by denying all boundaries—where and what is its end? The problem is a psychological one; as we have been seeing, it is also a generic and a tonal one. But it may be most useful, in a period when so many literary works revolved around questions of money, to see it as an *economic* problem. Honeywood is too sweet; he figuratively gives himself away.

From this perspective the most revealing line of the play is uttered by a good—a *sensible*—economist, Honeywood's fiancée, Miss Richland. "I see," she says, "that it is vain to expect happiness from him, who has been so bad an oeconomist of his own; and that I must disclaim his friendship, who ceases to be a friend to himself" (act 4; 5: 66). This theme of libidinal economy plays a subdued but crucial role throughout the play. Miss Richland is a capital friend and admirer, one whose interest (for Honeywood and for the other characters) grows continuously. Sir William, the admirable, rich uncle, recognizes her in the middle of the play as a kindred spirit: "it gives me great pleasure to find, that among a number of worthless friendships, [Honeywood] has made one acquisition of real value" (act 3; 5: 51). And in the last speech of the play Honeywood finally acknowledges that he must learn from her how better to husband his resources: "Henceforth, therefore, it shall be my study to reserve my pity for real distress; my friendship for true merit, and my love for her, who first taught me what is it to be happy" (act 5; 5: 81).

But how can the sensitive man become sensible? How do you define the ratio—the mean of reason—between generosity and reserve?[12] How do you compute the value of a heart? There is indeed one character in the play who perhaps knows himself and who reckons up his heart. But he will not tell us the value, and we should not believe him if he did: "Ay, Sir, [tenderness is] a perfect treasure. I love to see a gentleman with a tender heart. I don't know, but I think I have a tender heart myself. If all that I have lost by my heart was put together, it would make a—but no matter for that" (act 3; 5: 46). This is the bailiff speaking, and he is no more savory than Gay's Peachum or Fielding's Bondum. The value of his heart is what he can coax out of his prisoners, or—not to put too fine a point on it—what he can steal. Goldsmith himself, of course, made something of a career as a sponger, though I do not actually propose to argue that he conceives of identity in the fashion I shall attribute to Schiller, namely, as a stolen psychic capital. Yet the presence of the bailiff in the play at least reminds us how treacherous a task it can be to set up the law of the psyche. The mighty Johnson was surely better at it than the flighty Goldsmith, yet even Johnson's psychic economy creates only a perilous balance, as can be seen in the concluding lines of *The Vanity of Human Wishes*:

> These goods for man the laws of heav'n ordain,
> These goods he grants, who grants the pow'r to gain;
> With these celestial wisdom calms the mind,
> And makes the happiness she does not find.
>
> (lines 365–68)

A prudent economist—no prodigal enthusiast—can manufacture content. But it remains undecidable how genuine a product the balanced self is. For we cannot know whether "make" here has its licit sense, "to produce, as a cause" (sense 6 in Johnson's *Dictionary*) or its illicit one, "to form by art what is not natural" (sense 4). When even Johnson cannot in the end find "a healthful mind" (line 359), then a lost sheep like Honeywood certainly will be unable to find it, and if we believe the conclusion of *The Good-Natur'd Man*, then only a miraculous intervention can find the way for him.

It is surely this weak conclusion that has kept Goldsmith's play off the stage, for *The Good-Natur'd Man* is often as funny as *She Stoops to Conquer*, and it inaugurates many of the devices repeated in the later play, such as the inarticulate wooing scene and the comically confused pacing of the last act. But the conclusion lacks motivation. Without any forewarning, when Sir William reveals himself, the characters are suddenly transformed. Croaker abjures his sullen miserliness (allowing Leontine and Olivia to marry and indirectly freeing Miss Richland's inheritance so that she can marry Honeywood), Lofty abjures his hypocrisy (ending his rivalry with Honeywood and his claims on the latter's good-natured subservience), Miss Richland abjures her affected indifference to Honeywood, and Honeywood in his turn abjures his whole character. Such a happy ending is donated by the author, not earned; as Honeywood says, "A moment, like this, over pays an age of apprehension" (act 5; 5: 81). Audiences must long have felt that it is not so easy to make the man of feeling into a man.

One other theme that must concern us in Goldsmith's play is that of paternal authority. The theme is sounded most insistently by the absurd Croaker—father to Leontine; supposed uncle to Leontine's fiancée, Olivia; guardian to Miss Richland—who is constantly beset by fears of losing an authority he never really had. The absence of more effective parents is typical of the literature of the period, as is the conversion of the rich uncle into a good fairy at the end. And throughout the period individuation is associated with the breaking of paternal bonds. The Victorian hero typically establishes a family and often recovers or reconciles a lost or alienated father; the Victorian villain (Heathcliff, Bounderby, Bulstrode) is often forced to acknowledge his ancestry or his posterity. In either case the individual's identity is secured when he is raised or lowered to his allotted place in a social system. There is, however, on principle no system of sensibility. The family had served a mediating function, one's place in the domestic microcosm fixing one's place in the social macrocosm. The hero of sensibility denies the order and authority of the family in order to stake out the terrain for liberal feeling and free will; as Jacques Lacan would say, he forecloses the name-of-the-father. But no affirmation compensates for this denial. Parents are constantly getting lost in *The Castle of Otranto; Rasselas* (though written out of piety for the author's mother, like Pope's *Epistle to Dr. Arbuthnot*) contains no mothers and depicts fathers only as tyrants to be fled; Sterne, Smollett, and Goldsmith offer us at best only parodies of a stable family. Paternity represents an identity made, not found, and the hero of sensibility revels in an uncreating word that dissolves bonds not of his own making.

Yet in denying paternity, the hero transforms himself into a puny creature. He becomes, as we have seen, Miss Richland's pupil in true good feeling. But even worse, he becomes, in effect, the bride of his bride, when in desperation *she* offers *him* her hand. And the collapse of authority, that is, of the classifying or symbolizing power, leaves Honeywood speechless as well: "Heavens! how can I have deserved all this? How express my happiness, my gratitude!" (act 5; 5: 81). In truth, the play grinds to a halt not so much because there is no more to be done, but because there is no more to be said. Good nature etherealizes itself out of existence. This dilemma is echoed in the Epilogue, spoken not by Honeywood but by Miss Richland, who now wears the pants; here it is Goldsmith himself who is said to have become speechless and who presents the Epilogue as his feeble attempt to replace one he hoped to receive from some friend: "Our Author's friends"—no good-natured men they—"thus plac'd at happy distance, / Give him good words indeed, but no assistance" (5: 83).[13] Sensibility at the end is cowed and feminized, rather than emancipated.

The Man of Feeling: Wholes and Parts

My judgment of the destiny of sensibility is also, in its main lines, that of Henry Mackenzie, author of the lachrymose novelette *The Man of Feeling*. Mackenzie was the age's most sensible—and least sensitive—exponent of sensibility. In both his novels and his essays he criticized figures like Honeywood and praised moderation and tempered, thoughtful benevolence. Yet ultimately Mackenzie earns his place in our picture precisely because he was no more able to escape the aporias of sensibility than were his more flamboyant counterparts. Mackenzie knows what he would like to avoid, but (as I shall argue) he does not know where to take his stand: too many incompatible ideals attract the man of feeling. The rationalizing of expenditures, as I will explain, does not solve the mystery of personality any better than the other rationalizations we have examined. I quote in full Mackenzie's attack on excesses of sentimentality because I take its defensive violence to be a symptom of the seductive allure that such attitudes exercised on him; I quote it also because of its concluding recognition of sensibility as a form of madness:

> Be just before you are generous, is a good old proverb, which the profligate hero of a much admired comedy is made to ridicule, in a well-turned, and even a sentimental period. But what right have those squanderers of their own and other men's fortunes to assume the merit of generosity? Is parting with that money, which they value so little, generosity? Let them restrain their dissipation, their riot, their debauchery, when they are told that these bring ruin on the persons and families of the honest and the industrious; let them sacrifice one pleasure to humanity, and then tell us of their generosity and their feeling. A transient instance, in which the prodigal relieved want with his purse, or the thoughtless debauchee promoted merit by his interest, no more deserves the appellation of generosity, than the rashness of a drunkard is entitled to the praises of valour, or the freaks of a madman to the laurels of genius. (*Mirror*, no. 23; 1: 140–41)

If we turn from here to Mackenzie's other essays, we will find in both *The Mirror* and its sequel, *The Lounger*, a gallery of portraits of the various forms of sensibility—selfish, appropriate, and impulsive. Except in a few outbursts like the one just quoted, Mackenzie's judicious prose keeps his insecurity under wraps, but if we scrutinize the essays carefully, the paradoxes of sensibility keep returning upon us.[14] We cannot successfully give our emotions free rein, Mackenzie argues. We need to control them by keeping "refinement and delicacy of mind . . . within proper bounds"; "their natural effect"—if we know how to draw the line—"instead of producing uneasiness and chagrin, is to add to the enjoyments of life" (*Mirror*, no. 47; 1: 275). The enjoyments are the purely passive pleasures of sensibility—fellow feeling and benevolence. Yet they are not really enjoyments at all unless they have been naturalized, settled in the soul. You must earn your enjoyments, like "Mr. Stanley," as he is portrayed in the passage quoted and throughout the essay, or like Eudocius, a man of "pure good-nature," in *Lounger*, no. 34 (1: 236). That is to say, the enjoyments of good nature are not natural at all. What comes naturally is dissipation or indifference, such as Mackenzie portrays in Eudocius's opposite number, Clitander, who inherited his wealth, never learned its proper worth, and therefore cannot appreciate it. Feelings are like any other currency; they need to be stabilized, regulated, and given a value. Of "ordinary engagements and ordinary cares," Mackenzie writes in his most explicit use of an economic metaphor, "like metals in coin, it is not alone their intrinsic nature, but also that impression which they receive from us, that creates their value. It must be material, therefore, in the art of happiness, to possess the power of stamping satisfaction on the enjoyments which Providence has put into our hands" (*Lounger*, no. 34; 1: 232).

"Pure good-nature" does not come from nature, but from an "art of happiness" that keeps nature "within proper bounds." Mackenzie's moral sentiments are, in actuality, perfectly sensible and unexceptionable—"a real man of fashion has a certain *retenue*, a degree of moderation in every thing, and will not be more wicked or dissipated than there is occasion for"—and they descend from some of the most clichéd commonplaces of Enlightenment thought: "the highest good-breeding, and the most highly polished fashion, is the nearest to nature, but to nature in its best state, to that *belle nature* which works of taste, and a person of fashion is a work of taste, in every department require" (*Lounger*, no. 33; 1: 230). But the hoary ideal of *la belle nature* carries little conviction here. An aura of paradox and peril hovers around Mackenzie's writings despite the time-honored conventions of morality to which they adhere. As we read through the portrait gallery, it comes to seem natural, almost inevitable, that one will give away one's psychic health along with one's fortune (like Flavillus in Craig's essay in *Lounger*, no. 35) or else lock up the orifices of feeling with the key to one's treasure chest (like the avaricious old men of *Lounger*, no. 72). Extremes of sensibility abound, like the softhearted niece Emilia of *Mirror*, no. 101, who sacrifices herself in the footsteps of a deceased, miserable girl-friend, or the misanthropic hermit Hortensius, despondently cultivating his *ferme ornée* in *Lounger*, no. 9. It would be hard to imagine a more direct refutation than this last of the hollow rationalism of *la belle nature*, and indeed every paper praising the "unremitting bounty" of the natural scene (*Lounger*, no. 31; 1: 214) or the "pensive vacancy" and imaginative richness of the countryside (*Lounger*, no. 87; 2: 248) seems counterbalanced by an exposé of the splenetic Lorraine glass of the man of sentiment (Col. Caustic, also in *Lounger*, no. 31, who "stamps on the surrounding objects somewhat of the particular impression of his character"; 1: 216) or of the "brilliant fiction" underlying the rural ideal (*Lounger*, no. 89; 2: 260).

These contradictions are at the root of the delicate instability characteristic of the best of Mackenzie's prose. Mackenzie's age is marked by a "separation of conscience from feeling" (*Lounger*, no. 20; 1: 143), which we are now in a position to interpret as a separation of sense from sensibility. But we still need to explain the reasons for this separation and for the attractions of sensibility despite all the flaws that Mackenzie sees in it. And here Mackenzie will continue to help us, for just as he sees clearly the weaknesses of sensibility that are only implicit in Stolberg or Goldsmith, so he identifies the attractions that these authors and Diderot virtually take for granted.

One high point among the essays on sensibility is the essay on Hamlet, which Mackenzie's excellent biographer terms "the first romantic criticism of Shakespeare."[15] "The basis of Hamlet's character," says Mackenzie, "seems to be an extreme sensibility of mind" (*Mirror*, no. 99; 2: 261). His character is a balance of extremes, being both natural and cultured in the highest degree, "thus formed by nature, and thus modelled by situation" (2: 262). A powerfully driven character like Orestes becomes an abstract type who "interests us for the accomplishment of his purpose" (2: 263); but a powerfully divided figure like Hamlet, sensitive to all the slings and arrows of outrageous fortune, "one whom Nature had formed to be" a leader but who finds himself "placed in a situation" of weakness—such a figure interests us as a "person," and "we feel not only the virtues, but the weaknesses of Hamlet, as our own" (2: 262). Sensibility, in other words, equates for Mackenzie with humanity itself. The rational man is an ideal type who has achieved the ideal balance of nature and culture. But the sensible man is the type of the real; he is the mirror that reflects the whole world in its boundless variety and offers to everyman something he can recognize and call his own. Rationality is a narrow tightrope—"this isthmus of a middle state"—that few or none can tread; sensibility is a broad ocean where even if we are tossed about we can still stay afloat.

Behind these correspondences and metaphors, as behind the effusions of Diderot, Stolberg, and Goldsmith, there is, as we can now see, a distinctive logic of totalities. Inclusiveness becomes the standard. The shift from the early part of the century can be difficult to measure because certain long-established key terms can be adapted to the new norms; both an old Enlightenment interface and a new romantic interpenetration, for instance, can be called a coincidence of opposites, and a center can be both the single midpoint of balance on a line and the focal origin that generates a whole circle.[16] Yet we have seen how a logic of wholeness comes to judge a luminous ideal like *la belle nature* in terms of what the ideal rejects rather than what it encourages. Despite reason's preference for consistency, it is totality that matters emotionally for these authors. Anything less lacks true humanity.

The logic of wholeness is correlative to the broadening of the urbane sublime style that I described in Cowper. There I illustrated how neoclassical norms were expanded and stretched to the breaking point; here we see how neoclassical ideals not susceptible of expansion were rejected or silently ignored. In this chapter, however, I want to direct attention less to the process of expansion than to what came after. For we have seen in all the authors a fully developed sense of crisis; only in Mackenzie, the latest yet most traditional of the authors, was the crisis explicitly tied to its source in the logic of wholeness. I would like to suggest, then, that the crisis took precedence over the source or "cause" that "produced" it; people were worried before they knew why. We have in the Age of Sensibility another instance of the common pattern of an age preoccupied not with what satisfied it, but with what troubled it. That is why the discovery of the nature or root of sensibility in the logic of wholeness led not to an apotheosis of sensibility, but to the disappearance of the cult of feeling. Sensibility was a problem rather than an ambition; having seen through the problem, the authors would, in their various ways, naturally escape from its spell, "breaking the wand which summoned tears," to quote again the charmingly mystified phrase of Mackenzie's biographer.

We have seen how naturally the authors adopted economic metaphors for this crisis of sensibility. The logic of wholeness disturbed a logic of exchange; the conception of a *sensorium commune* was at odds with the conception of a balance of psychic faculties. As the spider of consciousness hovers in the center of her universal web, even the lightest vibration of emotion will provoke a flood of tears or a torrent of rapture. Such totalizing violence—manifested, notably, in the intolerable ranting of Sturm und Drang drama—disrupts the orderly functioning of the world-machine and calls all values into question. In seeking out the greatest possible responsiveness and the fullest self-development, the self loses its bearings.

If the world of empiricism is built of distinct parts rather than wholes, the first response of idealism, to build a world of undifferentiated wholes, will not work. Such supermonads, sensate mirrors of the universe, could be seen, from a later perspective, as nothing but empiricism writ large; in the attempt to see all, know all, and tell all, consciousness shatters the universe into an alphabetic dictionary or encyclopedia (so different from the systematic encyclopedias of Hegel or Spencer), into the fragmented narratives of a Sterne or a Diderot, into the broken personalities of *The Castle of Otranto* or *The Task*. The remnants of heroic couplet poetry keep the image of the past alive, but only as the forlorn world of Goldsmith's Aurora or else the fraudulent one of Crabbe's *The Village*. The totality absorbing all distinct individuals into a universe of quivering sympathies proves inevitably to be a world of indistinctness in which all gains are converted into loss: "Reason barters but sentiment is a surplus in the economy with no exchange value. It is therefore expensive, and poverty is bound to be its companion" (Todd, *Sensibility* 97).

Wordsworth's first masterpiece, the last great heroic couplet poem of the century, sings the swan song of both empiricism and the sensibility that emerged out of its bosom:

> But o'er the sooth'd accordant heart we feel
> A sympathetic twilight slowly steal,
> And ever, as we fondly muse, we find
> The soft gloom deepening on the tranquil mind.
> Stay! pensive, sadly-pleasing visions, stay!
> Ah no! as fades the vale, they fade away.
> Yet still the tender, vacant gloom remains;
> Still the cold cheek its shuddering tear retains.
>   (*An Evening Walk*, 1793 text, lines 381–88)

How can we account for the great calm of Wordsworth's poem? His conjuration of sensibility out of Enlightenment omits all the agitation that had been inseparable from sensibility. To be sure, sensibility had always foretold its own maturity, but its evocation of happy old men like W.G. and Benevolus in *Lounger*, no. 96 regularly seems to consist more of self-satisfied wish-fulfillment than of substance:

> I own I had acuter feelings some five-and-twenty years ago; but having now lived half a century, I am become a good deal less heroic, less visionary, and less tender than I was; yet I have not forgotten what my own feelings were, and I can perfectly understand what those of younger men are; I confess I like to see them as warm as I myself was at their age, and enjoy a sort of self-flattery in thinking that I have learned to be wiser, by being a little older than they. (*Lounger*, no. 96; 2: 332)

Mackenzie was 42 when he put these words into the mouth of his imaginary 50-year-old correspondent; if the 24-year-old Wordsworth sounds more realistic, this is because of the greater maturity not of the author, but of the concept. For in the very process of expressing itself fully and coming to know itself, sensibility paved the way toward resolving its own tensions and transcending its limitations.

The solution to the problem of sensibility arrives with the clear formulation of its nature. So soon as the underlying logic of wholeness that knows no difference becomes apparent, the tools for a more stable logic are at hand. The whole that in itself achieves neither equilibrium nor stable exchange does so when subdivided into parts. An economic solution offers itself to a problem of psychic economy, a solution definitely formulated by an economist in 1776, when the time was ripe, and readily adapted to all the various provinces of intellectual life. That principle is the division of labor. Lessing substitutes for Du Bos's reduction of the fine arts to a single principle the reduction of the several arts to their several principles; discussion of the senses shifts from questions of substitutability or hierarchy to questions of their distinctive individuality; [17] Greuze's absorption gives way (as Fried's *Absorption and Theatricality* shows) to the dramatic articulation of David's paintings; the poetic dithyrambs of sensibility yield to organic odes and conversation poems compounded of clearly demarcated parts; finally, the notion of a *sensorium commune* breathes its last to be replaced by a reinvigorated faculty psychology—all these are manifestations of the one recognition that a unified sensibility must compensate for its openness to the world by establishing internal boundaries. The whole self cannot be wholly engaged in all its actions and perceptions.

This does not mean that the notion of the unity of the self was abandoned. Quite the contrary, we have seen how the unity of the self as we understand it—as a greater unity of consciousness subtending the problematic unity of sensation—was first envisioned in the decade of Cowper and Kant. And gothic psychology demonstrates the preservation of this ideal of unity facing the shattering assaults of experience. Yet at the same time, the new conception is of a transcendental rather than an empirical unity of experience. There is, in reserve, a single self, but it is produced by and manifested through its parts (like the fragments of Walpole's Alfredo reassembled not into a single material body, but into the ideal totality of a narrative)—the different senses, categories of experience, stages of life, and social relations.

The Wealth of Nations has pride of place in elaborating the notion of the division of labor. But Adam Smith was already the author of the *Theory of Moral Sentiments,* and for him (unlike his predecessor Adam Ferguson) the notion is at bottom a psychological one.

Specialization is the specific nostrum to the anxieties of a world grown too large.[18] It is the connection of the division of labor to the problems of sensibility that leads Smith to incorporate the following sentence into his brief, seminal chapter on the topic: "In civilized society [man] stands at all times in need of the cooperation and assistance of great multitudes, while his whole life is scarce sufficient to gain the friendship of a few persons" (*Wealth* 1: 18). And like its roots, the fruits of the division of labor are, at least in part, psychological; it affects people's minds as well as their behavior: "The difference of natural talents in different men is, in reality, much less than we are aware of, and the very different genius which appears to distinguish men of different professions, when grown up to maturity, is not upon many occasions so much the cause, as the effect of the division of labor" (1: 19). If sensibility is the violent adolescence of romanticism, then the division of labor is its calm maturity; if sensibility is the serenade of the Enlightenment, then the partitioned world is the dawn song calling the newly ordered cosmos to work.

For sensibility the darkness with its attendant emphasis on feeling rather than sight may have been redeemed as the womb of imagination, or faery, or religious enthusiasm, but it was always a denial of real life; its representatives gaze blankly at the earth, though they may at last gaze with fulfillment up toward heaven, like Parnell in his "Night-Piece on Death" or the rapturous blind father of Stolberg's dialogue "Die Sinne" (*Gesammelte Werke* 10: 269–96). The Enlightened poet knew what he saw and named what he knew; the movement of sensibility beyond the bounds of Enlightenment led past evocation toward the unnameables, mad suicide and sin.[19] The mature greatness of *An Evening Walk* is that it ends neither with the triumph of night, as does *The Dunciad*, nor with the religious consolation of a resurrection, but instead with a new world made up of little worlds. There is no longer a picturesque scene, but rather a partitioned landscape humanized and divided by the discordant sounds of labor, "the still, sad music of humanity":[20]

> But now the clear-bright Moon her zenith gains,
> And rimy without speck extend the plains;
> The deepest dell the mountain's breast displays,
> Scarce hides a shadow from her searching rays;
> From the dark-blue "faint silvery threads" divide
> The hills, while gleams below the azure tide;
> The scene is waken'd, yet its peace unbroke,
> By silver'd wreaths of quiet charcoal smoke,

That, o'er the ruins of the fallen wood,
Steal down the hills, and spread along the flood.
  The song of mountain streams unheard by day,
Now hardly heard, beguiles my homeward way.
All air is, as the sleeping water, still,
List'ning th' aëreal music of the hill,
Broke only by the slow clock tolling deep,
Or shout that wakes the ferry-man from sleep,
Soon follow'd by his hollow-parting oar,
And echo'd hoof approaching the far shore;
Sound of clos'd gate, across the water born,
Hurrying the feeding hare thro' rustling corn;
The tremulous sob of the complaining owl;
And at long intervals the mill-dog's howl;
The distant forge's swinging thump profound;
Or yell in the deep woods of lonely hound.
  (*An Evening Walk*, 1793 text, lines 423–46)

Like any historical development, the emergence of the logic of partitioning out of the logic of wholeness, while a natural development, should not be thought an inevitable one. It is worth remembering that one great outsider, William Blake, resolutely continued the vein of sensibility. He rejected exchange and use and struggled to correct and convert the psychic economy of sensibility directly into a blinding vision of universal truth: "What it will be Questiond When the Sun rises do you not see a round Disk of Fire somewhat like a Guinea O no no I see an Innumerable company of the Heavenly host crying Holy Holy Holy is the Lord God Almighty I question not my Corporeal or Vegetative Eye any more than I would Question a Window concerning a Sight I look thro it & not with it."[21] But plainly Blake's "aching joys" and "dizzy raptures" (to borrow some phrases from "Tintern Abbey") were not of their time; they belong to that more adolescent stage of universal feeling when "nature . . . / To me was all in all." Here is Wordsworth's description of this stage, which I take to be a stage in culture as well as in individual development; in rereading the familiar words we may note the adolescent exaltation of sight into an apotheosis of sensibility and also the concluding economic metaphor, a buried yet unmistakable reminder of the way things work by the sober light of common day:

                    I cannot paint
        What then I was. The sounding cataract
        Haunted me like a passion: the tall rock,

> The mountain, and the deep and gloomy wood,
> Their colours and their forms, were then to me
> An appetite; a feeling and a love,
> That had no need of a remoter charm,
> By thought supplied, nor any interest
> Unborrowed from the eye.
>   ("Tintern Abbey," lines 75–83)

For loss of this exalted sensibility, Wordsworth tells us, "abundant recompense" has followed. And while the famous philosophical lines read like a paean to "all" in the glory of the setting sun, we can recognize that the all has now become a transcendent unity, "a presence," "something," somewhere. It is no longer "all in all," but now a latent all manifested in all its parts and all its places, in a world constituted by the partitioned labor of object and subject, "Of eye, and ear—both what they half create, / And what they perceive" (lines 105–6).

Stealing a Self: Schiller and Blake

The process of maturing came more easily for Wordsworth than for the writers of sensibility, and it did not always seem even to Wordsworth to come so easily, and with such bounty, as in the two poems I have just discussed (cf. Bahti, "Wordsworth's Rhetorical Theft"). This survey chapter should not conclude without a reminder that emancipation could often be costly or violent or both. It takes, indeed, no special insight to recognize the links between the farces of the 1770s and 1780s and the Revolution of 1789. And it is surely a mere truism to observe that if the Revolution initiated a new stage of European consciousness, this nevertheless could only have come to pass as the fruition of ideals and tendencies that had long sought expression. In England, to be sure, the crisis of sensibility, the search for consciousness, the problem of closure all seem to have found enough outlets to circumvent a final explosion. Yet there can be no question but that throughout Europe a revolutionary atmosphere preceded the Revolution. The only major literary work from a decade of growing nationalism to achieve a genuinely Continent-wide popularity, Schiller's play *Die Räuber*, was also the one that drew the final, revolutionary consequences from sensibility's precarious broadening or totalizing of Enlightenment epistemology. There was no peaceful—or at least no smoothly evolutionary—way out from the problems of psychological and aesthetic closure that had come to plague the European soul.

Suppose the relativistic mentality of the Enlightenment expanded to the point of positing the unrestricted relatedness of all things: a man would then be neither a citizen of a locality or country nor a member of a family or class, but would live in direct contact with the whole world. Schiller describes this condition in his major philosophical work of this period: "As in a prismatic glass a white beam of light divides into seven darker rays, so has the divine *I* split into countless sensate substances. . . . Should it please the Almighty henceforth to shatter this prism, then the dam between Him and the world would collapse, all spirits would be submerged in *one* infinity, all chords flow together in *one* harmony, all brooks cease in *one* ocean" ("Philosophische Briefe," *Werke* 5: 352–53).

Suppose next the community of man extended to embrace the entire world. One's identity would then not be a matter of one's perspective or one's position in a restricted sphere; it would depend on finding one's way rather than knowing one's place. Without a stable, central first principle to serve as the ground for knowledge, a man would be self-made: actively begotten by his deeds rather than passively begotten by his progenitors. But where identity thus loses its anchor, it is no longer proper to speak in any objective way of self-knowledge. Selfhood is now no more (and no less) than a feeling: the sensation of liberation as restrictions are surmounted and resistances overcome. All knowledge delimits; the identity of the citizen of the world is fabricated by a will to power that overturns the ordered structures formerly linking *conscience* to *connaissance* (or *Bewußtsein* to *Wissen*). This is the stance of Karl Moor's fiery Lieutenant Spiegelberg in Schiller's play:

> Let us first get into the great world. Paris and London!—where you purchase a box on the ear if you greet someone with the name of an honest man. And what a jubilee for the soul when you practice your handiwork on a grand scale. . . . Let me first warm up, you shall see wonders, your bird brain will turn over in your skull, when my pregnant wit goes into labor. . . . Accursed lethargy! (*Striking himself on the forehead*) That till now enchained my forces, blocked and strained my prospects; I awaken, feel who I am—who I must become! (*Die Räuber* 1.2, in *Werke* 1: 507)[22]

In the extremity of his ambition, it must be pointed out, Spiegelberg is not a new man, but an old man unleashed (see Steinhagen, "Der junge Schiller zwischen Marquis de Sade und Kant"). Up to the point of his murder by the loyal Schweizer his selfishness is not a romantic conscience like that of his captain, but rather the sensationalism (in both senses of the word) of a rationalist gone mad; as Moor responds at this point, "You are a fool. Your liquor is frothing and boiling out of your brain."[23]

Suppose, finally, the restricted economy of classical exchange and classical morality replaced by a generalized economy. As the play opens, Karl Moor has sent a letter of repentance to his father, but it is diverted by his evil younger brother, Franz, who is modeled on Edmund in *King Lear*. Franz, an even more corrupt rationalist than Spiegelberg, deceives his tenderly inclined father by substituting a faked grim rebuff. This action breaks the last ties of familial affection, the reciprocal devotion and dependence rooted in man's origin. "Is that a father's trust?" exclaims Moor when he recovers his senses after reading the fraudulent letter. "Is that love for love?" (1.2; 1: 514). Denied his place in this natural emotional exchange, Moor turns to a supernatural moral exchange, imagining himself as the avenging angel of the Lord. Denouncing the "Pharisees," the "counterfeiters of truth," he rejects all worldly accountability: "What I have done, I shall doubtless read in the heavenly book of accounts, but I will waste no more words with the pitiful stewards [of justice]. Tell them my handiwork is retribution [*Wiedervergeltung*, repayment]—Revenge is my trade" (2.3; 1: 553).

The robbers conceive of their mission with respect to the economy of goods as well as with respect to the economy of deeds. Imagining themselves to be the mysteriously powerful instruments of an authority greater than human society and human law, they practice a justice that is both retributory and distributive in a generalized economy that is thus both dispensing and disposing.[24] Or so at least they would like to think:

> Relieving rich skinflints of a third of the cares that hang around their necks and drive away their golden sleep, bringing stagnant money into circulation, restoring the equilibrium of goods, in a word, recalling the Golden Age, helping the good Lord from many a weary boarder, sparing Him war, pestilence, costly time, and *doctores*—look, that is what I call honest, I call that furnishing a worthy tool in the hand of Providence. (1.2; 1: 511–12)

This is, however, again the unworthy Spiegelberg prating. Much later in the play, discouraging a prospective robber in whom he sees an image of his purer self, Moor denies that Robin Hood is more than a lure to inflame a "childish fancy"; you cannot "purchase immortality with incendiary activities" (3.2; 1: 565). In some ancient or archaic realm perhaps things were different, but Schiller's play represents the dilemmas of modern consciousness—he protested vehemently against the director's insistence on staging the play as a medieval costume drama—and in the eighteenth century the recourse to banditry is, finally, a tragic counsel of despair. The citizen of the world is really an outcast of the universe, the general economy no better than a hoard amassed by nocturnal stealth and a secret stock of unexpressed virtuous intentions.[25]

The denial of paternity and of the name-of-the-father motivates the tragic action of the play (well analyzed in Koc, "Fathers and Sons," and set in a more general context in Préaux, "Le Motif des frères ennemis"). In the very first scene the spurious letter that Franz attributes to Karl climaxes in the lines "I seem to see your old, pious father . . . stumble, pale as death, back into his chair and curse the day on which *father* was first lisped toward him" (1.1; 1: 494). And at the end of the reading the only reaction of the father—the father who bears no name of his own in this play, only "Old Moor"—is, "My name! My honest name!" (1.1; 1: 495). "O father, father, father," beseeches the relentless Franz, "look round you for another name, or shopkeepers and street-boys will point their fingers at you after they have seen the portrait of your son in the marketplace in Leipzig" (1.1; 1: 496). One wonders why a change of name should cure the natural affinity visible in the portrait unless, to a rationalist like Franz, one's natural identity is inextricably bound to the categories that denominate and present it.

As a result of Franz's schemes Karl feels bereft of his natural identity. It is—as he proclaims in one of the truly notorious slogans of the time—a "slack castrate century." "The force of its loins has dried up, and now hops must help propagate the race." Modern men "barricade nature's wholesomeness with tasteless conventions . . . —[They] damn the Sadducee who doesn't attend church with enough diligence and calculate their Jew's interest at the altar—fall on their knees in order to spread their filth around" (1.2; 1: 503). As Karl says not long after, "I have no father left" (1.2; 1: 515), and for the remainder of the play Schiller hardly ever relaxes the revolutionary violence of a language that protests against the enfeebling of all ties through castration, dissolute masturbation, or—as in the case of the rationalist (crypto-Jewish) Spiegelberg—circumcision (1.2; 1: 504).

Yet the tragic paradox of Moor is that forceful self-reliance is the very reverse of his goal. He strikes out not to declare his independence, but to find the way back to his father. In a work that declares parricide to "break the bond of nature" (4.5; 1: 596) and to be, along with fratricide, "the greatest sin" (5.1; 1: 606), Moor is a prodigal son whose sole desire is to return to the bosom of his fathers: "Fatherland's earth! Fatherland's sky! Fatherland's sun," as he exclaims at the emotional opening of act 4 (1: 569). Schiller even weighed using "The Prodigal Son" as the title for the revised stage version of the play; in a suppressed early scene Moor defends his adherence to this tormented role in the face of Spiegelberg's scorn (variant to 1.2; 1: 919), and substitute father figures are everywhere: two pastors, the old servant Daniel, Karl himself as father to his band. The agony reaches a pitch in the last act when the disguised Karl at last confronts his repentant father. The latter apostrophizes the son whom he thinks lost for good—"I am not worthy of being called thy father"—and laments, "No son—no son left to press my eyes shut," while Karl deliberates and decides, "I can no longer give him his son" (5.2; 1: 610). Karl's painful decision to conceal his identity to the last is correct, for the father dies as soon as his son's identity is accidentally betrayed to him. No matter whose guilt broke the ties, they cannot be restored.

We are now in a position to understand why Schiller made the prodigal son a robber rather than, say, a spendthrift like Goldsmith's. For having lost his natural identity, Karl Moor sees no recourse but the attempt to steal one.[26] With nothing left that he can properly call his own, Karl resorts to appropriation and even to expropriation; breaking out is his desperate stratagem for breaking in again.[27] His brother is the one to perceive that Karl's boundless excesses are nothing other than a desire for acknowledgment: he himself, Franz scornfully says, "will one day die within his boundary stones, and rot and be forgotten, when the fame of this universal spirit [Karl] is flying from one pole to the other" (1.1; 1: 496).

Even in his most revolutionary mood Karl sees nothing natural coming from his actions: "The law has never made a great man, but freedom hatches colossi and extremities" (1.2; 1: 504). Unfortunately, this is not really what Karl wants, not, that is, what sensibility wants. And so his end is foredoomed. The little society of bandits he has gathered around him turns against its leader to enforce its own restricted economy of debts and obligations; they refuse to allow Moor to marry Amalia and establish a new family. Instead, he can only reassert his free identity by hatching a colossal extremity: he murders Amalia and then surrenders to the authorities. The end of Moor's outlawry is, as Hegel slyly phrases it in the title of the chapter of the *Phenomenology* that follows his discussion of the play, the reestablishment of "Virtue and the Way of the World."

It remains uncertain what moral we are to draw from the play, for there exist two substantially different versions of the conclusion.

In the original printed version the murder of Amalia is presented as an excess—"you have paid your debt with interest [*mit Wucher*]," says one of the robbers (5.2; 1: 616)—and the surrender reinforces what appears as an absurd stance of defiance. The hostile first reaction of the robbers to the surrender is to imprison the madman: "Put him in chains! He is raving." And their final reaction is an equally hostile distancing: "Let him go! It is megalomania. He wants to lay down his life for vain admiration" (5.2; 1: 617). In this version, in other words, identity is reduced from a stolen good to an empty, merely aesthetic illusion.

The alternative version—which can be briefly characterized as Schiller's redaction of Wolfgang Heribert von Dalberg's Mannheim staging—is greatly sentimentalized. Where, for instance, Franz originally hanged himself on stage rather than be captured by Karl's men, now there is a scene of reconciliation and forgiveness; where the devoted Schweizer originally shot himself in grief over the bungled capture, Karl now, in the long last speech of the play, declares him purged of all his crimes and exhorts him to become a good citizen. In line with this general softening, the murder of Amalia, which she now calls "sweetness" (5.2; 1: 933), is described as a proper payment, not an excess of interest (the original "Wucher" literally means usury); the robbers say "Bravo! bravo! That is redeeming his honor like a prince of robbers," and Moor replies with, "Bandits! we are even—My signature is torn up over this corpse—I give you yours back" (933). And this general rendering of accounts leads not to the hostilities of the first version, but to a mutual acknowledgment between Moor and his band and to an homage to the "rights of man" (934). Thus where the individual dissolves in the earlier version into hostility or the aesthetic distance of "vain admiration," in this version the individual dissolves back into the communal group.

Rather than regarding the printed version as authentic and the stage version as a way of appeasing the authorities, I prefer to remark on Schiller's ability to imagine—or at least his willingness to adapt to—alternative endings.[28] This may seem to be the opposite extreme from Goldsmith's inability ever to contrive a single plausible conclusion. But we may say that neither writer found the necessary and inevitable conclusion. The outcome of the drama of sensibility is not yet clear in these pre-Kantian, prerevolutionary, preromantic works. Identity in Goldsmith—as we shall shortly see—is faked, or borrowed (from Johnson), or aestheticized; in Schiller it is stolen, or aestheticized, or magnanimously conferred on one's associates; but in neither author is it truly found or truly made. Moor's surrender,

originally a gesture of tragic despair, becomes in the revision a shock-
ing and questionable self-abnegation: "And I too am a good citizen—
Am I not fulfilling the most dreadful law? Am I not honoring it?
Am I not avenging it?" (5.2; 1: 934). For all Moor's Shakespearian
grandiloquence, it remains at least until Schiller's fourth play, *Don
Carlos*, for the tragic hero to become a fulfilled personality.[29]

   Common to all the productions of sensibility examined in this
chapter has been a totalizing impulse. In the Enlightenment tradition perception builds bridges between the subject and a not fundamentally dissimilar object-world. For the writers of sensibility these
bridges become pathways to the universe, as perception strives to
grow into what Schiller calls "an embrace of the whole of nature"
("Philosophische Briefe," in *Werke* 5: 350). In the Enlightenment
tradition the end of perception might be termed cognition, a proper
alignment of the subject's understanding with the laws and processes of nature. In sensibility knowledge recovers its erotic dimension, as the subject moves toward engulfing the entire world: "The
whole of creation flows into his personality. If each man loved all
men, then each individual would possess the world" (5: 350). Such
a stance seems to be extrapolated from the idealism of Leibniz's
monads and Berkeley's intuitive understanding. Yet we have also
seen what dangers this flowing of the universe entails for the personality. Where all barriers between subject and object are overthrown,
the result can easily turn into a neo-empiricist submergence of the
subject in the ocean of reality. We become what we behold, or, as
Schiller phrases it, "we ourselves become the perceived object"
(5: 346).

   With this uncertainty in the outcome of sensibility comes the
recognition that something is awry with the homogeneity between
subject and object on which Enlightenment epistemology was predicated. The symmetry between perceiver and perceived is a terrifying
echo, a dreaded, deadly tiger that can only be framed by even greater
might and even greater daring.[30] Blake's Urizen, the all-bounding
one, shows us that the stake in sensibility is not feeling, but raw
power, the terrifying mastery of and by feeling in the dark night that
marks the outer limit of reason.

> But when the morn arose, her lamentation renewd,
> The Daughters of Albion hear her woes, & eccho back her sighs.
>
>   .   .   .
> Thy joys are tears! thy labour vain, to form men to thine image.
> How can one joy absorb another? are not different joys
> Holy, eternal, infinite! and each joy is a Love.
>
>   .   .   .

What are his nets & gins & traps. & how does he surround him
With cold floods of abstraction, and with forests of solitude,
To build him castles and high spires. where kings & priests may
    dwell.
    (*Visions of the Daughters of Albion* 5.1–2, 4–6, 18–20)

We become what we behold, the good-natured slogan of sensibility, echoes, of course, through Blake's *Jerusalem*. There, however, it occurs in the context of Hayley's well-meaning yet corrosive patronage of the poor painter; sympathy is revealed as the instrument of an unintentional tyranny, and sometimes of an intentional one:

Ah! alas! at the sight of the Victim, & at sight of those who are
    smitten,
All who see. become what they behold. their eyes are coverd
With veils of tears and their nostrils & tongues shrunk up
Their ear bent outwards. as their Victim, so they are in the pangs
Of unconquerable fear!

                                        (66.35–39)

In retrospect, such fearful symmetry may be seen to bisect the whole movement of sensibility. Strong feeling was from the start a mark of weakness, and sympathy a symptom of gullibility. The dreamer d'Alembert is commutative with the mathematician; all assertions of independence constitute acknowledgments of the framework of mutual dependence that is being transcended:

And the soft smile of friendship & the open dawn of benevolence
Become a net & a trap, & every energy renderd cruel,
Till the existence of friendship & benevolence is denied . . .
The open heart is shut up in integuments of frozen silence
That the spear that lights it forth may shatter the ribs & bosom
A pretence of Art, to destroy Art: a pretence of Liberty
To destroy Liberty. a pretence of Religion to destroy Religion.

                                        (38.25–27, 33–36)

Thus the robber seems fated to have been the culminating representative of sensibility. The man of sensibility dwells in a border region; his crossings—between self and other, subject and object, sorrow and joy—mark out the location of the boundary, and his freedom calls forth the inflexible law as its specter or shadow, as Hegel was soon to recognize. Whether or not the robber was a strictly inevitable figure, it is certain that Karl Moor captured the imagination of Europe as the distillation of the mood of the day.[31] It took decades to work through the implications of his commanding presence, and while I do not propose to do so here, one could scrutinize all the mysterious, sentimental, or violent borderers haunting Wordsworth's early poetry in connection with the antinomies of sensibility, the mysteries of personality, and the economy of the psyche.

Fredric Jameson has written about Schiller's *Letters on the Aesthetic Education of Mankind* that

> Schiller's profound originality, which will leave its mark on thinkers from Hegel to Freud, was to have . . . transferred the notion of the division of labor, of economic specialization, from the social classes to the inner functioning of the mind, where it assumes the appearance of a hypostasis of one mental function over against the others, a spiritual deformation which is the exact equivalent of the economic alienation in the social world outside. (*Marxism and Form* 87)

While the origin lay earlier, as I have shown, this is a penetrating and accurate insight into the conceptual basis of romantic psychology. Yet its evaluative tone misrepresents the thrust of history. To argue that the division of psychic labor is a deformation presupposes some prior Robin Hood age of the spirit when psychic forces existed in a healthy balance within a totally integrated community; as Jameson later writes (apropos of Sartre), "there cannot be alienation unless there was first something to alienate, some prior form of human relationship to serve as the object of distortion" (241). Any responsible history of romanticism will of course demonstrate that romanticism did not settle all questions. But it is wrong to imply that romanticism is the source of error, guilty of deformations that did not previously exist, the dark night of the spirit after the brightness of the Enlightenment. On the contrary, the Enlightenment had its own day with its own intellectual climate, its own unsettled weather, and its own night. Neither savior nor villain, romanticism was itself only another episode in the Great Year of the spirit that we call Western Civilization.

CHAPTER SIX

Goldsmith's Endings

Goldsmith has counted to many as the most agreeable writer of his age. His unproblematic texts have not proved rewarding material for study, particularly for critical practices geared to confronting and clarifying difficulties. Yet he was a fluent writer only in his hack work. Even after much struggle, he had to leave to Johnson the endings of his two major poems, and what little we know of his compositional labors suggests that what is easy for his readers did not come easily to him. If the central problems of sensibility were self-definition, self-regulation, and closure, then Goldsmith deserves to figure more prominently than he usually has as an index to the literary anxieties of his period. The present chapter is devoted to the concealed structural conflicts that necessitate those endings, and the two subsequent chapters concern the complex gestation of formal simplicity motivating the endings of *The Vicar of Wakefield* and *She Stoops to Conquer.*[1]

Boswell was and is Goldsmith's chief competitor for attention.[2] If sensibility is regarded as the cult of feelings, then Boswell is its hero. Since their publication, Boswell's journals have often served as a prototypical example of writing to the moment in the Age of Sensibility. "A man cannot know himself better than by attending to the feelings of his heart and to his external actions," Boswell writes at the start of his *London Journal* (Nov. 15, 1762, p. 39). As if to prove the point, the journals record Boswell's many moods, impulsive, splenetic, hypochondriac. Yet they do so imperfectly at best: "I find it is impossible to put upon paper an exact journal of the life of man. External circumstances may be marked. But the variations within, the workings of reason and passion, and, what perhaps influences happiness most, the colourings of fancy, are too fleeting to be recorded."[3] Not even Boswell wrote with the end of being Boswellian.

Rather, Boswell's avowed aim was to achieve "knowledge and moderation and government of myself" (*London Journal*, Jan. 13, 1763, p. 141). When an acquaintance suggests that a journal encourages Boswell to "hunt about for adventures to adorn it with," Boswell responds that "far from wishing for extravagant adventures," the journal is "a very excellent scheme if judiciously executed" for promoting "consistency of conduct" (May 25, 1763, p. 269). Sensibility is purgative—its pangs are a form of *Bildung* or apprenticeship in the mastery of life: "Upon my word my journal goes charmingly on at present. . . . I think, too, that I am . . . taking more pains upon it, and consequently writing it in a more correct style. Style is to sentiment what dress is to the person. The effects of both are very great, and both are acquired and improved by habit" (Feb. 9, 1763, p. 186). Hence Boswell writes against sensibility as it has been commonly understood, and in favor rather of the kind of psychic economics that my last chapter described: "The character worthy of imitation is the man of economy, who with prudent attention knows when to save and when to spend, and acts accordingly. Let me pursue this system" (ibid.). It is consequently a mistake to consider the spontaneous and open-ended journal form to express the truth of sensibility; it has meaning and appeal only as a record of the antagonist within, the negation to be overcome at the end of the epic of life. What William Dowling has written about the biography applies equally to the journals: they are struggles "to discover faith and order amid the moral disarray of the later eighteenth century."[4] A journal can never come to fruition and to completion. It cannot settle the problems of sensibility for the same reason that it cannot help raising them.

Hence I see the true drama of sensibility in its positive aspirations enacted elsewhere. Among all the writers of the period, Goldsmith is the one who confronts us most insistently, as he confronted himself, with the crucial dilemma: the difficulty of endings. The first page of his very first book, *An Inquiry into the Present State of Polite Learning*, announces that he takes "the decay of genius for granted" (1: 257), and throughout his career Goldsmith almost invariably associated development and refinement with increasing artificiality, dissoluteness, and decomposition.[5] The natural ending to

a Goldsmith plot is neither a comic reconciliation nor a tragic purgation and redemption, but catastrophe and chaos. In *The Vicar of
Wakefield* Goldsmith salvages a happy ending only by combining
practically every implausible trick in the whole book of romance. In
She Stoops to Conquer, likewise, only the sudden revelation that
Tony is of age prevents all plans from going sour and all the characters from being dispersed. Both of Goldsmith's major poems turn
near the end toward America, and though the descriptions of the
natural scene differ radically—tempestuous and noisy in *The Traveller*'s description of New York, silent and threateningly sultry in
the Georgia of *The Deserted Village*—both agree in calling the social conditions "murderous" (*Traveller*, line 416; *Deserted Village*,
line 356). At the end Goldsmith can foresee no good in the land of
the future. With this cast of mind the problem of a resolution becomes oppressive.

The aspirations to a happy ending first materialized in Goldsmith's verse narratives. "Edwin and Angelina" is pure romance,
ending with an entirely coincidental meeting of its two long-lost
lovers. The "Elegy on the Death of a Mad Dog" is pure spoof, with
the mad dog dying from having bitten the good man. From among
the minor poems, however, it is the early "The Double Transformation: A Tale" that exhibits Goldsmith's concerns in the starkest
form. This is a satire in Swiftean tetrameter describing Jack Book-
worm's abrupt marriage at thirty-six to the beautiful Flavia. Things
quickly run downhill, as always in Goldsmith: Flavia proves to be all
paint, a coquette abroad and a slut at home. When all seems hopeless, however, smallpox strikes, leaving Flavia with "but the rem-
nant of a face" (line 80) and costing her all her lovers. Suddenly, she
and Jack are thrown upon one another. He finds that disease dis-
figures her less than cosmetics, so that "Her present face surpass[es]
the old" (line 96), and she is driven to learn civility:

> With modesty her cheeks are dy'd,
> Humility displaces pride; . . .
> No more presuming on her sway
> She learns good nature every day,
> Serenely gay, and strict in duty.
> (lines 97–98, 101–3)

This must be the least promising cure for Swift's cynicism and the
most perilous genesis of good nature ever imagined. One begins to
wonder whether in the "Elegy on the Death of a Mad Dog," too,
Goldsmith did not intend to prove the man's virtue from the fact

that he was infectious.[6] Indeed, when one reads the last line of "The Double Transformation," one suddenly doesn't know what to think: "Jack finds his wife a perfect beauty" (line 104). The disease that made Flavia good turned the whole world so topsy-turvy that ugliness has become fair. Nothing makes sense any more. Perhaps Flavia is still no more dutiful than she is beautiful; perhaps Jack remains just as fond and as foolish—"dazzl'd" is Goldsmith's suspicious word (line 95)—as he was at the start. Despite its understated gentleness, it is an irony worthy of Swift.[7]

"The Double Transformation" may contain the only perfect ending that Goldsmith ever wrote—perfect because perfectly inscrutable. The clearer the outcome of a Goldsmith work, the more baffling is its origin and its relationship to the totality of the work. Therefore I want to examine Goldsmith's major works in detail in order to discern in each case what kind of stock-taking or coming to consciousness is reflected by the form and content of the conclusion.

The Traveller, or a Prospect of Society

Since Johnson was so intimately involved in the creation of Goldsmith's longer poems, it is natural to begin by comparing *The Traveller* with *The Vanity of Human Wishes*. Indeed, Goldsmith invites a direct comparison with the earlier poem by opening the last paragraph of his poem with the same find-mind rhyme that Johnson uses to open and also to close his last paragraph. It becomes apparent that Johnson is the more empirical and worldly, Goldsmith the more rational, the more concerned with mind, and hence ultimately the more inward. Where *The Vanity of Human Wishes* features a number of individual examples, *The Traveller* offers only general cases. Where Johnson, despite promising to "Survey mankind, from China to Peru" (line 2), in fact only hops around the circumference of Europe (Sweden, Moscow, Persia, the Greek states, the Holy Roman Empire—a borderland populated by "The fierce Croatian, and the wild Hussar," line 249—and, of course, Britain), Goldsmith surveys the major European civilizations systematically and crosses the ocean at the end. Yet the tone of his poem is far more personal, finally turning on a comparison of his feelings with his brother's. *The Traveller* moves toward a private, secularized alternative to Johnson's faith in a general providence guiding all mankind: "Vain, very vain, my weary search to find / That bliss which only centers in the mind" (lines 423–24). Everything thus far in the poem points precisely to the discovery of the individual consciousness as the solution to the problems of the commonalty. Indeed, the conclusion seems to confirm the poem's direction:

> Still to ourselves in every place consign'd,
> Our own felicity we make or find:
> With secret course, which no loud storms annoy,
> Glides the smooth current of domestic joy.
> The lifted ax, the agonizing wheel,
> Luke's iron crown, and Damien's bed of steel,
> To men remote from power but rarely known,
> Leave reason, faith and conscience all our own.
> (lines 431–38)

These concluding lines seem to grow inevitably out of the rest of the poem—even the consigned-find rhyme has been anticipated at lines 59–60—yet Johnson wrote all but the couplet concerning public evils (lines 435–36). How can we explain Goldsmith's reliance for his conclusion on the very man whose poem he was trying to answer?

The more closely we inspect Johnson's lines, the more at odds they seem with the poem. Throughout *The Traveller* Goldsmith has yearned for roots, for a "spot" to which he may be bound (the word occurs in lines 13, 30, 60, and 63). Traveling implies isolation; in one of the poem's many paradoxes the traveler calls himself "unfriended" in the first line, yet immediately says that his "heart untravell'd" (line 8) remains attached to his brother, "my earliest friend" (line 11). To the very end, his "weary search" (line 423) is for a home and a human circle. When he concludes by evoking "That bliss which only centers in the mind" (line 424), the verb prolongs the nostalgia for place, as we see from the ensuing question, "Why have I stray'd . . . ?" (line 425). The concern with nations in the poem—in contrast to Johnson's preoccupation with individual heroes and villains—partakes of a desire to establish identity that remains in contact with its particular clod of earth, its fatherland. Thus, Johnson's "in every place" betrays Goldsmith's hopes. Likewise Johnson's "Still to ourselves . . . consign'd" belies the wishful vision of a happy family with which this poem begins (in lines 11–22) and with which Goldsmith's novel and both plays conclude: for Goldsmith, "the smooth current of domestic joy" must make a show and not glide "with secret course," as Johnson says at the end. Johnson's "reason, faith and conscience all our own" are likewise secret, hoarded, invisible virtues; they can only be taken as negative ideals, the opposite of the understanding, hope and conscientiousness that Goldsmith practices or praises in the body of the poem. In these ways (and in others discussed by

Lonsdale in "A Garden and a Grave") Johnson's conclusion denies the manifest premises of the poem.

In many respects Goldsmith seems closer in sentiment to Gray than to Johnson. Goldsmith's praise of simple country living ought to have appealed more to the historian of "The short and simple annals of the poor" than to a committed urbanite like Johnson; and Goldsmith's great opening line, "Remote, unfriended, melancholy, slow"—three increasingly long adjectives completed by the burdened monosyllable—evokes the weary mood of the first quatrain of Gray's "Elegy." Yet there is a fundamental difference. Rejecting the uniqueness of fame and glory, the "Elegy" moves simultaneously toward universality and toward simplicity. *The Traveller,* by contrast, associates universality with the unhappy traveler's exile and with the troubled conditions prevailing across the globe; it envisions simplicity as the antidote to universality.

This observation illuminates the suture between Goldsmith's poem and Johnson's conclusion. Goldsmith's particular is simple without being individual; his general is embracing without being cosmic or universal. His thought remains within the fluid middle ground of the urbane sublime and shies away from the absolutes, oppositions, ironic underminings, and synthetic resolutions toward which Johnson presses. As the extensive view of Johnson's observation travels around the edges of the European experience, so do his individual consciousness and all-encompassing divinity alike lie beyond the horizon of what Goldsmith can imagine. Yet Goldsmith's poem secretly inclines toward them, despite his intentions.

Goldsmith's counterplot appears first in the remarkable tonality of his line, which projects an obscure force of resistance to the sociable reconciliations of the traditional heroic couplet. Consider the Dutch landscape, "Where the broad ocean leans against the land" (line 284). What is awry, burdening this line? Is it the emphatic adjective and verb that erode the prominence of the rational antithesis ocean-land—the adjective because of the displaced stress on the monosyllabic third syllable, the verb because of the ambiguous location of the caesura, which is felt equally before and after "leans"? Is it the discomfort of a suppressed punning relationship between broad and lean(s)? Is it that "land" is phonetically overpowered by the brighter "leans"? Goldsmith's strong lines seem dragged by a weight of language too inchoate to rise to the level of thought. One notices, to be sure, occasional pointedly individualizing ironies, such as the use of a rare run-on line where the verb is "stopt" (lines 347–48), or the displacement by a line of the inevitable Denham couplet, so that it no longer rhymes ("Though poor, luxurious, though submissive, vain, / Though grave, yet trifling, zealous, yet untrue," lines 128–29). But more characteristic is the less flamboyant, heavy line, like the first line or the great description of how we see opulence "In barren solitary pomp repose" (line 404), whose final halting (itself a phonetic expansion of the rhyme word "rose") forestalls any resolution of the irony in the long-delayed monosyllable, "pomp." The effect of "repose" here is not unlike the disturbing irresolution of Flavia's "perfect beauty" at the end of "The Double Transformation": time will not provide a reconciliation. And at an even more internalized, less conscious level there lies, I believe, a distinctive feeling for vowel patterning. Goldsmith appears on the one hand to use alliteration and other patterns of consonant repetition to integrate the lines, but, on the other hand, to tend toward vocalic differentiation (for example, back vowels in "broad ocean" contrasted with front and middle vowels in "leans against the land") to preserve separations. Vocalic echoes signal danger ("They please, are pleas'd, they give to get esteem," line 265), or else may occasionally urge toward unity what the consonants hold apart ("To men of other minds my fancy flies," line 281). Largely absent is the Johnsonian vowel harmony that gives peace to a troubled mind through the soothing repetition of a prevailing sound: front vowels as in Johnson's line 432, /o/ sounds as in his lines 433 and 437. Repetition of sounds in Goldsmith is barbaric ("And Niagara stuns with thund'ring sound," line 412), and it is not uncommon for there to be four or five different accented vowel sounds in a single line ("Where wild Oswego spreads her swamps around," line 411). Modeling our reading practice on Pope's wit or contrasting it with Johnson's ornate erudition, we are too prone to skim Goldsmith's couplets; read slowly, as they should be, they offer the rather grim effect of an irrational weight without stability.[8]

And that is, in truth, also the social vision that Goldsmith offers. As he looks around for a societal ideal, he sees how in each society the labor of many produces an ensemble that overwhelms the individual without generating a functioning totality or organized freedom. While the official aspiration of the poem is for a group of which the individual can become a part, its unacknowledged moral—unacknowledged by Goldsmith, at any rate—is that groups inherently absorb rather than integrate the individual. Goldsmith tells us that each national group has its curve of development, with a high point of coordination leading eventually to decadence. But what we see is a constant antithesis with no possibility of reconciliation; the general instability engulfs the particular. Behind the poem's social aspirations thus lies an almost Heideggerian anxiety—an unexpressed fear *of* and yet *for* the individual. A resolution needed to come by stealth and from an alien hand.

Structurally, the poem's instability results in part from the fact that it is almost entirely an imaginative vision of the speaker's. Since the imagination both internalizes and generalizes, it appears divided against itself: internalization creates a fictive particularity, whereas generalization ought to rest on a real universality. Yet both engulf the individual, the first by introjection into a vision, the second by insertion into a cosmos. Governed by a visionary consciousness, the poem tends toward making all consciousness visionary (and thus a covert projection of the traveler). But then the natural tendency of eighteenth-century diction turns the imaginative projection into a mere example. Thus the Swiss peasant knows himself happy because, like the traveler, his vision is clear: "He sees his little lot, the lot of all; / Sees . . ." (lines 178–79). Yet the poetic diction, with its telltale abstracting articles, dissolves the peasant into a type and disperses alert purpose into the manifold instinctive actions of myth:

> Chearful at morn he wakes from short repose,
> Breasts the keen air and carrols as he goes;
> With patient angle trolls the finny deep,
> Or drives his vent'rous plow-share to the steep;
> Or seeks the den where snow tracks mark the way,
> And drags the struggling savage into day.
>
> (lines 185–90)

Both larger and smaller than life, the peasant proves unreal at the end, until his happiness is rewarded by the even more imaginative, but even more imaginary, pilgrim: "And haply too some pilgrim, thither led, / With many a tale repays the nightly bed" (lines 197–98). Despite once praising "thoughtless realms" (line 255), the traveler remains a thinking individual committed to mind ("mind to mind," "The mind still turns," "To men of other minds," "Methinks," lines 257, 279, 281, 283; etc.). The observer imagines other observers, imaginatively projecting imagining individuals. This Chinese-box structure calls into question not just the durability but the very reality of individual, empirical experience. Thus near the end he sees the great British nobility—sees not only them but, in a surreal close-up, "their eye" (line 327)—and sees the peasant, another observer observed, "scan" not the scene, but something far more abstract, his "rights" (line 333). And this whole scene is itself unreal; he has been carried to Britain on wings of song ("Fir'd at the sound," "gentle music," lines 317, 322), and the very rights being surveyed are "imagin'd" (line 332). Finally, the traveler ends his description of Italy with the impoverished modern peasantry, again thinking:

> There in the ruin, heedless of the dead,
> The shelter-seeking peasant builds his shed,
> And, wond'ring man could want the larger pile,
> Exults, and owns his cottage with a smile.
>
> (lines 161–64)

The echoing vowels in line 162 forebode no good: we do not smile at the smiling peasant, except maybe in pity or contempt. The shed is not much to "own"; the peasant may *acknowledge* it, but can hardly be said to *possess* anything significant. The imagination is a poor investment, producing only illusions.

Nature is a second factor blocking a reconciliation of the particular and the general (or the individual and society). Nature is "a mother kind alike to all" (line 81), with a universality that ironically undermines any sense of loyalty to a particular group, family, or "kind."[9] Goldsmith's notion of a universal mother in a sense foreshadows Johnson's indifference to place, except that Johnson's "Still to ourselves . . . consign'd" leaves nature out of the picture, and his "smooth current" turns Goldsmith's myth into a merely metaphoric use of nature. For as the universal, nature by definition subsumes the particular into her broad sweep. "Lakes, forests, cities, plains extending wide" (line 35)—the human is submerged in the landscape; seen from "on high" (line 33), cities and even natural growths of the forest dwindle into vertical specks enclosed by an infinite horizontal.[10] The broadest perspective may make nature come alive ("Ye lakes, whose vessels catch the busy gale," line 47), but it reduces man to an ornament or a bubble on the stream of time ("Ye bending swains, that dress the flow'ry vale," line 48). The elevated perch produces a momentary exaltation, to be sure: "Creation's heir, the world, the world is mine" (line 50). Yet the traveler's possession is in its way no more secure than the Italian peasant's hut: if he possesses nature, the wealth will only enfeeble him: "As some lone miser visiting his store . . ." (line 51).

The imagination blocks individuation through reduction; it produces poverty or else the false glitter of "imaginary worth" (line 260). Nature, at the other pole, blocks individuation because its standard overreaches human power. In "florid" Italy "Man seems the only growth that dwindles" (lines 125–26). In Switzerland, where the mountains are higher, the buildings get lower (line 179) and life more "level" (line 221). Britain exchanges "Her useful sons . . . for useless ore" (line 398), showing how disproportionate is nature's currency to human labor. Any part smaller than the grand totality of nature will seem petty; indeed a closer look always shows corruption (lines 305–12), or a close approach is a symptom of danger (lines 205–8), or else "closer eyes" (line 99) prove effectively closed, yielding generalizations about mankind on the basis of a dark scene that is representative and not in any sense unique: "Like yon neglected shrub, at random cast, / That shades the steep, and sighs at every blast" (lines 103–4). "Yon" particularizes, but "at random" reduces the individual to a representative. The universal, natural standard precludes recognizing the value of any individual.[11]

The engulfing imagination and the enveloping nature combine to precipitate a crisis. It is initially a crisis of vision, as the traveler condemns the "blind" multitude (line 377) but then regrets his own power of sight, repeatedly reflecting on a vision no longer present, "Have we not seen . . ." (lines 397, 405). And the crisis is then projected onto an America grown morosely horizontal (wild Oswego's swamps) and terrifyingly vertical (Niagara's thundering sound). It is no wonder that so gruesome a vision terminates a poem in which vision is constantly going sour. But what is surprising is the way Goldsmith projects his anxiety onto an imaginary American double, as if unwilling to acknowledge the anxiety as his own and therefore unable to embrace some remedy lurking in the heart of the American Other:

> The pensive exile, bending with his woe,
> To stop too fearful, and too faint to go,
> Casts a long look where England's glories shine,
> And bids his bosom sympathize with mine.
> (lines 419–22)

The American's bosom could hardly fail to sympathize with Goldsmith's, since Goldsmith's bosom is the only place where he exists. Yet it remains for Johnson to articulate their secret agreement. It is not the meeting of two hearts—Goldsmith and his brother, the traveler and the exile—that would solve the poet's problems, but rather what is constantly getting overwhelmed in this poem, namely, the beating of a single heart. The perils enumerated by Goldsmith—the axe, the wheel, the crown of burning iron, and the steel bed—all threaten not society or family, but the lifelines of the individual;

consequently it would not be farfetched to read Johnson's "smooth current of domestic joy" as the most internal and private current of all, neither the currency of social exchange nor the flow of familial affections, but the life-preserving bloodstream itself. Indeed, though the poem begins by evoking the brother's family life—curiously elided in Goldsmith's dedication to his brother—the speaker concludes by condemning British freedom for destroying all social ties: "The self dependent lordlings stand alone, / All claims that bind and sweeten life unknown" (lines 341–42). An individual salvation is needed here, and not the social salvation that the whole poem has struggled to realize and shown to be in vain.

Goldsmith's eyes are turned away from the truth of his poem, and he does not, perhaps cannot, acknowledge that nature and society are always, at every point in their cycle, antagonistic to the very individualism that he yearns for them to nurture. Yet the poem contains signs intimating a covert recognition that its truth is at odds with its manifest content. The first sign is that the traveler is not, in the poem, a traveler at all. Instead he sits, and as he sits he looks, and then when he can no longer see, he imagines ("my fancy flies," line 281). The poem is a momentary respite in his restless journey, and his quietus comes from private thought. In a sense, "Still to ourselves in every place consign'd" does no more than name the situation of the speaker: it tells the poet that what he has instinctively done is in fact what satisfies him, even though he thinks that it was done in despair and that he would rather be moving than sitting. And the second sign, also distributed throughout the poem and hence perhaps overlooked as we read paragraph by paragraph, lies in the movement of thought. For the speaker looks south, then north, then west, then lets his thoughts take him ever further west. A revolution must complete the poem, a turning toward a sunrise of new origins and away from the sunset of civilization over the deadly American wilds. It is this revolution that Goldsmith is unwilling or unable to complete.[12]

But the speaker projects the completion that he himself does not consummate. Although the traveler does not turn east, his double does. What is the brightness that he sees or imagines shining there? I do not know, and I doubt that Goldsmith did either. Conceivably "England's glories" (line 421) would be the poets, heroes of the mind. We can be sure only that they are not her social achievements, since Goldsmith has told us at length (lines 399–412) that these are what drove the pensive exile out of Britain. But the exile turns in a direction that the traveler never faces, and he sees England in an altered light. He it is who represents the tendencies that the poet can only recognize when they are projected onto and by a fraternal figure. In a poem so divided against itself, it is the poet's other, Johnson and not Goldsmith, who speaks for the poet's own blind spot and gives utterance to the suppressed longing for an emancipated individual consciousness.[13]

The Deserted Village

Much in my reading of *The Traveller* is inferential. It depends on seeing the poem's proliferating figures of the oppressed as self-projections, with their woes as the residues of the speaker's psychic conflicts. Such a reading will always remain merely probable. But we can at least feel some confidence that Johnson read the poem along some such lines. For here is Johnson's conclusion to *The Deserted Village*:

> That trade's proud empire hastes to swift decay,
> As ocean sweeps the labour'd mole away;
> While self dependent power can time defy,
> As rocks resist the billows and the sky.
> (lines 427–30)

Since Johnson's *Dictionary* does not list "self-dependent," it is probable that he knew of no other occurrence than the "self dependent lordlings" in *The Traveller*, cited three paragraphs back. Johnson could hardly have risked so glaring a verbal clash with the earlier poem unless he sensed that Goldsmith harbored a secret sympathy for the freestanding nobility whom he had appeared to condemn. We can take the conclusion to *The Deserted Village* to be a public rebuke to *The Traveller* that masks a subterranean concord. We know from Boswell that Goldsmith was accustomed to such treatment from Johnson.

The relationship of the lines just quoted to *The Deserted Village* itself is perhaps more puzzling. For it is difficult to discern what in Goldsmith's text could be attached to the heroics of Johnson's conclusion. The whole cast of Goldsmith's concluding paragraph is feminine.[14] Having witnessed the devastation of the countryside, Goldsmith turns to Poetry for solace and hope. He calls Poetry "my solitary pride" (line 412)—"proud" is, of course, a negative term in Johnson's conclusion—and his "guide" (line 415); clearly, we cannot attribute "self dependent power" to the hesitantly "pondering" (line 397), self-pitying (line 414), shy poet. It is not the poet, but Poetry,

"Dear charming nymph" (line 411), whose voice may prevail "over time" (line 421). But Poetry is also not self-dependent; her job is to "Aid slighted truth" (line 423). And she is not a hard rock, but a voice that wanders from shore to shore, "On Torno's cliffs, or Pamba-marca's side" (line 418). Her mode is rather compliance than defiance.

Goldsmith's last couplet deepens the mystery, making it easy to see why he needed help, but hard to appreciate why he adopted Johnson's solution: "Teach him that states of native strength pos-sest, / Tho' very poor, may still be very blest" (lines 425–26). What is Poetry supposed to teach? There is no evidence in the poem that Poetry can provide any useful precepts. She does not remedy the ills of the turbulent countryside, any more than a rock calms the waves. Not even to Goldsmith has she been of any material use: "[Thou] found'st me poor at first, and keep'st me so" (line 414). Nevertheless, Goldsmith calls her the "source of all my bliss" (line 413). Evidently, she will teach not by precept, showing where to find a "native strength" of which the poem offers precious few instances, but by example. She is in herself the spiritual wealth that can compensate for the rigors of modern life. In using something so inert as a rock for his model of self-dependent power, Johnson seems to have acknowl-edged that native strength is a passive or reflexive quality rather than an active one. Yet it remains hard to see what legitimates Gold-smith's periphrasis, since he could as easily have written, "states of Poetry possest." He calls Poetry a "maid," a "nymph," a "guide," a "nurse," the aid to "slighted truth"; what makes her strong? And is Johnson completing or correcting Goldsmith's thought when he then calls her a rock with self-dependent power?

In one essential respect Goldsmith and Johnson clearly concur: in the desire to resist time. For Goldsmith the resistance comes from a wandering "voice prevailing over time" (line 421), for Johnson from a fixed rock whose "power can time defy" (line 429). Despite the contrasting tonalities, both may thus be said to find their salva-tion in space. Indeed, from the very start Goldsmith characterizes Auburn as a full landscape that is as free from the pressure of time as any earthly place can be:

> SWEET AUBURN, loveliest village of the plain,
> Where health and plenty cheared the labouring swain,
> Where smiling spring its earliest visit paid,
> And parting summer's lingering blooms delayed,
> Dear lovely bowers of innocence and ease,
> Seats of my youth, when every sport could please,
> How often have I loitered o'er thy green,

> Where humble happiness endeared each scene;
> How often have I paused on every charm . . .
> (lines 1–9)

Space in *The Deserted Village* is thus not Derridean *espacement,* the various effects of distancing and separation that make space into a mapping of temporal deferral. Space is rather the prior Kantian coordinate space in which we—and in which time itself—exist. The voice represents freedom of movement, the rock stability and endurance; both are modes of selfhood that cushion us from the fatal deterioration always attributed by Goldsmith to time. The task for interpretation will be to discern what kind of body or locus for bodies finds room in the poetic imagination.

The couplet itself is a narrow bed. Closed at the end and subdivided within, couplets can aspire to the firmness of a rock, but hardly to the expansiveness of a fervent voice. Those in *The Deserted Village* are lean and forceful—relentless as the pounding main and resistant as the cliffs of Torno and Pambamarca. Most often they function as units contrasting past with present. Time serves as the backbone for their articulation, as is readily seen from a series of paragraph beginnings: "Ill fares the land, to hastening ills a prey" (line 51), "A time there was" (line 57), "But times are altered" (line 63), "Sweet AUBURN! parent of the blissful hour" (line 75). Normally the couplets announced by such phrases reify differences; every syntactic variation merely confirms the basic pattern of contrasts and consolidates the sense of confinement to a moment, a situation, and a language.

The order of couplets is inflicted on a poet who claims to prefer "One native charm" to "all the gloss of art" and who seeks "Spontaneous joys" that "frolic [lightly] o'er the vacant mind, / Unenvied, unmolested, unconfined" (lines 254–58). In his preface to *The Traveller* Goldsmith had defended couplet poetry against the excessive refinement of Pindarics and blank verse, yet the couplets here have more in common ideologically with aristocratic enclosure than with Bohemian liberty. They serve the same function as a fence. In the old village the only fence we hear of belonged to the schoolmaster; he was stern but bumbling, and he built a "straggling fence" (line 193). But now, Goldsmith's *cri de coeur* tells us, the new fences that organize the landscape (no more "tangling walks, and ruined grounds," line 78) are depriving the populace of their national heritage:

> Where then, ah, where shall poverty reside,
> To scape the pressure of contiguous pride;

If to some common's fenceless limits strayed,
He drives his flock to pick the scanty blade,
Those fenceless fields the sons of wealth divide,
And even the bare-worn common is denied.

(lines 303–8)

The results of enclosure are many, but Goldsmith's concluding concern with poetic voice leads me to single one out here: the neat but empty parks of the aristocracy have deprived England of the possibilities of communication. The daughter is "silent" (line 377), the wife complains to a "silent" husband (line 384), and the exiles are relegated to a vast and "silent" land (line 350). The refinement of poetic style, it would seem, has parceled out and despoiled the vigor of the common language, producing a rank growth of empty words, barren of sense.[15]

The altered technique and tone can have little to do with actual changes in English society in the years since *The Traveller*. The earlier poem had already spoken of depopulation, and the dedication of *The Deserted Village* to Joshua Reynolds candidly admits to the fictive status of the problem: "I know you will object (and indeed several of our best and wisest friends concur in the opinion) that the depopulation it deplores is no where to be seen, and the disorders it laments are only to be found in the poet's own imagination." They are not to be found, it is worth noting, in *The Vicar of Wakefield* or in *She Stoops to Conquer*. Depopulation, after all, leaves emptiness in its wake, and a depopulated landscape reverts at least partially to a natural condition. Depopulation can no more "be seen" directly than can any other form of vacancy, and (continues Goldsmith) "this is not the place" to fill up that particular hole by "enter[ing] into an enquiry, whether the country be depopulating, or not; the discussion would take up much room." The mood of *The Deserted Village* may have more to do with psychological than with social concerns, for Goldsmith's brother had died in the interim (as the dedication mentions), an event that removed the utopian alternative in the earlier poem and perhaps intensified Goldsmith's sense of passing time. But whatever its real ground, depopulation evidently affected Goldsmith as a poetic problem: it constricts the imagination and creates a void to be filled in the right place and the right way.

The poetic task is thus to break through the bounds of the couplet to recover the humanity and the firm communicating voice that once belonged to the village preacher, Goldsmith's deceased brother. "As some tall cliff" (line 189) pierces the clouds into the open sky— the simile anticipates Johnson's conclusion—so the preacher rose above adversity, and so too, in his imaginative strength, must the poet do. Much freer in overall structure than *The Traveller*, *The Deserted Village* is memorable not for its diction, but for a new style of organization that resists the pregnant hollowness of that verbal "garden, and a grave" (line 302), the heroic couplet. The following pages will consider three features of that organization: verbal repetitions, catalogues, and imaginary portraits.

Typical of the poem's diction are lines like the following:

> These were thy charms, sweet village; sports like these,
> With sweet succession, taught even toil to please;
> These round thy bowers their chearful influence shed,
> These were thy charms—But all these charms are fled.
>   Sweet smiling village, loveliest of the lawn,
> Thy sports are fled, and all thy charms withdrawn;
> Amidst thy bowers the tyrant's hand is seen,
> And desolation saddens all thy green.
>
> (lines 31–38)

The semantic impoverishment is astonishing; not even namby-pamby Philips wrote so simply as this. The scarcely varied repetition of terms is a dike against change. Recirculation governs the lexical economy of the poem, attempting to convert linguistic poverty into a reserve of strength. Circling (with repeated words like "turn," "return," "around") also becomes thematically a sign of strength, with all the various circles knitting the village into a community. Yet repetition is rather a denial of time than the establishment of a space for life. If the circle suggests unity, it also suggests enclosure,[16] and it breaks open as it is enlarged: "Ah, no. To distant climes, a dreary scene, / Where half the convex world intrudes between" (lines 341–42).

Such intensity of repetition and such frequency of return thus have a double meaning: they evoke a world, but they do so in the mode of limitation. The repetition assures us of the emotional reality of the village, but at the price of suggesting a continuity between present deprivation and past circumscription. If the sports are fled, it was always their nature to be fleeting (since they involved races and quickly succeeded one another). If the charms are withdrawn, they were always shadowy and retiring. The repetitions frame a scene or series of scenes, but "scene" itself is a charged word that implies confinement; its negative connotations are revealed when Goldsmith turns to his satiric portrait of London ("Sure scenes like these no troubles ere annoy," line 323) and to his apocalyptic vision of the

American scene. Hence, though circling repetition defies time, it creates only the most restricted, self-limiting of spaces, either static or rapidly exhausting themselves in their race toward stasis. It is part of Goldsmith's logic that what "is seen" in each such imaginary "scene" is desolation and the dead or deadening "tyrant's hand." Repetition promotes what it would avoid: the inevitable decline from the old, confined and populated pastoral to the new, enclosed and depopulated one. And finally it collapses into pure nostalgia for a space, containing nothing:

> Do thine, sweet AUBURN, thine, the loveliest train,
> Do thy fair tribes participate her pain? . . .
> Ah, no.
>
> (lines 337–41)

An inventory of the repeated terms in the poem will confirm the point that initially space is created empty. One important group is purely emotive: adjectives like "sweet" and "lovely" and nouns like "pride" and "charms," to which "sport" should be added, since sports exist to please. There are the words for circling, the word "space," and other words and phrases connoting emptiness, such as "shade" and "vacant mind." The fullness of such a landscape is only emotional, not real. And there is one other term of which, as Roger Lonsdale notes in his edition, Goldsmith was "curiously fond" (676n), the word "train." Lonsdale glosses the word as "retinue," but clearly it means no more than the Thomsonian "tribe" (as in the lines just quoted) or "kinds." It is poetic diction, the "bare-worn common" (line 308) of the language. As a collective noun, it both ornaments and impoverishes, reducing individuals to a class or persons to personifications. Yet the term is also highly charged, for it serves as a constant reminder of a higher form of spatialization than can be found in mere repetition or the circling littleness of scenes that remain confined to closed couplets. Space is not just a circle, but also a line. And if the linearity of time is nothing other than the tragic fatality of history (line 135: "She only left of all the harmless train"), perhaps there may be a seriality of memory and imagination that will provide an enlargement from the chains of fate. If the counterplot of *The Traveller* insinuates an inner, individual solution to an outer, social problem, that of *The Deserted Village* necessitates an outer, spatial sense to compensate for an inner, temporal dilemma.

While Goldsmith's repetitions are empty, his catalogues are full. As the poem proceeds, the fullness grows demonic—the vain bustle of London and the exotic terrors of America. Eventually we will need to account for this demonic fullness. But for now I shall concentrate on the earlier, happier catalogues:

> How often have I paused on every charm,
> The sheltered cot, the cultivated farm,
> The never failing brook, the busy mill,
> The decent church that topt the neighbouring hill,
> The hawthorn bush, with seats beneath the shade,
> For talking age and whispering lovers made.
> How often have I blest the coming day,
> When toil remitting lent its turn to play,
> And all the village train from labour free
> Led up their sports beneath the spreading tree,
> While many a pastime circled in the shade,
> The young contending as the old surveyed;
> And many a gambol frolicked o'er the ground,
> And slights of art and feats of strength went round.
> And still as each repeated pleasure tired,
> Succeeding sports the mirthful band inspired;
> The dancing pair that simply sought renown
> By holding out to tire each other down,
> The swain mistrustless of his smutted face,
> While secret laughter tittered round the place,
> The bashful virgin's side-long looks of love,
> The matron's glance that would those looks reprove.
> These were thy charms . . .
>
> (lines 9–31)

We notice first the continual syntactic expansion. Goldsmith begins with two items per line, moving from passive to active or negative to positive, and from a pair of alternative locations (cottage and farm) to a pair (brook and mill) broadly suggestive of the range of village life, from cause to effect, from source of husbandry to its result. A full line is then devoted to the elevated church that surveys the countryside and two to the seats where the whole village comes together after the separated activities of the workday (women in the cottage, men on the farm, playing at the brook, working at the mill). After this, despite the stops with which the text is punctuated, the sentence keeps expanding, and the items from the dancing pair on achieve a syntactic independence hardly subordinated to any larger grammatical structure. The pair, the swain, the looks of love are no longer the terminable, goal-oriented activities of the "succeeding sports," and while the matron's reproving look has a goal, the iterative verb shows us that the goal is never achieved nor the action ended. Goldsmith's catalogue thus turns the activities of life into an expanding array of characters, a line without a direction. Such is the rhetorical mode of existence of a freestanding peasantry.

Yet just as repetition ultimately reduces the village to a lost point of origin, so too does what I shall call Goldsmith's double logic operate here. For the catalogue offers at best only a two-dimensional mode of existence. We are dealing here with types—not people, barely even personifications, but rather abstracted qualities and activities: the pastimes circle, the gambol frolics, sleights go round. Though it enumerates expansively, the catalogue also labels reductively. If the framing by repetition makes the village into mere scenes—pictures on a wall of blankness—we can now relate this limitation to a thematic issue, that of the gaze. What makes the catalogue possible in the first place is that the villagers exhibit only the most tangential and formulaic interactions. Watching and hiding, more in the shadow than in the light, the villagers, like the poet, abbreviate their judgments to a brief look at or away, a look many times repeated, but never enriched. The depths of village life, if it has any, lie in obscurity. Mere enumeration of entities breaks out of the limitation of the couplet for the group as a whole, but leaves individuals still caught within their two-line straitjackets.

There is as yet no poetry in the village, at least no poetry in the sense defined at the end either by Goldsmith (a wandering voice "prevailing over time") or, if my interpretation is convincing, by Johnson (a "self dependent power," a rock projecting into the sky). The next extended catalogue (lines 113–24) lists the sounds of the village, but even the human sounds resemble noises more than they do voices: "The swain responsive as the milk-maid sung" (this noise is paired with the cattle lowing to their young) and "the loud laugh that spoke the vacant mind." Emptiness and fullness are the governing categories, but the diversity of sounds can never rise to speech because the catalogue's attention wanders too quickly. There can be no continuity here; space is a collection of points rather than an expanse; the sounds are the "murmur" (line 114) of evening, and Miltonic echoes cluster to remind us that the catalogued world, no matter how full of elements it may be, is disorganized and already falling or fallen: "These all in sweet confusion sought the shade, / And filled each pause the nightingale had made" (lines 123–24). Sounds so disjunct could hardly be expected to endure, and the lines that follow the catalogue once again suggest how little hope there

could ever have been for the village: "But now the sounds of population fail, / No chearful murmurs fluctuate in the gale" (lines
125–26). Fluctuating sounds not of people but of population—the
abstract word encompasses cows, geese, and the dog, all of course
outdone by the nondomesticated nightingale—suggest only limited
reserves of native strength.

It is difficult to disentangle cause from effect. We cannot say
whether the village really lacked unity from the start or whether the
disappearance of the village caused slackening memory to disarticu-
late the sounds. The catalogue effect, if I may call it that, may be a
characteristic of village life or an artifact of the speaker. Particularly
in the catalogues, affectionate closeness is mingled with evaluative
distance in such a fashion as to suggest an inextricable complicity
of past scene, present view, and observer. The deictics—the most
emotion-laden place words in the poem—are the principal linguistic
source of this confusion; where "these" can be a distancing word
("These *were*," line 31) and "there" can suggest immediacy ("Up
yonder hill . . . / There as I past," "These all," lines 114–15, 123),
no distinct point of view emerges and thus no clear responsibility
for judgment. Ultimately I shall argue that this "sweet confusion" of
present and past, scene and speaker—so different from the first
appearance of the poem—is what constitutes Goldsmith's poetic
voice and enables the evocation of a past world within a present
prospect. Far from being ironic or destructive, Goldsmith's double
logic grounds the workings of the imagination: in the space of the
poem all times are unexpectedly consolidated, and the voice wandering through a landscape that is indifferently "here" or "there"
proves to have the stable firmness of a rock. The poet's voice prevails
over time by revealing as a fiction the view of temporal decline that
he has erected. Even the dedication addresses itself only to the current situation; Goldsmith professes to "believe those miseries real,
which I have attempted to display," but about Auburn he does not
even make any such tentative assertion.

Once again, the couplet carries the ideological burden. It was inherently satiric because it was inherently idealizing, and the unruly
real world could never live up to the pregnancy of the couplet form.
The development of a verse paragraph out of a couplet is always
fraught with difficulty. The more times an idea has been concisely
expressed, the more strained expression becomes, as when Pope's
Essay on Man 2.1–18 deviates from defining man as a mixed essence ("A being darkly wise, and rudely great") toward a crisis point

of dubious extremes ("In doubt to deem himself a God, or beast"). And insofar as the urbane sublime is a sociable style, the problem of filling the paragraph and illustrating the topic sentence is refracted into a vision of society falling away from its ideal. The nominalism of Goldsmith's catalogues fragments his picture of an integrated totality, thus infecting the description of an idealized space with the instability otherwise associated with temporal decline. A catalogued space is not yet the full space or the firm locus of real human experience. As Goldsmith's style transcends the couplet it has so completely mastered, so it must also explode the catalogue in order to validate the poet's imagination.

The brightest lines in the poem, and the most purely linear, are the description of the village inn:[17]

> Imagination fondly stoops to trace
> The parlour splendours of that festive place;
> The white-washed wall, the nicely sanded floor,
> The varnished clock that clicked behind the door;
> The chest contrived a double debt to pay,
> A bed by night, a chest of drawers by day;
> The pictures placed for ornament and use,
> The twelve good rules, the royal game of goose;
> The hearth, except when winter chill'd the day,
> With aspen boughs, and flowers, and fennel gay,
> While broken tea-cups, wisely kept for shew,
> Ranged o'er the chimney, glistened in a row.
> (lines 225–36)

Here the formal reifications of couplet rhetoric begin to break down in a foreshadowing of the miscellaneous style of Cowper. The careful balance of utile and dulce degenerates into the childish pairing of "The twelve good rules, the royal game of goose," and then into the incompatible alternatives of a warm fire or a decorated hearth. No longer is the catalogue framed by a concluding summary formula (such as "These were thy charms" or "These all in sweet confusion sought the shade") before the consciousness of loss intervenes. The poetic imagination thus comes to the fore at the moment when all the old structuring principles—social and poetic—have their hollowness exposed. Not all readers may wish to follow me in identifying the broken teacups as cup-lets, but the closing lines remain a clear picture of how catalogued linearity can come to echo the linear decline of society through time.

That broken ideal concludes the section of the poem devoted to portraying the personalities of the village. The bright interiors reflected the cheerful decadence of the inhabitants: "grey-beard mirth" and "village statesmen" circulating "news much older than their ale" (lines 222–24). In this section a different spirit breathes from the rest of the poem. The portraits are notable first of all for their length: twenty-four lines describing the schoolmaster follow a full fifty-six devoted to the preacher. The characters come alive as the idealized types in the general descriptions of the village and as the antitypes of London and America never do. Goldsmith portrays the schoolmaster in a Chaucerian diction full of particles, substituting the informality of the spoken word for the calculated writer's style of the remaining couplets. There is, further, a realism of content absent from the rest of the poem. Where the stories of real people are told, the village appears a much more mixed and imperfect place than in the opening tableaux. It has vagrants—a beggar, a ruined spendthrift, a broken soldier—it has the sick and dying, the scoffing unbelievers, it has naughty schoolchildren and a quarrelsome schoolmaster and parson. Finally, a set of themes and a form of action set off these portraits from the rest of the poem. The role- and game-playing of the villagers in the opening sections are here replaced by more enduring conflicts and struggles; the furtive glances in the shady wood are abandoned for careful observation in an atmosphere of—or tending toward—brightness; above all, mere chatter and noise give way to sustained conversation and narration. The village has become a lived space, populated by people acting like humans, a world of responsiveness and not of hide-and-seek.

The transition from the purely imaginary Auburn to this more fully imagined world comes when the speaker encounters an old beggar-woman, who evidently reminds him of the real people who have gone: "She only left of all the harmless train, / The sad historian of the pensive plain" (lines 135–36). This last line is the key and was early recognized as such, being chosen for illustration in the frontispiece of the first edition. It completes the opening movement of the poem, repeating the rhyme word of the first line. A land once blessed with "health and plenty" (line 2) has now become destitute. The mysterious, transferred epithet in "pensive plain" is the pivot on which Goldsmith's revival of the poetic voice turns: because the plain is empty, the old woman has little left to occupy her but memories. We can explain "pensive" by taking it in a causative sense (a pensive plain is one that makes people think); even so, the connection between vacancy and thoughtfulness remains close. This is,

THE

DESERTED VILLAGE,

A

P O E M.

BY DR. GOLDSMITH

The sad historian of the pensive plain.

L O N D O N:

Printed for W. GRIFFIN, at Garrick's Head, in Catharine-ſtreet, Strand.

MDCCLXX.

Title page of first edition of Oliver Goldsmith's The Deserted Village, *1770. Photo: Special Collections Division, University of Washington Libraries.*

however, neither an utter vacancy nor simply one more discovery of the isolated consciousness. The woman would not be a historian if there were not someone to relate stories to (represented in the frontispiece as an elderly traveler with a staff) and something to relate stories of. The plain is not completely empty, but retains traces of the former inhabitants (lines 137–38): "Near yonder copse, where once the garden smil'd, / And still where many a garden flower grows wild." ("Smil'd" echoes "smiling spring" in line 3, but the endurance of human touches replaces the slow round of the seasons in lines 3–4.) Such signs permeate this section of the poem, responding to the inquiring looks of the inhabitants past and present: the copse, the "few torn shrubs," the preacher's house, the "long remembered" beggar's beard, the soldier's crutch, the schoolmaster's fence (now lost), the thorn where the signpost used to be. The pensive plain is full of stories and—as the illustration shows—storied objects.

One might well be prompted to ask who the historian really is. Once the speaker has met the old woman, there is no way to tell whether the affectionate portraits are the woman's stories or those of the main speaker, who might point out "yonder copse" as he had pointed out the woman, "yon widowed, solitary thing" (line 129). In the frontispiece, indeed, no one speaks. The woman's mouth is shut, she points toward the village church, and the traveler gazes intently at her (and not at the scene). The landscape itself is full of significance and does not need a distinct chronicler to shape and transmit its stories.

We see here then—and the illustration captures beautifully the mood of the poem—a birth not of the solitary consciousness, but rather of a communal expressivity the more full and immediate for not needing to be expressed. This, too, is reflected in the contents of this section, where the preacher's smile and glow are just as effective as his formal sermon and his informal words of comfort. Goldsmith begins the poem by saying, "How often have I paused on every charm" (line 9), but only here does he and do his characters pause in fact, filling space with genuine speech culminating in the silence of genuine regard.

The poem's richness arises out of its conversion of loss into gain and absence into presence. Of course the story it tells of decline is false; of course Auburn never existed. The message of *The Deserted Village* is precisely *not* "The passage of time will tell," but rather "What counts is that which, scattered around us, endures and communicates." Circling, encirclement, concentration are forms of limitation common to the village and the park alike; thought feeds on the meaningful signs that survive the emptying out and opening up of everyday experience.

In its second half the poem grows yet more crowded, its view increasingly blocked and impoverished. Both London and America, in their different ways, are full and therefore oppressive, leaving little room for the human imagination. But just as the shallow pleasures of Auburn could be recuperated as a vacancy fondly retraced and brought to life by the imagination, so too can the inhumane wastes of London and America be repopulated by imaginative vision: "Even now, methinks, as pondering here I stand, / I see the rural virtues leave the land" (lines 397–98). Here, at the end, we find a second pensive historian, again converting loss into gain, as the landscape fills up with the virtues that are leaving it: "Downward they move a melancholy band, / Pass from the shore, and darken all the strand" (lines 401–2). We have yet one more catalogue arraying toil and care, tenderness and piety, loyalty and love. But then this catalogue pauses and dwells, no longer merely enumerating, but bringing to life the last of its members: "And thou, sweet Poetry, thou loveliest maid" (line 407).

In this poem fullness is always turning into emptiness as a result of the linear logic of the satirist (narrator of decline and cataloguer of lost glories), and emptiness in its turn is always creating space to be brought back to life by the poetic voice. The relationship between city and country is commutative: both are packed at times with "Vain transitory splendours!" (line 237); both grow full and decadent; in both wealth drives the populace away; both contain a "poor houseless shivering female" (line 326), as they have always contained vagrants and "ruined spendthrift[s]" (line 153). The end of the line for this inescapable loss is the demonic landscape of America. But signs multiply as the things signified disappear. Distance is the precondition for both *The Deserted Village* and *The Traveller*, and in both poems temporal and spatial distance alike ultimately acquire a semiotic function as the space in which meanings gather and circulate.

From this perspective the genre of both poems can be reevaluated. Both derive, of course, from the neoclassical formal verse satire.[18] Yet both, in different ways, introduce an instability into the form. Common to both Juvenalian and Horatian satire is a well-established persona; the speaker reproves a vice at length and then concludes by praising the correlative virtue. But in *The Traveller* the speaker turns inward at the end. A traveler who actually sits in one place and voyages only mentally, he does not remain a judging outsider in strange lands as does Lien Chi Altangi in *The Citizen of the World*. Instead, as he turns his thoughts to his native land, first-person singular pronouns multiply and he increasingly becomes the target of his meditations and, at last, as the pensive exile in America, the object of his own satire. Instead of turning against vice, the speaker in this satire finally turns, as we have seen, against his own earlier self. A literary form that had always embodied a corrective vision develops into a personal, self-correcting vision. In *The Deserted Village* the transformation of satire proceeds even a step further, for the concluding visionary apostrophe to Poetry transforms the poem from a satire to a sublime ode. Instead of a final judgment, Goldsmith introduces all the ritual formulas of sacred prayer.[19] We can measure the distance even from *The Vanity of Human Wishes* by noting that Goldsmith's conclusion introduces the personal voice that Johnson's sublime wisdom consoles. Johnson says, "Enquirer, cease" (line 349), whereas Goldsmith becomes an inquirer at the end. Johnson says,

> Still raise for good the supplicating voice,
> But leave to heav'n the measure and the choice
>
> Implore his aid, in his decisions rest,
> Secure whate'er he gives, he gives the best.
>
> (lines 351–56)

In Goldsmith's poem we hear the supplicating voice at length, without any secure answering repose.

One might hazard a guess that this generic wandering made conclusion difficult for Goldsmith. Goldsmith loses his formal bearings, or—to put it more positively—opens satire to a new range of possibilities, and he needs a foreign stabilizing hand at the end. In *The Deserted Village*, certainly, it is impossible not to hear a tone of imploring self-pity that persists even in the last lines written by Goldsmith: "Teach him that states of native strength possest, / Tho' very poor, may still be very blest" (lines 425–26). Johnson's similes right the balance by returning the satire to the great world of general nature.

Yet it is important to keep in mind the differences between the two endings. *The Traveller* is aimed toward a general reorientation and a rebirth of Britain, with the example of Goldsmith's brother in mind, and here Johnson's ending serves as a corrective, redirecting Goldsmith to the myth underlying his own text. In *The Deserted Village* Johnson's conclusion does not contradict Goldsmith's, but rather complements it, with a public exhortation to defy time corresponding to Goldsmith's private plea. As the main speaker's voice merges with that of the widowed matron in portraying the residents of the village, as satire joins with ode, so Johnson's couplets chime with Goldsmith's to create a space in imagination that never existed in reality.[20] By the double logic of the poem—a logic of mutuality and the correspondence of opposites—poetry is *both* a wandering voice and a firm rock. It is, indeed, a wandering voice (Goldsmith's phrase) insofar as it is Johnsonian satire, surveying mankind from China to Peru; and it is a resistant rock insofar as it remains Goldsmith's personal poem, expressing his stance and point of view. (Johnson's rock, we might say, is really the seat of Goldsmith's traveler, "plac'd on high above the storm's career," *Traveller*, line 33.) The merging of genres is a mechanism for change that we will see in many of the works to be analyzed subsequently. And the space of negations or of double logic, the space where a voice echoing in the void between rocks denies time in order to fill up the world with creatures that have the reality of an imaginative vision fulfilled— that space is what is properly called an aesthetic realm.

Throughout *The Deserted Village* Goldsmith has been straining to see. It is as if he were obsessed (as Johnson was) with Berkeley's contention that the so-called objects of sight are merely ideas, unrelated to the material objects that we touch. So long as we take Aurora to represent a lost dawn and the final "fare thee well. / Farewell" (lines 416–17) to be an adieu, we must regard Goldsmith as prey to a pseudo-Berkeleyan pathos. "The rigours of the inclement clime" (line 422) rhymes with "time" and figures time as the enemy, in the guise of mutability and unconstant weather. So it has always been, desolating Torno and Pambamarca and making even Aurora a "mouldering" "desert" (lines 48, 45). But the conclusion looks ahead, to the dawn of a new temperament and to a rock that will assert its presence without being kicked. Farewell then becomes as much a benediction as a valedictory. At the start "thy children leave the land" (line 50); at the end Goldsmith still "see[s] the rural virtues leave the land" (line 398). They have not left; they still "are there" (line 404), materialized through the labor of the poetic imagination. Johnson's defiant finale consummates the implicit argument of the poem in order to reaffirm the openness of a world in which people can fashion a life.

Because they never existed, because they offer an ideal image of a space that is connected to past and future only by the tenuous link of a transmitted vision and not by any developmental sequence or plot, Goldsmith's villages could legitimately be called the first purely aesthetic fictions in Western literature. The discussion of *The Vicar of Wakefield* will pursue this birth of the aesthetic in literature, contemporaneous with its birth in philosophy in Germany. But for now we can see the profound cultural importance of Goldsmith's character. His utter lack of seriousness is what qualified him to initiate a literature of pure imagination. Not even Gessner or Macpherson could ring the changes of a nonexistent world with all the craft and the disregard for plausibility that we see in *The Deserted Village.* Goldsmith's aborted endings are a final defeat for the literalism of the understanding—and a consequent triumph for a poetic creation speaking from amid the void.[21]

CHAPTER SEVEN

The Vicar of Wakefield:
The Invention of Plot

Although it has been argued that he didn't really think about it,[1] Goldsmith did at least write the end of *The Vicar of Wakefield*. Unlike the poems' conclusions, the novel's ending is thus merely an aesthetic problem. Since the day it was published, there has been general agreement that the problem lies in the plot, though with no consensus about what the problem is. The majority of readers have blamed the novel for an excess of action and a deficiency of control, while a few find the action a skimpy undergirding for Goldsmith's highly finished rhetorical and imagistic patterning. The characters, by contrast, are praised by almost all. Lovable, true to nature, they are said to be Goldsmith and his world brought to life on the page: his Victorian biographer says that Goldsmith "rested, with well grounded faith, on the vital reality of his characters" (John Forster, *Life and Adventures* 362). The critical blame and the critical praise are, of course, two sides to the same assessment, namely, that *The Vicar of Wakefield* is a quintessentially simple, naive, or transparent narrative. Somehow the artlessness with which the story is told serves to guarantee its immediacy, or, as one critic has written, "*The Vicar* may be popular to countless readers through the centuries because of rather than in spite of its faults" (Adelstein, "Duality of Theme" 321).

But what is a fault? Goldsmith himself prompted this whole age-old debate with the novel's brief Advertisement, which begins, "There are an hundred faults in this Thing, and an hundred things might be said to prove them beauties." Yet the Advertisement also immediately cuts the ground from under the debate: "But it is needless." In fact, the categories in which the novel has always been attacked and defended—unity of plot, depth of character—were precisely in the course of gestation as the novel was being written. They are not altogether irrelevant, but their relevance is problematic. Indeed, I shall argue that the "faulty" conclusion of the novel generates the categories by which its faultiness is judged: the fault, in this case, defines the norm. My general thesis about *The Vicar of Wakefield*, then, is that the break in tone at the end—the single, overriding fault to which so many readers reduce Goldsmith's "hundred faults"—is of revolutionary importance in establishing what is henceforth to be meant by a unified plot. And, correlatively, the shallow narration of Primrose defines what is henceforth to be meant by a "deep" or "rounded" character. Primrose narrates the whole novel, of course, but only in the last chapter does the narration break into the present tense—only here does Primrose, in a certain sense, become "present" and present himself to be judged—so that the end is crucial for the intersection of narration and character as well as for that of narrator and plot. It is the fault line that opens to disclose the novel's aesthetic perfection.

For *The Vicar* contains a simplicity embodied, yet not displayed. Transparency is the reverse of glitter; its clarity serves to hide the artistry that we would have it reveal. The novel's truth lies in its silences, secrets, and omissions, and ultimately in masquerade. The faults are the breaks in the disguise that show at last the true face of Goldsmith's achievement.

Plot

Despite the judgment of most readers, I think that it is a mistake to praise the characters and criticize the plot. After Goldsmith's Advertisement apologizes for the novel's "hundred faults," it proceeds to concentrate on inconsistencies in Primrose's character. According to the first reviewer, likewise, the novel's defects are said to lie in "the want of a thorough acquaintance with mankind" and in "limited knowledge of men, manners, and characters, as they really appear in the living world."[2] E. M. Forster has called it "a typical novel" in its surrender to the tyranny of plot. I intend to contest the judgment, but to endorse the description and even to enhance it: *The Vicar of Wakefield*, I shall argue, is not just typical, but prototypical, the first of its type.[3] It is the characters who are problematic, not the plot.

By plot here I mean specifically the selection and disposition of the incidents, or roughly what Gérard Genette has termed the *récit* (*Figures III* 71–72). (Aesthetic—rhetorical or stylistic—problems of the *narration*, such as the break in tone, will be discussed later, as these may be referred to defects of the narrator Dr. Primrose rather than to a lack of authorial control.) Improbabilities the novel has in abundance, to be sure, but then what prior narrative (apart perhaps from the intricate intrigues of Mme de Lafayette) had ever depended on material probability?[4] Surely the plot of *The Vicar* is not less probable than that of its main structural model, the *Book of Job*, a narrative that only a madman would assess by the yardsticks of plausibility and verisimilitude. Indeed what prior narrative, apart from *Tom Jones*, possesses a more unified plot than *The Vicar*, when measured by the accepted standard that all episodes should either be recapitulated (through the return of characters and final disposition of incidents) or resonate thematically at the end?[5] So rapidly and completely did the Gothic novelists, Austen, and Goethe (in *Elective Affinities*) establish this standard that we have almost completely lost our sense for the novelty of *The Vicar*.[6]

There is not much extrinsic evidence of Goldsmith's ideas about structure. In the late 1750s he reviewed four plays for *The Monthly Review* and *The Critical Review*. Here we find him saying that the moral "should be the ground-work of every fable" and that defects of plotting (along with the lack of a moral) "are all faults we could easily pardon, did poetic fire, elegance, or the heightenings of pathetic distress afford adequate compensation" (review of Home's *Douglas*; 1: 11). Yet Goldsmith's discussion tends to emphasize plot, which he is able to analyze with relative precision, whereas he tends to praise diction merely by extensive quotation.[7] In reviewing Murphy's *Orphan of China* Goldsmith articulates a simple yet significant principle of plot construction. Whereas Murphy "attempts to move us before his time," with "poignant anguish" as early as act 2, "Shakespear, Otway, and Rowe, seemed to have been perfect oeconomists of their distress (if we may use the expression) they were so sensible of a necessary gradation in this respect, that their characters frequently make their first appearance in circumstances of joy and triumph: they well knew that we are apt to pity the sufferings of mankind, in proportion as they have fallen from former happiness. Othello, therefore . . ." (1: 172). *Othello*, yes, and also *Romeo and Juliet*. But Shakespeare's plays, tragedies and comedies alike, more commonly begin in conflict, or with a sudden and early plunge into anguished difficulties. The review contains less an empirical observation of Goldsmith's than a predilection; the "necessary gradation" from happiness to suffering, equivalent to the gradual buildup of tension and long-range progression from tonic to dominant in the classical symphony, is an important new rule of structure in the period, and Goldsmith conscientiously adheres to it in his plays and major poems, as well as in his novel.[8] For even in a poem Goldsmith demands a graduated, overarching form that is necessary to give stylistic felicities their full effect:

> He who would write a perfect elegy . . . will here perceive beauty in distress, borrowing the language of nature and of passion, and adapting sentiments to the subject: the thoughts rising, as if of their own accord, without being sought after; the verse flowing with various harmony; the whole combined by a concealed connexion, yet seemingly without order: In short, our idea encreasing by just degrees to the end of the piece, like those landskips that rise upon the eye, till they seem to touch the skies. (review of Langhorne's "Death of Adonis," 1: 165)

Boileau's dictum "Un beau désordre est un effet de l'art" (*Art poétique* 2.72) was, of course, canonical throughout the century, but it remains noteworthy that Goldsmith interprets the maxim *ars celare artem* to mean that formal disposition should command the emotions.

It is consequently not "very probable that when Goldsmith began the story he had no very definite plot concocted" (Black, *Oliver Goldsmith* 81). The symmetrical division of the 32 chapters into two equal halves has been noted.[9] But the disposition of incidents is far more rigorously crafted than this simple observation acknowledges. For there is a regular four-chapter rhythm that prevails—and that must have been planned—from the very start. Chapter 5 is entitled (in part) "A New and Great Acquaintance Introduced"; the reference is to Squire Thornhill, of course. Chapter 9, "Two Ladies of Great Distinction Introduced," brings in the ladies of the town, Thornhill's accomplices in seducing Olivia Primrose. Chapter 13, which comes as mortifications are piling in upon one another, completes the inventory of villains, though the villain this time is only apparently one: "Mr. Burchell Is Found to Be an Enemy." Chapter 17 relates Olivia's abduction, the beginning of the second half of the novel. In chapter 21 Olivia is recovered and George Primrose, the eldest son, is lost, as the villainous Thornhill purchases a West Indies commission for him; Thornhill here secures the £100 bond that he will use at the end of this unit, in chapter 24, to send Primrose to jail. The plot takes a new direction in chapter 25, when the imprisoned Primrose first meets a consoling figure. Later in the chapter this proves to be the swindler Jenkinson, an enemy reborn as a friend, who eventually rescues Arabella Wilmot's fortune by attesting that Thornhill was legally married to Olivia. The melodramatic chapter 28, at the end of this unit, contains the novel's last miseries, Olivia's supposed death and George's imprisonment. In chapter 29 the mood suddenly and definitively shifts, first with Primrose's consolatory sermon demonstrating "the equal dealings of providence," and then with the rapid clearing of all storm clouds in the final three chapters of denouement. This unvarying rhythm of incident (more specifically of character positioning) coincides with a slower moral rhythm: in chapters 1–8 good and evil appear mixed; in chapters 9–16 evil is recognized (not always correctly) and rejected; in 17–24 evil triumphs over good; and in 25–32 good triumphs over evil, morally in 25–28 and materially in 30–32.[10] The arrangement is unexcelled in its elegant simplicity.[11]

Genre

I can best clarify the complex motivations for Goldsmith's symmetries by taking a detour. For Goldsmith tends his intrigues as Primrose does his gardens. In his prosperity the vicar leaves "the temporal concerns of our family . . . to my wife's management" (chap. 2; 4: 21). But in the poverty of their new residence he tends the garden himself, cultivating the plot with all the nice economy that Goldsmith devoted to crafting his novel: "Nothing could exceed the neatness of my little enclosures: the elms and hedge rows appearing with inexpressible beauty" (chap. 4; 4: 32). Primrose's taste, however, goes out for larger and freer prospects, and even though this is "a little neighbourhood" (chap. 4; 4: 31), it has been designed to enable him to indulge his fancy: "At a small distance from the house my predecessor had made a seat, overshaded by an hedge of hawthorn and honeysuckle. Here, when the weather was fine, and our labour soon finished, we usually all sate together, to enjoy an extensive landscape, in the calm of the even" (chap. 5; 4: 35). This is the setting upon which Squire Thornhill intrudes while hunting a stag, thereby initiating the dramatic action of the novel.

As there are two plots to Primrose's garden, so likewise are there two plots to the novel. The first is that of a meticulous farm—the careful plot of a moral fable, its message earned through the skillful tending of its author. The other, which comes to prominence at the end (on autumn evenings), its tranquility or "vacant hilarity" (chap. 5; 4: 35) subject to unexpected disruption, is a freer kind. The views here are broad, the structure looser, and the harvest of meanings collected without labor. This is the allegorical plot that seizes at once on "Primrose" as the first untended flower of the spring and on "Thornhill" as the path that attacks virtue and puts it to the test. Primrose is a rational gardener by necessity, but a sentimental, allegorical one by inclination (witness his concern for his daughters' names). And so was "Goldy," the impoverished and industrious country boy who has been so short-changed by his patronizing readers.

The loose allegorical plot resembles what we know as an English garden. But to Goldsmith it was something older and more exotic; he knew it as a Chinese garden. Lien Chi Altangi describes the gardens at Quamsi in letter 31 of *The Citizen of the World*. (The name is Latin for "how if," designating the hypothetical mode of existence of the aesthetic realm.) On the right in this "small" and "skillfully designed" space is a harsh and unattractive gate, "planned with the utmost simplicity, or rather rudeness," appearing antique to the point of decadence, and bearing the motto "Pervia Virtuti" (open to virtue). Meanwhile, on the left lies a gate marked "Facilis Descensus" (smooth is the descent [to Hell]), where "nymphs . . . beckoned the stranger to approach" and "all that lay behind . . . seemed gay, luxuriant, and capable of affording endless pleasure" (2: 136). The garden has a plot whose entanglements resemble those of the novel:

> As he walked farther on he insensibly found the garden assume the air of a wilderness, the landskips began to darken, the paths grew more intricate, he appeared to go downward, frightful rocks seemed to hang over his head, gloomy caverns, unexpected precipices, awful ruins, heaps of unburied bones, and terrifying sounds, caused by unseen waters, began to take place of what at first appeared so lovely; it was in vain to attempt returning, the labyrinth was too much perplexed for any but myself to find the way back. (ibid.)

At the last, however, Lien stage-manages or authors the rescue, suddenly clearing the heaped-up miseries of the victims: "In short, when sufficiently impressed with the horrors of what he saw, and the imprudence of his choice, I brought him by an hidden door, a shorter way back into the area from whence at first he had strayed" (2: 136–37). It is a stage machine that allows the unwary victim to escape and enjoy the primeval simplicity of a life of virtue.

The novel is a diptych much like the gardens at Quamsi. The first half, corresponding to the garden behind the right-hand gate, is an idyll. In this archaic realm time is inessential. The "primaeval simplicity of manners" entails a repetition of the same, merely conventional activities from year to year: carols on Christmas, Valentine morning greetings, Shrovetide pancakes, April Fool's jokes, Michaelmas eve nuts (chap. 4; 4: 32). While the events of the first half do follow one another, there is little more connection in the incidents than in these heterogeneous ceremonials: nothing is "experienced," nothing learned. In chapter 5 the ladies doff their finery and walk to church; in chapter 10 they make fools of themselves trying to ride. Burchell's sincere generosity in chapter 3 is forgotten by all when in chapter 15 he thwarts the girls' aspirations to a place in town. The Primrose women learn nothing from the coarse language used by the supposed ladies of the town in chapter 9, but then neither does the vicar: he yields to resentment at Burchell's interference with a plan he never favored, and he remains incapable of distinguishing sincere language from fraud. The vicar's insight into the town ladies' social pretensions fails to carry over to Jenkinson's intellectual pretensions at the fair: Jenkinson dupes Moses in chapter 12 and the vicar in the very next chapter. Indeed, this half of the novel is replete with foolish schemes, social and financial, not one of which ever matures, while real plot prospects from the itinerant son George and the reportedly bankrupt merchant are entirely forgotten. (George passes through London, where the merchant was, and Flanders, where he is later arrested, apparently without making any inquiries.) Pictures, faces, surfaces are abiding concerns of the whole family; the entire narrative consists of a succession of brief vignettes, with no more real depth or connection to be found in the family history than in the absurd history painting that they commission at the end of the first half. Living at a surprising remove from the church that ought to be the center of things, the Primroses accept visits and even marriage proposals from neighbors only because no one better offers. Life is as linear and meaningless and time as external in this unnamed village as in the imaginary Auburn that Goldsmith was to describe a few years later.

In the second half decline ensues, as always in Goldsmith. In a sense, the process is gradual; Primrose's standard response to difficulties has always been "to withdraw one more step, to diminish the area over which idyllic rules hold control until finally (chapter XXIV) it is reduced to his own soul: idyllism turned into stoicism" (Nemoianu, *Micro-Harmony* 51). Yet the character changes abruptly at the midpoint. In chapter 17 the family provokes Olivia's elopement with Thornhill by setting a deadline for her betrothal to Farmer Williams, and from here on out the pace of reversals increases.

If the first half of the novel is an idyll, the second half shifts to romance. Johnson's *Dictionary* defines "romance" (in part) as "a tale of wild adventures of war and love," and as in the left alley of the Chinese garden, the images are now of a regression to wild nature and elemental emotion. Disguise and even clothing are progressively stripped off; sentiment comes to the fore in the same chapter where worldly goods are destroyed and where the vicar lovingly evokes the sounds of nature ("the shrilling cock, and the deep-mouthed watch-dog, at hollow distance," chap. 22; 4: 130), and two chapters later he is paraded, inadequately covered, through the snow. (Note that each of the four elements in turn plays its role in causing the physical misfortunes suffered in the novel: the water in which Sophia almost drowns, the fire that consumes the family possessions, the cold snowy earth through which Primrose is compelled to walk to prison, and finally the "bad air" of the prison, chap. 28; 4: 153.) The family begins its trek from Wakefield to the new village when its fortune is lost; as honor, good temper, and any remaining material prospects go to waste, the march appears to continue and accelerate. George goes off as an adventurer to Europe and later as an ensign to the West Indies, Olivia is swept off by the squire and later by her illness and supposed death, Primrose is dragged away to jail. Time becomes, if not organic, at least a dominating consciousness.

In the second half of the novel we are no longer dealing with a linear array of plot elements. For the true shape of romance is not a line but a circle. One incident makes an adventure; it takes a second, superimposed incident—a co-incidence—to make a romance. A model is given by the famous ballad "Edwin and Angelina," recited in chapter 8 by Burchell (a romance figure who wanders through the idyll unrecognized, despite giving himself away with a pronoun slip in chapter 3). The first word of the romance, addressed by Angelina to Edwin, is in fact "Turn," and he soon responds in kind: "Then turn to-night, and freely share / Whate'er my cell bestows" (lines 18–19). At the end, likewise, the recognition is consummated in a series of turns:

> "Forbid it heaven!" the hermit cry'd,
>   And clasp'd her to his breast:

The wondering fair one turn'd to chide,
  'Twas Edwin's self that prest.

"Turn, Angelina, ever dear,
  My charmer, turn to see,
Thy own, thy long-lost Edwin here,
  Restor'd to love and thee."

Though there are plenty of adventures in the idyllic first half of the novel, such as the near drowning of the unwise "Sophia," it is in the second half that such incidents return to haunt the participants. George departs in the first half; in the second half he returns coincidentally to tell his tale, departs, and returns dramatically yet again. Early in the first part Primrose quarrels with Wilmot, and the engagement between their children George and Arabella is broken off; in the second part Arabella is fortuitously rediscovered, just in the nick of time to prevent her marrying the villain Thornhill. In chapter 10 comes the gypsy's apparently absurd prediction that Sophia and Olivia are to marry a squire and a lord; at the end it comes true. It is hardly necessary to enumerate all the other returns scattered throughout the second part. In chapter 17, adopting the mode of romance, the novel turns in a new direction, rounding back with a new intensity on the escapades of the first half.[12]

The generic shift supports the novel's redefinition of values.[13] In Goldsmith's relentless secularization of the Job story older values have eroded from within, revealing themselves to be mere worldly pretense. The result of foibles, rather than sins, the perils are resolved by a stage-managing *nobilis ex machina*. From the start the preacher treated prayer as part of the day's "proper ceremony" and "duty," which consisted in posing "bent in gratitude" to the Lord of serial time, "that Being who gave us another day" (chap. 4; 4: 33); eventually he develops "sensibility" (chap. 27; 4: 149) among the prisoners with a sermon promising "happiness" in a Heaven devoid of any real transcendence. Even the Devil, Thornhill, who originally swooped in behind the hounds to disrupt a Primrose family musicale, meets a suitably dandified *contrapasso* in being condemned to blow the French horn for a morose relative. As in *The Task*, the Enlightenment ideal of a rational society decomposes into contradiction, with "Thornhill," the decadent rationalist, confronting "Primrose" (a rose without thorns), whose empty sociability has become a shell, "some mechanical forms of good breeding" (chap. 4; 4: 33). Meanwhile, as we see in other works of the period, Enlightenment concerns like "prudence" yield to internalized values like conscience or "heart." George Primrose's career is paradigmatic, as he goes from picture buyer to actor. For, in general, the transparent masquerades of the first half, such as that of the ladies of the town, give way to dramatically staged concealments and revelations; and surfaces themselves gain a new depth, ironically when George's connoisseur-patron impetuously varnishes the picture he is touting (chap. 20; 4: 119), and more seriously, of course, as the virtue and steadfastness of the various family members is tested in earnest. Idyll is to romance as moral fable is to psychological allegory and as social virtue is to individual merit.

As a spokesman for archaic values, Primrose may be compared to "the sad historian of the pensive plain" in *The Deserted Village*. The poem, too, begins with vignettes and catalogues whose coherence is compromised by their linear or additive structure.[14] And in its second half, too, romantic narration replaces evocation, becoming increasingly affective and imaginary rather than realistic. In neither work is there a natural connection between the idealized past and its fate. Instead, *The Deserted Village* ends by appealing to an aesthetic dimension, "sweet Poetry . . . , prevailing over time," to furnish an image of the coherence lacking in experience. In *The Vicar* miraculous good fortune does allow a qualified return to past felicity. But in its improbable contrivances the ending achieves by a more complicated route what Goldsmith, with Johnson's help, was to achieve more directly in the later poem. The novel compensates for Primrose's failure—he is a "sad historian" indeed—by establishing a poetic space. Thornhill's French horn is not only the appropriate punishment for a wild huntsman, but also the romantic instrument par excellence, and it is worth remembering that Johnson also defined romance as "A lie; a fiction." If poetry first becomes aesthetic—primarily "sweet" and affective, rather than didactic—at the end of *The Deserted Village*, the end of *The Vicar* is the point where the novel makes a similar transition.

Narrator

To complement the account of the diptych structure, we need to consider the relation of the story to the narrator. When the novel changes character, the events that appeared in the first half to be disconnected genre images prove to belong to the romance by virtue of their adventuresome consequences or symbolic resonances. The placid, pedestrian narrator has thus falsified the nature of the story he is telling. He stubbornly retains his allegiance to the old value system, trying to relate sentiments and actions to time-honored social standards that have rotted away. But the story judges characters in terms of flamboyant breakthroughs and changes of heart. It refutes the narrator morally by virtue of refuting him structurally. Primrose's failure is the novel's triumph.

Departing from the common practice of the century, *The Vicar of Wakefield* is subtitled "A Tale," and not a history. The designation is all the more significant because the vast majority of Goldsmith's output—never incorporated into collections of his works—consisted of histories (and a natural history), which eventually earned him an honorary appointment as professor of ancient history at the Royal Academy. Although their scholarship may be negligible, these were not thoughtless undertakings, and the introductions express a conviction of the indissoluble connection among history, time, and experience. "Experience" is in fact the very first word of *A General History of the World, from the Creation to the Present Time*: "Experience," Goldsmith writes, "every day convinces us, that no part of learning affords so much wisdom upon such easy terms as history . . . ; in a well-written history . . . we profit by the experience of others without sharing their toils or misfortunes" (5: 277). And the preface to the projected history of the Seven Years' War confirms that the aim of history is "to show by what causes every event was produced, and in what effects it is likely to terminate" (*Works*, ed. Cunningham, 3: 401). History is a domain of knowledge, and it should steer clear of primeval times known to us only in the "picture" of "fancy," in "fables," and in the "fictions and conjectures" of "*Sanchoniathon, Manetho, Berosus,* and suchlike" (*Collected Works* 5: 279, 281). The historian and the fabulist have nothing in common.

In the novel, history lies under a cloud. Though Primrose early on arrogates to himself "the veracity of an historian" (chap. 1; 4: 19), he clearly does not mean to claim understanding of time and human action: at this point he merely tells us that his wife's gooseberry wine never varied and was loved by all. In the next chapter he tells us, more believably, that he is "careless of temporalities" and leaves "temporal concerns" to his wife (4: 21), and he proceeds to describe a typical day, not localized in time, wherein it was his wife's custom to give "the history of every dish" (4: 23). History proper makes its first appearance in the novel when Primrose meets the swindler Jenkinson at the fair. The whole encounter stands under the sign of fable: "no lovers in romance ever cemented a more instantaneous friendship," writes Primrose (chap. 14; 4: 73), and Jenkinson's history is characterized by talismanic repetition of his few bits of spurious knowledge. The names he repeats are the egregious Sanchoniathon, Manetho, and Berosus, together with Ocellus Lucanus, whose reported motto, "all things have neither beginning nor end," directly contradicts Goldsmith's historical concern with the causes and terminal effects of events. History fares little better in its second appearance, when Primrose attempts to amuse the fallen Olivia with the fable of Matilda. Set in a time of exceptional brutality—"Few histories can produce more various instances of cruelty, than those which the French and Italians at that time exercised upon each other" (chap. 23; 4: 134)—the story is pure fairy tale, free from sin or guilt, and "told us by a grave, tho' sometimes a romancing, historian" (chap. 23; 4: 133). Not only is this story thus an utter negation of the history from which it is supposedly drawn, but it is also singularly inept in application to Olivia's experiences: it is no wonder that Primrose's seduced and discarded daughter can find little consolation in the tale of a faithful wife who is restored to her beloved and long-lost husband through the agency of a son believed dead!

History as Primrose encounters it is reduced to irrelevance or fraud. The future looms only in the form of "agreeable reveries" (chap. 10; 4: 57), of foolish omens (ibid., where Primrose makes fun of a fortune-teller, but also chap. 2; 4: 23, where he cannot "pass over an ominous circumstance" at backgammon), or of intentionally ambiguous prophecy (chap. 12; 4: 65). There is no realistic sense of change, for this is a family that "seldom followed advice, [although] we were all ready enough to ask it" (chap. 12; 4: 66). Nor does Primrose display any more realistic a sense of the past: one wonders what "experience" could mean to a narrator who says in chapter 1, "we loved each other tenderly, and our fondness encreased as we grew old" (4: 18), but in chapter 2 that he is "convinced by experience that the days of courtship are the most happy of our lives" (4: 23). Images for the emptiness of the time line include the races that Jenkinson pretends he has won from the neighbor Solomon Flamborough (yet another figure of unwisdom, chap. 14; 4: 75) and "Henry II's progress," which was halted, according to a story that Primrose "could not avoid repeating," when the king encountered the abundant family of Count Abensberg (chap. 1; 4: 19–20). A family is a "little circle" (ibid.), its daily round of activities consisting of "a repetition of toil" in the morning and "vacant hilarity" at night (chap. 5; 4: 35).

Burchell tells his life anonymously, as a tale whose adventures "led . . . up to a romantic extreme" (chap. 3; 4: 29). And romance is equally Primrose's fate. He resists giving his daughters "romantic names" (chap. 1; 4: 20), but then gives in. Yet the name he would have preferred for one of them is Grissel, which he ought to have recognized as actually a far more romantic name than either Olivia or Sophia. What Primrose misleadingly calls "the history [!] of Patient Grissel" figures among the "ballads," "stories," "old songs," and "adventures" told by Burchell in a later chapter (chap. 6; 4: 39). If experience had any consistency for him, he should have remembered this when writing the first chapter. But it doesn't.

Primrose's ambitions are as a moralist. We have already seen that a moral patterning governs the surface structure of the 32 chapters, although the surface has been obscured by the turbulent coincidences of the romance. And Primrose, ancestor of Lewis Carroll's duchess, peppers his narrative with moralizing asides of dubious relevance and even more dubious validity. "I was ever of opinion," the novel begins (chap. 1; 4: 18), and that "ever" regularly marks the eternal verities of a would-be historian whose assessment of the facts at hand remains skewed. I count eighteen such aphorisms in the first half of the novel (including a rash at the end of chapter 5, but not including chapter titles), eleven of them including the telltale "ever," "always," or "seldom." By contrast, in the romantic, time-bound second half I count only five, of which one is a proverb concerning traveling rather than an original reflection (chap. 18; 4: 95), two are concerned with time and change (chap. 21; 4: 126, wisdom as "a slow defense against trouble," and chap. 23; 4: 133, "one vice, tho' cured, ever plants others"), and the two most general are uttered by George (chap. 20; 4: 113, "the looks of the domestics ever transmit their master's benevolence," and 4: 121, "riches in general" are "another name for freedom"). For the timeless, moral perspective does not even try to grasp the significance of events as they pass. The more fundamental time becomes, the more the history eludes the teller.

The book's homey warmth subsides in the second half not because Goldsmith loses control, but because the narrator is less and less able to reflect on events that involve him too directly. By the end, when the story reaches the present and all distance collapses, Primrose is rendered alternately irrelevant and speechless. His attention wanders to Thornhill, from whom he catches himself up with the expression, "But to return, for I am not apt to digress thus" (chap. 32; 4: 183); then he digresses to his wife's carving and catches himself up once again ("But notwithstanding this," chap. 32; 4: 184); then he confesses that "it is impossible to describe our good humour" and proceeds to demonstrate the proposition by reporting an utterly humorless joke of Wilmot's. But he "can't say" whether this was in truth wit or mere laughing, and indeed he exits with the declaration "my pleasure was unspeakable." At the end the narrator, an unwilling romancer and an unreliable moralist, self-destructs.[15]

What sort of interpreter is Primrose? In appearance, his deductions resemble the double logic that we have seen in *The Deserted Village*. He reasons by opposites, converting affirmation into denial and vice versa. Yet he is neither consistent nor successful in his attempts to penetrate motives and meanings. Typically, when he thinks at all, he interprets "by contraries" (chap. 5; 4: 37). Thus, in the incident where he uses this phrase, he assumes that Sophia despises Thornhill and that Olivia admires him because Sophia affects admiration and Olivia contempt. While Primrose is in fact correct in thus judging his daughters, it does him no good, for he still fails to anticipate or prevent Olivia's elopement. And when it comes to outsiders, his judgment fails utterly, though not in so simple a fashion that a mere reversal could correct his mistakes.

As an example of how the complexity of the world defeats the crude polarization of Primrose's assessments, one might adduce his gulling by Jenkinson. Not only does he neglect to interpret the swindler's pitch "by opposites," but his subsequent recoil in its turn fails to perceive the genuine human sympathy that Jenkinson will later manifest. "Being left to reflection," Primrose thinks as he leaves the fair, "I began to recollect that I had done wrong in taking a draught from a stranger, and so prudently resolved upon following the purchaser, and having back my horse. But this was now too late: I therefore made directly homewards" (chap. 14; 4: 75). But it turns out that neither a return nor an advance can successfully keep pace with time, and neither reflection nor prudence anticipates Jenkinson's conversion into Primrose's friend and benefactor. Circle and line are alike inadequate as models for the course of events.

Even more grievous is Primrose's misjudgment of Thornhill. The first time he hears Arabella mentioned in Thornhill's presence, Thornhill calls her "a fright" (chap. 7; 4: 42). Primrose makes no reference here to the principle of interpretation by contraries that he enunciated only a few pages earlier. Much later he at last applies the principle retrospectively, "when we received certain information, that Mr. Thornhill was going to be married to Miss Wilmot, for whom I always suspected he had a real passion, tho' he took every opportunity before me to express his contempt both of her person and fortune" (chap. 23; 4: 134). In this case, however, interpretation by contraries proves equally mistaken; for the unmasked Thornhill later confesses, "It was her fortune, not her person, that induced me to wish for this match" (chap. 31; 4: 176). We should beware of committing Primrose's error by taking either character's reversal entirely at his word. There are potentials for crass self-interest in Jenkinson's replacement of pretended by real benevolence and for mere spite when Thornhill reasserts his pretended contempt. Despite all the talk about "heart" in the latter parts of the novel, it would be naive to think that either villain now wears his heart on his sleeve. Motives remain too obscure or too variable for a principle of interpretation based on a simple contrast or an inversion of surface and depth.

"Reflection," for Primrose, has neither the pejorative connotations nor the sense of complexity that attached to the term earlier in the century. Clarissa is constantly accused of reflecting, that is, of casting aspersions, ruffling the smooth surface of polite manners. Primrose, by contrast, wants to reveal what lies under a placid surface. The best exterior is "transparent" (Arabella's complexion, chap. 2; 4: 23), and he says that "Mere outside is so very trifling a circumstance with me, that I should scarce have remembered to mention it" (chap. 1; 4: 20–21; but, a page earlier, "I was by nature an admirer of happy human faces"). He chooses his wife "as she did her wedding gown, not for a fine glossy surface, but such qualities as would wear well," including "pickling, preserving, and cookery" (chap. 1; 4: 18). Yet we have seen how little illumination Primrose's reflections cast and how rapidly they are outdistanced by events. Despite his careful selection of a spouse, the wife's husbandry proves to keep him badly; thus, after he peevishly throws the face washes into the fire at the end of chapter 6, they reappear in the window at the beginning of chapter 10, defending the ladies against the rude incursions of nature, lest the sun or the fire darken their white outside. The vicar appears more transparent and natural than Clarissa, but he too is a self-deceived schemer of sorts. In the competition of part and whole he remains a totalizer who sees an eternal meaning refracted in every incident.

Above all, it is Primrose's account of the prison that distinguishes his unimaginatively reductive logic from Goldsmith's productive imagination. The prison is an image that recurs throughout

Goldsmith's writings. An incarceration in 1754 providentially saved him from shipwreck and drowning (*Letters*, to Thomas Contarine, ca. May 6, 1754, p. 21); and facing prison again in 1759 he called it the home of "true society" (*Letters*, to Ralph Griffiths, Jan. 1759, p. 67). This brave defiance may have masked great trepidation, of course, but the fact remains that Goldsmith's essays, like *The Vicar*, uniformly treat the prison as an agent of (real or imaginary) good fortune.[16]

Goldsmith's reasons for praising prisons, however, are very different from Primrose's. The prison can relieve the anxieties of liberty for those, like Cardinal De Retz of essay 3 of *The Bee*, "who forget the cares of the world by being shut out from its ambition" (1: 387), as well as for the impoverished common soldier, in an essay that Goldsmith reprinted several times, who "found Newgate as agreeable a place as ever I was in in all my life" because "I had my belly full to eat and drink, and did no work" (*Citizen*, letter 119; 2: 461). To Voltaire it was "the school of wisdom" that taught him "the art of being a king" (3: 257); the semi-autobiographical Man in Black learned frugality in prison (*Citizen*, letter 27); and Lien Chi Altangi's son met his future bride there. Most interestingly, it is a place for artists like the author in *Citizen of the World*, who, "preferring a prison of my own chusing at home to one of my taylor's chusing abroad, . . . effectually kept my liberty by never stirring out of the room" (letter 30; 2: 133). In prison, where, as Goldsmith says, "the Poet, perhaps, has the advantage of all others" (*Memoirs of M. de Voltaire*, 3: 233), Voltaire began the *Henriade*; and Parnell, in solitude in Ireland, is compared by Goldsmith to "a famous painter, . . . confined in prison for debt, [whose] whole delight consisted in drawing the faces of his creditors in caricatura" (*Life of Dr. Parnell*, in *Works*, ed. Cunningham, 3: 415). In all these manifestations the prison, in Goldsmith's double logic, is the abode of life salvaged, reconsidered, or imagined, particularly in England, where "the peculiar strength of their prisons . . . argues their hardiness" (*Citizen*, letter 91; 2: 370). Indeed, one essay (*Citizen*, letter 73) compares all of life to a prison of which we grow fonder the longer we dwell in it.

For Primrose, on the other hand, the prison is the very opposite. In his logic of denial, prison reconciles us to death and fosters "in heaven all that superiority of pleasure which arises from contrasted enjoyment" (chap. 29; 4: 162). It is remarkable that none of the readers who delight in Primrose's foibles observe how chillingly vengeful is his sermon to the prisoners. He reconciles the prisoners to their state by denying the reality of life and by doing his best to deny time: "If we look back on past life, it appears but a very short span, and whatever we may think of the rest of life, it will yet be found of less duration; as we grow older, the days seem to grow shorter, and out intimacy with time, ever lessens the perception of his stay. Then let us take comfort now, for we shall soon be at our journey's end" (chap. 29; 4: 163). This is the preacher who thinks he has made the prison into a happy society, as he once thought he ruled over a devoted and peaceful family. Let those believe him who can.[17]

Lacking Goldsmith's imaginative fertility, Primrose reduces feelings to a quantifiable currency. A child's hospitality to Burchell (chap. 6; 4: 39–40) merits a larger lump of sugar (though no daughter of his would marry such "a man of broken fortune," chap. 6; 4: 40); "the honour of the family" equates to a guinea in the pocket (but it must never be used, chap. 10; 4: 57); and the prisoners are civilized by means of "fines for the punishment of immorality, and rewards for peculiar industry" (chap. 27; 4: 149). Such thinking levels the distinction between inherited status and accumulated virtue, just as it indifferently denominates the qualities that glue society together as "friendship and obedience" (ibid.). Far from increasing one's comprehension, compensation is, then, a sterile way of denying differences and extinguishing one's obligations toward one's fellow man or toward God. Even the philosophy of procreation that Primrose enunciates in the very first sentence seems half withdrawn in the closing tableau; now he sees fulfillment in a stable marriage of his children rather than in a profusion of descendants, and he ends his mortal career by reabsorbing part of his family: "My two little ones sat upon each knee, the rest of the company by their partners. I had nothing now on this side of the grave to wish for" (chap. 32; 4: 184). He is as mercenary in his way as Mrs. Primrose is in hers.

Telling tales rather than histories and interpreting by inversion rather than by implication are both signs of a failure to take time properly into account. What Primrose lacks is the principle of compensation implicit in the double logic of The Deserted Village. There nature intersects with imagination and with labor. By viewing absence temporally as loss, the poet imagines potential restorations and restores to vacancy the fullness of experience. The culture of the mind sees the landscape as field for cultivation; if it is empty, then it has been or can be worked. Understanding time as the form of life, the poem animates and poetizes space. But Primrose understands only substance. His educational methods and his moral precepts alike promote the status quo and block reform. We see the whole story through his eyes, but we cannot comprehend the book's tendencies if we rest content with that. Both structurally and conceptually it urges us to see through him, as a character among characters, in order to attain the proper scope for imaginative vision.

Character

I would not disagree with the many readers who have found the characters to be Goldsmith's great achievement. At the same time, the richness of the characters is inseparable from what Goldsmith and his first reviewer recognized to be their defects. Obviously they are not to be judged like those in the novels of Austen and her successors, whose characters grow and mature with time.[18] Goldsmith does not portray the interplay of intentions and actions—let alone of conscious and subconscious motivations—that makes a "rounded" character in the later sense. But through both its generic complexity and the vagaries of its narrative persona his novel does create the narrative presuppositions for a new kind of character that it is not yet prepared to embody.

In *The Vicar of Wakefield* the buffeting winds of fortune transform the traditional empiricist notions of character as a stable essence that is innate, remembered, or artificially created. Pastoral expresses nostalgia for a lost order; when time invades, character is transformed along with society. Goldsmith's histories exemplify the issues. Goldsmith refuses to narrate the "fabulous and uncertain" legends of early Greece because "man, plain historical man, seems to have no share in the picture." Tales devoid of life as it is experienced are to be rejected, for "while the reader wanders through the most delightful scenes the imagination can offer, he is scarce once presented with the actions of such a being as himself" (*Grecian History* 3). But history is as defective in its way as idyll. It gives the outside only—exploits and adventures, without depth. The Grecian history proper, for instance, begins (in chapters 2–3) with the artificial imposition of order by Lycurgus in Sparta and by Solon in Athens, and it narrates exclusively public actions, treating Socrates only as a military and political figure, Aristotle only as Alexander's tutor, and Plato only as the chronicler of Socrates' death. The domesticity of *The Vicar of Wakefield* is a corrective for the externality of history. With its combination of timeless idyll and timeful chronicle, the novel juxtaposes the pieces from which later authors will assemble narratives of action imagined and character transformed.

In narrating his history seriatim as a delightfully idyllic tale, Primrose cuts himself off from the life of his subject. Readers who love the quaint episodes above all else fall in with his manner of presentation. They praise the story as pure fable, like the "livre sur rien" imagined by Flaubert. But we have seen how superficial the narrator's perspective is. Essentially never alone, he concentrates on the actions of others and reports his own feelings chiefly when he is being urged to restrain them.[19] That leaves the episodes as so many stock incidents from farce and melodrama. They acquire their luster for the reader from the new light that surrounding accidents and events constantly shed on them. The twists and accidents of the plot continually shift the perspective and complicate our assessment.

Events take a course that none of the characters can control, finally not even Burchell. Moses, for instance, is made to look foolish in his debate with Thornhill (chapter 7) and even more foolish at the fair. But then Primrose is also swindled. And later the swindler Jenkinson proves to be a sheep in wolf's clothing. (But can we trust the sympathetic construction that Jenkinson puts on his life when he tells it in chapter 26?) Even within the fair scene judgment is already complicated by at least two associated considerations. The first is that Moses makes a good bargain for the horse. (At least his family consider it a good bargain. Can we trust them? The horse goes for a mere three weeks' combined wages calculated at the rate at which Mrs. Primrose has been desperately trying to engage her daughters to the two whores from town. Perhaps it's not such a good price after all.) The second is that, as readers are prone to forget, Moses is not the only one to make a mistake. Rather, he only falls for Jenkinson's swindle with neighbor Flamborough's concurrence. (But what kind of credulity leads Moses to call on Solomon for succor in the first place?) One function of the novel's reticent yet digressive conclusion is to leave the characters in suspense: the quarrels continue, Thornhill's villainy remains incompletely punished, and Burchell's eccentric and potentially destructive laxity is suspiciously forgotten. Goldsmith thereby frustrates interpretation. Character becomes an enigma, not reducible to appearances, impenetrable to the narrator's limited gaze.

To clarify the bearing of plot, genre, and narration on the construction of character in *The Vicar*, I want to draw on Jurij Lotman's brilliant essay "The Origin of Plot." The essay describes what Lotman calls the modern plot-text as a fusion of myth-texts and news-texts. I believe *The Vicar of Wakefield* to be the work where this fusion is consummated.

Myth-texts, according to Lotman, are cyclical, as is the primeval round of activities described by the vicar or, likewise, Goldsmith's

Auburn. In their pure state myths are about "me"; that is, they are the community's self-representation. They reflect the integrated relationships of all people in the interpenetrating roles of its actors. Their model in the novel is the inexplicable constancy unto death of Edwin and Angelina.

As myths are cast into narrative form, however, they become exempla, tales of somebody else. We can see this happening in *The Vicar of Wakefield* as the self-satisfied ensemble at Wakefield gives way to Primrose's narrative of various escapades by members of the family in which he is at best a reluctant participant. Furthermore, as Lotman also points out, such news-texts cast myths into linear form, such as we see in the idyllic half of *The Vicar* or in the catalogues of *The Deserted Village*. Its prototype is the picaro, who is driven by necessity and resourcefulness without ever establishing a nature in which he is at home. In *The Vicar of Wakefield* Jenkinson's rapid autobiographical narrative exemplifies the linear, picaresque model, which is characteristically irresolute in tone and form:

> When but seven years old the ladies would say that I was a perfect little man; at fourteen I knew the world, cocked my hat, and loved the ladies; at twenty, though I was perfectly honest, yet every one thought me so cunning, that not one would trust me. Thus I was obliged to turn sharper in my own defence, and have lived ever since, my head throbbing with schemes to deceive, and my heart palpitating with fears of detection. . . . The honest man went forward without suspicion, and grew rich, while I still continued tricksy and cunning, and was poor, without the consolation of being honest. (chap. 26; 4: 147)

The cyclic nature of myths means that the figures in them blend into one another, while news-texts begin to sort the figures out. At this stage of storytelling, however, the separation is imperfect, so that we tend to find character-doublings. Lotman instances these from *As You Like It*, and they represent the still primitive form in which character is represented in the first half of Goldsmith's novel. The children here come in three pairs; there are two eccentric Thornhills (with the 30-year-old uncle Burchell awkwardly close in age to his nephew), two ladies of the town, two indistinguishable daughters of neighbor Flamborough ("rosy daughters, flaunting with red top-knots," chap. 9; 4: 53). The last paragraph of chapter 1 is typical of this half of the novel, where the aging prose of Goldsmith's high style renders the underdeveloped characters of the linear news-tale:

The temper of a woman is generally formed from the turn of her features, at least it was so with my daughters. Olivia wished for many lovers, Sophia to secure one. Olivia was often affected from too great a desire to please. Sophia even represt excellence from her fears to offend. The one entertained me with her vivacity when I was gay, the other with her sense when I was serious. But these qualities were never carried to excess in either, and I have often seen them exchange characters for a whole day together. A suit of mourning has transformed my coquet into a prude, and a new set of ribbands has given her younger sister more than natural vivacity. My eldest son George was bred at Oxford, as I intended him for one of the learned professions. My second boy Moses, whom I designed for business, received a sort of a miscellaneous education at home. But it is needless to attempt describing the particular characters of young people that had seen but very little of the world. In short, a family likeness prevailed through all, and properly speaking, they had but one character, that of being all equally generous, credulous, simple, and inoffensive. (4: 21)

Clearly the vicar's homogenizing conclusion here is false. In chapter 6 the youngest children prove to be the generous ones, with Dick the most generous, for which he receives the largest lump of sugar. Both Moses and Olivia are credulous, but not equally so, since one figure is comic, the other tragic. George is simple in his stoicism, but not inoffensive, since he is eventually imprisoned for sending a challenge. And the suspicious reader might conclude that the inoffensive Sophia is far from guileless: she seems to begin angling for Burchell from the moment he fishes her out of the river, dropping artful hints about lovebirds (chap. 8; 4: 45), carrying on secret conversations with him (chap. 13; 4: 70–71), and generally paralleling the development that, in Burchell's case, leads "his simplicity to assume the superior airs of wisdom" (chap. 8; 4: 45). The type of mind that arrays incidents in a disconnected series casts the actors as types while concealing their true characters.

Finally, as idyll moves toward romance, the primitive doubled characters of the news-text become individualized. If the myth proper is a repetitive circling and the news-text is a line, Lotman says, then the plot-text that fuses the two can be thought of as a great circle. For, as we have seen, the romance is an apparent line that eventually rounds back upon itself. In terms of the characters, this means that their paths increasingly curve outward from the domestic center, distinguishing personalities and careers that once seemed identical or interchangeable. By the time the circles converge and the family reassembles, its members have been strikingly desynonymized, each with a fate emerging out of his or her character and actions. To Mrs. Primrose's horror the wedding banquet itself no longer offers a proper image of social order, for the adventurer George "proposed, that the company should sit indiscriminately, every gentleman by his lady" (chap. 32; 4: 184). One may imagine that even the Miss Flamboroughs will finally grow apart when one reads of the younger walking down the aisle with her likely future husband, Moses, while the elder makes do with Jenkinson, who is surely not her intended. With respect to plot, just as with respect to narration, the dissonances at the end may then be viewed as an opening toward a new kind of fictional structure. As Frank Kermode has written with reference to Turgenev and James, "The more elaborate the story grows—the more remote from its schematic base— the more [narrative] agents will deviate from type and come to look like characters" (*Genesis of Secrecy* 77). The novel had been the story of society and its outlaws; Goldsmith's ending clears a path for it to become the story of the shifting interactions of individuals.

Though one cannot imagine Goldsmith consciously approving, this lower-class Irish Tory here begins to make the novel into a democratic form. At the start the social order seems established: the laws operate, aristocratic privileges reign unabated, the preacher ministers to his flock. But the narrative rhetoric hints at its precariousness. Primrose's divided sympathies appear early on when he absurdly calls his family "the little republic to which I gave laws" (chap. 4; 4: 33).[20] In theory the family is governed by debate and "council" (chap. 5; 4: 37, and chap. 14; 4: 71), but Primrose's instincts are to issue "edicts" (chap. 4; 4: 34) and to become a "legislator" for the masses (chap. 27; 4: 149, in the prison). In chapter 19 he declaims warmly against democracy, yet at that very moment he is unwittingly consorting with Mr. Arnold's servant and making free with the master's property, and at home he surely exemplifies, without much effectiveness, precisely the evils that that harangue opposes: "I have known many of those pretended champions for liberty in my time, yet I do not remember one that was not in his heart and in his family a tyrant" (chap. 19; 4: 103). One could hardly expect a comedy narrated by so confused a politician to issue in a convincing triumph of the social order.

And indeed, as we move away from the familial idyll toward romance, we see individuals increasingly opposed to the society that nurtured them. In chapter 2 the Primrose family leave Wakefield accompanied by their grieving parishioners, whereas in chapter 25 Primrose feels obliged to disperse the crowd that is jeering at the sheriffs who are leading him to jail. In chapter 13 the family are assembled to hear little Dick tell the fable of the Giant and the Dwarf that he has just read. It concerns societies responding to external threats (two Saracens, three Satyrs carrying off a damsel, a company of robbers), and the catastrophe comes from personal betrayal. But in the story of Matilda that Primrose reads privately to Olivia (chapter 23) personal ties triumph over the gratuitous cruelties that rage within European society. By chapter 18 Primrose flees the mob rather than be seen publicly in the company of his new friends, the strolling players. Social relations continue, of course, but chiefly in the form of charity from the haves to the have-nots (the neighbors give clothes and utensils to the Primroses after the fire in chapter 22; Burchell and a reluctant Wilmot give money to the prisoners and "coarser provisions" to the villagers who are not invited to the banquet in chapter 31). And as the nature lover Primrose is increasingly confined indoors, the model that remains to him of a successfully integrated society is now found in the sentimental comradeship of the jail rather than in the communal enterprises of the fields. The wildness of romance tears asunder the firm social fabric of myths.

Thus the very narrative structure of the novel helps to engender a new thematic organization. It is the story of a group of individuals who depart from their social origins and create their fate by means of the cumulative effect of their actions. As the characters move further from the protective center of home, events become less predictable but more determining. Goldsmith highlights the transformation by presenting the story from the father's point of view rather than the son's.[21] The father is the source from which a story departs (hence he is typically enfeebled or even absent from the vast majority of eighteenth- and nineteenth-century plots); the son is the telos toward which the story moves. The son's story is one of fulfillment and emergence into his own; the father's story is one of watching others despoil him of his role, an impoverishment that echoes in the negatives of Primrose's penultimate sentence: "I had nothing now on this side of the grave to wish for, all my cares were over, my pleasure was unspeakable" (chap. 32; 4: 184). This unusual point of view confirms the form of *The Vicar* as a story of development and emergence.

At the novel's close Primrose's fortune has returned, restoring the father to the realm of pure romance. But he does not return to Wakefield. If George gets the girl he was originally expected to marry, she who was once betrothed to a scholar now weds a soldier. And apart from a cunning gypsy, nothing in early events or in the various omens and prophecies could have predicted Olivia's fate, a story, indeed, whose end remains to be written ("when he reforms she may be brought to relent," chap. 32; 4: 183). The same conditions apply outside the Primrose family (and the father's domain) as well. Jenkinson's role bears some resemblance to Nightingale, the repentant thief who saves Tom Jones and then becomes the honest man he had originally been. Yet Jenkinson, when he finally speaks "nothing but truth" (chap. 31; 4: 178), suddenly seems a new man with a character he had possessed neither in the cunning days of his youth nor more recently when he had contrived the tale of Olivia's death and imposed it upon the grieving father. The series of confessions at the end does not ratify what was inevitable from the start, as in *Tom Jones* and *The Castle of Otranto*, but rather serves to confirm the conditions that have subsequently emerged. The novel here becomes indeed the story of the new.

The Simple Form

As the above analyses have shown, the organization of *The Vicar of Wakefield* is far from elementary. As befits a transitional work that engenders a new stance out of an old one, the novel is notable for its conspicuous doublings. Idyll and romance, comedy and melodrama, literal and allegorical meanings, line and circle, the small round of stable society and the great circle of unstable adventure, and above all, of course, the two narrators, Primrose and Goldsmith—each of these doublings plays its distinct role in the complex economy of the novel. The improbabilities and inarticulacies at the conclusion mark the demise of a whole system or ideology of narration.

In *The Vicar* narration is no longer what organizes experience. In picaresque and in Puritan spiritual autobiography alike, retrospection, reflection, and judgment are the forces that give shape to an existence previously characterized by the tumults of adventure or passion. For decades the major novelists had been questioning the shaping force of writing. Especially in *Roxana* Defoe ironizes the moralizing viewpoint by truncating the conclusion. Richardson's writing to the moment turns judgment into a restless and never-ending crisis of self-confidence. Fielding's omniscient narrator distances the story from its meaning, benevolently in *Tom Jones* (where the narrative reveals an essential goodness in Tom, though we can never know whether Tom himself recognizes it and definitively con-

quers his dangerous impulsiveness), coldly and almost cynically in
Amelia.[22] Goldsmith's bumbling Primrose, by contrast, is effectively
swamped by the story he tells. The product is less flamboyantly
radical than Sterne's explosion of both narrator and story, but no less
revolutionary in its own way.

For throughout the analysis a new concept has emerged, guiding
and regulating experience in ways that the inherited forms and
genres of writing no longer did. That concept is time, considered as
an inward force. The time of the Renaissance, the external mutability or mythic power of transformation that ruins or redeems human
structures and earthly essences, had dissolved into the timeless cult
of ruins and the nostalgic melancholy of Walpole and the graveyard
poets.[23] Time, of course, becomes a constructive shaping power in
Tom Jones, but it remains an external and dramatic rather than a
psychological time. In *The Vicar of Wakefield*, as we have already
begun to see, time emerges as the form of life itself, the succession
of events, rather than the mere sequence of chronicle or the order of
judgment.

One need only review the opening sentences of the chapters to
remind oneself how the narrative is saturated with the modulations
of lived time, so very different from Fielding's clockwork titles and
frequently generalizing or even aphoristic incipits. Most often they
feature a "now" or a "soon," less often the more complex "when" or
"after." Evening and night give their emotional coloration to the
start of chapters 11 and 12; morning marks a constantly varied new
beginning in chapters 7, 8, 22, 24, 26, 27, and 32. Even the sermon
begins with a "when" (chap. 29; 4: 160), whereas the changeless conditions of chapters 1, 2, and 5, and the timeless first sentences of the
crisis chapters 17 and 18 serve as foils to offset the flow of life. Just
as *Tristram Shandy* proclaims the manifold overt powers of time, so
Goldsmith's novel begins quietly to demonstrate the hidden psychological power of time—the power that matures schemes and heals
rifts, the power of planning and the power that spoils plans, the
power of memory with its reflective second thought and the power
of oblivion, the forgetting that forgives.

Above all, time means openness, possibility, uncertainty. Mr.
Thornhill's "time is pretty much taken up in keeping his relation,
who is a little melancholy, in spirits [i.e., happy, or drunk?], and in
learning to blow the French-horn. My eldest daughter, however, still
remembers him with regret; and she has even told me, though I
make a great secret of it, that when he reforms she may be brought
to relent" (chap. 32; 4: 183). By keeping her thoughts to herself

Sophia may be protecting from ridicule a tenderly budding Christian virtue or else repressing a yearning for retributive justice, but there is no way to tell which; the slow, silent movement of time finally teaches the man of God the strangely amoral lesson not to judge.

Time is thus a great simplifier. Intricate though its structure is, the novel is devoid of the complex layerings of consciousness and of symbolic elaboration that later novels have taught us to expect. This has led to the impression that of all the influential masterworks of our literature, *The Vicar of Wakefield* is the simplest and most naive. It is taken (to evoke another Flaubertian ideal) to be life itself making an appearance on stage. We are not surprised to find Goethe, in the tenth book of his autobiography, commingling the Primrose family with the family of Friederike Brion, calling himself George and her siblings Olivia and Moses, and using the real immediacy of Goldsmith's novel as an excuse to exclude fiction: "I would here insert [the story 'The New Melusine']," he writes, "if I did not fear harming with fancy's wondrous games the rustic reality and simplicity that pleasingly surrounds us here" (*Werke* 9: 446). Yet it is also precisely Goethe who acknowledges the craft underlying Goldsmith's simplicity. "It is strange," he writes in a letter to Karl Friedrich Zelter on Dec. 25, 1829, "that Yorick should incline rather to that which has no Form, and that Goldsmith should be all form, as I myself aspired to be when the worthy Germans had convinced themselves, that the peculiarity of true humour is to have no Form."[24] Goldsmith's simplicity is the product not of careless ignorance, but of a distillation that rids the work of dross. "Humour" in Goethe's usage and that of his contemporaries is a more ethereal mode than "wit," and the phrase "ganz Form" assigns the novel to the highest aesthetic sphere, rather than the lowest popular sphere.

Goethe knew his craft, and we ought therefore to credit an anonymous *Critical Review* contributor with more than idle flattery when he writes along similar lines: "He [Goldsmith] appears to tell his story with so much ease and artlessness, that one is almost tempted to think, one could have told it every bit as well without the least study; yet so difficult is it to hit off this mode of composition with any degree of mastery, that he who should try would probably find himself deceived" (in G. S. Rousseau, *Critical Heritage* 45−46). This judgment of Goldsmith's hidden art reappears in some comments of George Eliot, another novelist who was an undeniable master of her craft:

> Images and pictures . . . are the primitive instruments of thought. Hence it is not surprising that early poetry took this way,—telling

a daring deed, a glorious achievement, without caring for what went before. The desire for orderly narration is a later, more reflective birth. . . . The only stories life presents us in an orderly way are those of our autobiography, or the career or our companions from our childhood upwards, or perhaps of our own children. But it is a great art to make a connected strictly relevant narrative of such careers as we can recount from the beginning. In these cases the sequence of associations is almost sure to overmaster the sense of proportion. Such narratives *ab ovo* are summer's-day stories for happy loungers; not the cup of self-forgetting excitement to the busy who can snatch an hour of entertainment. But the simple opening of a story with a date and necessary account of places and people, passing on quietly towards the more rousing elements of narrative and dramatic presentation, without need of retrospect, has its advantages. . . . The opening chapters of "The Vicar of Wakefield" are as fine as any thing that can be done in this way.[25]

"Summer's-day stories" is Eliot's name for idylls. Her account reminds us of Goldsmith's achievement in this vein of easy, consecutive narration without retrospect. It also reminds us of the other half of Goldsmith's achievement in begetting the novel, as his romance plotting rounds things off to forestall the sprawl that typifies the idyll. The simplifying discovery of time as the form of experience was not a simple discovery. One does not have to resort to *Tristram Shandy* or *Nostromo* to demonstrate how difficult it is to tell a simple story in order; even Defoe's narratives, or Fielding's, or Austen's exhibit a degree of intricacy in the management of the time line that is entirely foreign to Goldsmith. The other great masters of fictional time manipulate time and make us conscious of it; only in Goldsmith is time the dominant yet utterly unconscious medium of life, the in-itself of a narration that seems thoughtless precisely because it is "all form."

Eliot's "without retrospect" is the key to Goldsmith's handling of time. There is no background information to be filled in, except insofar as characters like Burchell and Jenkinson tell their own histories, not without distortion. Hence *The Vicar* is a narrative without omniscience. It is also a narrative without depth: the pluperfect tense expresses the conditions of the narrated events rather than either remote sources or distance and contrast. There is also no retrospective reflection by the narrator; he does not in any material way link the time of the narrative with what precedes it, or his own present state with the time of the narration. This is, then, a narrative without judgment. Nothing interrupts the immediacy of events that Primrose recalls with flawless accuracy and yet with perfect innocence, and hence there is no surprise when the narrative suddenly breaks into the present tense. This is a first-person narrative in which memory plays no shaping role, and regardless of the verb tense employed time always functions in the form of presence. "Without retrospect" appears to be a negative characteristic, but in fact it establishes what all readers have felt to be the real-life immediacy of the narration.

The narrative would not function in this way with more complex characters. "Without retrospect" describes the life of the characters as well as the form of the narration. They live without learning and, as I have shown, without "experience" because they too know time only as presence. It is curious that while Primrose as narrator seemingly never forgets, neither Primrose as character nor any of the other characters seems ever to remember anything. George and Arabella disappear from the stage with nary a tear and reappear with only the most perfunctory of recognition scenes. "I don't know what were my feelings on this occasion; for they succeeded with too much rapidity for description," says Primrose upon recognizing his "speechless and immovable" son (chap. 19; 4: 105). If the revival of the past is not beyond articulation, as here, it is reduced to cliché, as when Primrose stutters his amazement to the reborn Olivia, "whose silence only spoke her raptures" (chap. 31; 4: 178). Really, even forgetting is too complex a term for the temporal consciousness of the characters; in this novel, though plots mature, characters are either simply present or absent.[26] Primrose, who after all is the narrator, shows glimmerings of a more sophisticated time sense at the moments when resentment and grief flare up, for these are modes in which the past lives on in the present. But these are also the emotions immediately suppressed, spontaneously or at the counsel of others.

To live virtually without a past also means to live without a future. The fondness for omens and prophecies betrays a consciousness too primitive really to think ahead. It would not be quite true to say that no thought whatsoever is given to things to come, but it is true that the future is not functionally distinguished from the present. "The journey of my daughters to town was now resolved upon," one chapter begins (chap. 14; 4: 71), as if thinking of a cause of action were sufficient to bring it about. The family then resolves to sell the second horse—Moses's unfortunate misadventure having recently resulted from a similar thoughtless resolution—as if there were no real impediment hindering the accomplishment of the family's intentions, or no distinction between end and means. The collapse of the pretentious makeshift carriage that precedes selling the horses offers an even more striking instance of the reduction of the future to an imagined presence. "I own their present mortification did not much displease me," says Primrose about his women, "as it would give me many opportunities of future triumph, and teach my daughters more humility" (chap. 10; 4: 60). The daughters don't in fact learn humility, and we are certainly not shown any of these future triumphs. So far as appears from the narrative, at any rate, these anticipations never come to pass. Nor need they. For in this book present "opportunities" displace actions to come: the future, here as throughout the novel, is entirely absorbed into the present.

Finally and most remarkably, Goldsmith completes the reduction of time to presence by excluding all forms of prolepsis. Not once does Primrose warn us of future reversals or console us with the knowledge that crises will ultimately be resolved. He offers no retrospective explanations. There is no allusion to the narrator's stance as he writes or to his motivation for writing. "I was ever of opinion," he begins the novel, without identifying himself, and indeed the very name Primrose is only mentioned by or in connection with the swindler Jenkinson. (Jenkinson addresses him in chap. 14; 4: 73, and chap. 25; 4: 142. In chap. 31; 4: 174, George is called Capt. Primrose while Jenkinson is dressing his hair.) The story is thus cut free from its moorings in a way that would never be possible given an authoritative third-person narrator or a first-person narrator sure of his identity and of the concluding position from which he relates his adventures. The vicar is not an unreliable narrator in the ordinary sense, but he could be called a vanishing narrator, with no distance from the events he describes. Countless ironies thus pass him by. By "accident," as he tells us, "one of the company happening to mention" Arabella's name, the Primrose family hear Thornhill express contempt for her (chap. 7; 4: 42). At the time there was no clue to a connection between Thornhill and Arabella, but the two later turn up engaged, and one might surely suspect that the companion was trying to gall Thornhill by mentioning her name. Yet Primrose reports the byplay without remark. He also omits any of the foreshadowing that the inserted poems and tales openly invite.[27] George and Arabella are eventually to be reunited like the long-lost lovers Edwin and Angelina (chapter 8). Like the Dwarf who accompanies the Giant in Burchell's unmistakably monitory fable, Primrose courts danger by consorting with Thornhill (chapter 13). Rejecting the pure poetry of "The Dying Swan," Primrose asks Billy in chapter

17 to sing the "Elegy on the Death of a Mad Dog," yet he fails to acknowledge the prophetic truth contained in this piece of doggerel, which anticipates the failed attack by the town dog Thornhill on the man of God. The history of Matilda in chapter 23 may be inappropriate for the current plight of the victim of seduction, as we have seen, but it will apply to Olivia differently later on (and also to Sophia's much earlier brush with drowning), when she becomes, like the general in the story, a dead child restored to life. And, finally, in singing "When Lovely Woman Stoops to Folly" Olivia comes close to announcing the scheme she will soon employ:

> The only art her guilt to cover,
>   To hide her shame from every eye,
> To give repentance to her lover,
>   And wring his bosom—is to die.
>   (chap. 24; 4: 136)

There are lessons to be learned, conclusions to be drawn from all of these insertions, as from the countless other dramatic ironies of the novel. But they are lessons and conclusions of the story itself, not of a narrator who passes over all such hints in silence. Goldsmith conspicuously refuses to cast Primrose in the storyteller's usual roles of soothsayer or dying swan.

The reduction of time to presence in no sense reduces the importance of time. On the contrary, it reduces the importance of the narrator in order to emancipate the story. Time is rendered at once simple and fundamental. The narrative becomes not what Zola was to call "a corner of creation seen through a temperament," but rather a slice of life pure and simple, a corner of creation freed from any filter of temperament. The narrating consciousness is bracketed in order to make the events themselves coextensive with the experience they beget.

This is to my mind the greatest achievement of *The Vicar of Wakefield*, indeed Goldsmith's greatest achievement. It helps to explain the mystifying international popularity of a small novel that was extravagantly admired without ever being thought well composed. Quite simply, *The Vicar of Wakefield* is the work in which story becomes completely equivalent to plot. There is no narrator shaping events, and yet no events remain unshaped or unassimilated to the whole. The judgment of the *Critical Review* contributor is naively stated, but unassailable: it is surely no mean feat to compose a plot in which every incident counts and that requires neither backtracking nor dramatic concealment to tell effectively. Incidents gain their greatest significance by being seen precisely as and how they occur. Life is not a series of events doubled by a consciousness that gives them their meaning; it is, rather, a series of inherently significant events. What happens is what matters.

Goldsmith's achievement is so radical a simplification of action that it has remained beneath notice, recognized instinctively by many readers, but consciously by none. He naturalized plot, making it so transparent that even the work's obvious external symmetries have been overlooked. To be sure, the artful disposition of events into units of four chapters—indeed, the very notion of chapter divisions—appears to be at the other pole from the artlessness of a plot in which each incident is immediately in place, without need of arrangement.[28] Yet in this case the appearance of spontaneity and the appearance of order are mutually reinforcing, for the point of the narrative is that order is what comes naturally. Likewise the two modes of the narrator's temporality are mutually reinforcing. Primrose is simultaneously immersed in the timeless immediacy of events and in the timeless eternity of judgments, a dual allegiance that is reflected in the curious grammar of his opening words, "I was ever." And just as there is no contradiction in this novel between art and artlessness, form and spontaneity, so there is no contradiction between the present moment and the eternal moment, event and meaning. All that separates them is the thin wall of consciousness, and as Goldsmith's narrator dissolves into insignificance, so too do any barriers to the hegemony of action.

The suppression of consciousness in *The Vicar of Wakefield* (like, and yet quite different from, that in Diderot's *Rêve de d'Alembert*) seems diametrically opposed to the discovery of consciousness in *The Castle of Otranto* and *The Task*. The tight organization of *The Vicar* and *The Castle of Otranto* could hardly differ more from the disjointed structures of Sterne and Cowper, though at the same time it seems hardly legitimate to compare the moody tautness of Walpole's novel, produced by a supernatural fatality, with Goldsmith's blithe naturalism and ironic undermining of transcendence. In its implicit celebration of action per se *The Vicar* has perhaps most in common with the work of another *arriviste* to whom I shall later turn, Beaumarchais, yet the Frenchman's immoral and opportunistic radicalism would have been profoundly antipathetic to Goldsmith. We have seen forces of decomposition at work within *The Task* and *The Vicar of Wakefield*, and when we turn to examine the preromantic period as a collectivity, we see the crisis of orientation writ large. Even Sterne and Goldsmith, these twin heroes of the feeling heart so often linked by later generations, seem to have had little in common, either artistically or biographically, beyond a certain zest for high life. How can we argue that there was a common project and intentionality linking figures not just diverse, but in appearance utterly contradictory? I have already used the term "farce" to characterize the period, and it would seem that the only consistency to be found is one of surprise and an almost magnetic repulsion of similar poles. It would be hard to think of another period whose major works have had so little in common with one another. Perhaps this is one explanation for the difficulty in composition experienced by authors and the paucity of masterpieces in the period.

Yet in a fundamental sense all these works are linked. Whether consciousness disappears into meaning-impregnated action (as in *The Vicar of Wakefield*) or action is sublimated into an effective consciousness (as we shall see in *Tristram Shandy*), whether form becomes invisible because it grows transparent as in Goldsmith or opaque as in Sterne, whether nature is spiritualized into a moral ambience or spirit naturalized to manifest a judgment on human actions—in all these cases, despite their difference, the boundaries between transcendence and immanence, mind and body, unconsciousness and consciousness are broken down. In its own way each such work is a totalization, and whatever principle becomes dominant immediately comes into a relationship of equivalence with all others. We need only survey the theme of the secret motive in *The Vicar of Wakefield* to illustrate how freely values circulate in the economy of works in this period. It is a surprising theme, given both the novel's emphasis on externals and the superficiality of Primrose's understanding. But then it turns out that the explanation in terms of secrecy is the one that lies readiest to hand and that it makes the sequence of actions rather than the expressed intentions the conveyor of meaning. As the possessor of secrets, the deep or inward self links all the discrete present moments of the novel, and yet the secret self proves merely the sum of its actions after all. Secrets are known as secrets by giving themselves away: "My eldest daughter," Primrose confides to the universe in the last and most unguarded occurrence of this motif, "has even told me, though I make a great secret of it, that when he reforms she may be brought to relent" (chap. 32; 4: 183).[29] With no successful partition between outside and inside, Goldsmith's characters wear their hearts on their sleeves, exactly as do those of Sterne and Walpole.

I have discussed the totalizing impulse of sensibility as an economic problem, and that analysis is just as true of Goldsmith as of other writers. To the very end, as Robert Hopkins shows (*True Genius*), Primrose remains a hopelessly bad reckoner. Labor is divided within the family, to be sure, with the wife handling things material and the husband things spiritual. Yet they are both such bad economists that the division utterly fails. The novel's plot is propelled largely by the family's total loss of its financial resources and material possessions. But the failure to manage money is just as clearly a synecdoche for the complete failure to manage life. The Primrose family live life from moment to moment, in the fashion that Mackenzie repeatedly exposed, giving no heed to past or future. With no boundaries and yet no scope, they share an essential trait with the characters of all the other, so diverse masterpieces of the period. That trait is impulsiveness. Feeling induces movement, wish prompts action, without intervention or restraint.

One may argue whether the morality of *Tom Jones* is based on benevolence or prudence, and one may of course object (as Johnson and others did) to Fielding's morality, but there is no doubt that the book addresses moral issues. No one that I am aware of has ever expressed moral outrage at *The Vicar of Wakefield* (as distinguished from its title character), and the reason is perhaps that moral questions depend on a complexity of temporality or of psychology that has been refined out of the novel. One might say that Primrose is rewarded at the end for his good heart (though it might be objected that Primrose, unlike, say, Job or Tom Jones, is too stupid to *choose* the good), but it is hard to take Burchell seriously as an agent of divine justice.[30] Nor would it be easy to say for what virtues beyond good looks George is finally rewarded. Primrose has a morality, of course, a small-minded stoicism that preaches ataraxia on earth as a prelude to epicurean bliss in heaven. But Primrose clearly doesn't know what he is talking about, for in the chapter following his sermon he quotes the first and shortest of Seneca's moral essays, *De Providentia*, with no recognition of the gulf separating his passive submissiveness from the Roman's muscular fortitude. Rather than align ourselves with the teller's confusions, we would do better to acknowledge freely that this is an impulsive book, totalizing in the additional sense that it is totally self-contained, a delightfully pure fable, with no meaning beyond its story. At the conclusion of Karl Philipp Moritz's "Über die bildende Nachahmung des Schönen" (1788), the most important essay in aesthetics from the decade preceding Kant's *Critique of Judgment*, we read, "Mortal lips may speak no sublimer word about the beautiful than: *it is!*" (*Schriften* 93). Such a dictum can explain the glamour that Goldsmith's early readers perceived in a book they acknowledged to be so insignificant. For in the precise sense of preromantic aesthetics, Goldsmith's novel is the paradigm of literary beauty.

The Vicar of Wakefield has, first of all, the dimensions of an aesthetic object. One of Moritz's favorite terms is *Verjüngung*, which means both reduction in scale and rejuvenation. Beauty dwells in a narrow pastoral or idyllic realm that is forever young because forever isolated from events. These currents in Moritz's thought remind one of the name Primrose, of the putti sitting on the vicar's knee in the final tableau, of the vivid immediacy within the transparent past tense of the narration: the archaic world of fable lives always within us. But even more, they may call our attention to the curious fact that *The Castle of Otranto* and *The Vicar of Wakefield* could plausibly be viewed as the first two major novels to be set entirely in imaginary locales. Walpole and Goldsmith were, of course, noted observers of the contemporary scene, yet in their novels they have given us symmetrically timeless worlds, one a historical Otranto that could never have been present, the other a modern village that, by reducing the real world to the foolishness of the Whistonian controversy and the politics of the hoaxing butler of chapter 19, effectively remains outside of history.

For Moritz, in addition, beauty is self-contained. The line of beauty is a small circle that imitates the infinite circle of nature. Consequently the work of art lives as an organism does within its skin, through the complex interrelationship of its parts. *Tom Jones* could be said to precede *The Vicar of Wakefield* in the complex symmetry of its construction.[31] But *Tom Jones* is a large and increasingly worldly book: the characters' collective pilgrimage to London may be said to follow the great circle of nature and not the reduced circle of art. It is, rather, in Goldsmith's novel where the purely aesthetic notion of plot as return, reabsorption, and restoration emerges. Far more clearly than Fielding, Goldsmith anticipates Moritz's prescriptions in constructing his plot, as he does in his idyllic setting. His plot-text, with its gradual bending of line into circle, is the perfect example to concretize the abstract discussion in Moritz's essay "Die metaphysische Schönheitslinie" (1773):

> In our impulse to imitate the highest beauty in creation, which is perfect within itself only in its totality, we give to what in nature seem to us *straight lines*, or merely *divergent* means, a gradual inclination toward one another, precisely as if we wanted to model on the great, immeasurable circle a smaller one within it on a reduced scale. . . . These curved lines are thus what we wish

to call the lines of beauty, and the lines in the immeasurable circle that appear straight, the lines of truth. Beauty would thus be truth in a reduced scale. (*Schriften* 154–56, Moritz's emphasis)

An aesthetic plot is arbitrarily cut out from the infinite flow of events. What one individual is able to see as a self-contained story with a beginning, middle, and end will look to another incomplete or even incoherent. To God all times are present in an eternal moment, but humans see things successively, and in an order that can be deceptive ("Zeit und Ewigkeit," *Schriften* 36–37). Whereas, we might infer, a sublime text would have a God-like omniscient narrator, a human-scaled work needs a particular focus or perspective around which it crystallizes: "To view every beautiful work of art as a self-contained whole, it is necessary to find the *point of view* within the work itself through which every detail presents itself in its necessary relation to the whole" ("Bestimmung des Zwecks einer Theorie der schönen Künste," *Schriften* 122). Lotman observes that it was only at an advanced stage of development that the beginning and end of a plot became identified with the beginning and end of a life, that is, that the focus of plot became the life story of a person ("The Origin of Plot" 179–83). In Goldsmith's novel the personal narrator gives us the necessary perspective from which the events appear complete, whereas Burchell's story, for instance, lacks a beginning and Olivia's an end. A personal narrator, as George Eliot saw, cannot give us his complete life history—Tristram Shandy is the narrator who tries to combine beautiful self-containment with sublime totality, and inevitably fails—but Primrose gives us the appropriately scaled-down, beautiful version of the complete plot, which is the story not of a life, but of a career. The earliest event of the narrative is his ordination; the last is the accomplishment of his human destiny, leaving him "nothing new on this side of the grave to wish for" (chap. 32; 4: 184). There are no opening vistas in this conclusion, but rather the last fulfillment of a life as seen from the inside.

The Carnival Text

The simplification of narrative does not dispel all problems. It remains troubling, for one thing, that the perfect work of art should necessarily end in such darkness. Moritz's aesthetics is predicated on a series of negations—exclusion, boundedness, the withholding of meaning—and only a few years after he began writing, he was overtaken by the Kantian revolution that restored to the work of art the grandeur that Moritz withheld from it. We have seen how the formal perfection of Goldsmith's novel depends on the failure of the narrator at the end: the novel is concluded when Primrose loses focus and has nothing more to say. *The Vicar of Wakefield*, further-more, belongs to a succession of intricately structured works writ-ten around this time—including *Rasselas, The Castle of Otranto*, and *Werther*—that are strictly limited in scale: masterpieces to be read in an evening.[32] In addition, there is a problematic asymmetry to Goldsmith's achievements. On the one hand there is the perfec-tion of plot closure accomplished in the novel; on the other, there is the open-ended notion of character projected by the novel, though not developed in it. The vicar's narration renders the plot with a con-tinuous immediacy and presence that makes it seem timeless. Causal connections that would define a necessary sequence are frequently elided, such as the missing explanation for the family's leaving Wakefield, which gave rise to the famous missing-chapter hypothe-sis. Yet the depths excluded from the plot return in the sense of growth and change in the hidden motivations of the characters. Time is moment in the discontinuous, tableau-like scenic structure of Primrose's narration, but flow in the deep structure of Gold-smith's novel. One might also well claim *The Vicar of Wakefield* (along with *She Stoops to Conquer*, as the next chapter will show) as the prototype for romantic organic form. If the work has never been acknowledged as such, that is perhaps because organic form, too, is here generated as a contradiction rather than as a synthesis. With re-spect to plot, the novel's organic form appears in the well-understood guise of self-regulation and self-limitation. But with respect to char-acters the organic form appears in the equally essential but normally overlooked form of self-differentiation. In every respect the novel shows us two faces that seem at once inseparable and incompatible.

It is no wonder that *The Vicar of Wakefield* remained a unique achievement, for analysis shows it to be a crisis text, poised in a balance that one could hardly imagine repeated. The elements of the romantic universe appear assembled here, but in the form of perpetually unreconciled oppositions. The idyllic absorption of the characters is here a pure externality; the melodramatic theatricality of the plot points to the inwardness that turns romance into roman-ticism;[33] yet the two modes do not interpenetrate, but coexist side by side in the two halves of the novel. Time as moment and as flow; form as limitation and as differentiation; action as the visibility that unifies plot by excluding considerations of character and character as the invisibility that unifies plot by motivating it—such are the structuring duplicities of this deceptively self-effacing novel.

Behind Goldsmith's simplicity, then, lies an astonishing profusion. My stress on the novel's unity will have surprised those who have been accustomed to regard it as planless; undoubtedly it will still surprise those who have in mind its episodic and digressive presentation. To be sure, the episodes all have clear thematic functions, as other critics have pointed out and as I have further illustrated. Still, at one level the impression given by this crisis text is one not of unity, but of remarkable diversity. Of the three inserted poems, one is a ballad, one a song, one a parody. Inserted stories include a fable, a historical exemplum, Burchell's "character," George's "history" (chapter 20, title), and Jenkinson's epitome. One chapter is a sermon; another contains what is tantamount to a periodical essay. The disputes between Thornhill and Moses (chapter 7), between the Primroses (chapter 10), and between Burchell and Mrs. Primrose (chapter 15) are examples of the little comic scenes that further vary the narrative mode. Moritz's essays suggest that totalization can function positively in this period only in combination with limitation and not as a cosmic ambition, and it would surely be an exaggeration to call *The Vicar of Wakefield* an encyclopedic novel. But one would be hard put to find such diversity of presentation in so small a compass in any other novel in English, or indeed, any Continental work preceding the novels of the German romantics who so revered Goldsmith.

Terry Castle has recently described the pervasive topos of the masquerade in eighteenth-century fiction. In a society governed by fixed forms, the masquerade was the locus where identity could be denied so as to make change possible.[34] *She Stoops to Conquer* opens on a discussion of the costumes of the town, and while it *contains* no masquerades, it could plausibly be said to *be* one, with many of the characters in disguise and with the license and inverted hierarchies typical of the carnival. And *The Vicar of Wakefield* is even more clearly a carnival text. Its giddy formal profusion is pervaded by images of disguise and by scenes of humiliation of the proud and of those who are (or, like the Dwarf, think they are) high and mighty. As the romance plot upsets the placid surface of the idyll, so does the formal turbulence obscure and impede the simplicity of the novel's organization. Time and again Goldsmith's writings advert to the difficulties of passage. The road from Wakefield to the modest new village is barred by dangerous rapids. The gate from the Garden of Pleasure to the Garden of Virtue is hidden amidst a labyrinth of "frightful rocks . . . , gloomy caverns, unexpected precipices, awful ruins, heaps of unburied bones, and terrifying sounds, caused by unseen waters" (*Citizen*, letter 31; 2: 136). "Unquiet waves . . . of the darkest hue" in the Ocean of Doubts, giving "a lively representation of the various agitations of the human mind" (*Citizen*, letter 37; 2: 160), lie between the happy Valley of Ignorance and the even more idyllic Land of Certainties. And so, likewise, have we seen how the achievement of a simple form results from a confused and difficult process.

Goldsmith's infrequent letters give unreliable testimony of his feelings, and it is not possible to reconstruct the state of mind in which *The Vicar of Wakefield* was produced.[35] It is tempting to regard his breakthrough as a costly undertaking that led the author to bestrew the book's path with the litter of discarded forms; certainly none of the insertions conforms very well to what little we know of Goldsmith's principles of form, centering on the gradual buildup of tensions. But whether or not we see the book's form as the reflection of a psychic process such as the two *Citizen of the World* essays describe, we would do well to see in it the condensation of the corresponding historical process. It is a revolutionary book, and its flood of radical innovations did not ensue as the logical next step building smoothly on earlier works.[36]

I do not at all mean to suggest, in the fashion of Thomas Kuhn, that there is no logic of innovation; quite the contrary, my whole book is an attempt to understand the factors that promoted literary change and the processes that guided the course of development specifically toward romanticism as we know it. But I do mean that the logic of crisis and revolution differs from the logic of incremental growth. To a consciousness dominated by problems rather than possibilities, development must come, as Kuhn suggests, from outside, by way of a change in paradigms or, as literary critics call them, forms. But we can see, in the later eighteenth century, *how* these innovations have been discovered through combining or borrowing forms or else through exploding or inverting them by taking them to extremes. The status of literature as we customarily define it today—fictional narrative, poetry, drama—had become uncertain. There were no stable forms that could be renewed simply through variation (like satire for Pope or the novel for Scott), nor a stable style to which traditional forms could be adapted so as to renew them (as Wordsworth and others renewed the various lyric genres in the romantic style). Indeed, there were no major writers in the period whose main occupation was the creation of literary works (in the modern sense), as it had been, say, for Pope, and was again to be for Wordsworth and Scott. Creation in the later eighteenth century was a risky business, psychologically as well as economically, and innovation came from experimenters and exaggerators who were not confined by the conventional forms of writing and the norms of a conventional literary career. To be a significant writer meant not to be a writer at all in the traditional mold.

Of the two kinds of innovators, it makes more sense to see Goldsmith as an experimenter. The last fact that I wish to bring into view in this section is the variety of his achievement. No other major author in English has been equally successful in writing drama, prose fiction, and verse.[37] The diversity of Goldsmith's carnival novel is matched by the diversity of his experimenter's career, and the career, like the novel, is comparable only to those of Continental romantic authors. And these (Goethe, Pushkin, Hugo, and some others) were fluent experimenters grounded in a stable style, whereas Goldsmith's experiments cost him infinite pains. (Goldsmith would have recognized Voltaire as his predecessor—really the only one—in mastering the different literary genres, but posterity has not ratified the judgment of the eighteenth century.) One might argue that Shakespeare and Milton succeeded powerfully in narrative, lyric, and dramatic verse, even though not in prose. But this argument only confirms Goldsmith's stature. He is usually considered nowadays a slender talent, an eighteenth-century Mrs. Gaskell, say. He was, rather, an extraordinarily robust talent working an infertile soil. (Studies appearing since I drafted this incautious remark have convinced me that she was too.) One did not need to be a political revolutionary in order to be a revolutionary figure in literature or philosophy; indeed, it often seems as if one kind of revolution could be a satisfactory substitute for another. In France society acted out its problems; in Germany and in England it thought them through. But one could not be a great literary creator in this period and be a settled figure.

The New Critical essay that first analyzed the patterns of disguise in *The Vicar of Wakefield* concludes by asking, "But, when all is said and done, does the *Vicar of Wakefield* really 'mean' anything?"[38] At first the question seems merely perverse or cowardly. Yet it should continue to haunt any discussion that takes cognizance of Goldsmith's intense formalism (which we have also seen in his versification) and of the care he lavished on the elaboration of purely imaginary worlds. In an age of farce, of conclusions in which nothing could be concluded, and of the empty signs of a school for scandal, the urgent need was not for meanings but for forms into which meanings could plausibly be cast. Goldsmith is an inventor of paradigms, projecting a new kind of spatialized story whose beginning, middle, and end are all surveyed from a timeless controlling vantage point, and a new kind of temporalized character that develops without a fixed essence. We have lost sight of Goldsmith's achievements because he created a language without discovering a message, or because, to put it less metaphorically, others were soon to obscure his achievements by filling in the paradigms far more richly than he had done. But, even more, his achievements are hard to appreciate because they take the revolutionary form of masquerade, deceit, and unresolved antithesis. In order to accomplish anything at all, Goldsmith found himself accomplishing too much at once, in a work that never seems to find its bearings and that succeeds only because it ends so badly. It *is*, then, a meaningless work, or one that outruns its meaning; we may take that to be not a defect, but a reflection of its situation. If there was to be a next step, it would have to result from becoming conscious of the author's situation—such as with the more pointed fictionality of Auburn—but above all from directly facing the antinomies of the revolutionary work. If he was to continue constructing plots, Goldsmith would have to learn the art of reconciling contradictions. And that is the task of *She Stoops to Conquer*.

CHAPTER EIGHT

She Stoops to Conquer: From Farce to Organism

The Art of Reconciling Contradictions

"The art of reconciling contradictions" is old Mr. Hardcastle's phrase. He desires it, and he also doesn't believe that it is possible. "But if young Mr. Brazen can find the art of reconciling contradictions," he says, "he may please us both." But then he adds a skeptical, "perhaps" (act 3; 5: 161). Remaining truculently divided within yourself is not the way to end a dispute. Tory though he is, one can hardly take Hardcastle to be Goldsmith's spokesman, any more than the other tyrannical fathers of Goldsmith's plays or—it had better be admitted—of his novel. Yet Hardcastle is the only father who is also an uncle; he has a solidity and a generosity absent from Croaker, Primrose, Wilmot, Sourby (in *The Grumbler*), and several negligent fathers portrayed in essays.[1] In this effervescent farce—two early reviewers use the word (in G. S. Rousseau, *Critical Heritage* 122, 126)—Goldsmith edges toward a happy combination of the opposing forces of earlier works.

Goldsmith's own early reviews had enjoined a gradual building of excitement. In establishing contradiction as its central issue *She Stoops to Conquer* appears to violate that injunction. Whereas a classical comedy might begin with a monologue and a modern sentimental one with a discussion of plans, rumors, uncertainties, problems, or worries (such as the good-natured disagreement between Sir William and his servant about Honeywood's character in *The Good-Natur'd Man*), *She Stoops to Conquer* opens abruptly on a violent quarrel. The conflicts of old versus new, country versus city, England versus France are broached in the first scene and traverse the whole play. In act 1 we hear that Kate wears clothes for town outings in the morning and rustic housewife's clothes in the evening. In act 2 it becomes evident that identical actions have contradictory meanings in houses and in inns. An elaborate menu ("made dishes" like those "at the French ambassador's table," 5: 139) shows a host's generosity, but a landlord's avariciousness; urging one's servants to drink freely (Jeremy, in act 4) is an insult to a host, a courtesy to a landlord. In act 2 we learn of Marlow's divided nature and witness the "sober sentimental interview" (5: 148) between him and Kate, still wearing her fancy clothes; in act 3 she assumes a fake identity as an alluring country wench, and he shows his dashing side, in the process assuming the false names Rattle and Mr. Solomons (5: 172).[2] By the end of act 3 identity and contradiction become indistinguishable even in language when we hear Hardcastle explode, "I tell you I'll not be convinced. I am convinced" (5: 175). The confusion grows too great to bear, until Hardcastle, in one of the greatest exploitations of an ancient topos, exclaims, "I no longer know my own house. It's turned all topsey-turvey" (act 4; 5: 180).[3] Contradiction splits open the identity of the person and of that which is most properly his, his domicile.[4]

The contradictions between characters that open the play thus lead to both intentional and unintentional contradictions within characters.[5] The knowledge of who a man is, which is intimately bound up with where he stands (and how old he is), is called into question by the jolting action of the play. Yet the splitting apart of the shell of the self opens an internal space that first makes genuine self-knowledge possible. At the start of the play identity is no more than one's role, and one's dwelling a haphazard house. The thoughtless characters know truly neither who they are nor where they belong. Should Hardcastle use the word "home," he would give away that his mansion is not an inn. But of course he has no such intimate relationship to the house: after he uses the word "home" once with his wife in the first scene and once with the servants in the first speech of act 2, it does not occur again until Mrs. Hardcastle has been shaken up by her wild ride, when "home" suddenly clusters as the focus of one's being.[6] As if the *I am* only comes into being as a result of the *I think*, the characters find themselves and their places by questioning them. Without that they are merely "Anthony Lumpkin, Esquire, of BLANK place," and "Constantia Neville, spinster, of no place at all" (act 5; 5: 215).

The site of *She Stoops to Conquer* is, if possible, even more remote from reality than Auburn or than Primrose's village. Yet in the
blank of this place, within the space opened by contradiction, the
play stages the emergence of domesticity and inwardness, sincerity
and simplicity. Thus between the elegant city Kate, whom he does
not see at all, and the pert country Kate, whom he sees too appe-
titively, a new, true Kate appears to Marlow: "What at first seem'd
rustic plainness, now appears refin'd simplicity. What seem'd forward assurance, now strikes me as the result of courageous innocence, and conscious virtue" (act 5; 5: 210). The values of selfhood
are latent from the start, particularly with the unsocialized Tony,
whose only loyalty is to himself: "As for disappointing *them*, I should
not so much mind; but I can't abide to disappoint *myself*" (act 1; 5:
110). And the instant that characters are alone, the veil falls, and
frankness prevails. The numerous brief soliloquies that speckle the
action are little islands of sincerity where unaffected thoughts and
feeling find expression. But though Hardcastle is the first figure to be
alone on stage, it is chiefly Tony and the divided characters Marlow
and Kate who pause and look within in these moments of temperate
reflection. Finally, in act 5, with the appearance of Sir Charles Marlow, with the discounting of fortune and station in favor of love and
virtue as the basis for marriage, and with the investigation into
Kate's and Marlow's sincerity (the word falls three times on 5: 199–
201) the new values begin to prevail generally on stage.

The emergence of this new ideal follows a course similar to
those of *The Vicar of Wakefield* and *The Deserted Village*. In this
sense the play does observe the gradualness enjoined by Goldsmith,
but transferred from the plane of action to that of theme and image.
An episodic series of scenes at the start evokes rustic manners in a
largely idyllic vein. We hear much of the little daily cycle of activities, such as the ladies' "afternoon's walk round the improvements"
(act 1; 5: 115) and the rounds of drinking at the Three Pigeons. Then,
when the plot gets under way, its comic foolery is insistently linear:
Tony sends Marlow and Hastings to the supposed inn by sending
them "streight forward, till you come to a large old house by the
road side" and again, almost at the curtain of act 1, "streight forward" (5: 124). Later, when the plot thickens and mistake turns to
confusion and mystery, the play begins to suggest a different mode.
"My chief aim," says Kate, "is to take my gentleman off his guard,
and like an invisible champion of romance examine the giant's force
before I offer to combat" (act 3; 5: 169). Earlier this had not seemed
to Marlow a world where, "like an Eastern bridegroom, one [might]

be introduced to a wife he never saw before" (act 2; 5: 130), but things change as night approaches. Disguise, theft, and abduction bring Aunt Pedigree's prison into view, then madness ("We shall have old Bedlam broke loose presently," act 4; 5: 192; "I'm so distracted with a variety of passions, that I don't know what I do," act 4; 5: 194), unbearable anguish ("The torture of my situation is my only excuse," act 4; 5: 195), and their paradoxical preromantic correlative, reverie. Tony is distracted during the frenzy at the close of act 4 and awakens only to deliver the curtain speech; the stage direction reads, "From a reverie" (5: 195). However fancifully, Tony illustrates the pull toward romance when he compares his mother in the horse-pond to a mermaid (act 5; 5: 204). And in some of its most memorable expressions the line of the play becomes a farcical equivalent of the great circle toward which all of Goldsmith's major works tend. "What's that goes round the house, and round the house, and never touches the house," asks Tony when the women are finally enticed beyond the bounds of the estate. He takes them, as he describes, on his wild-goose chase, and then, "with a circumbendibus, I fairly lodged them in the horse-pond at the bottom of the garden" (act 5; 5: 203). By this point we are ready for the magical revelation that duly arrives in the appropriately bureaucratized guise of an *ex machina* birthdate.

But of course this low mimetic or parodistic form of romance is hardly compatible with the dignified values of inwardness that the play is set up to engender. It tears apart a work that nearly ends with a sentimental family tableau like that in *The Vicar of Wakefield*. For here, where the contradictions ought to be finally appeased, we confront a persistent dissonance. While not a two-author conclusion like those of the poems, it is a two-genre conclusion that telescopes the genre mixing of *The Vicar of Wakefield* and *The Deserted Village*. First, Constance and Hastings repent of their elopement and return to express submission; they have decided to wait until Tony's majority before marrying. Lest there could be any doubt about the type of conclusion that stresses sincerity, pity, family responsibilities, and mixed emotions, Mrs. Hardcastle gives it its proper name: "Pshaw, pshaw, this is all but the whining end of a modern novel" (act 5; 5: 215). It isn't quite the end, however. Kate continues to torment Marlow at the back of the stage. And then, forthwith, the sentimental fusion bursts apart, dethroning the mother and placing the children in command after all: "Witness all men by these presents, that I, Anthony Lumpkin, Esquire, of BLANK place, refuse you, Constantia Neville, spinster, of no place at all, for my true and lawful wife" (ibid.).[7] With the mother's whining novel giving way to the son's antique farce, Tony's negations invert the values just established. "Tony Lumpkin is his own man again," we hear; Mrs. Hardcastle's final catcall, "My undutiful offspring!" deflates the pious congratulations of Sir Charles and Hastings; and the emergent shrew Kate Hardcastle (the name is one of a whole network of Shakespearian allusions in the play) returns to front and center without ceasing to be what Marlow calls "my little tyrant" (5: 216). Though "to-morrow" the sentimental old Hardcastle plans, like Burchell, "to gather all the poor of the parish about us" (ibid.), on stage the social reintegration typical of comedy dissolves into farce's cosmos of eccentric luminaries.

Sentimentality was "modern" in Goldsmith's day. Picking up an important strand in the text, the early reviewers agree that *She Stoops to Conquer* depicts an archaic or fictive world. Like David Garrick in his prologue to the play, they recognize that Goldsmith has abandoned the modern sentimental comedy. In the victory of the younger generation they find a victory of the old comedy (in G. S. Rousseau, *Critical Heritage* 118, 123), and most of them deplore it. Thus, according to William Woodfall, in the *Monthly Review*, the diversity among the characters falsifies the "general politeness" and "sameness" to be found in modern manners (ibid., 116). But we have seen how problematic and even sterile the modernity of sensibility could appear in this period. Goldsmith spoofs the sentimentality of the bashful Marlow on every occasion, of course. In the wooing scene between Marlow and Kate he mercilessly parodies Johnsonese at its most sentimental. And he both typifies and ridicules the closed economy of sensibility in the person of the authoritarian mother who tries to suppress the circulation of goods and emotions by forbidding an exogamous marriage. To move beyond sensibility is thus actually to move ahead. The double ending of the play differs from those of the earlier works by clearly signifying a temporal advance. The younger generation's new-found self-assertion upstages the romantic morality of sincere communication toward which the play had seemed to tend. Decisiveness, not submissiveness, becomes the order of the day: to be oneself is to know *and to act* oneself in distinction from all others.

Movement thus supplants the aestheticizing stabilization that concludes Goldsmith's earlier works. Several early reviewers complain in particular about Goldsmith's handling of time; their objections, however misguided, recognize the distinctive foregrounding of time in the later acts, both through words and through the breakneck pace leading up to the revelation of Tony's premature coming-of-age. The play's title, with its romantic suggestion that humility will prevail, is quoted by Kate in the middle of act 4 (5: 186), but the final speech quotes the original title—which became the subtitle—suggesting the preeminence of time: "the Mistakes of the Night shall be crowned with a merry morning" (5: 216). Bypassing in the confusions of the last two acts its romantic guise as reverie or inner sense, time comes to seem an irrational force that is always felt and never understood. To that extent, at least, it is possible to see in the double conclusion the dawning of a sense of time as an individuating power. Individuation was already a force in *The Vicar of Wakefield*, but only in a cognitive or narratological sense: as the vicar proceeds with his storytelling we come to recognize the differences between pairs of characters, but we do not see the characters on their escapades, when they are asserting themselves. In *She Stoops to Conquer* individuation acquires a genetic sense: as the characters act, in time, they become themselves. The aesthetic mode suspends contradictions. While encompassing much of the fictive, aestheticizing air that we have seen in earlier works, *She Stoops to Conquer* undertakes something different, a genuine attempt at resolving contradictions rather than wishfully abolishing them.

The Contradictions of a Reconciling Art

It is strange that such an ideology of youthful advance comes wrapped in so traditional and so perfectly self-contained a form. Though the early reviewers all accuse the play of lacking unity, it is clear that Goldsmith went to remarkable lengths in order to unify the play. The buoyant ending, it will be recalled, is pulled out of a hat when Hardcastle reveals that his stepson, Tony Lumpkin, is of age; as a result, Tony is free to reject his cousin Constance Neville, and she in turn can then marry her lover, Hastings. However, unlike the surprise restoration of Primrose's and Arabella's fortunes, the play's romance conclusion is foreshadowed from the first page, with Hardcastle's wisecracks about his wife's and Tony's ages. The speed of the conclusion is initially prepared by Tony's first line, "I'm in haste, mother, I cannot stay" (act 1; 5: 109); then it is motivated by the news that Marlow is to arrive shortly and to be followed soon after by his father (5: 110); and it continues to be evoked throughout the play by, among other things, the name of Constance's lover, Hastings. Even the bit just before the end when Tony dupes his mother and deposits her in a horse-pond is anticipated in a remark of Hardcastle's, "I'd sooner allow him an horse-pond" (5: 108). And Mrs. Hardcastle's remark in her second speech about the "old rumbling mansion, that looks for all the world like an inn" (5: 107) sets the stage for the trick that Tony plays on Hastings and on Kate Hardcastle's suitor, Marlow. Goldsmith continues to use incidental motifs such as embroidery or reading and writing, together with echoing stage devices like teasing at the rear of the stage (Constance in act 2; 5: 142, and Kate in act 5; 5: 213), to impose a type of unity unknown in his earlier works.

What unifies *She Stoops to Conquer* is, on the first level, repetition. To be more specific, it is backward repetition: a motif that is functional at the end gets prepared in an incidental way earlier on. This is not a causal, organic unity: Tony does not dump his mother in the horse-pond *because* Hardcastle mentions one in the first scene. Rather, it might be called a semantic unity: the Hardcastles inhabit a tight little world where every detail has its place and its significance. But the contradictions that plague this world destroy its cozy significances. Of these the most far-reaching, as we can now see, is the contradiction of the two conclusions. The first conclusion is regressive; the eloped couple return home and revive the unity of the household by restoring something resembling the *status quo ante*. But this is a wrong conclusion, reflecting a world whose meanings have all been backwards, or fictive, motivated by the selectivity of art rather than the fecundity of life. The true conclusion is the one that will follow from the presuppositions of the plot, not the one that will fall back upon them. If the (metonymic) progress to the new generation merely confirmed a (metaphoric) substitution by making the young into new parents who adopt the values of the old, then one could say that *She Stoops to Conquer* instances Roman Jakobson's famous formula by projecting "the principle of equivalence from the axis of selection into the axis of combination" ("Closing Statement" 358). But the double ending disjoins the two axes. At the end the play fulfills the demands of syntactic development, even at the expense of semantic reassurance. The contradictory ending perpetuates the contradictions that pervade the play because contradiction opens up the space in which things happen—she stoops to conquer.

Signification is a form of repetition, insofar as the significance coincides with the object of signification. In this play Goldsmith has fully mastered the formalism of such correspondences. But the perfected form is too hard and confining, too sterile (like the bashful Marlow) or too incestuous (like Mrs. Hardcastle's proposed marriage between the cousins Tony and Constance), and it breaks free at the end. When J. Craddock's Epilogue for Tony, as Goldsmith's note tells us, "came too late to be Spoken" (5: 217), the author seized the opportunity by the forelock: he wrote an Epilogue for Kate that quotes Shakespeare's Seven Ages of Man speech and that recasts Kate's spontaneous improvisations as a generic biography. On the face of it, one would not have thought *The Mistakes of a Night* the equivalent of the story of a life, but so Goldsmith will have it at the end: "Such, thro' our lives, the eventful history" (5: 105). Repetition and contradiction are both static modes, but their combination engenders the form of temporality that I have called individuation.

Naming becomes a prominent individuating force. Rather than classifying, as traditional or tribal names do (see Lévi-Strauss, *Savage Mind*, chaps. 6–7), the names in this play promote self-assertion. The alliance of Hastings with Constance Neville illustrates how names break free of categories. "*Mrs. Hardcastle*. Constance, why Constance, I say! *Miss Neville*. I'm coming. Well, constancy. Remember constancy is the word" (act 4; 5: 195). In this instance constancy is indeed the word. But constancy to what? Constancy to Hastings could be seen as mere thoughtlessness. For Hastings is a sentimental totalizer with no regard for limited resources and divided motivations: "Love and content will encrease what we possess beyond a monarch's revenue" (act 5; 5: 208). His unwavering urgings to flee surely do not warrant the designation "prudent choice" (act 5; 5: 213) that Sir Charles gives him shortly afterward. In fact his actions exemplify what could only be called a hasty constancy, as his very words confirm: "Such a tedious delay is worse than inconstancy" (act 5; 5: 208). Miss Neville, by contrast, changes her mind. She opts for the virtue that Sir Charles attributes to Hastings, who seems not to possess it: "Prudence once more comes to my relief, and I will obey its dictates" (ibid.). A better economist than Hastings, she is constant above all to her jewels. Fortune is, of course, notably fickle, and in this instance the goddess rewards Miss Neville's constancy to her by relenting. The names are reliable guides to the problems that the characters confront; the solutions come through contradictions and reversals of meaning. "A pair of large horns over the door" may be the sign of the house (act 1; 5: 124)—that is to say, if the house were an inn, then Hardcastle's trophy would be a sign—but any spectator led by this sign to anticipate a bawdy comedy in the old style would have been sorely disappointed. Signs exist in this work to be complicated and corrected, without copulation in either the physical or the grammatical sense. Tony is oafish at the start, but by the end he is no longer a lump, though some of his kin may be. Names are that from which time may lead us to differ.

A sign, or a name, in this play, comes to signify only as it develops its potential for individuation. Otherwise it grows stale, like the outworn platitudes that Hardcastle is prone to utter, following Primrose's lead.[8] Garrick ridicules these in his Prologue in terms that show, in contrast to his misjudgment of *The Good-Natur'd Man*, how well he understood what kind of play Goldsmith had written:

> But why can't I be moral?—Let me try—
> My heart thus pressing—fix'd my face and eye—
> With a sententious look, that nothing means,
> (Faces are blocks, in sentimental scenes).
>
> (5: 102–3)

Properly speaking, neither a person, a work, nor a sign bares its inside or wears its heart on its sleeve. The face (or the surface) is the boundary, not the revealer of meaning.

Platitudes and sincerity are both faces of sentimentality because both are transparent and unreflecting. Yet they are incompatible modes. They coexist in this play, which has never heard of the division of labor (see Hardcastle's futile attempt to assign tasks to the servants at the beginning of act 2) so as to show forth the self-contradictions of sensibility. If Hardcastle is sincere, the young folk are, in their various ways, opportunistic; if they are sincere, then the older generation are, in their various ways, rigidly conformist. Correspondence theories of meaning make no sense out of a play that, indeed, many of Goldsmith's contemporaries felt lacked a center.

But in fact the play directs us toward neither platitude nor sincerity, neither conventional nor unconventional sentiment. These are incidental motifs that appear only intermittently. The face, not the heart, the complexity, not the simplicity of meaning are its standard-bearers. "Am I in face to day?" (act 1; 5: 114), asks Kate, in the first occurrence of the word after the prologue. The *OED* says that the expression means to look one's best, by analogy with being in voice. This passage is, however, the only citation of what may well have been a striking coinage and not a timeworn phrase. To be in voice means to show one's powers. But to be in face means, at least in part, to conceal one's emotions. Being in face is a brave or a cowardly way of denying sincere reflection: "Well, if he refuses, instead of breaking my heart at his indifference, I'll only break my glass for its flattery. Set my cap to some newer fashion, and look out for some less difficult admirer" (act 1; 5: 113). And it is also a way of repressing sentiment: Constance responds to Kate's concern about face by echoing in advance the comment about "the whining end of a modern novel": "Has the last novel been too moving?" (act 1; 5: 114). Kate's whole effort with Marlow is to get her face seen, not her heart; she wants not to be felt, but to be known, as an individual, distinct from the class of high ladies or low barmaids to which he assigns her. "I don't think I shall venture to look in her face," he says (act 2; 5: 130); she first meets him "with a demure face, and quite in his own manner" (act 2; 5: 143) and emerges "certain he scarce look'd in my face the whole time" (act 2; 5: 148); and she disguises herself because "I shall be *seen*, and that is no small advantage to a girl who brings her face to market" (act 3; 5: 169). Her stratagem begins to pay off when, as the stage direction says, he "looks full in her face" (act 3; 5: 170).

The point is not that the face is the person, or the marble index of the mind. On the contrary, it is the sign of the distance at which we always stand from the person, even from ourselves when we see our own face in a mirror.[9] "There's a mahogany table"—says Hardcastle scornfully to Marlow, thinking he has been impudently imposed on and after first offering Marlow a set of *The Rake's Progress*—"that you may see your own face in" (act 4; 5: 183). Constance praises Tony's "bold face," and he her "hazle eyes" (act 4; 5: 188), in order to fool Mrs. Hardcastle by courting "before her face" (act 4; 5: 187). Her slightly more honest praise of Tony, however, is for the frankness of his affronts—"He falls out before faces to be forgiven in private" (act 2; 5: 153)—and Marlow, too, is at his best when his face is at its most forbidding: "This house I no more shew *my* face in" (act 4; 5: 185). At this point he begins to respond to her tears—not sincere tears, of course, but signs that are recognized to the degree that they are artful—which is altogether better than when he "said some civil things of my face . . . , mentioned his heart, gave a short tragedy speech, and ended with pretended rapture" (act 5; 5: 201).

The honesty of the face that shows what one means and wants others to apprehend is far preferable to the affected sincerity of the undisciplined heart. Seeking an honest alliance, rather than an elopement, Kate also honestly confesses her attachment to fortune. Kate's railing is the triumph of honesty over the affected modesty and affected licentiousness of Marlow; it expresses her willingness to overlook both the high and the low faults that mar his character in appearance, once his true temperance at last shines forth. Hardcastle, likewise, becomes a truth-teller at the end, revealing Tony's age, which policy has kept secret all these years out of a mixture of moral and mercenary motives. And though Tony, with his "natural humour, that pleasant, broad, red, thoughtless . . . bold face" (act 4; 5: 188), knows how to lie, to deceive, and to steal, he nevertheless remains an unwavering supporter of individualities. He does not know how to corrupt or manipulate others for his own benefit; he is not self-serving.

Kate brings together the play's two key terms near the end, when she offers to her father and Sir Charles Marlow to "convince you to your face of my sincerity" (act 5; 5: 201). Her expression is deceptive, since she proceeds to convince them by placing them behind a screen and acting out a scene with Marlow that they are in no position to understand. The face of sincerity here is something quite different from the voice of the heart, and the conviction produced is of a different order from that produced by conventional truth-telling. The face brings forward, but it also alters and individualizes sentiment; it puts inwardness on stage, turns passion into action, and realizes through a process of conversion. The honest face adapts itself to its situation, and it has a power and freshness that it may maintain by practicing restraint or even concealment: "As the times are, there comes rarely forth that thing, so full of authority, or example, but by assiduity and custom, grows less, and loses. This, yet, safe in your judgment . . . is forbidden to speak more; lest it talk, or look like one of the ambitious faces of the time; who, the more they paint, are the less themselves."[10]

Honesty is the value that looms over the work's horizon. The term appears three times. In its first occurrence it refers to the sincerity of heart that can gild any action, no matter how disreputable: Tony, defending his having pilfered for Constance the jewels that will eventually be hers by inheritance, says, "An honest man may rob himself of his own at any time" (act 3; 5: 162). In the term's second occurrence it refers to the brazen face that covers up debauchery with a facade of equity: Marlow, speaking of Kate the presumed barmaid, says, "There's nothing in this house, I shan't honestly *pay* for" (act 4; 5: 178). But finally, at the end, it appears in a passage strongly marked as a turning point and as the only mention of Hastings's royal Christian name: Sir Charles becomes the first of the older generation to praise the Hastingses' elopement, in the words, "my honest George Hastings. As worthy a fellow as lives, and the girl could not have made a more prudent choice" (act 5; 5: 213). If worth is inner merit, prudence points toward outward stability, and honesty becomes at last the explicit resolution of the contradictory values.

But when we look at how honesty operates in the play, we are forced to concede that there is more to reconciling contradictions than merely finding the term in the middle. The truth of face is the product of multiple deceit on the fluid stage of comedy. Face acts honestly by being, not by saying; when it does speak, its saying is a negation that unsays affectation. Marlow and Kate unsay their pretended identities; Constance and Hastings unsay their elopement; Hardcastle unsays the lie about Tony's age so that Tony can unsay his inheritance. Honesty, as the face of sincerity, is thus above all the denial of role. The role-playing has established a dialectic that runs from the opening of the play to its first, sentimental conclusion.[11] The second conclusion goes beyond this dialectic to its truth, which is grounded in the unspoken. We move here in the domain of Heidegger, which is perhaps less surprising if we consider the degree to which Heidegger's thought was an exploration of what lies behind romanticism, as *She Stoops to Conquer* certainly does. I cite at length a passage from Heidegger's "The Origin of the Work of Art" that analyzes perfectly what is at issue here:

> The open place in the midst of beings, the clearing [*Lichtung*], is never a rigid stage with a permanently raised curtain on which the play of beings runs its course. Rather, the clearing happens only as this double concealment. The unconcealedness of beings—this is never a merely existent state, but a happening. Unconcealedness (truth) is neither an attribute of factual things in the sense of beings, nor one of propositions.
>
> We believe we are at home in the immediate circle of beings. That which is, is familiar, reliable, ordinary. Nevertheless, the clearing is pervaded by a constant concealment in the double form of refusal and dissembling. At bottom, the ordinary is not ordinary; it is extra-ordinary, uncanny. The nature of truth, that is, of unconcealedness, is dominated throughout by a denial. Yet this denial is not a defect or a fault, as though truth were an unalloyed unconcealedness that has rid itself of everything concealed. If truth could accomplish this, it would no longer be itself. This denial, in the form of a double concealment, belongs to the nature of truth as unconcealedness. Truth, in its nature, is untruth. We put this matter this way in order to serve notice, with a possibly surprising trenchancy, that denial in the manner of concealment belongs to unconcealedness as clearing. The proposition, 'the nature of truth is untruth,' is not, however, intended to state that truth is at bottom falsehood. Nor does it mean that truth is never itself but, viewed dialectically, is always also its opposite.
>
> Truth occurs [*west*] precisely as itself in that the concealing denial, as refusal [*Versagen*], provides its constant source to all

clearing, and yet, as dissembling [*Verstellen*], it metes out to all clearing the relentless trenchancy of error. Concealing denial is intended to denote that opposition [*Gegenwendige*] in the nature of truth which subsists between clearing, or lighting, and concealing. It is, the opposition [*Gegeneinander*] of the primal conflict. The nature of truth is, in itself, the primal conflict in which that open center is won within which what is, stands, and from which it sets itself back into itself. (*Poetry, Language, Thought* 54–55, translation slightly modified)

She Stoops to Conquer points toward a truth that, like Heidegger's, is compounded of unsaying and displacement (which are connotations of Heidegger's *Versagen* and *Verstellen*). Goldsmith unmasks the dialectical art of resolving contradictions as a homey, repetitious, sentimental self-confirmation of the "familiar, reliable, ordinary." The associated *Lichtung* is, we may presume, the rustic illumination of an inn on a dark night. But the genuine illuminations of truth are different and more unsettling (perhaps a better translation yet of the intention behind *Verstellen*). There is conflict and victory, but not peace; the opposition that opens onto truth persists as a turning against (*Gegenwendigkeit*). Thus does Kate turn to renew the combat at the end of the play, and likewise Tony. One could wish for no better illustration of the way that the assertion of truth is rooted in denial.

Heidegger has to struggle to define a truth that is grounded in untruth without being falsehood, I suggest, because he is working around a gap in the German language. He means honesty, as we can see from his choice of a gruffly realistic, almost farcical painting (Van Gogh's *Old Shoes*) to lead off his discussion. But the German language splits honesty into the inward look of honor (*Ehrlichkeit*) and the outward face of frank speech (*Redlichkeit*). Having one word for both, we forget or are mystified by the complexities that the concept harbors. But we can recover our sense for them by returning to a period in English when honesty was itself problematic. In the eighteenth century it is characteristically a snickering term. It designates both forthright sociability and self-reliant inwardness, and it rarely if ever occurs without an implicit or explicit awareness of the cleavage between the two.[12] That is why, even though the word has a long history, honesty can still loom as a missing value over Goldsmith's text. Truth in this sense does not merely exist, shining either by its own radiance or else by a reflected glow, but instead "comes on" (*west*) in a complex, theatrical performance. This kind of truth is two-faced, though our habitual ease in making assertions conceals what a miracle it is when we can be true both to the permanence of our identity and to the fickleness of the world. Goldsmith's double ending stages for us the complexities of conceiving truth as honesty rather than as manifestation or correspondence and thus makes a new value accessible to thought.

As an action, addressed to its own time, *She Stoops to Conquer* projects a series of emergent values. First comes sincerity, associated with simplicity and reunification of the family, as a dialectical resolution of the multiple duplicities and contradictions of the play. This is a modern value whose origin Goldsmith demonstrates from behind the facades of Enlightenment sociability. Next comes face, character, individuation, as a value without which sincerity would be sterile and timeless. And barely articulated, but indispensable, is the third value that is yet to emerge, the value of honesty. Honesty is the honorable ground (or essence, or being) of face, and it is the frank, speaking face of sincerity.

In Goldsmith's earlier works the imperfect endings suggest a stable terminus in some ideal to be imagined. For this reason I have spoken of a mythic structure in *The Traveller* and of the birth of the aesthetic in *The Vicar of Wakefield* and in *The Deserted Village*. Authorial control is greater at the end of *She Stoops to Conquer* and leaves a more palpable—certainly a more freely acknowledged—irresolution; consequently, it is plausible to regard the terminus here more concretely as an ideal to be discovered. We have more of a sense of sequence in the double ending here; more of a sense of contradiction in the earlier endings. The terminus of *She Stoops to Conquer* will be found on the level of its problems; the formal contradictions will produce a formal resolution, rather than the earlier annihilation and sublimation of reality. Formally, the first ending is built on repetition and total integration, the second ending on contrast, discovery, emergence. What *The Vicar of Wakefield* enacts in its split between compact plot and changing characters *She Stoops to Conquer* works out entirely on the level of form, in the split between sentimental comedy and farce.

Thus Goldsmith moves even closer here to the romantic conception of organic unity. Boundedness and growth, self-regulation and self-differentiation, the soul and the life force: these two sides that are perfectly fused in the living organism are the two faces that exist back to back in *She Stoops to Conquer*, the more clearly seen for still remaining distinct. Each of Goldsmith's works is unique for a different reason; each work hovers on a threshold and thereby opens a door, and this unrepeatability limited his output and eventually his fame. Mere chance left *She Stoops to Conquer* as the last of his works, and there is no telling what Goldsmith might have gone on to write, whether his genius for analysis would have continued to discover new problems and to project their solutions under a veil, or whether a genius for synthesis might have emerged.[13] But it seems appropriate that Goldsmith's last major work should be the one to define the formal terms by which the formal irresolution that had always plagued him would at last be resolved.

CHAPTER NINE

Sheridan's Semiotics

Et ait eis Jesus: Omnes scandalizabimini in me in nocte ista. . . . Petrus autem ait illi: Et si omnes scandalizati fuerint in te, sed non ego. Et ait illi Jesus: Amen dico tibi, quia tu hodie in nocte hac, priusquam gallus vocem bis dederit, ter me es negaturus. At ille amplius loquebatur: Et si oportuerit me simul commori tibi, non te negabo.

Mark 14:27–31

Neoclassicism

How does a traditionalist like Sheridan fit into a history of inventions and innovations? If novelty as such were the concern of this book, then he would figure less prominently than, say, Smart and Chatterton. These acted in truly disruptive roles, creating works that were bound to seem not just unprecedented, but even to a large extent unmotivated. But novelty like theirs washes out. Writers who seemed not of their time (this includes Macpherson and the German Sturm und Drang writers as well as Chatterton) created a sensation while they appeared exotic, but as soon as their relation to their contemporaries became apparent, the luster vanished. Those more deeply exceptional—Smart or Blake—remained ignored until an audience emerged that felt a kinship with them. Quirks masquerade as discoveries or discoveries as quirks; either way, novelty as such expresses mere difference. Its relationship to time and hence to history remains in abeyance.

About Sheridan, by contrast, there was nothing sensational, except his success.[1] Yet his deep roots in the past respond to a profound engagement with the historical place of his works. What matters, to be sure, is not that he was old-fashioned. Greatness does not come that handily. But Sheridan's masterpieces are distinguished by their reflections on an essential historical paradox: the old forms prove their vigor by having lasted long enough to grow feeble. By rethinking their grounds, he can recover a source of energy missed by more rebellious writers. Like the proverbial pygmies standing on the shoulders of giants, Sheridan and his French counterpart Beaumarchais add only a little to their predecessors—so little, indeed, that the most thorough scholarship has missed some innovations that I will be pointing out—yet they see further in all directions. Hence perhaps it comes that they could exercise a political influence—progressive in Sheridan's case, revolutionary in that of Beaumarchais—greater than most of the flamboyantly radical authors.

One is struck in Sheridan by a curious yet powerful ambivalence toward innovation. Nostalgia is his governing mode: youth is sought by turning back, whereas advance leads only into decadence and old age. Age is a burdening consciousness for Sheridan's numerous old husbands, who know their frailties in a way that their ancestor, Wycherley's Pinchwife, does not. *"Youth's the season made for joy,"* sings Sir Anthony Absolute with touching sentiment in *The Rivals* (4.2, p. 125), and old Uncle Oliver is rejuvenated by young Charles Surface, the polar opposite of Goldsmith's alternately depressive and foolish Charles Marlow. Sheridan's generally progressive politics were complicated by a streak of caution that was manifested on the one hand in excessive loyalty to party, on the other hand in hesitancies toward promoting a Regency or in a merely ironic support of impossible parliamentary reform (see Moore, *Memoirs* 2: 323, 55; 1: 196–97). Yet we find Sheridan changing careers, changing friends, remarrying (it "must have been like a renewal of his own youth," writes Moore, *Memoirs* 2: 189), and spending prodigally in the effort to keep life from growing stale. Sheridan's literary career was, of course, extraordinarily precocious. He developed astonishingly early, and he was capable of composing and revising with almost instantaneous speed. Yet he was also slow, deliberate, a compulsive rewriter, strangely impeded in impromptu utterance (ibid., 319–22). Whether or not we accept the judgment that *The School for Scandal* falls off at the end, we cannot escape from the obsessive tinkering and the neurotic reluctance ever to issue an authoritative text for most of the plays, leaving us with one of the worst textual muddles in English letters. Goldsmith forced endings upon his works; Sheridan withheld finality from his.

As a psychological clue to Sheridan's reluctance either to develop or to stay put, we may take the poignant conclusion of a fragmentary review of Chesterfield's letters, written by Sheridan in 1774, at the age of 23, just as he was completing *The Rivals*: *"There are on every subject few leading and fixed ideas; their tracks may be traced by your own genius as well as by reading:—a man of deep thought, who shall have accustomed himself to support or attack all he has read, will soon find nothing new: thought is exercise, and the* mind, like the body, must not be wearied."[2] Sheridan was certainly not shy about work, particularly when the work consisted in a speech to be delivered on an occasion prompted by others and not to be preserved for posterity.[3] Rather, the review seems to suggest a more specific fear of undertaking and completing a task, of erecting a monument, as if the self contained a stock of assets that it would be death to waste.[4] This condition anticipates the curse of belatedness that began to haunt Johnson as he toiled and aged. Sheridan stands as the last of a line of melancholy prodigies in the later eighteenth century. Their careers had been self-thwarted by madness (Smart, Collins) or suicide (Chatterton), but Sheridan's, most forbiddingly of all, by an act of the will.[5]

The very strength of Sheridan's resistance to closure, seriousness, and innovation can hence be seen dialectically as an acknowledgment of these forces. Such is the experiment that I undertake in this chapter. It is not a study of what Sheridan's burlesque knowingly omits, for the alternatives that the age was aware of can readily be found in the satirical rantings of Matthew Bramble and the sentimental pantings of Sterne. Rather, it is an examination of what Sheridan was unable to exclude and, more importantly, of what forces he mobilized in his preemptive strike against innovation.[6]

As John Loftis has pointed out, Sheridan's lighthearted farces and burlesques have always embarrassed serious critics of later-eighteenth-century literature.[7] If the heir of Congreve does not do anything new, formally, then it seems as if his plays certainly cannot have anything to say.[8] Loftis points out autobiographical elements in the plays, but these are always veiled, and Mark Auburn (particularly in his analysis of Charles Surface) identifies a movement away from realistic characters and plots. The plays are thus neither confessional nor mimetic documents. We risk being left with praise of clever lines (chiefly in scenes that do not advance the plot) and of vivid minor characters, with here a Spanish plot, there a device from George Colman, yonder a line from Wycherley or a character from Congreve. A familiar thesis based on Goldsmith's essay on sentimental and laughing comedy had asserted that the mission of *The Rivals* and then of *She Stoops to Conquer* was to cure the unrelieved sentimentality of the stage with laughter. But not even that thesis survives. Auburn has now demonstrated how all plays of the period mixed sentiment and humor in varying proportions, including Sheridan's plays and even Goldsmith's.[9] The great comedies of the age stand opposed not to feeling, but to flabby, spiritless writing: the attack on sentimentality is at bottom an attack on dullness. Goldsmith—together, by implication, with Sheridan—advocates plays that are the liveliest possible expression of the spirit of the age.

Such assertions of meaninglessness, of mixed modes, and of the contemporaneity of the old-fashioned comprise analyses without synthesis. Yet if we attend closely to their terms, they can ground a richer account of Sheridan's historicity. Loftis advances the argument by defining the spirit of the age as neoclassical. The designation is not new, but Loftis alters its import by stressing a break with the seventeenth century. Sheridan's plays, he argues in effect, are not a late flickering of seventeenth-century neoclassicism, let alone of the classical Greek and Roman tradition, which had by then receded into the misty background: they are neoclassical more because they come after these earlier classicisms than because they revive them. There no longer appears to be a direct line to Plautus and Terence: *Amphitryon* comes to Sheridan through Molière and Dryden, among others, the *Aulularia* through Molière's *L'Avare* and Fielding's *The Miser*. And Loftis's brilliant insight, though not stated in these terms, is that even the seventeenth century is, from Sheridan's perspective, classical and not neoclassical. "Sheridan represents the end of an era in dramatic history as clearly as Dryden represents its beginning," and "Sheridan wrote his plays with a more restrictive and specifically neoclassical conception of the genre of comedy than that of Dryden when he wrote his plays."[10] The later seventeenth century is a problematic origin for Sheridan, not an unmediated ambiance. His works show us the figure of the virile youth as an enervated poet.

Basically, as Loftis shows in detail, Sheridan worked at self-consciously normalizing the comic form. He eliminated ambiguities of tone (tragicomedy) and moral ambivalence, quietly strengthened observance of the unities of time and place (though not so much as Goldsmith), tightened the relationship between different strands of the plot, and replaced the often rather casual closure of Restoration comedies with a perfect resolution of all plot complications. Restoration comedy obeyed instinctively, so to speak, the spirit of the rules of representation as it understood them, and consequently it did not need to observe them to the letter. To a latecomer like Sheridan, however, the spirit of the rules was transmitted through the letter, whose authority was reinforced by an epigone's impulse toward perfection of the form. The very sense that he is consolidating, not creating, a tradition entails an altered relationship to it, breathing a different, more self-conscious and time-bound spirit. It is no coincidence that the titles *The Rivals*, *The School for Scandal*, and *The Critic* make these plays preeminently into representations of competition, in the latter two cases promoting a theme that is more typically subordinate in Restoration comedy.[11] As we shall see, Sheridan's neoclassicism covertly struggles against the very classicism to which it swears allegiance.

Classicism and Consciousness

If we turn back from Sheridan to survey the plays of the second half of the seventeenth century, we can see what sorts of restraints the classical theater practiced so spontaneously that it did not need to work at them. (I follow Loftis's example by taking both English and French comedy into account.) Restoration drama is far more varied than that of Georgian England. Yet its freedom coexists with limitations that were hardly acknowledged. These limitations have nothing directly to do with the Aristotelian rules—which were controversial in Dryden's day as in Johnson's—though they do have something to do with the spirit behind the rules and with the grounds on which the rules were debated. Classical (seventeenth-century) drama channels and guides consciousness. Georgian comedy practices more rigid inhibitions in response to energies that threatened to overwhelm the unstated decorums of the form.

Here is a representative seventeenth-century view of the theater:

> A good Play shu'd be like a good stuff, closely and evenly wrought, without any breakes, thrums, or loose ends in 'um, or like a good Picture well painted and designed; the Plot or Contrivement, the Design, the Writing, the Coloris, and Counterplot, the Shaddowings, with other Embellishments: or finally, it shu'd be like a well contriv'd Garden, cast into its Walks and Counterwalks, betwixt an Alley and a Wilderness. Of all Arts, that of the Dramatick Poet is the most difficult and most subject to censure; . . . the Poet must write of every thing, and every one undertakes to judge of it.[12]

By reconceiving both plot and imitation in terms of design and pattern, the "classical" dramaturgy of the seventeenth century effectively excludes the spectator from reflection. It makes little difference whether the play is imagined as a seamless fabric that separates or an artful garden that incorporates; in either case, the ideal is an imperturbable construction that sheds active scrutiny. In classical dramaturgy, as the last sentence quoted above hints, admiration preempts judgment.

The portraits of foibles and vices in the classical theater are idealizations; they must delight and instruct without infecting the spectators. Hence we ought to take more at face value than we customarily do monitions like this one of Uranie in Molière's *Critique de l'école des femmes*: "Everyone ought to watch without embarrassment all the ridiculous pictures shown in the theaters. They are public mirrors in which you must never confess to seeing yourself; and you tax yourself out loud with a defect if you are scandalized at being reproached" (*Théâtre* 1: 500).[13] A pure mimesis is an empty reflection in an inviolate surface. To be sure, Mrs. Flirt is obviously teasing, or even taunting, when she tells the audience in the Epilogue to Wycherley's *The Gentleman Dancing-Master*, "Hippolita is not like you at all" (*Plays* 234). The stated exculpation of the spectators masks covert accusation. Yet behind both lies the heightened artificiality always found in epilogues, where the actors come forth as actors to solicit applause for their performance. It is a complex maneuver, but the end is disidentification, curtaining the staged action off from life.[14] Other epilogues, of course, evoke Flecknoe's garden rather than his picture or his fabric: they rail darkly at the audience and implicate it in the vices and follies of the characters. "Stay away," is the implication. "The Visor-Mask sells Linnen too i'th' Pit," Wycherley writes in the Epilogue to *The Plain Dealer* (*Plays* 508), and that for *The Country Wife* warns spectators against imitating art: "you Essens't Boyes," he writes, "Encourag'd by our Womans man to day, / A *Horners* part may vainly think to Play; / . . . But Gallants, have a care" (*Plays* 353–54). Life does not appear on stage. It often fails to appear offstage too, but the message of such utterances, if we can take them at their word, is that we should make our lives unlike what we see. The Restoration dramatist is therefore being less disingenuous than it seems when he denies that his play contains any immorality; for the stage exists to purge vices, that is, to drain them of any connection to the world of experience.

Both space and time are negated in classical representation. We need to bear in mind that the French word *unité* means unit as well as unity. The play represents a unit of space, of time, and of action, rather than an expanse, a flow, or an action that rejoins life. Subtending all the endless debates concerning the formal, the logical, and the psychological aspects of the unities is an unstated consensus on the unitary, self-contained character of dramatic representation. Even when Dryden's Neander attacks the unities in "Of Dramatic Poesy," he stresses the importance of a unified plan, with a single focal character, "managed so regularly, that the beauty of the whole be kept entire" and achieving "a labyrinth of design" like Flecknoe's garden; likewise he insists on short speeches in order to preserve the distinctness of the units of his complex plays, for "a long sober shower gives [grief and passion] leisure to run out as they came in, without troubling the ordinary current" (*Essays* 1: 73, 72). Time should be a series of moments without flow: this principle underlies both Corneille's *liaison des scènes* (the stage must not be empty between scenes because all characters must converge within the same unit of time) and the attack on it (linking the scenes creates an impression of flow rather than unitization).[15] Only in exceptional cases, as when Horace is thrashed between acts 4 and 5 of Molière's *Ecole des femmes*, is there a sense of time passing outside the moment of representation.[16]

Even when the seventeenth century attacked the unities, it did so in the name of formal logic, not in that of experience. Sir Robert Howard writes in his Preface to *The Great Favourite* (1668):

> If strictly and duely weigh'd, 'tis as impossible for one stage to present two Houses or two Roomes truely as two Countreys or Kingdomes, and as impossible that five houres, or four and twenty houres should be two houres and a halfe as that a thousand houres or yeares should be less than what they are, or the greatest part of time to be comprehended in the less; for all being impossible, they are none of them nearest the truth or nature of what they present, for Impossibilities are all equal, and admit no degrees.
> (in Spingarn, *Critical Essays*, 2: 109)

In content this is the same argument that Johnson used to crush the unities a century later. Johnson's spectator, knowing that he is not witnessing the real Thebes, is free to imagine himself experiencing the events in the Thebes of the imagination. "Time," writes Johnson, "is, of all modes of existence, most obsequious to the imagination," and the drama "is credited . . . as representing to the auditor what he would himself feel, if he were to do or suffer what is there feigned to be suffered or to be done" ("Preface to Shakespeare," in *Works* 7: 78). Howard differs by couching his argument in the mode of rational judgment, thus underscoring the rationalistic, nonexperiential, and unitized character of classical drama. The consequences of Howard's seemingly Johnsonian objections, as Dryden drew them in his "Defence of an Essay of Dramatic Poesy," are anti-Johnsonian. Dryden uses the word "imagination" even more frequently than Johnson, but he associates it with the reduced images that the playwright makes by holding a mirror up to nature. The theater is not the realm of factual truth, and therefore certainly not the realm of the truth of experience as it is for Johnson, but rather the realm of reflection, understood by analogy and exposed to judgments of rational plausibility and proportionality: "Fancy and Reason go hand in hand; the first cannot leave the last behind" (Dryden, *Essays* 1: 128).[17]

The soliloquies merit further consideration. In them we find most clearly reflected the nature of the dramatic spectacle. Pre-classical (Elizabethan and Jacobean) soliloquies preponderantly concern the speaker's environment. They can be introspective, but they can also be declarative, explanatory, projective, or judgmental; thus, they convey to the audience a perspective on the world of the play. (In the early Restoration, numerous examples of these types can be found in Etherege's first two plays, before he came under the influence of Molière.) Neoclassical soliloquies, as we shall see, are also representations "to the auditor" (to repeat Johnson's phrase), but of the speaker rather than of his world, in the spatial and temporal expanse shared by the imaginary characters and the spectator's imagination. Classical representation, by contrast, is a closed circuit, a mirror reflecting the speaker back to himself. The spectator, as if in another world, communes with himself and at best merely eavesdrops on a world outside the space and time of his experience.[18]

The defective mode of soliloquy, while not the most common, best reveals its function in classical dramaturgy. Soliloquies such as those in the nurse's eavesdropping scene in *Love for Love* and Margery Pinchwife's letter-writing scene in *The Country Wife* deform imperfect self-reflection into one-way communication. Far from confiding in the audience while other characters are offstage, the speakers in such scenes want to talk to themselves and fail even at that. Soliloquy here aims at being an exercise in domination; it is an assertion that wants not to be answered back. To speak is to stop the action and to control the scene,[19] and to have one's soliloquy interrupted is to lose one's balance, as happens to Margery Pinchwife.

More customarily, of course, soliloquy is a self-scrutiny. Leonidas's soliloquy at the end of act 3, scene 1, of Dryden's *Marriage a-la-Mode* shows explicitly the tenor of such soliloquies in the period: they do not affect to bare the character's insides and share his emotions with the world, but rather reestablish the closed circuit of an individual's communication with himself. Leonidas soliloquizes:

> 'Tis true, I am alone;
> So was the Godhead ere he made the world,
> And better serv'd Himself, than serv'd by Nature.
> And yet I have a Soul
> Above this humble fate. I could command,
> Love to do good; give largely to true merit;

All that a King should do: But though these are not
My province, I have Scene enough within
To exercise my vertue.

(*Works* 9: 272)

The situation here remains Cartesian. All experience is representation: the royal stage of action or the private stage of speculation. Leonidas's being is his thinking; his isolation merely displaces the locus of representation from the social world to the internal commonwealth.

Classical speech makes its own scene by commandeering presence. Again the import surfaces most instructively where the mode starts to break down, in Molière's later comedies. These scrutinize the moral frivolity implicit in the worldlessness of classical dramaturgy. The title character typically labors to maintain the empty order of a self-mirroring world, while the dramatist's aim is now to open the world to transcendent moral values within the traditional epistemology of cognitive reflection. Molière's art reached a crisis in the earliest play in this mode, *Tartuffe*. The scandal aroused by the play at court may be understood as a reaction to Molière's revival of the etymological link of the actor (*hypokrités*) and the hypocrite. The work equates acting and representation with lying, in a profound and profoundly troubling re-creation of the archaic forms of mimesis among the Greeks.[20] This play has no soliloquies, undoubtedly because Tartuffe can only exist as a public figure; his essence is to lie, and one cannot lie to oneself. But one might also say that the classical soliloquy is pure representation, and that soliloquy is impossible in a play whose essence is to call classical representation into question. Were Tartuffe himself to have a soliloquy, for instance, he would have to confide in or delude the audience; in either case the partition that creates the comic illusion would be broken and with it the play's *raison d'être*, which is to portray the questionable character of the comic illusion.

Subsequent works then experiment with the form. The famous long soliloquy of Harpagon at the end of act 4 of *L'Avare*, for instance, has in its alarmed, self-questioning, paratactic rhythms much in common with Figaro's great monologue of self-examination in *Le Mariage de Figaro*. Harpagon enters crying, "Stop thief!" and his gaze might seem necessarily to fall on the audience, breaking the illusion, when he exclaims on the empty stage, "How many people are assembled! I do not cast my glance on anyone who does not cause me suspicions, and all seem to be my robber. Eh! what is being talked about [*de quoi est-ce qu'on parle*] there? Of him who has robbed me?

What noise do I hear [*quel bruit fait-on*] above?" Who could *on* be if not the spectators? But Molière salvages the integrity of classical representation by showing Harpagon's questioning—so much like Figaro's penetrating rationalism at first glance—as the discourse of madness. Thus his speech ends, "I want to hang the entire world; and if I don't find my money, I shall hang myself after." And much earlier in the speech Harpagon has already muddied beyond remedy the question of whom he is speaking to by distractedly addressing none other than himself: "Stop. Give back my money, rogue. . . . [*He seizes his own arm.*] Ah! it is I. My mind is troubled, and I do not know where I am, who I am, and what it is I do" (*L'Avare* 4.7, in *Théâtre* 2: 302). He is thinking aloud, after all, not issuing an appeal. Molière shows the limits of classical form by testing yet refusing to transgress them.

The classical soliloquy is, properly, not an act of communication at all, but a *tirade* staking out a position that resonates through the theater. Congreve formulates the classical theory of the soliloquy in the Epistle Dedicatory to *The Double-Dealer*. He emphasizes the wall between the actor and the audience, who exist in different worlds. But in the hesitation of his account—first saying, then denying, that the character speaks to himself in soliloquy—he seems to be groping for a way to distinguish what happens on the stage from *any* world of experience, even a fictive one. The soliloquies are thus evidence for the thorough abstractness of classical representation:

> The Audience must observe, whether the Person upon the Stage
> takes any notice of them at all, or no. For if he supposes any one
> to be by, when he talks to himself, it is monstrous and ridiculous
> to the last degree. Nay, not only in this Case, but in any Part of a
> Play, if there is expressed any Knowledge of an Audience, it is
> insufferable. But otherwise, when a Man in Soliloquy reasons
> with himself, and *Pro*'s and *Con*'s, and weighs all his Designs: We
> ought not to imagine that this Man either talks to us, or to him-
> self; he is only thinking. (*Comedies* 115)

The members of the audience are "conceal'd Spectators of the Plot in Agitation"; the spectacle, that is, remains cut off from the world that it imitates.

The worst thing that can happen to a soliloquizer is to be heard, above all to be heard by those whom he cannot hear in his turn. This is what happens to Harpagon in the other soliloquy in *L'Avare*: "[*Here the brother and the sister appear in quiet conversation.*] O Heavens! I must have betrayed myself: my ardor must have carried me away, and I believe that I have spoken out loud while reasoning

by myself" (1.4, in *Théâtre* 2: 249).[21] What is true of soliloquies is
also true to a considerable extent of dialogues: the speeches are not
so much communicative acts as jockeyings for position. The final
tableau represents the closing, stable determination of position for
the characters; even the dance of cuckolds that concludes *The Country Wife* in an apotheosis of inconstancy is nothing like the uncertainties remaining at the end of *She Stoops to Conquer* or the taunting vaudeville that concludes *Le Mariage de Figaro*. In this light
it appears that the normal mode of speech toward which classical
drama strives is performative; the characters speak not so much to
be heard as to call a situation or an ordering of existence into being.

    If classical theater aims at stabilizing time and fixing conscious-
ness in the mirror of representation, Sheridan's world, by contrast, is
continuously unsettled by both elements. The remainder of this
chapter will be devoted to discussing this proposition. Sheridan's
world is marked by time in a way that is foreign to his models and
different from Goldsmith's world. The mark of time, as we have already seen, is upon his characters; their consciousness is preeminently a consciousness of this mark; and Sheridan's evasions and
obliquities are his attempt to deflect its fatality. From this perspective the deepest issue in *The School for Scandal* will appear to be the
process of marking itself, that is, the constitution of meaning, and
its ultimate concern a reconstituted meaning that frees character
from the constraints of a sense that appears senselessly imposed
from without.

The Marks of Time

We may begin by noticing Sheridan's soliloquies. Whether as recollections or as schemes, these are predominantly concerned with the
stream of time and with the urgent desire to change its direction.
They are by no means pauses for self-reflection like Goldsmith's
soliloquies, for there is no reserve of true character in Sheridan. On
the contrary, Sheridan's figures, when we see them unbuttoned, are
chronically anxious: "Suspense is at all times the devil—but of all
modes of suspence, the watching for a loitering mistress is the
worst—but let me accuse her no longer—she approaches with one
smile to o'erpay the anxietyes of a year" (*Trip to Scarborough* 5.1;
p. 610). In a moment like this—and there are many in Sheridan—
Hardcastle's art of reconciling contradictions is not even in prospect,
and we will see that the books on such a character are in fact never
balanced. The most introspective monologues are represented by

the one that fills the "dispiriting . . . interval of expectation" while Louisa waits for her lover Antonio to appear in *The Duenna* (2.4; p. 258). Oppressed by the pure weight of time, Sheridan's characters are given to aimless stalling.

Even the exception proves the rule. The soliloquy just mentioned gives way to an ode to time: "What bard, O Time, discover, / With wings first made thee move." Indeed, most of *The Duenna*'s exquisite songs function as solo performances that manifest the pulse of time. With rhythms less supple and more imperious than Dryden's—anapests for the comic passions, iambs for the serious ones, and feminine endings wherever a momentary triumph over the pounding heartbeat of time is in prospect—their texts protest against a power that their music makes irresistibly present.[22] *The Duenna* is, to be sure, the most radiant of Sheridan's works, troubled neither by money woes nor by swordplay, and for once its final chorus fulfills the wish for a truce with time:

> Thus crown'd with dance and song,
> The hours shall glide along,
> With a heart at ease, merry, merry glees
> Can never fail to please. (3.7; p. 283)

This operatic conclusion is, however, a unique wish-fulfillment in Sheridan, who can otherwise envision no escape from time, unless perhaps in one of his fits of drunkenness, and no end but in decrepitude and death.

For, indeed, time is passing even as the character strives to distance himself from his experience.[23] This is not always equally evident, but commonly enough to permit a generalization concerning the unstopping current of time. Often the soliloquy is actually a dialogue not with other speakers, but with events occurring as the soliloquy proceeds: "so! the door opens—yes, she's coming" (*Duenna* 2.2; p. 249), or "I hear a door open and some one coming" (*Trip to Scarborough* 4.3; p. 608). Sometimes the rhetoric approximates one of Richardson's letters in its attempt to seize the fleeting moment:

> Julia!—my soul—but for one moment:—I hear her sobbing!—
> 'Sdeath! what a brute am I to use her thus! Yet stay.—Aye—she is
> coming now:—how little resolution there is in woman!—how a
> few soft words can turn them!—No, faith!—she is *not* coming
> either.—Why, Julia—my love—say but that you forgive me—
> come but to tell me that—now this is being too resentful:—stay!
> she is coming too. . . . No—Z——nds! she's *not* coming!" (*Rivals*
> 3.2; p. 108)

A soliloquy like this frustrates our judgment just as the characters are frustrated. When a creature like Faulkland speaks the foregoing, who is to say where sentiment ends and spoof begins? In this changing world the true rivals are neither a man and his enemy, nor a man and his friend, nor even the separate masks of the dissembling wooer, but finally the impenetrably conflicting moods of his mind.

On account of his discomfort with time, almost everything in Sheridan is unseasonable. His own life was an unending mixture of "hurry and procrastination" (*Letters* 1: 210).[24] His characters, likewise, are hardly ever at one with themselves. The proliferation of disguises is remarkable even for the comedy of the period, and the lack of a unifying presence makes his characters often seem both remote from one another and comically lost to themselves: they have a way of soliloquizing absurdly even when in company. Mrs. Malaprop's wild eccentricities make her right on the mark in this offbeat world: "Well, Sir Anthony, since you desire it, we will not anticipate the past;—so mind, young people—our retrospection will now be all to the future" (*Rivals* 4.2; p. 124). And Dr. Rosy declaims pathetically on a similar subject to an increasingly unwilling listener:

> *Doctor.* Heaven send we succeed better at present—but there's no
>   knowing.
> *Lieut.* Very true.
> *Doctor.* We may, and we may not.
> *Lieut.* Right.
> *Doctor.* Time must shew.
> *Lieut.* Certainly.
> *Doctor.* We are but blind Guessers.
> *Lieut.* Nothing more.
> *Doctor.* Thick sighted mortals.
> *Lieut.* Remarkably.
> *Doctor.* Wand'ring in error.
> *Lieut.* Even so.
> *Doctor.* Futurity is dark.
> *Lieut.* As a Cellar.
> *Doctor.* Men are Moles—
>   [*Exeunt; the Doctor pondering.*]
>
> (*St. Patrick's Day* 2.3; pp. 183–84)

In another text the final stage direction reads, "Lieutenant forcing him out." In the paradigmatic conjuncture of the doctor's blind truth and the soldier's wilting vigor, Sheridan gives us a moving emblem of the debilities of consciousness and of time.

In Sheridan's belated world, time lurks as the impregnable antagonist. His plotting therefore differs equally from the seeming carelessness of Restoration comedy and from Goldsmith's perfect crafts-manship. In what seem like forecasts of the way Sheridan's own marriages soured, *The School for Scandal* ends with Charles's re-fusal to promise to reform and *St. Patrick's Day* with the prospect of lifelong quarreling for Justice Credulous and his wife.[25] Goldsmith's concluding dissonances are carefully positioned at the peripheries of his world—America in the poems, a relative's side table in the case of the French-horn-blowing Ned Thornhill, stage rear while Kate Hardcastle taunts Marlow—whereas Sheridan's remain front and center. And while Goldsmith treats time as a hostile power, it is for him something external to be overcome by imaginative withdrawal into the recesses of selfhood, whereas for Sheridan it courses through all of life, most immediately present and most irresistible at the very moments (soliloquy and conclusion) when the inner self comes to the fore.

We do not find, then, in Sheridan, the carefully integrated or-ganic structures that make Goldsmith's works into artifacts of jewel-like precision. *The School for Scandal* began as two independent sketches, known to posterity as "The Slanderers" and "The Teazles," and with all his tinkering Sheridan never achieved a perfect fusion of the gossip plot that dominates the first two acts and the last with the sentimental plots in acts 3 and 4. To be sure, *A Trip to Scar-borough* revises Vanbrugh's *The Relapse* in the direction of greater unity of plot and setting, as well as greater moral decorum. Yet even though he preserves Loveless's marital fidelity and ultimately lets him repent of his flirtation with Berinthia, Sheridan withholds the promised scene of confession and reconciliation that would make the action truly pause at the end.

More revealing yet is Sheridan's early sketch for a dramatic adap-tation of *The Vicar of Wakefield* (*Dramatic Works* 801–3). The text shows Sheridan's neoclassicism at work, both by plunging at once in medias res, with Thornhill confiding to Arnold his intention to se-duce Olivia, and also, even more, by the cast of characters, whose contrasting pairs heighten the symmetries already present in the novel.[26] And it shows Sheridan's neoclassic belatedness in its preoc-cupation with time. In three pages of printed text we learn more about the past history of Ned Thornhill's, Moses's, and Olivia's feel-ings than in the whole of Goldsmith's novel. Source, development, and projection become the very fabric of the characters' lives:

> It seems last year at some of the wat[e]ring places her ladyship['s] reputation began [to] suffer a little so that she thought it prudent to retire a little, till people learn'd better manners, or got worse memories she soon got acquainted with this little family and as

> the wife is a prodigious admirer of quality, became in a short time
> very intimate an[d] as she imagined she might one day make her
> market of the girls, has much ingratiated herself. (802)

A speech like this is so crowded with unfolding situations that the young dramatist's invention is soon exhausted. Yet flawed as such a beginning is, Sheridan adhered to this mode throughout his career, pruning its excesses but preserving its basic tendencies. Time is increasingly of the essence in his dramatic expositions from *The Duenna* on. He rejected outright the static exposition of what is—he ridiculed such a scene in *The Critic*, deleted an equally ridiculous one from his Kotzebue adaptation *Pizarro* (see *Dramatic Works* 643–45), and, in turning *The Relapse* into *A Trip to Scarborough*, omitted Vanbrugh's first scene, whose opening soliloquy expresses Loveless's contentment—while perfecting the animated exposition of what has been and may be, at a moment of crisis.

Fortune is always on the move in Sheridan. (This is, of course, also true of fortune in the economic sense; fortune hunting is a key motif in most of the comedies, and both in the plays and in his own life Sheridan was more concerned with the acquisition of money than, in Goldsmith's fashion, with its proper distribution.) Vanbrugh's Loveless opens *The Relapse* "content with fortune" (1.1.12; p. 9), in the scene Sheridan omitted, and his Fashion closes the next scene by calling fortune "a bitch" (1.2; p. 18); to the classical dramatist time is either wholly in our possession or altogether hostile. But Sheridan's Fashion calls her "a jilt" (*Trip to Scarborough* 1.1; p. 576); beholden unto us yet eluding our grasp, she occupies a border region of desire, of aroused and deluded expectations. In the half-cadences of Sheridan's comedies time is both true and unpredictable—true *because* unpredictable, one often feels, like Sheridan's humor. Justice Credulous's sudden conversion at the close of *St. Patrick's Day* is paradigmatic. All comes out well, though with mixed auguries for the future, by virtue of this unprepared acknowledgment of the truth:

> *Doctor.* You're right, Lieutenant.
> *Justice.* Is he?—why then I must be wrong.
>
> (*St. Patrick's Day* 2.4; p. 192)

Sheridan's dramaturgy rests on this unpredictable rightness of time that startles chaos into meaning. This does not mean that Sheridan's plays lack unity. But their unity is one of discovered theme or idea, rather than one of self-contained motif and plot structure. At the end, not a pattern but a meaning emerges, the truth of scandal that disrupts the complacent illusions of Enlightenment rationalism.

Sheridan shares with many in the romantic generation a faith in the equivalence of time and truth. But for him it remains an embattled faith. Time's truths unsettle him, and the affirmations that he fights through to in *The School for Scandal* are hard won and fragile. Like the romantics at a few critical junctures—Wordsworth fleeing the Revolution (*Prelude* 6.692–94) and Keats meditating on history in the nightingale ode—Sheridan assimilates telling to tolling: what time teaches tells against us. But precisely because it was problematic, time's language becomes the focus of more intense concern for him than was ordinarily to be the case in the next generation.

From his first beginnings Sheridan had been renowned above all for the brilliance of his language. This brilliance is never without a certain conscious obsessiveness. In *The Rivals*, Bob Acres originates "the *oath referential,* or *sentimental swearing*" (2.1; p. 96), and Mrs. Malaprop's *faux dits* are most often slips into grammar or the body of language—Lydia is "an object not altogether illegible" (1.2; p. 86); "Female punctuation forbids me to say more" (2.2; p. 101); "I laid my positive conjunctions on her" (3.3; p. 109); and so forth—rather than into sexuality like those of Sterne, scatology like those of Smollett's Win Jenkins, or merely random morphological confusion like those of Termagant in Arthur Murphy's *The Upholsterer* and Mrs. Tryfort in Frances Sheridan's *A Journey to Bath*, Sheridan's putative sources. While the central focus of *The Rivals*, as of *St. Patrick's Day* and *The Duenna*, is on identity, language was destined to be Sheridan's main concern. A consideration of the various strands of Sheridan's treatment of the movement of meaning in these plays and in *The Critic* will lead to a study of their interweaving in *The School for Scandal*. As we turn to consider the thematic unity of *The School for Scandal*, our guiding concern will be texts and the transformations by which time marks them.

> A clock.—Hark!—[*clock strikes.*] I open with a clock striking, to beget an aweful attention in the audience—it also marks the time, which is four o'clock in the morning, and saves a description of the rising sun, and a great deal about gilding the eastern hemisphere. (*Critic* 2.2; p. 521)

Thus begins Puff's ill-starred tragedy, *The Spanish Armada*, the butt of *The Critic*. Unlike the dialogue or, indeed, the opening tableau, with its two sentinels fortuitously snoozing, the initial stage effect escapes censure by Puff's auditors. And well it might, for it precisely duplicates the opening of *The Duenna*, which continued to be extremely popular: "Past three o'clock! soh! a notable hour for one of my regular disposition to be strolling like a brave thro' the streets of Seville!" (*Duenna* 1.1; p. 229). Thus does the infatuated Lopez begin his soliloquy, and an early autograph manuscript specifies the intended staging: "A Piaza before Don Jerome's House—The morning breaking—Clock strikes 3. Enter [Lopez]" (219). Puff's gong is, it would seem, his one competent piece of stagecraft, unforgotten even by the worst of bunglers, in a dramaturgy inescapably marked by time.

Under what conditions is life marked by time? Again the exception represented by *The Duenna* clarifies the issues. The mark that "saves a description" for Puff is a textual surrogate. *The Duenna* gives us both time and text, the latter supplementing the former when the servant yields center stage to his master. During Lopez's monologue Don Antonio enters with his companions to serenade his beloved, and he furnishes, at least in abbreviated form, a description of the dawn such as Puff had elided: "The breath of morn bids hence the night, / Unveil those beauteous eyes, my fair," he sings (1.1; p. 230). Louisa has not been counting the hours, but now she hears his "numbers"; she takes the poetry to be the very figure of dawn. In the utopian spirit of *The Duenna* Sheridan gives us the perfected equivalence of text and time:

> Waking I heard thy numbers chide,
>   Waking, the dawn did bless my sight,
> 'Tis Phoebus sure that woos, I cried,
>   Who speaks in song, who moves in light.
>   (ibid.)

Phoebus is, however, a poetic fancy, and Don Antonio's party are in masquerade in what is yet another of the period's farcical carnival texts. Time and text happily coexist only in the operatic context of an idealized or illusory timeless moment.

For in truth neither time's mark nor life's text can endure. The text that Puff's strike of four renders superfluous returns with ludicrously mock-heroic vengeance a short time after:

> Now has the whispering breath of gentle morn,
> Bad Nature's voice, and Nature's beauty rise;
> While orient Phoebus with unborrow'd hues,
> Cloaths the wak'd loveliness which all night slept
> In heav'nly drapery! Darkness is fled.
>   (*Critic* 2.2; p. 529)

And as time is constantly dissolving back into text, so conversely the true mark of a text lies in being tragically ruined or comically exploded by time. Texts are not susceptible of being fixed, for if the words don't change, the sense does. "Dearest," Sheridan thus writes to his second wife in a rare comment on his own work,

> I enclose you a Letter and a Newspaper professing to *publish* for the *first time some* verses of mine to Mrs. (now Lady) Crewe. They are inaccurately printed but on the whole I certainly wrote them but had *forgotten* . . . them. . . . I never yet own'd or allow'd the printing of anything Play Poems or Speeches but two things to both which I put my name—. . . . When I look at these ver[s]es Oh! how it reminds me what an ardent romantic Blockhead nature made me! . . . N.B. I was not then 25—by the way She was in truth the Handsomest of the set. . . . I have lost the Paper with the verses. I'll get it tomorrow. (*Letters* 3: 202–3)

Much was enduring, for better or worse, in Sheridan's life and character, but not words.

Scandal's Text

Sheridan's delight in names surfaces in the opening speeches of *The School for Scandal*, where we hear at once of Mr. Snake and Mrs. Clackit and of "Lady Brittle's Intrigue with Captain Boastall" (1.1; p. 359).[27] Later in the scene, when Mrs. Candour and Crabtree enter the room, a veritable onomastic cascade begins. In another dimension the onomastics run through the drafts, where we can pursue the spectacle of Sheridan's constant alteration of the characters' names, to a degree for which it would be difficult to find a parallel even in Dickens.[28] Virtually all are speaking names—many with literary precedents to boot—and the question immediately arises, which comes first, the designation or the meaning. Did the names, that is, follow Sheridan's conception of the characters, or did his conception of the characters follow the names? What is the status of signification in a world of Clackits, Sneers, and Backbites? Are the polished facades of the drawing room more than mere words?

These questions lead in two not unrelated directions, first toward facades and surfaces, and then toward drawing and pictures. With a central trio named Surface, the action apparently moves toward revealing what lies underneath. Since the outside is shallow or false, we are led to suppose that the inside is deep and true. But Sheridan teaches us otherwise. Unlike the characters in the earlier plays, those in *The School for Scandal* do not actually wear disguises; even the newly arrived Uncle Oliver wears his own clothes and face while he pretends to be Mr. Premium and Mr. Stanley. But they all conceal their real natures or at least work hard at doing so. The screen scene—arguably the most famous scene in English drama since Shakespeare—features a surface that hides an embarrassing truth. Hung with maps, the screen is covered and converted into a kind of shallow depth by signifiers that are imposed on it.[29] The screen's true purpose is not to provide knowledge but to prevent it, for Joseph uses it in front of his window to block off the inquisitive gaze of a neighbor lady. The screen, in short, signifies a static two-dimensional knowledge that refuses depth. Thomas Moore plausibly objects to this ruse, since "by placing Lady Teazle between the screen and the window, [Joseph] enables this inquisitive lady to indulge her curiosity at leisure" (*Memoirs* 1: 165). In the real world Moore's objection would apply, but in Sheridan's artificial world of screens and maps no depth can ever be penetrated, and we shall see that even when the screen falls no "truth" is revealed. Originally there were two screens hiding the two Teazles (*Dramatic Works* 292). Sheridan's alteration removes some of the implausibilities of the scene (were there to have been two windows and two neighbor ladies?), but it also strengthens the thematic network of the play, as do many of his changes, including the alteration of the name Pliant to Surface. In the final version Sir Peter hides in a closet while his wife is behind the screen: the one sham depth, where clothes are taken off and kept out of sight, becomes the equivalent of another, where a true body is hidden from one gaze and exposed to a second. There is nothing but falsehood in the depths.

The language of society is the ultimate sham. In scandal's school the stories seem never to be true. Quite the contrary, stories exist for the sake of embellishment, as in Crabtree's example of Miss Letitia Piper:

> "Miss Letitia Piper, a first cousin of mine, had a Nova-Scotia Sheep that produc'd her Twins." "What!" cries the old Dowager Lady Dundizzy (who you know is as deaf as a Post) "has Miss Piper had twins?" this Mistake as you may imagine threw the whole company into a fit of Laughing;—however, 'twas the next morning everywhere reported and in a few Days believ'd by the whole Town, that Miss Letitia Piper had actually been brought to Bed of a fine Boy and a Girl—and in less than a Week there were People who could name the Father, and the Farm House where the Babies were put out to Nurse. (1.1; pp. 368–69).

Such ostentatious tale-telling is a surface display that obliterates a retiring, sheepish truth. The scandal machine goes into operation again in the last act, after the Teazles emerge from hiding to confront one another in the screen scene. It decides that Sir Peter has been wounded in a duel, either by sword or by shot. It is only momentarily confounded when he appears in person; then it retorts by promising to spread malicious stories of "how hardly you [Sir Peter, in this case] have been treated" and "how Patiently you bear it" (5.2; p. 431). Scandal and truth stand in very much the same relationship as do language and the mark of time; reality constantly effaces language, and language just as perennially regenerates itself to mask reality.

The closer scandal comes to truth, the more dangerous it becomes. Just as no one could much believe in Puff's garish portrayal of dawn, so scandal has little force when it becomes too overt. Thus Mrs. Clackit, as Snake tells Lady Sneerwell at the beginning of the play, "generally designs well—has a free tongue and a bold invention—but her colouring is too dark and her outline often extravagant" (1.1; p. 360). But the risks are greater when language approaches a transparency that might at last dissolve sign into reference. Even poor Puff seems to have some glimmering of this blankly radiant ideal, for he lets his polychrome dawn—

> The strip'd carnation, and the guarded rose,
> The vulgar wall flow'r, and smart gillyflower,
> The polyanthus mean—the dapper daizy,
> Sweet William, and sweet marjorum,—and all
> The tribe of single and of double pinks—

dissolve into the sentimentalism of a "white handkerchief" that appeals to a "milk-white day" (*Critic* 2.2; pp. 529–30). In *The School for Scandal* it is Mrs. Candour whose whiteness most effectively blackens reputations, though she refrains from any tangible smear or sneer. Candor was a quality highly esteemed by Sheridan (in contrast, say, to Hume and Chesterfield).[30] We meet it constantly throughout his works, beginning with the Preface to *The Rivals*, with its repeated appeals to the "candour and judgment" or the "candour and liberal attention" of that "candid and judicious friend," the public; his political letters, likewise, assiduously profess unswerving fidelity and sincerity. Yet we may feel that he protests too much when he effusively thanks the first-night audience of *The Rivals* for disliking the play, and his political opponents regularly suspected him of double-dealing. Language reaches its most dangerous point with candor's blankness, when we can never feel secure whether reference has completely absorbed the sign or the sign has totally undone reference.

Thus we define the semiotic crisis in Sheridan. If Goldsmith's humor arises largely from the reversal of expectations that turns the world topsy-turvy, Sheridan's derives largely from the evaporation of meaning into meaninglessness. A sign is true when it points toward something else, outside it or within its depths. For Sheridan—if I may be forgiven so abstract a formulation, which will shortly be backed up by a quotation—the truth of a sign lies in its noncoincidence with itself. Truth in reference always appears as a breaking, a scandal, rather than as the frank honesty aimed at by Goldsmith: Sheridan's characters point in order to embarrass. As the distance decreases, so does the reference. In the whiteness or self-effacement of candor the sign moves closer to its referent, the speaking character approaches her object. But this only redoubles the scandal, for truth vanishes as it draws nigh, and we enter the world of the slanderers, where blame is praise (or at least jealous admiration) and praise is blame.[31] Sheridan says this most explicitly at the conclusion of one of his earliest productions, a spoof on a wretched poetaster entitled *Clio's Protest, or The Picture Varnish'd*:

> We pretty Sciolists in verse,
> For ever make each other worse;
> By turns this license take and give,
> —The Muses' known prerogative.—
> This once allow'd—'tween you and me,
> Great *Pindar*, there's no enmity.
> But if my satire seems uncouth,
> As back'd by that foul monster, *Truth*,
> And you (true Bard!) are therefore vex'd;
> —Be quit—and *praise* me in your next.
> (*Plays and Poems* 3: 118)

Here, as in the plays from *The Rivals* on, opposition is true friendship. To be sure, this motif is less pervasive in *The School for Scandal* than earlier, but it emerges in the scene where the enemy brothers Charles and Joseph join hands to evict their true friend Uncle Oliver. Correspondence is at odds with truth.

Whether in paintings or in utterances, time erodes resemblance. The "mimic pencil" is but "magic," not real.[32] To be sure, the hand of time invoked in Sheridan's monody on Garrick improves a painting. Yet in the context of a poem on the ruins of time and the disappearance of the actor's achievement, on the perpetuation of grief by funerary sculpture and the enhancement of sculpture by defacement (lines 35–38), Sheridan's praise of time's varnishing remains notably cautious.[33] And the poem called "A Portrait" that customarily prefaces *The School for Scandal* (the poem to Mrs. Crewe that Sheridan kept losing) displays even more elaborately the transiency both of verbal and visual signs. On the one hand the desperate poet tells us that "all words were faint" and could not "paint" "the Peril of her Lips" (lines 63–64). The truth of utterance lies in silence. On the other hand, thought falsifies meaning in stabilizing it, for it halts free movement and violates the charming unpredictability of genuine expression. The more we read Sheridan's shimmering description, the more puzzled we become as to where the true Mrs. Crewe lies:

> And Thou—who *seest* her speak—and dost not *hear*,
> Mourn not her distant Accents 'scape thine ear,
> *Viewing* those Lips—thou still may'st make pretence
> To judge of what she says—and swear 'tis Sense;
> Cloath'd with such Grace, with such Expression fraught,
> They move in meaning, and they pause in Thought!
> But do'st thou further watch, with charm'd Surprise,
> The mild Irresolution of her Eyes?
> Curious to mark—how frequent they repose
> In brief Eclipse, and momentary close?
>
> (lines 67–76)

"Grac'd by those signs—which Truth delights to own" (line 101), Mrs. Crewe is the perfected sign; in blazoning her, Sheridan reaffirms the mobility by which all true signs make their mark.

Much in Sheridan's dramaturgy confirms the lability of the sign. He suggests and withholds meanings at one and the same time, reducing signification to insinuation. He borrows characters, lines, and plot motifs at once to affiliate and to distance himself—reviving Congreve, say, but also cleaning him up or replacing him. And his allegorical names, those that allude and do not merely signify, are similarly duplicitous. Benjamin and Joseph, Moses and Snake let us glimpse a biblical drama: scandal as the modern manifestation of evil, in a world where virtue triumphs and the anointed younger child is elevated at last. And uncle and nephew adumbrate a drama of historical reconciliation wherein the once deadly enemies Charles and Oliver are reconciled and enter a glorious future under the empire of Love: "Tho'—thou, dear Maid; should'st wa[i]ve thy Beauty's Sway, / —Thou Still must Rule—because I will obey" (5.3; p. 441). How the play tantalizes us to read such significances in it! And yet how inchoate any such allegorization remains. A paradigm from the Latin Bible lies behind the themes of scandal and negation (see the epigraph at the head of this chapter—the King James Bible translates the Greek and Latin "scandalize" with "offend"). But however suggestive the thematic parallel, the wrong character is named Peter. "It doesn't follow that one is to be an absolute Joseph either," says Joseph at one point (4.3; p. 417), denying his own name. It would be a fantastic enterprise to allegorize *The School for Scandal.* Yet by his explicit hint of so scandalous a hermeneutical procedure, Sheridan reminds us what designs signs have on us.

From as early as *The Picture Varnish'd* Sheridan's comic strategy depended heavily on exploding signs or on covering them up. His first three plays all turn on faked or forged letters, and Snake opens *The School for Scandal* by describing his disguised submissions to the newspapers and closes it, for all intents and purposes, by admitting that he has forged letters between Charles and Lady Teazle. Charles's mercenary servant Careless is indifferent to texts—"Word, Note—or Bond 'tis all the same to me" (3.3; p. 400)—Lady Teazle's "Note of Hand" is no better than a joke (3.1; p. 392); the moneylender Moses, despite his name, will "never Meddle with Books" (3.3; p. 402); and only the hypocritical Joseph pretends any liking for them, "dozing over a stupid Book" as a sign of total idleness at the beginning of the screen scene (4.3; p. 413). (Joseph further condemns himself by admitting his preference of a fake moral surface, "sentimental French Plate," to a genuine depth, "the silver ore of pure Charity," 5.1; p. 426.) Even Crabtree gets into the picture, with his antiliterate fantasy that an imaginary duel has "wounded the Postman" (5.2; p. 429). Charles, of course, has already sold the family plate (a silvered surface), among which Oliver particularly regrets the signed objects, "all the Family Race cups and Corporation Bowls!" (3.3; p. 402), and he now sets to work on the pictures. He expresses his contempt for signs and becomes "an ex post facto Parricide" when he appropriates the family genealogy as the auctioneer's gavel (4.1; p. 405). Names invoke stubborn typologies and the dead hand of the past; Sheridan's attack verges (as his life did at moments) on a full-scale oedipal rebellion.

Yet the play's two great climaxes in act 4 are designed to reassert a certain depth and truth to signs. Charles redeems himself by exempting the picture of Uncle Oliver from the general rout of his possessions,[34] and Joseph condemns himself when the screen falls and Sir Peter and Lady Teazle emerge from the shadows to confront one another. To be sure, Charles overlooks the resemblance between the youthful portrait and his elderly uncle, and the unmasking of Joseph is nearly overwhelmed in turn by the slanderers' proliferating gossip.

Another act follows, time takes its course, and justice outbids deceit (without the agent's being specifically named) by purchasing Snake's confession in order decisively to repel the slanderers. Interpretation will need to take account of this extended denouement rather than merely regretting it, as criticism has tended to do ever since the early reviews. But first we need to reflect on act 4 and on the true signs that emerge there.

Act 4 seemingly replaces the deceptive and artificial signs of language with the genuine and natural signs of visual images. As soon as he is apprised of his nephews' situation, Oliver resolves "to make a trial of their Hearts" (2.3; p. 386). If the picture and screen scenes—together, perhaps, with Oliver's trial of Joseph's charity in act 5, scene 1—showed forth a hidden, stable essence of character, then the concluding scenes would become a mere cleanup operation. The unvarnished truth has appeared, and it remains only to remove the loose flecks of dirt and grease, personified by the slanderers. Before her husband enters the room, Lady Teazle claims to "know the integrity of my own Heart" (4.3; p. 411). Joseph speaks even more pompously of "the Heart that is conscious of its own integrity" (4.3; p. 414). And then Sir Peter in his turn begs Joseph to "set my Heart at rest" by testing the purity of Charles's motives (4.3; p. 417). If language could ever stabilize meaning for Sheridan, it would be here.

But the language of depth has become discredited through overuse. Hypocrisy having been detected at last, depth should now coincide with surface, feeling with action, sign with sense, in characters of rectified integrity. "Sir Peter," says Lady Teazle, "the Tenderness you express'd for me . . . *has penetrated to my Heart* and had I left the Place without the Shame of this discovery—my future Life should have *Spoke the sincerity of my Gratitude*" (4.3; p. 422, my emphasis).

Yet the replacement of verbal lie with visual truth is not so simple. There is no unvarnished correspondence of picture with reality, revealed in a flash and enduring for ever. Sheridan nowhere allows a distinction like C. S. Peirce's between icons and indices, or natural and artificial signs. In view of these invariable principles of Sheridan's semiotics, we should not be misled by the grand tableaux of act 4 of *The School for Scandal*. They are sentimental recognition scenes in the bad sense. Oliver's reconciliation with Charles exemplifies the good-natured, totalizing economics of sensibility: "Well—well—" as the uncle says, "I'll pay his Debts—and his Benevolences too" (4.2; p. 410). And the unmasking of Joseph becomes a sentimental apotheosis of inwardness, as Lady Teazle's invocation to sincerity gives way to Sir Peter's valedictory to Joseph: "and so I leave you to your Conscience" (4.3; p. 422). Yet despite the obvious sentimentality it makes sense both conceptually and theatrically to acknowledge a strong element of burlesque in these scenes. Even as they unroll, comedy has its revenge: while Oliver overflows with benevolence, the servant Trip continues negotiating an annuity offstage with Moses, and Sir Peter's closing sentiment cannot prevent Joseph from continuing his hypocrisies as he exits. The stage undermines scandal and sentiment alike, very much along the lines laid out by the Tenth-night Prologue to *The Rivals*:

> Is grey experience suited to her youth?
> Do solemn sentiments become that mouth?
> Bid her be grave, those lips should rebel prove
> To every theme that slanders mirth or love.
>   (lines 19–22)

In act 4 sentiment grows sententious and begins to sound a little too much like scandal; act 5 is needed to return us to a proper sense of life's irrationality.

Ultimately the term that matters to Sheridan is not integrity or sincerity but heart. "Odd's heart" becomes Oliver's oath (5.2; p. 430, and 5.3; p. 437); Lady Sneerwell distinguishes her heartfelt passion for Charles from Joseph's merely interested attachment to Maria (5.3; p. 434), and Maria resentfully concludes (on the basis of a forged letter) that Charles's heart is given to Lady Sneerwell in return (5.3; p. 438). The point about a heart is its impulsiveness and unpredictability. Self-knowledge becomes not a guarantee of sincerity or fidelity, but almost the reverse. If Joseph "knows himself," Sir Peter says, "He will consider it as the most perfect Punishment that He is known by the world" (5.3; p. 437). Snake does know himself, and he asks and receives permission to continue his career of deceit and dishonesty. And Charles likewise, in his self-knowledge, confirms the inconstancy of the true heart: "Why as to Reforming Sir Peter I'll make no Promises" (5.3; p. 441). The pretense of act 4 is that nothing changes: Charles and Oliver are linked by the same affection as ever; Joseph, if he ever was an absolute Joseph, is one still; and even servants can fix their income in annuities. In the denouement of act 5 time makes its mark. In truth nothing is constant. As we have heard much earlier, Mrs. Ochre cannot hold back her wrinkles, nor can Mrs. Evergreen successfully "repair the Ravages of Time" (2.2; p. 378). A fixed demeanor is a denial of life. Mrs. Candour remains the most egregious example, followed by Joseph in his endeavors to "put a little Charity into my Face" (5.1; p. 423). But Sir Peter's protest against fixity in the middle of the play is perhaps the most poignant expression of this theme: "Plagues and Tortures! can't I make her Angry neither! O I am the miserablest Fellow—But I'll not bear her presuming to keep her Temper—No she may break my Heart but she shan't keep her Temper" (3.1; p. 394). The heart manifests its spontaneity in its protests against the mask of civility; the signs of life are always untimely in a world that survives by change and flux. The eventual loving reconciliation of the old husband and his young wife becomes Sheridan's emblem for the power to create meanings through the vitality of a changing existence.

The Desiring-Machine

Comedy is frequently a conservative mode that promotes social cohesion. In particular, critics customarily contrast the reaffirmation of traditional moral values of marriage and family in Georgian comedy to the libertinism of plays like Wycherley's *Love in a Wood* or Vanbrugh's *The Provoked Wife*. Thus, at the end of Sheridan's play, the trio from the older generation (Oliver, Sir Peter, and the faithful servant Rowley) reestablish their authority over the youthful trio that remain (Charles, Maria, Lady Teazle). Charles's financial extravagance hardly seems to matter, though the undependable Mrs. Candour pretends that "The Town talks of nothing else" (1.1; p. 365); and the sexual gossip that actually dominates the slander scenes is altogether frivolous. Indeed, Sheridan mutes the seduction motif even below the level of other contemporary plays. Lady Teazle remains careful of her chastity, reminding Joseph in private that "I admit you as a Lover no further than Fashion requires" (2.2; p. 384). In other plays of the period fashion avers no such scruples—"people of fashion marry," says Miss Tittup at the beginning of Garrick's *Bon Ton; or, High Life Above Stairs*, "but I should think very meanly of myself, if after I was married, I should feel the least concern at all about my husband" (*Plays* 2: 257)—and Murphy's *The Way to Keep Him* actually shows us two aggressive philanderers making advances to women, one aided by the woman's husband, the other while being spied on by his own wife. It proves to be all talk, in conformity to the decorum of the age. But in Sheridan not even the talk risks so much.

Yet around the borders of a comedy like *The School for Scandal* lie the potentially more explosive modes of farce, masquerade, burlesque, and satire. The irrepressible energies of Sheridan's play outrun its moral commitments.[35] The screen scene in act 4 is notable for its rapid-fire series of entrances and discoveries. The scene in Joseph's library that concludes act 5 (books again, with their problematic connotations) brings an even more rapid series of exits, first when Oliver is almost pushed offstage, and then when the villains, Lady Sneerwell, Joseph, and Snake, leave in quick succession. Only six characters remain onstage at the curtain, out of a speaking cast of twenty (fifteen named characters, two unnamed servants, one maid, and two gentlemen).[36] Time's dispersive movement is only partially counteracted by the pulling together of this virtuous band: the Teazles "intend" to be happy (but will they be?); Maria looks happy but withholds even "a word" of consent to her engagement; and Charles, in addition to promising nothing, presents himself as a spectacle of abasement, "an humbled Fugitive from Folly" (5.3; p. 441). The last stage direction reads, "Charles and Maria apart"; George Colman's Epilogue for Lady Teazle exudes a spirit of enervated valedictory; and indeed the last line of Sheridan's own text speaks of death: "For even Scandal dies if you approve." It seems to me mistaken to play the final ensemble in too triumphal a tone.[37]

But where, indeed, does Scandal live in *The School for Scandal*? The essential principle confirmed by the ending is the nonconformity of sign and significance. We learn at the end that slander (*médisance*, as the French say) will continue unabated, that lying can be a way of life, and that solemn protestations are meaningless. Charles does not renounce virtue, but rather the appearance or pretense of virtue, and Snake does not resent having done a good deed, but only having been seen doing it. It is hardly an exaggeration to say that the true scandal of the play comes with Sheridan's remarkable threefold dismissal of moral pieties at the end—the rejection of social integration as the unreconstructed slanderers leave the stage, Snake's rejection of rectitude, and Charles's rejection of the conventions of sincerity. It is not the slanderers, Lady Sneerwell and her accomplices, who are the school for scandal but the play itself, as Sheridan uncovers and schools us in and for a scandal deeper than the idle dissipations of undesirables.[38] That scandal, rooted in the nature of language, comes, as I hope to show, from the depths of the unconscious.

Comparison with some of Sheridan's sources illuminates his concerns. Before settling on the name Surface, Sheridan had earlier called his central characters Pliant and Plausible. The former name is also found in Congreve's *Double-Dealer*, whose villain is a sanctimonious wooer like Joseph Surface; the latter name is also found in Wycherley's *Plain Dealer*, which features a scandalous college not unlike Sheridan's.[39] *Médisance* in Wycherley, however, is raillery rather than slander: it is as often general (directed against the world or the court) as particular, and it is a prime example of the performative nature of discourse on the classical stage. In the artificiality of Restoration comedy, raillery is referential only in appearance; its real purpose is entirely tactical and self-interested. As Wycherley's Plausible says in the first scene: "I, like an Author in a Dedication, never speak well of a man for his sake, but my own. . . . But if I did say or do an ill thing to anybody, it shou'd be sure to be behind their backs, out of pure good manners" (*Plain Dealer* 1.1, in *Plays* 378–79). The worldly characters agree that such talk is the way of the world and that no one believes either raillery or flattery. Language only works if it contradicts experience: "telling truth is a quality as prejudicial, to a man that would thrive in the World, as square Play to a Cheat, or true Love to a Whore" (Freeman in 1.1; pp. 385–86). No one overlooks the strictly negative character of all such discourse, though it falls to the plain dealer, Manly, to state its nature most plainly: "O, Friend, never trust, for that matter, a Womans railing; for she is no less a dissembler in her hatred than her love: And as her fondness of her Husband is a sign he's a Cuckold, her railing at another Man is a sign she lies with him" (5.2; p. 495).[40] The sole law of signs is unreality; not even the law itself can escape, as we hear the Widow Blackacre and her lawyer jabber in their phantasmagorial law-French about Pere, Mere, and Fitz.

If consciousness in classical drama takes the form of a timeless, rational picture, Wycherley's last play is a proleptic coming to self-awareness of the classical discourse of consciousness. Language here knows itself to be pure negation and abolishes itself in the process. (Early in act 2 Eliza already says, "methinks we ought to leave off dissembling, since 'tis grown of no use to us; for all wise observers understand us now adayes, as they do Dreams, Almanacks, and *Dutch Gazets*, by the contrary," 2.1; p. 401.) At the end the plain dealer is vindicated; when his young sailor-boy proves to be the loving Fidelia, he is promoted from paternal ship's captain to husband, becoming now "Manly" indeed. The war of negations between law and desire—that is, between superego and id—yields to a language of sentimental exchange. One could further examine the connotations of the cabinet given to Fidelia, the orphan girl from the north, and of the jewels proffered to Olivia and struck down by her, but enough has already been said to show how *The Plain Dealer* is a fable of the oedipalization of discourse. As such it represents a precocious limit of classical representation; it is no wonder that Wycherley wrote no more plays and that the belated Sheridan at last came to reflect on what the earlier author had wrought.

Onto this conflict between language and truth that is drawn from Wycherley and Congreve and that is central to "The Slanderers" (the scandal plot of the completed *School for Scandal*), Sheridan grafted the conflict between the sexes and the generations that is central to "The Teazles" and the love intrigue in the completed play. Sheridan approaches this second conflict in the spirit of Georgian comedy rather than that of the Restoration; satisfaction, for instance, is much more a motive force than is power. The relationship between these two conflicts is, on the face of it, far from obvious. Slander is a problem of language, while scandal is one of sexuality. Why should the slanderers have essentially nothing but sex on their minds? Why should Sheridan's love plots hinge so regularly on false letters and signs and his old maid (Mrs. Malaprop) be so obsessed with language? Why should Sheridan have unified his play by compounding and crossing its themes in this way, rather than through the simplification and regularization of plot for which Goldsmith offers a model?

Slander is the negation of love. The relationship between the two plots, in other words, echoes the negative relationship between sign and significance developed in Sheridan's Restoration sources. Desire is crossed by law, and both appear in illicit forms: forbidden or foolish desire versus censorious prudery. The slapstick of the Restoration—as, indeed, that of Goldsmith and Sheridan's other contemporaries—is essentially a realization of juvenile instincts and fantasies: Tony Lumpkin's coming-of-age. But in the last act of *The School for Scandal* the instincts mature into drives that find an outlet beyond the repressive sublimations of social comedy.

My occasional adoption of Freudian terminology, here and elsewhere in this book, should not be misconstrued. I do not mean in any way to suggest that it is true or that it in some fashion validates the literary text to which it is applied. If anything, I would like to hold the reverse: literary works whose value is not in doubt authenticate and often enrich the analytical languages (psychological, philosophical, economic, or whatever) that can successfully be applied to them. In this case, however, and typically, my justification is more historical and less grandly metaphysical. It has become commonplace to recognize that Freud's intellectual foundation and culture were thoroughly romantic. But as the heir to the eighteenth century in all the ways I have been discussing, romanticism absorbed into its synthesis the problematic strains of the culture that preceded it.

Through a romantic filter the Enlightenment will thus tend to appear as an underdeveloped, immature, or even infantile romanticism. Wordsworth makes no bones about such a view, nor have traditional, undialectical accounts of "preromanticism." A more dialectical approach will recognize the essential difference of precursor stages and will also be aware that the romantic filter is increasingly partial as the historical distance increases: romantic (or Freudian) readings of, say, *Hamlet* visibly reshape the play. But insofar as Freud is still a romantic theorist of culture, it is plausible to expect his analysis to reflect important strains of Enlightenment culture in the guise of an immature stage of development.

Freud's essay on negation links the problems of language and desire both conceptually and genetically. Negation, according to Freud, originates as a censorious superego that allows unconscious desires to surface by blithely denying them. It gaily says, "Now you will think that I mean something insulting, but I really have no such intention" (*Gesammelte Werke* 14: 11). This primitive negation is, unmistakably, what Sheridan calls Candour. As it develops beyond hypocritical candor, however, Freud's negation plays a pivotal role in the emergence of the superego and of mature sexuality. For negation is the first manifestation of the death instinct (or, as Freud here calls it, the destructive drive) in its conflict with the libido. Its development leads from pure condemnation (*Verurteilung*), which "is the intellectual surrogate for repression" (12), to judgment (*Urteil*). Time is an element here, since condemnation postpones thought, whereas judgment, which directs perception and thought, "is the intellectual action . . . that puts an end to the postponement of thought and makes the transition from thought to action" (14). In permitting both delay and the choice that puts an end to delay, "the creation of the negation symbol has permitted to thought a first degree of independence from the consequences of repression and thus also from bondage to the pleasure principle" (15). Slander, in the form of a malicious candor, ultimately leads to controlling the pleasure principle, instituting morality and foreclosing scandal.

Lest these terms seem an unwieldy way to unravel a play as ethereal as Sheridan's, I want to look at Sheridan's other group of sources, the sexual farces of the decades preceding *The School for Scandal*. For in these cruder plays the psychosexual content is far more overt. It would be unthinkable, for instance, to overlook the anxiety about masculine potency evident in the frequent brandishing of swords, particularly since the participants, like the daring young men in a modern beer commercial, practically never actually indulge.[41] In Murphy's *The Old Maid* (1761), a play to which I shall return, there is a delightful sequence in which Clerimont, Captain Cape, and Harlow argue heatedly about Miss Harlow. In lightning succession Cape draws on Clerimont then puts up, Harlow on Clerimont, Clerimont on Cape, and Clerimont on Harlow; finally the rich uncle, Heartwell, arrives to put a stop to the charade. In Garrick's *Bon Ton; or, High Life Above Stairs* (1775), there is a gratuitous sequence where Sir John Trotley, the moral rich uncle from the country, complains of London pickpockets. This rather feeble gentleman has been robbed of "my hanger from my side" and in return receives the loan of a "sword" (2.1, in *Plays* 2: 273). Evidently his hanger did not make enough of a prick. Garrick approaches outright obscenity when the heroine of *The Irish Widow* (1772), posing as her military brother, "loosens her knee-bands" before drawing, "for the advantage of lunging" (act 2, in *Plays* 2: 178). Even here, however, the transvestism, coupled with the rivalry for the widow's hand between the fainthearted but tightfisted Whittle and his vigorous nephew, assures a resonance that transcends mere buffoonery.

Still, sex never rises above the level of badinage in these plays. The badinage is often coarser than Sheridan's, to be sure, but the strictly sexual element remains symbolic (latent or repressed). The unmistakable reality is a conflict of roles, of generations, and of drives. In *The Old Maid* Clerimont, like a fairy-tale prince, falls in love with Mrs. Harlow when he glimpses her at a ball. Thinking she is unmarried, he sues for the hand of "Miss Harlow." The real Miss Harlow, the repulsive old maid of the title, jilts her fiancé, the respectable and mature Captain Cape, while all the other characters remain stupefied at Clerimont's ardent pursuit of such a hag. At the end Clerimont discovers his error. Both suitors stalk off the stage followed by the old maid. As in *The School for Scandal* there remains a reduced band of now more settled characters, the Harlow couple and Clerimont's good-natured country uncle, Heartwell, who provide a moralizing close. At the beginning the old maid haunts the household as an Ate, or figure of discord, but by the end, when she banishes herself "from the world for ever" (Murphy, *"Way" and Other Plays* 280), her role has been simplified into that of a life-denying force. Pluto is evicted from the realm of Venus:

> In vain the *faded toast* her mirror tries,
> And counts the cruel murders of her eyes;
> For ridicule, sly-peeping o'er her head,
> Will paint the roses and the lillies dead;

And while, fond soul! she weaves her myrtle chain,
She proves a subject of the comic strain.

(281)

Thus the play is predicated on a confusion of eros and thanatos, not without relation to that of the Harlows' Richardsonian forebear. The abusive condemnations of the opening mature into judgment at the end. Yet knowledge and judgment arrive at a cost: both suitors are driven offstage, and their future success—even their future allegiance—remains undetermined.

Hardly a comedy of this era comes without its controlling father or rich uncle, and the old maid plays a role in most as well. These figures appear in many shades—selfish or benevolent, stingy or generous, frigid or lusty. But whether they renounce their desires or demand renunciation from others, whether they withhold affections and subventions or learn to restrain misplaced affections, whether they act gently or harshly, they are all figures of negation; and should fulfillment come, it would take the form (as in Sheridan's *Duenna*) of one dried prune yoked to another.

Murphy provides a paradigm for a sterile, "pre-Freudian" negation in his schematic and almost plotless two-acter, *Three Weeks After Marriage* (1764, revised 1776). Here the father, Drugget, has a passion for formal gardening. He perverts natural forces into their antithesis: his garden "is all art; no wild nature here" (*"Way" and Other Plays* 298). He cuts his topiary into a grotesque and morbid assemblage of shapes, "a fine Dutch figure, with a scythe in his hand, and a pipe in his mouth" (197); the giants Gog and Magog ("the shape of two devils," as a servant says, 298); "a fine tree of knowledge, with Adam and Eve in juniper; Eve's nose not quite grown, but it's thought in the spring will be very forward [not even Drugget's shears can excise the lusty innuendos of spring!] . . . , with the serpent in ground ivy" (301–2). The motto on his sundial is "*Tempus edax & index rerum*" (296); the same figure, so to speak, mows and shows. This garden of death, lest its significance be overlooked, abuts the London road, where it is choked by the dust of commerce and greed. Drugget's elder daughter has married a nobleman with whom, after three weeks of marriage, she squabbles constantly. His younger daughter is courted by two suitors. One, Lovelace, as confused in his drives as *his* Richardsonian forebear,[42] is after money, and he thinks that the way to the daughter's dowry is through her parents: he would make love by courting death. Unfortunately, in accord with the deadly spirit of negation, nothing that pleases

Drugget pleases his wife. Faux pas are inevitable, and when Drugget sees Lovelace unmasked and his elder daughter bickering with her lord, he is induced to resign the younger one to her loving and natural suitor, Woodley. Drugget's valedictory, however, forebodes misery to all: "Though, mercy on all married folks, say I!—For these wranglings are, I am afraid, what they must all come to" (329). *Edax & index*: things are exhibited when they are cut off. Except in some fairy-tale "millennium" such as the Epilogue evokes (330), this play presents marriage as a razor-sharp divide between nature, whose element is desire, and consummation or consumption, whose element is death.

The motto *edax & index* suggests the contiguity of the satiric and the semiotic functions, or of condemnation and judgment. The final element in this picture of farce before Sheridan is *tempus*. Despite Drugget's sundial, time is inorganic to Murphy's farce: not only do the effects of marriage appear in an extremely brief time (reduced in revision to three weeks from an original six), but the outcome is determined early in the second act, so that dramatic development is short-circuited. A better play, *The Clandestine Marriage* (1766), by Garrick and Colman, takes place four months after a happy secret wedding between Lovewell and Fanny Sterling. The authors compound the jilting motif of *The Old Maid* with a suggestion of incest when Lovewell's friend Sir John Melvil bribes Mr. Sterling to release him from his engagement to the shrewish elder Miss Sterling in favor of her younger sister, Fanny. The wealthy aunt, Mrs. Heidelberg, whose only interest is in getting Miss Sterling a noble husband, and Melvil's lascivious uncle, Lord Ogleby, contribute to the pattern of negations in an elaborate conflict between the forces of love and those of death. Meanwhile Melvil (whose name, though not his overt actions, suggest Congreve's double-dealer) plays an ambiguous role between the friend he unwittingly betrays and the sisters whose rivalry he greatly exacerbates. But here time comes into play, both in the form of the delay in announcing the secret marriage and in that of the impending crisis moment toward which the play's rapid action skillfully builds. As a result there is a more successful resolution of the play's oedipal crisis, and slander (such as Mrs. Heidelberg's outburst, "Would you connive at your daughter's being locked up with her sister's husband? [*Cries out.*] Help! thieves! thieves, I say!" 5.2, in Garrick's *Plays* 1: 325) fails to develop into scandal. The cost, however, is a series of emasculations—Lord Ogleby and Sir John Melvil renounce their wooing and Sterling and the formidable Mrs. Heidelberg their social ambitions—while the elder sister seems faced with spinsterhood. Love can succeed when it masters time, but it still must take its revenge on a host of witting and unwitting enemies.

Georgian comedy represses overt sexuality in favor of bawdy innuendo combined with sentimental moralism. But it appears that this repression is its way of absorbing and working out issues of Restoration comedy. The Restoration problems of language and of sexuality both appear in suspended or sublimated form (the allusion of a name or the exaggerated antisexuality of a spinster); language and sex thereby acquire a considerable homogeneity as part of the generalized problem of negation. *The School for Scandal* fulfills this development, bringing the hidden semiotic issue back into the foreground. With time at last taking its rightful place as the medium of resolution, far more fully even than in *The Clandestine Marriage,* the problems for once achieve an orderly clarification in a plot that marches forward toward a convincingly motivated conclusion. No longer does the final reintegration depend on the unprepared changes of heart that make possible the concluding felicities of so many Georgian comedies, including Sheridan's earlier plays. But the resolution is not without its own cost. Sheridan's neuroses and the fact that, despite many projects, he never again wrote a full-length comedy, are two of its symptoms: Sheridan's masterpiece unleashed energies beyond his control.

Sheridan's response to his Restoration and Georgian background may be sketched out in the following way: the relationship of scandal to slander takes the form of a temporalized negation that ultimately generates judgment by regularizing and redistributing the conflicts of drives, of sexes, and of generations. Negation becomes a medium of knowledge by converting desire into an indicator: signs acquire depth and become shareable. A problem of instincts is sublimated into a psychic capacity.

The School for Scandal begins with slander. Naively, slander appears to have a denotative relationship to scandal: slander is the signifier that names scandal as its signified. Of course we know implicitly that slander is not a disinterested intellectual activity, and Sheridan carefully reminds us of the fact. One circulates scandalous rumors in order to accomplish personal ends. Sheridan's characters are virtuosos of gossip, and truth is irrelevant to their purpose: "Wounded myself," says Lady Sneerwell, "in the early Part of my Life by the envenom'd Tongue of Slander I confess I have since known no Pleasure equal to the reducing others, to the Level of my own injured Reputation" (1.1; p. 360). Motivated by past trauma and aimed at future injury, slander has no relationship to the present. It doesn't even matter if the slander is factually accurate, for its real focus is character though its reference is behavior and external action. "Peace, Sir!" says Amanda in *A Trip to Scarborough*, "I will not even listen to such slander—this is a poor device to work on my resentment, to listen to your insidious addresses. No, Sir; though Mr. Loveless may be capable of error, I am convinced I cannot be deceived so grossly in him, as to believe what you now report" (5.1; p. 612). Slander is thus a prime example of performative language. A slander is uttered in the hope that it may become a scandalous truth (like Miss Piper's twins, or Sir Peter's duel), or at least that it may promote scandalous behavior.

When slander grows into scandal, however, it vanishes. It may be that the mendacious slander is less awful than the scandalous truth, as when the little French milliner behind the screen evaporates in favor of Lady Teazle. But even if the slander proves strictly accurate, it still vanishes, for then it is no longer slander, but truth. Slander is nonreferential language, uttered in the hope of affecting the future and with no relationship to present circumstances. It is neither true nor false, but a language of pure negation, existing to be believed and disbelieved at once: "Face your enemies: nay, you shall outface them too. Why, what's the difference between truths and untruths, if you do but stick close to the point? Falsehood would scarce ever be detected, if we had confidence to support it" (*The Jealous Wife* 5.1, in Colman, *Plays* 99).

There is, as we have seen, little confident affirmation in Sheridan's dramaturgy. But time plays a positive role, nevertheless, in changing the nature of negation. In Freud's essay negation begins as a symptom of the conflict between eros and thanatos and ends as the sign through which thanatos expresses itself, in sublimated form. The development in Sheridan's play is related, though not identical. Beginning as an empty form, the disembodied chatter of slander that occupies so much of act 1, time becomes the embodiment of negation in action. At the beginning a denial of time—or, more accurately, of the present—negation becomes by the end the form of time: "Why as to Reforming[,] Sir Peter[,] I'll make no Promises— and that I take to be a proof that I intend to set about it" (5.3; p. 441). Noncommitment in the present is here taken as an indicator of commitment to a future that is not like the present. If signs in general are predicated on the nonidentity of signifier and signified, in the valid sign negation takes the pragmatists' temporalized form of a possible future correspondence. Signs at the beginning of the play lie on the surface. Slander "plants a Thorn in another's Breast"; "the malice of a good thing is the Barb that makes it stick" (1.1; p. 364). By the end these pinpricks have become swords and bullets that penetrate to the quick. After the screen collapses in Joseph's library, the anonymous letter acquires a signatory, Snake, whose future career is thus put in jeopardy. The picture of Oliver acquires a subject, though one grown unrecognizable with age. The chatter in act 1 is entertaining but desultory—entertaining, perhaps, precisely because nothing is at stake. That in act 5 is swift and excited. Even slander is caught up in real life as Sheridan's play discovers a temporal depth and an energetics of the sign.

Eros, as Freud describes it, is a state of psychic excitement; thanatos one of psychic equilibrium. Between them there develops a rhythm of animation and relaxation, the acquisition and release of energy. As he describes negation, it progresses from a state of conflict between the drives to one of order in their disposition. Negation, that is, becomes a mechanism regulating the economics of the soul. In a schematic form this development is the subject of the comedies written between 1768 and 1776 by Hugh Kelly. Particularly relevant to Sheridan is the first and best of these, *False Delicacy*, the play in whose favor Garrick rejected Goldsmith's *Good-Natur'd Man*. Brilliantly conceived, though rather stiffly written, the play is a set of variations on a single theme. "Delicacy" refers to the negative functioning of language: the delicate person refrains from uttering desires, lest others feel obliged to satisfy them, and delicately interprets the utterances and silences of others accordingly, by contrasts. Some ridiculous situations ensue where young people resist their inclinations and ally themselves, or nearly do, with partners for whom they have no affection. Delicacy is thus an overrefined moral sense that comes into conflict with desire. In general it internalizes inherited, partly unspoken social codes, but in particular it reveres the Fifth Commandment and the dead hand of paternal injunction.[43] In the end common sense triumphs. Either good fortune or friendly contrivance leads the negations to cancel one another out, and love is rewarded within a general framework of triumphant moral piety. The multiple plots inevitably bring to mind the economic aspect of psychic health, since one age-old issue is that of properly distributing the women among the eligible men.[44] Kelly's comedies—and many by his contemporaries—are fables of the establishment of psychic health in a world that hardly distinguishes society from family or from the commonwealth of the individual mind. As such they are troubled above all by the uncertainty whether the denouements are to be considered natural and descriptive or miraculous and utopian.

The School for Scandal disperses and generalizes the rivalries found in the more mechanical comedies of Sheridan's day. The sibling rivalry between the Surface brothers remains, with the older sibling punished by ostracism as in The Old Maid,[45] but there is no consistent opposition between the sexes or the generations. Nor is thanatos an expressed concern, as it was to be, for Sheridan, only in the mediocre tragedy Pizarro. We know—from Pope, for instance— that in a scandalous college "At ev'ry word a Reputation dies" (Rape of the Lock 3.16), but Sheridan alludes to this topic only by inversion, when he kills off scandal in the last line of the envoy, "For even Scandal dies if you approve."[46] Sheridan's negative pole is not the repressive paternal moralism of the death or destruction drive.

To the energy of desire Sheridan opposes something less readily sublimated than thanatos and therefore more insidious. The young Charles is full of life; in the drinking scene (3.3), he extols champagne over the spiritless and flavorless Spa water of his degenerate age. And old Oliver calls himself "as hale and healthy as any Man of his years in Christendom" (3.3; p. 401). But the slanderers who chatter and bicker so much, and chiefly about sex, seem enfeebled in action. Mrs. Candour surely refers to her own kind when she describes "a sort of puny sickly Reputation that is always ailing yet will outlive the robuster Characters of a hundred Prudes" (1.1; p. 368), and it would be hard to forget the image of Joseph Surface, the eternal utterer of languid sentiments, pretending to "doz[e] over a stupid Book" in the screen scene (4.3; p. 413). Yet the scandalous college never dies; it continues its activities, offstage, to the end of the play and presumably to the end of time. It is not inert, but rather a continuing wasteful dispersal of energy. To quote Charles's very words in the drinking scene, "their conversation is become just like the Spa water they drink which has all the Pertness and flatulence of Champaine without its Spirit or Flavour" (3.3; p. 397). (As will be remembered we have already met with flatulence as the farcical outlet for constipated sensibility; see above, p. 84.)

In Sheridan, that is, negation appears in the form of entropy. Slander's almost random naming of names aims at bringing all of society down to its level and into its orbit: Lady Sneerwell, for instance, joined the scandalous college because she had once been its victim, and thus the miasma spreads. And Joseph's inexhaustible sentiments are equally random. In his mealy mouth the praise of slander can follow as blandly and immediately on the blame of

slander as "Oh, Certainly I do!" follows on "Indeed I do not."[47] Sentiment is a form of utterance with indifferent or interchangeable content. Hence, Sheridan effectively truncates many of Joseph's sentiments, leaving them as nominations without predication or point.
Even faithful old Rowley catches the bug at one point: "Nay, Sir
Peter—He who once lays aside suspicion—" (5.2; p. 433). And so
long as Lady Teazle remains infected, the Teazles illustrate yet another variety of the entropic cycle, finding their satisfaction in being
dissatisfied:

> *Sir Peter.* Very—well, Madam—very well—a separate mainte-
> nance—as soon as you Please. . . . Let us separate Madam.
> *Lady Teazle.* Agreed—agreed—and now—my Dear Sir Peter we
> are of a Mind once more we may be the happiest Couple—
> and never differ again, you know; ha! ha!
>
> (3.1; p. 394)[48]

Thanatos is a parental injunction that is eventually subverted
by the mute glances and actions of eros. Entropy also speaks, but
it lacks the effectiveness of the commands of thanatos. Thanatos
speaks in negative imperatives. Entropy, as we have seen, utters performatives, or, more precisely, what it hopes to make performatives.
But, as we have also seen, its speech is predicated on the inescapable
noncorrespondence of sign and significance in the present. We can be
reminded of this by the soliloquy of Sir Peter's that concludes the
quarrel scene: "Plagues and Tortures! can't I make her Angry neither! O I am the miserablest Fellow—But I'll not bear her presuming
to keep her Temper—No she may break my Heart but she shan't
keep her Temper" (3.1; p. 394). She could look calm if he knew that
she was really angry, but so long as she looks unhappy she may be
successfully working her hostile aims. Nothing will satisfy the point-
lessly disordered husband.

Eros counteracts parental oppression by arousing an energy so
firmly bound to its object that it cannot be rooted out. Entropy, however, does not seek to destroy energy, but to enfeeble it through generalization: the pansexual badinage of scandal flirts with everyone
and consummates affairs with no one. Restoration libertinism must
therefore always recognize the antithetical power of genuine passion, whereas the fashionable dalliance of Georgian comedy threatens to reduce all passion to its own level: "—to Day Mrs. Clackit
assur'd me Mr. and Mrs. Honeymoon—were at last become mere
man and wife like the rest of their acquaintances" (1.1; p. 365).[49] One
can flirt even with one's spouse. It is a mistake, therefore, to under-

stand Sheridan's conclusion as a triumph of love. Charles and Maria have not yet married. Their wedding, like the Teazles' conjugal happiness, remains a future hope, while the text emphasizes character and its resolves. Charles acknowledges himself in Rowley's debt, but the loyal servant accepts future merit in lieu of present payment: "deserve to be happy—and you overpay me" (5.3; p. 441). So long as a debt has not been retired, the currency remains in circulation; so long as satisfaction lies in the future, the energies to procure it remain free and available. Love that is bound to a present object may prove no more constant than gallantry; this is the risk portrayed by the fickle heroes of Cumberland's *West Indian* and Murphy's *Know Your Own Mind*. The true counterforce to entropy, by contrast, is the free energy, directed outward and to the future, that is known as desire.

A realized present, a satisfied love, an embodied meaning is debilitating, not animating. This is the scandal into which Sheridan's play schools us. In semiotic terms this means that although words command meanings (an English speaker cannot help thinking of a horse upon seeing the letters h-o-r-s-e or hearing the sounds /hors/), complete utterances fall short, leaving a residue of dissatisfied desire. Proper names, in this respect, are more like utterances than like words. They too are a kind of free or shifting signifier: a Joseph need not be a "Joseph." In his play with names and with hints of allegory Sheridan creates a craving for interpretation that is the foundation of meaning. We must want signs to have an inside and we must work at penetrating them, or else they will remain mere surfaces. The slanderers understand one another too well because their talk is insignificant; a true sign signals the desire for the generation of meaning.

Both the psychological and the semiotic terms for this are given in a letter written by Sheridan to his close friend Thomas Greenville in September 1772 (*Letters* 1: 43–47). Sheridan was a notably moody correspondent, and one needs to exercise caution in attributing general significance to any one letter. But this one so perfectly captures the underlying concerns of *The School for Scandal* and, in its paradoxes, so fully motivates the shifting moods of the man and the work that we are surely justified in singling it out. "I have almost doubted," Sheridan writes,

> whether I am not most happy when I have some real trouble of my own, to employ as well as distress my Mind. . . . If [a man] has an object in view (however desperate) he may be comparatively happy in the *Pursuit*. But what is his State who is unhappy—he knows not why, who has no pursuit, and who were it possible to

bid him name his wish and he should have it, would answer that he wanted nothing. . . . Believe me when I am most melancholy—when I am poring over Nature's large volume of affliction, I turn to the page of Love (tho' a blotted one) for consolation. I find there it is too much cause for vexation, but were it a blank to *me*, I should be ten time more miserable. I am sick and without society—my love is almost the only Feeling I have alive "Amo ergo Sum"—is the confirmation of my existence.

And yet circumstances have placed Sheridan in the situation where his love cannot be spoken, or at least not in a way that leads toward satisfaction; for uttering his love merely envelops him in an endless chain of self-denying signifiers of desire: "To tell her *why* I am right is to plunge into the wrong:—to tell why I did *resolve*, is to break my resolution, yet to deny her and not excuse my denial is a hard mortification.—I am determined," he writes, "not to write."

Amo ergo Sum. Sheridan's happiness and his pursuits are inseparable. He sees himself before his wedding like Charles Surface before his, as a desiring-machine. The term emerges naturally out of the logic of Sheridan's creation and fits readily into the context of his post-Cartesian anthropology. I have borrowed it, however, from a modern source: *Anti-Oedipus*, by Gilles Deleuze and Félix Guattari. Deleuze and Guattari see desire, much in the way that it emerges from Sheridan, as an alternative to Freud's confining oedipal moralism. Meaning, for Freud, is given with the self-mirroring structures of society and of the psyche, and it is predetermined, at least in general outline, by the nature of the inescapable conflicts between parents and children, ego and id. But for Deleuze and Guattari—and for Sheridan—desire is primary, and the structures and boundaries that fixate meanings are derivative repressions. What matters is energy and change, and not identity, except to the extent that identity is redefined as the force of time that produces meanings and objects.

Although the *Anti-Oedipus* does not use these terms, the issue may be described as an attack on the notions of identity as role and of semiosis as classification. Not even the role of sincerity is acceptable—least of all that, after Joseph Surface has discredited it—for there is no solid core of the self to which one might remain faithful. Instead, there is the moving heart, with its flux and its appetency, defining the inner self by what it desires and engenders outside. Sheridan needs to have his "object in view" and to be always moving after it. "Desire does not lack anything; it does not lack its object. It is, rather, the subject that is missing in desire, or desire that lacks a fixed subject; there is no fixed subject unless there is repression. Desire and its object are one and the same thing" (*Anti-Oedipus* 26).

"The essential thing is the establishment of an enchanted recording or inscribing surface that arrogates to itself all the productive forces and all the organs of production" (*Anti-Oedipus* 12). It seems to me that Charles Surface is such a surface. Critics have often remarked on the odd construction of the play that keeps its hero offstage until the last scene of act 3. (*The Man of Mode* partly anticipates *The School for Scandal* in keeping its title character offstage until the same point, but Sir Fopling Flutter is in no sense Etherege's hero.) Charles's delayed appearance is only justifiable if he emerges as an electric force that galvanizes the action. What matters at the end is not his engagement, but his reformation—except that, since he refuses to name and thus to fix his reformation, it is better to say his reformed direction. The engagement to Maria is secondary. She becomes the agent or organ of his reformation, but she is not its cause in the manner of a Petrarchan beloved. As Charles says in the envoy—and the emphasis on the word of desiring-production, though not Sheridan's, is found in the received text—"Thou Still must Rule—because I *will* obey" (5.3).

I do not want to inflict on the defenseless Sheridan the whole terminology and mechanism of *Anti-Oedipus*, but it is suggestive to apply the terms of that book to the play's substitute for epiphanic Petrarchan love-magic. For Charles becomes what the authors term a "miraculating machine" ("machine miraculante," which might also be punningly translated as "ass-staring machine"). The body, according to the authors (and here they have Marx in view), "falls back on all production, constituting a surface over which all the forces and agents of production are distributed, thereby appropriating for itself all surplus production and arrogating to itself both the whole and the parts of the process, which now seem to emanate from it as a quasi cause. Forces and agents come to represent a miraculous form of its own power: they appear to be 'miraculated' by it" (10). The essential action of the play is that Charles learns to channel his desire so that it can engender his future world in the form he signifies. The requited love for Maria—whose hallowed name suddenly seems to ring true—is the magical surplus value that overflows from the labor of his desire.[50]

"Reading a text is never a scholarly exercise in search of what is signified, still less a highly textual exercise in search of a signifier. Rather it is a productive use of the literary machine, a montage of desiring-machines, a schizoid exercise that extracts from the text its revolutionary force" (*Anti-Oedipus* 106). I do not propose that every literary work is amenable to such a schizo-lecture. But *The School for Scandal* began with a split personality—as two almost entirely independent fragments—which it never entirely lost. We have already considered Goldsmith's difficulties with endings from a different perspective, and what we may call the "orthodox" Freudian formulation of the problem of sexuality in the comedies of the mid–eighteenth century failed to evolve a convincing resolution.[51] The analysis in *Anti-Oedipus* may help us to see why, for the authors reveal the oedipal structure as a circle with a foregone conclusion, such as we surely always feel in the denouements of these comedies. Sheridan's play ends differently, by precipitating the entropic dross in order to purify the ore of desire, yet with no pretense of a purely affirmative, sublimating resolution. The play thus reveals and rediscovers the force that begot the oedipal triangle, and that the triangle must hide in order to perpetuate itself.

I do not know to what extent Sheridan was by nature a schismatic, though it is suggestive that he supported the American Revolution, opposed merging the Irish and English parliaments, contributed materially to the breakup of the Whig party, and indeed prided himself throughout his career on his independence from any party line. What his masterpiece does show, at any rate, is the way that he transmuted his belatedness into an earliness, that is, into an explosive sense of how much time can, or could yet, do, provided that it once break free of established patterns. If Goldsmith painfully evolves the earliest models of the organism as a growing thing, Sheridan gives us, in Charles Surface, a powerful image of what it takes to grow up, of what growth signifies and how.

Finally, then, adroit as Sheridan was at manipulating the theatrical conventions of his time, there is an important sense in which the received image of him is true: Sheridan's mastery does not mean that he was a timely writer. The play possesses a revolutionary force that overthrows convention and refuses to profess allegiance to paternal injunctions and to values that have grown stale. Yet it continues to embody its revolutionary force in a form that was recognizably antique in all the ways that Loftis and Auburn have shown. One suspects that the revival of classic form not only supports the novel statement but in some obscure way was even a necessary condition for it to emerge. It remains clear, in any case, that the emergence was at best only partial, hedged around by conventional understanding, and that Sheridan, for whatever reasons, never even tried to renew what he had begun in the play.

We have to turn to a more agitated, revolutionary climate to see farce complete the logic of Goldsmith and Sheridan by asserting its power of renovation. When Figaro marries Suzanne, he avails himself of the freedom of uttering his desire that Sheridan forecasts, and thereby completes the conquest whose conditions Goldsmith outlined. What is at stake is the awareness of what farce can achieve. The categories that Beaumarchais masters in the crowning play of its kind are performance and consciousness. The comedy of language in a restricted exchange among the characters gives way to an unrestricted—and irresistible—comic exchange mediated by signs and achieves a direct relationship between the action on stage and the consciousness of the audience. The new beginning becomes a reality when the whole problem of semiosis is transcended by a play that, at least in retrospect, seems to aspire to what it soon achieved, the condition of music.

CHAPTER TEN

Beaumarchais's Stagecraft

Sheridan and Beaumarchais

"Calumny, Doctor, calumny," says the conspirator Bazile to Dr. Bartholo, early in the last act of *Le Barbier de Séville*. "Things must always come to that" (4.1; p. 341). No one I know of has suggested that Sheridan was influenced by Beaumarchais. But if Sheridan read the play—either in 1775 or, more likely, in the English translation that was dedicated to him in 1776[1]—he cannot have failed to be struck by Bazile's school for scandal:

> Calumny, Sir? You hardly know what you scorn; I have seen the most upright men nearly laid low by it. Believe me, not the most arrant mischief, no horrors, no absurd tale, but the idle of a great town will adopt it, if you go about it correctly; and we have people here of such skill![. . .] At first a gentle sound, skimming the earth like a swallow before the storm, murmurs *pianissimo* and skips off, and sows the poisoned dart as it runs. One mouth receives it, and *piano, piano* slips it adroitly into your ear. The evil is done, it sprouts, it climbs, it trudges, and goes like the devil *rinforzando* from mouth to mouth; then suddenly, no knowing how, you see Calumny arise, whistle, swell, grow in front of your eyes. She darts forth, stretches her wing, whirls, envelops, seizes, drags, bursts and thunders, and becomes, thanks to Heaven, a general cry, a public *crescendo*, a universal *chorus* of hate and proscription. Who the devil could resist?[2]

Who, indeed, can stand up to scandal? Bazile's stepson, Figaro, is a resistant devil, as we learn on more than one occasion.[3] But even

Figaro needs a powerful helping hand from fortune (see his speech praising chance in *Mariage* 4.1; p. 452). The battle is fought as much between powers as between men, and slander continues to enjoy a quasi-mythic status not unlike that in *The School for Scandal*.

The outer and inner affinities between Sheridan and Beaumarchais run much deeper than one eye-catching speech. Both men were the children of successful members of the middle class. Born in 1732, Beaumarchais was the son of a noted watchmaker, André Charles Caron. As precocious as Sheridan, he first made his reputation in 1753 by inventing a new escapement, which led to membership in the Académie des Sciences and eventually, as things went in those days, to an appointment as harp master to the king's daughters. In 1757 he adopted the name Beaumarchais from a property of his first wife's, henceforth signing himself Pierre-Augustin Caron de Beaumarchais. Around 1761 he composed some *parades*, short farces in a bizarre, conventionalized patois, designed for private performance; none of these was published for over a century, and they are without historical significance. In 1767 and 1770 two dramas were performed, bourgeois moralities in the manner of Diderot. The first, *Eugénie*, was quite successful (as was Mrs. Elizabeth Griffith's English version), but not the second, *Les Deux Amis*. Beaumarchais's two masterpieces, *Le Barbier de Séville* and *Le Mariage de Figaro*, were staged in 1775 and 1784, both after considerable delays and both with enormous international success. But Beaumarchais turned his back on his genius in favor first of a grand opera, *Tarare* (1788), successfully set to music by the royal composer Salieri, then a somber drama about an older Figaro and Almaviva, *L'Autre Tartuffe, ou La Mère coupable* (1792), which held the stage for the first half of the nineteenth century. He always talked about his comedies as trifles and as mere preparations for *La Mère coupable* and for a further sequel that he did not live to write. Like Sheridan, in short, Beaumarchais wandered from genre to genre, feeling insecure about comedy, drawn to popular forms and to melodrama, and hesitant in general about completing dramatic projects.

Like Sheridan, too, Beaumarchais seems to have been a born man of the theater. He could not become an impresario, and indeed his engagement with the practical affairs of the theater was largely limited to leading a successful authors' revolt against the financial practices of the Comédie Française. But his texts contain numerous technical innovations that bespeak an overriding concern with stage effect: entr'actes to occupy the intervals, extensive descriptions of costume and (in *Le Mariage de Figaro*) of the personalities of the characters and the appropriate acting style, and lavish stage directions (the provision of which was a practice begun by Diderot and enriched by Beaumarchais, who developed a system for suggesting the stage blocking in the text). Beaumarchais's plots, like Sheridan's, are patchworks of hoary topoi; like Sheridan he excels at quick repartee—this is also true of the dramas, if they are compared with Diderot's—and at the effective use of props, mime, and music. This is a theater of gestures and actions—including certain kinds of verbal actions—not of communication and ideas.

Beaumarchais's comedies, like Sheridan's, were very far from being the focus of his activities. They seem almost instinctive products of a genius writing under the conditions of a particular era. Both authors actually made their careers in politics. Although Beaumarchais, as a bourgeois, could not be a legislator, his obvious oratorical gifts found a substitute outlet in a series of lawsuits and in countless polemical pamphlets. His employment was in diplomacy, where his political liberalism, his fidelity to superiors, his backstage maneuvering, and the stubborn streak that led to an extended exile in his later years and to relative poverty at the end are all characteristics that strikingly resemble Sheridan's.

Such affinities between the two authors run far deeper than in most cases of demonstrable influence and color every aspect of their works. The plays of both authors revel in changing names, in misleading documents and letters, in hollow proverbs.[4] The scandal of reference is a crucial problem in both, one that Figaro's long speech on the word "God-dam" (*Mariage* 3.5; p. 433) attributes preeminently to the English. In both playwrights the skepticism toward language in turn implicates convention, authority, and, eventually—more explicitly in Beaumarchais than in Sheridan—the structure of society. (Politics and drama are also intermingled, with different allegiances yet similar ambivalences, in Sheridan's friend Burke.) All external signification not rooted in inner determinations becomes subject to scrutiny and attack.

Even while both authors observe the letter of the three unities (as classically interpreted), the focus on consciousness utterly transforms their spirit. Full use is made of the precedent of shifting locales within a single general area because the unity of place has come to be sensed far more as a unifying aura and symbolic decor—the library, say, or the garden with pavilions—than as a ground for the rational plausibility of the action. Rationalistic unity of plot is preserved—just barely—in the sense that a focal problem presented at the beginning is resolved at the end. But the plot articulations are relatively weak in both authors. Whereas Goldsmith intensifies plot unity in the direction of organic unfolding, both Sheridan and Beaumarchais employ a more episodic organization. The classical flow that builds toward a single climax and denouement disappears in favor of "a plot that is comfortably spun out . . . , tied and untied without interruption along a host of comic situations" (Preface to *Mariage*, in *Oeuvres* 375–76). Underneath the classical trappings, then, incident is more important than what Corneille calls *suite* (connection). Fundamentally, unity of plot, like unity of place, becomes a question of maintaining a single mood, as is signaled by Beaumarchais's rejection of tragicomedy (mixed mode) in favor of drama (middle mode) and by Sheridan's preference for laughing over sentimental comedy.

Beaumarchais resembles Sheridan, finally, in treating time as a transcendental force. In the previous chapter I suggested that Corneille's *liaison des scènes* was intended to promote coherence and to underscore the unitary character of the action. In *Eugénie* (and also after act 3 of the *Barbier* and act 2 of the *Mariage*) Beaumarchais adds a *liaison des actes* that seems a mere extension of the principle, but really undermines it: "Theatrical action never resting, I have thought that one might try to link an act to the one that follows it by a pantomime action that would maintain, without wearying it, the attention of the spectators, and would indicate what happens behind the scene during the entr'acte" (*Eugénie*, note to first Entr'acte, 154). Corneille's rule is that each scene in a given act must include at least one character from the preceding scene: unity of action is thus inseparable from continuity of character. Beaumarchais's entr'actes, like his occasional silent scenes and his numerous portrayals of reverie, represent characters existing outside of the dramatic action. The neoclassical perspective objects to these as an irrationality that distorts the current of time: they are said to have "the inconvenience of rendering flagrant the difference between the supposed real time of the action and the time of representation" (Scherer, *Dramaturgie* 67). From a more sympathetic perspective, we might say that Beaumarchais represents two modalities of being, the measured but intermittent time of consciousness and articulated speech, and the unceasing though unmeasured underlying flow of an intuitive time of feeling.

In Sheridan's plays time does not stop for soliloquies; in Beaumarchais's it does not stop even for changes of scenery. For Sheridan time is allied with writing, and as it passes it makes its mark on the characters. There is little sense in Beaumarchais of aging and of the mark of time, perhaps only in the hardening of roles found in *La Mère coupable*, the last of the Figaro plays. But pace is all-important— some scenes carry indications such as "This scene moves rapidly" (*Eugénie* 3.7; p. 173)—and so is time of day: the progress of the sun governs the shifting decor and mood, especially in the two comedies. In somewhat different ways, then, these playwrights do not strive to govern time and to encapsulate action, but rather allow time to govern the flow of sensation. All three unities are transformed from principles of cognition and rational segmentation into wellsprings of feeling and emotional reference. Thus do the two playwrights share a situation and a project of reevaluating human consciousness rooted in the general crisis of the word in the period.

Paradoxes of the Comedian

But how do you put inwardness on stage? What is entailed in representing moods or performing feelings? "I was not slow," Beaumarchais writes in the first paragraph of the preface to his first play, "to feel that I was wrong to wish to convince by reasoning in a genre where one must only persuade by feeling. So I passionately wished to be able to substitute example for precept" ("Essai sur le genre dramatique sérieux," in *Oeuvres* 119). But realizing his desire, he continues, is fraught with difficulty and even peril: "This is an infallible means of making disciples when it succeeds, but it exposes the unhappy failure to the double distress of missing his aim and of remaining charged with the ridicule of having presumed on his strength." Later, in the preface to his last play, he writes with more apparent confidence, but also more strangely, about the paradoxes of his enterprise: "I composed it . . . with the cold head of a man, and the burning heart of a woman, as has been thought of Rousseau. I have noticed that this combination, this moral 'hermaphroditism' is less rare than is thought" ("Un Mot sur 'La Mère coupable,'" in *Oeuvres* 600–601). A new and uneasy balance must be sought between feeling and reason, emotion and expression, example and precept. Virtue, meaning, and succession or discipleship all become equally imperiled by a logic that succeeds, finally, only when it decides to substitute acting for life.

Beaumarchais's theories seem above all designed to mark his departure from the precedent of the century's great reasoner, Voltaire. Beaumarchais was closely associated with Voltaire's name as editor of the great Kehl edition of Voltaire's works, which began to appear in 1784. The sentimentality of Voltaire's theater must have appealed to Beaumarchais, and Voltaire's most important comedy, *L'Enfant prodigue* (1736), was on a subject dear to the hearts of Diderot and his successors. But Voltaire's overriding concerns are judgment and justice, and feeling in his play remains strictly subordinated to reason. Voltaire still understands unity of action as applying to plot rather than mood: servants included, there are only eight characters, and only one question is resolved (will Lise marry Fierenfat or Euphémon?). But the tone shifts from farcical at the beginning to pathetic or even tragic in the later acts, and Voltaire's preface contains an attack on generic purity and a defense of tragicomedy that are directly answered by Beaumarchais's "Essai sur le genre dramatique sérieux."

In contrast to Beaumarchais, Voltaire refuses to distinguish feeling from its articulation. As is typical in French classical theater, a confidante is present to express emotions, that is, to expose what is within. In one striking exchange the mistress, Lise, exclaims:

> Comment chercher la triste vérité
> Au fond d'un coeur, hélas! trop agité?
> Il faut au moins, pour se mirer dans l'onde,
> Laisser calmer la tempête qui gronde.
> (*L'Enfant prodigue* 2.2, in *Oeuvres* 4: 27)

> How can the sad truth be sought, alas, in the depths of so frantic a heart? The storm must cease to growl before one's reflection can be seen in the waves.

But the confidante Marthe will not allow her mistress to evade self-expression in this way:

> Comparaison n'est pas raison, madame:
> On lit très bien dans le fond de son âme,
> On y voit clair; et si les passions
> Portent en nous tant d'agitations,
> Fille de bien sait toujours dans sa tête
> D'où vient le vent qui cause la tempête.
> (ibid.)

> Comparison is not reason, madame: the depths of the soul can easily be read, the view is clear; and if passions agitate us so much, a daughter of virtue always knows in her mind from where the storm-wind blows.

Against her servant's clear-sightedness, Lise's protest, "Et moi, je ne veux rien savoir" (ibid. "As for me, I wish to know nothing"), is both transparent and ineffective. She wants not to know her feelings because they seem hopeless, and she consequently wants not to feel them. But in Voltaire's comedy feelings can no more be kept down than can the knowledge of feeling that is inseparable from them.

Beaumarchais's intention to reverse such emotional rationalism could hardly be more evident. Concealment was a mode of life for him—Bégearss in *La Mère coupable* apparently reflects the author's experience when he says that politics is "as deep as Etna, [and] seethes and rumbles for a long time before bursting out" (4.4; p. 650)—and it is a dominant theme in both the comedies. Feelings in particular exist to be cherished in secret. Thus, *Eugénie* concerns the heroine's secret marriage with Lord Count Clarendon, which is also—this is the secret of the feelings that he keeps from her—a sham marriage. The sign of her feeling is her pregnant condition, which for the moment remains concealed. But the pregnancy is also the ideal symptom of the paradox of expression that Beaumarchais confronts from the beginning of his career. "Oh! how dear it would be to me if it did not expose me," Eugénie exclaims (1.9; p. 151). For Beaumarchais a feeling expressed is a feeling betrayed. Inside and outside, emotion and expression are antithetical by nature, and never more so than at the moment of conception or engendering that ought to link them.

The next play, *Les Deux Amis*, leaves no question that Beaumarchais values feeling above reason. "Where reason falls short, feeling must triumph," as the good father soliloquizes in this work (2.4; p. 219). But the play enacts an antinomy. Feeling, whether enveloped in "silence" (3.4; p. 235) or embodied in an "interior voice" (3.5; p. 236), is imperceptible by nature. Hence it needs reason to speak for it.

Les Deux Amis is a proto-Kantian fable of the conflict between the two friendly but irreconcilable forces of the soul: the heartfelt benevolence of Mélac, who secretly covers the debts of his friend Aurelly, and the rational justice of Aurelly, who insists on scrupulous repayment. At the start the play makes much of its setting, the day when all accounts are settled, and thus establishes an allegorical resonance for the problem of reconciling Mélac's silent feeling with Aurelly's manifest reason. But the king, who is the principle of reconciliation, has grown remote. In the earlier *Eugénie* Clarendon, the sham husband, is actually about to be married at court, and Eugénie's father feels a personal relationship to the paternal king: "And why should he reject me? He is a father. I have seen him kiss his children" (4.3; p. 178). *Les Deux Amis*, by contrast, takes place in Lyons, far from Paris, and the king is represented only by the devious and morally equivocal tax collector, Saint-Alban. Virtue and benevolence ultimately make a spectacular show in the final tableau, on a day that, as the daughter says, "has enlightened me about all my feelings" (5.6; p. 260). But the display of feelings does not so much reconcile them to reason as put reason to rout. First we learn (in 3.5) that Aurelly is not Pauline's reasonable and affectionate uncle, as he had pretended, but her adoring, illegitimate father. Then in the last scene Saint-Alban, who had passed for a dutiful servant of the laws, suddenly changes heart and acts in a private capacity, as generous benefactor. Beaumarchais at times expressed a particular fondness for this play, perhaps because its allegory so exactly represents the paradox that virtue can only find expression by transforming its nature into sentimental loving-kindness. But if the allegory is exact, it is by the very same token crude; there is no blunting, blending, or mediating of the conflicts. It is too forthright a representation of the reserves of feeling, and hence it never held the stage.

The sign of virtue is reason, but reason no more coincides with virtue than does a word with its meaning. The only true expression of virtue is silent. As a consequence of this logic, many of the most expressive and affecting moments in Beaumarchais are wordless: reveries, silent scenes, pantomimes.[5] Though the action rarely stops—it is notable how much business there is in Beaumarchais's soliloquies, for instance—the flow of language pauses to allow a vision of what lies within. And when for once the action also stops, in "a small interval of time without movement" between acts 3 and 4 of *Eugénie* (176), or when even the orchestra is subdued to a remote murmur (in the following entr'acte, 189–90), then muffled feelings become powerfully evident. Soliloquy, by contrast, risks appearing as posturing or as a mere rationalization of feeling, with the speaker implicitly debating either with the spectators or with himself (as noted by Conesa, *La Trilogie de Beaumarchais* 52–55).

The classicizing Scherer recognizes the decline in rational self-awareness in the eighteenth-century theater and reports—wrongly—a corresponding decline in the importance of soliloquies.[6] In fact Beaumarchais does not so much reduce soliloquy as turn it in a new, unclassical direction. Quite apart from his having written, for Figaro, the longest soliloquy in the traditional French repertoire, it should not escape notice, for instance, that soliloquies open the first three acts of the four-act *Barbier de Séville* and close acts 2 and 3, nor that Figaro and Almaviva are given long soliloquies in acts 1 and 3, respectively, of *Le Mariage de Figaro*.[7] In *Le Mariage de Figaro*, at least, Beaumarchais develops the soliloquy into a direct correlative of the paradox of signification. If the relation of feeling to its expression is by nature problematic, then the natural, isolated expression of the heart will concern problems of articulating and knowing feeling. In soliloquy after soliloquy the main characters in *Le Mariage de Figaro* come forward, less often to debate, to scheme, or to bare their insides, than to express confusion: "I no longer know what I came to fetch" (Suzanne, 1.6; p. 390). "What am I doing at this moment?" (the countess, 2.25; p. 429). "The thread escapes me. . . . Where did I go astray? In truth, when you flare up, the best regulated imagination goes mad, like a dream" (the count, who is *"alone, walking in a dream,"* 3.4; p. 431). "Who knows? perhaps he will [kiss] me back" (Fanchette, 5.1; p. 467). Such are the questions and doubts that the main characters share with us in private, and most of the remaining soliloquies differ only by expressing somewhat less readily quotable frustration. Figaro's great soliloquy of self-questioning and disillusionment is not the anomaly that Scherer claims, but a fulfillment of the author's tendency to regard all confidences, confessions, and self-scrutiny as self-baffled.

So far I have considered two paradoxes of representation. One is moral: the impossibility of expressing virtuous motivation without compromising its purity. The second is semiotic: the impossibility of reconciling the natural, immediate, or internal relation of sign to significance with the arbitrariness, freedom, or externality that makes it a sign. But in examining Sheridan's context we have already seen how a problem of utterance can be correlated with a conflict of generations, that is, with problems of begetting and rearing. However arbitrary it may be, the association of these two domains has a long history, reaching back at least as far as early medieval juxtapositions of the Latin *semen* (seed) with the Greek *seme* (sign). In our period this third, psychological paradox is most often presented as an impossibility of transmitting social values without stifling independence. Oedipus is, paradoxically, both the ultimate in freedom, in murdering his father, and also the ultimate in bondage, in fulfilling the prophecy to the letter. We have seen how the minor English dramatists of the period suffer from the worst aspects of the oedipal paradox: both the sign and the son, when they are most free, wind up repeating identically the paternal dictates. Concealed or dubious paternity (as in *Tom Jones* and *Tristram Shandy*, respectively) provided a means for the son to eclipse the father. But we remain in want of a father worthily represented by a son who is not simply a shadow or pale reflection of him.

Voltaire's *Enfant prodigue* follows the old dispensation unreservedly. In the absence of his elder son, thought to be imprisoned or dead, the despairing father almost marries the son's beloved to his thoroughly despicable younger brother. The younger brother, a *président* (magistrate), represents the letter of the law, while the elder brother is its spirit, that has come temporarily into conflict with the letter. When he returns at the last moment, he proves to have returned in every respect to paternal values, and he is allowed to claim his rightful inheritance and his bride, "the unhoped for return of the rights of blood and the rights of love" (5.7; 4: 100). Whereas in *The School for Scandal*, for instance, an uncle indulges a younger brother's follies while leaving a hypocritical elder brother unpunished, in Voltaire's play the father punishes the hypocritical upstart and rewards the rightful heir who has repented of the freedom for which he was imprisoned. Despite being couched for much of its length in the register of feeling, the play thus reaffirms all the traditional sanctions.

In Diderot's *Fils naturel*, by contrast, it is the father who is the prodigal, having been shipwrecked under a false name, at the cost of his fortune. Without knowing that they are brother and sister, his two children have been tormented by a mutual passion that they have struggled to resist. The father's return saves them from the threatened incest, and he bequeaths them instead to a sister and brother who have long loved them. But liberation is dubious and bittersweet at best, for the father's destiny is to be fulfilled through his death: "It is time for you to live, and for me to stop; tomorrow, if Heaven wills it, it will be without regrets" (5.5, in *Oeuvres complètes* 10: 80). The father's curtain line points the paradox of paternity. "May Heaven," he says to his natural son and his lawful daughter, "which blesses children by their fathers, and fathers by their children, grant you ones that resemble you, and that will repay you the tenderness that you have for me" (5.5; 10: 81). As a moral issue reciprocity is unproblematic here. But Beaumarchais's veritable mania for illegitimacy carries a disturbing biological pathos. The father's desire to liberate his children is complicated by the tacit anxiety for ocular proof not only that they really are his, but that they look like it. "Oh how cruel it is . . . how sweet it is to be a father!" as Diderot's next play concludes (*Le Père de famille* 4.12; 10: 322).

A child who resembles you, physically and morally, can also represent you. Representation becomes dangerous, however, when the son engages in an illegal duel to defend his merchant father's honor against a slur by a military officer. This is the subject of Sedaine's

Philosophe sans le savoir, the most successful *drame bourgeois.* Falling on the day of the sister's wedding, the secret duel threatens to destroy the cohesion of the happy family that it seeks to defend. All is resolved in the end, when the offending officer also proves to be a son who recognizes the sanctity of fathers. But first the merchant resigns himself to the necessity of the duel and sends his son off with approbation but, significantly, without an embrace. A gap threatens to open between the father who needs defending and the son who defends him. This is the only remarkable scene in a play whose popularity surely rested on its blandness. (It, too, enjoyed a well-received English translation by Mrs. Griffith.) But the paradox of a self-destructive representation was too strong for the censors, who insisted on a revision that prevailed for over a century, namely, that the father disavow the duel to be fought on his behalf. For a truly effective representation ultimately undermines and replaces the father, or the authority of which paternity is the sign.

Later, in 1787, it became possible for Beaumarchais to put on stage the consequences of filial representation in an opera about popular resistance to a tyrant who is not a compliant father to his people. Here a chorus of Europeans sings a hymn to free love:

> Si le dur hymen est chez nous
> Bien absolu, bien despotique,
> L'amour, en secret, fait de tous
> Une charmante république
> *(Tarare* 3.4; p. 555)

> Hymen with us is strict, absolute, despotic, but love, in secret, makes of all a charming republic.

In this play sons elect a popularly chosen father, the hero Tarare, who triumphs over the despot as well as over the intended successor, the son of the ambitious and manipulative high priest. As middle-class drama edges toward democracy, it begins to appear that the only qualified fathers are those who are sons of nobody.

Beaumarchais's plays repeatedly address the paradox of paternity, but they solve it no more than the paradoxes of the heart and of the sign. *Eugénie* features a secret pregnancy and a sham marriage; *Les Deux Amis,* a father who pretends to be an uncle. As in most Georgian comedy the sentimental plights in both plays are cured only by unprepared changes of heart, leaving the remaining plays to pose similar issues with increasing insistence. Almaviva steals Rosina away from her protector, Don Bartholo. Figaro, the son of nobody, imagines a noble ancestry, but proves to be the bastard off-

spring of Marceline and of Bartholo, who spurns him, and he is
adopted at length by Bazile, the foolish music-master who weds
Marceline.[8] And in the sequel, *La Mère coupable*, Almaviva and
Rosina each confess to having an illegitimate child. Beaumarchais
stands *Le Fils naturel* on its head, for here too the purported brother
and sister are in love, but the play leaves open the possibility of their
marriage. Indeed Beaumarchais defended the apparent incest in a letter (to M. Martineau, 14 Messidor, Year V [July 2, 1797], in *Oeuvres*
1176–79), and actually planned to represent it in a further sequel.
Despite the impression left by Jean-Pierre de Beaumarchais's nice
survey of the topic ("Enfant naturel, enfant de la nature"), paternity,
inheritance, and family continuity only grow more perplexed with
the years.

There is, however, a fourth, specifically theatrical paradox. It
comes to Beaumarchais from Diderot, and it is the ground on which
Le Mariage de Figaro actually triumphs. The theater, in Diderot's
view, had degenerated into the empty posturings of tragedy and the
equally empty frivolity of comedy. His reform was intended to return to a middle ground of serious truth.[9] Tableau and not *coup de
théâtre*: the theater was to rid itself of theatricality in order to become a picture of real life. If this sounds paradoxical, it is, and was so
from the start, long before *Paradoxe sur le comédien*. Representation was to be reversed. Instead of imitating life on stage, the play
was to be the reality, with the actors imitating the events of the text.
Le Fils naturel, in particular, is presented as an episode, falling between a narrative of the surrounding events and a lengthy discussion
("Entretiens sur *Le Fils naturel*") in which the main character,
Dorval, criticizes the text. Instead of a dramatis personae and cast,
the play is headed by a list "of the names of the real personages of
the play, with those of the actors who might replace them" (*Oeuvres
complètes* 10: 18). The profuse stage directions have the character of
a narrative intended to bring the text alive for a reader, and the performance is presented not as an imitation or even as a commemoration, but as an incarnation that cancels the mortality of ordinary
existence:

> There is no stage to be erected here, but the memory of an event
> that touches us is to be conserved, and rendered as it happened
> [. . .] We would renew it ourselves, every year, in this house, in
> this chamber. The things which we have said, we would say them
> again. Your children would do the same, and theirs, and their de-
> scendants. And I would survive myself, and I would go and con-
> verse thus, from age to age, with all of my offspring. (10: 16)

Diderot was a greater genius at setting problems than at solving them. Between conquering mortality and repeating the fixed text of the past, between reanimation and perpetuation, there is an incompatibility that is difficult to reconcile.

The evidence that Diderot produced only a paradox and not a dialectic of representation lies in the works themselves. Dorval insists afterwards that a true play should consist of pictures (*tableaux*), not *coups de théâtre*; but beforehand he approves of his father's intention precisely to bring the events alive and not to present mere portraits: "Dorval, do you think that a work that should transmit our very ideas, our true sentiments, the speeches which we have given in one of the most important circumstances of our lives, is not more valuable than family portraits that show only a moment of our faces" (10: 16). In fact, the conflicting demands are met very differently in Diderot's two plays. *Le Fils naturel* heaps misfortune upon misfortune to keep interest alive—Dorval calls it "a house that I fill with disorder" (2.5; 10: 36)—and the mood is continually agitated. *Le Père de famille* is much longer, but has much less action and consists largely of sentimental tableaux. Furthermore, Diderot is notably unsuccessful in the effort to find a stable middle tone. The serious diction of the earlier play sits awkwardly on basically farcical situations such as Dorval's proposing to his beloved Rosalie on behalf of his friend Clairville (a motif also used in Goldsmith's *Good-Natur'd Man* and Murphy's *Know Your Own Mind*) or Constance's thinking that Dorval's unfinished love letter to Rosalie is meant for her. Diderot's ideology allows for no distinction between the subject and the norm of representation, which are supposed to be equally and perfectly natural. But in practice the ideal of a simple and universal subject proves incompatible with the ideal of a striking, pregnant action. Universality of plot is objective and entails a generality that can appeal "in all times and peoples" (*Le Fils naturel* 10: 131); universality of action is subjective and entails a concentrated focus "on particular instants" because "we must all be completely intent on the same thing" (10: 86). The play must conform to all forms of experience at the same time that it forces all consciousness into its mold.

Unable to reconcile these demands, Diderot abandoned original composition for the theater. But shortly after the premiere of *Le Barbier de Séville* he embarked on a new dramatic project that was to occupy him for a number of years.[10] Far from resolving the paradoxes of representation, the new play is of interest here because of its greatly more explicit acknowledgment of them. M. Hardouin, the central character of *Est-il bon? est-il méchant?*, is a playwright and a schemer. He is confronted in turn by a series of individuals with various problems. After promising a play, he dupes a friend into writing it; he improves a widow's pension by pretending to have fathered her son; he persuades a mother to approve her daughter's marriage by forging letters that compromise the daughter; and he even manipulates his reluctant lawyer into settling a lawsuit. Clearly, there is no unity of plot here, but instead a unity of character that shines through the plurality of plots. (Nearly all the soliloquies belong to the central character, as in *Le Fils naturel*; *Le Père de famille* is antithetical in this respect, as in others.) Yet the character remains mysterious in the representation. The soliloquies are externalizations, and neither the audience nor the other characters nor even Hardouin himself can get access to his "true" nature. The title reflects the moral paradox with which we began, and it is echoed in the closing dialogue, which acknowledges paradox as the precondition of dramatic universality:

> *Mme de Chepy.* Is he good? Is he bad?
> *Mlle Beaulieu.* One after the other.
> *Mme de Vertillac.* Like you, like me, like everyone.
> (scene 18, in *Oeuvres complètes* 25: 479)

Such is the legacy of theatrical frustration over which Beaumarchais's revolutionary masterpiece emerges victorious.

The Action of *Le Mariage de Figaro*

From the perspective of *Le Mariage de Figaro* it is evident that Diderot's revolt against classicism was incomplete. Both Beaumarchais and Diderot turned from the *drame* to loose-jointed farces about marriage and dubious paternity, theatrical deception and incompetent shysterism, held together by a curiously inscrutable schemer. But, as the "Entretiens sur *Le Fils naturel*" makes clear, Diderot remained under the spell of the dramatic unities. Unity of time and place serve ultimately to guarantee unity of action: one place and one time concentrate attention on one thing. And unity of action entails further concentration, not on the incidents themselves, but on an idea that underlies and unifies them: "The art of plotting consists of linking the events so that the alert spectator always perceives a reason to satisfy him" ("Entretiens," in *Oeuvres complètes* 10: 86). According to the Aristotelian doctrine of imitation, as classically understood, the incidents of the plot are merely signifiers pointing to an invisible, ideal "action." The unities thus ultimately rest on a subordination of the body of the work to its soul, as intuited by the mind of the spectator who knows how to concentrate and to judge. Even *Est-il bon? est-il méchant?* is unified less with respect to the inscrutable character of Hardouin than with respect to an action that determines the time frame of the play, the preparations for a party for the absent Mme de Malves, and to the indispensable idea behind the action, in this case, social integration based on mask and pretense. In a classically self-contained reflection, Diderot's paradox represents its own duplicity.

Beaumarchais does not subordinate incident to overall effect in this way. Only with difficulty, and with considerable apologies for act 5, can a classical orientation defend the play's unity.[11] In truth there are, as in *The School for Scandal*, two actions. One occupies the central acts. Its question is whom Figaro is to marry. It climaxes in act 3 with the discovery that Marceline cannot enforce his agreement to marry her because she is his mother, and its denouement comes with the pantomime in the middle of act 4 (scene 9), where Figaro and Suzanne are formally presented to the count as bride and groom. This action, however, is a digression from the problem that dominates the first and last acts, namely, whether the count will exercise his seigneurial right after Figaro and Suzanne marry. This in turn is a curious action because its goal is negative—not even the renunciation of the old custom, but merely the confirmation of a prior renunciation. Finally, it is the idiot judge, Brid'oison, who unties the knot in an outburst of wonderful inarticulacy:

> *Count.* And you, Don Brid'oison, your opinion now?
> *Brid'oison.* O-on everything I see, Sire? [. . .] My-y faith, for me, I
>   don't know what to tell you: that is my way of thinking.
> *All together.* Well judged!
>
> (5.18; p. 486)

The choral response makes this beyond question the moment corresponding to the classical expectation of a removal of obstacles and a social reintegration, and the judge's stammering makes it, equally beyond question, a parody of the classical expectation of an ideal depth to the action.

Traditionally, climax is clarification: clouds lift, understanding is achieved at last, and the dialectic breaks through to its resolution. There is no such moment of transcendence to *Le Mariage de Figaro*. Instead of a single overriding action, each act has a different focal incident. Indeed, the first act has two focal incidents, the game of hide-and-seek, with the same chair concealing both the count and Chérubin, followed immediately by the first crowd scene, where Figaro tries to shame the count into authorizing his wedding. In the second act Chérubin is locked in the countess's closet and then, with Suzanne's help, escapes out the window. Act 3 is the trial concerning Figaro's conditional promise to marry Marceline, climaxing with the discovery of his ancestry. Act 4 is the presentation of Figaro and Suzanne, complete with dancing and festivities and accompanied by intriguing about hanky-panky to follow. Finally, the last act is the masquerade in the darkened garden.

Each act swells to a grand and increasingly tumultuous crowd scene. But the crowds disperse almost as suddenly as they come. All acts except the last actually conclude with a reduced group of one to three actors onstage. The rapid activity of Beaumarchais's long text resembles less a wave rising to a climax than a series of breakers with their residual outflow. Even the concluding vaudeville, with its succession of self-interested verses for each of the main characters, is far from a picture of social integration. It is the idiot judge who stammers out the last judgment about "the people" as a whole:

> Qu'on l'opprime, il peste, il crie;
> Il s'agite en cent fa-açons;
> Tout fini-it par des chansons
> (5.19; p. 489)

> If you oppress them, they rage, they cry; they shake themselves a hundred wa-ays; all e-ends with songs.

As Beaumarchais says in his long, moralizing Preface, "instead of pursuing a single vicious character . . . , the author profited from a light composition or rather formed his plan in such a way as to put into it a critique of a host of abuses that desolate society" (360–61). With so pervasive a sense of fragmentation, and with irresponsible song substituting for earned insight, it finally makes little sense to ask about the unity of the action.[12]

The real generic affinities of *Le Mariage de Figaro* lie instead in a hitherto unexamined direction. In the discontinuous, episodic rhythm of the action, in its focus on the schemes of a vagabond of uncertain parentage, and in its irreverent atmosphere, the play has far less in common with classical comedy than with the picaresque novel.[13] Like Diderot, Beaumarchais often used the term *roman* to designate his plays. The elaborate stage directions and the extensive character analyses that for the first time in the history of drama accompany the list of dramatis personae are as much for a reader's benefit as for a director's or spectator's. But even a spectator confronts the play as a reader, rather than as a mere witness of the action. The characters—even Figaro, in this play—plot and counterplot in mutual bafflement, while the audience knows all.[14] A striking instance of this generic shift is found in another of Beaumarchais's technical developments, the abundant use of stage whispers in which one character speaks to another so as not to be heard by a third. Where the whisperer is managing an intrigue, he may be prompting his partner's responses or actions. Scherer discusses the stage whisper only with respect to this kind of character function, for which there are precedents in Molière, and he relates it to the unstable "third space" in which characters hide or escape, that is, to its role in furthering the main action (Scherer, *Dramaturgie* 172–81; for Molière see, for instance, *Dom Juan* 2.4 and *L'Avare* 3.6–7). But stage whispers can also mark a parallel action running alongside the main action (as in *Mariage* 2.20; p. 422), or they can be associated with a cascade of asides emphasizing the separateness of characters despite their attempts to manipulate one another (5.5–6; pp. 472–74). In general, then, this technique works to fragment the action further, not to forward it. The characters live by keeping secrets from one another, and only the audience remains as omniscient perceiving consciousness.

The action of classical drama is subordinated to a unifying idea or thought (Aristotle's *dianoia*) that becomes more or less fully manifested to the characters at the end. We have seen how *The Vicar of Wakefield*, with its thoughtless narrator, transforms the unifying category from idea to experience. *Le Mariage de Figaro* displaces unity in a different direction. With plot now subordinated to episode, there is no longer a unity of action, that is, a moral or an experiential unity. Instead, there is an epistemological unity; the characters are constantly surprised or mystified, but the action remains coherent for those who stand outside it in a position to understand the interplay of the numerous intrigues. The epistemological emphasis is most striking in the two recognition scenes, in acts 3 and 5. Deceptive writing is at issue in both: Figaro's illegible agreement with Marceline to repay her and/or to marry her, and the message arranging an assignation with the count in Suzanne's handwriting, but actually dictated by the countess. In a parody of sentimental recognition scenes, act 3 treats the identifying mark as a writing on the flesh—"this hieroglyph on my arm," as Figaro calls it (3.16; p. 445)—that voids the now-unenforceable contract. And both scenes feature Brid'oison, the foolish and incompetent judge. There hardly remains a question of righteousness in these scenes, only of gaining knowledge of what has been done and what is possible.

Beaumarchais's long, moralizing Preface has always seemed disingenuous. Even if one accepts his reasoning, it somehow doesn't matter. For these characters have no depths to be defended or attacked. Though the stage is often crowded and grows increasingly dark, this is a transparent spectacle.[15] In contrast to Sheridan's in *The School for Scandal*, Beaumarchais's characters often remain bewildered about who was hiding in the chair, or in the closet, or beyond the window, let alone who is in which pavilion; yet the audience sees and knows all. The introductory analyses of the dramatis personae draw attention to the style of acting and emphasize that all must remain on the surface. On the count: "The corruption of his heart must not detract from the *bon ton* of his manners." On the countess: she "must show only a suppressed sensibility or a very moderate choler; nothing above all to degrade her amiable and virtuous character in the eyes of the spectator." (The already planned sequel was to reveal both her passionate exchange of love letters with Chérubin and the child she bore him, but we must suspect no such depths here.) On Figaro in particular: if the actor "saw anything in the role but reason seasoned with gaiety and with sallies, especially if he put the least burden in it, he would debase" the part. Only in the case of Chérubin—the dreamy youth who is ultimately driven out of the ceaselessly active world of Beaumarchais's "mad day"—does the analysis point toward, rather than away from, inner depths: "Timid to excess before the Countess, otherwise a charming rascal; a restless, vague desire is the ground of his character" (379). The essay prefixed to *Eugénie* had attacked comedy because of its immoral tendencies: "Despite the moral, the spectator too often is surprised into interesting himself in the scoundrel against the honest man, because the latter is always the less amusing of the two" ("Essai sur le genre dramatique sérieux," in *Oeuvres* 127). *Le Mariage de Figaro* does not escape this charge through identification with an honest man against the scoundrel, for there are no moral characters in the play. Instead, the analyses of the roles show Beaumarchais's intention to avoid identification altogether. The audience sits in amused detachment overlooking characters who have no depth and whose soliloquies repeatedly express only confusion as to what lies within them.

As with many comedies, it could be said that the morality of *Le Mariage de Figaro* is "the reverse of what it should be" (ibid.). Such reversals are an integral part of the topos of the inverted world (*monde renversé*) that pervades the comedy. Governing one's master, punishing by marrying, transvestism—these are examples of the intentional exchange of roles and the accidental exchange of gifts prompted by Figaro's morality. "To take revenge on those who harm our projects by overthrowing [*renversant*] theirs; 'tis what all do; what we ourselves are going to do" (*Mariage* 2.2; p. 402). It would be a mistake, however, to regard these frolics as prompting immorality. The axis of concern remains knowledge and ignorance, not good and evil, and Figaro's madness mounts an attack on truth, not on virtue. Suzanne, to be sure, insists that she has "only one" truth (4.1; p. 453), but she happily encourages her mistress to lie "without letting it show" (2.24; p. 428). Figaro, meanwhile, has "several" truths (4.1; p. 452), and he can gaily tell the truth without letting it show: "in your place, in truth, Monseigneur," he frankly confesses, "I should not believe a word of all we have told you" (2.20; p. 422). Such inversions undermine moral systems in favor of a situational pragmatics: the play is not immoral, but it may well be considered amoral. Its texture amounts to a policy of devaluation, or *Entwertung aller Werte*.[16]

These are the negative aspects of Beaumarchais's revolutionary farce. It resolves the first three paradoxes of the comedian by cutting right through them. There is no paradox of inward expression because the characters have no inside. There is no paradox of paternal devotion and filial revolt because paternity is just a joke. There is no morality, and hence no moral paradox. But the play also has its constructive side. Theatricality is not dismissed after the fashion that Diderot proposed. On the contrary, it becomes all-important.[17]

One of the most striking effects of the play in production must be the materiality of the stage. The texts of all of Beaumarchais's plays minutely specify the costuming; and the colorful crowd scenes of *Le Mariage de Figaro*, the music, and the elaborate choreography make it a lavish visual spectacle. Most plays of the period engage in a comedy of words—perhaps with an occasional sword—but *Le Mariage de Figaro*, even more than *The School for Scandal*, is at least as much a comedy of objects. A room and a costume are the subjects of the opening exchange between Figaro and his bride, and the great scenes focus on a chair and a sheet, on a window and a closet door concealing a noisy object, on a ribbon and a pin, on all the papers in Figaro's pocket, on a single paper that cannot be read, and of course on the great procession of masqueraders, the darkened garden, the trees, the pavilions, and the torches. Things are the effective powers in Beaumarchais's world.[18]

But is not the spoken word precisely such a powerful object in Beaumarchais's play? "With *God-dam* in England, you lack for nothing anywhere," Figaro expounds in a famous speech that had originally been hissed in *Le Barbier de Séville* and then enthusiastically received when transferred to the more suitable atmosphere of *Le Mariage de Figaro*. "Do you want to try a nice fat hen? enter a tavern, and just make this gesture at the waiter. (*He turns a spit.*) *God-dam!* they bring you a piece of salted beef without bread" (3.5; p. 433). Curious throughout Figaro's whole rhapsody is that *God-dam* both fails and succeeds: it never communicates a meaning, but it always evokes a warranted response: "Do you meet one of those lovely lasses who go daintily mincing, eyes lowered, elbows to the rear, and hips gently wriggling? put your fingers coquettishly all together on your mouth. Ah! *God-dam!* she straps you one quick as any seamstress. Proof that she understands" (ibid.).

Written words are the worst. Written messages always go astray, and precisely thereby exert their force. None of them is properly signed: the count forgets to sign Chérubin's commission, Suzanne's coded message to the count is sealed with her pin, and of course the contract, to be completely honest, would need to be signed "mother" and "son," or at least would need a proper last name from Figaro, who has none.[19] A signature guarantees the ideality of writing, making it a surrogate for a person's voice, captured for all to perceive—especially if the signature is Almaviva (living soul). But the absence of a signatory disturbs both voice and message. A letter that is improperly sent and that goes astray—on this Derrida and Lacan agree—returns us to the essential materiality of the word. Is it *et* or *ou, ou* or *où?*—these are the issues that the document flings back at its readers in Beaumarchais's parody of a meaningless and unenforceable, an *unspeakable*, piece of writing.

Both plots of *Le Mariage de Figaro* concern the enforcement of an agreement. Whereas the written agreement is both illegible and invalid, the count's oral agreement to abandon his seigneurial right proves inescapable. Not the message but the action of pronouncing it prevails. Beaumarchais specifies tones of voice, from the whispers of conspirators all the way to the yelping of the usher in court, as carefully as he does costumes and gestures. Language for him is not a sign system subordinated to a signifier that it shadows; it is in itself one of the realities that structure our existence, his "basic substance," the "cornerstone of his comic dramaturgy."[20]

It is a curious world, this, in which normal priorities are reversed. "If I did not otherwise know it, scoundrel, your physiognomy, which accuses you, would already prove to me that you lie," says the count. But Figaro puts a stop to this verbal attribution of a signifying power to his face by responding, "If it is so, then it is not I who lie, it is my physiognomy" (2.20; p. 421). Acts are ambiguous, objects can be tampered with, looks are fleeting, but the spoken word remains. "I was light in my conduct, it is true, Monseigneur," Chérubin declares, "but never the slightest indiscretion in my words [. . .]" (1.10; p. 398). Beaumarchais's looking glass makes such an argument irrefutable.

The successful characters in the play enforce what Figaro calls their "truest truth" (4.1; p. 452) by controlling reality with words. The great art and wit of dialogue consists in contradicting and mystifying your interlocutor, haunting him in such a way that your own words cannot return to haunt you. Figaro almost gets trapped, for instance, when he covers for Chérubin by claiming to have sprained his ankle jumping out the window. And the count repeatedly falls victim. "Ah! Monseigneur, listen," Fanchette taunts him in front of the assembled company, "every time you come to kiss me, you know you always say, 'If you will love me, little Fanchette, I will give you whatever you want'" (4.5; p. 456). It is easier to undo what has been done than to unsay what has been said. Willy-nilly, the semiotic function of speech here is fully absorbed by the performative, in ways that undermine the commanding rationality to which classical discourse aspires.

The spectrum of *She Stoops to Conquer* leads from impersonation through denial to a revelation of the wordless truth of the heart. That of *The School for Scandal* encompasses chaos and flow, entropy and desire, babble and defiance. *Le Mariage de Figaro*, finally, with its focus on costume and gesture, setting and prop, tone of voice and the act of utterance, ranges from tumult and senseless dispute to silence or the externalized matter of language. And "all e-ends with songs" (5.19; p. 489). Wordsworth eventually made readers familiar with ways that language can be effective without communicating or even without having a meaning:

> Whate'er the song the maiden sang
> As if her song could have no ending . . . ,
> The music in my heart I bore,
> Long after it was heard no more.
>   ("The Solitary Reaper," lines 25–32)

Such a language need not even belong to humanity. It could be the voice of nature herself: "Black drizzling crags that spake by the wayside" (*Prelude* 6.631). The great farces of the prerevolutionary decades remain resolutely social in their milieu and do not yet attribute transcendent powers to a guiding spirit of nature. But they all probe beyond the limits of what the community can know and say.

Their silences and negations enact resistance to imposed norms and characters. They affirm the rights of man to the pursuit of happiness.

In this sense the innate theatricality of language as performance conquers the paradoxes of representation that Diderot so beautifully formulated but could not resolve. And in this sense, likewise, *Le Mariage de Figaro* can be said to participate in the same project as *The School for Scandal* and indeed to complete it. From the calumny speech in *Le Barbier de Séville* onward, the Figaro trilogy can well be considered a school for scandal. Indeed, Beaumarchais teaches a more radical lesson than Sheridan's conversion of scandal into eros. By moralizing *Le Mariage de Figaro* and following it with a tearjerker in defense of conjugal infidelity, illegitimate children, and sibling incest, he encourages us to believe that scandal, quite simply, doesn't exist. The characters themselves have no consciousness; even when not actually daydreaming, they are left perpetually confused by the mad action. And none of them, not the count, nor even Figaro, can successfully stage-manage the comedy by himself: "Chance has done better than us all, my little one: So goes the world; you work, you plan, you arrange on one side; fortune achieves on the other" (4.1; p. 452). But the action, as "read" by the audience, is as fully transparent, naive, and free from mystery as Primrose's narration without retrospect in *The Vicar of Wakefield*.

The more material the language and the action become, the more the characters evaporate into the effervescence of farce. Once again, then, we see contradictory forces at work in the period. Early eighteenth-century urbanity knows only relative qualities; in the great chain of being body merges without interruption into mind. Not so in the comic conflicts of Goldsmith, Sheridan, and Beaumarchais. They assault the genial core of eighteenth-century diction. Tony Lumpkin's drinking scene (1.2) turns what his companions call gentility into airy spirits (the Three Pigeons) and erotic physicality (Bett Bouncer); Joseph Surface distills from linguistic polish an unction that deprives urbanity of its substance; and Figaro's glibness, by relegating the flowery aura to castles in Spain, purifies the original core of urbanity—the jargon of the cit who is in the know.[21] Closely related as the latter two plays are, consequently, Sheridan's looks nostalgically backward toward obsolete idealisms (religion, hierarchy, love), whereas Beaumarchais's faces ahead toward revolutionary materialisms. Thus do the farces bestow upon us the problem of rethinking the relationship between body and spirit in our period. The most sensational and influential literary text of the period focuses precisely on this relationship. Consequently, it is to *Tristram Shandy* that I now turn.

CHAPTER ELEVEN

Sterne's Stories

O ye POWERS! (for powers ye are, and great ones too)—which enable mortal man to tell a story worth the hearing,—that kindly shew him, where he is to begin it,—and where he is to end it,—what he is to put into it,—and what he is to leave out,—how much of it he is to cast into shade,—and whereabouts he is to throw his light!—Ye, who preside over this vast empire of biographical freebooters, and see how many scrapes and plunges your subjects hourly fall into;—will you do one thing?

Tristram Shandy 3.23

From among all the works of its era, *Tristram Shandy* was uniquely influential. Yet its uniqueness remains a disquieting problem for the literary historian.[1] Not only does the novel compose a class of one, but so likewise do its three most apparent offshoots, *Jacques le fataliste*, *Wilhelm Meisters Wanderjahre*, and *Sartor Resartus*. To the extent that there is a "line" or "school" of Sterne, it descends down byways of European literature, through Jean Paul and Hoffmann to the early works of Stifter, or through Foscolo to Tarchetti. And to the extent that unquestionably major novelists drew explicitly on Sterne, such as in the copy of Trim's flourish that stands at the head of Balzac's *Peau de chagrin* or the Aged Parent's fortifications in Dickens's *Great Expectations*, they risked normalizing him into something resembling an amiable humorist.[2] Whereas the tradition has made Goldsmith's achievements almost invisible by fully absorbing them, it has parried Sterne's thrusts without blunting their vigor. He therefore retains a fascination and a mystery for critics that other authors of the period have lost.[3]

Sterne's writing grows out of a familiar Lockean epistemology. It respects not only the surface structure of associations, but more importantly the deep structure of the urbane sublime, based on relativism and omnicomparability. "Things are great or small by comparison," as Sterne preached in one sermon (*Sermons*, sermon 15; 1: 251), and this entails as a consequence "that the supreme good, like any other good, is of a relative nature" (sermon 29; 2: 140). In drawing this conclusion Sterne passes from an epistemology, or logic of knowledge, to a psychology, or logic of the soul: "and, consequently, the enjoyment of it must require some qualification in the faculty . . . something antecedent in the disposition and temper, which will render that good a good to that individual" (ibid.). No ordering of the novel will ever be definitive, but mine takes its cue from this passage, or bridge, from epistemology to psychology. Sterne's hobbyhorse drives rational knowledge toward the camp of emotion and feeling.

The old urbane tolerance of contradictions remains an ideal. But Sterne speaks of urbanity only in contexts that test it emotionally by conjoining it with beggary, forcing it to choose between two equally polluted paths, or, in general, carrying it to excess.[4] In French contexts, above all, feelings run high and threaten to overwhelm all the sweet reasonableness of Lockean reason: think of the Sorbonne disputation, the choplogic of the French posts, and the unanswerably laconic debates of the *lits de justice*. Yet these *lits*, and the French domain in general, are also a locus of amours and a desirable refuge from Northern frigidity. York is in the Danelaw, and Sterne signals his novel's direction early on by killing off the Danish jester who is also the eponymous minister of the place (Yorick being, in effect, York with an I in the middle). Recognizing that lying-in at home can prove dangerous to the race, the novel is under way toward a new dispensation. Beyond reason and fact, and toward story: such could be Sterne's motto.[5]

The drive toward emotional narrative is ever-present in Sterne's sermons.[6] A sermon is a piece of reasoning. But its effect varies with the disposition and temper of its listeners. Yorick's sermon drives Trim to distraction by reminding him of his brother's plight in the dungeons of the Inquisition. Walter endeavors to palliate the despair by assigning the discourse to the realm of imagination: "I tell thee, *Trim*, again, quoth my father, 'tis not an historical account, 'tis only a description" (*Tristram Shandy* 2.17; p. 162). Slop—a foolish Catholic who does not know how to listen to a Protestant sermon—would deny truth to the exemplum altogether, with the implication that a true history should be an antinovel or a story against stories: "'Tis only description, honest man, quoth *Slop*, there's not a word of truth in it." But, "—That's another story, replied my father" (ibid.). Story differs from history, but it is not necessarily less true. Properly understood, an exemplum moves away from the pedantic truisms of philosophy and the facts of history toward the truths of the heart: "Such an example, I say, as this, is of more universal use, speaks truer to the heart, than all the heroic precepts which the pedantry of philosophy has to offer" (*Sermons*, sermon 15; 1: 249).[7] In a century of wars and religious controversies history can become too painful to face: the truths that console and save arise from the realm of fiction.

In writing about *Tristram Shandy* one can build on powerful readings by earlier critics. I single out here Richard Lanham's account of the novel's roots, Eric Rothstein's of its organization, and Sigurd Burckhardt's of its tendency.[8] As the novel's finest critics to date, all three authors stress aspects of play: the ludic tradition, the interplay and loose adjustment of parts, the parodic law of gravity. But their readings remain partial in the way that they parcel out among them what is central to all of them, the novel's temporality, its past (Lanham), present (Rothstein), and future (Burckhardt). In attempting to synthesize the spirit of these three readings, I posit Sterne's playfulness, which I do not discuss again because many others have discussed it so well. But I also view the novel as something other than mere game. Not for Sterne the suspensive play of the gothic, nor, certainly, the free-wheeling yet ultimately anxious strategies of farce, which he decisively rejects in chapter 15 of volume 5: "Had this volume been a farce, which, unless every one's life and opinions are to be looked upon as a farce as well as mine, I see no reason to suppose" (443, and cf. the imprecation against "farcy" in 5.1; p. 408). While the novel seems to be thrown whimsically together from bits and pieces, its fragments convey the aura of overflowings from a divinely ordered whole and carry with them the constant impetus to interpretation and hermeneutic reintegration.[9] I want to try trusting Tristram's view (3.23) that disorganization is a problem rather than an achievement. The novel then appears as the consequent search for a narrative economy, rather in the way that the problem of sensibility provoked the search for a psychic economy. The parts need to be distributed so as to tell a whole story. *Tristram Shandy* is not a connected narrative, of course, but it does incorporate stories, in whole or in part, on the way toward figuring out how to tell its central tale.[10] It might be called an integrative novel—not an integrated one, but one that keeps the aim of integration in view. It builds bridges, coordinating elements, forms, and levels of discourse that simpler narratives filter out. Finally, in the last half of the last chapter, it succeeds in doing once the one thing that crowns its uniqueness—to tell a synoptic story.

We need then to begin examining what constitutes a story for Sterne. What is its mode, what are its parts—its ends and beginnings and middles—what kind of knowledge does it provide, what alternative to outmoded rationalism? From the storytelling we can move to the novel that tells the story—its shape, its genre, its relation to some of its forebears. And then we will return to the story that the novel successfully tells, tracking the novel's fulfillment and the inimitable model that it transmits to posterity.

Knots and Threads

> L——d! said my mother, what is all this story about?—A COCK and a BULL, said Yorick—And one of the best of its kind, I ever heard. (9.33; p. 809)

It would be hard to imagine a criterion according to which any of the novel's stories, this one included, is among the best of its kind. If we consider the cock-and-bull story to be the novel's consummation, we impose an odd teleology that takes the chance end of an unconcluded novel as its goal. But in a class of one, fulfillment and therefore teleology take on a new meaning. After surveying the ludic forebears described by Lanham, the period's procedures of analogy and modification that Rothstein lays bare—as applied with Sterne's characteristic constant interchange of literal and figurative, thematic image and plot motif—and Burckhardt's law of gravity—the tendency of all things in the novel to sink and to lose thrust as they do so—something else still remains to be examined: the novel's historicity, its movement or intentionality, as it processes its materials and generates its meanings through the life of its forms. In a novel where "shut the door" is an open invitation to the "curious and inquisitive" to eavesdrop (1.4; pp. 5–6), there is naturally no closure. But it becomes possible to speak of an open teleology that lies in the activation of possibilities and not in the perfected repetition of a type or mode.[11] That is why its unique non-ending can function as a model disclosure.

In arguing that the novel's end is the key to (or perhaps the keyhole through which we can glimpse) its aim, I will merely be applying to it Sterne's own view of teleology as we find it in his sermons:

> Some, indeed, from a superficial view of this representation of things, have atheistically inferred,—that because there was so much of lottery in this life,— . . . that the providence of GOD stood neuter and unconcerned in their several workings, leaving them to the mercy of time and chance to be furthered or disappointed as such blind agents directed. Whereas in truth the very opposite conclusion follows. For consider,—if a superior intelligent Power did not sometimes cross and overrule events in this world,—then our policies and designs in it would always answer

according to the wisdom and stratagem in which they were laid, and every cause, in the course of things, would produce its natural effect without variation. Now, as this is not the case, it necessarily follows . . . that there is some other cause which mingles itself in human affairs, and governs and turns them as it pleases; which cause can be no other than the First Cause of all things, and the secret and overruling providence of that Almighty GOD. . . . For undoubtedly,—as I said, it should seem but suitable to nature's laws, that the race should ever be to the swift,—and the battle to the strong;—it is reasonable that the best contrivances and means should have best successes;—and since it often falls out otherwise in the case of man, where the wisest projects are overthrown,—and the most hopeful means are blasted, and time and chance happen to all;—you must call on the Deity to untie this knot:— . . . in respect of GOD's providence overruling in these events, it were profane to call them chance, for they are pure designation. (*Sermons*, sermon 8; 1: 131–33)[12]

Designation reinterprets accidents as signs and thus establishes a hermeneutic teleology; that is, it rejects predictable mechanical determination in favor of a sense of the end as that which guides our understanding of the whole, from its beginning. The integrative word available in English that covers the whole span from beginning to teleological aim and hermeneutic understanding is "conception": the end provides us our conception (understanding) of the conception (purpose) that proves to have been at work from the conception (origin). As we shall see, it is not entirely by chance that the end and the beginning of the novel both tell cock-and-bull stories about problematic conceptions: the final cause is also the First Cause, and only the delivery can reveal the hidden truth of insemination. And yet the end cannot be given from the start by any kind of predestination, lest the itinerary be collapsed into the mere prehistory of a foregone conclusion. "Honor thy father and mother" must, to be sure, be the conception of a story concerned to discover all that can be known about a conception; but Walter, Yorick, and Toby all err in asking Trim to repeat the Commandment instantaneously, upon a "word of command" (5.32; p. 469), as if founding causes are always known immediately and without reflection. Trim understands the Commandment better, for he can only arrive at his end (which is not an ultimate end, but the fifth of ten), as if serendipitously, by beginning at the beginning (5.32). He really knows it because he doesn't know it by itself, but only in context. We must learn, like Trim, to conceive our causes.

Going straight to the point gets you nowhere. The straight line is either a mystery, "the path-way for Christians to walk in!" (6.40; p. 572), or, more often, a closeout, as in

——————————————————— Shut the door. ———————————

(1.4; p. 6)

or, "drop the curtain, *Shandy*—I drop it—Strike a line here across the paper, *Tristram*—I strike it" (4.10; p. 336). Sterne flaunts his lines at us, as he does so many of the chimeras that beset the human imagination. But lines are bloodless abstractions. (Sterne's countless dashes, as in the above quotation, are little lines that emblematize the failure of directness by inconclusively interrupting a portion of utterance.) The line of causes or the chain of associations fragments a story into its parts, giving us something more like a vector analysis than like an integrated path, motions rather than meanings. The line is the mystified, metaphorical reduction of the stories that we experience.[13]

In actuality, the course of life is jagged and roundabout, governed by the freaks and capricious buffetings of association (6.40; p. 570). Providence works secretly within, not in a line that all can see, but as a thread that is woven into the fabric of human destinies. (Goethe's Ottilie may have learned this lesson from Sterne.) Of the many chapters that Sterne promises to write (4.9; p. 335), two that he withholds are the chapter of wishes (remembered at 3.1; p. 186) and the chapter of knots: purpose and its entanglements remain hidden. "You must call on the Deity to untie this knot," as the last-quoted sermon says, for human reason stretches only to "cutting the knot . . . instead of untying it" (4.7; p. 332, Walter Shandy apropos of Toby's purported demonstration of divine providence). However "intricate are the mases of this labyrinth!" (2.3; p. 103), however much the author finds himself "entangled on all sides of this mystick labyrinth" (6.37; p. 565), it is "nonsense to break the thread" of discourse, particularly when it is, as here (5.3; p. 422), a discourse on last things, death and divine providence. A story without a thread is mere burlesque: "as an appendage to seamstressy, the thread-paper might be of some consequence to my mother,—of none to my father, as a mark in *Slawkenbergius*" (3.42; p. 285).

But Tristram is compounded differently from Slawkenbergius: "Whenever my brains come to be dissected, you will perceive, without spectacles, that [my father] has left a large uneven thread, as you sometimes see in an unsalable piece of cambrick, running along the whole length of the web, and so untowardly, you cannot so much as cut out a ✽✽ . . . , but it is seen or felt" (6.33; p. 558). What Cervantes calls "the carded, twisted, and reeled thread" (*Don Quixote* 1.28: "e rastrillado, torcido y aspado hilo") of a story may be "unravelled" at the end by "the teeth of time" (*Tristram Shandy* 7.21; p. 607). But the teller's or interpreter's proper activity is the more delicate one of disengaging the thread of meaning without destroying the texture:

> But this rich bale is not to be open'd now; except a small thread or two of it, merely to unravel the mystery of my father's stay at AUXERRE.
> —As I have mentioned it—'tis too slight to be kept suspended; and when 'tis wove in, there's an end of it. (7.27; p. 618)

As the blissful end of the journey to France approaches, allegorical images of disentangling and reweaving accumulate: "a sun-burnt daughter of Labour rose up from the groupe . . . ; her hair . . . was tied up in a knot, all but a single tress. . . . Tie me up this tress instantly, said Nannette, putting a piece of string into my hand—It taught me to forget I was a stranger—The whole knot fell down— We had been seven years acquainted. . . . 'the duce take that slit!' . . . I would have given a crown to have sew'd it up—Nannette would not have given a sous" (7.43; pp. 649–51). And another appears as the end of the whole novel approaches: "My uncle *Toby* laid down his pipe as gently upon the fender, as if it had been spun from the unravellings of a spider's web—" (9.31; p. 803). This is a proper respect for the providential complexities of life.

By gathering up all these threads, we have moved toward the delicate, hermeneutic teleology of the novel. Providence and chance stand in league over against necessity, and in the chapter of chances (4.9) providence works, not through calculated secondary causes, but through the minute accidents that ply their inconspicuous path through experience. The end of volume 6 dreams of a linear narration, but the opening of volume 8 (which was written before volume 7) corrects the dream by depicting "straight lines, and stoical distances" as the death of imagination in the frigid North (8.1; p. 655). Ratiocination, which is linear and stepwise, is neither the order of real experience nor the truth of stories that live. The turn from rationalist epistemology to psychology makes meaning not a "heavy moral" that rests on the "vicious taste . . . of reading straight forwards" (1.20; pp. 66, 65), but a continually emergent conception that floats atop the narrative. Teleology is not far from cast of mind, a flexible guiding principle rather than a rigidly determining one.

To a certain degree, consciousness was always considered to be a retrospect and stock-taking. For Locke it is discretely accumulative, as perception is added to perception to furnish the storehouse of the mind. For Leibniz, who is closer to Sterne in this respect, the never-ending stream of *petites perceptions* that strike us day and night, awake and asleep, become cognitions whenever the mind halts long enough to take notice of them. But no one before Sterne had so rigorously scrutinized the temporality of consciousness. Plunged in the tide of experience, consciousness tries to stop and take stock, but it is never freed from movement. It is difficult to separate from story, that is, from the movement of its objects. That is the true meaning of what critics often refer to as the double time-scheme of the novel, which encompasses not just two speeds, but two kinds of time. The narrated time is ever-present but broken into discontinuous and inauthentic fragments, for the narrator can shift at will from one piece of his history to another. Meanwhile, underneath, the narrator's time passes without interruption, but normally unnoticed. He becomes aware of himself, his body, and his world at moments when the narrative is interrupted or blocked. In *Tristram Shandy*, as in a play, a pause in the action is a moment of reflection, and, as in Sheridan's plays, reflection gives access to the continuum that grounds all possible experiences.[14] *Tristram Shandy* may indeed be the first autobiographical fiction that does not treat the events as warning exempla or present the narrator as a judging consciousness at a remove from his past experience. Previous autobiography had always separated life and opinions, but here they come close to merging in a book whose subject is Tristram's conceptions.

We may look, then, at Sterne's endings to see how understanding is born:

> I danced myself into Perdrillo's pavillion, where pulling a paper of black lines, that I might go on straight forwards, without digression or parenthesis, in my uncle Toby's amours—
> I begun thus—
>
> END of the SEVENTH VOLUME
>
> (7.43; p. 651)

The ideal beginning of understanding would be a cutting off from all that precedes; from the confused train of thoughts and feelings it would abstract the black lines of a cold literalism. "—But softly—" the companion volume corrects,

> for in these sportive plains, and under this genial sun, where . . . every step that's taken, the judgment is surprised by the imagination, I defy, notwithstanding all that has been said upon *straight lines** [Sterne's footnote states: *Vid. Vol. VI, p. 570] in sundry pages of my book—I defy the best cabbage planter that ever existed . . . to go on cooly, critically, and canonically, planting his

cabbages one by one, in straight lines, and stoical distances . . . in this fertile land of chivalry and romance, where I now sit, un-skrewing my ink-horn to write uncle Toby's amours, and with all the meanders of JULIA's track in quest of her DIEGO, in full view of my study window. (8.1; p. 655)

Sterne's pauses do not sharpen the focus, but complicate it as the narrator takes renewed cognizance of space, of body and soul (erotic cabbages and stoical distances), and of his own situation. Heidegger speaks in this connection of a *Sammlung in den Ort*, but the place where Sterne re-collects himself is the irregular expanse of the living earth rather than Heidegger's focal hearth. Imagination overtakes judgment: pausing for thought brings awareness, not order and certainly not decorous syntax. Sterne removes us from the mechanism of habitual associations in order to plunge us into the swirl of life.[15]

The end of every chapter is such a turbulent pause.[16] "To the end of the chapter" is Sterne's expression for continuing along an unswerving course (1.10, p. 22; 8.22, p. 701; 9.13, p. 763). The end of the chapter interrupts the course and thus frees imagination from habit: "Imagine to yourself;—but this had better begin a new chapter" (2.8; p. 120). Tristram's ideal is to join with the reader in sympathetic communion over the events of the story; he hopes "to halve this matter amicably [with the reader], and leave him something to imagine, in his turn, as well as yourself" (2.11; p. 125).[17] But usually he is more truculent. He may bait the reader, challenging inventiveness:

> If I thought you was able to form the least judgment or probable conjecture to yourself, of what was to come in the next page,—I would tear it out of my book.
>
> END of the FIRST VOLUME
>
> (1.25; p. 89)

Or, more typically, he may provoke a blush. The normal Sternian aposiopesis is, self-evidently, not an opportunity for logical processes to take over, and not often an invitation to blithe fancy. Rather, it interrupts the mechanisms that drive us, the *idées fixes* and *idées reçues* that ordinarily beset our brains. Pauses lower the sights from reason or understanding—pure mentalism—to imagination, the matter of mind:

> 'Tis all . . . devils' dung— . . . I would not touch it for the world— —
>
> O Tristram! Tristram! cried Jenny.

O Jenny! Jenny! replied I, and so went on with the twelfth chapter.

CHAP. XII.

—"Not touch it for the world" did I say—
Lord, how I have heated my imagination with this metaphor!

CHAP. XIII.

Which shews, let your reverences and worships say what you will of it (for as for *thinking*—all who *do* think—think pretty much alike, both upon it and other matters)—LOVE is certainly, at least alphabetically speaking, one of the most [there ensues an alphabet of love]. . . . But in short 'tis of such a nature [that] "You can scarce," said [my father], "combine two ideas together upon it, brother Toby, without an hypallage"—What's that? cried my uncle Toby.
The cart before the horse, replied my father—. (8.11–13; pp. 670–72)

If all share a view of love at the end of the chapter, it is that the horse of the passions goes before the chariot of the soul. And in this case, that's where things belong. The horse in point is no hobbyhorse but the Widow Wadman, as capricious and beloved a nag as Yorick's horse in volume 1: "She stood however ready harnessed and caparisoned at all points to watch accidents" (8.13; p. 672). At the end of the chapter a healthy animal thinks of accidents, not of logical consequences or artificial orderings like the alphabet.[18]

Consciousness in Sterne is thus the antithesis of reason. Reason is order, logic, logos. Nothing is so irritating as an interruption, for that calls attention to the horizon limiting the power of reason: "Now there is nothing in this world I abominate worse, than to be interrupted in a story." "Speaking of my book as a *machine*, and laying my pen and ruler down cross-wise upon the table, in order to gain the greater credit to it—I swore it should be kept a going at that rate these forty years." But the interruption is inescapable: "DEATH himself knocked at my door" (7.1; p. 576).[19] Self-consciousness, like the hot chestnut in Phutatorius's private parts, halts the progress of thought with a painful warmth best cured by the proper application of printed paper, that is, of language in its material form (4.27–28). Blush and all, Sterne's self-consciousness is a mode of participation, not of detachment: "For consider, Sir, as every man chuses to be present at the shaving of his own beard . . . and unavoidably sits overagainst himself the whole time it is doing, in case he has a hand in it—the Situation, like all others, has notions of her own to put into the brain" (9.13; p. 763).

The proper objects of thought are irregularities and minute individualities. Gestures typically prompt a pause for thought—above all in *Sentimental Journey*—and the narrator who goes halves with the reader pauses particularly over half-gestures and partial nuances, below the level of conceptualization, such as Trim's "angle of 85 degrees and a half" (*Tristram Shandy* 2.17; p. 140). The novel is rich in such critical half-tones that "shew us . . . how the arts and sciences mutually befriend one another" (ibid.). As "a man of science" Tristram applies "the painter's scale" to rate outlines, composition, coloring, expression ("13 and a half") and design (1.9; p. 16); discourse stops "for four minutes and a half;—five had been fatal to it" (3.1; p. 186); Toby looks "for half a minute" (6.28; p. 548); and of course the nuns of Andoüillets with their mules and Tristram with his ass save their souls by dividing words in half (7.25; p. 613, and 7.32; p. 632). One of Sterne's neologisms captures perfectly the aim of such hovering halfway between thought and observation, in its most characteristic form as the body's imagination: "(as all the blood in his body seemed to rush up into his face, as I told you) he must have redden'd, pictorially and scientintically speaking, six whole tints and a half, if not a full octave above his natural colour" (3.5; pp. 191–92). The other, opposing neologism, connoting the divorce of science and art, or mind and body, is "philosophating" (7.38; p. 640), though Tristram's abstraction here is fortunately interrupted after "half an hour." Scientintical philosophation would be a grandly Rabelaisian way of describing Sterne's critique of pure reason.

Sterne regularly turns his ridicule on immortal essences, bodiless minds, idealized emotions. ("*If you will turn your eyes inwards upon your mind*," Walter Shandy pontificates in a pseudophilosophical discourse upon time, until Toby interrupts by exclaiming, "You puzzle me to death," 3.18; p. 224). Walter foolishly dotes on abstractions and èven copulates "out of *principle*" (2.13; p. 134), yet, says Tristram, he always called passions *ass* (8.31; p. 716). (Tristram is wrong here, for Walter continues to speak of "passion," 8.34; p. 723, and 9.33; pp. 806–7). Such substitutions pile up: Toby can only conceive of things in material representation, but his materials reduce and etherealize war, leaving him the most peaceable of mortals. The pugnacious Walter, on the other hand, seems to have difficulty distinguishing words from weapons. Hobbyhorses can be either mental or bodily tics, and Sterne's own hobbyhorse, his pen, is clearly both at once. Depending on one's penchant one can lean to one side or the other, as in this exchange between matter and energy:

> So much motion, continues he, (for he was very corpulent)—is so much unquietness; and so much rest, by the same analogy, is so much of heaven.
>
> Now, I (being very thin) think very differently; and that so much of motion, is so much of life, and so much of joy—and that to stand still, or get on but slowly, is death and the devil— (7.13; pp. 592–93)

Such altercations are among the commonest features of the novel, and they lead to no resolution (see Van Ghent, *The English Novel* 97). For the end of *Tristram Shandy* is to forestall ends and to give their due to both the warring factions of the human personality. There are no autonomous realms either of body or of spirit: "A Man's body and his mind, . . . are exactly like a jerkin, and a jerkin's lining;—rumple the one—you rumple the other" (3.4; p. 189). "The soul and body are joint-sharers in every thing they get" (9.13; p. 764). Sterne's metaphysics rejects any Cartesian dualism.[20]

Thus do the continuities of Sterne's text provide the ground under the rift that we have seen between Sheridan and Beaumarchais. Sterne keeps both the idealism of passions and the materialism of actions in suspense. For Tristram mind is always desire: his opening words are "I wish," and he has uncanny penetration of the way that desire contaminates all our reasoning processes. And body for him is always pure action: he has equal penetration of the ways that our gestures and movements escape from the control of our intentions. Both mind and body are defective modes of existence—a future without presence, a present without orientation—and Tristram's obsession with the multiplicity of the past is a reflex of his inability or reluctance to link present (body, action) with future (mind, desire). The farces explore the deficiencies of one or the other. Yet the deficiencies are also what allow the two to coexist in Sterne's curious and characteristic state of combative disengagement. For a body without desires—and this is surely the trait that links most of Sterne's very disparate men, the variously asexual Shandys as well as the selfless Yorick and Trim—does not ever really run athwart of a mind without presence (a trait that could be considered to link the shadowy and back-room women).

Sterne shares with Sheridan and Beaumarchais a belief in time as an inner sense that is the constitutive category of human experience; he differs from them in treating time not primarily as it is felt (age versus youth, energy versus aimless bustle or sloth, as in Sheridan) nor as it is manifested in behavior and sedimented in objects (as in Beaumarchais), but rather as what might be called a preconception. We cannot conceive of time without getting lost, yet we retain a sense of the unmeasurable directedness of experience in general; this obscure sense allows us to distinguish between the modalities of present and future, or body and mind, to hold them in suspense and, ultimately, to reconcile them.

At this point, the relationship between Sterne and Goldsmith, whom posterity regularly linked together, may appear more problematic than that between Sterne and Sheridan or Beaumarchais. For Sterne's sprawling comprehensiveness seems to lie at the other extreme from Goldsmith's idyllic reductions. We have seen how the repressions and negations of Goldsmith's narrator contribute in essential ways to creating the notion of an experience: by neglecting loose ends such as the tangential adventures of subordinate characters and by suppressing all comparisons back and forth along the time line, he becomes able to disengage a single thread and follow it through its various modes from beginning to end. Tristram, by contrast, forgets nothing. As his narrative grows increasingly comprehensive, it lays its comprehensibility on the line. The problem becomes ever more acute in the later installments; here Tristram's birth moves to the background, epistemology (birth and naming) modulates into psychology (war and love)—the open window in the unfinished *Tristrapaedia* (5.16 and 26) is the transition—and, in ways that we shall see, the relativism of Enlightenment thought gives way to protodialectical contrasts. By the later parts of the novel the gestures toward closure seem futile, straws in the wind that are not taken seriously even by the narrator at his most credulous:

> —But this rich bale is not to be open'd now; except a small thread or two of it, merely to unravel the mystery of my father's stay at AUXERRE.
> —As I have mentioned it—'tis too slight to be kept suspended; and when 'tis wove in, there's an end of it. (7.27; p. 618)

Yet the next chapter begins, "—Now this is the most puzzled skein of all" (7.28; p. 621). The very last chapter, before introducing the cock-and-bull story, recurs to the problems of beginnings and endings as it pits praise of procreation against Walter's exaltation of murder. As the extremes push ever further apart, the totality of experience encompassed in Goldsmith's narrative becomes ever more difficult to conceive. Yet, miraculously, this chapter, and with it the novel, turns back to story at the end. My analysis will likewise turn now from consciousness and its entanglements to stories, their contexts, and their articulations, with the aim of eventually bringing Sterne and Goldsmith back together again.

Stories Before Sterne

Sterne uses words with abandon. He liberates speech from all attempts to confine it. The written word, fixed on paper, is a travesty, good for lighting pipes or curing testicles (4.26 and 28). But in the speaking, a sermon acquires the personal resonance that it neither has nor was intended to have as a written text. Even in the mechanical act of translation words come alive, for colorful elaborations and double entendres cannot be kept out of the English of "Slawkenbergius's Tale," and other innuendos are refracted from the English back into the Latin. ("Nudâ acinaci" and "vaginam . . . habilem," vol. 4; p. 290, are conventional Latin, but a proper rendering cannot prevent improper English associations from creeping in.) Acting in the spirit of Trim's flourish, he flings defiance at all those who would keep language conventionally tied down to the impersonal page.

Yet like so much in *Tristram Shandy*, its free speech is shadowed by death. The novel opens with conception followed almost too quickly by birth, and threatens to subside into a lifelessly routine account of setting and circumstance: "In the same village where my father and my mother dwelt, dwelt also . . ." (1.7; p. 10). It really only takes wing with its second beginning, the account of Yorick's death. Yorick was the public, official, so to speak, canonical Sterne. By killing him off so early, Sterne makes *Tristram Shandy* into a kind of posthumous novel, liberating it from the rigors of conventional form. The narrator becomes a ghostly ventriloquist and—a creation perhaps unparalleled in the history of fiction—an omniscient first-person reporter, with perfect recall even of scenes at which he was never present (cf. Hamburger, "My Uncle Toby"). Sterne comes alive, disseminated in bits and pieces into most of the novel's men (cf. Dowling, "Tristram's Phantom Audience").

The living words, then, spring from dead forebears. Sterne's iconoclasm needs to be understood, more than it has been, in relation to the icons that it breaks. Unlike its rootless descendants, *Tristram Shandy* stakes out a definite field of battle. Not for Sterne the bizarreness that makes *Jacques le fataliste* reach out to the metaphysical, nor the play of inclusion and exclusion that renders dubious the ontological status of the stories in *Wilhelm Meisters Wanderjahre*.

Tristram's village is positioned even though unnamed; it is not Carlyle's Weissnichtswo. Sterne's undertaking can usefully be understood not just as a defiant antinovel, but as a *prise de position*, through a comparison with his two most immediate predecessors, Fielding and Johnson.

Against a backdrop of scholastic learning and of a greater world recently at war, the great Author's freedom unfolds in a restricted setting.[21] "By [the] word *world*," as Tristram says at the outset, "I would be understood to mean no more of it, than a small circle described upon the circle of the great world, of four *English* miles" (1.7; p. 10). "Nature, though she sport[s]—she sport[s] within a certain circle," and even when the novel moves outward to France, it remains bounded by the awful imprecation *"Make them like unto a wheel"* (7.13; p. 592). Within that Shandy circle are found a weak father, an uncle retired from the military, a brother with whom there is latent competition for the family wealth, a shadowy mother, a formidable aunt (Aunt Dinah), a preacher and pedagogue, and some unreliable servants. The characters differ notably in prominence and in value, but in the distribution of roles there is considerable agreement with that other sprawling eighteenth-century microcosm, the Western family of *Tom Jones*. Fielding's novel, of course, migrates to London, whereas in *Tristram Shandy* a false pregnancy (a misconception) forecloses that expansion from the start. Sterne never mentions the recently deceased Fielding, but one of his great achievements lies in freeing the novel from the model of the older author. Sterne's central subject could be termed the matter of Fielding.[22]

Both Fielding and Sterne begin with the forms of the picaresque. And both recognize that picaresque is a debased version of romance. Fielding aims to reinvent picaresque with artistic shape, narrative refinement, and cultural resonance so as to restore it to the dignity of romance and, indeed, of epic. Sterne, by contrast, both distills and reduces the old genres. The romance of the two lovers gets itself told in a page (7.31; pp. 627–28); the story of Trim and the Beguine "contain'd in it the essence of all the love-romances which ever have been wrote since the beginning of the world" (8.22; p. 704); and the very language of romance emerges for brief moments, lowered both figuratively and literally, enriched with diminutives, langorous yet unsustained:

> The day had been sultry—the evening was delicious—the wine was generous—the Burgundian hill on which it grew was steep—a

> little tempting bush over the door of a cool cottage at the foot of
> it, hung vibrating in full harmony with the passions—a gentle air
> rustled distinctly through the leaves—"Come—come, thirsty
> muleteer—come in."
> —The muleteer was a son of Adam. I need not say one word
> more. . . . Slinking behind, he enter'd the little inn at the foot of
> the hill. (7.21; pp. 608–9)

We have seen how Sterne's self-consciousness is an embarrassed
pausing for thought at a point when the various strands of time are
gathered into a knot; here he keeps pausing over a situation such as
is often encountered by Tom Jones, turning Fielding's grand periods
into paratactic pantings. In competition with Fielding, he searches
for an inner psychological truth that will escape from the tragic destinies of the great world. Calling his novel *The Life and Opinions of*
rather than *The History of*, he attacks history in defense of story.

Yet Tristram's stories, as one hardly need point out, bear little
resemblance to Fielding's. They do not distinguish adequately—or
at all—between progression and digression, connection and distinction (that is, wit and judgment), or body and mind (event and significance). The stories attempt articulations—*into* scenes and *of*
meanings—but they get entangled in their own complexities. Consequently they do not organize, discern origins and causes, or get
inside of things. Stories told consecutively—whether inserted narratives like "Slawkenbergius's Tale" (vol. 4), the christening of Francis I's son (4.27), the tale of Amandus and Amanda (7.31), the stories
of Le Fever (6.6–10) and of Trim's brother Tom (9.4–7), or else segments of the main narration such as the incident of Phutatorius's
chestnut (4.27)[23] and Trim's amours with the Beguine (8.19–22)—
mostly concern war or disaster. (Trim's story, the apparent exception, evokes an irrepressible nostalgia for an unrecoverable past.)
The comic tales and incidents, by contrast, are fragmented. The two
major framing stories, Tristram's birth and Toby's amours, set the
tone, and the most striking triumph is perhaps the journey to France
in volume 7, where the antagonist Death gets lost amid all the narrative complications. In a world where a sentence is a struggle or a
condemnation and the end of a sentence is death, comedy presupposes interruption: the story of the king of Bohemia (8.19), a fairy-
tale comic conflict with a happy ending, is never told, and the comic
progress of the abbess of Andoüillets contains its own *mise en*
abyme, the gardener or muleteer who gets lost "in the vortex of his
element" (7.21; p. 610). Abandon becomes abandonment, as Sterne
systematically clears his own path. For Sterne's reductions are also

refinements, his fragmentations also analyses that lead to a reconstituted vision of narrative.

Three patterns of organization come into view as the novel proceeds. The first is Burckhardt's law of gravity, the book's downward tendency, toward matter and the body—for instance, toward mules as bedrock creatures from which there can be no descent (ibid.). This tendency is activated whenever Sterne literalizes metaphors or, as one says (3.23; p. 244), "drops" them. He gladly turns ideas into specks of narrative: Toby would not hurt a fly (2.12; p. 130), flesh is dirt (5.9; p. 435), radical moisture is ditch water (5.40; p. 481). Literalizing stories increasingly prevail as the metaphor of reading as traveling funnels into a travel narrative, as pervasive ideas of combat and sexual jesting issue in the erotic combats between Toby and the Widow Wadman, and in general as Toby, the creature of instinct and material existence, gains in prominence at the expense of Walter, the creature of speculative ideas.

Second, at the same time that it literalizes, *Tristram Shandy* also articulates contrasts with increasing dramatic clarity. Such articulations are both thematic (Walter versus Toby, male versus female, English versus French) and formal (chaotic main narration versus consecutive inserted stories, narration versus authorial intrusion, narrative present versus narrated past). The accumulated contrasts give a sense—again quite different from any in *Jacques le fataliste*— that Tristram lives in an ordered world, no matter how disordered his stories. Events may not be distinct, but meanings increasingly are.

The third pattern that structures the book as a whole, in addition to literalization and articulation, might be called consolidation. Wayne Booth has pointed out how the last chapter brings all the main characters together for the first time in the entire novel.[24] This conclusion fulfills a tendency present from early on. For most volumes of the novel move in a curve from isolation or exclusion toward social collectivities. Volume 1 moves from conception in the privacy of the bedroom (chap. 1) and from the homunculus or fetus (2) to the Sorbonne disputation (20), simultaneous activity above and below stairs (21), and the consoling effect of visitors (25). Volume 2 begins with Toby's history, not even mentioning his servant Trim until chapter 5, and ends with Trim's reading of Yorick's sermon (17), followed by Obadiah's entry (18) and a general discussion of childbirth among the principal men (19). Relinquishing the trajectory from individuals to collectivities, volume 3 moves from things —Walter's India handkerchief (1–6), knots (7–10), forceps (13–17), Toby's smokejack (19–20), hinges and jackboots (21–22)—to people and their bodies—Dr. Slop's nose-bridge (which Toby mistakes for a drawbridge, 23–26), Tristram's nose (26–32), and, in the concluding chapters, family history (33) and Walter's perspective on European culture (36–38). This brings us to "Slawkenbergius's Tale"; from here, at the start of volume 4, the great crisis of Tristram's naming gradually ebbs until it disappears altogether when the characters fall asleep in the middle of the volume (4.15, corresponding exactly in position to 3.20, where the characters also fall asleep); then the volume rises to the great banquet scene (26–30), before concluding atypically with the deaths of Dinah and Bobby and with reflections by the author. Volume 5 features in its first half separate reactions to Bobby's death (Walter's oration in chap. 3, Trim's in 7–9), leading to the exits of Walter (13) and Toby (14); its second half focuses on Walter's reading of the *Tristrapaedia* to the assembled household (30–43), the scene having been prepared by the massed entrance of Toby's forces (23) and subsequently to be punctuated by Slop's waddling in (39). Volume 6, again varying the pattern without fundamentally departing from it, represents growing sociability: it begins with calamity (the burning of Slop's wig, chaps. 3–4) and war and death (the story of Le Fever, 6–9), moves to Toby's war games after chapter 20, declares peace in 29, and enters upon the subject of love, beginning the story of Toby's amours in 36–39. The French journey in volume 7 begins, of course, as a solitary escape and ends with a village festival. Volume 8 is entirely taken up with Toby's and Trim's amours; these gradually gain steam as the parties come closer together, and in the last chapter (35) Mrs. Shandy—active for the first time, having been abandoned in a dark passage in 5.5, and not really remembered in 5.11–12—joins her husband to call on Toby, the visit foreshadowing the general gathering at the end of the last volume. Though the novel could hardly be said to tell the story of socialization, the rhythm of assembly is maintained, with variations, throughout.

The novel thus has a special kind of unity. For totality it substitutes the image of totality. It nostalgically evokes Fielding's norms at the moment when Tristram describes the assembled Shandy family:

> I believe in my soul, (unless my love and partiality to my understanding blinds me) the hand of the supreme Maker and first Designer of all things, never made or put a family together, (in that period at least of it, which I have sat down to write the story of)— where the characters of it were cast or contrasted with so dramatic a felicity as ours was, for this end [i.e., for entertainment]; or in which the capacities of affording such exquisite scenes, and

the powers of shifting them perpetually from morning to night, were lodged and intrusted with so unlimited a confidence, as in the SHANDY-FAMILY. (3.39; p. 279)

The composition here suggests Fielding's principle of dramatic construction based on pairs of antithetical characters, depicted scenically; the "unlimited confidence" of Tristram's "supreme Maker and first Designer" is reminiscent of the comic control of Fielding's narrator; and it seems to me that the phrase "from morning to night" in Tristram's mouth may also signal a yearning toward Fielding's precisely articulated time schemes. Yet the passage also forecasts the organizational principles destined to govern *Tristram Shandy*: narrative literalization, articulation by dramatic contrasts, and the rhythm of assembly. Beginning with conception, then, the novel passes beyond Fielding's ideal of completeness and moves instead toward comprehension. It becomes a self-conscious microcosm in which, though absent, story can be known for what it is. In the for-itself of narrative, as has been written in another context, "the parts or fragments . . . exclude the Logos both as logical unity and as organic totality. But there is, there must be a unity which is the unity *of* this very multiplicity, a whole which is the whole *of* just these fragments: a One and a Whole which would not be the principle but, on the contrary, 'the effect' of the multiplicity and of its disconnected parts."[25] Just when Lord Kames was producing his *Elements of Criticism* (1761), Sterne was schooling readers in the elements of story.

Tristram Shandy shares the fragmented "effect of unity" with its exact contemporary *Rasselas*. By comparing the two books we can continue to highlight the positive and constructive sides of Sterne's imagination. (Sterne was in the middle of the imperfect first draft of volumes 1 and 2 when *Rasselas* was published in April 1759, and the letter to Robert Dodsley of October 1759, in which Sterne speaks of his revisions, mentions *Rasselas* as the model for the physical format of his book.) Like Sterne, Johnson reworked and reduced the matter of Fielding, though Johnson's reduction had more to do with form than with content. Both *Rasselas* and *Tom Jones* fall into three equal parts: in each work the first part, set in a childhood paradise, ends with an escape that cites Milton's Adam (*Tom Jones* 7.2; p. 331: "The world, as *Milton* phrases it, *lay all before him*"; *Rasselas*, chap. 16, p. 47: "I have here the world before me"); the second part contains stories and adventures (in the countryside in Fielding and partly so in Johnson), including a notable evening encounter with a disillusioned hermit; the third part consists of rapidly accumulating incidents and disclosures in the city, concluding with a return up-country.[26] In Johnson, however, as in Sterne, the quest for story collapses from its very idealism: there can be no resolution in either novel of the continual pendulum swings between mind and matter. (Hence the futility of debating whether Rasselas finally returns to the Happy Valley.) Indeed, Rasselas's own failures at eliciting completed life stories from others should warn us sufficiently against wishing to complete his; the ideal of permanence can be equated, as Earl Wasserman points out, with a conclusion in which, for all eternity, nothing is concluded.[27]

Johnson, like Sterne, comes to prefer comprehension over conclusion, as his characters realize when they praise variety in chapter 47. Only in the delirium of imagination is a life story ever completed, whereas consciousness arises, as in Sterne, when an obstacle, an occurrence, an incident, an object interrupts the dream of reason. A mountain intervenes, bringing to Rasselas "the consciousness of his own folly" (chap. 4, p. 11), or a teacup falls, startling Rasselas into awareness of the "obvious" (chap. 4, p. 12; this use of the word approaches its etymological sense, as when Imlac in chapter 10 speaks of "those characteristicks which are alike obvious to vigilance and carelessness," p. 28). Sober, conscious understanding, with all its imperfections, arises from "useful hints . . . obtained by chance" (chap. 4, p. 12) through the collision of mind with matter. At the end, then, *Rasselas*, like *Tristram Shandy*, replaces the epicurean imaginative satisfactions of *Tom Jones* with more astringent, fragmentary images of totality. The characters "return home" to see a sacred marriage of heaven and earth ("the beams of the moon quivering on the water," chap. 44, p. 116);[28] the floods return, but this time in a real spring rather than the magical eternal spring of the Happy Valley. The last chapter, like the end of *The Vanity of Human Wishes*, combines resignation with an upswing whose strength cannot be separated from its indefiniteness: the turn upward and back toward home is an image of what every life should be and none ever entirely is.

One may conjecture that Johnson resented Sterne so bitterly because of the way that Sterne represented his repressed inclinations. Johnson's stoicism aspires to a spiritualizing refinement of matter, attempting to reconcile mind and body without acknowledging the body's role. The perspective is so grandly general, the flux of time so sweepingly cosmic as to reduce physical concerns to insignificance. In the famous poem devoted to Dr. Levet, the doctor's daily round of toil is the grim time of the body, punctuated "By sudden blasts, or slow decline." Yet he dies by neither—"with no throbbing fiery pain, / No cold gradations of decay"—and the perfectly rounded iconic poem, with its descent to "misery's darkest caverns" in the middle stanza and subsequent reascent to bright day, images a transcendent immediacy of the eternal moment: "Death broke at once the vital chain, / And free'd his soul the nearest way." The rhyme at the end echoes the first stanza, and the redemptive "and" is the soft transition that magically repairs all the ravages of time. Leave off the redemption and you have a life little different from Yorick's, except for the pressure of its greater length. The minuteness of daily toil and corporeal struggle was the element in which Johnson lived and which his literary work sought to conquer, yet the strategies of resistance to life—the fragmentary evocation of wholeness, the disproportionate reductions of a whole life to 35 lines of poetry and of these 35 lines to one final line of release—have much in common with Sterne's embrace of life.

The flux of time is the founding problem of both Sterne's and Johnson's novels; "time is not a whole, for the simple reason that it is itself the instance which prevents the whole" (Deleuze, *Proust and Signs* 143). But whereas Johnson tries to reduce time through a cosmic perspective, Sterne reduces it, equally effectively, by dwelling. The two authors are related as telescope to microscope, or as heavenly abode to earthly habitation, the one a type of the other.[29] Time stops for Sterne not in a glimpse of eternity, but in a stilled moment when the heart shines forth: "When *Tom*, an' please your honour, got to the shop, there was nobody in it, but a poor negro girl, with a bunch of white feathers slightly tied to the end of a long cane, flapping away flies—not killing them.—'Tis a pretty picture! said my uncle Toby" (9.6; p. 747). In such pictures, throughout both of Sterne's novels, consciousness captures time for the sympathetic imagination. One such is the unforgotten moment years past when Toby refused to kill a fly (2.12; pp. 130–31); another is the locket with Eliza's picture that Yorick, as he says on the first page of the *Sentimental Journey*, will treasure until death; a third is the imaginary portrait of the captive at the center of the same work. These pictures are cessations of life ("Let me stop and give you a picture of the corporal's apparatus. . . . The corporal— —Tread lightly on his ashes," *Tristram Shandy* 6.25; p. 544), escapes or little deaths whose blanks, like the white pages of 6.38 (pp. 566–67), are to be filled by strokes of the pen or the brush. Sterne's exaltation of Hogarth and Reynolds is surely based, at least in part, on his sense of pictures as small enclosures where, at last, consciousness comes to rest, as it never can for Johnson.[30]

Pictures, Sterne tells us, are composed of the fine lines, shadings, and nuances of a pencil that is ever on the move: pictures are the medium of a work that is progressive and digressive at once (1.22; p. 80). At one point Tristram presents Trim as the figure of linear progress, "without wit or antithesis, or point, or turn, this way or that; but leaving the images on one side, and the pictures on the other, going strait forwards as nature could lead him, to the heart" (5.6; p. 429). But Trim's digressive flourish (9.4; p. 743) later refutes this picture of him as an antipictorial straight man; in the scientintical novel picture and gesture (the point or turn of the body) are more often the roads to the heart. Sterne's contest of line and picture has much in common with Diderot's debates concerning *coup de théâtre* and tableau, as well as with the alternation between picaresque elements and essayistic character sketches in Johnson's Eastern tale. But in Johnson the picture is a tragic enclosure, and the line at least points toward an open future, whereas Sterne's lines, as we have seen, become limits and barriers:

> Could a historiographer drive on his history, as a muleteer drives on his mule,—straight forward;—for instance, from *Rome* all the way to *Loretto*, without ever once turning his head aside either to the right hand or to the left,—he might venture to foretell you to an hour when he should get to his journey's end;—but the thing is, morally speaking, impossible: . . . there are archives at every stage to be look'd into, and rolls, records, documents, and endless genealogies . . . —In short, there is no end of . . . unforeseen stoppages. (1.14; pp. 41–42)

The past rises up, like an unfathered vapor, to block off the road to the future; it is not by accident that *Tristram Shandy*'s greatest offspring are all novels of baffled traveling. But almost at the very end of the novel, in the humble and redemptive story of the imbecile Maria and her goat, we finally find a perfected emblem of the heartfelt moment when soul and body meet to defy both progress and its consequent mutability: "That moment she took her pipe and told me such a tale of woe with it, that I rose up, and with broken and irregular steps walk'd softly to my chaise" (9.24; p. 784).

Even more than history then, Sterne's true antagonist is the movement of time itself; as Martin Battestin has written, Tristram wants "to stop the clock, by which previous narratives had been regulated" and "to release us from the bondage of time."[31] This is the deeper sense of Yorick's early death and of the conception of the book as a posthumous novel. It carries Sterne beyond both Fielding and Johnson, whose stories remain beholden to the passage of days, and brings and finally shows us what constitutes his closeness to Goldsmith. For the affect of Maria's silent tale closely resembles that of the broken teacups and the closemouthed, sad historian of the deserted village. Sterne's chapters are broken and irregular steps toward a tale that never gets told, never can, indeed never should, for the completion of a tale is the end of life.

Toward the end of the novel the breakings grow increasingly violent, as at the segue from the story of Maria and the "excellent inn at Moulins!" (9.24; p. 784) into "CHAP. xxv. When we have got to the end of this chapter (but not before) we must all turn back to the two blank chapters, on the account of which my honour has lain bleeding this half hour—I stop it, by pulling off one of my yellow slippers and throwing it with all my violence to the opposite side of my room" (785). The concluding breakings and turnings back glorify story, but only as a lost art on a blank page, nostalgically sought in a continually receding past. Sterne's incessant flow of talk sounds very remote from Goldsmith, but the two authors are brought together at the moments when Sterne stops or abandons speech. Tristram's microcosm, like the vicar's, is an aesthetic space, beautified through alienation and perfected through its refraction in a consciousness that knows all and judges nothing.[32]

Bull or Cock?

Tristram's dyschrony is the perfect complement to the vicar's unreflected sequentiality: both novels expose the folly of trusting to time. (A deep gulf, by contrast, separates Tristram from his professed imitator, Mackenzie's man of feeling, for whom pity is inseparable from *pietas* toward the past and from pious future intentions.) Tristram's past lies in the unreality of play, and his future is split between the gravitational tendency described by Burckhardt and the iconoclastic intention that I have been outlining. One moment in the story of Maria hints at both futures:

> I swore I would set up for Wisdom and utter grave sentences the rest of my days—and never—never attempt again to commit mirth with man, woman, or child, the longest day I had to live.
> As for writing nonsense to them—I believe, there was a reserve.
> (9.24; p. 784)

By this point, Sterne has little in reserve for us apart from the final rupture, the cock-and-bull story, with its grave nonsense. Almost at the last instant the trajectory from tendency to intention is rehearsed when Toby's gravity—"My uncle Toby laid down his pipe to intercede for a better epithet"—provokes Yorick's fractious levity—"and Yorick was rising up to batter the whole hypothesis to pieces" (9.33; p. 807). In connection with the novel's abrupt end, furthermore, it would not be amiss to recall how, for a woman, gravidity must end in tearing or cutting from her womb the offspring she has conceived. I want to conclude by examining at length the revolutionary transformation of the time sense in Sterne's conclusion, reflecting as I go on the relations between wisdom and nonsense, or closure and rupture, or the male and the female principles, that is, on what has been called, apropos of Kantian aesthetics, "le sans de la coupure pure" (Derrida, *Vérité* 95–135).

The cock-and-bull story, says Yorick, is "one of the best of its kind" (9.33; p. 809). It is time, at last, to scrutinize its kind. It is certainly not a beast fable. Nor is it a "story" in the sense of a shaped narration like Fielding's or a self-contained experience like Goldsmith's. It also appears to possess none of the features abstracted by *Tristram Shandy*: it does not literalize, but depends on a continuing dubious analogy between man and beast; its effect is confusion rather than articulation ("L——d! said my mother, what is all this story about?" ibid.), and it moves toward litigation rather than social integration. In its fragmentary character and its themes of love, birth, and conflict it resembles the other inserted stories of *Tristram Shandy*, yet it is an interruption rather than a digression and an incident rather than an illustration: its kind, if it has one, lies within the purview of Yorick's reading and outside the novel.

The closest generic analogues to the cock-and-bull story that I am familiar with may be found in the *Decameron*.[33] Not in one of Boccaccio's hundred tales but in the frame occurs an incident by which the role of the tales can be measured. It is the quarrel of Licisco and Tindaro in the Introduction to the Sixth Day.[34] In Boccaccio, as in Sterne, the assembled company is interrupted by a servant bringing a dispute for judgment. The dispute in both authors involves a legal matter concerning sexual competence among males and sexual precocity among females (Squarotti, "La 'Cornice'" 151–52). To be sure, one incident involves people, the other animals, but both concern bestiality (a key term of Boccaccio's) and civility, that is, the relation of man to animal or soul to body. And both terminate abruptly with only the female (woman's or cow's) case having been presented. In addition, the cock-and-bull story has an affinity with what might be called Boccaccio's ass-and-gosling story. This is the tale of Filippo Balducci and his son that is told, again as part of the frame, in the Introduction to the Fourth Day. It tells of a youth brought up in seclusion on Monte Asinaio (the Mount of Asses) who is taken to town and immediately conceives an inordinate desire for the women he sees, even though his father calls them goslings.[35] The story—incomplete, like the cock-and-bull story—forms part of a defense of poetry: the Muses are women, and therefore (as the story illustrates) no man can help loving them. Taken together, the Boccaccio stories form a context that permits us to define the genre of the cock-and-bull story: it is an hors d'oeuvre. Neither altogether part of the work nor altogether separate, it sets the tone and defines the standards. The end is an odd position for an hors d'oeuvre, but no odder than the locations of Sterne's Dedication and Preface.

Suppose, then, that we consider the cock-and-bull story to be an exemplary defense of poetry, part of Sterne's outwork or prefatory matter. Such an exemplum is both more and less than an ordinary story: more because it compounds narration with an element of reflection; less because it is not simply a story, and is thus only imperfectly a simple story.[36] Its odd terminal position proves appropriate because Sterne's consciousness naturally pauses to knit its imperfect knots at the end of the threads of experience.

One thread that Obadiah knits back into the skein is the story of the abbess of Andoüillets (7.21–25). This story haunts Tristram as no other interpolation does: "I declare I am interested in this story, and wish I had been there," he exclaims as he tells it (7.21; p. 608). This is the other episode in the novel for which an analogue exists in the *Decameron*. Tristram's story concerns two salacious nuns[37] who undertake a journey to the hot baths of Bourbon, accompanied by a young gardener who serves as their driver. The muleteer, having drunk more than he can handle, remains behind at an inn, and the nuns are unable to coax the stubborn mules up the next hill. They resort to the two-syllable epithets that are supposed to get all mules moving, saving their consciences by dividing the syllables between them. The ruse fails, however: "They do not understand us, cried Margarita—But the Devil does, said the abbess of Andoüillets" (7.25; p. 614). Now this is a curious conclusion, since the story is supposed to illustrate how the two words will coax even the puny French horses to move (7.20). The story's unresolved conclusion, leaving the nuns stranded halfway uphill, suggests a negative moral: as a mule, being only half a horse, is not merely puny but sterile, so half an oath is powerless to engender action. Sterne does not draw this moral, however, and he ends on an evidently deliberate suspension or dissonance. The story thus turns into a loose thread or a meaningless unit, pure filler, again (like Sheridan's monologues) occupying empty space while the action silently advances.[38] The story remains in Tristram's memory, that is, as an uncompleted utterance, (female) words waiting to be inseminated with a (male) meaning.

The analogue in Boccaccio for Tristram's story is the tale of Masetto da Lamporecchio that opens the Third Day of the *Decameron*. Masetto is also a gardener for a convent who becomes, in the sexual sense, the driver, first of two nuns, then of the whole sisterhood. (Boccaccio uses the verb *cavalcar*, to bestride.) He has gained access by feigning dumbness, and he breaks his silence only when, sated with his nightly labors, he has to reach an accord with the abbess. Boccaccio's issues are silence and speech, night and day, power and impotence, bestiality and humanity. Masetto's silence allows him to amass a reserve of domination over his social and moral superiors, and then he judiciously breaks his silence to negotiate the difficult conversion of his burdensome nighttime interest into a stock of daytime capital, eventually dying rich and the father of many "little monks."

Tristram's story complicates Boccaccio's dualisms. He is concerned not with radical oppositions, but with marginal or halfway states: chronic infirmity, evening, moderate inebriation, venial sins, the general mulishness of life that refuses to coalesce into any distinct patterns. In terms of language—the central issue of Sterne's story as of Boccaccio's—the focus is again not on speech and silence, but on half-words and discourse that does not rise to the level of intelligible articulation. Tristram's true subject here, in short, is noise.[39] The story contains, in fact, a whole chapter of noises, arising from various organs, spiritual and physical:

> Get on with you, said the abbess.
> —Wh —— ysh—ysh—ysh—cried Margarita.
> Sh —— a—shu-u—shu——u—sh — aw—shaw'd the abbess.
> —Whu—v—w—whew—w—w—whuv'd Margarita, pursing up her sweet lips betwixt a hoot and a whistle.
> Thump—thump—thump—obstreperated the abbess of Andoüillets with the end of her gold-headed cane against the bottom of the calesh—
> The old mule let a f—— (7.22; pp. 610–11)

Tristram Shandy has been called a musical novel,[40] but when too many sounds are threaded along a line, the result must surely be discord: "a taylor sat musically at it, in a shed overagainst the convent, in assorting four dozen of bells for the harness, whistling to each bell as he tied it on with a thong" (7.21; p. 607). The whole life of Andoüillets is disheveled in just the way the jangling of the harness must be: "a couple of lay-sisters were busied, the one in darning the lining, and the other in sewing on the shreds of yellow binding, which the teeth of time had unravelled" (ibid.).

We meet here the lower end of the great chain of being—not nonexistence, but chaos and disorder; not an abyss, but a midpoint from which ascent proves impossible; not inorganic matter, but hybrid monsters that are "not . . . in a condition to return the obligation *downwards*" (7.21; p. 610; in theory this incapacity should apply to nuns as well as to mules, and there are indeed no "little monks" in Tristram's story). As dissonant in imagery as in form, the scandalous little story presents the bottom line of existence as a formless entropy or codeless noise. It is a peril that Sterne recalls to us at every recurrence of Toby's anarchic *argumentum fistulatorium*, which is used at intervals throughout the novel to refute all possible logics and is heard for the last time as the merest undertone of inescapable disorder only two chapters before the end.[41] And it reappears unmistakably in the cock-and-bull story itself, when Walter echoes Margarita's noise: "Wheu — u —— u —— cried my father; beginning the sentence with an exclamatory whistle" (9.33; p. 808). Boccaccio's concern in telling a story is to reach a satisfactory mean between opposing forces; Sterne's is to define or articulate a formless force.[42]

A loud quarrel between Walter and Toby precedes the cock-and-bull story. In a more Rabelaisian moment than any in the Andoüillets story, Walter extols the phallic brutality of war over love, which he views as an activity both monstrous (it "makes us come out of our caverns and hiding-places more like satyrs and four-footed beasts than men," 9.33; p. 806) and beneath conceptualization (occurring in the dark, it is "to be conveyed to a cleanly mind by no language, translation, or periphrasis whatever," ibid.). The story proper then begins, like that of Licisco and Tindaro, with a noisy interruption, "a complaint, which cried out for an immediate hearing" (ibid.). The movement toward articulate order within the story thus recapitulates a movement from Rabelaisian debate to Boccaccesque story within the chapter, as well as the whole novel's progress from dark conception toward articulation. But it is not easy to see how that movement can be said to arrive at its goal. An hors d'oeuvre is, after all, a formal disturbance, neither inside nor outside the meal, and a cock-and-bull story is by definition a rambling, shapeless narrative.

Though the case is presented to Walter, he does not decide it. His bull, who originated the problem, has become, if not a monstrosity, at least mulish in its inability to return the obligation downward. It needs a dose of levity if it is to rise to the occasion. So does Walter: "as he went through the business with a grave face, my father had a high opinion of him" (9.33; p. 808). But Walter is a poor judge. Just before the end we are told that he tended "to force every event in nature into an hypothesis, by which means never man crucified TRUTH at the rate he did" (9.32; p. 804). He remains captivated with the archaic and unwholesome mixtures of myth from which a rational legal order has finally cleared civilization: "this poor Bull of mine . . . might have done for *Europa* herself in purer times" (9.33; p. 808). The allusion to a conquest of Europe is hardly innocent in the mouth of a warmonger like Walter. But then, from the start his authoritarian regulation of time and of sexuality constituted a primitive violence; by giving him an estrous period, it made him more like a beast than like a man. At the end we shall see his disastrous mixture of anarchism and authoritarianism rebutted by the cock-and-bull story.

Like the bull that is supposed to service the whole parish, Walter's logic is indiscriminate. The story (as told by Tristram, though he wasn't born yet when it occurred) begins in Walter's mode, with a vague precision of time based on a groundless association of ideas: "Obadiah had led his cow upon a *pop-visit* to him one day or other the preceding summer—I say, one day or other—because as chance would have it, it was the day on which he was married to my father's housemaid—so one was a reckoning to the other" (9.33; p. 807). Given this bizarre beginning, the task of the story is to make distinctions, to know its day, and to demarcate one thing from another. And despite one's initial impression, it does adumbrate a series of distinctions on the basis of which both knowledge and judgment become possible: the distinctions between cows and women, between bulls (who can be barren) and cows (who can't), between hairless (premature) and hairy (full-term) babies, between men and bulls, between town (i.e., common) bulls and private bulls. As originally put, the case is a confused tangle; the ensuing interrogations are a (disheveled) cock-and-bull story because they don't narrate the incident in a clear sequence, but they are a good (cock-and-bull) story because they disentangle the issues along the way toward a possible adjudication. Out of life's tangled knots of phenomena, the cock-and-bull story draws a sense of arrangement.

But it is not a man's rational ordering. In line with its scientintical spirit the novel, as Sterne left it, ends with a particular instance, not with a general outlook or a philosophating moral reflection. If the novel as a whole is an abstract expansion of the general shape of a story, the cock-and-bull story is an abstract reduction of the volumes and of the novel: like them, it moves from birth to love, from village life to the great world, from private quarrels to public conflict (the myth of Europa, the forum of Doctors' Commons), from epistemology to social psychology (the concern for the "poor Bull" and its "character"). Consciousness comes to itself on the basis of such minute particulars. A conception is a begetting and, ultimately, a birth, rather than a Hegelian *Begriff*, or all-encompassing grasp. This is the law of story (and of consciousness) that I have not yet enunciated and that sets Sterne the revolutionary apart from Fielding and even from Goldsmith: not only must story literalize, articulate, and gather, but above all it must change. Rounded forms and reflective apologias are not for Sterne. The cock-and-bull story restores "case" to its etymological sense as a fall: moving far from the canons of traditional logic, it refigures consciousness as the story of the emergence of an individual, rather than as an assignment of facts to general categories.

An anecdote is the microcosm of a microcosm, or a knot of knots. As the great world shrinks into a little village and its deeds into anecdotes, story approaches the condition of picture. Though devoid of descriptions, the cock-and-bull story is unmistakably gestural; the "broken and irregular steps" of the story are marked by Obadiah's prayer, by his address to Walter Shandy with a nod in the direction of the bull, by his pointing at his hair (the story's moment of exemplary self-consciousness), as well as by Walter's successive orientation toward Obadiah, toward Slop, and toward Toby. Its captioned snapshots seemingly permit us to take the measure of each moment. Yet the pictorial composition of the group constantly shifts, as each of the characters present gets actively involved with the story at a different point. This segmentation of the story into moments, like that of a book into chapters, raises questions of composition. Just as the problem of sensibility could only be solved by a division of psychic labor or an economy of the soul, so Sterne's problem demanded a chrono-economy or distributed temporality for its solution. Sterne criticism has not succeeded in integrating the time line of the novel because, finally, that cannot be done: its seriousness is its play; its structure is its multiplicity.[43]

Tristram envies pictures as moments of arrested truth. Seeking to master time, he begins the novel like a man, calculating and reckoning. But increasingly the times of the narrative overwhelm the calendar's regulative power. There is no way of rationalizing and reconciling the three temporal dimensions of a story: writer's time, reader's time, and character's time. The tangled strands of time differ in length, pace, and density, as well as in mere date. Fielding, it is true, had already recognized the multiple determination of actions, but he had treated all causes as equivalent and equally proximate. His narrative therefore remains, in Sterne's terms, not really a story, but a succession of pictured events, each with its own swirl of motivating causes.[44] A man totalizes narrative, as sensibility totalizes feeling. What is needed is rather a non-euclidean multidimensionality of narrative. As a storyteller Tristram fares no better than his—let us start to admit it—putative father.

The story's problem, like the novel's, is synchronicity and comparative chronology. In Sterne's "ronde des durées" (to cite Henri Fluchère's beautiful and untranslatable phrase)[45] three principal temporal dimensions coexist: the rapid development of the scene itself, the time of gestation and birth, and the slow pendulum of cultural development from the age of myth to the age of Doctors' Commons. A story somehow correlates the volatile flux of emotions, the measurable time of the clock and the sun, and the inexorable but glacial pace of culture. Within each mode of time a whole gamut of nuances and values coexist. The emotions determining subjective time range from Obadiah's impetuousness (the story begins with his interruption) to Mrs. Shandy's lethargy (her interruption ends it), with the other characters' moods presumably falling in between, some more clearly marked than others. The time of pregnancy is calculated in months from an indefinite beginning ("one day or other"), while in an allied register the time of waiting is calculated in named days and numbered weeks. Chronologies eddy in dubious consequence: what period in the fetus's development is measured by the three weeks' growth of Obadiah's beard? Does Walter's historical sense measure the distance from ancient culture to modern or from myth to reality? And the modes interpenetrate: history's inexorability comes into view as the months of pregnancy are counted, while rapid shifts of emotion accompany the weeks and days of waiting for the cow to go into labor. These complications make it impossible to speak in terms of a rational three-dimensional geometry of determinants on the order of the positivists' milieu, moment, and race. Instead, the story becomes an exemplum or pictorial schematism of the non-euclidean multidimensionality of narrative. Its articulations, its literalizations, and its gathering of parts serve to unfold the incalculable mystery of time.[46]

The subject of the cock-and-bull story is the timing of a conception. That subject sends us back to the very first chapters of the novel. Tristram, like Obadiah, is at pains to calculate the moment of conception from circumstantial evidence that he pursues with unmatched obsessiveness. He never names his real fear, but he hints unmistakably at it.[47] By his calculations his father can only have lain with this mother on the first Sunday of March 1718, and he was born on November 5. Readers do not always observe that this account makes him an eight-month baby, but Tristram had made the calculation, for he calls the term "as near nine kalendar months as any husband could in reason have expected" (1.5; p. 8).[48] He seems, however, less than fully reassured. His father's mechanically regular sexual activity has one weighty consequence: "It was attended but with one misfortune, which, in a great measure, *fell* upon myself, and the effects of which I fear I shall carry with me to my *grave*; namely, that, from an unhappy association of ideas which have no connection in nature, it so *fell* out at length, that my poor mother could never hear the said clock wound up,—but the thoughts of some other things unavoidably popp'd into her head" (1.4; pp. 6–7, my emphasis). Why does sexual regularity intimate a fall? Among the beasts who inhabit Doctors' Commons neither frailty nor impotence is a moral defect; if the two-legged bull loses his character, it must be from cuckoldry.

The crux, precisely as with Tristram's birth, lies with the gestation period. If Obadiah's wife gave birth early, then the cow's time may not be up. But the baby is hairy and therefore full-term; consequently the cow is overdue and the bull is impotent. What thoughts, Tristram must have wondered, popped into Mrs. Shandy's head on the first Sunday of February, during Walter's attack of sciatica? Might she not have paid a pop-visit to some two-legged town bull whose character (as sexual prowess) was better than Walter's and (as morality) also worse?[49] It is more than a little dubious at the end of the story what a good character would mean. The insinuation is not lost on Mrs. Shandy, who chooses this moment to cry out: "L——d! said my mother, what is all this story about?" (9.33; p. 809). What indeed! Yorick, ever the friendly counselor, hastens to reassure her that it is just a cock-and-bull story, a tale with no point. But even his intervention at this moment points to an agitation in need of calming. In its oblique way the story thus permits concerns to surface that have been passed over in silence hitherto. Reading the story, for instance, we might wonder in retrospect why the novel gives us so much information about the infant Tristram's nose, but none about his hair, around which questions of prematurity obviously circled.[50] Now we begin to discern, if only in a transferred and partly metaphorical context, what Tristram does *not* ask in inquiring about his birth. Mrs. Shandy's question voices Tristram's anxieties.

Tristram is damned if he is and damned if he isn't. *The Life and Opinions of Miss Sukey Shandy* (1760) early recognized the hints of illegitimacy (which would further link Tristram with Tom Jones) and made light of them. The graver fear is of the impotence that haunts the men of Shandy Hall.[51] Now the pen may be mightier than the sword—Slawkenbergius's stranger, having but a "short scymetar [*acinaces*]," has "lost his scabbard [*vaginam*] . . . and will not be able to get a scabbard to fit it in all *Strasburg*" (vol. 4; pp. 289, 291)—but the aging author's anxiety as he writes his first volume is unmistakable. Though Sterne, like Walter, had certainly fathered a child by his wife, the years took their toll. When he was diagnosed in 1767 as having a venereal illness, Sterne wrote indignantly (*Letters*, to the Earl of Shelburne, May [2] 1, p. 343), "I have had no commerce whatever with the sex, not even with my wife, added I, these fifteen years." The thought recurs a full seven months later, in connection with an allusion to the novel: "I might indeed solace myself with my wife, (who is come from France [the realm of warm sexuality in Sterne's letters, as in his book]); but in fact I have long been a sentimental being—whatever your Lordship may think to the contrary.— The world has imagined, because I wrote Tristram Shandy, that I was myself more Shandean than I really ever was" (*Letters*, to the Earl of ———, Nov. 28, 1767, pp. 402–3). For both Sterne and his narrator, writing becomes the inadequate compensation for sexual deficiency.

An eternal victim, Tristram can neither write nor do what he wants. As he says in a chapter beginning "IT is with LOVE as with CUCKOLDOM," "I begin with writing the first sentence—and trusting to Almighty God for the second" (8.2; p. 656). Among all Sterne's men, Yorick, sentimental being though he may be, is the only one to show even flickers of spontaneous sexual activity. Thus looms another implication of Yorick's early death. Sexuality is of course the great unwritable; it is in the reader but never in the author, who always covers it under a dash or an aposiopesis, or masks it as the subverbal noise of half-words like "bou-bou-bou" and "ger-ger-ger." Eugenius—properly born, clean—designs a startlingly brief epitaph for his friend Yorick, and one ought to wonder what lies under the printer's noise,[52] those two pages of black ink (1.12; pp. 37–38) that lead Tristram back from Yorick's grave to thoughts of the midwife. The silence at Yorick's death is as awkward as that in volume 4 at the death of Tristram's properly born brother Bobby. The controlling, male writer remains equally apprehensive about sexuality and about legitimacy.

The rather unsavory hors d'oeuvre served up at the end belongs as much to the male domain as does the ill-fated chestnut at Didius's banquet in volume 4. In what sense, then, can Mrs. Shandy be said to be in the picture? What part do women's meanings play in men's stories? Finally, it is not strictly correct to say that *Tristram Shandy* ends with a cock-and-bull story. It ends, properly speaking, with Mrs. Shandy's question about the story and with Yorick's judgment (cf. Booth, "Did Sterne Complete *Tristram Shandy?*" 545–46). The strangeness of his judgment should not escape notice. For, properly speaking, this could hardly be called a cock-and-bull story at all, let alone a story about "A COCK and a BULL," capitals notwithstanding. (Yorick says both things in this bizarre end, both that the story is about a cock and a bull and that it is a cock-and-bull story; thus he confuses form and content as might a bad story—say, a cock-and-bull story—but surely no good story.) The bull plays a distinctly peripheral role, as does the cock (Obadiah, unless the cuckold Walter is meant); an unbiased reader—but can one be neutral about sex?— would really have to call this a hen-and-cow story. The novel's gravitation toward the female, the unique, the microcosm of a microcosm, is Tristram's self-sacrificing reaction to his complex of sexual anxieties. What Mary Poovey has called the paradoxes of propriety, including women's eloquent silence and pointed indirection, reach a comic apotheosis at the novel's triumphant conclusion.[53]

The end of the novel shows us Toby defeated in war, Walter silenced in shame, Yorick a living ghost, and Tristram crucified. Widow Wadman, alone among the living main characters, is safely out of this excruciating scene, and Mrs. Shandy suffers in silence. The woman's question, "what is all this story about?" puts an end to the story and reasserts its unanswerable skepticism toward all reductions or inflations of story into meaning. The woman's side is the dark side, the side of the body and its sexual energies. A bull may be barren, but never a cow: this may be dubious in the real world, but it seems to hold for Sterne's people as well as his animals. The procreative power lies entirely with women: Mrs. Shandy and the Widow Wadman, the midwife who beats the clumsy Dr. Slop to the punch, the hyperactive women of Strasburg set aflame by the stranger's nose. (And by a nose, Tristram tells us, he means nothing but a nose.) In woman's body and in her good time the trajectory from conception to generation is traversed.

For women remain the custodians of time. One example is Nannette, with her hair both tied up and untied, who captivates Tristram as if "we had been seven years acquainted," "who had stolen her voice from heaven," and whose circling song (a "roundelay") leads to an "insidious" dance that infects Tristram with its demonic energy, making it possible to abandon his "Plain Stories" and turn at last to the great story of Toby's amours (7.43; pp. 648–51). The Widow Wadman is another as she marshals her inner forces for a "nine months" campaign (3.24; p. 246) that prepares the only unqualified success, or conception with a happy issue, in the book. Men wind the clock, but as with pens, they are at least as much slaves of its mechanism as masters of it. The Widow Wadman's nine months, by contrast, hints at an inward and unmeasured time of the body and of instinct that only women possess. Dr. Slop, to be sure, having been warned by Walter that Mrs. Shandy's time is up, happens to amble by, as "'twas natural and very political too in him" (2.10; p. 124), just as Mrs. Shandy is giving birth, but he has forgotten his tools, and he misses the delivery. None of the men seems to be aware that Mrs. Shandy has gone into labor, for they merely calculate the time, whereas she truly knows her time, and so does the midwife, who is there when she is needed, poorly skilled (resembling in this the cock-and-bull story) but at least equipped and prepared.[54]

"—Endless is the Search of Truth!" (2.3; p. 103). Others who are more adept can pursue the psychocritical implications of Tristram's occultations.[55] A philosophical criticism will keep the question of truth before it as it reflects on the way Sterne concludes upon the frayed ends of a story. To end thus, as to end with woman, is, of course, to defer truth endlessly. But where, after all, could truth ever be found? It is both untangling and knotting up, both analysis and synthesis, and since it cannot be both at once, it can only be approximated in an infinite process. Woman's romantic and open-ended stories may thus be closer to truth than man's logical short circuits. Walter Shandy treads a path of error when he recommends a *petite canulle* as the highroad to human dignity (1.20).

Finally, the intention of *Tristram Shandy* is to overturn story and not to define it. Story cannot be defined. In this sense, the old Shklovskian truisms about the novel as metafiction and antifiction are indeed true, but with a hitherto unrecognized power. For the

novel does not simply invalidate itself in its last two lines; it remains a search for story and a defense of poetry. But the end of the
end, the denouement of the knot of knots, confirms what should
have been evident all along: a good story must break its bounds.
Pure fiction is as airy as a puff of smoke; a true story, belonging to
the endless search for truth, must be a vehicle of knowledge spilling
over beyond its fictionality.

At the very moment Sterne was writing, Goldsmith was perfecting the form of the closed story, through the filter of an incorrigibly
self-deluding, aestheticizing narrator. We have seen how Tristram is
infected by the vicar's aestheticism. But *Tristram Shandy* is ultimately wiser than its narrator. The exemplum proves an example
after all, for all stories—all those in *Tristram Shandy*, at any rate—
are not well-wrought urns, but unbounded cock-and-bull stories,
opening in one direction onto the great world of England in the 1760s,
in the other onto the pinpoint searchlight of consciousness. As space
is co-original with time, so the form of stories is inseparable from an
energy of signification that effaces their limits.[56] In this anecdote
that is both more and less than a perfect story, Tristram succeeds at
last in clueing us in to an original trauma that he has never risked
mentioning. Sterne succeeds in evoking the multiple local and long-
range determinants and resonances of a momentary event. Mrs.
Shandy succeeds in provoking an open-ended reflection on the meaning of it all. Aesthetics and hermeneutics, formalism and deconstruction, man and woman are coupled in an interminable and
unanswerable dialogue.

We return in this last twist of the dialectic to the problem of the
class of one, or of the relationship between cock-and-bull stories and
stories in general. The cock-and-bull story carries to its limit the
transformation of conception from a rational ordering to a covert
and multifarious disposition. That limit is occupied by Mrs. Shandy.
But just what kind of limit, what kind of close, is it? Are Mrs.
Shandy's open-ended question and Yorick's concluding reassurance
part of the anecdote or not? Are they a reflection on half a chapter, or
on the whole novel? Who speaks what, who knows what? What is
transmitted, what reconstructed, what purely imagined? What was
said then, what only now written? How does Tristram know all of
this, and what is the status of his report? Early in volume 1 Tristram
divulges his sources—"To my uncle Mr. *Toby Shandy* do I stand indebted for the preceding anecdote," "another small anecdote known
only in our own family," "it appears, by a memorandum in my father's pocket-book, which now lies upon the table" (1.3–4; pp. 4, 6,

7).[57] After that, we mostly can only speculate. In the last chapter, even more than in the rest of the book, the absence of quotation marks renders the narrative perspective impenetrable. In the eighteenth century, as novel and drama moved closer together (in Walpole's Aristotelianism, for instance, or Beaumarchais's picaresque disjointedness, or Diderot's dialogue narratives and narrated plays) the status of fictional language became ever less certain. By omitting quotation marks, Sterne effaces the internal boundary between immediate speech and mediated writing, but the result is confusion rather than combination. In this way, his termination—whether willfully or accidentally—issues a provocation to successors who might wish to harness his achievements. To find the limits of story, to define its class and capture its energy, it would be necessary to have a clear and simple narrative perspective.

Tristram Shandy's itinerary runs from the obfuscating determinations of man's logic to the obscure indeterminacy of woman's intuition. The itinerary is the meaning; nowhere in its scale of values is there a point of neutrality or of measure. There is no purgation in Sterne's world: his stories comprise what is unforgotten and will not let us rest. It would not quite do to say that the enemy is clarity or enlightenment, for these values are nowhere represented in a novel that portrays even Locke as the spokesman for a psychological irrationalism. But we may sense a return of the repressed.[58] What Sterne does not even bother to oppose because it does not exist and never has—that is the outer boundary delimiting and defining story. Simple and clear is the one thing that Sterne's stories are not—and that a perfect story therefore would be, could one exist.

Simplicity After Sterne

It would be no more irresponsible a generalization than any other to claim that simplicity was the central literary problem in the last decades of the century. The popularity of the epistolary novel with multiple correspondents reflected the fragmentation of perspectives both as a breakthrough in literary form and as a psychological dilemma. Indeed the letter by its very nature coupled spontaneity with artifice, immediacy with analysis, speech with writing in a tangle whose unraveling lies on the horizon of these novels. Frances Burney's *Evelina* (1778) is a case in point. The orphaned Evelina, who is destined to find, almost simultaneously, a father, a brother, and a husband, is described as a character of "genuine simplicity, . . . singleness of heart, . . . guileless sincerity."[59] It is possible to feel that somewhere outside the correspondence there may be some recognizable truth to this claim, in particular as Evelina approaches the indescribable climax: "I cannot write the scene that followed, though every word is engraven on my heart: . . . he drew from me the most sacred secret of my heart!" (letter 76, pp. 326–27). At the moment of truth, writing and speech coalesce in a perfect and unrepeatable utterance. But the worldly norm is altogether different, even for Evelina. Here is the "genuine simplicity" of her everyday behavior, as she analyzes the typical density of its gestures in another letter: "I told him, frankly, that it was not in my power, at present, to see him, but by accident; and, to prevent his being offended, I hinted to him the reason I could not receive him as I wished to do" (letter 70, p. 294). In a society where utterances, gestures, and even silences are so multiply coded, clarity and simplicity of perspective remain a utopian dream—or a cock-and-bull story.

The great comic picaresque of the period, *Humphry Clinker* (1771), is another class of one that brilliantly solves the problem *Tristram Shandy* never even allows itself to pose. By composing an epistolary novel whose hero writes no letters, Smollett creates a figure whose purity transcends the entanglements of the word. From the scatological Win Jenkins to the splenetic Matthew Bramble the correspondents are laid out along a scale that stretches from discontented naïveté to jaded oversophistication, with no neutral point of common sense. But over against these observers Smollett places a collection of picaresque characters, including Lismahago, Wilson, and Martin, as well as Humphry Clinker. These characters are actors rather than writers, and their actions have a simplicity of motivation that keeps them free from any genuine danger. It is not necessary to retrace the whole course of the novel here in order to understand the outcome: around Humphry as the center of purity the whole cast coalesces in a series of reconciliations. The different regions of Britain become peaceably linked, as do the different social classes (Matthew Bramble's son Humphry marries a servant, while his sister Tabby marries Lismahago, who, at least among the Indians, counted as royalty). Religion comes to terms with freethinking, the picaresque form with the epistolary, the past with the present, speech with writing.

Humphry Clinker remained an isolated triumph. Its characters were often copied, but in form and style it had nothing like the impact of Smollett's earlier novels (see Giddings, *Tradition* 151–83). Perhaps it proved a dead end because of the very complexity of its construction of simplicity. As Eric Rothstein has demonstrated, it is among the most finely wrought novels of the period, but it paid a price for its artistry. Rather than purging the turbulence of Smollett's earlier novels, *Humphry Clinker* transmutes it, reimagining accident in the guise of metamorphosis. But this means that the action is simple only if the novel is seen on the mythic level, where all the events appear to be equivalent reflections of a common principle of transformation and its associated image of water. And character is simple less in the reduced form of the naked body than in a totalizing form where all are linked to all: it is the simplicity of the mongrel, rather than that of the purebred.

The grim little diptych called *A Simple Story* published in 1791 by Elizabeth Inchbald is named by antiphrasis: there is little that is simple about it, but it does cast a searchlight on the problem of simplicity. It is a tale, in its first part, of stubborn pride and self-deluding flirtation, in its second, of parental tyranny and blind filial submission. Especially in the first part, to be sure, the swirling characters and incidents increasingly prove to be false obstacles that vanish effortlessly to permit a concentration on a single love bond. Beneath the comic dramatist's delight in repartee and gesture there does seem to be a gradual revelation of the simple emotion of love, triumphant over all. But what kind of story can pure feeling generate? In the aftermath of Richardson and Rousseau, any expression instantly contaminates pure feeling, and the only truth lies in silence: Miss Milner, we are told at one point, "loved too sincerely, to reveal it to the object" (2.3; p. 110). Yet the gestures that should reveal the interior are no more reliable than the words that social convention required always to mask feeling. Although purportedly "each understood the other's language, without uttering a word," the lovers who have long since mutually declared and confirmed their love continue at risk of a tragic irony in which a "just construction" construes signs to indicate "total indifference" (2.11; p. 181). Only an unprepared change of heart by Lord Elmwood's confessor restores the love marriage that is nearly aborted at this point. For when signs are unstable, the only truths to which they give access must be just as turbulent.

It is impossible to love simply, sincerely, or "with moderation" (2.5; p. 130). Love always appears as "the rapid emotion of varying passions" (ibid.), and the frequent glimpses we get of "the real passion of love," as it is inwardly experienced, are all of "agonizing torment" like "the tortures of the rack" (2.4; p. 119). The first half of the novel (vols. 1–2) ends with the marriage of love between Lord Elmwood and Miss Milner, but the second half shows the prospect

of simple bliss to have been an illusion. Instead, the outcome justi-
fies Lord Elmwood's earlier forebodings of "domestic wrangles—a
family without subordination—a house without oeconomy—in a
word, a wife without discretion" (2.7; p. 142). Nothing lasts: while
the husband tends to his West Indian estates, the wife betrays him,
for there is no economy of love, and the only simple story is written
to the moment and cannot dependably endure. This first tragedy sets
a discouraging precedent; the second, and more sadistic, tale seems
to have a stable, happy ending, but no assurances are given of the life
ever after: "Whether the heart of Matilda, such as it has been described, *could* sentence [Rushbrook] to misery, the reader is left to
surmise—and if he supposes that it did not, he has every reason to
suppose their wedded life was a life of happiness" (4.12; p. 337). A
simple story is a fairy tale concocted in the deluded imagination of
the gullible reader.

Where does a history look beyond these false hopes and dead
ends? Inchbald wrote the play, *Lovers' Vows*, that almost wrecks
Mansfield Park. Accounts of the eighteenth-century novel often
lead up to the triumph of Austen, and there is much in her perfection of story forms, with their architectonic distribution of the plot
across the chapters, in her fluid yet precise narrative perspective, in
her purification of words, and in her ways of revealing consciousness
through spoken monologue and written letter that would make her
appropriate here. To balance out the generic perspectives, I have
chosen instead to end with Wordsworth. Wordsworth's great autobiographical novel in verse owes much to *Tristram Shandy* in its chaotic overlay of incidents and chronologies and much to *The Vicar of
Wakefield* in its gallery of sentimental and sarcastic portraits. Yet
his prefaces trumpet the doctrine of a conscious simplicity of subject matter and expression. Above all in Wordsworth's language, the
poetry of the spoken word, the inherited problems are resolved or
even left behind. Nature and history no longer oppose mind, but are
subsumed in its movements.

The simplicity of romantic poetry was not easily won.[60] It was
never comfortably extended into large forms and comprehensive
perspectives (perhaps such extension was most nearly achieved in
Goethe's brief epic, *Hermann und Dorothea*), and it condenses most
successfully in the images that seem to be the carriers of so much of
Wordsworth's power. The images of freedom—the free flow of waters and the wandering voices of birds—are the ones that have most
often captured the imagination of Wordsworth's readers. But I prefer
to focus my attention on the most stable element of Wordsworth's

landscape. That is his stones. My subject is not the inscribed stones, the epitaphs in which language seeks its own negation, but that negation itself, the blank stones—not even distinctively black or white or mottled, like Sterne's all-too-eloquent, coded blanks, but gray—that are the empty pages of the imagination where all is possible.

CHAPTER TWELVE

Wordsworth's Old Gray Stone

Thou art Peter, and upon this rock I will build my church.
Matthew 16: 18

The rock is the gray particular of man's life,
The stone from which he rises, up—and—ho,
The step to the bleaker depths of his descents.
Wallace Stevens, "The Rock," part 3

For one throb of the artery,
While on that old grey stone I sat
Under the old wind-broken tree,
I knew that One is animate,
Mankind inanimate phantasy.
W. B. Yeats, "A Meditation in
Time of War"

Toward Hope

At the depth of his confusion about how to tell his story, Tristram appears lost in time. It is one of Sterne's most notorious spots of dyschrony: "A cow broke in (to-morrow morning) to my uncle *Toby's* fortifications, and eat up two ratios and half of dried grass, tearing up the sods with it" (3.38; p. 278). The scientintical spirit (Tristram's ubiquitous "half") here comes a cropper; the narrator who wants to be everywhere at once and yet have everything in its place is perplexed by a cow that literally dis-courses as it overruns the mock fortress. To the end Tristram remains haunted by a cow and never acquires the naive simplicity he yearns for. Sterne's legacy is the problem of finding an unfortified, undemarcated time on which discourse can be nourished at her ease.

One of the sonnets of William Lisle Bowles contains a usage similar to Sterne's. In "Dover Beach" Bowles writes that "many a lonely wanderer," about to set off into the wide world,

whilst the lifted murmur met his ear,
And o'er the distant billows the still Eve

      Sail'd slow, has thought of all his heart must leave
      To-morrow.

Its position in the line makes Bowles's "to-morrow" as emphatic as Sterne's, but it is less startling because the sense of time is more diffuse. Though Bowles's early sonnets concern his own trip to the Continent, their slow and mazy rhetoric softens and generalizes the experience. In his other, less interesting poems, time either dissolves into a vast infinitude (as in the "Monody, Written at Matlock") or remains a majestic force that dwindles man into insignificance (as in "The Philanthropic Society"), so that forgetfulness is left as Bowles's favorite defense against time's gloomy power. But the sonnets are poems of memory, devoted to finding an accommodation with time.

    As Wimsatt's well-known account of the River Ichin sonnet reminds us, Bowles was no dialectician (Wimsatt, "Structure" 105–7). His 1837 Introduction says that "fourteen lines seemed best adapted to unity of sentiment": the sonnets (originally published in 1791) evoke simple feelings rather than complex ones. His sense of genre, accordingly, is entirely affective, not structural: "I thought nothing about the strict Italian model; the verses naturally flowed in unpremeditated harmony, as my ear directed, but the slightest inspection will prove they were far from being mere elegiac couplets." No amount of retroactive justification, however, will make the sonnet a pristine and uncomplicated form. The strict Italian model is predicated on a turn or break between the octave and the sestet, and Bowles must have associated elegiac couplets with regret at time passing. Bowles does not ignore the generic complexities that he calls to our attention, but rather avoids them; unity of sentiment is the achievement of the sonnets in overcoming formal and temporal discontinuities.

    Bowles's 1805 Preface calls the sonnets "occasional reflections which naturally arose in his mind, during various excursions, undertaken to relieve, at the time, depression of spirits. They were, therefore, in general, suggested by the scenes before them; and wherever such scenes appeared to harmonize with his disposition at the moment, the sentiments were involuntarily prompted." Poetry of the moment, then, written to escape from unhappy memories: "in youth a wanderer among distant scenes, I sought forgetfulness of the first disappointment in early affections" (1837). Yet the momentary disposition, to be effective, must be prolonged, and the forgetfulness remembered. The original fourteen sonnets, Bowles confesses, were only written down three years later, salvaged from among many other effusions that had been forgotten, and mended and corrected. And half a century after the experiences, he still remembered the original effusions, and at long last restored the texts to their spontaneous first state. His more pretentious poems typically reduce to a simple opposition between man and time, whereas the "simple" sonnets, with their "softened image of the past" ("On Leaving a Village in Scotland") blend past and present, forgetting and remembering, discontinuity and continuity.

Two examples will illustrate Bowles's simplicities. Here, first, is the sonnet "The Rhine":

> 'Twas morn, and beauteous on the mountain's brow
>   (Hung with the clusters of the bending vine)
>   Shone in the early light, when on the Rhine
> We bounded, and the white waves round the prow
> In murmurs parted:—varying as we go,
>   Lo! the woods open, and the rocks retire,
>   As some gray convent-wall or glistening spire
> 'Mid the bright landscape's track unfolding slow!
> Here dark, with furrowed aspect, like Despair,
>   Frowns the bleak cliff! There on the woodland's side
>   The shadowy sunshine pours its streaming tide;
> Whilst Hope, enchanted with the scene so fair,
> Counts not the hours of a long summer's day,
> Nor heeds how fast the prospect winds away.

Bowles's world here seems as shot through with contrasts as Sterne's: woods open / rocks retire; gray wall / glistening spire; bleak cliff / streaming sun. Yet the syntax is befuddled; "Shone" seems to lack a subject, the function of "As" in line 7 is inscrutable, and it is uncertain whether "unfolding" modifies "track" or "wall" and "spire."[1] Line 4 suggests energetic progress; "murmurs" and "slow" suggest passive reverie. The landscape is partitioned like one of Akenside's, but sun and shadow seem inseparable, and Hope apparently reckons both forms of darkness equally "fair." Personification fluctuates between the dramatic vividness of eighteenth-century convention and the psychological dreaminess of the romantics. And all is sustained by what is crucial in Bowles, a sense that time is both fast and slow, passing and enduring. To Wordsworth Bowles's achievement may finally have seemed a mere trick of the deceiving elf Hope, a self-deluding know-nothingism ("Counts not . . . / Nor heeds") rather than an objective penetration of time's mysteries. Still, Bowles establishes the conditions that must be satisfied by a lyrical reinscription of the problem of time onto the speaking face of things.

"The River Wainsbeck," which explicitly acknowledges the precedency of Akenside in a note, struggles even more consciously with temporality.

> While slowly wanders thy sequestered stream,
>> Wainsbeck, the mossy-scattered rocks among,
>> In fancy's ear making a plaintive song
> To the dark woods above, that waving seem
> To bend o'er some enchanted spot, removed
>> From life's vain coil; I listen to the wind,
>> And think I hear meek Sorrow's plaint, reclined
> O'er the forsaken tomb of him she loved!—
> Fair scenes, ye lend a pleasure, long unknown,
>> To him who passes weary on his way;—
>> Yet recreated here he may delay
> A while to thank you; and when years have flown,
> And haunts that charmed his youth he would renew,
> In the world's crowd he will remember you.

Bowles combines imperfect rhymes[2] with internal echoes (ear-hear, making-meek, plaintive-plaint) to break through the logical articulations of the form. He struggles to convert the "enchanted spot" into a spot of time, with an obscure sense of the epitaphic quality that became essential for Wordsworth. Recreation here means exemption from ravaging time, but it also means re-creation (or renewal by emerging from dreaming fancy into real existence), hence the sudden projection ahead from present "delay" to rapidly flying future years. After the insistence of "removed," "reclined," "recreated," and "renew," even "remember" seems to yield up a buried etymology, as the faceless crowd is re-membered—repopulated—by the persons and personifications that haunt memory like the voices of wind and rocky brook. Unlike Wordsworth Bowles cannot separate simplicity from the indefiniteness of his shifting modal constructions. But the scant room of a sonnet saves him from enquiring too closely; it therefore leaves him free at least to imagine the unity of past sensations with present sentiments, of an experience with a memory, and of a miraculous yet natural landscape with a fanciful yet natural state of mind.

The problem of the spatial and temporal continuities that Bowles evokes could not long remain separated from the problem of expressive continuities that he evades. His best sonnets are pure atmosphere from which the concrete meanings have been distilled out, or defecated, as Coleridge would have said. Their virtues vanish (except in the notable Wordsworthian meditation "Combe-Ellen," published in 1798) as Bowles follows the impulse toward greater descriptive precision and ultimately sandbags the flow of inspiration in his dreary historical epics. Paradoxically, language retains its connecting power only so long as it is disjoined from reference. Bowles's achievement of simplicity could well inspire the early romantics, but they would still need to make simplicity meaningful.

Sheridan had shown one way to create meanings, through his representation of the semiotics of desire. The objects of desire are part of us in a way that the objects of knowledge are not, and so long as meanings are a function of desire, they remain bound to the self. But comedy is a utopian mode whose outcome is not readily translatable back into experience; hence, Sheridan discovered nondisjunctive signs only in ideology, not in practice. In Georgian comedies where the resolutions resulted from a change of heart, social reintegration depended on a more or less radical discontinuity of character. Sheridan avoids the change of heart, but at the cost of a discontinuity of behavior that is potentially at least as troubling. For the Surfaces and the Teazles to live happily ever after, Charles's profligacy and Lady Teazle's flirtatiousness must be not so much forgiven as utterly forgotten, which seems unlikely in the world of Scandal. The risk of a relapse remains strong, despite Sheridan's attempt to neutralize it by rewriting Vanbrugh's comedy of that name. The semiotic continuities of desire are thus not only cut off from the past, but also connected to the future by the most fragile of threads. Character is bonded to time not by memory, but only by the precarious utopianism of hope (cf. Sheats, *The Making of Wordsworth's Poetry* 33–41).

Faced with disruptive forces in society and in consciousness, the individual clings to hope as his delicately reforming power. But finding genuine continuities is not easy. "'Tis I," we read in the ninth and last stanza of James Beattie's "Ode to Hope" (in Chalmers, *English Poets* 18: 545–46),

> 'Tis I, who smooth the rugged way,
> I, who close the eyes of Sorrow,
> And with glad visions of to morrow
> Repair the weary soul's decay.

The wound to consciousness evoked by the Eton College ode is recalled in Beattie's ode:

> Ye days, that balmy influence shed,
> When sweet childhood, ever sprightly,
> In paths of pleasure sported lightly,
> Whither, ah whither are ye fled!

And the social wounds that Sheridan was to represent are akin to those in Beattie:

> Lo, wizard Envy from his serpent eye
> Darts quick destruction in each baleful glance;
> Pride smiling stern, and yellow Jealousy,
> Frowning Disdain, and haggard Hate advance.

But though the eighteenth century identifies the problem, it is unable to find the solution it so readily names. Beattie's epiphany overcompensates: "Lo, from amidst affliction's night, / Hope bursts all radiant on the sight." Sublime totalization is, as ever, a false and even dangerous economy; the "glad visions of to morrow" give way before dazzling visions of a life after death, as the ode concludes "In rapture too severe for weak mortality." Burnout likewise besets Thomas Campbell's popular couplet poem, *The Pleasures of Hope* (1799), where the "passion-kindling power" and "rapture-lightened eye" of "prophetic Hope!" lead digressively yet inescapably through "Nature's mazy plan" toward a destructive apotheosis: "Thou, undismayed, shalt o'er the ruins smile, / And light thy torch at Nature's funeral pile" (pp. 38, 39, 41, 44, 71). So easily can romantic aspirations baffle themselves.

Hope will be the vehicle for constructing a self at once simple, continuous, and yet embedded in lived time. But it must be a hope shorn of the excesses of enthusiastic extravagance.[3] In a splendid essay in existential phenomenology, Gabriel Marcel has described hope as that form of patience that never suffers because it knows how to take its time.[4] In hope, thus experienced, there is no anxiety about facing the future because there is no worry about losing the past; the repetitions of memory offer a permanent consolation by making time an expanse that is at our disposal rather than an onrush of events that befall us. Marcel compares hope to a release from a prison, namely the prison of selfhood and immediate self-involvement. Though Rousseau does not call this hope, it is the mood in which he writes, in the Fifth Reverie, "I have often thought that in the Bastille and even in a dungeon where no object should strike my sight, I should still be able to dream agreeably" (*Rêveries*, in *Oeuvres* 1: 1048). The possibility of hope in prison is, of course, the constant obsession of gothic novels, as of theatrical works like Beethoven's *Fidelio* or Inchbald's *Such Things Are*, and the metaphysical imagery of the confined and released spirit shines through with beautiful ease when Wordsworth's Matthew expostulates with him to heed "that light bequeathed / To beings else forlorn and blind." Whether

found in books or in the speaking face of things, such hope is inseparable from the community of humans and the language that makes
community possible.

I am not aware that anyone has charted the course of hope in the
romantic poets, even though it is the indispensable pendant of the
familiar romantic melancholy. For Wordsworth hope is preeminently a virtue of immature youth, before exposure to the disrup-
tions of experience. The adult may "dare to hope" ("Tintern Abbey,"
line 65), but only the boy hopes naturally: "When linked with
thoughtless Mirth I cours'd the plain, / And hope itself was all I
knew of pain" (*An Evening Walk*, lines 31–32). Hope is the condition of those whose world lies all before them, as melancholy is that
of those behind whom the gates of life have been closed. The pathos
of hope is the impossibility of realizing the future or retaining the
past: hope conjures up a continuity in experience that is by definition always getting lost. This is the great subject of the romantic
ode. The odes are hopeful poems, most frequently appeals to a fading
divinity, Psyche, autumn, or evening. The success of the appeal is
also the validation of the hope; romantic odes are thus all implicitly
odes to hope, as the ground without which the utterance cannot
make contact with its object.

Among the major romantic odes, I know of only one that names
its underlying goal directly, Friedrich Hölderlin's elusive and neglected "An die Hoffnung." If hope is the implied or correlative subject of all romantic odes, then the ode addressed to hope itself can
plausibly stand as the generic poem, defining the norm of poetic diction in the period:

> O Hofnung! holde! gütiggeschäfftige!
>   Die du das Haus der Trauernden nicht verschmähst,
>   Und gerne dienend, Edle! zwischen
>   Sterblichen waltest und Himmelsmächten,
>
> Wo bist du? wenig lebt' ich; doch athmet kalt
>   Mein Abend schon. Und stille, den Schatten gleich,
>   Bin ich schon hier; und schon gesanglos
>   Schlummert das schaudernde Herz im Busen.
>
> Im grünen Thale, dort, wo der frische Quell
>   Vom Berge täglich rauscht, und die liebliche
>   Zeitlose mir am Herbsttag aufblüht,
>   Dort, in der Stille, du Holde, will ich
>
> Dich suchen, oder wenn in der Mitternacht
>   Das unsichtbare Leben im Haine wallt,

Und über mir die immerfrohen
Blumen, die blühenden Sterne, glänzen,

O du des Aethers Tochter! erscheine dann
Aus deines Vaters Gärten, und darfst du nicht
Ein Geist der Erde, kommen, schrök', o
Schröke mit anderem nur das Herz mir.

O, Hope! gracious! kindly employed!
Who scornest not the house of grief,
And, glad to serve, Noble one! between
Mortals rulest and heavenly powers,

Where art thou? little have I lived; but my evening
Breath grows cold. And quiet, like shadows
Am I now here; and already songless
Slumbers the trembling heart in my breast.

In the green vale, there, where the cool spring
Daily rustles from the hill, and the lovely
Meadow blooms timelessly up to me in the autumn day,
There, in the stillness, gracious Hope, will I

Seek thee, or when at midnight
Life surges forth invisible in the grove,
And above me the everglad
Flowers, the blooming stars, gleam,

O thou, daughter of Aether! come forth then
From thy father's gardens, and mayst thou not
Come a spirit of earth, fright, oh
But fright with other guise my heart.

Hölderlin based the structure of his major odes on a doctrine of "modulation of tones." Almost the only certainty about his elaborate and opaque theory is that it focuses attention on the shifting registers of the poetic voice.[5] Yet here the speaker seems unvaryingly inert. Hope is the spirit of mediation (lines 3–4), whereas the speaker lives in a separated world, a sleepy, shadowy "here" set over against a flowery "there." The thrice-repeated "schon" (lines 6–7) indicates his situation in a motionless limbo; a brilliant pun reminds us how the paradisal meadow ("Zeitlose") is timeless "to me," whereas for hope even eternities exist in a world of time, "daily" (line 10; cf. "am Herbsttag" and "in der Mitternacht," lines 12–13). Hope visits "those who grieve," since even grief implies a consciousness of change. But the speaker who lacks hope can only utter the empty and disoriented outburst, "Where art thou?" (Cf. "Dem Sonnengott," where "Wo bist du?" is the drunken call of the soul buried in a sleep beyond grief). There is no content to the call issued by the man without hope, since only with hope come time, life, meaning, reality itself. Hope is the "spirit of earth," or, if not that, it bears the indistinct "other" that rouses the sleeper. The related ode "Ermunterung" specifies this other as the "spirit in man's word" that "on the fine day, shall name itself again by name, as formerly." The "other" of hope is the disjunction between presence and absence or sign and significance that makes expression possible. Without it there is only an apparently toneless, uninterpretable utterance by a speaker "without song."

"An die Hoffnung" is simplicity itself. What Hölderlin's theory would call its naive character (its personal diction and pastoral imagery) makes it a poem of essences. "Gesanglos" (line 7) implies the timorous speechlessness of infancy, reflecting a speaker without enough experience to have emerged from the narcissistic possessiveness of "*Mein* Abend," "*mir* . . . aufblüht," and "über *mir*" (lines 6, 11, 15). Yet there is no irony in attributing to this speaker a perfectly modulated ode. For hope is a narcissistic, self-begotten quality that "new-proclaims itself," "knows itself," "unfolds itself," "names itself," "finds itself," and "expresses itself," as we read in the stanza ends of the two versions of "Ermunterung." To call on hope is already to live in hope. Hence Hölderlin is able to negotiate a brilliant turn from the "ideal tone" (purified erotic mood) of the third stanza of "An die Hoffnung" to the "heroic tone" (groping and striving) of the fourth stanza. There is perhaps no other romantic poem that so unobtrusively and yet so decisively crosses the threshold from pure desire ("will ich," line 12) to pure absorption in the object of desire ("Dich suchen," line 13). The speaker who lives beyond change still lives in time; though he slumbers, he is not dead, and "schon" belongs to the realm of time in general, if not to that of measurement. The ode's stasis, in short, is the elemental medium of movement.

Several factors in "An die Hoffnung" narrow the distance between static hopelessness and the movements of hope. The cold of evening (lines 5–6) is, in romantic iconography, not very different from the cool of autumn (line 11), and stillness is found on both sides of the great divide (lines 6, 12). "Athmet kalt" (line 5) in some other context might be a witty periphrasis or an anguished oxymoron signifying death-in-life, but here it circumscribes the condition of quiet slumber in which hope dawns. The ode to hope—that is, to the poetic voice—is thus predicated on a minimal diction representing a threshold condition: "nicht verschmähst," "wenig," "Schlummert," "das unsichtbare Leben." On the threshold of hope, subject

310   *Wordsworth's Old Gray Stone*

merges with object, action with passivity, consciousness with unconsciousness. The songless trembling of the slumbering heart—
reminiscent of Coleridge's lines in "The Eolian Harp," "the mute
still air / Is Music slumbering on her instrument"—is a merely potential fear that in itself hardly differs from the invisible movement
of life. Yet little needs to be changed in order to bring the fear to
light—at least to the star-gleam of that Ariel or aerial spirit of hope.
For how little is hope? Its invisibly migrating life—less than ether in
person, not even a breeze of earth—resembles that of the faintly
gothic "Winds . . . from the fields of sleep" in Wordsworth's Intimations Ode. The fear that hope brings is already present in the trembling heart, needing only the uncertain difference of an indefinable
"other" to startle it into wakefulness.

In his mature poetry Hölderlin was always a master of the hidden metaphor, the assimilative simile, and the static transition. His
diction is a model of the simplicity that early romantic poetry generally hoped to achieve. Simplicity is an unexpected term to apply to so
notoriously hermetic a poet, but less so if it is understood as intransitive self-containment and as reduction of syntax to the bare bones
traditionally discussed as "harte Fügung" (see Adorno, "Parataxis").
In its curious way this is a poetry of understatement—or, as Wordsworth might have said, the under-song of an under-consciousness
—whose subtlest yet greatest effects are often phonetic. At the very
moment when Hölderlin calls his heart "songless," he is playing a
melody on richly modulated sibilants; later, the symmetrical asso-
nances of *Dort-holde* and *Stille–will ich* lead up to the rhymed
couple of *ich-Dich*,[6] and the next stanza issues in the relaxed disjunction between the alliterating *Blumen-Blühenden* and the as-
sonating *Sterne-glänzen*. Amid varying syntax, the phonetic weight
is always on the last line of the stanza, culminating in the sturdy
double spondee at the end of the poem. The vehicle of hope is an
unseparated, unfallen consciousness dwelling at the heart of language. Sign recovers its roots in song.

Toward Wordsworth

It will be the argument of this chapter that the old gray stone is the
ground and anchor of Wordsworth's hopes and the figure of his
simple style, resolving the compositional obstacles analyzed in the
previous chapters. The interpretation will thus continue the trian-
gulation—begun in the discussions of Bowles, Beattie, and Hölderlin—of an image, an attitude, and a style. The old gray stone is a nostalgic figure.[7] In the old days, as will be remembered, such a stone

stood in the Hawkshead village square, "the goal / Or centre" of village sports, before an assembly room replaced it (*Prelude* 2.33–40; Wordsworth repeats the phrase "the old grey stone" in line 88). And on it, or one like it, the young Wordsworth used to sit "and dream my time away," playing Peter to his beloved teacher Matthew ("Expostulation and Reply"). And yet his games and daydreams remained vital to the mature poet. The gray particular, I shall argue, is the animating One, the mysterious "living stone" from which "newborn babes" imbibe "the sincere milk of the word" and themselves become "lively stones" (1 Peter 2: 2–5). The momentary throb, which is Yeats's equivalent of Hölderlin's heart's trembling, never seizes the aged scholar's "inanimate phantasy." But we find it frequently in the quatrains of the young Wordsworth: the "thrill of pleasure" in "The human soul that through me ran," occurs at the "moment" when "Our minds shall drink at every pore / The spirit of the season" or when we receive "One impulse from a vernal wood" and drink the "spirit . . . breathed / From dead men to their kind." The inorganic rock embodies a unity both greater and less than that of the solitary organism. It "emblems," as Geoffrey Hartman has written, "energies in man and around him that . . . cannot be subdued to the self" (*Wordsworth's Poetry* 154).

It is not easy for us to reconstruct the degree to which all the poems of Wordsworth's Great Decade were meditations in time of war.[8] But behind even his simplest poems lurks a certain pressure of time, sensed in the urgency of the moment or in the exaggerated linkage of youth and age: "A pair of friends, though I was young, / And Matthew seventy-two" ("The Fountain"). I will not pretend to decide whether this pressure of time that Wordsworth registers was caused by revolutionary events, or they by it. Suffice it to say that, when relaxed, Wordsworth keeps the pressure in the background: the golden glow of memory restores the bond between Wordsworth and "the grey-haired man of glee" (ibid.) with only occasional hints of the craziness that the later Yeats was to reveal in such a figure,[9] while the "living calendar" of "To My Sister" dispenses chronologies with an abandon that Sterne could only have envied—"the first mild day of March," "each minute," "morning," "one day," "the year," "the hour of feelings," "one moment," "years," "long," "for the year." Here the redbreast's song converts time into something like the music of the spheres: the "temper" of today is its scale, and "the measure of our souls" is clearly no chronometry, no "joyless forms," but a melodious pulse that is "tuned to love." Time weighs on a man's life, but "time grows upon the rock" (Stevens, *The Man with the Blue Guitar*, stanza 11), and when Wordsworth sits on the

312 Wordsworth's Old Gray Stone

stone, he comes into contact with the source of time and is, for a time at least, at ease.

"Expostulation and Reply" and the other quatrain poems where the rock figures confidently look forward in a Rousseauistic spirit of primitive fellow-feeling to the round of the seasons and the dispensations of nature. The Rousseau in question is the recluse who, following the "night of stones," retired to the Île de St.-Pierre. This was a brief episode in Rousseau's life, but it forms the culmination of the *Confessions* and the central subject of his last work, *Les Rêveries du promeneur solitaire*. Buried alive on his green and pleasant stone— the epitaphic dimension of the old gray stone will occupy us later on—Rousseau dreamed his time away, feeding his mind in a wise passiveness, alone and yet (in Wordsworth's strange collocation) "conversing as I may."[10] Entering his societal limbo, to be sure, Rousseau abandoned all hopes, but "hope" always meant for him concrete expectations, which were invariably frustrated, and he claims that it gave way to an Augustinian confidence in God and in destiny that he describes at the end of the Second Reverie: "all is due to return to order at the last, and my turn will come sooner or later" (*Oeuvres* 1: 1010). St. Peter's rock, for him, is the place where he overcomes his tragic social persecution by recalling past bliss and anticipating its future repetition. At its best, the effect is produced by a kind of soul-writing that unwrites itself at the moment of ecstasy: "Amid such riches how was I to keep a faithful register? In wishing to recall so many sweet reveries, instead of describing them, I fall back into them. It is a state that is brought back by remembering it" (1: 1003). Whether internal or written, the memorial converts fate into faith by converting time from a resistless advance to a restful expanse.

Wordsworth's and Rousseau's experiences on their spots of rock thus help show us why their spots of time are also spots of eternity. The word "spot," indeed, is misleading, for just as the small rock is always perceived as part of the universal earth, so too what Hartman has called Wordsworth's centroversion is regularly encompassed by an unlimited spatial expanse, "all this mighty sum / Of things for ever speaking." Even the haunted spots are embedded in a vast landscape and accompanied, amid their terror, by an element of release. The stone is ageless; its temporality is of that which endures, and this is the ground for romantic hopes, as they "connect / The landscape with the quiet of the sky," linking a social and geological entity that changes slowly or imperceptibly with a meteorological and theological one that changes momently or never.

The old gray stone is, of course, more natural and less pretentious than a rock of faith. On the stone one may sit and collect or recollect oneself, taking time as it is offered. Ease is of the essence in combating despair, and religious and transcendent concerns are consequently muted in these poems to the point of near inaudibility. Even a term like "pantheism" seems too fraught to describe their utterance. Hartman, seconded by Bloom, has made it customary to read Wordsworth in the light of his moments of sublimity and prophecy. But though hope is less grand than prophecy, it is, like its corollary love, more of a "universal birth" ("To My Sister"), and hence more fundamental to human experience. Marcel calls it "a memory of the future" ("Sketch" 53) with "the power of making things fluid" (41), whereas "the prophetic consciousness [is] in danger of becoming obliterated to the extent that it seeks to pass itself off as second sight" (61). Prophecy brings things about, whereas hope lets them happen.

The power of hope is thus also a power of pausing. So Wordsworth pauses when he confronts the Boy of Winander, or when he is halted, "Like angels stopped upon the wing by sound" (*Prelude* 14.98). It does not come from above, like intermittent prophecy, but from below, "A fixed, abysmal, gloomy, breathing-place" (14.58), ever present, if we can only quiet our appetites enough to hear it. "If," says Marcel, "however feebly, we remain penetrated by hope, it can only be through the cracks and openings which are to be found in the armour of Having which covers us. . . . Thus, and only thus can the breathing of the soul be maintained, but under conditions, alas, of irregular action and a dangerous uncertainty often on the increase so that it is always in danger of being blocked like the lungs or the bowels" (62). Snowdon is the greatest stone in Britain and, one surmises, in the solid mist that seems to threaten blockage of the lungs and bowels, perhaps the grayest, and the ascent in book 14 of *The Prelude* reads like a momentary prophecy of enduring hope. For here, in a sublime image, Wordsworth intuits a time extended like space, just before time ends altogether,

> with the generations of mankind
> Spread over time, past, present, and to come,
> Age after age, till Time shall be no more.
> (14.109–11)

Such it is "To hold fit converse [1805 text: communion] with the spiritual world" (14.108), and just such, but more humble and more sustained, is Wordsworth's achievement as he sits at Hawkeshead, "conversing as I may." Goldsmith, we may remember, disposes perfectly of time in the idyllic flow of his narrative; Sheridan discerns its force in the animation of his monologues; Sterne intuits how to master its complexities, but no preromantic author could be said to step far enough outside time to under-stand or over-look it. Wordsworth's pauses and conversations are thus also conversions—as Coleridge too wanted his anxiety-filled conversations to be—and that not in the isolated moments of Miltonic grandeur that so often regulate current Wordsworth interpretations, but in the permanent, colloquial flow of the more typical Wordsworthian simplicity.[11] The Wordsworthian colloquy is the mystery whose emergence, tied to the topic of stones, I now wish to trace.

Toward the Great Decade

The Vale of Esthwaite

There is little ease or simplicity in the surviving fragments of Wordsworth's earliest major effort, known as *The Vale of Esthwaite*. Gentler parts may have been quarried for later poems, but what remains hectically endeavors to load every rift with ore. While the simple style quiets the eye to allow us a glimpse into the life of things, here we have a gothic superabundance of signifiers—sound and fury, not seeming to signify much. In *Prelude*, book 14, the shepherd's dog "once" interrupts misty musings with a "small adventure," soon "over and forgotten" (lines 21–27), in a brief, subhuman reminder of romance, whereas a similar dog in *The Vale of Esthwaite* is a center of attention and a "guiding sound" (lines 14–19). Here "the stream's loud genius" is not loud enough for the overwrought poet, who converts it, in one of the few recorded variants, to "the torrent's yelling spectre" (line 35). The incessant motion and noise reflect a fear of vacancy that undermines the poem's few approaches to calm. "Peace to that noisy brawling din / That jars upon the dirge within" (lines 398–99), he calls out at last, the noise interfering with a none-too-restful self-awareness. Music here is a strain in both senses: "But ah! fond prattler, ah! the strain / No more, as wont, can sooth my pain; / Cease, cease" (lines 402–4). Yet the plea for quiet is self-defeating in its intensity, betraying a poet who cannot stand much silence:

> or rouse that sullen roar
> As, when a wintry storm is o'er,
> Thy rock-fraught heavy heaving flood

Sounds dear, and creeps along the freezing blood.
'Tis dear.

(lines 404–8)

I admit to confusion at the last phrase, but I think the confusion was Wordsworth's first of all. However terrifying the gothic mode, he cannot live long without it, as if the blood of terror were the life-blood itself. "Still art thou dear, fond prattler, run" (line 414), as an iconic line has it, where "prattler," canceling the muteness of "still," and "run" canceling its repose, leave only its adverbial function as an intensifier of temporality itself. Time's flow as such is not enough, but must be continually created by external stimuli. The general marker of gothic emotions is also the general marker of temporal impulse: "I started," writes Wordsworth at the moment when the immobility of a seizure ("I the while / Look'd," "my fear-struck mind") is converted into a frantically active fit ("and with wild af-fright / Turn'd," lines 210–23; cf. "start" in lines 71, 123, 327, 368, 392). Action lacks all continuity of momentum, just as utterance lacks all continuity of expression; *The Vale of Esthwaite* is a place where meanings are forever being born, but never successfully transmitted.

Intensity is inseparable from tumult in *The Vale of Esthwaite*. If its violence seems always at least partly directed against the poet, that is because consciousness denatures the objects it seeks to de-scribe and because their elemental persistence seems in return to challenge the power of the mind. Intelligibility is the enemy of en-ergy, and only a sensual disequilibrium keeps the economy of the self going. Coming from an eighteenth-century sensibility, the psy-chic economy of the poem seems unimpeachable, however impover-ished its intellectual content: there must be no halt to the flow of sensation, of syntax, or of tears.

Flow on, in vain thou hast not flow'd,
But eased me of a heavy load;
For much it gives my heart relief
To pay the mighty debt of grief,
With sighs repeated o'er and o'er,
I mourn because I mourned no more.

(lines 428–33)

In the third stanza of the Intimations Ode "relief" counteracts "grief" to make Wordsworth "strong" again, but here the same rhyme ex-presses a solidarity that leads Wordsworth to speak of his "little heart" (line 434) and to go on to wish for his own death. And even death would not put a pause to grief, but only (via an allusion to Gray's "Elegy," lines 458–59) transmit it to a friend and thereby generalize the flow. The poem yells without articulating and breaks without demarcating, in a boundless narrowness that makes the Vale of Esthwaite a kind of imprisoning universe.

In a brilliant essay written from the perspective of Wordsworth's mature verse, Geoffrey Hartman has attempted to discern an incipient, incomplete dialectical structure within these early fragments (*Wordsworth's Poetry* 76–89). By parceling their utterances into opposing realms—mildness and sternness, sound and sight, nature and mind, repose and apocalypse—he is able to trace the origin of "a confict never to be quieted" in Wordsworth's verse (89). But to see the beginnings of romanticism in these undisciplined, preromantic effusions requires doing some violence to the texts. The Miltonic octosyllables do not indicate "a precarious interplay of opposing moods" (76), but rather a soupy fusion of allegro and penseroso in a poem that, for instance, sees "fancy in a Demon's form" (line 548). The poem's spectrum, Hartman says, is gradually reduced "to black and white" (p. 81), but the lines that he quotes (lines 95–102) actually progress to the two mixed yet hardly opposed tints of gray and brown. Though Wordsworth begins and ends in the equivalent "lingering" of dawn and dusk (lines 7, 512), he dwells on the more than Miltonic intensity with which he flees the clarity of noon.[12] He links grave and person, for selfhood is an obscure chaos, and he wants to make its darkness visible.

Hartman again adopts the perspective of the mature Wordsworth when he writes (about *Descriptive Sketches*) that Wordsworth "often, of course, bogs down in static personification" (108). Yet so common a characteristic of Wordsworth's early style should not be written off. The poet compulsively overdramatizes entities that are hardly dramatic in themselves. He is desperate to give them proper names and to make them speak. Meaning appears here as a kind of surplus value of being, as if in singling an object out for description the poet were issuing an appeal to it and demanding a response. Yet it is a factitious value that violates the object, saddling it with a voice not its own and insisting that it act when its nature is merely to be. Thus the early fragment "Beauty and Moonlight," beginning "High o'er the silver rocks I roved," turns the entire landscape into a fragmented image of a woman's countenance and body. But however delicate and tactful Wordsworth tries to make his flickering personification, the strain of voicing the image never leaves him alone: "True, true to love but false to rest, / So fancy whisper'd to my breast" (lines 11–12). Whose fancy is this, we may wonder, as we wonder about the fragment's unearthly perspective generally: is it a dictation from above (personification piled upon personification in a ghostly gothicism), or is it an internal voice, never quite articulate enough to carry conviction? The life of things—and in particular of those rocks that already litter Wordsworth's versescape—is never quite their life, but always too great or too small for them. Personifications persist so long as Wordsworth cannot convince himself of the adequacy of an organic view of nature; the discomfort we feel with them cannot be separated from their mission.[13]

Gray remains Wordsworth's progenitor here.[14] He bequeathes to the peripatetic young poet his idyllically redemptive sense of space. Yet Wordsworth pits space against time in a way that Gray never did, taking seriously the hauntings and death that ply urbanely around Gray's vision:

> I saw
> A dark and dreary vale below,
> And through it a river [? strong]
> In sleepy horror heav'd along,
> And many a high rock black and steep
> Hung brooding on the darksome deep,
> And on each sable rock was seen
> A Form of wild terrific mien.
> Ha! that is hell-born Murder nigh
> With haggard, half-reverted eye,
> And now aghast he seems to stare
> On some strange Vision in the air,
> And Suicide with savage glance
> Started from his brooding trance,
> Then sunk again, anon he eyed
> With sullen smiles the torpid tide;
> And moody Madness aye was there
> With wide-rent robe, and shaggy hair.
> That streamed all wildly round his f[ace]
> (*Vale of Esthwaite*, lines 379–97)

This is Gray writ large, amalgamated from the Eton College ode (source of the phrase "moody Madness") and from "The Bard." Yet the energy has been drained from Gray's "fury Passions." The neat quatrains and Collins-like statuesque personifications suggest a struggle to master the mode. Sight is multiply refracted—he sees Murder seeming to stare at a vision; "brooding" comes to mean looking vacantly; even "aye" seems to be pulled by homophony into the orbit of vision—but without ever fully awakening. It is as if stern nature were forever threatening to collapse into mildness, "sleepy horror." The violence, then, is that of consciousness itself. Murder and suicide are hardly distinguishable, for the self seizes itself in seizing the world; and madness is the essence of mood in a world where vicissitude is life and consistency is torpor. The key to the passage is Murder's extraordinary "half-reverted eye," a conflation of the "forward, and reverted eyes" of Gray's "Ode on the Pleasure Arising from Vicissitude" (line 32); for Wordsworth's strain here arises from a feeling that the eye (or the I) can only look outward if it can simultaneously look inward, and vice versa. It is not a comfortable posture.

The struggle to affirm consciousness in the face of brute nature is inscribed in the pun I-eye-aye. Even more deeply buried, and more essential, is the pun on "mien." A heightened, more threatening face, the mien is also what gives the wild landscape its meaning. Personification increasingly concentrates on the face, but more specifically on eyes and mouth as the source of consciousness and expression respectively. In this early verse, then, we see a frenzied effort to avoid vacancy. Etymologizing "chaos" as "yawning gap," Wordsworth seeks to fill in the wastes. The mode remains preromantic, looking backward as well as inward ("half-reverted"), as it labors to justify and fulfill the presuppositions of Gray's style.

For the eighteenth century consciousness is identical with attention and arises conjointly with the objects of attention. Personification is rarely completely objectified, that is, disjoined from the human agents affected by it; Gray's "fury Passions," for instance, are seen in relation to the children they are expected to beset. Wordsworth's personifications are more questionable spirits, diminished and alien, a challenge to perception and not a part of it:

> On tiptoe, as I lean'd aghast
> Listening the hollow-howling blast
> I started back—when at my hand
> A tall thin Spectre seem'd to stand
> Like two wan wither'd leaves his eyes
>
> . . .
> His bones look'd sable through his skin
> As the pale moonbeam wan and thin
> Which through a chink of rock we view
> On a lone sable blasted eugh.
> (*Vale of Esthwaite*, lines 325–33)

The specter is compared to leaves in a reversal of the normal order of personification, yet this order is reversed again by the modals "seem'd" and "look'd." The issue in confused visions like these—dark and pale at once—is not the content of the personification, but its status. The midcentury poets meditate on the soul by means of personifications; the early Wordsworth meditates on personification itself, staring at eyes that stare back, a poet confronting the mystery of his own animating inscriptions ("And on one branded arm he bore / What seem'd the poet's harp of yore," lines 334–35). He is looking about him for the substratum of meaning.

And so the ever-present rocks of these early poems are figures for what makes figurations possible. They are the mass of substance through whose chinks we glimpse spirit, the seat of the monsters, the articulating interruptions that give a voice to the stream. "From every rock would hang a tale" (line 495): already at this early stage Wordsworth feels the urge to solidify meaning. Later Wordsworth will learn to see the mien in the stone, the story of darkness itself. But these early rocks are featureless: they are not yet the stable essence of the living earth, but the dark foil that makes the light visible. So far there are only barren contrasts that undermine the Enlightenment synthesis, pitting action suicidally against its double, meaning; life against matter; existence against being; or (in the incoherent image quoted above) organic skin against inorganic bones. The urbane sublime caves in, as it were, producing a chaos haunted by obscure, superstitious yearnings: "Perhaps my pains might be beguil'd / By some fond vacant gazing child" (lines 490–91).

An Evening Walk

Worries about vacancy are central to Wordsworth's first major publication, *An Evening Walk*. Again reading retrospectively, Hartman emphasizes Wordsworth's effort to preserve the continuity of being in the face of prophetic fears of apocalyptic disruption. He does not mention the invocations to hope that frame the poem (lines 31–42, 407–22, also 255). The ethos is not fundamentally defensive: gothic nightmare seems less a problem than sleep. Death is a quiet, not a violent, cessation, and the supernatural is treated lightly, as a childish regression that, at its worst, threatens not madness but melancholia, a "tender, vacant gloom" (line 387). The "aërial music" (line 436) of evening keeps the walker going, but only as a reminder of new dawns and awakenings, "Where we, my friend, to golden [1836 text: happy] days shall rise" (line 419). Continuity, or the avoidance of apocalypse, is not enough in itself; it serves rather as a hopeful reminder of the progress and productivity toward which the poem points.[15]

Man here is a laborer. But even work is no salvation; it is a hollow and repetitious round whose emblem is the "blasted quarry" that empties out the earth itself: "How busy the enormous hive within, / While Echo dallies with the various din!" (lines 143–44).[16] The workmen in the poem lack one essential hope for the future without which all other labor is vain, namely families and offspring. The hopeless female beggar's children die in her arms, whereas the blithe or proudly idle birds and animals conjugate and propagate. Hartman finds the juxtaposed pictures of the lordly swans and the desolate beggar "unduly empathic" (p. 96), but the rhetorical inflation is functionally precise as a way of linking the emblems. The magical parent swans, in their "moveless form of snow" (line 206), act as vainly as the human mother, though in a different sense, and remain as remote from real life. One empty circle confronts another, the unvarying round of generations and the unprofitable round of daily chores. The noises that pervade the poem, culminating in "the slow clock tolling deep" (line 437), may be compared to the heartbeat of time, but its lifeblood is missing.

The separation of (human) labor from (animal) procreation points up the absence of a conception of productive labor. In an even more drastic sense than in Gray's evening "Elegy," this is a world in which nothing is made. It contains a proto-organic vision in much the same way as *She Stoops to Conquer*, juxtaposing undirected change against unchanging repetition, though with emphasis on the natural rather than the social realm. There is none of the unfolding that defines organic development. A reverie that never awakens, *An Evening Walk* could be called a meditative or musing poem in search of life.

There is a reflexive dimension here. For one kind of making that would satisfy the poem's needs is that of a poetic creator. The poem's mode is georgic and rambling, but as in most georgic, one senses a yearning for the grander continuities of epic. As the poet's world broadens out to encompass martial superstitions and social woes, Spenser, Milton, and Du Bartas (whose creation is, I think, echoed at lines 345–46), there is a gradual shift toward a vatic tone. The shift is most evident in the unpublished 1794 revisions. (At many points in the poem the 1794 version is the most forthright, as if Wordsworth could let his problems rest once he had fully articulated the poem's tendency.) This text incorporates at its conclusion an evocation of Druidic bards, beginning, "But, in the poet's vision, shapes sublime / Obscurely shadowed, solemnize the time," and recalling heroic battles between the Celtic heroes and the Romans (1794 text, lines 725–36; see also this text's lines about war, 358–409). The poet wishes to project society as the organism whose emergence gives meaning to the manifestations of life.

But for the georgic, nature remains the more valid context for the life that Wordsworth seeks. In the glancing lights that mark evening's arrival (lines 329–44) one misses the composed image of a grand mythic body found in Collins. But then Wordsworth's nature here is almost entirely the realm of living beings. Unlike, for instance, the *Guide to the Lakes*, which opens by describing the primeval terrain, *An Evening Walk* humanizes the countryside from the start, a landscape of "bridge, rude church, and cottag'd grounds" (line 11). The poet is rarely far from signs of human habitation—which the *Guide* was largely to describe as desecrations of the scene—and never far from animal life, treading the grass, breaking the mirror surface of the water, disturbing the silence of contemplation. Epic history holds little promise for this poet, but an even grander history might hold more: around the poem's horizon lurks the earth itself as the ultimate created object and the ultimate organic being. Again the 1794 text tries to address what earlier and later versions omit:

> A heart that vibrates evermore, awake
> To feeling for all forms that Life can take,
> That wider still its sympathy extends
> And sees not any line where being ends;
> Sees sense, through Nature's rudest forms betrayed,
> Tremble obscure in fountain, rock and shade,
> And while a secret power those forms endears
> Their social accents never vainly hears.
> (1794 text, lines 125–32)

From the first four lines of this passage it is easy to see why one might take continuity and the avoidance of apocalypse as the poem's central issues. But the continuation shows that the mere endurance of natural "forms" is not enough for the poet and that growth and change are essential to life.[17] Already this early, sense and power are charged words for Wordsworth,[18] the former implying meaning as well as perception, the latter life and intelligence as well as brute force. As nature is the universal society, so the life of things—of water, rock, and trees—is the subject of the universal epic, the poem of nature.

To become a romantic, then, Wordsworth needed to make himself into a geologic poet. He lacked, of course, the geological training that Goethe and Novalis were acquiring in Germany at almost the same time (let alone the astronomical training that was the favored alternative of most of the German romantics), but he did not lack the interest. In a third passage from the 1794 text we can discern the ultimate aim of Wordsworth's early personifying style, which is to capture the whole cosmos as a single, sentient and living force—not just the "meanest flower that blows," but the meanest pebble, as well as the most distant star:

> How different with those favoured souls, who, taught
> By active Fancy or by patient Thought,
> See common forms prolong the endless chain
> Of Joy and grief, of pleasure and of pain.
> With them the sense no trivial object knows;
> Oft at its meanest touch their Spirit glows
> And, proud beyond all limits to aspire,
> Mounts through the fields of thought on wings of fire;
> But sure with tenfold pleasure they behold
> The powers of nature in each various mould;
> If like the sun, their [   ] love surrounds
> The [   ] world to life's remotest bounds.
>
> (1794 text, lines 203–14)

Wordsworth's forebear here is the scientific Thomson, especially the exalted appeal that concludes "Autumn":

> O Nature! all-sufficient! over all
> Enrich me with the Knowledge of thy Works;
> Snatch me to Heaven.
>
> (lines 1352–54)

Thomson's panorama, however, is more clearly stratified and graduated. A Thomsonian phrase like "endless chain" seems out of place when Wordsworth collocates it with joy and grief, or pleasure and pain,[19] and Thomson's "Profound of Time" is a rational spectacle of "Motions, Periods, and their Laws" ("Autumn," line 1357), rather than a historical pageant of "Whatever man has been and man can be" (*Evening Walk*, p. 163). Wordsworth's enterprise encompasses far more than Thomson's; his "all" is more appetitive, and his gradations ("beyond all limits," "Mounts," "tenfold") are much less convincingly regulated. As a result, Wordsworth is acutely sensitive to the excesses of sensibility. He concludes the passage with some compensatory "yets":

> Yet not extinguishes the warmer fire
> Round which the close domestic train retire;

If but to them these farms an emblem yield,
Home, their gay garden, and the world their field;
While that, more near, demands minuter cares,
Yet this its proper tendance duly shares.
                    (1794 text, lines 215–20)

"Close domestic train" is another Thomsonian phrase, but the immediate linkage of the local to the universal presents a problem, requiring a suitable disposition of the self, its interests, and its activities.

To become a poet of earth thus entails a proper care of the ground. Reverence and tendance go hand in hand, as do feeling and thought. A phrase like "the world their field" suggests cultivating Nature herself, but by exploring and understanding rather than by gardening her, as Cowper would have desired. The 1794 passage just quoted is followed by a paragraph, found (with variations) in all versions of the poem, that appears to be concerned with the sights and sounds of evening, but whose real subject is the circumspect, sometimes perilous use of earth and its products: first potters, and later a peasant and a timber wain are seen on a dangerous cliff path; a single horse and an oblivious flock of sheep under a sheltering wall are briefly illuminated, the brook breaks blithely over its rocky bed, chapel bells call to evening, sounds remain from "the hammer'd boat" and, at last, from the distant quarry. In 1793 the paragraph (lines 109–24) followed directly upon a reference to "Th' unwearied glance of woodman's echo'd stroke" (line 107); in revision this disappears, but a new, more earthy reference is added to the "industrious oar" of the charcoal barge, which initially precedes the scientific passage and then, when that is omitted, leads immediately to the potters. The excesses of sensibility are surrounded and eventually conquered by industry.

At the end of the poem Wordsworth rewrites the paragraph about earth and industry. Here the streams sing to the poet, a hare alert to danger replaces the horse and sheep, the boat is a ferry, a forge replaces the quarry, and one "slow clock tolling deep" substitutes for the three bells in the low chapel. Where the early passage featured a busy road and communal activities of man and beast, now we have a less danger-filled but also more solitary field of labor. At the end of my discussion of sensibility I have already spoken of the beautiful partitioning of this landscape, no longer subject to the rational, geometrical unification of sight. Sound dissolves the tyrannical orderliness of the visual realm, as with the confused orientation in line 440, "And echo'd hoof approaching the far [1836 text: nearing the distant] shore." The noises are intermittent and of indeterminate significance ("The tremulous sob of the complaining owl," line 443, becomes, in the late text, "The sportive outcry of the mocking owl"), giving the landscape an emotional spaciousness that transcends the merely geographical. Yet costs and needs remain in this remarkably self-aware poem. The poet who has begun, like Goldsmith's traveler, roving "Far from my dearest friend" (line 1) is now at last on "my homeward way" (line 434). But there is little hominess about the last paragraph, and the isolated sounds of the last lines grow ever more restless. If this is Wordsworth's home, then his home is to be the ever-broadening expanse of the ear, and not the eye's bounded circle. Nearness and distance, repose and alertness, melancholy and hopeful expectancy come together in the "spiritual music" (1836 text, line 377) of Wordsworth's cadence. To make his home the broad earth, to make his community the diverse universe of separate beings, to make his history the history of the earth— these are the tasks that confront the poet on his long road home.[20]

Descriptive Sketches

It is then no surprise poetically—whatever the biographical motivations may have been—that the poet of the Lakes next turned outward to celebrate the most ancient and sublime mountains within his purview. On the surface the last of Wordsworth's early triptych of descriptive couplet poems, *Descriptive Sketches*, seems to be a blind alley in his development, what with its exotic subject matter, its clotted style, and its extreme idealization of Swiss mountain life. But the poem turns out to be a productive detour, forming an essential part of Wordsworth's stylistic development. Here the poetry of man is stifled, but the poetic life of an inhuman nature takes its place. It is not by chance that the 1793 text of the poem contains, in a martial context, the earliest reference in the Wordsworthian corpus to "old grey stones" (line 359), and the phrase is perhaps the more noteworthy for occurring casually, part of a general recognition that nature itself is born, matures, ages, and dies.

Descriptive Sketches was Wordsworth's most ambitious work to date (though the lost original of *The Vale of Esthwaite* appears to have been longer), with a greater range of poetic and historical reference than earlier poems, and with a more explicit background of war and of the pageant of society's development. But the conclusion seems to turn back into the path of *An Evening Walk*. Beginning with line 632, "Gay lark of hope thy silent song resume," it returns to the central topic of the earlier poem (the image closely resembles that in *An Evening Walk*, lines 407–12), to which there are only sentimental allusions earlier in the poem. Line 767 then echoes a Milton quotation earlier used in *An Evening Walk* (line 30). But above all the last four lines seem to complete the movement of both poems together. The earlier poem, like Goldsmith's *Traveller*, begins, "Far from my dearest friend, 'tis mine to rove," and ends with the poet on his "homeward way"; he is still alone throughout *Descriptive Sketches*, yet he ends the poem at home and in company: "Tonight, my friend, within this humble cot / Be the dead load of mortal ills forgot" (lines 810–11).[21] This temporary respite is not the end of the poet's quest, but it does mark a resumption, perhaps conscious, perhaps not, of the main line of his development.

The poem is so bookish that one wonders whether Wordsworth need ever have left his library to write it. Society hardly exists in the land he describes—except when invasion is being resisted. Otherwise, despite an occasional small and none-too-lively festivity— "ringlet-tossing Dance" rhymes at one point with "powerless trance" (lines 98–99)—the largest human context is the family, and the normal situation is isolation. Man is here less a laborer than a pastoralist; he is normally aged or young rather than in the prime of life, and the poem's most active figure, the chamois-hunter, dies in the solitude of his hostile terrain. Man's job is to watch and wait, and if he has nothing to watch and to wait for, he does not even beg, but merely exists. The inert style may be unappealing, but it functions to represent the inhospitable environs. Formulaic and heavily nominal, it is as craggy as the Swiss mountains. Indeed, the style is almost too successful. The journey to the Alps takes Wordsworth to a place where conversation is hardly possible, and where meaning comes not from other men, but from the weight of words themselves. He undertakes an allegorical journey, "While chast'ning thoughts of sweetest use, bestow'd / By Wisdom, moralize his pensive road" (lines 29–30), and the fearful rush of personifications all but overwhelms the human voice. A mere typographer's trick suffices to moralize the scene, creating an irresistible superhuman agency: "On the high summits Darkness comes and goes, / Hiding their fiery clouds, their rocks, and snows" (lines 205–6; in 1845 and after "darkness" is lowercase, and the second line is omitted). The vision of the poem is so grand, and so labored, that man dwindles into insignificance.

That is the poem's weakness. But it is not unrelated to its strength and to its place in Wordsworth's development. For the personifications have their own distinctive character. The poem, to be sure, is not devoid of static personifications of passions and moral sentiments, particularly toward the end. But in the more interesting parts the features of nature itself are personified. These are not the empty abstractions of the romantic caricature of personification, but eighteenth-century heightenings; when darkness becomes Darkness, feeling is intensified, and nothing is lost. There is a constant effort to read the significance of the landscape; it becomes the bearer of meanings, and not just an object of perception. The names attached by humans to the landscape—"the mystic streams of Life and Death" (line 73), or "Huge Pikes of Darkness nam'd, of Fear and Storms" (line 564)—are forms of such personification, as are mythical constructs like "the infant Rhine" (line 185). They all belong to a nature that is intrinsically expressive.

Reading *An Evening Walk* after *Descriptive Sketches*, one notices the relative informality of much of the earlier poem's diction; there a man speaks, to men or to nature ("Erewhile, I taught, 'a happy child' / The echoes of your rocks my carol wild," lines 19–20). *Descriptive Sketches* sacrifices the colloquial or spontaneous elements, but though we miss a man speaking to men, we should at least recognize the presence of mountains speaking to mountains, "Black drizzling craggs, that beaten by the din, / Vibrate, as if a voice complain'd within" (lines 249–50), or "An idle voice . . . / Of Deep that calls to Deep across the hills" (lines 432–33). Wordsworth repeatedly calls the Alps a "desert," at one point quoting Petrarch and footnoting him (lines 164–65). But where Petrarch, without Laura, hated the desert, Wordsworth claims to love it. In Switzerland man dwindles into insignificance, while nature grows into significance; the voice is inhuman, but proves on inspection to be at least an attempt to capture the language of nature. The stones are beginning to wax eloquent:

> Is there who mid these awful wilds has seen
> The native Genii walk the mountain green?
> Or heard, while other worlds their charms reveal,
> Soft music from th' aërial summit steal?
> While o'er the desert, answering every close,
> Rich steam of sweetest perfume comes and goes.
>
> (lines 418–23)

Descriptive Sketches reverses what in Wordsworth's time was still, if precariously, the traditional hierarchy of the creation. Even in the most idealizing passages there is a heavy dose of condescension. The Golden Age has been preserved because the society has not changed. But these are just relics: "by vestal Nature guarded,

here / The traces of primaeval Man appear" (lines 528–29). There is
something pitiable in these fragments of man's former glory:

> There with his infants man undaunted creeps
> And hangs his small wood-hut upon the steeps.
> And old men talking at the shady door
> Like patriarchs sit with long beards thin & hoar
> While solitary forms illumined stray
> Turning with quiet touch th[e] pale green hay.
>   (lines 293–94 and variant, p. 165)

Such persistence is at best a negative virtue; the Swiss have been
diminished by their failure to advance. But social growth and the
changes produced by man mask the slower rhythms of nature.
Where man's life stagnates, the life of nature emerges. In *Descriptive
Sketches* Wordsworth first learned to see nature "with voluntary
power instinct" (1805 *Prelude* 1.407).

In the mild pastoral valleys nature is timeless or asleep. Among
the crags and on the heights it comes alive: "From such romantic
dreams my soul awake, / Lo! Fear looks silent down on Uri's lake"
(lines 283–84). In 1845 Wordsworth changed "Fear" to "sterner pleasure," part of a general purge of the most characteristic elements of
the 1793 text. But fear is the essential emotion permeating the text.
Fear is the sign of man's confrontation with time. There is also time
among human habitations, of course, but pastoral time makes little
difference, and no one seems to care much about its passing. The
Grison gypsy, as Wordsworth says, "On viewless fingers counts the
valley-clock, / Followed by drowsy crow of midnight cock" (lines
227–28). But the heights give a panorama of a greater time, too large
and powerful to measure or regulate: "More high, to where creation
seems to end, / Shade above shade the desert pines ascend" (lines
289–90). The terrible drama of creation comes into view, amid the
"living rocks" (line 581) that belong to what Wordsworth learns to
recognize as "the endless Alp of life" (line 593).

In *Descriptive Sketches* Mont Blanc is already what it was to remain for all the romantics, the emblem of that greater time of nature
as well as of the overwhelming power of creation. From a distance
the mountain in its setting already presents a temporal spectacle
larger than man's view ordinarily comprehends: "Here all the Seasons revel hand in hand" (line 687). But its heights make visible an
even more immense power, at once oceanic and glacial:

> Six thousand years amid his lonely bounds
> The voice of Ruin, day and night, resounds.

> Where Horror-led his sea of ice assails,
> Havoc and Chaos blast a thousand vales,
> In waves, like two enormous serpents, wind
> And drag their length of deluge train behind.
>   (lines 692–97)

While there is plenty of physical danger in Wordsworth's Alpine excursion, that is the least of Wordsworth's fears. The "voice of Ruin" proclaims a greater horror for all who come within its spell. With a stone in one hand and a shell in the other, Wordsworth was later to revive that horror in a nightmare set in another desert, foretelling "destruction to the children of the earth / By deluge, now at hand" (*Prelude* 5.98–99). The featureless stone there is Euclid's *Elements*, the perfection of man's rational mind, "undisturbed by space or time" (5.105). But the oceanic forces that have stranded the shell and molded the rocks embed the abstract timelessness of reason in a temporal fatality, making both stone and shell alike into "emblems for the past and future products of the intellect" (Kelley, "Spirit and Geometric Form" 579). The terror in the apocalyptic voice, then, lies in the confrontation with a mysterious temporal power greater than reason can comprehend, such as that of a mountain "That dallies with the Sun the summer night" (*Descriptive Sketches*, line 691).[22]

Eventually Wordsworth learned how to draw strength from nature's violence. In his dream emblems the poet of *The Prelude* was to find "A joy, a consolation, and a hope" (1805 text, 5.109—the 1850 text is different, but still speaks of exhilaration and soothing). But in *Descriptive Sketches* the plenitude of time overshadows and darkens the mind of man: "Glad Day-light laughs upon his top of snow, / Glitter the stars above, and all is black below" (lines 700–701). It is no wonder that the poem proceeds beyond this evocation of nature's shattering blackness to an impassioned appeal for freedom. The late texts preserve the appeal because its underlying motivation is less a transiently political one than an enduring psychological dilemma. Somewhat inconsistently, a different passage in the 1836 and later texts reconciles the two times, that of man and that of the mountain, or the two minds, that of human and that of divine reason. It says that the voice of the Deep "accords the soothing sound / Of drowsy bells" (lines 371–72) and lets the two "Blend in a music of tranquility" (line 378). But originally the greater voice was "Broke only by the melancholy sound / Of drowsy bells" (lines 434–35). The epistemological task of the next few years was to bring the cosmic and geologic clocks into accord with the social and psychological clocks. Nature had to be humanized or, as one might also say, naturalized. It cannot be a question of avoiding apocalypse, for nature is apocalyptic in its essence, as it manifests the might and the totality of time. And, indeed, Wordsworth's poetry continued to be full of apocalyptic moments like the Arab Dream or the sublime sunset of *Descriptive Sketches* (lines 332–47). Rather, the task was to turn apocalypse to use, to master and control it so as to convert time from the drowsy tinkling of bells—a self-negating fourth dimension within the geometrical uniformity of reason—into the mighty form of change.

Descriptive Sketches remains too bookish to achieve this aim. Its chief inspiration, indeed, was not so much the landscape itself as a book of travels, Ramond de Carbonnières's version of William Coxe's journey to Switzerland. Wordsworth's footnotes repeatedly acknowledge Ramond, and it is well known that he borrowed Ramond's portrayals of the mountain settings and of the Golden Age of Switzerland. But Ramond's real originality and fascination was his view that the time of the earth is visible in high mountains. "Time," as Wordsworth might have read in Ramond's other major work,

> which skims over the rest of the earth, here imprints profound vestiges of its passage; and while elsewhere it hides from us the rapidity of its course by sweeping us along more rapidly than most of the objects that surround us, in the mountains it unfolds what is frightening about this speed by shaking, under our eyes, an edifice that seemed unshakable to our weakness, and by changing, in our presence, forms that, from a distance, we were accustomed to consider eternal. . . .Time seems to stop when it gives existence, when it develops it, when it sustains it; one only learns that it passes when one sees it destroy its work.[23]

From a book Wordsworth learned how apocalypse prints its mark on eternity.

The signs are there for all to read, in print, and in nature. For the voice of nature is bookish too.[24] Wordsworth saw deep calling to deep, for instance, in the Psalms, long before he saw or heard it in the Alps. Yet an unresolved tension remains between the living landscape and the signifying landscape. "That mountain nam'd of white" (line 690), Wordsworth calls Mont Blanc. It speaks by manifesting its own name in its appearance. But the name speaks of the blankness of the human imagination in the face of nature's dazzling spectacle. The poem is less frantic than *The Vale of Esthwaite*, but there is still a superabundance of signification. Nature personifies

itself in every feature. There is too much imprinting, and insufficient reserves of vital meaning. And so, when Wordsworth returned
to the old gray stone, he coupled it with an appeal to Matthew to
leave his books.

The Borderers

In the mid-1790s Wordsworth experimented with gothic modes. In
terms of his stylistic development the main undertakings of these
years, the Salisbury Plain poems and *The Borderers*, are even more
aberrant than *Descriptive Sketches*, and he withheld them from
publication for almost half a century. They depend on a perplexing
double alienation, from nature and from society: their wasted landscapes force the nature poet's gaze back onto human destinies, yet
the humans in these no-man's-lands are homeless outcasts. In undertaking his play, as in the so-called "Fragment of the *Gothic Tale*"
(*Borderers*, pp. 750–57), Wordsworth may originally have sought to
write a conventional poetry of effect, employing atmospheric setting
and melodramatic narration to call forth an emotional frisson and
a universal sympathy. Nature generally appears in *The Borderers*
as a realized emblem of its own meaninglessness, all ruins, deserted
cairns, and beacons that illuminate nothing. Such motifs in a sense
consummate the sign character that Wordsworth had always been
prone to attribute to nature, but at the cost of natural agency as well
as of intelligibility. Yet the accumulated surprises inevitably put
consciousness on the alert. The sharply profiled spectacles of guilt
and sorrow seem to demand an accounting of responsibility. In his
revisions, and particularly with the addition of the essay analyzing
Rivers's character, Wordsworth was gradually drawn to organize its
sensational effects into comprehensible patterns. The wedge that
Wordsworth drives between feeling and knowledge, man and nature,
subject and object throws his conceptual task into high relief, even
as it generates intolerably conflict-laden texts.[25]

The famous lines declaring that action is transitory while suffering is permanent highlight the dilemma. They were published separately well before the rest of the play, in the epigraph to *The White
Doe of Rylestone*. There the emphasis is on suffering and endurance.
Some added lines speak of hope and a patient movement toward re-
generation: one must live the consequences of one's actions. In the
play, however, Rivers, the villain, intends something different from
what the words in themselves say: he is encouraging Mortimer to
choose momentary evil actions in preference to eternal submission.

Even in 1798 the lines ought thus to have left readers as perplexed as they do Mortimer (who responds, "I do not understand you," *Borderers* 3.5.66). Obsessed by a past he is driven to repeat, Rivers acknowledges only moments without consequence and eternities without cause, whereas consciousness properly operates within time by making connections and drawing distinctions. At the last minute, in the printer's copy for the 1842 revision, Wordsworth changed the reply to the "Action is transitory" speech into "Truth—and I feel it" (the first revision had been "Your drift I know not"), in an implicit reaction to the intolerable conceptual impasse. Caught between such irreconcilable conditions of fixation and of movement, Wordsworth's gothic mode renders in its most blatant form "The unimaginable touch of time" ("Fragment of a *Gothic Tale*," line 66).

I suggest, therefore, that the alienated consciousness depicted in these unpublished works represents an aberration, and not a necessary component of the Wordsworthian imagination. As a transitional work placed in a border setting and composed in the hybrid genre of the closet tragedy or dramatic poem, *The Borderers* rests particularly uneasily on its premises. Despite Wordsworth's attempts at psychological penetration, the tragic action is externalized in a cumbersome fashion. In the absence of a narrator to complicate our perspective through a mixture of sympathy and judgment, we are left with characters who fulfill their destinies in the same way as Darkness or Mont Blanc. Functioning as personifications of moral qualities, they harangue: there is little room for dialectical interchange and dramatic collision where action is irresponsible and suffering appears permanent and unmotivated or predetermined long before the stage action begins. Walled off from one another in almost complete incomprehension, they cannot help revealing themselves to the audience in the purity of their plight. The fatalism that pervades the play is thus less an article of belief than a condition of form.[26]

The play is of interest here because of its insight into this crisis of expression. On the borderlands—where meaning approaches a gothic haunting of sound by sense and where revelation of character coincides with inscrutable fixation—the swift hand of destiny that brings death to Rivers (though his name suggests an onward flow) is no different in its effect from the hereditary fatality and timeless wanderings allotted to Mortimer (though his name suggests death rather than deathlessness).[27] Action and suffering—in the form of expression and comprehension, or of a joint binding to intention and to origin—seem as unhappily identified in every utterance as they are in the characters and incidents of the plot. In the 1842 version (a more successful revision than those of the early poems, probably because there was less personal investment in the original text) the victim Marmaduke identifies the dilemma in his valediction to the villain Oswald:

> When seas and continents shall lie between us—
> The wider space the better—we may find
> In such a course fit links of sympathy,
> An incommunicable rivalship
> Maintained, for peaceful ends beyond our view.
>
> (lines 2274–78)

The pious conclusion is alien to the original text, but only if "ends" is taken in too complacently temporal (or political) a sense, as an earthly predestination. For, more broadly conceived, the darkness of a link both indissoluble and incommunicable where sympathy and alienation meet is of the essence from the inception of the tragedy. Mortimer takes his homeless future to be a mute expiation for the original sin of hearkening to Rivers:

> I will go forth a wanderer on the earth,
> A shadowy thing, and as I wander on
> No human ear shall hear my voice,
> . . . and all the uncertain way
> Shall be as darkness to me, as a waste
> Unnamed by man!
>
> (5.3.265–71)

The only alternative seems to be the ranting babble that composes the play and that re-erupts at the end: "Confused voices—several of the band enter—rush upon Oswald and seize him." (The original version contains an even more graphic sequence of stage directions: "Confused noises are heard with uproar," followed by "Voices" shouting "—Hola.—There! there! Huzza!") The conclusion thus leaves us with a world ranging between speechlessness and noise, a tragic redaction of the spectrum we have already seen in Sterne.

But that is not all there is to the play. In the couplet poems it was possible to discern an inarticulate yearning for forces of expression, nature, and time that lay beyond the young poet's grasp. *The Borderers,* for the first time, offers a positive image for man to counterbalance the dissolution it portrays. For the figure that interpretations have tended to slight, the blind old Herbert, offers a purified vision of natural expressivity.[28] He is a figure of mystery rather than of inner conflict. He unhesitatingly retells his history (1.1.150–78; a crude expository device, yet, as Richardson notes in *Mental Theater* 34, thematically appropriate in contrast to the uncommunicative-ness of the two young men), and he readily signs his name (2.1.128). Yet he flees noise (1.2.50–59) or tames it (3.3.73–79), favors a "gentle voice" of "quiet hope" (3.3.61, 97), and barely protests when Mortimer abandons him on the heath (3.3.138–40, 142, and 145, re-duced in 1842 to two half-lines, "Oh, Mercy!" and "My blessèd Child!" lines 1405 and 1408). He fuses the roles of Lear and Glouces-ter, becoming a spectacle of helpless suffering and the focus of pity while hardly needing to utter a word. You only need to look at him to know him: "His face bespeaks / A deep and simple meekness," says his daughter (1.1.136–37), who also says later, "Could I behold his face, could I behold / The terrible pleading of that face of his" (3.5.131–32). It is a dark, "blasted face" (1.1.153), and part of its mystery is its ability to communicate wordlessly and even in the obscurity of night: "'Twas dark, dark as hell—yet I saw him—I tell thee I saw him, his face towards me—the very looks of Matilda sent there by some fiend to baffle me" (2.3.287–89). This masklike, mute eloquence has much in common with the stony gothic resistance to demonic persecution, such as is found in Godwin's *Caleb Williams*, which was much in Wordsworth's mind at the time.[29]

One could not exactly say that Herbert is an old gray stone. But it is precise to say that, in accordance with the norms of Words-worth's style in the period, Herbert *personifies* the old gray stone. The beggar identifies his role most unambiguously:

> but yesterday I overtook
> A blind old grey-beard and accosted him . . .
> If you can melt a rock he is your man.
>
> (1.3.71–75)

Though tinged with resentment, envy of the old gray stone remains his primary emotion, for he has just finished confessing, "I'd rather be / A Stone than what I am" (1.3.48–49). Herbert sits on a stone (3.3, s.d.), and is drawn to stones as to his home (4.1.2; 5.2.21–28). His enemy Rivers, by contrast, experiences rocks as the site of "most hellish orgies" (2.1.118) and of death (4.2.22–28), as a curse ("ten years' visitation of the stone," 4.2.176), and as a hostile power that can be ruined at the sound of his voice (5.3.252–55). While guiding Herbert, Mortimer hears "delicious" words echoed off a stone that are inaudible to Rivers (2.3.23–28), though later on he is corrupted into Rivers's hostile attitude ("I would cleave a stone,"

5.3.208]. Herbert is the only character whose name is unchanged throughout all the revisions; it associates him with St. Herbert of Derwentwater, who also lived among stones, as Wordsworth tells us in a poem of 1800. The stones are the signs of Herbert's subhuman weakness, but also of his nearness to nature and to God.

Through Herbert's blind trust Wordsworth undermines Rivers's fatalism. If he suffers, then, by Rivers's own account, he must also endure. The rock of faith and the hopefulness of romantic expression are not yet much in evidence in this product of Wordsworth's disillusion with revolutionary utopianism. But there is a sense in which they lurk at least half-understood within the text. For Herbert's visage seems, as Keats says of Moneta, "deathwards progressing / To no death." Reports of his lingering agonies fill much of the last two acts. Yet accusations and confessions of murder alternate with images of a corpse at peace, of sleep, rebirth, and natural cycle. The slowing of action at the end—except when Rivers is abruptly seized—contrasts effectively with the frenzied accumulation of on-stage deaths, including the murder of the father, at the end of Wordsworth's model, Schiller's *Die Räuber*. Violence remains offstage, and it is a violence of recognition rather than of action, as when Matilda is reported to have screamed at the discovery of her father's corpse. There is no moment of death, hardly even a moment when death is fully acknowledged. On the contrary, there is a gathering feeling that Herbert's spirit—the life of the stone—cannot die. He becomes an image of himself ("The dead have but one face," 5.3.45), and he imparts his stony nature to the unfortunate daughter ("I have cased her heart in adamant," 5.3.102) and to the deluded, spiritually innocent murderer ("This scrip [the accidental, negligent cause of death] . . . / Doth lie upon my bosom with a load / A mountain could not equal," 5.3.112–15). Mortimer inherits the stony, "dead" life of the blind man as he accepts his destiny to wander over the earth:

> and all the uncertain way
> Shall be as darkness to me . . .
>
>   . . .
>
> . . . till heaven in mercy strike me
> With blank forgetfulness—that I may die.
>   (5.3.269–75)

The earth becomes the purgatorial realm of the soul awaiting release.

Herbert's curse and Mortimer's, to be sure, have something in common with that of the Ancient Mariner, another old, stony graybeard. But by splitting the wanderer into two, an old man who is allowed to die and the younger scapegoat who substitutes for him,

Wordsworth replaces Coleridge's nihilism with signs anticipating fulfillment through a slow yet patiently awaited redemption. The Mariner passes with preternatural swiftness, "like night, from land to land," as he compulsively retells his story. Mortimer's story is to be inscribed on a warning monument (5.3.262–63), while he shuns society and becomes a moving darkness. He is a figure as eerie yet as natural as night itself.

Externalization in *The Borderers* entailed a heightening of inwardness rather than the usual dramatic extroversion. Hence, as Wordsworth seems to have sensed, in contrast to Coleridge, it had to be an unperformable play. Even monologue can only point to the core of human suffering, without truly expressing it, as when Mortimer soliloquizes at the beginning of act 3, scene 5:

> Deep, deep and vast, vast beyond human thought,
> Yet calm—I could believe that there was here
> The only quiet heart on earth.—In terror,
> Remembered terror, there is love and peace.

The setting here is "the Wood on the edge of the heath," and one can feel sure that Wordsworth was not thinking of a stage wood and a painted heath. Paradoxically for so garrulous a text—perhaps, indeed, because the text is so garrulous—what counts in *The Borderers* is appearance and gesture, and above all the hauntingly expressive look of the blind man.[30] Wordsworth experimented with drama as a way of reinvesting literature and language with the immediacy of life. But life meant for him a quiet heart and a loving memory. And so its natural expression was in an unspoken drama, representing silence itself and intimately involved with the natural landscape, which could hardly be imported live into the theater. It points directly toward Wordsworth's envy for the silent permanence and peace of landscape painting, in the line that reaches its exquisite apogee with "Peele Castle," a hoary pile at once deep, vast, and calm.

And Beyond: The Stony Likeness

Wordsworth's itinerary toward the threshold of romanticism thus generates as a series of negations and absences the conditions to be met by his mature style. Wordsworth was slowly learning what it means for consciousness to take its time. Confronting a semiotic disjunction when meaning takes the form of haunted personifications, he gradually tames it to the point where meaning can be treated as a growth out of the soil of thought. The disjunction of practical reason—the suddenness of action in its "starts"—provokes a search for a flow of time so grand and so steady that it cannot be broken. Finally, an epistemological disjunction affects the locus of the search: is time to be found within or without, in the subject or in the object? And here the discovery, in which the spirit of Berkeley is as important as that of Kant, concerns an interpenetration of man's mind and nature's matter. The sound of the bells tolling through the early landscapes—and also, for instance, through book 6 of *The Prelude* (1805 text, lines 84–87, 623–24)—shifts Wordsworth's attention from places and things to "A motion and a spirit" that "rolls through all things" ("Tintern Abbey," lines 100–102). I have not attempted to trace extrinsic roots for these various concerns, in which philosophical, scientific, historical, and even biographical instabilities mingle indissolubly.[31] Rather than pointing backward, the growth of the poet's style points ahead, teleologically, toward the resolutions that Wordsworth, as a great poet, more convincingly attained than did a minor figure like Bowles.

Heidegger analyzes the central problem bequeathed by the romantics as that of fundamental ontology, or of the nature of being. A romantic designation for it (in Kant, say, or Humboldt) is that of anthropology, or of the nature of man. Under either designation, the worry that links the various stylistic disjunctions is that of the endurance of identifiable essences—personal identities, species types, political institutions, or moral values—under conditions of internal and external change. The ground of consciousness must be sought in a continuity glimpsed beneath all the disjunctions and abysses of experience. Through images of growth and flow and interpenetration Wordsworth learns to evoke the moving permanences that would ally creation with life.

But these are just images after all. The most famous utterances of Wordsworth's Great Decade remain mystic projections of the unknown objects of unsettled desires. Phrases like "a motion and a spirit" are magical in context and, to some, ludicrous out of context, precisely because their value is relational rather than substantive or doctrinal. They are constructed, not found solutions. Hence the poetic energy and power that readers so often feel at the very moments when they least know what Wordsworth is saying. For that is where the drive of Wordsworth's style is most palpable.[32]

There remains, then, the crucial issue of finding in experience what Wordsworth has projected in imagery. How can what is thought be related to what is seen, what learned to what discovered, past knowledge to present insight? Perception too has its disjunctions, its half-creations (see "Tintern Abbey," lines 107–8). Nature is both a gallery of images, free and spontaneous as the fleeting clouds, and a repertory of inscriptions, simple in their unchanging majesty. Is there a way that it can be both at once?

With the "inward eye" ("I Wandered Lonely as a Cloud," "Suggested by a Picture of the Bird of Paradise") and with the "speaking face of earth and heaven" (1805 *Prelude* 5.12) Wordsworth approaches a conception of continuous revelation. Apocalypse is not avoided but, on the contrary, grafts its sublimity onto the ordinary fabric of existence. God's message needs neither proclamation nor registration, for it is "like the wild growth / Or like some natural produce of the air" ("It Was an April Morning"). The overly bookish young poet discovered, within him and around, an eternal, living, natural, and hence unwritten book in which all, even the unlettered shepherds, could read, now and in the future ("Years after we are gone and in our graves," as the last-cited poem says). This is God's folio; its pages are the luxuriant "foliage of the rocks," and the volume, the rocks themselves, living memorials of the Creation.

An old gray stone is the face of nature. Geological processes have etched, molded, and colored many of the stones that we see or that we mine. They take their character from their history. But the stones called "old"—old even in the geological perspective—are worn beyond characterization. The incised features of a young stone slowly weather away to an unimaginable purity. The Wanderer in *The Excursion* comes closest to defining what an old gray stone is, though he remains too superstitiously attached to particularities to ally himself with nature's oldest and most naked forms:

> Among these rocks and stones, methinks, I see
> More than the heedless impress that belongs
> To lonely nature's casual work: they bear
> A semblance strange of power intelligent,
> And of design not wholly worn away.
> Boldest of plants that ever faced the wind,
> How gracefully that slender shrub looks forth
> From its fantastic birthplace! And I own,
> Some shadowy intimations haunt me here,
> That in these shows a chronicle survives
> Of purposes akin to those of Man,
> But wrought with mightier arm than now prevails.
> (*Excursion* 3.80–91)

Here, in the book entitled "Despondency," there remain traces of local ties. But the tendency of Wordsworth's thought is toward a universal spirit, broadly diffused and not merely dialogic but, in every sense, colloquial. Even here, therefore, the setting generalizes the inscription, which is actually an unwritten imprint on a "barren . . . tablet" (3.61), and glorifies the place for the utter featurelessness of its sky:

> —Voiceless the stream descends into the gulf
> With timid lapse;—and lo! while in this strait
> I stand—the chasm of the sky above my head
> Is heaven's profoundest azure; no domain
> For fickle, short-lived clouds to occupy,
> Or to pass through; but rather an abyss
> In which the everlasting stars abide;
> And whose soft gloom, and boundless depth, might tempt
> The curious eye to look for them by day.
>
> (3.92–100)

The style of *The Excursion* indiscriminately juxtaposes the elevated and the ordinary. Note here the jingle of "abyss" and "abide," along with the phrase "pass through" where "traverse" would have maintained the prevailing level; elsewhere we find imagery like "A lowly vale, and yet uplifted high" (2.329), and diction like "Feebly it tinkles with an earthy sound" (3.31), which both distills and parodies the "soft inland murmur" of "Tintern Abbey." Hence the "design" of a "power intelligent" does not forestall the Wanderer from apostrophizing contemplation, fifteen lines later, as an undifferentiated realm of "height or depth," where "the scale / Of time and conscious nature disappear, / Lost in unsearchable eternity!" (3.108–11). Wordsworth has passed beyond the ironic condescensions of *Descriptive Sketches* to this stony and inexpressive grisaille.

The term for the rubbing out of distinctive features is effacement. Its etymology suggests that Wordsworth countenances a visage even when there are no characteristic marks. The fulfillment of the Wanderer's vision is deferred until the blank apocalypse that climaxes the whole poem:

> That rapturous moment . . .
> When these particular interests were effaced
> From every mind.
>
> (9.588–90)

Here is found the final leveling:

> From that exalted station to the plain
> Descending, we pursued our homeward course,
> In mute composure, o'er the shadowy lake,
> Under a faded sky.
>
> (9.756–59)

Effacement is complete: "No trace remained / Of those celestial splendours" (9.759–60). Heaven's architecture solidifies the blank— "grey the vault" (9.760)—as the sky is emptied for a moment of all its signs of day and of night: "Pure, cloudless ether; and the star of eve / Was wanting" (9.761–62). The gray vault yields all too soon back to the more conventional glitter of the stars, but for a moment "this communion with uninjured Minds" has brought "renovation" and "healing to a wounded spirit," turning it toward "delightful hopes" and, in the very last line of the whole poem, toward "future labours" (9.785–96). "Composure" is also the term with which Cowper responded to Collins. Wordsworth's healing vision, which retains so many elements of the "Ode to Evening," but which descends from the heights and eliminates all mythological mediation, even that of the evening star, is the culmination of a half-century-long movement of style.[33]

The old gray stone is what would now be called a visage under erasure.[34] The erasure, however, is not a deprivation, but a purification and fulfillment. Individual history dissolves back into universal history; particular markings vanish before the featureless blank— Derrida calls it an "archi-écriture"—that marks the stones as mere stones:

> Here on their knees men swore: the stones were black,
> Black in the people's minds and words, yet they
> Were at that time, as now, in colour grey.
> ("The Black Stones of Iona")

Grayness is essence, the face of the stone in itself, behind whatever might have been inscribed on it. It is the color of inwardness, the mind or soul of physical nature. The self-portrait of Wordsworth sitting on the old gray stone introduces the "Poems of Sentiment and Reflection" in his collection: the old gray stone favors meditation because it is the closest we can come to an image of thought itself, abstracted from its contents.[35]

I have already discussed the use of the phrase "old grey stone" in *Descriptive Sketches* (where it is pluralized), in "Expostulation and Reply," and in book 2 of the 1850 *Prelude*. It also occurs in a 1798 elegy for Matthew, "Address to the Scholars of the Village School of ———"; in a poem written in 1824, "Written in a Blank Leaf of Macpherson's *Ossian*"; and in two unpublished manuscript versions of an inscription for Rydal Mount, written in 1830, that begins, "In these fair vales"; as well as in the sonnet with which I shall conclude. "Grey rock(s)" or "grey stone(s)" occurs in five other published texts, in the 1805 and 1850 *Preludes*, and in a manuscript variant to *The Excursion*. In most of these cases a word like "old" or "hoary" occurs in close proximity, as it also does in "Composed at Cora Linn," where the "central stone" is called both "Yon time-cemented Tower" and "Yon grey tower." Finally, four of Wordsworth's most representative poems contain, as does *The Borderers*, a figure representing an old gray stone: *The Thorn* (which is "old and grey" and "Like rock or stone"), *Michael*, "Hart-Leap Well," and "Resolution and Independence." Wordsworth was not reluctant to reuse a striking phrase or image once or twice, but he was notably fussy about more frequent repetition. I doubt that there is any comparable phrase or image that he returned to so many times over such a period of time. With these facts in mind, I will turn to a beautiful, neglected sonnet of 1815 in which the old gray stone is again central:

> Mark the concentred hazels that enclose
> Yon old grey Stone, protected from the ray
> Of noontide suns:—and even the beams that play
> And glance, while wantonly the rough wind blows,
> Are seldom free to touch the moss that grows
> Upon that roof, amid embowering gloom,
> The very image framing of a Tomb,
> In which some ancient Chieftain finds repose
> Among the lonely mountains.—Live, ye trees!
> And thou, grey Stone, the pensive likeness keep
> Of a dark chamber where the Mighty sleep:
> For more than Fancy to the influence bends
> When solitary Nature condescends
> To mimic Time's forlorn humanities.
>   ("Mark the Concentred Hazels")

As the generic concern of the Renaissance sonnet is the relation of reason to passion, so that of the Wordsworthian sonnet is the relation of thought to feeling.[36] While the Great Ode addresses "Thoughts that do lie too deep for tears," the sonnet meditates on the emotion touched by "solemn thought" ("It Is a Beauteous Evening"), or on a returning thought of grief ("Surprised by Joy"). In the "Dedication" to the "Miscellaneous Sonnets," the group that includes "Mark the Concentred Hazels," the association of stones and thoughts is as explicit as anywhere in Wordsworth:

> Happy the thought best likened to a stone
> Of the sea-beach, when, polished with nice care,
> Veins it discovers exquisite and rare,

Which for the loss of that moist gleam atone
That tempted first to gather it.

(lines 1–5)

Wordsworth's thoughts are always at some remove from the oceanic gleam of transcendent perfection. Their birthplace is a Platonic Idea, an intimation of immortality spared by the touch of time. But their destination is more humble:

That here,
O chief of Friends! such feelings I present
To thy regard, with thoughts so fortunate
Were a vain notion.

(ibid., lines 9–12)

The gleam fades into the light of common day, and the veins—so the pun hints in line 12—get rubbed out. And so they come to rest in what the ensuing sonnet ("Nuns Fret Not") calls "the Sonnet's scanty plot of ground," as if in the gray uniformity of the tomb.[37] Such is the telos of thought.

What, then, is a thought in its mature fulfillment?[38] That is the question that will guide the interpretation. In "Mark the Concentred Hazels," Fancy, with its dancing lights, plays the same role as "the feeling . . . like a bubble blown / For summer pastime into wanton air" in the dedicatory sonnet: it is also evoked in the "toys of fancy," "bright liquid mansions" "in miniature" that dance on the surface of the Duddon in the twelfth sonnet devoted to that river ("Hints for the Fancy"), or in the morning light on the Meuse that Wordsworth contrasts to "grey rocks clustering in pensive shade" in "Between Namur and Liege," sixth of the "Memorials of a Tour on the Continent, 1820." How is the likeness of thought "more" than these delusive reflections of fancy? What constitutes a *"pensive likeness"*? How do the vertical interplay of height and depth, the horizontal contraction and expansion, the sensations of confinement and release contribute to the picture of the mind's operations that Wordsworth's sonnet gives us?

The spirit in this hazel bower corrects the excesses narrated in "Nutting." There a surplus of eager hope, abetted by overly fanciful mimicry of costume, had led to a mutilation of the grove. Here, by contrast, the scene is respected and there is no defacement. The exclamation "Live, ye trees!" shows that Wordsworth had learned his lesson from the earlier occasion, when the trees "patiently gave up / Their quiet being" ("Nutting," lines 47–48). "Nutting" is another illustration of the maxim that action is suffering ("I felt a sense of pain," line 52), whereas the bower of the sonnet seems beyond both. But we must then ask where the life of the scene resides. The trees bear no injuries, but we are also not told that they bear any fruit comparable to the "tempting clusters" of "Nutting" (line 20). The fertile trees of the earlier poem form a "virgin scene" (line 21) with respect to human knowledge, but their "beds of matted fern, and tangled thickets" (line 15) testify to the abundant life of the forest community. The bower of the sonnet is infinitely more cloistered. Indeed, it is more cloistered even than a third pensive bower that is described as the resort of monks in one of the "Ecclesiastical Sonnets" (1.21) entitled "Seclusion":

> Within his cell,
> Round the decaying trunk of human pride,
> At morn, and eve, and midnight's silent hour,
> Do penitential cogitations cling;
> Like ivy, round some ancient elm, they twine
> In grisly folds and strictures serpentine;
> Yet, while they strangle, a fair growth they bring,
> For recompense—their own perennial bower.

Death and life tangle in "Seclusion" as, rather differently, in "Nutting." But in "Mark the Concentred Hazels" sexuality is reduced to an intangible personification by coy beams and wanton wind, and even these are almost completely excluded. Euphemism keeps death at bay, but only barely, as the emphatically positioned "repose" and "sleep" hover on the verge of nonexistence. The solemn late style nearly stifles the speaking voice and finds little room for the living, thinking mind. Sterility seems the price to be paid for preserving the virginity of the scene.

The sonnet presents what Harold Bloom has called a scene of instruction. The first word, "Mark," signals the pedagogical intention, which only creeps in at the very end of "Nutting." In "Wordsworth and the Scene of Instruction," Bloom has written brilliantly of Wordsworth's fear of writing, encompassing under the concept of writing all traces in the landscape and memorial fixations on the past. But in this hazel bower Wordsworth encounters what his poetry had long sought, an unwritten writing.[39] The stone, if it is an image of mind, is a tabula rasa. Despite the opening word, this is an unmarked scene. The "Mark" is in truth not a mark—for to mark the trees might risk disfiguring them indeed—but a remark. Yet no historic chieftain made the spot remarkable; the scene is not memorable because of an inscribed mark or trace, an impress or a signature. Rather, the scene is a constellated image with a focal or hearth-like character. The trees surrounding the stone make an instance of what Kant, in the *Critique of Judgment*, called purposeless purpose, and they become a figure of mind by a structured interplay of parts rather than by an act of initiation or a mark of originary difference. The key word is "concentred." The rejected opening of "Nutting" had spoken of "the concentration of your groves" (line 43); by echoing this discarded piece of writing while burying the decisive pun, Wordsworth elicits from the grove an image of mind without specifically designating it as such.[40]

Any mark is already a remark. The "re-" is elided because it is understood, and it is understood because it is universal. As an implication posited in this as in every scene of instruction, the "re-" haunts the poem in two respects. It represents first of all the belatedness of understanding: the force of time is felt in the pervasive repetitions, "image," "likeness," and "mimic." And, second, it is felt in the intensity with which the apperception confronts the scene. The personifications are lyrical ghosts like those of "Yew-Trees" (the poem that precedes "Nutting" in Wordsworth's arrangement).[41] What rises to the belated consciousness in such a scene of pure thought is more than a thoughtless first glimpse, could any such exist: it is "The light that never was, on sea or land" ("Elegiac Stanzas"), or "life that breathes not," "the memorial majesty of Time / Impersonated in thy calm decay" ("Address to Kilchurn Castle, Upon Loch Awe"). As an undertone of the pedagogical "Mark," here apparently spoken by no one and to no one, we can hear the acknowledgment that consciousness is a glorious but ghostly afterthought.[42]

A pair of late sonnets, "Near the Lake of Thrasymene" and "Near the Same Lake," from the "Memorials of a Tour in Italy, 1837," recur to the mutual impact of consciousness and scene. Their terms confirm Wordsworth's sense of the belatedness of thought. In antiquity, he says, Hannibal's victory over the Romans had marked and wounded the spot. But the spot's power over the mind outlives the marks of battle that have long since been effaced: "Of that day's shame, / Or glory, not a vestige seems to endure." *Saucia tellus*, the earth marked by battle or labor, is a witness to man's degradation. Effacement actually elevates humanity here, as also in "Mark the Concentred Hazels" and in "Elegiac Stanzas" ("A deep distress hath humanized my Soul"), for

> So may all trace and sign of deeds aloof
> From the true guidance of humanity,
> Thro' Time and Nature's influence, purify

Their spirit; or, unless they for reproof
Or warning serve, thus let them all, on ground
That gave them being, vanish.
            ("Near the Lake of Thrasymene")

Vanish, but not utterly. Something yet remains, something that is not a mark or testimonial, yet a vague reminiscence that "deeds aloof" once were marked here: "vanish to a sound." The second sonnet evokes this sound, the ghostly presences that haunt the scene in thought, not exactly prompted by the murmur of the brook or by its bloody name yet somehow lingering in both:

What wonder if at midnight, by the side
Of Sanguinetto or broad Thrasymene,
The clang of arms is heard, and phantoms glide,
Unhappy ghosts in troops by moonlight seen.
            ("Near the Same Lake")

The "vanquished Chief" is one of the unburied dead; no traces of his presence survive, yet there are traces of the traces, re-marks of the vanished marks through which meaning accretes to the scene. Understanding is epitaphic because it is a second-order reflection that comes about only when fixed signs sink back into the watery depths of the mind; as Frances Ferguson says, "The mind insists on the validity of the original passion through being unable to find words for it" (*Wordsworth* 13). "We murder to dissect," writes Wordsworth in a famous poem against books spoken from the vantage of the old gray stone ("The Tables Turned"). But it is a secondary poem—a reply, as it were, to "Expostulation and Reply"—and, despite the "freshening lustre" of the sun and the air of spontaneity, it portrays a belated, evening scene and opens by uncannily echoing Macbeth's witches. Even this poem, then, hints that wisdom and truth arise from an arduously gained and ghostly simplicity; hence its perhaps surprising inclusion among the "Poems of Sentiment and Reflection." "Let Nature be your Teacher," advises this scene of instruction, "and bring with you a heart / That watches and receives." Mark and remark your world.

It makes little difference whether we say that thought teaches, or animates, or personifies. Conceptually it does the first, imagistically the second, rhetorically the third. It is important to understand the connection, lest we misunderstand what it means when Wordsworth writes that Nature is a Teacher. For his attack on personified abstractions in the Preface to *Lyrical Ballads* is really an attack on abstraction, not on personification. Misunderstanding of its aim has led to two grave errors.[43] The first is the failure to recognize that personification is a normal device of Wordsworth's style. The second and graver error is the assumption that personification somehow affects the meaning of the utterance. Yet it is evident that a Tomb or a Stone is not materially different from a tomb or a stone, and the same, in Wordsworth's usage, is true of Fancy, Nature, Time, and, for that matter, Chieftain. Capitalization intensifies presence but does not modify concepts, any more than, according to Kant, existence alters the essence of a thing. As Wordsworth clarifies in the 1802 revision of the Preface, personifications are "a figure of speech occasionally prompted by passion" (*Poetical Works* 2: 390): they are an index to the energy of the scene or of the observer's response rather than a mark of some quality in the objects.[44]

When Wordsworth, in his epitaphic mode, speaks of hauntings and ghostly presences, therefore, he should be understood psychologically rather than materially. The capitals are not empty abstractions, but signs of life that attest to the soul in the machine of nature. Yet the life is not to be found in the objects and concepts themselves, which are but the flesh and bones of the system of nature. The capitals are the products of an overflowing energy, but the energy flows between them, not within, in the composed animation of the scene. In "Mark the Concentred Hazels," it is the verbs that carry the emphasis and, one might say, that cause the nouns to be capitalized. After the initial imperative, they come mostly at the end of the line and in the rhyme. The two infinitives, occurring in what amount to conditional constructions, are transitive, as are the words "enclose" and "framing" that help to set the scene, but the remaining verbs are intransitive or, like "finds repose" and "likeness keep," inactive. The poem, then, portrays action without suffering, and it does so because the scene has grown into its meaning in the course of emerging, through the grave, into a world beyond alteration. The poet has learned the lesson of "Nutting": "with gentle hand / Touch—for there is a spirit in the woods."

There is no transitivity here—no transition, no transformation. But the damping of action is a release into time, not, as one might fear, a release from time. Part of the violence of "Nutting" is the necessary confinement of the action to one day "from many singled out"; transitive action forces attention to the moment or, at most, to the brief span of its occurrence. (Hence, as Baker says in *Time and Mind* 47, "the virgin scene is already raped by the eye that sees and the consciousness that counts.") But in the sonnet the temporal consciousness, even broader than Sterne's or Bowles's, ranges from the momentary through the diurnal to the biological, the historical, and the eternal, encompassing Time itself in the last line. And the verbal actions, similarly, range from the intermittency of "play / And glance" through the slightly more sustained gusts of the wanton wind to the continuity of "grows," the different degrees of perduration of "Live" and "keep," and then, through "sleep," to the moral relationships specified by "bends" (a verb of physical movement used metaphorically) and by "condescends" (a metaphorical derivative from a motion verb).

Such highly nuanced sensitivity to verbal aspect is a hallmark of romantic style.[45] It is made possible by a perspective that concentrates on what Kenneth Burke's *Grammar of Motives* terms "scene," that is, on conditions and contexts rather than on actions. An old gray stone could earlier have served as the metaphorical pretext for a poem (think of the "rime petrose" of Dante), but certainly not as its subject. Wordsworth writes a poetry of powers rather than agents and of movements rather than deeds. To do so is in one sense a simplification or reduction, as is most glaringly evident in *The Prelude's* merely personal and mythic perspectives on the French Revolution. But in another sense it is an enrichment, as forms of life, of movement, and of time itself come into view that are inaccessible to the restless consciousness for which being is always doing and acting:

> Think you, 'mid all this mighty sum
> Of things for ever speaking,
> That nothing of itself will come,
> But we must still be seeking?
> ("Expostulation and Reply")

In time of war, of course, the meditative stance that is willing to let things come of themselves, unsought, might be a particularly rare commodity. Yet what seems difficult or even problematic in its contemporary environment can also be seen historically as the natural outgrowth of Fielding's increasingly complex sense of the long-range contexts that nourish actions, of Goldsmith's simplified and idealized foregrounding of time over individual will, and of Gibbon's vision of the rootedness of history in character and in local setting.

To help characterize what is distinctive in Wordsworth's achievement, I will interpose a representative lyric by John Langhorne, from the middle of the eighteenth century. Though not a particularly good poet, Langhorne was a favorite of Wordsworth's as a fellow countryman (see the evocation of "These uncouth rocks, and mountains grey!" in Langhorne's "Ode to the Genius of Westmoreland," in Chalmers, *English Poets* 16: 465), as a sentimental depicter of the miseries of the poor (*The Country Justice*), and as a celebrant of memory and of fancy's mimic power. This last quality is in evidence in "An Ode to the River Eden" (1759), bringing it close to Wordsworth's sonnet in theme, if not in spirit:

> Delightful Eden! parent stream
>   Yet shall the maids of Memory say,
> (When led by Fancy's fairy dream,
>   My young steps trac'd thy winding way)
> How oft along thy mazy shore,
> That many a gloomy alder bore,
>   In pensive thought their poet stray'd;
> Or, careless thrown thy bank beside,
> Beheld thy dimply waters glide,
>   Bright thro' thy trembling shade.
>
> Yet shall they paint those scenes again,
>   Where once with infant-joy he play'd,
> And bending o'er thy liquid plain,
>   The azure worlds below survey'd:
> Led by the rosy-handed Hours,
> When Time trip'd o'er that bank of flowers,
>   Which in thy crystal bosom smil'd:
> Tho' old the god, yet light and gay,
> He flung his glass, his scythe away,
>   And seem'd himself a child.
>
> The poplar tall, that waving near
>   Would whisper to thy murmurs free;
> Yet rustling seems to soothe mine ear,
>   And trembles when I sigh for thee.
> Yet seated on thy shelving brim,
> Can Fancy see the Naiads trim
>   Burnish their green locks in the Sun;
> Or at the last lone hour of day,
> To chase the lightly glancing fay,
>   In airy circles run.
>
> But, Fancy, can thy mimic power
>   Again those happy moments bring?
> Can'st thou restore that golden hour,
>   When young Joy wav'd his laughing wing?
> When first in Eden's rosy vale,
> My full heart pour'd the lover's tale,
>   The vow sincere, devoid of guile!
> While Delia in her panting breast,

With sighs, the tender thought supprest,
  And look'd as angels smile.

O goddess of the crystal bow,
  That dwell'st the golden meads among;
Whose streams still fair in memory flow,
  Whose murmurs melodise my song!
Oh! yet those gleams of joy display,
Which bright'ning glow'd in fancy's ray,
  When, near thy lucid urn reclin'd,
The dryad, Nature, bar'd her breast,
And left, in naked charms imprest,
  Her image on my mind.

In vain—the maids of Memory fair
  No more in golden visions play;
No friendship smoothes the brow of Care,
  No Delia's smile approves my lay.
Yet, love and friendship lost to me,
'Tis yet some joy to think of thee,
  And in thy breast this moral find;
That life, though stain'd with sorrow's showers,
Shall flow serene, while Virtue pours
  Her sunshine on the mind.
            (in Chalmers, *English Poets* 16: 428)

"Maids of Memory" was a fashionably innovative designation for
the Muses in 1759 (Sitter, *Literary Loneliness* 120–36). But memory
cannot be redemptive where the defining characteristic of time is
that it passes. Hope, for Langhorne, does not connect present with
future, but instead simply contradicts the present ("Hymn to Hope");
meditation does not connect the landscape with the quiet of the sky,
which remains an Edenic and utopian "golden vision"; and likewise
memory does not connect the past with the present, but only reminds us of the difference. Fancy's mimic powers reduce as they reflect, demoting Father Time to an irresponsible child, diminishing
bodies to body parts, shying away from deep or dark emotions.
Fancy's "mimic beauties," as Langhorne writes in "Elegy II" from
"The Visions of Fancy," make "the visionary scenes appear / Like
the faint traces of a vanish'd dream" (in Chalmers, *English Poets* 16:
422). Hence in the "Ode to the River Eden" there is an unbridged gap
separating the gentle and largely intransitive movements attributed
to nature and to the poet in the natural landscape from the animated
and largely transitive actions of the spirits that are mirrored in
Fancy's eye. The personified abstractions vitiate the poem as Wordsworth's do not because they represent agents that remain disjunct

from the scene. Body and mind are separated by the constructed and incompatible forms of time in which each exists, and the attempt to reconcile life that "flows" with virtue that "pours" must consequently remain delusive. A poetry like Langhorne's moralizes allegorically for lack of a unifying vision.

Wordsworth's mastery of time—more precisely, of the multiple modalities of time—is thus the correlative of the unity of his consciousness with respect to the scene. In emphasizing relationships over entities, he views the scene as a whole. In a further development of Goldsmith's aestheticizing stance, Wordsworth's reflective marking converts the scene into a picture. The transitive action-verbs of the poem all belong to the aesthetic sphere: "enclose," "framing," "mimic," along with the "mark" of rapt attention and the privative "seldom free to touch" that evokes the imagination's *noli me tangere*. The bower is a contemplative space that becomes a "pensive likeness" by virtue of its constitution. Isolation and unification go hand in hand; whereas a poem about chiseling marks in a vocal "living stone" speaks of "the brotherhood / Of ancient mountains" ("To Joanna"), here the mountains are "lonely" and nature is "solitary." "To Joanna" is a poem of recollection and of social and natural collectivities, all of which are forms of unification to be sure, but defective forms, not free from irony and self-deprecation. The greater concentration of the sonnet gives a perfected image of mind in its fundamental encounter with the primeval blankness of time itself.

The shape of the encounter in the sonnet warrants comparison with that in the poem with which this study began, Gray's Eton College ode. Both poems open with attentive, almost ritualized observation from a distance, and both slide gradually into empathic identification and visionary moral pathos. Unlike Gray, who keeps a certain ironic detachment even while addressing Father Thames, Wordsworth swells into earnest apostrophe at the beginning of the sestet. Yet the sonnet too remains reflective. Sound doublings—the inner rhymes and assonance of lone[ly]-Stone, [mountai]ns Live–[pe]nsive l[ikeness], trees-keep—are the marks of the reflective consciousness. And unlike Cowper's self-negating ice-garden, the concluding double imitation—nature mimics time, which apes human action—confirms a human countenance hidden in the scene in much the same way as in Gray's "brow / Of windsor's heights." In these respects the two poems are remarkably similar allegories of human destiny and ambition.

But between the two poems a revolution has taken place in the relation of man to nature, that is, of thought to its objects. Returning to Gray from Wordsworth, one is struck by the linearity that the mind imposes on his scene. The "silver-winding" Thames represents the course followed by nature left to itself, silent and remote. But humans subordinate the flexibility of the "pliant arm" and of the "rolling circle" to the purposeful transgressiveness of running, cleaving, chasing, and flying; they are met with a "baleful train" and an inflexible "piercing dart," and though the poet says that they are whirled from high, we know that by this desperately ironic parody of childhood sports he really means hurled.[46] The advance of time forms the internal articulation of most of the stanzas—most subtly in the fifth stanza, where the crybabies of line 43 seem to teeter on the verge of puberty when we get to "buxom" and "of vigour born"— and more obviously of the poem as a whole, in its progress from ancient history through personal recollection into the present and on to the grim future of conflict, defeat, and death. Similarly progressive is the descent of the eye as it reads the scene, from the heights down to the Thames Valley and into the visionary abyss of "the vale of years beneath."[47] The sense of an implacable march into an opposition between man and nature is self-generated, and only Gray's skeptically urbane reserve keeps him from being crushed by it.

Wordsworth's thought, to echo his own brilliant pun, does not align but concenters. In the Eton College ode Gray lectured his reading public from his elevated natural pulpit opposite the college buildings, "speaking clearly to the wise," in line with the motto to "The Progress of Poesy." But Wordsworth, in his increasing absorption, bends the scene of instruction around until it becomes a scene of self-instruction, with the speaker as both pedagogue and pupil.[48] Gray's ode retains the directness of an ocular demonstration. It is significant, by contrast, that Wordsworth's sonnet is not an occasional poem, but rather oscillates between the specificity of "*Yon old grey Stone*" and the generality of "noontide *suns*" or between the momentary immediacy of "beams that play / And glance" and the unspecified duration of "moss that grows." To be sure, Wordsworth, and likewise Coleridge, wrote many occasional poems. But even in "Tintern Abbey," the prototype of the scene of instruction according to Bloom, the very specific occasion ("July 13, 1798") is attached to a vaguely specified landscape ("a few miles above Tintern Abbey"), and the emphatic presence of the scene dissolves before concentric circles of hypothetical meditation: the pedagogical assurance of "I have owed to them" (line 26) fades into the self-questioning of "Nor less, *I trust*, / To them I *may* have owed another gift" (lines 35–36).[49] Gray reads the scenic code from top to

bottom and from past to future. Wordsworth's landscapes may suggest traces of textuality (thoughts "impressed" on the scene by the
steep and lofty cliffs), but the logic of effacement supervenes. The
"plots . . . lose themselves," the "little lines . . . run wild," and the
natural text becomes a pretext, the occasion an overflowing spring of
meditation at the center of thought.[50]

The first half of line 9 is the anchor of a typical Wordsworthian
sonnet and its point of greatest expressivity. "In the better half of
[Milton's] sonnets," as Wordsworth wrote in a letter of 1833 (cited in
Poetical Works 3: 417–18),

> the sense does not close with the rhyme at the eighth line, but
> overflows into the second portion of the metre. Now it has struck
> me, that this is not done merely to gratify the ear by variety and
> freedom of sound, but also to aid in giving that pervading sense of
> intense Unity in which the excellence of the Sonnet has always
> seemed to me mainly to consist. Instead of looking at this com-
> position as a piece of architecture, making a whole out of three
> parts, I have been much in the habit of preferring the image of an
> orbicular body,—a sphere—or a dew-drop.

Source at once of variety and of unity, the structural center of the
sonnet is the point where the line of thought rounds back on itself to
make a perimeter. There are, of course, many cases where this kind
of turn degenerates into mannerism. None, I think, is finer or more
revealing than the overflow in "Mark the Concentred Hazels."

The overflow from the bower is reminiscent of the ecstatic outward view over "the grand terraqueous spectacle, / From centre to
circumference unveiled," in the middle of two other embowered
meditations, "Lines Left upon a Seat in a Yew-Tree" of 1797, and
"Written with a Slate Pencil on a Stone, on the Side of the Mountain
of Black Comb," published in 1815 (from which the quotation comes).
The sonnet's greater concentration and lower perspective, however,
make its expansion more startling.[51] Here the eyes seem less involved
than the mind, as it hypothesizes the necessary conditions of a meditation. The two inscriptions just mentioned are explicit addresses to
a passerby, and the related "View from the Top of Black Comb" is a
group vision, whereas the sonnet's overflow is the point where the
speaker confronts his own isolation. He begins the sonnet descrip-
tively and, as it seems, demonstratively. The interruption in the
middle of line 3 launches an explanation that merges into the imaginative projections of the second quatrain. The octave, that is, reflects the movement of thought in response to the present scene. It

is in the nature of such thought to digress increasingly from direct observation as it weaves its web of explanation and commentary. The prosody is one sign of thought's inability to control its own elaborations: the only line in the first half that forms a complete syntactic unit is line 7, locus of the image of death, whereas after the overflow the sonnet has a closed couplet followed by three relatively self-contained lines. The overflow is the mind's acknowledgment that thought has gone astray and needs to be enclosed, hence the view upward to the confining mountains, rather than downward to the boundless ocean as in the inscriptions. Also typical of Wordsworth's sonnets is a linkage of the overflow to the rest of the sestet. In "Mark the Concentred Hazels" the word "lonely" links the overflow to the adjectives "solitary" and "forlorn" in the last two lines. With this word, feeling—the characteristic subject of a Wordsworthian sestet as thought characterizes the octave—enters the poem. We can conclude, then, that thought for Wordsworth is centrifugal until feeling comes in aid with the enveloping recognition of the mind's isolation and its need for containment.

The sonnet corrects and completes the doctrine of book 2 of *The Prelude* (a meditation prompted by the disappearance of the old gray stone). Here, in the poem's most famous expression of pantheistic one-life sentiment, Wordsworth denies any disjunction or need for containment:

> From Nature and her overflowing soul
> I had receiv'd so much that all my thoughts
> Were steep'd in feeling; I was only then
> Contented when with bliss ineffable
> I felt the sentiment of Being spread
> O'er all that moves, and all that seemeth still,
> O'er all, that, lost beyond the reach of thought
> And human knowledge, to the human eye
> Invisible, yet liveth to the heart.
> (1805 *Prelude* 2.416–24)

But this consoling, Coleridgean faith, Wordsworth concedes, may be "error" (2.435, followed first by an apostrophe to mountains and mountain waters that corrects the oceanic rapture of lines 427–28 and then by a propitiatory address to Coleridge that concludes the book, lines 466–84). There is also a draft passage that strives to describe the lonely digression of thought toward the confining mountains: as he watched the clouds, Wordsworth says, he

> Laboured the subtile process to detect
> By which, like thoughts within the mind itself,

They rose as if from nothing, and dissolved
Insensibly; see with the lofty winds
These hurrying out of sight in troops, while that,
A lonely One upon the mountain top,
Resteth in sedentary quietness,
Faint answers yielding as my thoughts inquired
By what subjection he was fix'd, what law
Stay'd him, and why alone he linger'd there
Crowning that regal hill.

(*Prelude*, p. 53)

But Wordsworth evidently felt this passage to be out of place in book 2. As an *éminence grise*, or shadow minister, the sonnet's reposing Chieftain, like the Leech-Gatherer,[52] may be considered a reworking of the "lonely One" resting on the regal mountain in the lines just quoted.

If we take the sonnet to be a compact and mature portrayal of the course of thought and of its relation to feeling, then we can draw from it an account of the romantic response to the preromantic crisis of expression. Neoclassical thought is concerned to place its object in the contiguous scales of nature and of ideas, and its fundamental mode, as I have argued, is comparison. When the sonnet says "more than Fancy," by contrast, it is distinguishing, not relating; whether the phrase refers to imagination, reason, or grace, something is designated that is undefinable yet, clearly, fundamentally different from fancy.[53] Neoclassical nature is created as a chaos and organized by the perceiving mind; mind and matter are thus not alien, but complementary aspects of the universe.[54]

Romantic nature, however, is organized in itself. Mind searches for its essence, but the order of mind is fundamentally opposed to the order of nature, as inside to outside.[55] Wordsworth can only hazard "dark guesses" as to the "alliance" of mental abstractions like geometry with the "laws of Nature" (1805 *Prelude* 6.135–49), and his dream that geometry is identical with the stone leads to a nightmare from which he wakes in terror. The mind is "beset / With images, and haunted by itself" (1805 *Prelude* 6.179–80), the former because images mediate, in the fashion of Kant's schematism of the understanding, between the forms of nature and the categories of mind, the latter because all such mediations are in part projection.[56] Thus in the sonnet the speaker proceeds through a series of veiled negations ("protected," "seldom free") to arrive at the haunted image of the tomb as his first approximation to an adequate comprehension of the scene before him. Yet the very character of the scene that attracts the observer is its life, the unmarked yet remarkable life of the old gray stone and of the intact moss, in interchangeable supremacy with the concentered trees.

Framing images is the natural activity of the mind.[57] "Framing" suggests the fixation that the mind imposes in its effort to isolate, identify, and name the scene. While the image invariably misses the mark, the mind recognizes in its isolated and isolating function an affinity with the activities of nature. It feels itself framed by a natural horizon that confines and isolates but also incorporates it. Feeling may thus be called the life of thought—its horizon of selfhood—as thought is the form of feeling. The "sentiment of Being" is a self-recognition bridging the gap between the forms of the understanding and the flow of life. It takes only a dash, with no further conjunction, to reorient the speaker from the dead Chieftain to the living trees. The life of the poem is in this striking yet unostentatious dash. Up to this point the typically meandering syntax has followed a generally associative course, threatening to go off track like an eighteenth-century meditation; but this high romantic transition unites connection and correction, refinement and revision, to constitute a new dialectical "sense of intense Unity." The content of the thought is fixed from here on out, with "dark chamber" merely rephrasing "gloom" and "Tomb."

But the operation of thought changes. The crux is the substitution of a "pensive likeness" for the framing of a "very image." In contrast to an "image," a "likeness" is an approximation growing out of the asymptotic relationship of mind and nature. The mind no longer suffers even the partial negations and distinctions of the octave: the tomb is now a chamber, and the defensive warding off of the outside world suggested throughout the octave is absorbed into the hopeful neutrality of "keep." "Likeness," of course, means a visage as well as a comparison. And the term "pensive," evoking at once activity and mood, reflects the movement toward coalescence of the observing mind and the stone. "Pensive" is a word that Wordsworth uses for thoughts that are "steep'd in feeling." It is applied to a living emblem that happily haunts the mind, such as the White Doe of Rylestone, after it has supplanted the divisive banner whose image was imprinted by human hands ("pensive Visitant," line 1919), or to Yarrow, insofar as it is not merely dreamt or merely seen ("Yarrow Visited," line 24, and "Yarrow Revisited," line 106). Insofar as "pensive" implies possessing a will and not just a melancholy appearance, "pensive likeness" could serve as a periphrastic definition of personification—the comparison of an object or a concept to something that thinks. Yet personification, as Wordsworth has learned to master it, is purged of its disjunctiveness. It is easy to feel a potential intentionality in verbs like "enclose" and "protected," or a potential sensorium in "wantonly" and "lonely," but the only separated agent that the poem names is the Chieftain, who is both imaginary and dead—an icon of the imagination's gentle triumph over its own errors.[58]

Wordsworth's visionary stance is thus, in fundamental ways, the opposite of Gray's. Where they are identified, the personifications of the Eton College ode are static and picturesque. Association in the ode means that the speaker does not control the direction of his own thoughts, which drift along the stream of time, feeling increasingly powerless. With the possible exception of Ambition, the "fury Passions" (Anger, Fear, Shame, etc.) are different forms of entrapment by the past. The linearity of time and the rigidity of the defenses against time are equally destructive. The only escape is a denial of the vision ("No more; where ignorance is bliss") in a return to the opening (in this case to the Greek motto, whose ἱκανή—"enough"— foreshadows the "no more" of the conclusion). Some such circularity, with a concluding retreat or return, is the structural norm for eighteenth-century poems, most obviously in the round of Thomson's *Seasons*. Wordsworth's personifications, by contrast, do not bind him. The bower is an aesthetic space, but unlike eighteenth-century pictorial modes it remains in movement; the personifications interact with one another and with the speaker, without compulsion. The movement into vision is an increasingly flexible and reflective cooperation with time. Its general course is teleological rather than circular, arriving at its goal with the last word, the phonetically and semantically surprising "humanities," the reverse of the commonplaces with which eighteenth-century poets liked to finish.[59] If we study neoclassical poems to see what holds them together despite their meandering, we read romantic poems to see toward what, despite their obvious organic focus, they develop.

I take time's humanities to refer to the richly varied temporal relations that are present in living nature and that are perceptible to a feeling consciousness not limited to rational measurement. I take nature's humanities to refer to the equally rich, not merely geometrical, spatial sense reflected in romantic style, here particularly in the profusion of prepositional relations (upon, amid, in, among, in lines 6–9) that replace the axial gradations and polarities of the eighteenth-century landscape. "Humanity" in Wordsworth's usage refers to what I have called the democratic spirit of his vision and of this style. In the poem entitled "Humanity," another meditation on the quintessence of stonehood—the "STONE OF POWER," which is a rock that "rocks, or seems to rock"—he defines the spirit as the "poetry of things" and as the glorious

> blending
> Of right affections climbing or descending
> Along a scale of light and life, with cares
> Alternate; carrying holy thoughts and prayers
> Up to the sovereign seat of the Most High;
> Descending to the worm in charity.
>
> (lines 27–31)

In the sonnet the democratic mingling results from the low and sunless perspective, which parallels the humble stone with a Chieftain, which links trees and stone like the more famous line "With rocks, and stones, and trees," and which seems to equate might and depth. In *The Prelude* Wordsworth claims such leveling as a distinctive trait of the Lake District (1805 text, 9.217–35); he features it in the dedicatory sonnet to his whole collection ("If Thou Indeed"); and he celebrates it in the sublime mode in the "Vernal Ode," written in 1817.[60] The progression from marking to "humanities" may be taken to define the fundamental ethos of the sonnet, and, I would argue, of romantic style in general. The spiraling course of a Wordsworthian meditation draws out the resources of the mind and penetrates the scene, discovering a wealth of active forces and factors that allow the apparently inert stone of the earth to be revealed as a suitable habitation for human beings. To this end cooperate all the features of nuance and variation, of phonetic reinforcement, of semantic enrichment, of unification and transition that I have been describing, not, to be sure, as the denumerable elements of a manner, but rather as the resources of romantic style. "Outer and inner landscape," as Paul Böckmann has written about the similar intentionality of German romantic lyric, "intermingle and refer to the unified mood of a fulfilled poetical life" ("Formen der Stimmungslyrik" 441).

But does not Wordsworth retract the entire gain by calling time's humanities "forlorn"? "Mimic" is also not a positive term in Wordsworth's usage—it evokes the London of book 7 of *The Prelude*, for instance—and Nature's condescension to mimic forlorn time sounds like an unpromising gestation for the hopeful final plural. To be sure, it was never uncharacteristic of Wordsworth to take the long way around to good cheer, and particularly not after 1805. In this case, if time alone ("forlorn") sufficed, then nature would not be needed in order to engender humanities, and if nature alone ("solitary") sufficed, then the poetic consciousness that Wordsworth sometimes called the "point of vision" would not be needed. Humanity lies neither in matter, which is fixed, nor in movement, which cannot be fixed, but in the understanding that generates the accord of matter and movement, energy and form, variety and unity. All preceding states are necessary prerequisites, but also defective, derivative forms, apparent mimics of a perfection that they are in the process of constituting. The noblest art, as Wordsworth evokes it in the "Essay, Supplementary to the Preface" of 1815, produces an "accord of sublimated humanity" (*Poetical Works* 2: 429). But it often reaches the heights through exalting an embowered gloom: "There is also a meditative, as well as a human, pathos; an enthusiastic, as well as an ordinary, sorrow; a sadness that has its seat in the depths of reason, to which the mind cannot sink gently of itself—but to which it must descend by treading the steps of thought" (2: 428). "Forlorn": the word is like a bell; its still, sad music is both peal and appeal, both accord and strain, oration forever bound to commemoration.

If there is one thing that the phrase "old gray stone" should call to mind, it is that for Wordsworth essences are never fixed.[61] Even the most featureless matter is alive and has arrived at its present, passing state as the result of many changes. Humanities are always forlorn because always changing, but it is the sublime glory of humanity to recognize time—though time has no essence and no visage—in all its multiplicity. I recall the force of the missing "re-" in Wordsworth's "Mark," which is the action of time and of consciousness as they meet in the mimic iterations of his conclusion. I recall the missing pupil in his scene of instruction, which is himself, reborn as he rethinks the panorama before him. And I call to mind that a likeness, which is not an identity or a "very image," is also a difference. Consciousness is the name of the difference between man and nature that allows man to recognize in nature the glory nature cannot recognize in itself for lack of man's faculty of sublimated recognition.

Wordsworth also used the word "humanities" in a long draft for book 8 of *The Prelude*. (The plural seems to occur only one other time, in line 127 of "Liberty.") Here once more, Wordsworth is at his most explicit in a suppressed passage, as if reluctant or finally unable to fix in a philosophical formulation a doctrine whose essence is the unfixability of consciousness. Here, then, at length, is Wordsworth's finest meditation on the asymptotic relationship of man and nature, on likeness as difference, on false framing and imaging, and on the subtle processes by which these are unbound to form true, more humble images of a greater humanity:

And in this season of his second birth, . . .
He feels that, be his mind however great
In aspiration, the universe in which
He lives is equal to his mind, that each
Is worthy of the other; if the one
Be insatiate, the other is inexhaustible.
Whatever dignity there be [   ]
Within himself, from which he gathers hope,
There doth he feel its counterpart the same
In kind before him outwardly express'd,
With difference that makes the likeness clear,
Sublimities, grave beauty, excellence,
Not taken upon trust, but self-display'd
Before his proper senses; 'tis not here
Record of what hath been, is now no more,
Nor secondary work of mimic skill,
Transcripts that do but mock their archetypes;
But primary and independent life,
No glimmering residue of splendour past,
Things in decline or faded. [   ]
What hidden greater far than what is seen,
No false subordination, fickleness,
Or thwarted virtue, but inveterate power
Directed to best ends, and all things good
Pure and consistent. If upon mankind
He looks, and on the human maladies
Before his eyes, what finds he there to this
Fram'd answerably? what but sordid men,
And transient occupations, and desires
Ignoble and deprav'd? Therefore he cleaves
Exclusively to Nature as in her
Finding his image, what he has, what lacks,
His rest and his perfection . . .
So doth he measure the vast universe,
His own by right of spiritual sovereignty.
    Yet who can tell while he this [?] path
Hath been ascending, in apparent slight
Of man and all the mild humanities
That overspread the surface of the heart,
What subtle virtues from the first have been
In midst of this, and in despite of [?]
At every moment finding out their way
Insensibly to nourish in the heart
Its tender sympathies, to keep alive
Those yearnings, and to strengthen them and shape,
Which from the mother's breast were first receiv'd?

The commonest images of nature—all,
No doubt, are with this office charg'd.
(*Prelude*, pp. 575–77)

The time has arrived to feel the force of this great passage of philosophic verse, together with the great sonnet that resolves its "humanities" into images. Not much is left these days of the old humanist and naturalist Wordsworth. First admired, then scorned, the poet whose heart loved and lamented the fates of all things great and small has been reborn in recent decades as a powerful and relentlessly self-aware critic of all the illusions of his own mind and heart. Yet in the process the ends of Wordsworth's critical reflexivity have been too often overlooked. In his spots of time the deconstructive critic finds a usurping letter that murders spirit (Kneale); the Marxist critic—with equally rich nuance, and not all that differently—finds a tyrannizing fetish that endangers community (Simpson, *Figurings*). But both these modes subscribe to a kind of neo-Shelleyanism that finds poets strong in their weakness. (See the Shelleyan essays in Bloom et al., *Deconstruction in America*, or the Shelleyan manifesto in Simpson, *Figurings* 117–19.) If they are right to find complexities that were overlooked by the antiquated exponents of the cult of feeling, it is not because the Ideological Unconscious breaks through the shell of Wordsworth the Simple. Rather, Wordsworth was there first, putting deconstruction and critique in their place, as he put feeling in its place.

The passage I have just quoted at length is my evidence that Wordsworth's poetry traverses these itineraries of contemporary critical thought. In this "season of his second birth," Wordsworth looks through deconstructive "difference," "secondary" imitation, and writing that hollows out its origins, then through human domination and servitude, and toward a natural power of seemingly awesome sublimity, yet ultimately working within, "insensibly," and without the "slight" inflicted by a totalizing sensibility. The key is his replacement of humanity by humanities. No longer an idea, but a set of practices—the "office" of "subtle virtues"—Wordsworthianism here comes into its maturity.

My book, to an extent, tells the story of the maturing of that style. It narrates the rites of passage that chasten and subdue sensibility into romantic humanism. The conception of a transcendental time and space and of a transcendental ego, the birth of an aesthetic imagination, the mastery of plot and character development, the assemblage of an order of the organic, the emergence of will and of action as the primary categories of selfhood, the disposition of the multiple temporality of the event—I have described how "Mark the Concentred Hazels" refracts these preromantic developments, and it would not be absurd to find them subsumed and, as it were, hushed, in the untold yet somehow exemplary life story of the sonnet's undead Chieftain. For what is at stake are the elements of a life according to the coordinates of human consciousness.

Yet to say that this book tells a single story—that it eventuates in a single image that fuses all of its components—would be false to my aim. It would return the book to the pseudoteleology of the old preromanticism I have aimed to correct. It would be a reduction of history to aesthetics. We may yearn for such an emblem, but time's humanities—time's forlorn humanities—deny it to us. Hence I would stress the multiplicity of the strands knotted up so brilliantly in the concluding plural of Wordsworth's sonnet. History's rites of passage do not fix energies, but rather release them. Nature may be "solitary," but "the Mighty" who "sleep" within her "dark chamber" are plural, and so are the "trees!" that construct time's emblem. The mind, Hume said so many pages back, is a republic or commonwealth, and fulfillment comes only in the never-subdued form of a commonwealth of objects, of values, of forces, and of persons.[62]

And of poems. For what would be most spurious about the pseudoteleology I have striven to avoid would be the illusion that Wordsworth's meanings can be successfully channeled by a selection of texts. Foregrounding a poem that other critics ignore has enabled me to project a certain image of Wordsworth's development and of the development of eighteenth-century literature toward Wordsworth. Criticism inevitably makes such choices. It is licensed to do so. Licensed, but not authorized. Debates over canons and canonicity arise when license is taken for authority, teleological opening for pseudoteleological closure, humanities for humanity. My personal canon may or may not carry conviction, but it cannot command assent. The meaning of Wordsworth, of romanticism, of history can and should not be controlled by marking and remarking any icon, however hallowed, however central.

Consequently, I would not have this book understood to be telling a story—not, at least, if a story means a package neatly tied up. It has endeavored instead to release the energies confined and concealed by the late Wordsworthian simplicity. The condensation of the lines and fields of history in a particular framed image is, I think, more than an illusion of Fancy, but less than a protected, eternal resting place. Others have construed the forces of history in this period and these poets differently, and should and will continue to do so. It is in refusing to lie still, it is in the unquiet graves dug by even so subdued a work as "Mark the Concentred Hazels," that poems find their life. May it ever be so.

CHAPTER THIRTEEN

Touchstones

... what Matthew Arnold called "touchstones," a notion now obsolete
beyond imagining ...

Cynthia Ozick, *New Yorker*, Nov. 20, 1989

The foregoing chapters lay claim to constituting a history of the origins of literary romanticism in Britain. *A* history, certainly not *the* history. They are far removed from the pretended completeness of chronicle, for chronicle implicitly levels and sometimes even explicitly denies the proposition that history is what matters. Without selection history has no shape; we should be condemned to relive the current events of two centuries past. What matters is, by contrast, what stands out in hindsight. Not long ago showing the conventionality of *The School for Scandal*, the traditionalism of *Le Mariage de Figaro*, or the contemporaneity of *Lyrical Ballads* was an outstanding task; thanks to scholars who have performed these labors—and on whom I have depended heavily at times—we can turn our attention to a better informed account of what distinguished those works from their contemporaries. Better informed, in every case, than the authors themselves were. Not even Wordsworth, at first, knew what he had wrought. Whether following private judgment or that of the mass of readers, the historian remains committed to one form or another of the maxim, by their posterity shall ye know them.

But these chapters, despite some appearances to the contrary, are also far removed from Hegelian ideologies. Their eddying themes and their currents meandering across generic and national boundaries are far from systematic, and their localized focus keeps them firmly rooted in the past. No transcendent Absolute is revealed; no hypostasized Present orients the flow.[1] I have already commented in

Chapter 1 on the intentionality, that is, the directionality of history in its movement toward the future. But it is not solely by chance that in writing a prehistory of romanticism I have virtually skipped over Wordsworth's Great Decade. For the flowering, or the actualization, of romanticism is not part of a history of romanticism; it is the moment when that history pauses in the sun, though other histories may have begun or progressed there. Instead, the history I have written ends in a sonnet that is, again not solely by chance, an epitaph happening to hark back to the original genius of romanticism, Robert Burns. That sonnet would be less interesting and less moving were it merely a static end point or confluence; instead, it participates in other histories, notably that called Biedermeier, of which others have written and will write again.

Chronicle aspires to universality, Hegelianism to centrality. My history pretends to neither. Yet it is not therefore a vulgar nominalism. There are foci, though there is no focus. The error committed by chronicle and by synthetic history alike lies in the assumption that history exists apart from the works that make it. Time, for both of them, is an outer sense. History becomes a revelation—of abstract sequence, of abstruse meaning. But a bible, if it contains a revelation, is surely also an event. The bibles of history are the books that have made history. I presume, therefore, that *books do not exist in history, but that history exists in books.* History is a mode of production or of invention, not of revelation. Where my reading is dialectical, it has, if it is worth anything, learned much from Hegel, but little if any from "Hegelian" historicism. It presumes that writers probe and discover and that they have a medium in which they do so. Their discoveries constitute time in the active mode. Their medium is also time, but sedimented: the past that becomes a living past—a past for us and not merely a past in itself—only insofar as a future is made. Without probings and discoveries, there is no time; without a future, no past, but only the indistinguishable grains of a sandy present.

Thus history, in my view, is preeminently the history of works. History has goals because works do, but it is not unified by them. Time, like tide, is incremental, as wave upon wave sweeps up the shore. Much comes to rest in Wordsworth (and in Coleridge as his anti-self), but far from everything, even everything in England. Regarding Germany, by contrast, I have elsewhere found the goal of a certain romanticism in an image (the ellipse), and not in the works of a single writer or movement. I see no reason to mistrust the conventional wisdom that the unity of a period is an outsider's over-simplification. Yet I find such a terminal simplification at least subjectively necessary in confronting the teeming multiplicity of my own period of study: the Wordsworthian perspective identifies nodes of resonance in what might else seem self-canceling energies. Time flows unevenly yet without pause. But the stories we tell—that is, the books we write—seek a shape with a beginning, middle, and end, and hence assume some form of the tripartite schema of context, elaboration, project. Whether or not that is the form of time, it is the form of historical narration, as understood in this book.[2]

To orient my concluding reflections, I shall adopt a label from the past and call my work a history of touchstones. Despite the common misunderstanding exemplified by the essay from which my epigraph is drawn, Matthew Arnold did not mean by "touchstone" a monolith like *Tristram Shandy*. But then neither do I, for I do not consider masterpieces to be monoliths. My touchstones, like Arnold's, are the points where the work's energies burst into life. Should that touchstone be a nameless tomb in a country churchyard or a ubiquitous old gray stone, so much the better, for then it runs little risk of defacement. But should it be as fluid as the rising Nile of *Rasselas* or as full of hot air as a cock-and-bull story, it more readily escapes the contrary danger of encapsulation. The touchstone functions as a kind of talisman: it stays firmly in place, but you touch it and move on, healed of your infirmities. (Ketcham, "That 'Stone of Rowe'" 175, cleverly calls Wordsworth's "stones of power" "Stone Age lie detectors.") It gives you what Arnold, in "On the Modern Element in Literature," calls an "intellectual deliverance" (*Prose Works* 1: 19) by uniting solidity and vigor.

Arnold's prose would tease us—or often badger us—out of thought. Yet I propose to examine his theory of touchstones not merely because so many of mine too are stones, but rather because the thoughts that his writings conceal are the best guide I have found to my own motivations in this book. My case will rest not on Peter, but on Matthew, and on Michael.

There is indeed much that is curious about Arnold's conception. The notion is as absurdly simpleminded on the face of it as it was baleful in many of its effects. Yet it may serve as a touchstone of touchstones, releasing energies perhaps unsuspected by its author, in a movement beyond culture and also beyond disinterestedness. It is also a theory of romanticism rooted in a conception of simplicity, and relevant here for that reason as well. For Arnold's great quarry—one of them, at least—was Wordsworth. Yet why is it, I cannot have been the first to ask, that the greatest Wordsworthian touchstone concerns, precisely . . . not touching a stone? "And never lifted up a single stone"—what magic seized Arnold in that line where the most ordinary of men speaks to his fellows? Neither prosody, syntax, nor imagery elevates Wordsworth's prosaic utterance in any obvious way to the dignity Arnold attributes to it.[3] Structural function perhaps does, if we can agree that this humble touchstone is also a capstone. But what could have drawn Arnold to *Michael*? What turned the peasant's burden into the educator's lodestone?

If we are to elaborate an account of touchstones as a theory of the history of poetry, then we must confront the paradoxes of Arnold's text. It does him an injustice if we sever his touchstones from their context. To lift up a single stone means to remove it from the pile. And that is something that Arnold and Wordsworth both extol Michael for not doing. The same critic who specializes in isolating lines or stanzas as proof-texts insists on the integrity of whole works and refuses to excerpt for his anthology even that most excerptable of poems, *The Prelude*. He celebrates life, yet celebrates poetry as the criticism of life. He praises Wordsworth as the poet of joy, yet repeatedly cites professions of stoic perseverance or insensibility as the greatest examples of truly classic poetry. All this—and more to come—from a writer who claims to "detest paradox" (*Prose Works* 3: 528, variant of 3: 247). There is a pathos in all this too troubling for tragedy. "How much more striking, in general, does any Englishman,—of some vigor of mind, but by no means a poet,—seem in his verse than in his prose!" (3: 239), writes the English poet turned essayist, and though he was occasionally capable of striking prose (as in the sarcastic and evocative Preface to *Essays in Criticism*), his normal mode was drably emphatic. Arnold is a moving exemplar of the condition depicted in Tennyson's *Idylls of the King* as the "sublime repression of himself" ("Dedication," line 18).

I conclude from these observations that Arnold was a great essayist precisely to the extent that (apart from sincere modesty topoi) he did not say what he meant. He does not exactly fall into the line of those for whom the classic does not exist (see my essay "The Classic Is the Baroque"), but it remains for him utopian and untouchable. "The Study of Poetry" promotes real estimates as opposed to personal and historical ones, yet in the essays devoted to individual writers it is invariably the criticisms that are "real" and that are counterbalanced by defenses either historical (the writer did what his age and context made possible) or personal (the writer did what his character traits made possible). Arnold rarely writes at length on the few genuinely classic authors, for they cannot happily stand up to a scrutiny that measures rigorous blame against scant praise. (Dante fares reasonably well in the biographical "Dante and Beatrice" and Homer in "On Translating Homer"—though not in "On the Modern Temper in Literature"—but "Milton," "A French Critic on Milton," and "A French Critic on Goethe" are, in parts, little less than scathing.) Moreover, he repeatedly evades opportunities to write on the classic: "Neither will my limits allow me to make any full application of the generalities above propounded" ("The Study of Poetry," in *Prose Works* 9: 172); "detailed proof of the assertion must be reserved for another occasion" ("On the Modern Element in Literature"; 1: 28). Sometimes the excuses are more candid: "We may feel the effect without being able to give ourselves clear account of its cause" ("Milton"; 11: 331); "Alas! the grand style is the last matter in the world for verbal definition to deal with adequately" ("On Translating Homer"; 1: 188, and see also 136–37 and 159). The classic resists analysis because it depends on a semidivine grace that remains out of our grasp. "In His will is our peace" is one of the touchstones from Dante; in another we find the word "impietrai," "of stone I turned within"; in the third, the phrase "non mi tange," "toucheth me not" ("The Study of Poetry"; 9: 169). It takes "tact" to appreciate classic touchstones (9: 168). Tact is a touch that respects the integrity of the object, purifying us by leaving it, so to speak, intact. It was, for instance, the saving grace of that "beautiful and *ineffectual* angel" Shelley ("Shelley"; 11: 327); "these few lines, if we have tact and can use them, are enough even of themselves to keep clear and sound our judgments about poetry" (9: 170). If we have tact, then why, we might wonder, do we need touchstones?

More than an insufficiently mixed metaphor is at issue here. Arnold was nice enough in his diction to be held accountable for the fact that a touchstone is not the real thing, but only a tool for testing the genuine article. Properly, if Arnold really found his favorite passages representative, he ought to have called them standards or else, "taking an expression from the builder's business, . . . points de repère" ("Johnson's *Lives of the Poets*," in *Prose Works* 8: 307–8). But a standard is available for all to use, whether or not they have tact. And representativity and democracy make Arnold nervous, touchy. "The *esprit démocratique*," he writes in praise of Renan's forceful criticism of life, "is admirably touched [i.e., struck down]; but touched not less admirably is . . . the cherished ideal of vulgar liberalism, the American type" ("Renan's *La Réforme intellectuelle* . . ."; 7: 49). The logic of the touchstone is different from builder's logic. It suggests that the classic purchases its brilliance at the expense of remoteness and intangibility. The classic remains remote in time and, more often than not, foreign; it must already be alien if it is to be inalienable, beyond aging if a timeless essence.

In "The Literary Influence of Academies" the problem becomes acute. Here Arnold associates poetry with English genius and prose with French quickness and flexibility. But without quickness and flexibility, without intelligence, simplicity, and measure, that is, without prose (Arnold argues) a perfect merger of style and idea or an achieved classicism is impossible. The argument of the essay is that classical prose must be written on the French model, but its subtext is that a classicism in poetry is inconceivable. And the evidence is the essential historicity of genius: Shakespeare and Milton were allowed to degenerate into Pope and Addison, for only an Academy of Prose can preserve the standards of culture. This argument finally makes comprehensible the plainness of the greatest lines of verse, including "And never lifted up a single stone." Their poetic quality is both untouchable and unaccountable for the simple reason *that they have none*. Genius (an English trait) has the brilliance of precious metals, but wears away with time; only prose can test genius, and hence only prose can endure. "To get rid of provinciality," Arnold writes—but this is also to get rid of genius and poetry—"brings us on to the platform where alone the best and highest intellectual work can be said fairly to begin. Work done after men have reached this platform is *classical*; and that is the only work which, in the long run, can stand" (*Prose Works* 3: 245). "Work done"—here Arnold forgets that he means to be writing only about classical prose and reveals that, in truth, the essay is about the possibilities of classicism in general. And nothing about classicism leaves Arnold comfortable. "We must not make of too much importance" this stage of culture, he writes, yet it "is, nevertheless, indispensable" (ibid.). The platform on which classicism stands, which makes even works of genius "immortal," if only "by moments" (ibid.), is indispensable, but not very important. It is only a few pages later that Arnold added the note about detesting paradox; perhaps so, but his criticism, with its pervasive self-suppression, lives off it.

In practice there is a restless mutuality about touchstones. "The Study of Poetry" ends by discussing Burns. "The poetry of the great classics [is] a sort of touchstone" (9: 187) by which to evaluate Burns's fire, his "touches of piercing, sometimes almost intolerable, pathos" (9: 186). But Burns too is a touchstone; for evaluating, say, Shelley, "no contact can be wholesomer than the contact with Burns" (9: 187).

At the threshold of modernity, on the borders of England, writing in a semi-alien language, Burns faces two ways. Hence Arnold also uses him, without fully acknowledging the strategy, as a stepping-stone, paradoxically placed last in the essay, to give us intimations of the greater and truer classics behind him. Touchstones can be eternal truths that measure our fallen condition, but mostly Arnold's essays give us highlights from defective poets as beacons toward the greater sweetness and light of the Untouchables. Whichever way we look, the touchstones are reminders precisely not of eternity but of the essential historicity of our existence.

The greatness of *Michael*, for Arnold, must have lain in its reticence. It is memorable for the stories it does not tell. We might compare it to *Anna Karénine* (as Arnold called it, preferring to read a modern classic in a foreign tongue), about which Arnold is more explicit. The novel's chief distinction is that it avoids prurience; it does not "put in touches" dictated by "the goddess Lubricity" (*Prose Works* 11: 292). Burns—once again serving a strategic function—tells him that the hardness of authors, like Flaubert, who dwell on indecencies, "*petrifies feeling*" (ibid., Arnold's emphasis). Arnold must have valued *Michael* for its refusal to relate the sordid history of Luke's dissoluteness, the "heavy news" (line 443) that the poem epitomizes in one brief sentence (lines 442–47). Wordsworth's untouched stone, we may infer, stands for a fundamental lightness or tact in his narration. Wordsworth's "style of perfect plainness" derives from Burns the "weight and force" that render it "bald as the bare mountain tops are bald" (9: 53, 54). But "obstacles . . . hinder or delay his due recognition by others," obstacles that are "removable," but that for now are "the poetical baggage which now encumbers him," "obstructions" that Arnold proposes to "clear away" (9: 41–42, 44). "Let us lay aside every weight which hinders our getting him recognised," Arnold concludes (9: 55), leaving it heartily uncertain what kind of stone, or airy mountaintop, is left us to rest on at last. The "And never" of his favorite line is the eternity of a classic and patriarchal idyll, an impossible Platonic ideal in whose shadow we consume our days.

Wordsworth does not even bother to tell us that the stones of the deserted sheepfold are old and gray. It would be too heavily emphatic to insist upon so inescapable a fact. They symbolize all too inevitably the passage of time.[4] The "And never" of the touchstone is the essence of the classic in its proper form as an eternal denial. Yet the repressed temporality stubbornly returns by way of reminders and reminiscences. For all of nature is pregnant with emergent meaning. The heap of stones is a sign of the destroyed cottage—or, to be more precise, an icon, since the one unlifted stone evokes the "single" house that formerly existed "on a plot of rising ground" (lines 132–33). The cottage was an icon in its turn, known by its light as "The Evening Star" (lines 139, 476), "a public symbol of the life / That thrifty Pair had lived" (lines 130–31). The evening star is, of course, a transient representative of greater lights in the natural and moral heavens (Hartman, "Evening Star"). It is intermittently "constant" and "regular" (line 136) in witness to the unremitting constancy of the couple, "Thus living on through such a length of years" (line 140). And their labor in turn depends on a proliferation of signs: Michael "had . . . learned the meaning of all winds" (line 48), and the landscape,

> like a book, preserved the memory
> Of the dumb animals, whom he had saved,
> Had fed or sheltered, linking to such acts
> The certainty of honourable gain.
> (lines 70–73)

The classic is perduring, but not timeless, and it exists within a context of displacements, substitutions, spoliations, and restitutions that constitute the life both of people and of things.

Despite its apparent quietism, the poem exists from the opening lines onward in a mode of confrontation: I and you, the sublime labor of ascent up Green-head Ghyll and the pastoral repose of the "hidden valley" meet "face to face." The confrontations continue and expand to include Michael and Luke, cottage and sheepfold, narrator and scene, and, as has recently been shown, Jewish and Christian consciousness.[5] The classic repose at the end is conclusive and retrospective; it sums up a completed action. But action itself is prospective; Michael's labor is sustained by "hope" and "forward-looking thoughts" (line 148). Closure takes on the cast of legend: the narrator qualifies Arnold's favorite line with the phrase, "and 'tis believed by all" (line 464), just as he turns another stone into a legend in "The Thorn" ("But all and each agree," line 207). The heap of stones is not telic, though it is teleological; it reminds us of the force of human aspirations that can never come to rest in a finished work. Five lines after "And never lifted up a single stone," the narrator says without consciousness of contradiction, "He at the building of this Sheep-fold wrought, / And left the work unfinished when he died" (lines 471–72).

The term "deconstruction" comes too readily to mind in connection with Michael's stones. Nothing, after all, is undone by the patriarch's neglected labors. No sheepfold was erected, and hence none has been demolished. "And never lifted up a single stone" is a negation free from irony; in its pure sequentiality without consequence, it bears the mark of Wordsworth's noble simplicity and high seriousness. With the colloquial ease of syntactic polysyndeton ("and" occurs nine times in lines 455–65) and rhythmic enjambment (e.g., "From time to time / Did he repair," lines 460–61) the vision slides irrecoverably into the past. Yet the versification delicately preserves the distinction between the perfective and preservative modes of time found at the ends of lines ("wrought," "died," "have been wrought," "is left," together with the aestheticizing "was he seen" and "may be seen") and the imperfective modes and forms of transiency that populate the beginnings of lines ("and left," "survive" [i.e., outlive], "was sold," "is gone," "that grew"). No single ordering encapsulates the whole moral, neither that of the fullness of time nor that of its destructive power. The poem concludes in a composed openness—not that of an idealized classic structure, but also not a collapse.

The pastoral of *Michael* teems with stories at its periphery: Luke's urban entanglements, the wondrous success of Richard Bateman that spans birth and death in a single sentence (lines 258–70), family histories of Michael's nephew (lines 209–17) and the prosperous London relative (lines 247–50), other unspecified "domestic tales . . . / Of Shepherds" (lines 22–23) and "incidents . . . / Of hardship, skill or courage, joy or fear" (lines 68–69), tales of the "Forefathers" (line 368) and, long before them, of our biblical ancestors. It is tempting to rewrite *Michael* as the complete story of a tragedy caused by the father's perverted affection for property (Bushnell, "'Where Is the Lamb'"). But it is not told that way. The life of the poem lies in its desultory and ruminating progress ("At random and imperfectly indeed," line 32), a tale without a moral, centered not on products finished, but on "remains" (line 480). If we dissever deconstruction from destruction, we can return to the former term its proper meaning. Deconstruction resides hopefully at the origin, in a heap of stones barely discernible from the natural wilderness that surrounds them. The stones are a project and a story, the one because the other, and because no completed structure has enclosed the space or put an end to the tale. A regulated incoherence lies at the birth of thought.

Thus does Arnold's touchstone become mine as well, in what I take to be Arnold's own, albeit suppressed, spirit. The Wordsworthian "and," like those of Homer and the Hebrew Bible, reflects the on-going, unfinished business of life, which is, according to Arnold, Wordsworth's one great theme. In his stiffer, Miltonic moods Words-worth envisions a perfect marriage of mind and matter in a poem "On man, on nature, and on human life" (first line of Prospectus to *The Recluse*, quoted by Arnold, *Prose Works* 9: 44 and 45). But at his most characteristic he departs ever so slightly from nature to em-phasize the human pulse, writing now "On man, the heart of man, and human life" (*Michael*, line 33). When most himself, he has, ac-cording to Arnold, no style, yet something indefinably distinctive and greatly expressive of the whole of life. The touchstone is the to-tality in the part, the norm in the distinctive trait, the structure as aggregate, the joyful future hatched by the epitaphic past.

These are the senses in which I have studied a literary epoch through its touchstones. Expression reaches fruition in the gesture that initiates a movement by laying aside a problem. Arnold is right and consistent in his paradoxical insistence upon the integrity of the whole from which the touchstone comes. The error of the old no-tion of preromanticism lies in the detachability and hence the inert-ness of the elements composing it. In an indifferent setting a heap of stones is just a weight that does not matter. But if you find the same formless grayness after climbing Green-head Ghyll, it gives you a lift with the shock of a discovery that points toward the stars. Touch-stones must be approached properly, tactfully. In each of the works and traditions studied here I have been concerned with emergent values. After centuries of asking what literature teaches and decades of asking what it is, we are only beginning to learn how to ask the question of what literature does.

Touchstones are passages. According to Arnold they must com-bine truth of matter with diction and movement. We underestimate the force of words in the critical tradition such as *movement* and *power* if we aestheticize or psychologize them. If touchstones are passages, the works from which they come are the rites of those pas-sages, staging the progress of discovery through which they chan-nel us. If we are willing to read Wordsworth's prose with a trust not always accorded to it, we can find at the peroration of the "Essay, Supplementary to the Preface," a noble expression of the dynamic mission of poetry: "Every great poet . . . has to call forth and to com-municate *power*. . . . Of genius the only proof is, the act of doing well what is worthy to be done, and what was never done before. . . . Genius is the introduction of a new element into the intellectual universe: or, . . . the application of powers to objects . . . in such a manner as to produce effects hitherto unknown" (*Poetical Works* 2: 428). The great enemies of genius are stasis, the inertia of conventionality and popular wisdom, Coleridge's fixities and definites. "Remember, also, that the medium through which, in poetry, the heart is to be affected, is language; a thing subject to endless fluctuations and arbitrary associations. The genius of the poet melts these down for his purpose; but they retain their shape and quality to him who is not capable of exerting, within his own mind, a corresponding energy" (ibid.). Wordsworth's rhetoric in this, his finest programmatic declaration, falls little short of the excitement whipped up by Shelley a few years later. Understood is the notion that the poet reforges not just the consciousness of the race, but indeed the very tools of consciousness. If he melts down the language, he must also reshape it, though without Shelley's overheated nervousness about popularity. Poetic effects are "complex and revolutionary"—this is bold language for 1815—hence, "can it be wondered that there is little existing preparation for a poet charged with a new mission to extend its kingdom?" (ibid.).

Great poetry is rarely easy, and there is no simple way to account for its achievement. It is "charged with a mission"; in an age of modern warfare and of electricity, "charged" suggests an explosive combination of matter and energy. "Rock" is, for our purposes, another such primal word, antithetically a stable noun and a dynamic verb. I have already commented on the rocking stones of "Humanity." But in connection with Wordsworth's intuition of the mysteries of poetic form, I should note also the poem written in 1816 where the stones become the ocean in an ecstatic vision of fixity and flow:

> The Original of human art,
> Heaven-prompted Nature, measures and erects
> Her temples, fearless for the stately work,
> Though waves, to every breeze, its high-arched roof.
> And storms the pillars rock.
> ("A Little Onward," lines 35–39)

Essence flows into essence as trees become temple, winds waves, stones seas, building book, and poems "Holy Writ" that yields "passage . . . / To heights more glorious still, and into shades / More awful" (lines 51–54). With Wordsworth and Arnold we can, for good measure, triangulate Wallace Stevens's "The Rock." For Stevens's gray rock at "The starting point of the human and the end," "point A / In a perspective that begins again / At B," provokes the mind to "adduce / Its tranquil self," which, by the process of adduction, must be C, "the main of things." This "main," focal C would be— as Wordsworth called the "headlands, tongues, and promontory shapes," in alternate versions of a line in *The Prelude*—"the Sea, the real Sea," "the main Atlantic" (1805 text, 13.48–49; 1850 text, 14.46–47). J. Hillis Miller, in reflecting with too rigidly binary a logic upon the "cure of the ground" in Stevens's poem,[6] missed the under-currents that make it another theory of the flux of life within all great works, tinged with sadness at what all advance leaves behind:

> The poem makes meanings of the rock,
> Of such mixed motion and such imagery
> That its barrenness becomes a thousand things
>
> And so exists no more.

It is nearly twenty years since Miller called for an essay to be written on Wordsworth's stones.[7] My analyses certainly take up that challenge. But I think they also show why the topic has been ne-glected. If we rigidly oppose stone to shell, land objects to water objects, concretion to movement, form to force, then we shall not readily discern the buried life of the things of earth. The false alter-natives have been with us for a long time, perhaps from the begin-ning. "Wordsworth went to the lakes, but he was never a lake poet. He found in stones the sermons he had already written there." So wrote Oscar Wilde nearly a century ago in "The Decay of Lying" (*The Artist as Critic* 301). But there is no such fixity in stones. They are not objective correlatives for the simple reason that they are not objects. As pure matter they are a substratum waiting to receive an idea; as scattered fragments of a totality they lack a distinct identity. Hence our inability to grasp the mystery of a line like "With rocks, and stones, and trees." Stones are pre-objects or post-objects: pre-objects because from them we hew shapes or quarry building blocks, post-objects because of the effacement of profile or the crumbling of the terrestrial mass that produces them. The last thing they do is to reflect back our face or our preconceptions.

If my conclusion has dwelt in metaphor, that too is in the spirit of the touchstone. "If we are asked to define this mark and accent in the abstract," we read in Arnold's "The Study of Poetry," "our answer must be: No, for we should thereby be darkening the question" (*Prose Works* 9: 171). Touchstones are to be illustrated and exempli-fied, not defined. "Rolled round in earth's diurnal course," stones are tropes—synecdoches of earth whence they come, metonymies of buildings whither they are headed, and, if they are touchstones, an-titheses of precious metals that they disfigure themselves in testing.

They are *there*—all around Wordsworth in the Lakes—but only as subsisting *Dasein*, duration without significant presence until they are used. The uses of stones are, to be sure, enormously varied, but the uses of touchstones are very precise. I would add to Arnold's account only what is, indeed, implicit in his concern for creating an educated public, namely that literary touchstones test the mettle of their readers just as they do that of their tradition. I remain with a metaphor for literature rather than a conceptual definition—that is, with a descriptive phenomenology rather than an explanation—because of the main point to which I return, that literature is a mode of acting, and not a mode of being.

From metaphor to example. "Spinoza and the Bible"—to my mind the finest of Arnold's literary essays, though far from the best known—does not deal with a literary figure at all, but with an author whose antiliterary form makes him the ideal touchstone of the literary. In revealing Spinoza, the outcast of the temple, to have built in his works a mansion of the Lord, in revealing the philosopher *more geometrico* to have been in touch with the spirit of poetry because his edifice drives with fervor toward a future stability, Arnold gives, I think, his one substantive account of the grand style:

> A philosopher's real power over mankind resides, not in his metaphysical formulas, but in the spirit and tendencies which have led him to adopt those formulas. . . . Propositions about substance pass by mankind at large like the idle wind, which mankind at large regards not; it will not even listen to a word about these propositions, unless it first learns what their author was driving at with them. . . . This object of the author is . . . that which is most important, that which sets all his work in motion, that which is the secret of his attraction for other minds, which, by different ways, pursue the same object. (*Prose Works* 3: 175)

More clearly than in Arnold's other essays, we see here the fundamental beliefs, which have motivated my analyses as well, namely, that a significant work is by nature a project or enterprise, and that the kernels that attract us to it, its touchstones or lodestones, are those passages that are its passageways toward the future, the driving drift. Such a work is a vibrant edifice. Arnold is surprised to find this dynamism in Spinoza and recognizes it, perhaps, all the more readily where it stands out in relief. And, indeed, the relief proves, in the last analysis, not merely to facilitate recognition of literary quality, but to be essential to it. For there is a double mission in literature. The perfect, classic touchstone is an unmoved mover that remains intact even while it affects its readers. The author discomposes, but then also recomposes, reading "my Father's house" as the goal of his "genuine sacred transport," his "immortal longing" (3: 182). "Spinoza first impresses Goethe and any man like Goethe, and then he composes him; first he fills and satisfies his imagination by the width and grandeur of his view of nature, and then he fortifies and stills his mobile, straining, passionate, poetic temperament by the moral lesson he draws from his view of nature" (3: 177). Arnold's own touchstone passages have a pathos of finality that links them to the philosopher's moral lessons.[8] Literary or philosophical touchstones reveal a power that is held in reserve; they are the ground on which the work stands, when all is said and done.

Touchstones, as I conceive them, are parts of a whole—passages from works, or works from epochs. But they are not parts in the sense of separable unities or of representative samplings. They are, rather, condensations and embodiments of the forces animating the whole. In one sense the whole contains the part, for the part loses all finality if it is not embedded in a language, a tradition, a context, and an expressive vehicle. But in another sense the part contains the whole. It is a seat of expression, where the work's energies come together. To the extent that the energies are intentional it is a telos; to the extent that they are temporal it appears as a last, or latest, thing, whether or not it is the end of the work. ("For not every thing that is last claims to be an end, but only that which is best," Aristotle, *Physics* 2.2, 194a32–33.) History does not make itself; it is made in the works of men. Within those works, the touchstones are both a final resting place and the horizon of the new. A deficient historical sense has often encouraged either a merely appreciative attitude that emphasizes the untouched, pristine remoteness of the past, or else a merely hermeneutic one that emphasizes the actuality with which it touches us. The old notion of preromanticism combined both forms of a historicity, seeing a static yet skewed contemporaneity linking the curious lore of Thomson and Wordsworth. Arnold, by contrast, never doubted the historicity of the classic, even while praising its timeless value.[9] Among recent critics, it is the marxists who have insistently pointed out how authors are most authentically themselves at the points where, even unwittingly, they break free of traditions and preconceptions. Every significant work participates, at moments, in the avant-garde.

What kind of organism, then, is the work of literature? Work is production. The literary work generates and differentiates. We must distinguish the integrity of the work, which is its power of forming contexts and of generating innovations from within, from excessively limited notions of unity, all simple consonances and unisons. Harmony of some sort there surely is in any great work, but a strenuous harmony that takes dissonances in stride. Integrity is earned; the work of genius (as Kant says) obeys laws, but it also makes the laws it obeys. There is no impermeable boundary to a living, breathing organism. The law is without and within, time is without and within, history is without and within. No model simpler than Freudian introjection can describe the individuation of the literary work; no model simpler than Freud's layered self can describe its unity. And that means, as Freud increasingly recognized, that models for the individual cannot be rigorously distinguished from models for the community, the race, or the species. Psychic processes are also historical processes; the organism is life in action, at whatever level.

Organic history is agglutinative. As an agglutinative language builds by compounding, without distinguishing word from phrase, so, in history, single works are communities of parts, while large-scale enterprises cooperate in making a single statement. The work, *l'oeuvre*, can equally be a particular composition or the sustained product of a life or an age, and in any case it is also always the labor of production as well. Two of my chapters deal with broad movements and issues, one with Goldsmith's lifework, three with individual masterpieces in the context of their authors' production and their tradition, and one with *Tristram Shandy* considered apart from Sterne's other major work. In each case what matters is the sustained concern with a subject, leading toward an articulation of essential possibilities. Each subject can be considered a touchstone for concerns in the period; and the analysis, a passage toward resolution of the touchstone. The subjects selected have been an aggregate of terms that shaped discourse in the period: self-consciousness, pure space and time, feeling, closure, the aesthetic, story, synthesis, sign, action, experienced time, and finally, in Wordsworth, the fusion of all such concerns under the rubric of simplicity.

The literary touchstone is a passage from a causality of conditions to a causality of goals. In the touchstone the possible becomes actual, with its genuineness proved, the implicit becomes conscious, the object becomes a subject. The touchstone changes the question, with respect to its particular topic, from a retrospective one (what makes consciousness, feeling, closure, etc.?) to a prospective one (what can consciousness, feeling, closure, etc., make?). In the touchstone the two sides of the question are held in balance. There it appears to have the purified form of a question of definition, that is, of essence (what is consciousness, etc.?). Hence the touchstone possesses an aura of containment or repose that we variously term perfection, autotelism, or reflexivity. A suspension of forces masquerades as a relaxation, a release of potential as a repose from power. It seems a spontaneous outgrowth of the imagination, an unfathered vapor or a mountain-birth, returning upon its unknown source:

> How shall I paint thee?—Be this naked stone
> My seat, while I give way to such intent. . . .
> To dignify the spot that gives thee birth
> No sign of hoar Antiquity's esteem
> Appears, and none of modern Fortune's care;
> Yet thou thyself hast round thee shed a gleam
> Of brilliant moss, instinct with freshness rare;
> Prompt offering to thy Foster-mother, Earth!
> (Wordsworth, "The River Duddon,"
> sonnet 3)[10]

Yet in fact the touchstone is a moment of breakthrough. Many currents circulate within any work; the touchstone channels them, becoming, in the passage of history, one of the stepping stones toward the future:

> stone matched with stone
> In studied symmetry, with interspace
> For the clear waters to pursue their race
> Without restraint.
> ("The River Duddon," sonnet 9,
> "The Stepping-Stones")

If I had to coin a term to identify my approach, it would be "postdialectical." From a dialectical history I retain the guiding conceptions of an interplay of opposing forces, of the interdependence of form and content, and of consciousness as the main agent in reaching a synthesis. I follow the mainstream of the dialectical tradition in regarding history as the grand march of intellect. Yet I value consciousness as much for what it saves or restores as for what it produces.

For Hegel consciousness is negation: it is the antithetical *for us* that stands opposite the thetic *in itself* and draws what is outside into the mind. The grand march of intellect then entails a necessary element of rejection: it produces the future by denying the past and comprehension through dissatisfaction with mere, uncomprehended presence. Hegel's consciousness is an imperialist, its march a campaign, its aggressiveness inscribed in the metaphors of seizing and grasping (*begreifen, auffassen*) that describe its activity. Often, however, the workings of consciousness and of time seem to me more varied. Instead of production, they often take the form of eduction, drawing out threads implicit but unrecognized in the past. No sharp line separates two guises of advance, revolutionary initiation and gradual emergence. The motive may as well be a potential as a problem, the mechanism as well a syn-opsis, or viewing together, as a syn-thesis, or putting together.

Many of Hegel's terms have a generous ambiguity that evokes numerous possibilities, yet they seem to me not generous enough. *Aufheben* evokes preservation as well as suspension or cancellation, but only preservation in storage or by laying aside, as one conserves fruit or reserves tickets, and even then mostly only in the past participle. It is not an active preservation and employment. *Zugrundegehen* evokes grounding, but only as a pun on its principal meaning, destruction. And the English "resolution" has a whole range of meanings—including courage, decision, and clarification—that are unavailable to the German *Versöhnung* (reconciliation). The literary work comes to consciousness not so much by seeing through past errors as by collecting, "reading with" its tradition, "gathering together" the threads that compose its texture, which it makes the web of history. We have seen the process of collection repeatedly in the works analyzed. Even the "art of resolving contradictions," the dialectical art as such, takes in Goldsmith's play the form of a clarification of focus as in a microscope, displaying the contrasting groups front and center at the end; it does not become an *Aufhebung* or quietus.

Perhaps Tony Lumpkin's "circumbendibus" is not a bad description of the postdialectical mode, a looser, more flexible, even more whimsical curve than the Hegelian spiral. Contradiction and reconciliation, problem and solution, provocation and response are part of the historical process, but only part. Consciousness is not only the negation that impels the intellect restlessly forward, but also the synopsis that comes after, gazing from the present backward as well as forward, preserving and projecting. It makes or it finds, but either way it "invents"; its patterns are given by the material or imposed by the force of personality, but either way they are images. Consciousness as invention and as imagination, not as concept and logic—that is the watchword of the postdialectical mode. Literary invention sifts the infinite data of human experience to forge an image—more than a sign, less than a system—wherein history is reflected, focused, and mastered.

Arnold called poetry the criticism of life, and it is clear that, without necessarily meaning anything very precise, this phrase at least means something postdialectical and collective rather than confrontational. From the Muse comes music: the touchstones, when struck, or when they strike us, sound the keynotes of our existence.

Envoi

It is the trick of thinking to be either premature or behindhand.
George Eliot, *Daniel Deronda*, chap. 54

Few authors, I suppose, abandon a project of this length to its fate
without mixed feelings of relief and regret. The relief looks forward,
to a season of newer and fresher concerns, and it looks backward, to
a finally achieved ordering of its thoughts and materials, however
imperfect, after years of struggle. The regret looks backward, to
omissions, defects, and errors that will never cease to haunt, and it
looks ahead to the time when texts that are now old friends will be
left behind and new and strange acquaintances must with difficulty
be won over. To the relief, the immediate past has a long prehistory
and the future is an impending respite—still impending as I write
this, in anticipation of future emotions—of limited duration. To the
regret, the past reaches out with long arms across the present, and
the future looms large and uncertain. Neither past nor future is a
single dimension; the different emotions are also different dura-
tions, impinging differently on the fleeting present.

Feelings of presence and possession there surely are too. But for
me at least, satisfaction is transient and unstable. It waxes and wanes,
subject to moods and outside influences. And the work itself is more
uniformly present to a reader who confronts it in a single encounter
than to the author with whom it has grown and aged, refreshed in
parts, obscured or forgotten in others. A reader necessarily begins by
assuming that the book is all of a piece, equally sincere in all parts,
evenly meditated, uniformly significant. The author knows better.

A work of this nature will never rise to the dignity of history. For
those, increasingly few, who take it off the shelves, it will be present

for a while and then fade rapidly back away into absence. It will be judged by simple categories: right or wrong, original or familiar, consistent or contradictory, adequate or skimpy, interesting or dull. The fond author hopes that it will affect the way readers think, but knows it will not so affect many, nor much, nor long; he will perforce be gratified if it but succeeds in altering for a while some judgments and conclusions. Such is the weakness of human enterprise. Yet to the author the book lives. That may be cause for triumph in the case of works that are historical, that live for their readers. In a work like this it is the ground only for pathos. The work lives with the fragility of an organism that its maker is too weak to protect. We might yearn for classic utterance, timeless perfection, eternal truths. But these are not in our grasp. The turbulent currents of temporality swirl through even our most cherished dreams. Until—

> *I sought, and soon discovered, the three head-stones on the slope next the moor—the middle one, grey, and half buried in heath—Edgar Linton's only harmonized by the turf, and moss creeping up its foot—Heathcliff's still bare.*
>
> *I lingered round them, under the benign sky; watched the moths fluttering among the heath and hare-bells; listened to the soft wind breathing through the grass; and wondered how any one could ever imagine unquiet slumbers for the sleepers in that quiet earth.*

THE END

Reference Matter

Notes

All translations of passages from foreign language titles are mine. Full information on the sources cited in text and notes is given below in Works Cited.

Introduction

1. The history of the term "preromanticism" has been traced by Scouten in "The Warton Forgeries" and earlier, for French and Italian literature, by Jonard in "Una nozione che non esiste: 'Preromanticismo.'"

2. Van Tieghem, *Le Sentiment* 66. The passage is repeated in almost identical words on p. 86: it is, characteristically, the critic, not the poet, who tries too hard.

3. See the critiques of "preromanticism" by Jean-Louis Diaz, Roger Fayolle, and, especially, Françoise Gaillard, together with the editor's presentation and the ensuing discussion, in Vialleneix, *Le Préromantisme* 11–94. Not all the papers in this symposium heed the warnings. The old habits also survive in the typescript lectures by Klein reproduced under the title *Anfänge der englischen Romantik 1740–1780* (Beginnings of English Romanticism 1740–1780).

4. A case in point is Wesling's "Augustan Form: Justification and Breakup of a Period Style." Following a curious anatomy of period characteristics, Wesling concludes that, while "it is absurd to call the period 1750–1795, by retrospective reasoning, pre-Romantic" (418), its poetry does reveal "the historical condition of an incipient modernity" (417). Replacing preromantic with premodern is surely, on any account, to substitute the greater historiographical evil for the lesser. I need not stress how many critics claim this kind of anticipation for their favorite authors.

5. Closest to my approach is that suggested by Nemoianu in *A Theory of the Secondary* 125–26: "Throughout the [eighteenth] century, several literary and cultural transactions consisted in probing the limits of the [neoclassical] model and breaking down its limits, altering and qualifying it. . . . In retrospect, such qualifications seem to justify the use of 'pre-Romanticism' as a unifying historical category, although these departures were mostly separate. The core of a high-Romantic alternative model was constituted when, say, around 1790, these autonomous modifications connected with an almost audible click. It appeared when the changes—exoticism, historic nostalgia, subjectivity, and so forth—that had accumulated in the eighteenth century combined and were perceived as pertaining to a kind of center. This central or unifying principle was expanded consciousness: expansion in time, expansion in space, expansion in variety, expansion in depth." My analyses corroborate and flesh out all the aspects of this admirably precise summation. The only difference—but it is a substantial one—is that the historical process appears to me more dialectical than Nemoianu suggests. The romantic "click" comes only in part from adding together dispersed preromantic initiatives; it comes far more from resolving problems that the preromantic authors imaginatively projected.

6. A book, excellent in its way, that illustrates the spirit of traditional versions of preromanticism even though it does not use the term, is Sheats's *The Making of Wordsworth's Poetry, 1789–1798*. Taking his terminal year as the Wordsworthian norm, Sheats scrutinizes the earlier poems to identify period commonplaces and foreshadowings of things to come. He denies that Wordsworth's "poetic character under[went] fundamental change" (41) and claims that "the schoolboy" already possessed, in embryo, "the ideas of the mature man" (42). In "Wordsworth's Old Gray Stone" (Chap. 12 below), I reread many of the same poems with an eye to ideas lying beyond the horizon of the work. Each poem, on this reading, is coherent in itself, and there is an internally motivated progression from each to the next; whereas for Sheats the early poems are incoherent, subsequent works sort out their facets in order to reiterate and elaborate the "romantic" themes, and the development is, in many cases, motivated externally by relations with France and by the inaccessibility of Annette Vallon.

7. For a particularly fine account of the resemblances see Barrell and Guest, "On the Uses of Contradiction." Barrell and Guest, however, attack the good faith of the poets for evading a kind of dialectical thinking that my Chap. 2 argues was not available to them.

8. See Arac, *Critical Genealogies* 57–80, and especially Simpson, *Wordsworth's Historical Imagination*, which concludes coincidentally by calling for a study of Wordsworth's late style such as I have undertaken here. More general considerations from a marxist perspective can be found in McGann, *The Romantic Ideology*, esp. chap. 9; from a deconstructive perspective, though not focused on romanticism, in Miller, "Deconstructing the Deconstructors."

9. See my essay "Romanticism and Enlightenment."

10. My sense of the settling-in of romanticism in its later phases resembles that of Nemoianu in *The Taming of Romanticism*, where much of interest can be read about the "rehabilitation of the eighteenth century" (34).

11. The best New Criticism and structuralism, however, respect historical dialectic. Thus, for instance, Lévi-Strauss, *The Way of the Masks* 144: "The originality of each style . . . stems from a conscious or unconscious wish to declare itself different, to choose from among all the possibilities some that the art of neighboring peoples has rejected. This is also true of successive styles. The Louis XV style prolongs the Louis XIV style, and the Louis XVI style prolongs the Louis XV style; but, at the same time, each challenges the other. In its own way, it says what the preceding style was saying in its own language, and it also says something else, which the preceding style was not saying but was silently inviting the new style to enunciate."

12. Chap. 11 of McGann's *The Romantic Ideology* discusses this topic in relation to Shelley.

13. In *The Visionary Company* Bloom notes that the "prayer thus heralded [in line 121, 'And this prayer I make'] is never quite expressed in the rest of the poem." An expected "that" clause, however, is likewise missing in line 65. By focusing on "prayer" alone, Bloom implies that "vision" transcends experience; by comparing the two lines and taking account of the implicit context, we can recognize that "vision" is, rather, a generalized sense of the structure of future experience. "Vision" is, in Kant's terms, transcendental but not transcendent. Having failed to recognize that the romantic vision always was conditioned, the later Bloom feels anxiety when he discovers the past that conditions it.

Chapter One

1. For a beautiful and carefully documented study of the way texts shape their readers, see Klancher, *The Making of English Reading Audiences*.

2. I am far from wishing to impugn the power of nonintegrative criticism, especially from kinds of marxist, gender, and ethnic studies that have articulated subaltern and subversive voices within texts and that have often rehabilitated works other than the traditional and (in the later eighteenth century) exclusively male canon that I focus on. For a programmatic call relevant to this historical period see the introductory chapter of Armstrong's *Desire and Domestic Fiction*. Although it may be only a difference in temperament that leads me to feel that you join history whenever you join battle with it, my discussion of Marilyn Butler later in this chapter gives an example of how historicist criticism often undermines its own premises, and my review of *The New Eighteenth Century* illustrates how alternative or oppositional histories can turn into essentializing oppositions to history.

3. See also my review essay "What's in a Text?" where I have argued that the work of Jerome McGann likewise testifies to the priority of textual constitutions over ideological determinants.

4. See the debate between Martin Heidegger and Emil Staiger on Eduard Mörike's line "Was aber schön ist, selig scheint es in ihm selbst" (from the poem "Auf eine Lampe"), in Staiger's *Die Kunst der Interpretation* 28–42.

5. Cf. Ehrmann, "The Death of Literature."

6. Even in the writings of the later Walter Benjamin, one of the great forebears of today's cultural materialists, one can read the following: "To know the history of the revolts, the uprisings, and the civil war means nothing; in all of that the Revolution shows only . . . its external and natural side. . . . But to let one's feelings be penetrated by it as were those of its contemporaries means seeking out its terrors elsewhere. They are in the words." The passage is quoted with approval from a book under review, Ferdinand Brunot, *Histoire de la langue française*, vol. 9, pt. 2; *La Révolution et l'empire: Les Événements, les institutions et la langue*, in Benjamin, *Gesammelte Schriften* 3: 563.

7. Nietzsche, *Werke* 1: 140, 145, 191. The German from p. 145 is this: "Sie erdachten den Begriff des Epigonen-Zeitalters, nur um Ruhe zu haben und bei allem unbequemen Neueren sofort mit dem ablehnenden Verdikt 'Epigonenwerk' bereit sein zu können." In the quotation from p. 191, "anstößig" means offensive (to the Philistine), but conceals within it the impulse (*Anstoß*) that makes textual production possible.

8. For this notion of style see in particular Granger, *Essai d'une philosophie du style*.

Chapter Two

1. Hume calls poets "liars by profession" in the chapter "On the Influence of Belief," *Treatise* 121. As Trilling shows in *Sincerity and Authenticity*, the ideal of sincerity only emerged with Diderot, Rousseau, and Goethe.

2. Hurd, *Letters on Chivalry and Romance*, letter 10, p. 89. Another locus classicus for the artificiality of art is Batteux, *Les Beaux Arts* 1.2, and see also Abrams, *The Mirror and the Lamp* 18–19. Harold Bloom's view that poets lie against time is in this tradition.

3. Wimsatt, "The Augustan Mode in English Poetry," *Hateful Contraries* 64.

4. Hughes, "Language, History and Vision." See also Hughes's sequel, "Restructuring Literary History," and Gossman, "Literary Scholarship and Popular History." Related, but cruder, is the account by Horkheimer and Adorno in *Dialektik der Aufklärung* 7–41.

5. The quoted words are all used prominently by Weiskel in chap. 2 of *The Romantic Sublime*, a sophisticated restatement of the traditional view, based (as is often the case) on Locke and the theorists rather than on Hume and the poets. More supple, and argued from actual poetic practice, is Price, "The Sublime Poem." Price, however, neglects the sociability and the retreat from transcendence that I discuss below.

6. The best description of the urbane sublime style, to my knowledge, is still Richards's account of a very belated example, Longfellow's elegy "In

the Churchyard at Cambridge," in *Practical Criticism* 175–76: "If this interpretation of the poem is right, 'rude' is simply an acknowledgment of the social convention, not in the least a rebuke. . . . The last verse is not a grim warning or an exhortation, but a cheerful realization of the situation, not in the least evangelical, not at all like a conventional sermon, but on the contrary extremely urbane, rather witty, and *slightly* whimsical. . . . If there is any character in poetry that modern readers—who derive their ideas of it rather from the best known poems of Wordsworth, Shelley and Keats or from our own contemporaries, than from Dryden, Pope or Cowper—are unprepared to encounter, it is this social, urbane, highly cultivated, self-confident, temperate and easy kind of humor."

7. For a classic statement of the satirists' seriousness, see Bredvold, "The Gloom of the Tory Satirists." Chap. 2 of Rothstein's *Restoration and Eighteenth Century Poetry* is an excellent anatomy of period style. The fullest reading of Pope along relevant lines is Jackson's excellent *Vision and Re-Vision*. Cohen's unsystematic but important essay, "The Augustan Mode in English Poetry," includes an account of asymmetry and emotional intensification (i.e., movements toward sublimity) within Pope's couplets. For a carefully nuanced comparison of Thomson with Pope (good on similarities and differences, though with insufficient acknowledgment of Pope's diversity) see Sitter, *Literary Loneliness* 175–88. Finally, for the persistence of satire in Gray, Cowper, and Crabbe, see Carnochan, "Continuity," though I shall argue that these poets all depart from the urbane basis that they grow out of.

8. Cf. the echo in Greville's "The Man of Pleasure," in Pearch, *A Collection of Poems* 1: 314: "In Pleasure's ray see Nature shine, / How dull, alas! at Wisdom's shrine! / 'Tis folly to be wise.' / Collusive term, poor vain pretense, / Enjoyment sure is real Sense / In philosophic Eyes." Spacks has drawn attention to some additional ironies of Gray's final couplet in *The Poetry of Vision* 101–2; her discussion (91–95) of the delicate humor of the "Ode on the Spring" is also useful. On Gray's view of childhood see Micklus, "Voices in the Wind," and Fry, *The Poet's Calling* 69–71. On Gray's detachment see Griffin, "Gray's Audiences."

9. I borrow the observation concerning quasi-personification in stanza 5 from Schlüter, *Die Englische Ode* 85–86. On the inherent flexibility of eighteenth-century personification see Spacks, *An Argument of Images* 133–46, and, more broadly, cf. Chapin's hesitant conclusion in *Personification in Eighteenth-Century Poetry* 133: "The use of personified abstractions as figures of vision is never, accordingly, with most eighteenth-century poets, entirely serious."

10. McIntosh has a good analysis of the Addisonian voice as it pervades eighteenth-century prose in *The Choice of Life* 122–43. David Durant's "Vanity of Elevation" interestingly surveys the tension between naturalness and elevation in poems by Collins, Johnson, Gray, Goldsmith, and Smart; it does not recognize how dramatizing isolation becomes a means of communicating and sharing isolation, turning poetic objects into poetic processes.

11. See Fletcher, *Allegory* 70–146, especially the section on "kosmos," 108–20. Relevant to urbanity, despite his solemnity, is Fletcher's statement "Leveling and lowering is then a primary function of kosmos, no less than its elevating function" (159).

12. See Krieger's essay "Samuel Johnson: The Extensive View of Mankind" for a reading of *The Vanity of Human Wishes* along similar lines. In Johnson, of course, the fabric of assurance (the urbane and witty flexibility) begins to come apart.

13. Pater, *Marius the Epicurean*, chap. 4, describing the Academy where Marius learns Greek: "While all their heart was in their limited boyish race, and its transitory prizes, he was already entertaining himself, very pleasurably meditative, with the tiny drama in action before him, as but the mimic, preliminary exercise for a larger contest, and already with an implicit epicureanism. Watching all the gallant effects of their small rivalries—a scene in the main of fresh delightful sunshine—he entered at once into the sensations of a rivalry beyond them, into the passion of men, and had already recognized a certain appetite for fame, for distinction among his fellows, as his dominant motive to be" (27–28).

14. Virgil, *Aeneid* 8.47, trans. Dryden, in Dryden, *Works* 6: 610.

15. None of these sources is cited in Lonsdale's notes (Lonsdale, ed., *Poems*)—nor is Swift's "On Poetry," lines 207–8, which implicates Gray in the "human fate" (Eton College ode, line 56) of the victims that he would like to keep at a distance. Here are three of the relevant passages. Tickell, *Oxford*, lines 345–52 (Chalmers, *English Poets* 11: 133): "See how the matchless youth their hours improve, / And in the glorious way to knowledge move! / Eager for fame, prevent the rising Sun, / And watch the midnight labours of the Moon. / Nor tender years their bold attempts restrain / Who leave dull Time, and hasten into man, / Pure to the soul, and pleasing to the eyes, / Like angels youthful, and like angels wise." Thomson, *The Castle of Indolence* 1.48.1–6: "Or are you sportive—Bid the Morn of Youth / Rise to new Light, and beam afresh the Days / Of Innocence, Simplicity, and Truth; / To Cares estrang'd, and Manhood's thorny Ways / What Transport! to retrace our boyish Plays, / Our easy Bliss, when each Thing Joy supply'd." Thomson, *Liberty* 1.280–85: "How chang'd, how vacant, VIRGIL, wide around, / Would now your *Naples* seem? Disaster'd less / By black *Vesuvius* thundering o'er the Coast / His midnight Earthquakes, and his mining Fires, / Than by Despotic Rage: that inward gnaws, / A native Foe— a foreign, tears without." Dryden's imitation of Horace's ode, too long to quote, is Gray's principal structural model, gradually drifting from "soft *Etesian* Gales" to "A train of Ills, a ghastly crew, / . . . lash'd on by Fate," and to "audacious Crimes" against "the Gods" (Dryden, *Works* 3: 77–78); a fuller reading would show the Eton College ode to be a palinode to Dryden's poem.

16. For "inly gnaws" cf. the passage from *Liberty* quoted in the preceding note. For "vitals" and "rage" cf. *Liberty* 3.335–39—"Near this great Aera, ROME / Began, to feel the swift Approach of Fate, / That now her Vi-

tals gain'd: still more and more / Her deep Divisions kindling into Rage / And War, with Chains and Desolation charg'd"—and 4.122–28 (where again the artist is implicated in the general ruin)—"Added to these the still continual Waste / Of inbred Foes that on thy Vitals prey, / And, double Tyrants, seize the very Soul. / Where hadst thou Treasures for this Rapine all? / These hungry Myriads that thy Bowels tore, / Heap'd Sack on Sack, and bury'd in their Rage / Wonders of Art."

17. Cf. Pope's letter to Walsh, July 2, 1706: "To bestow heightening on every part is monstrous: Some parts ought to be lower than the rest," etc. (*Correspondence* 1: 19). Similarly, in commenting on the proper way to translate Homer, Pope states in the Postscript to his translation of the *Odyssey*: "To read thro' a whole work in this strain is like traveling all along on the ridge of a hill; which is not half so agreeable as sometimes gradually to rise, and sometimes gently to descend, as the way leads, and as the end of the journey directs" (*Poems* 10: 388).

18. Perhaps this deficient attention to immediate context may excuse the insensitive attack on Thomson in Sherbo, *English Poetic Diction* 158–80.

19. There has still not been enough attention paid to the "deeply buried and always reticent" puns in Pope's nonsatiric verse. (The phrase is Mack's, "Wit and Poetry and Pope" 32.) Like one of Thomson's inverse decorums, for instance, the sublime, neoplatonizing treatment of nature in the *Essay on Criticism* is prepared by a rarefied pun that suggests the mutuality of high and low: "Would all but *stoop* to what they *under-stand*" (line 67, hyphen added). This principle of compensation is ubiquitous in the verse of the period; see, for one instance, the humble graves that "heave the crumbled Ground" in Parnell's "A Night-Piece on Death" (line 30), while the monuments of the rich are undermined by hollowness and irony; for another, see the theology of Smart's Seatonian Prize hymns, where, as Donald Marshall has written, "The style is sublimely obscure, but courteously explicates itself" ("The Development of Blank-Verse Poetry" 222).

20. This line is misleadingly emended in Sambrook's text but correctly reported in his Appendix D.

21. "One of the more permanent functions of the word [honest] . . . was to soften the assertion of class, or contrariwise to maintain the assertion in a softened form" (Empson, *Structure* 200).

22. Cohen, *The Art of Discrimination*. More useful in application to literary works is Cohen's essay "On the Interrelations of Eighteenth-Century Literary Forms."

23. Thomas Warton, "Ode on the Approach of Summer," in Chalmers, *English Poets* 18: 106.

24. For some additional remarks on the historical significance of Gray's enumerations see Tillotson, "Methods of Description." Siskin's *Historicity* 94–124 is a nice discussion of the way that eighteenth-century additive organization turns into romantic temporal flow and development, which he aptly calls a "positing of growth as continuous revision" (103). Where, how-

ever, he sees "epistemological and ultimately spiritual limitations" in eighteenth-century "fragments whose sum approaches but cannot equal the
whole" (102), I see a "middle state" that is not impelled toward totalizations.

25. Thomson, *Seasons*, pp. 303–5. See Cohen's valuable discussions of
Thomson's punning, which he calls "illusive allusion," in *The Unfolding of
"The Seasons"* 39–40 and passim (consult index). I will not detail here all
my points of agreement and disagreement with Cohen's commentary, but I
would like to call attention to the excellent pages on sociability (252–92)
and to what seems a misleading treatment of summer as a fiery season.

26. Typical of the poets' conscious preference for loose over rigid forms
is Gray's criticism of Buffon's "Love of System, . . . the most contrary Thing
in the World to a Science, entirely grounded upon experiments, & that has
nothing to do with Vivacity of Imagination" (letter to Wharton, Aug. 9,
1750, *Correspondence* 1: 329). For more documentation see Greene's witty
essay "Logical Structure."

27. Cf. also Goldsmith's *The Citizen of the World*, letter 50 (*Collected
Works* 2: 212), which praises the "ductility of the laws" in England. Goldsmith argues that there can be more liberty and looser enforcement of the
laws in aristocratic England than in a democracy because the state is stronger
by nature. Barrell, in *English Literature in History*, gives a fine account of
the flexible comprehensiveness of politics, society, and language in the period and of the unsettling dynamic that eventually bequeathed to the romantics a "crisis of social knowledge" (209); chap. 2 (51–109) concerns
Thomson and John Dyer.

28. In *Graces of Harmony* (118–36) Percy G. Adams comments copi-
ously on Thomson's "attractive," "ear appealing," "pleasing" sound effects.

29. On the underlying sociality of Richardson and Chatterton, two
other writers who seem to privilege the solitary self, see Cox, *Stranger*
59–81 and 99–112.

30. On Collins as a light or sociable poet see Sypher, "The *Morceau de
Fantaisie*"; Johnston, *The Poetry of William Collins*; Sitter, *Literary Loneliness* 136–45; and, best of all, Spacks, "The Eighteenth-Century Collins."
Despite its deconstructive rhetoric, Finch's discussion of the volatility of
presence in Collins's invocations has a related import; see "Immediacy in
the *Odes.*" Knapp highlights the saving theatricality of the "Ode to Fear" in
Personification and the Sublime 87–97. It has not been customary to see a
unifying plan in the odes; thus Quintana, "The Scheme of Collins's *Odes,*"
separates the odes into two distinct groups, poems about poetic kinds and
patriotic poems. Similar in spirit to my account and fuller, with different
details, is Rothstein, *Restoration and Eighteenth Century Poetry* 155–57.

31. Pope is again comparable. His form too is social even when the content is at its most personal. Neither he nor Collins could rest content with
the pilgrim's heedless hum, and repeated statements in his letters show that
even the retreats to the isolation of his garden had a quasi-social function, to
"converse with myself." As Patey has well said, "Art and life, the public and
the private, the corporate and the personal are continuous for the Popean

self" ("Art and Integrity" 369). Like Young, who was taken for the author of the anonymous *Essay on Man*, Pope aimed to promote man's self-knowledge as a creature of a "middle state," in his varying relation to higher and lower spheres. Indeed, in his gloomier moods Pope could sound much like a more gifted Young, conceding that human reason is nothing more than heightened imagination and that optimism is a corollary of despair, as in the following letter to Caryll, July 13, 1714 (*Correspondence* 1: 236): "Half the things that employ our heads deserve not the name of thoughts, for they are only stronger dreams or impressions upon the imagination; our schemes of government, our systems of philosophy, our golden words of poetry, are all but so many shadow images and airy prospects, which arise to us but so much the livelier and more frequent as we are more overcast with darkness, wrapt in the night, and disturbed with the fumes of human vanity." Patey contrasts Pope with Young (as does Price, *To the Palace of Wisdom* 345–51), though conceding at one point that the difference is a matter of "degree" (377). Jackson's "Thomas Gray: Drowning in Human Voices" criticizes dichotomized readings on the way to an interesting discussion of Gray as wayfarer: "The distinction between public and private is voided in the very fact that voice is equally and simultaneously one and the other" (371). Barrell, "The Public Figure and the Private Eye," is a sensitive probing of the diction of Collins's "Ode to Evening" in the same spirit.

32. Likewise James Hervey writes in "Meditations Among the Tombs": "How *short* the transition, from time to eternity! The partition, nothing more than the breath in our nostrils; and the transition may be made, in the twinkling of an eye" (*Meditations* 18). On the transition past death see McKillop, *Background* 22–25, and Chipka, "Stranger" 541–66.

33. The continuity of thought and feeling is well discussed in Brissenden, *Virtue in Distress* 22–55.

34. The strains on the eighteenth-century synthesis can be observed in Lowth's *Lectures* (delivered in Latin in 1741–50, published in 1753). In lecture 14, "The Sublime," Lowth says, in pointed contrast to the lines of Young just quoted, "In a word, Reason speaks literally, the Passions practically" (1: 308). Much in the *Lectures* points toward this kind of dissociated sensibility, which is linked to what Lowth calls the "sublime of language." Yet he begins by saying that Hebrew, lacking vowels, "has remained altogether silent" (lecture 3; 2: 66). There is also much in the *Lectures* that continues the "sublime of sentiment" deriving from Boileau and the more fluid sensibility of the earlier part of the century, such as the account of mixed style in lecture 26 and the flexibly classicizing formal analyses, in lectures 30–34, of the *Song of Solomon* as an epithalamium and of *Job* as an imperfect tragedy.

35. This essential fluidity of eighteenth-century thought has of course not gone unnoticed—see, for instance, the parallels cited by Carnochan in *Lemuel Gulliver's Mirror for Man* 128–29—but the full consequences are rarely drawn. Thus, Brower's "Form and Defect of Form" intelligently yet, in my view, mistakenly dichotomizes eighteenth-century poetic procedures;

he can be corrected by Cohen's "Association of Ideas." For a recognition of eighteenth-century relativism leading to a large-scale and penetrating attack on its numerous forms, see Bachelard, *Formation*. On the relation of art and nature see Battestin's excellent essays on eighteenth-century pastoral, in *The Providence of Wit*, chaps. 2 and 4; one might also cite lines like Parnell's "And all the Nature, all the Art, of Love" ("Hesiod: Or the Rise of Woman," line 56), as well as the same poem's reference to "native Tropes" (line 62), a characteristically fluid notion that would only involve a problematical dialectic if found in an author later than Rousseau. On the admittedly vexed question of the "poetry of statement," Hume's opinion in "Of the Standard of Taste" needs to be considered: "Every kind of composition, even the most poetical, is nothing but a chain of propositions and reasonings; not always, indeed, the justest and most exact, but still plausible and specious, however disguised by the colouring of the imagination" (*Essays* 240).

36. Siskin, *Historicity* 68–77, is an excellent discussion of how personification in eighteenth-century poetry "helps to figure both the sense of a universal human community, whose uniformity is the basis for all communication, and the sense of a select literary community that is grafted upon it" (71). The ensuing account of Wordsworth's attack on personification (77–84) is one-sided; see my discussion of the topic in Chap. 12 below, "Wordsworth's Old Gray Stone." Maclean, "Personification but Not Poetry," argues that personification fails in its aim of evoking pure imagination and that in eighteenth-century poems horizontal description often stands in for imaginative elevation. The diagnosis is true for the most part, but the essay does not address the question of what effect the personifications then do have in practice. It should be juxtaposed to Davie's claim in "Personification" for an innate tendency of language to tap natural energies.

Chapter Three

1. "Intuition" is the conventional English translation of Kant's term *Anschauung*. It does not mean intuition in the customary sense; for present purposes it can be considered a synonym of perception.

2. Jago, *Edge Hill*, bk. 1, in Chalmers, *English Poets* 17: 290.

3. The excessive individualism of later satire is a major theme of Lockwood's *Post-Augustan Satire*.

4. Although the special achievements of Gray's "Elegy" and Collins's "Ode to Evening" are not sufficiently singled out, there is a sensitive discussion of preromantic darkness in Lipking, "Quick Poetic Eyes."

5. The pronoun "thee" in line 93 of the "Elegy" is famously ambiguous. I follow Wimsatt, "Horses of Wrath," in *Hateful Contraries* 43, in believing that the ambiguity cannot be an accidental blemish; it functions, rather, to deindividualize the speaking voice. The comparable ambiguity that Collins introduced in revising his ode ("its last cool Gleam" in line 32) may be less finely calculated, but serves a similar function in diffusing what had been a definite personality: in the first version the pronoun "they" re-

fers specifically to Evening. I cannot accept Lonsdale's specification, in his notes (Lonsdale, ed., *Poems*), that "'its' more probably refers to Evening's 'car,'" since a "shadowy Car" cannot plausibly "gleam."

6. The definite article implies, first, belonging to an already known world (*the* curfew, vs. *a* curfew, which would anticipate subsequent clarification) yet, second, general rather than particular (*the* vs. *this*). On the kinetics of the definite article see Weinrich, *Sprache in Texten* 163–76 and 186–98, and Guillaume, *Langage* 143–66.

7. Cleanth Brooks points out the impropriety of the word "annals" in *The Well Wrought Urn* 111. The proper, altogether unpretentious term is "journals." Cf. *Spectator*, no. 317 (3: 156): "One may become wiser and better by several Methods of Employing ones self in Secrecy and Silence, and do what is laudable without Noise or Ostentation. I would, however, recommend to every one of my Readers, the keeping a Journal of their Lives for one Week." The poem gives us, of course, only one, unwritten and truncated journal, in the swain's account of the youth.

8. Edwards, *Imagination and Power* 128–29. I follow, rather, Hutchings, "Syntax of Death."

9. In his *Criticism on the Elegy* 40, John Young nicely holds Gray's "whiggish prejudices" responsible for the "fairy land" aura of poetic vagueness in the political stanzas.

10. Scalia developed the notion of the "sublime in basso" in unpublished remarks at the conference "Il Sublime: Creazione e catastrofe," Univ. of Bologna, May, 1984. See the related discussion by Franci in the published proceedings ("Sulla soglia").

11. Cf. the interesting Freudian account of Gray in Jackson, "Thomas Gray and the Dedicatory Muse." Jackson argues persuasively that "the generative ground of vision [is] death" (287), but he imposes too dialectically negative a sense of death on Gray, for whom "death is a shaper" that "provides a dynamic impetus," with no "suggestion of a misanthropic or 'misbiotic' attitude" (Nemoianu, *A Theory of the Secondary* 121). There has to be a self—in the full romantic sense—before there can be, as Jackson says in his essay, a "betrayal of the self" (286). Cf. also Peter Brooks, *Reading for the Plot* 34, apropos of Rousseau's *Confessions*: "To imagine one's self-composed obituary read at the Judgment Day constitutes the farthest reach in the anticipation of retrospective narrative understanding. It is one that all narratives no doubt would wish to make." With the greater generality of the lyric, the "Elegy" satisfies this yearning, but in the form of a narrative of no one in particular in an unbounded space that is liberated from "the geometrical sense of plotting" (Brooks 24). Gray's spatializing can be highlighted by contrasting the "Elegy" to the time-saturated imitation by J. Cunningham, "An Elegy on a Pile of Ruins," in Chalmers, *English Poets* 14: 443–45, esp. lines 133–36: "Vain then are pyramids, and motto'd stones, / And monumental trophies rais'd on high! / For Time confounds them with the crumbling bones, / That mix'd in hasty graves unnotic'd lie."

12. See Wright's Berkeleyan reading ("Stillness and the Argument of

Gray's Elegy"), which finds an ironic reversal in death, weakly overruled by the Epitaph—another suggestive account that goes astray by treating (eighteenth-century) continuity and flux as (romantic) dialectical contradiction.

13. I owe to Steve Dillon the observation that "born[e]" in the funeral procession, line 114, is an ironic echo that undermines the positive associations of birth in the gem and flower stanza, lines 54–55.

14. Cleanth Brooks's reading, "Gray's Storied Urn," in *The Well Wrought Urn* 105–23, attempts to salvage his notion of a poem as a self-contained organism by using the first 116 lines to contextualize the Epitaph. He is perceptive enough to concede that "I am not altogether convinced" (121), for, indeed, the Epitaph breaks free of all such bounds. He is answered by Bateson ("Gray's 'Elegy' Reconsidered," in *English Poetry* 127–35). Bateson gives the best compact account of the poem's inconsistencies in structure and ideology, concluding that the familiar, revised ending betrays Gray's genuine position "in the central social tradition of his time" (56). My analysis of flux in the poem is intended to show how it can seem both organic and inorganic, romantic and Augustan, strong and weak: its conclusion transforms the conditions of thought, but not yet the contents of thought. In a thought-provoking though sketchy essay ("Gray's 'Elegy'"), Bygrave calls this "a kind of repressed dialectic of self and society" (173) whose "displaced name . . . is not death but 'Romanticism'" (174).

15. Rzepka, however, takes the "Elegy" as the founding text of his study, *The Self as Mind* 2–9, in a section called "The Body Vanishes: Solipsism and Vision in Gray's 'Elegy.'" Rzepka discusses well the persons in the poem as personifications of the speaker's psychic state. But though he sees the poem's task as "to reunite inner and outer" (8), he sees inwardness and "visionary solipsism" (9) as its sole subject. He overlooks the tradition—from Berkeley to both Kant and Coleridge—for which outness is as much a mental construct as inwardness.

16. On Gray's instability see Cox, *Stranger* 82–98, and (in passing, about Gray as a typical figure of the period) Blom, "Eighteenth-Century Reflexive Process Poetry."

17. Observing the poem's prevailingly negative rhetoric, the disappearance of the "I," and the persistent sense of passing, Anne Williams (*Prophetic Strain* 93–110) reads its mood as resignation to "passing on," i.e., to mortality. Yet she sees a movement at the start through fadings and endings toward "a kind of resurrection" in stanza 4 (100). I take that movement of release to be general and fundamental in the poem. Sacks, in his brief and reluctant treatment of the "Elegy" (*The English Elegy* 133–37), berates it as a "poem about the dying of a voice" (136) that leaves the poet "enshrined in a highly literary, even divine obscurity" (137). My discussion may help to clarify why Gray's masterpiece is refractory to the experiential, individual psychology that forms the basis of Sacks's book. Sacks begins, it may be further noted, by questioning Gray's relevance to his topic, since the title "Elegy" (rather than the original "Stanzas") was due to Gray's friend William Mason. Why mention this, since "elegy" appears in the title of no other

poem that Sacks interprets? Perhaps Gray's impersonality, so forcefully ac-knowledged by Sacks's resistance, should be understood in terms of generic self-reference—an elegy on the elegy, and specifically on indulgence in grief and mourning, whose travails are one of the labors that Gray's ease ("haply," "one morn I missed him") conspicuously spares us.

18. This exclusion is the unrecognized reason why, as Empson says in his commentary on the poem, "one could not estimate the amount of bour-geois ideology 'really in' the verse of Gray" (*Some Versions of Pastoral* 5).

19. Evening must "compose the composer," as Wendorf says in *William Collins* 130. But he takes composition in a pictorial rather than a mu-sical sense, arguing that there is little movement in the poem, "a poem-as-process that gradually evolves into a poem-as-product" (134). This is, as he accuses Collins of being in "How Sleep the Brave," unrealistically hopeful.

20. In *The Figure in the Landscape* 165–71 Hunt likewise concludes that Collins is reluctantly pictorial—particularly significant from a critic who specializes in literature and the visual arts. Also instructive is McKil-lop's clear-sighted struggle to salvage the notion of Collins as a painterly poet in "Collins' *Ode to Evening*."

21. Herder discusses *Würfe* and *Sprünge* in folksongs, but with the primitive passions of odes clearly in mind ("Auszug aus einem Briefwechsel über Ossian und die Lieder alter Völker," sect. 9, in *Sturm und Drang: Kri-tische Schriften* 534–39); Bloom's terms (*Figures* 7), while applied to a range of Coleridge's verse, likewise seem to me too apt to pass up.

22. See Merle C. Brown, "On William Collins' 'Ode to Evening.'" Brown also comments well on energy and on balance in the poem, though I do not think, as he does, that these two qualities add up in this case to ener-getic balance.

23. I adapt my sense of the relation of ode to hymn from Fry's ground-breaking study *The Poet's Calling* 4–10.

24. I take "train" here to mean attendants, as it does in the similar con-text of the "Ode to Fear," lines 9 and 24. The train is shrinking because Eve-ning has disrobed as she vanishes into the bare night sky, and most of her attendants have gone to bed with her. "Shrinking" could, of course, also mean cowering with fear. My contention is that to do Collins justice we must take all plausible readings into account, and that we get the most con-sistent picture if we attribute the emotive alternatives to the speaker and the literal ones to the controlling poet.

25. Imagination had better use a footnote to run rampant. I have little hesitation in hearing an echo of "thy darkning Vale" in "the gradual dusky Veil": the place of Evening is really her attire in its changeableness. But is it legitimate, in "May not unseemly with its Stillness suit," to hear an allu-sion to the seamless vestment later torn by Winter's noise? The indirection of these lines ("May not un- . . . ," and the like) seems in any case an appro-priate rhetorical dress for Evening, or, to put it in Collins's terms, fitting "Numbers" for his "willing Feet."

26. Sherwin, *Precious Bane* 116, speaks of "Evening out of extremes,"

which is not quite the same. Sherwin's is the reading that most forcefully identifies Evening with speaker as his romantic self-image, and speaker with poem.

27. See Weinsheimer, "Give Me Something to Desire," which also raises the issue of originality, to which I come in a moment.

28. In *The Poet's Calling* 102–13, Fry has brilliantly related the belatedness of the "Ode on the Poetical Character" to the textualized solidity of the woven cest. I think that the "Brede *ethereal* wove" of "Evening," further dissolved by the partial echo of "*wavy* Bed," evaporates the problem. In "Poetical Character" scenes are "curtain'd close" behind a "veiling Cloud"; in "Evening" it is ambiguous whether the "gradual dusky Veil" is drawn open or shut. Other images that are freed from menace because they are duple, at least in affect, are "folding Star arising" ("folding" means shutting up or welcoming home) and the shadowy car that is prepared so late in the game. The "Ode to Evening" does not continue, but corrects the debilities of the poetical character.

29. On animistic vividness see Jackson, *The Probable and the Marvelous* 39–88. Jackson overlooks the special character of the reticence in the "Elegy" and the "Ode to Evening." I would not, on the other hand, exclude as he does Johnson's *The Vanity of Human Wishes* from the period style. He distinguishes it as historical, but it is no more so than Collins's political odes or Gray's "Progress of Poesy," and no less animist (e.g., "And detestation rids th'indignant wall"), though it is more orthodox. In this connection see Sitter, "To *The Vanity of Human Wishes.*"

30. In pp. 284–86 of "Societal Models" Nemoianu argues that the "Elegy" negotiates this passage: "We witness the highly dramatic moment of the transubstantiation of an abstract epistemological subject into a living, breathing person." "Gray is . . . so extreme in his love of temperance that he becomes an extremist of non-expansion, and thus a Romantic." (This argument is not reproduced in the revised version of the essay printed in *A Theory of the Secondary.*) The difference between our readings is tonal; in particular, it depends on whether the Spenserian diction that describes the youth is felt to be conventional and generalizing or specific and individualizing. Perhaps it is best to call the "Elegy" a pivotal work that is amenable to being made romantic by a romantic reading.

Chapter Four

1. For thematic surveys of Cowper's problems of self-assertion see Binni, *L'Idolo e il vero,* and Goldstein, *Ruins and Empire* 87–94.

2. Cf. Cowper's *Conversation*, lines 289–90: "But we that make no honey, though we sting, / Poets, are sometimes apt to maul the thing."

3. See pp. 66–72 of Blom, "Eighteenth-Century Reflexive Process Poetry," which relates Cowper's shifting perspective to that of other poets of the century, in contrast to the more limited and controlled verse of *The Prelude.*

4. Boswell, *Life of Johnson* 4: 13. According to Lévi-Strauss, gourds, watermelons, and similar plants that are dry outside and moist inside figure in South America "as an emblem for a deceiving god" who mediates between nature and culture (*From Honey to Ashes* 101–3). The Northerner would inevitably include their relative, Cowper's "prickly and green-coated gourd" (3.446). Beginning from this point, one might well undertake a full-scale "ethnographic" analysis of *The Task*, treating each paragraph as a separate "myth." (Since I wrote this, Priestman's fine book on *The Task* has performed such an analysis.) Norrman and Haarberg's *Nature and Language*, a wide-ranging but myopic book devoted to the literary use of cucumbers and their relatives, suffers from a constricted notion of symbols as one-to-one codes, sometimes ambiguous but never dialectical. While they find their chosen images often "clustering around the subject of *sex*" (101, their emphasis), they misread Cowper's preoccupation with cucumbers in the letter of his that they quote as a sign of "total boredom" (44). *The Task* is not mentioned.

5. Davie gives a more urbane account of Cowper's cucumbers in *Purity of Diction* 56–58. But cf. Cowper's letter of Feb. 8, 1783, to Rev. John Newton: "You will suppose me a Politician; but in truth I am nothing less. These are the thoughts that occurr to me while I read the News paper, and when I have laid it down, I feel myself more interested in the success of my early Cucumbers, than in any part of this great and important Subject. . . . [A]ll these reflections are absorbed at once in the anxiety I feel for a plant the fruit of which I cannot eat when I have procured it" (*Letters and Prose Writings* 2: 105). The letters show that Cowper spent a great deal of time in his greenhouse, particularly during the extraordinarily cold weather of 1782–83, often entertaining friends and family in its protected simulation of a natural environment.

6. Feingold, *Nature and Society* 121–92, teases out a number of the fundamental contradictions, concluding that they testify to the integrity of what he calls "an essentially modern poem" (158). Marshall's straightforwardly sacramental reading, on the other hand, misses the tensions that beset Cowper's "central, unifying statement" of testimonial to the divine logos ("The Presence of 'the Word'" 486).

7. For a good discussion of Hume and Wordsworth on personal identity see Langbaum, *Mysteries* 25–47.

8. "I believe no one, who has any practice of the world, and can penetrate into the inward sentiments of men, will assert, that the humility, which good-breeding and decency require of us, goes beyond the outside, or that a thorough sincerity in this particular is esteem'd a real part of our duty. On the contrary, we may observe, that a genuine and hearty pride, or self-esteem, if well conceal'd and well founded, is essential to the character of a man of honour" (Hume, "Of Greatness of Mind," *Treatise* 598). The locus classicus for this widespread view is Lord Chesterfield's letters to his son, but similar sentiments can even be found in Kant's lectures on pedagogy, first delivered in 1776–77.

9. House discusses Cowper's influence in *Coleridge* 70–73 and 78–79, to which can be added the information assembled in Matheson, "Influence."

10. The earliest citation of this construction in the *OED* dates from 1841: "and when at last he was conscious." If not established earlier, this usage may have been popularized by William Hamilton's *Lectures on Metaphysics* (first delivered in 1836, published in 1858), where it occurs in the definition of "conscious" (lecture 11, pp. 110–11) and repeatedly in the latter half of the discussion of consciousness (lectures 17–19). For the unmodified *attributive* use the *OED*, following Johnson's *Dictionary*, cites an example from 1725: "thinking or conscious beings."

11. The commonplace eighteenth-century view is succinctly stated in the *Encyclopédie*, s.v. "Conscience," with acknowledgment to Locke: "Perception and *consciousness* are really but one single operation under two names. Insofar as this operation is considered solely as an impression in the soul, we may retain the name of *perception* for it; and insofar as it alerts the soul to its presence, it may be given that of consciousness." In the Cartesian tradition, as represented by the third of Malebranche's *Entretiens*, consciousness and reason are opposed as body to soul. Two discussions of romanticism that bring out the continuing tension between consciousness as the indefinite sense of being and consciousness as rational awareness are Hartman, "Romanticism and Anti-Self-Consciousness," and Cohn, "Kleist's 'Marquise von O . . .'" See also Brunschvicq, *Le Progrès de la conscience* 1: 260–352; Engelberg, *The Unknown Distance*, chap. 1; Lewis, *Studies in Words*, chap. 8.

12. Contrast Thomas Burnet, *Remarks upon an Essay Concerning Humane Understanding* (London, 1697) 9, qtd. in Fox, *Locke and the Scriblerians* 130: "I do not understand how the Soul, if she be at any time utterly without Thoughts, what it is that produces the first Thought again, at the end of that unthinking Interval." Fox adduces this passage to correct my claims for Cowper's originality, despite the manifest contradiction between Burnet's empirical conception of a consciousness that is never "without thoughts" and Cowper's transcendental conception of a soul "that does not always think." The rest of his book contains much valuable information on the post-Lockian identification of selfhood with consciousness. In another valuable study, "Towards a Profile of the Word 'Conscious,'" Hagstrum argues (29) against my claim for Cowper's novelty in this passage. He is correct that it remains possible to construe "conscious" here in the older, empiricist fashion. It is the conception of waking dreams, not necessarily the term as such, that is revolutionary in Cowper, though I continue to find the syntactic highlighting of "conscious" remarkable, and perhaps facilitated by the whimsy that Hagstrum correctly points to in Cowper's lines.

13. Priestman points out a number of these self-projections in *Cowper's "Task,"* including the thresher of 1.355–66, who "both is and is not a self-projection" (60), and the covertly autobiographical elements in bk. 2 (71–83).

14. Another important transitional work published in the 1780s, Thomas Reid's *Essays on the Intellectual Powers of Man*, also posits a generalized consciousness as a precondition of attention (for instance in the distinction between consciousness and attention in essay 1, chap. 5, proposed as a correction of Locke). Like Cowper and unlike Kant, Reid does not analyze the mechanisms of consciousness, and in fact essay 2, chap. 15, declares consciousness to be unanalyzable. Reid's imagery, too, is comparable to Cowper's: "By his reason, he can discover certain abstract and necessary relations of things; but his knowledge of what really exists, or did exist, comes by another *channel*, which is open to those who cannot reason. He is led to it *in the dark*, and knows not how he came to it" (*Works* 330, my emphasis). The earlier *Inquiry into the Human Mind* (1764) still treats consciousness as a *late* stage of perception (*Works* 107).

15. Cowper discovered Collins while writing *The Task*; see his letter to Rev. John Newton of March 19, 1784 (*Letters and Prose Writings* 2: 224–26).

16. See further the subtle analysis of the ambivalences of Kant's *Träume eines Geistersehers* in Weissberg, "*Catarcticon.*"

17. The quoted sentence concludes the first half of Kant's essay; the anticlimactic second part contains a satirical account of Swedenborg's spiritualism, a confession that in the opening chapters "I deceived my reader in order to benefit him" (A 116), and a call to judge men by the moral standards of this world.

18. Nancy, "Logodaedalus." The essay shows that Kant regarded bad writing as a sublime ascesis through which philosophy presents itself "pure" and unadorned (comparable to the way that phenomena are the self-presentation of noumenal objects). The conclusions of this essay are further developed and in some respects corrected in the baroque intricacies of the book entitled *Logodaedalus*. The brief "Metakritik über den Purismum der Vernunft" by Kant's friend and first reader, Johann Georg Hamann, remains the most brilliant dissection of Kant's style and philosophical "roots" (in both senses). The text, one of Hamann's most difficult and all but unquotable, will be found to contain many of the themes of my analysis: the subversive relationship to Hume; the inconsistency of the stylistic norm, which undercuts Kant's Archimedean claims; the co-originality of thought and feeling; and even the association Kant-Mercury. Some help in reading Hamann's essay is given by Gruender, "Langage et histoire."

19. The identical phrase appears in Kant's *Critique of Pure Reason* B 369 (the following quotations are taken from this paragraph), and in his *Critique of Judgment* B 54, footnote.

20. The principal audience addressed are the philosopher-teachers who are to interpret his doctrine to the people. This is evident from the pedagogical orientation of the lengthy "methodologies" that conclude each of the three critiques and is made explicit in the opening sentence of the *Prolegomena to any Future Metaphysic*. Tonelli's "Wiederaufleben" surveys the sources of Kant's neologisms and emphasizes their utility in command-

ing authority by differentiating Kant from his contemporaries. See also Lady Welby's comment: "Kant, for instance, complained bitterly of the defeating tendency of language in his day, as compared with the intelligent freedom of the vocabulary and idiom of the 'classical' Greek, who was always creating expression, moulding it to his needs and finding an equally intelligent response to his efforts, in his listeners and readers—in short, in his public" ("Significs" 81a).

21. Cf. Hamann, "Language is the *center of the misunderstanding of reason with itself*" ("Metakritik," *Werke* 3: 286). See also numerous comments on Kant's style in Puder, *Kant*, a brilliant study despite what seems a forced and incorrect general thesis, derived from Adorno, that individualism represents the traditional stratum and the social basis the innovation in Kant's thought.

22. A relevant detail is Rousseau's ambivalence toward the Latin language, which may be compared with Kant's inconsistent attitude and Cowper's ironic one. For an analysis of the central question of Rousseau's deconstruction of empiricism see de Man, "Allegory of Reading (*Profession de foi*)" (originally titled "The Timid God: A Reading of Rousseau's *Profession de foi du vicaire savoyard*"), *Allegories of Reading* 221–45. The analysis focuses on the problem of judgment, but Rousseau's "timid voice" (a phrase from the first version of the *Contrat social, Oeuvres* 3: 287), like Cowper's "STILL SMALL VOICE," belongs to conscience.

23. The words *sentir* and *sentiment* occur, for example, six times on the most famous page of the fifth of the *Rêveries, Oeuvres* 1: 1046–47. It should be noted, however, that far from being a state of heightened receptivity, this is a feeling that abolishes feeling, "which leaves in the soul no vacancy that it feels the need to fill."

24. Marmontel, "Leçons d'un père à ses enfants sur la métaphysique," *Oeuvres* 17: 196, my emphasis.

25. "While in Descartes thought unveils existence but establishes us in being, in Rousseau the feeling of existence installs us in being as a presence to the world and to the self" (Burgelin, *La Philosophie de l'existence de J.-J. Rousseau* 124).

26. Raymond, *Rousseau* 216. See also Starobinski, *Rousseau* 99–101; MacCannell, "Nature and Self-Love"; and Tripet, *La Rêverie littéraire*. I have pursued the discussion into another domain in "Mozart and After."

27. Cf. the famous lines in Wordsworth's *Prelude* 2.397–402, echoing Rousseau: "From Nature and her overflowing soul, / I had received so much, that all my thoughts / Were steeped in feeling; I was only then / Contented, when with bliss ineffable / I felt the sentiment of Being spread / O'er all that moves and all that seemeth still." Verneaux effectively demonstrates but refuses to acknowledge the co-originality of intellectual and sensible consciousness in his naively rationalizing study, *Le Vocabulaire de Kant* 2: 131–32. Though taking Malebranche rather than the more likely Rousseau as a source, Verneaux points out (2: 162) that Kant uses the phrase "Gefühl meines Daseins" exactly once, in the *Prolegomena* (published in

1783, the year after Rousseau's *Rêveries*). For a scrupulous semantic comparison and contrast of Rousseau's usage with Wordsworth's see Sabin, *English Romanticism and the French Tradition* 103–24.

28. *Herders Briefe* 388 (letter to Jean Paul, Nov. 1798). See Adorno, *Negative Dialektik* 209–92; Derrida, "Economimesis" and *Verité* 21–168.

29. Horace, *Odes* 1.10: "Mercuri, facunde nepos Atlantis, / qui feros cultus hominum recentum / voce formasti catus."

30. Starobinski, *Rousseau* 236–37. By beginning with the pure self-consciousness that was historically and biographically an end point, Poulet's otherwise splendid chapter in *Studies in Human Time* (158–84) smooths out the disturbed and disturbing side of Rousseau's achievement.

31. As Dawson writes in a nice essay on Cowper as alienated artist, focusing on books 3 and 5 of the poem, "Cowper's favoured oppositions show a repeated tendency to turn on him" ("Cowper's Equivocations" 30).

Chapter Five

1. See Bredvold, *The Natural History of Sensibility*, esp. chap. 1; there is an excellent delineation of Diderot's position in chap. 2. For a more literary emphasis, packed full of information and ideas though inadequately synthesized, see Todd, *Sensibility*.

2. "This I have experienced to be the case with all pleasure arising from inanimate beauties, and from every thing that may be termed an object merely of taste; they all terminate in themselves, and lead to weariness and satiety. . . . Many a time have I felt a craving void in my heart, and how to fill it up I knew not" (*Lounger*, no. 9; 1: 71, by Craig). Bogel's *Literature and Insubstantiality* concludes (210–25) by associating sensibility with Freud's melancholia as a kind of object-loss without the object's ever having been there. His evidence in chap. 4 (74–135) of a quest for an idealized past provides interesting support for his analysis. Still, it seems reasonable to say that the ego in this state is even less confident of itself than of the world around. My broad area of agreement with Bogel is in treating sensibility as a problem, not a goal. My broad area of disagreement is in seeing breakthroughs toward a solution in authors he discusses either differently or, in the case of Goldsmith and Sheridan, not at all.

3. Add to this list of works published between 1760 and 1780 *Le Neveu de Rameau*, titled merely "Satire II" in the manuscript. On farce as a historiographical category see Mehlman, *Repetition and Revolution*.

4. "Exuberant wit" is New's term for this characteristic mood; see, in his fine essay on Sterne's anxiety of influence, the "abundance of food" imagery cited from Lowth and Johnson ("Sterne, Warburton" 256–57).

5. Frye, "Towards Defining an Age of Sensibility"; Blake's poem, "When Klopstock England Defied" (*Poetry and Prose* 491–92), is dated by Erdman c. 1797–99.

6. See Fox's essay "Locke and the Scriblerians," or the expanded book version.

7. Diderot's farcical leveling is redeemed in a figure like Wordsworth's Lucy: "No motion has she now, no force; / She neither hears nor sees; / Rolled round in earth's diurnal course / With rocks, and stones, and trees."

8. The conclusion of this statement, "et sur laquelle il siège, écoute, juge et prononce," could equally well be translated, "and on which it holds its sessions, examines, judges, and decides." Even Diderot's diction manages to avoid any clear lines between sensation and thought.

9. It is possible to contextualize the excesses in Diderot's text by treating the work as a system rather than a process. The most recent attempt is Dixon, *Diderot, Philosopher of Energy* 133–87. Dixon argues that Diderot upholds definite, qualitative distinctions between latent and active energy and between the materialism of universal energy that he accepts and the pantheism of a vital force that he rejects. It is not implausible to treat the dialogue in this fashion as a debate that settles into such rationalizing doctrines consistent with less notorious works of Diderot. Still, the thrust and irrepressible vitality of the writing resist such treatment, in part by leaving much that "is not clear," as Dixon says of the uncertainty regarding the vitality of molecules (171).

10. Likewise, in England, *The Looker-On*, no. 62; 2: 308–18, uses the word "benevolence," but argues that true sensibility lies in right action, not in right feeling.

11. I would like to signal in passing a little-read yet splendid prize essay by Herder, "Vom Erkennen und Empfinden der menschlichen Seele: Bemerkungen und Träume" (1778), which attempts to turn the contradictions of sensibility to account by evoking it as the mysterious origin, the dark core of life, using Herder's familiar concept of force. Unfortunately, what might have become a powerful epistemology relapses for the most part in the second half of the essay into social questions. To the best of my knowledge Herder never again linked so closely the individual with the generic aspects of the problem—sensation with sentiment—and the relationship between psychology and sociology remained a vexing issue, perhaps not really formulated in a tractable manner before the generation of Durkheim and Weber.

12. Cowper raises this question in his poem "The Poet, the Oyster, and the Sensitive Plant," with the crustacean representing the pole of reserve and the mimosa the pole of reactivity. But neither pole, as Cowper's poet complains, balances its books properly: "Disputes, though short, are far too long, / When both alike are in the wrong; / Your feelings, in their full amount, / Are all upon your own account." Presumably Cowper intended to show the poet as a better bookkeeper, though few will find his lesson worth much: "The noblest minds their virtue prove / By pity, sympathy, and love." Cowper, like Goldsmith, was better at stating the problem of sensibility than at solving it.

13. The same actress later spoke the Epilogue to *She Stoops to Conquer*, but there she spoke in character; here, on the other hand, she speaks as a surrogate for the enfeebled author.

14. The best sections of Sheriff's *Good-Natured Man* (81–102), a sketchy anatomy of character types, concern satire and paradox in Mackenzie's essays and in *The Man of Feeling*. Mullan's far more intensive study, *Sentiment and Sociability*, remains beset with the instability of sensibility to the point of exaggerating Mackenzie's misanthropy (114–36); he is more successful dealing with the paradoxes of public virtue in Richardson (57–113).

15. Thompson, *A Scottish Man of Feeling* 207. Thompson continues by evoking Mackenzie's paradoxes: "Here was a man who was shrewd enough to see all the faults of a philosophy which had underlain his own literary triumph; and yet, at the moment when he was writing the clearest exposé of sentimentalism in eighteenth-century criticism, he was inaugurating romantic criticism of Shakespeare and bringing the sentimental tale to perfection!" Yet Thompson proceeds by lapsing into metaphor and abdicating the interpreter's duty to interpret: "Perhaps he wanted once more to 'wring the heart' before breaking the wand which summoned tears" (208).

16. I have discussed the shift from a center of balance to a center of wholeness with respect to Herder in *The Shape of German Romanticism* 27–32. I mention in passing there Pope's anticipation of the development; this has been well analyzed by Fabian in "Pope und die goldene Kette Homers."

17. While this change in the discussion of the senses is not explicitly analyzed, it is implicit in the materials collected in Modiano, "Coleridge's Views on Touch and Other Senses."

18. Alfonso's curse, in *The Castle of Otranto*, precedes *The Wealth of Nations* in representing the disproportion between consciousness and its world: "*the castle and lordship of Otranto [shall] pass from the present family, whenever the real owner [shall] be grown too large to inhabit it*" (chap. 1, p. 51). In Walpole's life we see the universalizing tendencies of sensibility mastered through being trivialized into connoisseurship—the collection and appreciation of all kinds of antiquities.

19. See, in Robert Blair's *The Grave*, the lines "Self-murder!—name it not" and "Oh! where shall Fancy find / A proper name to call thee [Sin] by, expressive / Of all thy horrours?" (in Chalmers, *English Poets* 15: 66, 67). The last figure evoked by the poet before his plunge into blank despair is the miser; here commerce is not man's salvation but the worst of society's evils. Salvation is foreseen at the end when "the conscious soul" (15: 68) shall arise and know its mate, but this will happen only at the Last Judgment, not on earth.

20. For a different treatment of economy see Heinzelman, *Economy*. His book concerns production, accumulation, compensation, wealth, and value, and complements my discussions of disposition and distribution. The featured texts in his chapter on Wordsworth (196–233) are *Michael* and *Home at Grasmere*.

21. *Vision of the Last Judgment* 95, in Blake, *Poetry and Prose* 555. The comparable image (perhaps Blake's source?) in early eighteenth-century

criticism omits the monetary reference and speaks of meditation where Blake speaks of vision: "As for Example, the Sun mention'd in ordinary Conversation, gives the Idea of a round flat shining Body, of about Two Foot Diameter. But the Such occurring to us in Meditation, gives the Idea of a vast and glorious Body, and the top of all the visible Creation, and the brightest material Image of the Divinity" (Dennis, *Grounds* 17). Damrosch compares the Dennis and Blake passages in *Symbol and Truth* 51–52.

22. Spiegelberg's outburst prefigures Schiller's fascination (some fifteen years later) with the work of Fichte, who was still in his teens when *Die Räuber* was written. Spiegelberg represents very precisely what was to become the negative pole in Fichte's dialectic: the self that denies all limits in the effort to attain a fully active consciousness of self. As so often happens, literary representation precedes philosophical articulation; or a state of mind prompts an idea, rather than the reverse.

23. Staiger, *Friedrich Schiller* 55, finely describes the pathology of unleashed selfhood: "Whoever thus claims freedom as the Palladium of the person, whoever thus puts forth the ego as the highest meaning and goal of human life and then leaves it to the enjoyment of his own potential, runs the risk that in the long run no one will be prepared to recognize him, that his idol, the self, writ no matter how large, will acquire the privative meaning of the private and will sink at last in the abyss of his inward privitude."

24. Shell discusses the alternatives of dispensation and disposition in "The Golden Fleece." The former, he suggests, is the more political and the more sublime in its morality, the latter more administrative and prudential. He calls for a return to the Aristotelian integration of the two. That the two orders jostle in Schiller's play is one more sign of its status as a crisis text.

25. See Hegel's famous analysis of the play in the *Phänomenologie des Geistes* (Phenomenology of Mind): "The heartbeat for the weal of humanity therefore passes over into the raging of crazed self-conceit, into the fury of consciousness to maintain itself against its destruction, and this by throwing the perversion that it is out of itself and endeavoring to regard and express it as an other. It thus expresses the general order as a perversion of the law of the heart and its happiness, inverted and manipulated to the nameless misery of deluded humanity by fanatical priests, carousing despots, and their servants who compensate themselves for their abasement by abasing and oppressing those below them" (271–72).

26. Taking Schiller's economic language literally, Bohm argues in "Possessive Individualism" that "self comes to be constituted and affirmed through ownership, through having property" (32). His social reading of the problems of individualism, like my psychological reading, finds them unresolved in the play. Hinderer, "Freiheit und Gesellschaft," documents the case that early Schiller and the Sturm und Drang generally are more fundamentally concerned with anthropological (individual and psychological) questions than with political and social ones.

27. Karl's "suppressed fantasy of action" is well captured in Mattenklott, *Melancholie* 173–74: "For the characterization of this expression, of the expression of freedom against convention, of self-determination against

heteronomy, of fraternity against complicity, it is historically significant that it must be sought and found in the outlaw's criminal gesture of provocation. Deeds, Schiller's *Räuber* insinuates, are—at least for now—only thinkable as crimes." (For an earlier, but less concise formulation of essentially the identical view of the play, see the essay "*Die Räuber*" by Mattenklott's frequent collaborator Klaus Scherpe.) Mattenklott's historicist reading converges with mine at the end, where the contention that the play reflects a "transitional society" (179) is absorbed into the view that its primitive emotions express the dissolution of Enlightenment order.

28. Schiller's wavering is a featured topic of Michael Mann's excellent reading of the play in *Sturm- und Drang-Drama* 71–121, which takes much fuller account of the compositional history than I can do here. Neubauer, "The Freedom of the Machine," concerns the play's inconsistent alternation of mechanist (determinist) and of materialist (vitalist) language.

29. My account of this moment of crisis in the economy of selfhood should provide an entrée into Liu's chapter "The Economy of Lyric" (*Wordsworth* 311–58). Liu's study of *The Ruined Cottage* traces four strands of development: (1) from New Critical humanism based on a falsely redemptive view of the "richness" of symbolic imagery to the fragmented mode ("disassociated souvenirs and bric-a-brac," 313) of the lyric, as implied by the hidden "wealth" of the daffodil vision ("I . . . little thought / What wealth the show to me had brought"); (2) from an economy of independent producers based on an economics of trust to an economy of piecework based on debt and capital accumulation; (3) from patronage as the poet's means of support to economic professionalism as the writer's; and (4) from identity based on theft—especially in *The Borderers*—through identity based on misgiving and forgiveness to identity as gift. Even though the fit between the explicit marxian analyses 2 and 3 and the tacitly Heideggerian analyses 1 and 4 seems imperfect, Liu's work unquestionably greatly advances understanding of these issues.

30. This is not a usual reading of Blake's "Tyger." For instance, Shaviro, "Striving with Systems," says "the 'symmetry' is that imposed by the container or frame" (239). Yet he later seems to approach my reading when he writes, "The making of the tyger is no less awful and awe-ful for being a self-referential metaphor" (245). Hazard Adams does read "symmetry" as I do, though not "fearful": "The tyger is formed on the anvil of inspiration, which is the eye of man and God, but it is also a symbol of the very same eye that created it, for Blake believed that men are what they behold" (*William Blake* 73).

31. On the reputation of *Die Räuber* in England see Parker, "In Some Sort."

Chapter Six

1. Bridgman, "Weak Tocks," surveys problematic endings in Collins, Cowper, Goldsmith, Johnson, and Gray, with nice examples and a breezy reluctance to generalize.

2. Woods, "Boswell's Presentation of Goldsmith," argues, however, that Boswell was more sympathetic to Goldsmith in life than the *Life of Johnson* makes him appear.

3. *Boswell in Search of a Wife*, July 29, 1769, p. 258. At best, this entry continues, the journal helps postpone the decay of sensation. "However, what I put down has so far an effect that I can, by reading my Journal, recall a good deal of my life." See also the March 1783 essay, "On Diaries," in *Boswell's Column* 330–37.

4. Dowling, "Boswell and the Problem of Biography" 93. Braudy writes suggestively, but one-sidedly, about "the threat of an ending" in midcentury fiction, in "The Form of the Sentimental Novel" 12.

5. The exception is the latter half of *The Citizen of the World*, beginning with letter 73 ("Life Endear'd by Age"), where Goldsmith makes partial amends for the pessimism of the earlier letters. Thus in letter 95, Lien Chi Altangi consoles his son in these—to be sure, equivocal—terms: "The life of man is a journey, a journey that must be travelled, however bad the roads or the accommodation. If in the beginning it is found dangerous, narrow and difficult, it must either grow better in the end, or we shall by custom learn to bear its inequality" (2: 380).

6. There are three possible aetiologies for the mad dog's death. The first is that the dog was really mad, though the man's goodness preserved him from disease; this is unlikely in view of Goldsmith's then-popular essay questioning the prevalence of canine madness (*Citizen*, letter 69). The second is that the man was the really wicked and ill one who infected the dog; this would not explain why the man recovered. The third is that the man infected the dog, but equates illness with goodness, as in "The Double Transformation." The wicked dog (who bit the man) cannot tolerate the disease whose nature is virtue.

7. Downie, "Goldsmith, Swift" 134–37, finds "The Double Transformation" a "trite" (136) and feeble imitation of Swift. I think he missed the joke.

8. Hopkins, *True Genius* 66–95, notes echoes, such as the /s/ sounds that suggest happiness, which he finds the theme that unifies the various levels (national, domestic, and individual) of *The Traveller*. Wallace Cable Brown gives a more nuanced account of Goldsmith's consonant patterning in *The Triumph of Form* 142–60, but neglects the vowels. Other discussions of Goldsmith's versification are Mahony, "Lyrical Antithesis," who discusses the way that sound echoes sense in *The Deserted Village* to bring "into focus not only the fact of change, but that of changing" (36), and Piper, "Musical Quality," whose self-confessedly "impressionistic" account asserts a "distinctive musical quality" (272) that is an "enrichment" (267) of the same poem. Mahony's and Piper's essays both suffer from inaccurate examples.

9. See above, p. 29, for this common eighteenth-century resonance of the noun "kind" in the adjective.

10. Fabricant, "The Aesthetics and Politics of Landscape," is an excel-

lent discussion of the ideological tensions implicit in the elevated perspective. Pp. 65–68 concern *The Traveller.*

11. Davie, "Notes," argues persuasively that *The Traveller* espouses explicitly monarchical views, and that *The Deserted Village* implies a like stance, despite its more generalized rhetoric. In setting up an idealized Nature as the measure of human affairs, however, Goldsmith ultimately makes *any* political stance unstable.

12. Rogers, "The Dialectic of 'The Traveller,'" follows a good account of oxymoron and contradiction in the poem with a claim that Britain, as "concentrated oxymoron," provides a "cultural myth" of a "middle course" (123). The attempt to take oxymoron as resolution underplays the strain at the end of the poem, in particular by omitting reference to the American episode.

13. In *Ruins and Empire* 95–113, Goldstein has a fine discussion of Goldsmith's critique of expansionism and of his sense of being personally implicated in the problems of his society. I am persuaded by his arguments that the poet finds no escape from the dilemma, yet, as I have been trying to show, the poem knows better.

14. Anne Williams (*Prophetic Strain* 111–22) discusses the abandoned female figures throughout the poem, in which she discerns suppressed oedipal resentments. Though she distinguishes Poetry from the others, she finds no resolution: the poem remains divided between neoclassic pastoral objects and romantic feeling. Feingold, *Moralized Song* 139–86, follows her in concluding that "Goldsmith's poem is preromantic in the sense that it realizes lyric intentions in a way not entirely compatible tonally and structurally with its didactic ones," 185. The best account of Poetry's dilemma is Simpson, *Wordsworth's Historical Imagination* 22–25. In what follows I argue that the poem's divisions, which are genuine, serve in a positive way to construct an imaginative space, distinctively represented by the figure of Poetry.

15. Love, "Goldsmith's Deserted Village," finds unconscious ironies that produce "amiable limitations" (58) in Goldsmith's narrative voice. This is surely too tame a description. Nor am I convinced by his claim that the first half of the poem is proto-romantic pastoral while the second half is sentimentally moralized Miltonism. Eve's "sweet reluctant amorous delay" (*Paradise Lost* 4.310), for instance, is writ large throughout the opening description of Auburn. Goldsmith's fear of fall is more earnest than Love allows (hence the initial loitering in the tag end of summer), and his poetic resurgence more individual, complex, and hard-won.

16. In applying Eliade's mythological constructions to Auburn, Barfoot's essay "*The Deserted Village*" underplays the restrictiveness of Goldsmith's circles.

17. Much of this description, with its veneer of brightness, derives from the gloomy "Description of an Author's Bed-chamber," Goldsmith's earliest extant original poem in heroic couplets.

18. For the definition of formal verse satire see Weinbrot, *The Formal Strain.* Quintana, in *Oliver Goldsmith* 129–36, calls *The Traveller* a pros-

pect poem and *The Deserted Village* a pastoral. These are satisfactory descriptions of the contents, but not of the form: *The Traveller* does not intersperse description with episodes of history, myth, and prophecy, and *The Deserted Village* does not narrate a rustic episode.

19. Lonsdale, "Garden" 27, nicely says that *"The Deserted Village* enacts the collapse of the very poetic conventions in which it might have sought refuge"—namely, pastoral, georgic, country-house poem, Whig panegyric to commerce and liberty. He calls it a progress poem that finally progresses beyond its speaker's situation. He does not note the concluding ode formulas, with their specific reorienting effect.

20. We may add to these fusions in *The Deserted Village* Macaulay's charge—in my reading a strength of the poem, not a weakness—that Auburn is half English, half Irish.

21. My reading converges here with that of Raymond Williams, *The Country and the City* 74–79, except that I find aestheticization a more self-aware and even heroic maneuver than he does. Miner's "Making of *The Deserted Village*" implies the ideological valence of the aesthetic by combining a survey of doctrines with a New Critical conclusion that the final apostrophe asks Poetry "to do what the poem has in fact been doing all along, . . . making the poem a sustained metaphor for its own purpose" (138). On the other hand, both sides in the continuing debate as to whether Goldsmith's writing is rhetorical (typified for this poem by Storm's "Literary Convention") or personal (typified by Feingold's *Moralized Song* 139–86) posit an unrealistic dissociation of thought from feeling and of language from life.

Chapter Seven

1. Golden, "Image Frequency" 476: "The last five chapters seem to have been thrown off in haste, with the author . . . unconcerned about inconsistencies or finish." This tone was struck from the beginning; one of the earliest reviewers writes, "But pray, Dr. Goldsmith, was it necessary to bring the concluding calamities so thick upon your old venerable friend; or in your impatience to get to the end of your task, was you not rather disposed to hurry the catastrophe?" Anonymous, *Critical Review,* in G. S. Rousseau, *Critical Heritage* 47.

2. Anonymous, *Monthly Review,* no. 34, May 1766, in G. S. Rousseau, *Critical Heritage* 44.

3. E. M. Forster, *Aspects* 95. Forster goes on to say, "In the end even the author feels he is being a little foolish," but the sentence he quotes is Primrose's, not, in the sense that Forster means it, the author's.

4. Cf. the Vicar's reflections in chap. 31 of the novel: "Nor can I go on, without a reflection on those accidental meetings, which, though they happen every day, seldom excite our surprize but upon some extraordinary occasion. To what a fortuitous concurrence do we not owe every pleasure and convenience of our lives. How many seeming accidents must unite before we can be cloathed or fed" (*Collected Works* 4: 174).

5. I will not discuss the unique case of *Tom Jones* at any length here, though I have examined it in a paper presented at the MLA in 1982, "Imitation of Action: Toward a Theory of Plot," whose analysis I hope to publish at a later date. For now, suffice it to say that *Tom Jones* is at least as dependent on coincidence as *The Vicar of Wakefield*. And while Fielding's novel is, arguably, less episodic than Goldsmith's, this greater compactness of the *récit* is purchased at the cost of a far greater disjunction between the *histoire* (Tom's life) and the *narration* (Fielding's omniscient narrative presentation). *The Vicar* remains the novel that establishes (even though it does not altogether exemplify) the standard that a plot should be simple and unified. For a good discussion of problems of compactness in *Tom Jones* see Homer Obed Brown, "*Tom Jones*: The 'Bastard' of History."

6. According to Rothstein's convincing analysis in *Systems of Order and Inquiry*, the effective norms of eighteenth-century plotting are not recapitulation and thematic resonance (the principle that all parts must come together in the end, as in classical symphonic form, which was also emerging in the 1760s), but rather analogy and modification (the principle that each part reflects on its neighbors, as in the sequences and ornamented repetitions in baroque music). Rothstein's book does not discuss *The Vicar of Wakefield*, though it does analyze one of Fielding's novels, *Amelia*, and indeed Rothstein has elsewhere contributed to showing the unifying thematic relevance of what has always appeared to be among the least integral of all the book's themes; see Weinbrot and Rothstein, "The Vicar of Wakefield, Mr. Wilmot, and the 'Whistonian Controversy.'"

7. Thus Goldsmith identifies three separate faults of Home's plot: "the unfolding a material part of the plot in soliloquy; the preposterous distress of a married Lady for a former husband, who had been dead near twenty years; the want of incidents to raise that fluctuation of hope and fear, which interest us in the catastrophe" (1: 11). Likewise his praise of *The Siege of Aleppo*, by the otherwise worthless Hawkins, singles out "the opposition of character, the variety of the distress, and the unexpected catastrophe" (1: 204), and Goldsmith blames Hawkins's mock epic *The Thimble* in general terms for its want of humor, but with considerably greater specificity for its silly plot (4: 299–300). For the use of quotation see the review of *Douglas* (4: 322), but more especially the review of Murphy's *Orphan of China*, where essentially all Goldsmith has to *say* in favor of the verse, amidst four pages of quotation, is the following: "But to do the writer ample justice, we will lay one scene against all his defects; and we are convinced, that this alone will turn the balance in his favour" (1: 173); "a strength of thought, a propriety of diction, . . . embellished by a justness of sentiment" (1: 178); "This is finely conceived, and exquisitely executed" (1: 179).

8. Bäckmann, *This Singular Tale* 247–51, is an excellent survey of the theory of graduated distress in relation to dramatic form. Two important predecessors in fiction are *Roderick Random*, whose Preface objects to the sudden transitions of *Gil Blas*, and *Tom Jones*, which favors having the "great Man . . . rising . . . by Degrees" (1.1; pp. 33–34).

9. Quintana, *Oliver Goldsmith* 109, also points to a balance of the first

three chapters against the last three. He is followed by Bäckmann, *This Singular Tale* 40–49, whose schema (diagrammed on 43) highlights changes of locale rather than the character patternings I discuss below. Bäckmann's book is a valuable survey of forms, motifs, and conventions in the novel.

10. An instance of this moral rhythm is the contrast between the end of chap. 5, where Primrose is wary of Thornhill, in doubt of his ability to discern good from evil, and the end of chap. 9, where Primrose judges decisively. Note the parallels. Chap. 5: "I would have proceeded, but for the interruption of a servant from the 'Squire, who, with his compliments, sent us a side of venison and a promise to dine with us some days after. This well-timed present pleaded more powerfully in his favour than any thing I had to say could obviate. I therefore continued silent, satisfied with just having pointed out danger, and leaving it to their own discretion to avoid it. That virtue which requires to be ever guarded is scarce worth the centinel" (4: 38). Chap. 9: "The ladies seemed very unwilling to part from my daughters; for whom they had conceived a particular affection, and joined in a request to have the pleasure of their company home. The 'Squire seconded the proposal, and my wife added her entreaties: the girls too looked upon me as if they wished to go. In this perplexity I made two or three excuses, which my daughters as readily removed; so that at last I was obliged to give a peremptory refusal; for which we had nothing but sullen looks and short answers the whole day ensuing" (4: 56).

11. For a general discussion of arrangement in novel plots, see my essay "Plan Vs. Plot."

12. Paulson, *Satire* 269–75, clearly identifies the change in genre (though he places it one chapter late), but confines his commentary to the first half and neglects the structure and functions of the second half.

13. The shift in values is best analyzed in James H. Lehmann, "*The Vicar.*" See also Battestin, *The Providence of Wit* 193–214.

14. Cf. Knoblauch's analysis of the concept of coherence in "Coherence Betrayed."

15. Defenses of Primrose as amiable humorist or as insightful moralist include Sutherland, *Art of the Satirist;* Hilliard, "Redemption"; Thomas Preston, "Uses of Adversity"; and, worst of all, Jefferson, "*The Vicar of Wakefield.*" Attacks include Jaarsma, "Satiric Intent"; Hopkins, *True Genius* 166–230, and Dussinger, *Discourse of the Mind* 148–72.

16. I have noted an exception only in a passage of the *History of Animated Nature* deploring bird cages (*Works,* ed. Cunningham, 4: 421), probably taken over from one of Goldsmith's sources. On prisons in *The Vicar* see Bender, "Prison Reform."

17. Madelin's essay concerns the insubstantiality of the religious element in the novel ("*The Vicar of Wakefield* et l'apologétique des augustéens").

18. The most thorough study of Austen's characters, following Hardy, *A Reading of Jane Austen,* is Morgan, *In the Meantime.* The most penetrating study is Weinsheimer, "Theory of Character: *Emma*"; the most pro-

vocative is Bruns, *Inventions* 11–24. Harvey's *Character and the Novel* is mostly concerned with subsequent complications, but see pp. 118–21.

19. In chap. 28 Primrose goes on a long, solitary journey to locate Olivia, but he is never alone for more than half a sentence of his narration. Typical reports of feeling are, "The leaving of a neighbourhood in which we had enjoyed so many hours of tranquility, was not without a tear, which scarce fortitude itself could suppress" (chap. 3; 4: 27) and "My sensations were even too violent to permit my attempting the rescue. . . . [My wife's] gratitude may be more readily imagined than described" (chap. 3; 4: 30–31). One senses behind the Vicar's inarticulateness the lack of an economy of sensibility that would make feelings determinate and therefore narratable.

20. Johnson's only definition of "republick" is "Commonwealth; state in which the power is lodged in more than one." Goldsmith's *Grecian History* is free from the political confusions of Primrose's phrase.

21. Spacks, *Adolescent Idea* 59–65, analyzes the psychological debilities of the paternal narrative perspective in *The Vicar*. On generic ramifications (paternal narrative as antiromance) see Bäckmann, *This Singular Tale* 110–11; on patriarchal ideology see the chapter on this issue in Dussinger, *Discourse of the Mind*.

22. See the beautiful analysis of *Amelia*'s distanced narrator in Rothstein, *Systems of Order and Inquiry* 154–67.

23. See the fine discussions in Goldstein, *Ruins and Empire*, esp. chaps. 6–7.

24. Goethe, in G. S. Rousseau, *Critical Heritage* 278. The terms for my discussion of this passage are set by Preisendanz, *Humor*.

25. George Eliot, "Story-Telling," in her *Leaves* 240–43. This essay is excerpted in G. S. Rousseau, *Critical Heritage* 63–64, but it is misleadingly cropped.

26. Goldsmith's relations with his own family seem likewise to have been almost entirely devoid of temporal depth or continuity. As with the "artlessness" of the novels, there may be complex explanations for Goldsmith's naive *bonhommie*. See the good presentation by Balderston in Goldsmith's *Letters* ix–xxiii.

27. See Hunting's essay "The Poems in *The Vicar of Wakefield*," which argues for the superiority of illusion to reality in the novel.

28. Hopkins evidently relies on this distinction between the sequence and the disposition of events when he persuasively assigns the chapter titles to Primrose rather than Goldsmith (*True Genius* 217–19).

29. Not only is this an open secret, but in the absence of actions it is also an uncertain truth: "she *may* be brought." Here is an anthology of occurrences of the motif that illustrate, with little need for context, the open darkness and ironic seriousness of secrecy in the novel: "I still found [my daughters] secretly attached to all their former finery" (chap. 4; 4: 34). "Either curiosity or surprize, or some more hidden motive, held my wife and daughters to their seats" at Thornhill's first appearance (chap. 5; 4: 36). "Prompted, perhaps, by some secret reasons, I delivered this observation with

414 Notes to Pages 172-79

too much acrimony" (chap. 6; 4: 40). "As for secret reasons, you are right: I have secret reasons, which I forbear to mention, because you are not able to answer those of which I make no secret" (Burchell in chap. 13; 4: 70). "'Excuse me, madam,' returned [Thornhill], 'they [his reasons] lie too deep for discovery' (laying his hand upon his bosom); 'they remain buried, rivetted here'" (chap. 16; 4: 85). With multiple ironies we find Olivia at the crisis saying of Thornhill, ingenuously or disingenuously: "Yes, pappa, . . . but he has his reasons for this delay: I know he has. The sincerity of his looks and words convince me of his real esteem. A short time, I hope, will discover the generosity of his sentiments" (chap. 17; 4: 86). Here the concealment makes his true character an open book, even in some degree to Primrose, and no readers can ever have been misled, though Primrose briefly is, when Thornhill urges him "by all means to keep [the elopement] a secret" from the Wilmots (chap. 21; 4: 123). "But Sir," says the oath-violating Olivia, concluding this inventory of maladroits when she confesses to her father, "will that be right, when I am sworn to secrecy?" (chap. 21; 4: 127–28).

30. Privateer's essay "Goldsmith's *Vicar of Wakefield*" treats Burchell as an artist who becomes an "artificer of Order" (34). If Burchell is to be glorified, then it must evidently be in partial recognition of the novel's aesthetic dimension.

31. The best discussion of patterning in *Tom Jones* is Alter, *Fielding* 99–139.

32. *Rasselas* is another work, like *The Vicar of Wakefield*, whose unmistakable symmetries escaped mention for two centuries: see Rothstein, *Systems of Order and Inquiry* 23–43, and also Emrys Jones, "The Artistic Form of *Rasselas*."

33. My terms here are those of Fried, *Absorption and Theatricality*.

34. Castle, *Masquerade and Civilization*. In his rather critical Epilogue to Charlotte Lennox's *The Sisters*, Goldsmith explicitly suggests absolutizing the masquerade: "What if I give a masquerade? I will. / But how! ay there's the rub! (*pausing*) I've got my cue: / The world's a masquerade! the masquers, you, you, you" (lines 10–12).

35. We do know, however, that Goldsmith's literary works, unlike his histories, were composed with painful slowness.

36. I am arguing against the gradualist model of generic change presented in Fowler, "The Life and Death of Literary Forms."

37. Braudy, "Recent Studies" 550, mentions that Goldsmith's generic experimentation was the subject of a question in the Graduate Record Examination, but I have not noted any published comments on its significance.

38. Dahl, "Patterns of Disguise" 104. I have torn Dahl's question from its context, where he asks only whether the book means specifically his proposed interpretation. But in spirit his reversal has the larger import of questioning the relationship between form and meaning, or analysis and interpretation, in general.

Chapter Eight

1. Since paternal incompetence is a condition of plot interest rather than a fact of life, it is no contradiction that nothing detrimental is conveyed about a peripheral father, the farmer Flamborough in *The Vicar of Wakefield*. Lien Chi Altangi is, of course, a devoted father, but he is an Oriental, with values the inverse of those in England, and his behavior and his traveling to exotic countries and writing affectionate letters while his scion gets into trouble make him more like an uncle such as Sir William Honeywood than like a father. Finally, though Sir Charles Marlow has a heart of gold, he still behaves toward his son like an inquisitor. I take it as a sign of latent tensions that the only lines addressed by Sir Charles to his son are the following: "And you never grasp'd her hand, or made any protestations!" (act 5; 5: 199), and "I can hold it no longer. Charles, Charles, how hast thou deceived me! Is this your indifference, your uninteresting conversation!" (act 5; 5: 212). And Marlow, in return, quivers in the only speech he addresses directly to his father: "As heaven is my witness, I came down in obedience to your commands. . . . I hope you'll exact no further proofs of my duty" (act 5; 5: 199). *The Grecian History* depicts Philip as a devoted father to Alexander, but Goldsmith seems suspicious that a good father stifles his son: "That discipline which prevailed in [Alexander's] army, was produced and cultivated by his father; but his intemperance, his cruelty, his vanity, his passion for useless conquests were all his own" (316).

2. Naming is another of the motifs that unifies the play. Marlow, thinking he is wise when he is not rattled, here invents the members of the Ladies Club, "Mrs. Mantrap, Lady Betty Blackleg, the Countess of Sligo, Mrs. Langhorns, old Miss Biddy Buckskin" (act 3; 5: 173). In his embarrassment he later calls himself "the Dullissimo Maccaroni" (act 4; 5: 184). When Tony, in act 4, can't read Hastings's note about the elopement, Constance seizes it and pretends to read, but Tony is so taken in by the names she invents, Shake-bag Club and Goose-Green, that he gives it to his mother to read in extenso. The complex issue here is the motivation of names, as with the rooms at the supposed inn that are imagined by Kate, the supposed maid: "Attend the Lion, there.—Pipes and tobacco for the Angel.—The Lamb has been outrageous this half hour" (act 3; 5: 169). One wonders, then, whether Colonel Wallop and Dr. Drowsy (act 2; 5: 137, and act 4; 5: 188) are really names or just characterizations. And this leads to the issue of speaking names among the acting roles, which will be discussed later.

3. Donaldson analyzes many of the prior examples of the topos in *The World Upside-Down*.

4. Cf. the exchange in act 4: "*Hardcastle.* I say this house is mine, Sir; this house is mine, and I command you to leave it directly. *Marlow.* . . . This, your house, fellow! It's my house. This is my house. Mine, while I chuse to stay. . . . *Hardcastle.* . . . To come to my house, to call for what he likes . . . , and then to tell me, *This house is mine, Sir.* . . . Pray, Sir, (banter-

ing.) as you take the house, what think you of taking the rest of the furniture? . . . *Marlow*. Bring me your bill, I say; and I'll leave you and your infernal house directly" (5: 182–83).

5. For discussions of the conversion of differences between into differences within see Barbara Johnson, *The Critical Difference*.

6. "*Hastings*. And so you have at last brought them home again?" (act 5; 5: 203); "*Tony*. By my guess we should be upon Crackskull common, about forty miles from home" (act 5; 5: 204); "*Mrs. Hardcastle*. But who, my dear, could have expected to meet you here, in this frightful place, so far from home?" (act 5; 5: 207).

7. As a sentimental name Neville means new city; Tony here etymologizes it as a farce name meaning no city. On the "synthesis" that displaces narrative and "gently consummates the mild hegemony of the theater," see also the insightful pages in Christensen, *Practicing Enlightenment* 35–36.

8. Hardcastle: "I could never teach the fools of this age, that the indigent world could be cloathed out of the trimmings of the vain" (act 1; 5: 111). Primrose: "I don't know whether such flouncing and shredding is becoming even in the rich, if we consider, upon a moderate calculation, that the nakedness of the indigent world may be clothed from the trimmings of the vain" (*Vicar*, chap. 4; 4: 34).

9. On face (in contrast to voice) as the "organ" of humanity's "eccentric positionality," see Plessner, *Lachen und Weinen*, in *Philosophische Anthropologie* 53–54.

10. Jonson, *The Alchemist*, dedication. Face is the name of the alchemist's henchman in this play of transmutation. I am grateful to Gerald Bruns for reminding me of Jonson's play and of the Heidegger passage below.

11. Indeed, I have somewhat overstated my case in saying that Constance and Hastings unsay their elopement. Language remains stiff and formal here, with a limited role, for instance in contrast to Marlow's abjuration, "O, curse on my noisy head" (act 5; 5: 213). In the case of Constance and Hastings it would be more accurate to say only that they un*do* their elopement, and thus they don't really emerge out of the sentimental ending into the farce ending.

12. In connection with my discussion of honesty, see Empson, *Structure*, chap. 9. Smollett's *Roderick Random* is another good locus for studying the complex eighteenth-century usage. In chap. 7 of *A Thousand Plateaus* Deleuze and Guattari develop a more abstract concept of "faciality" that can be used, with discrimination, to elucidate the face of Goldsmith's landscape. The horse-pond at the edge of the property and at the vortex of Tony's circling represents the black hole or eye of tyrannical subjectification that "deterritorializes" (in this case satirically, by soiling all pretensions) and "reterritorializes" (by instilling guilt at the parents' humiliation and thus prompting the reestablishment of the moral order). The white wall of authoritarian significance is, perhaps, represented by the front of the

stage, where the characters come to enunciate their—and the author's—meanings.

13. It is, however, worth taking note of the ending that Goldsmith wrote for *The Grumbler*, an abridgment and adaptation of a farce by Sir Charles Sedley that Goldsmith prepared in 1773 to benefit the actor who played Tony Lumpkin. The last line, addressed by Octavio's loving uncle, Wentworth, to the misanthropic father, Sourby, is "recover then that Serenity of mind which as a sensible Man you must condemn yourself for losing, and endeavour to promote the happiness of others [i.e., Octavio and Clarissa, who have tricked Sourby into permitting their engagement], and by so doing secure your own" (29). The editor rightly calls this "the declaration of good intentions and moral sentiments usually found as an end-speech in the plays of this period" (xviii). But Sourby's part concludes differently, with ranting about the "Charming Scene of uproar and Confusion" that he gleefully foresees (28); Octavio then pleads for favor without response, and Wentworth precedes his surely vain invocation of serene sensibility by a realistic condemnation of the way Sourby's "turbulence of temper" tends to promote a "general dissatisfaction" (29). I see no evidence here to project a development in Goldsmith beyond the disruptive greatness of his breakthroughs toward a greatness of reintegration.

Chapter Nine

1. Hogan, "Plot, Character, and Comic Language," discusses the conventionality of Sheridan's best-known plays and concludes that he, like Goldsmith, has "a sunny good nature deriving from a benevolent tolerance" and from an "attitude" of "charm" (281).

2. Qtd. in Moore, *Memoirs* 1: 92, italics in Moore's text. Moore mentions a page numbered 232 in this brief fragment: how many fragments the fertile and improvident Sheridan must have lost or else left uncollected, and now scattered throughout the world and (in many cases) unpublished!

3. Alone among his speeches, those against Hastings, Sheridan's most sustained and greatest oratorical triumph, were in fact stenographically preserved, rather than more conventionally reported and edited, but this fact remained unknown until well after his death.

4. The psychic economics here are those, again, of Charles Surface, who preserves his youth by speedily giving away to old Mr. Stanley money that could satisfy "a Hosier and two Tailors" (4.2; p. 410). "Justice is an Old lame hobbling Beldame," he exclaims, "and I can't Get her to keep pace with Generosity" (4.1; p. 409); and cf. Moore, *Memoirs* 2: 333–34, applying this line biographically. It is as if settling the debt or having done with the work would turn any textile or text into a shroud.

5. I do not want this generalized suggestion to erase individual variations. The midcentury, for instance, also exhibits some prodigies (the Wartons, or Klopstock in Germany) who proceeded to churn out increasingly undistinguished verse for a lifetime. Crabbe's career, even later than Sheri-

dan's, is another instructive case; after the stylistically exhausted, self-pitying poems of the 1780s, he maintained a public silence for over a quarter of a century, but seems to have continued to write in private, until he started publishing his collected verse exposés of Aldeburgh in a very different climate. The foiled careers of romantic poets, on the other hand, do not seem self-thwarted in the same way. The tuberculosis of Keats, the drowning of Shelley, and the madness of Hölderlin seem either purely accidental or else actual fulfillments of deep-seated currents in their lives and works. Even Pushkin's fatal duel echoes, as if typologically, the poet Lensky's death at the hands of Eugene Onegin.

6. This would be an appropriate, because unexpected, moment to invoke Harold Bloom. "We must see the object, the poem," he writes, "as in itself it really is not, because we must see not only what is missing in it, but why the poem had to exclude what is missing" (*Agon* 18). Bloom's importance for the present study is not in his idiosyncratic mechanisms of interpretation (which in any case he hardly wishes to share with, let alone impose upon, others, as he says on p. 38), but rather in his sense for the powerful intricacies, the complex, inward personality of time itself as the ultimate agonist.

7. Throughout this chapter I will frequently refer to and freely draw from Loftis, *Sheridan*, and Auburn, *Sheridan's Comedies.* These two scholars' reports on the plays produced during Sheridan's lifetime are indispensable in situating Sheridan in his literary culture and in correcting time-honored misconceptions. Elmar Lehmann accomplished a similar project in his virtually unknown book on Goldsmith's comedies, *"Not Merely Sentimental."* He bogs down in detailed comparisons and contrasts of too many moments in too many sources and analogues, but the opening survey (29–65) of the development of character and motif types from the Restoration into sentimental drama is excellent.

8. Paradigmatic of the approach to Sheridan evoked in this paragraph is Andrew Schiller's essay *"The School for Scandal."* At least, Schiller says, the play "is remarkably free from 'offense.' . . . Even the villains cannot be debauched when the final curtain rings down" (704). True, but, as I discuss later, they are also neither redeemed nor effectively punished. Similar in spirit but more critical of Sheridan's alleged emptiness is Holloway, "The Rivals."

9. The contemporary function of Goldsmith's essay was first clarified by Robert D. Hume in 1972; see (in reprint) "Goldsmith and Sheridan." For an even more detailed investigation that takes account of the differences between published texts and acting versions, see Bevis, *The Laughing Tradition.*

10. Loftis, *Sheridan* 74, 79. Hannaford, "The Shape of 18th Century English Drama," documents the degree to which, before 1760 and to a lesser extent thereafter, old plays dominated the repertoire. For a general period concept of neoclassicism there is much of value in James William Johnson's essay "What Was Neo-Classicism?" although Greene's sharp rejoinder, "What Indeed Was Neo-Classicism," offers essential qualifications.

11. In Etherege's *Man of Mode*, for instance, the figure strongly identified with scandal-mongering is Medley, the only young character not involved in love intrigues.

12. Richard Flecknoe, "A Short Discourse of the English Stage" (1664), in Spingarn, *Critical Essays* 2: 93.

13. In a related spirit the Preface to Vanbrugh's *The Relapse* says, "I do therefore, with all the humility of a repenting sinner, confess it wants everything—but length" (3). Vanbrugh concedes that there may have been some indecencies in the performance, but surely none in the text. His apology is fully consistent with Uranie's image of the text as a blank mirror.

14. Seventeenth-century dramatic theorists certainly called for the spectator to participate emotionally in the spectacle. But, as Rousset shows (*L'Intérieur et l'extérieur* 165–82), it regarded the effect as a collective hallucination, rather than a merging of worlds. Reiss, who lays out the materials admirably (*Toward Dramatic Illusion* 138–55), confuses the issues by using the anachronistic terms "identification" and "empathy." The classical theory of absorption presupposes that the spectator leaves his true self behind when he enters the imaginary world of the theater. That accounts for the gaps that Reiss notes: "Somewhat surprisingly, the relationship between play and spectator [in connection with verisimilitude] is only slightly touched on and almost never clearly developed in the theoretical writings of the seventeenth century" (140), and the "desire to cause the spectator to confuse his emotions with those of the stage character is usually left implicit" (142). Both lacunae occur for the reason that the spectator vanishes to the degree that the illusion takes over. And that illusion is not the end, but the means toward a purgative reflection: "It is clear that [Rapin's] ideal is a theater which, while emotionally placing the spectator in the play—not simply in sympathy with the characters but empathically involved in the action—also provokes him to reflect upon what he feels" (141).

15. Lapp, *Aspects of Racinian Tragedy* 38–65, argues persuasively that "Racine is concerned . . . with indicating a *movement in time*" (44, Lapp's emphasis). The consciousness of a past gathering in stages toward the present and of an impending future indeed characterizes Racine's inflection of the unity of time. That consciousness, however, only becomes perceptible as it funnels into the dramatic present. Time passing turns into time moving coherently only at the instant of crisis when the plot falls into place. Lapp's argument thus in fact corroborates my thesis of the unitary character of *dramatic* time in the classical theater.

16. See Poulet, *Studies in Human Time* 97–130, which makes fine distinctions among the modes of timelessness in the three classic dramatists. Of particular relevance to the present chapter is the conclusion that "there is no temporal movement in Molière" (103). The same could be said, as well, of Congreve's *Love for Love*, where everything whirls with such giddy rapidity, in a world surrounded by the pounding main and permeated by lunacy, that the flow of time loses all meaning. As Sir Sampson says in 2.5, "No matter for the time; prithee, Brother *Foresight*, leave Superstition—

Pox o'th' time; there's no time but the time present, there's no more to be said of what's past, and all that is to come will happen" (*Comedies* 246).

17. Shortly afterwards Dryden suggests that the theater is less than reality (not imaginatively richer, as for Johnson) by means of an artful correspondence of his modest argument and his image of diminution: "I am almost fearful of illustrating anything by similitude, lest he should confute it for an argument; yet I think the comparison of a glass will discover very aptly the fallacy of his argument, both concerning time and place. The strength of his reason depends on this, that the less cannot comprehend the greater. I have already answered, that we need not suppose it does; I say not that the less can comprehend the greater, but only, that it may represent it; as in a glass, or mirror, of half-a-yard in diameter, a whole room, and many persons in it may be seen at once; not that it can comprehend that room, or those persons, but that it represents them to the sight" (*Essays* 1: 129–30).

18. Howard, for instance, attacks tragicomedy because "'tis probable the Audience may not so suddenly *recollect themselves* as to start into an enjoyment of the Mirth or into a concern for the Sadness" (in Spingarn, *Critical Essays* 2: 100, my emphasis). Dryden's Neander answers the argument in the same terms: "[Lisideius] tells us, we cannot so speedily recollect ourselves after a scene of great passion and concernment, as to pass to another of mirth and humour, and to enjoy it with any relish: but . . . [a] continued gravity keeps the spirit too much bent; we must refresh it sometimes, as we bait in a journey, that we may go on with greater ease" (*Essays* 1: 69–70). Both sides of this debate focus on the self-alienation of the audience in its absorption with the spectacle.

19. Thus Etherege's *The Man of Mode* opens—in an interval between Dorimant's passions—with the play's only soliloquy, which begins by quoting two lines of Waller concerning the immobility of the sun and which ends with the phrase "Hey!—who waits?" signaling that the servant Handy has been standing motionlessly by (act 1; p. 8). Soliloquies are also fixating devices in Molière's early plays; see the fine analysis of *L'Ecole des femmes* in Relyea, *Signs* 12–35. Marin compactly summarizes the underlying semiotic issues in *Food for Thought* xi–xxi.

20. Cf. Relyea, *Signs* 52: "Seeing is not knowing. . . . In fact, according to Cléante, the more pronounced the signs, the more likely they are to be deliberately deceitful." The ancient development is beautifully sketched by Freydenberg in "Proiskhozhdenie."

21. Congreve appears to echo Harpagon in the Epistle Dedicatory: "this Man . . . is only thinking, and thinking such Matter as were inexcusable Folly in him to speak. But . . . the Poet . . . is willing to inform us of this Person's Thoughts; and to that end is forc'd to make use of the Expedient of Speech, no other better way being yet invented for the Communication of Thought" (*Comedies* 115).

22. On the music of Dryden's lyrics, see Miner, *Dryden's Poetry*, chap. 7.

23. Sheridan resembles Sterne in his anxious sense of time. Cf. *Tristram Shandy* 1.22; p. 80: "tho' my digressions are all fair, . . . yet I constantly take care to order affairs so, that my main business does not stand still in my absence," and 3.12; p. 213: "But in suspending his voice—was the sense suspended likewise? Did no expression of attitude or countenance fill up the chasm?—Was the eye silent? Did you narrowly look?—I look'd only at the stop-watch, my Lord."

24. Much of the sparse interest in the three volumes of letters derives from the recurrence, throughout Sheridan's whole life, of the phenomena of untimeliness. Good fortune blessed one such occurrence, when *The School for Scandal* opened at the tail end of the London theatrical season and was held over well into the summer. But see, for instance, the urgent yet inconsequential correspondence that followed the burning of the Drury Lane Theater in 1809.

25. Sir John and Lady Brute remain an unenviable couple at the end of Vanbrugh's *The Provoked Wife*, but the effect is quite different. After an aside in which, thinking aloud, Sir John determines his future stance, he declares, "jealousy's a mark of love; so she need not trouble her head about it, as long as I make no more words on't" (109). Further arrivals and revelations, to be sure, complicate the picture in the closing pages, but the tone remains far from that of the penultimate speeches of *St. Patrick's Day*: "*Bridget*. This day's Adventure, Lovee, will be a good scolding Subject for you and me these ten years. *Justice*. So it will, my Dear—tho' we are never much at a loss" (2.4; p. 192).

26. In particular Primrose's six children appear to be reduced to two boys and two girls: Sheridan's Moses is a bumpkin who has attended the university, fusing Goldsmith's George and Moses, and I presume that the unidentified Steven (who appears directly after Moses at the end of the list of male characters) was to replace the two younger boys. The pairings in the dramatis personae are fluid, to be sure, presumably in order to give variety to the basic structural contrasts. The list of men begins with Primrose and Burchell, the bad father and the good uncle; Burchell is followed by his nephew Thornhill, Thornhill by his companion Arnold (who plays a cautionary role to Thornhill's impetuosity in scene 1 of the text); the list concludes with two farmers and two sons. On the women's side, Mrs. Primrose stands alone, contrasted horizontally to her husband and vertically to her two named daughters, and the three Primrose women in their turn are opposed to the two unnamed ladies of the town.

27. Frances Sheridan's *A Journey to Bath* also begins with a flurry of naming. But the people named are the characters about to appear on stage, and the naming accompanies a mechanical summary of their situation. It is a textbook case of the kind of static exposition that Richard Sheridan's inventive fancy rejects.

28. Sichel reviews the name changes in *Sheridan* 1: 568–69.

29. An engraving of 1777, reproduced as the frontispiece to vol. 2 of the *Dramatic Works* (though it was intended for vol. 1 according to the List of

Illustrations), shows the screen painted (not hung) with maps; an engraving of 1788, reproduced in Sichel, *Sheridan*, facing 1: 548, shows it blank. Even the engravings thus problematize the relationship of sign to surface.

30. According to Randolph's essay on the term, "candor," by Sheridan's time, "was no longer an honest word, but a mealy-mouthed cant term, unlovely as Sheridan's Mrs. Candour herself, serving only to gloss over rank hypocrisy on the part of both satirists and readers" ("Candour" 61). Outside of satire, as she shows, the term was not necessarily smutty. Her essay helps to sort out a word that Empson finds "confusing" (*Structure* 310) and to correct the political and chronological distortions of Davie's essay "An Episode in the History of Candor."

31. Mrs. Candour is so dangerous because she never fixes her position; candor's signs are as inconstant as a weathervane. Compare the villain Melvil in Arthur Murphy's *Know Your Own Mind*, who combines Mrs. Candour's bland scandalmongering with Joseph Surface's hypocritical moralizing, thereby effacing the distinctiveness of each. Murphy's play premiered three months before Sheridan's and may have influenced it, though the compositional history of both plays is too complicated to allow any firm determinations.

32. *Plays and Poems* 3: 213 reports the variant "magic" for "mimic" in line 23 of Sheridan's "Verses to the Memory of Garrick"; it is not noted in *Dramatic Works*.

33. Here are Sheridan's lines, early in the monody: "E'en Beauty's Portrait wears a softer Prime, / Touch'd by the tender Hand of mellowing Time" (lines 29–30). They need to be compared with their source, the far less qualified conclusion of Dryden's "Epistle to Sir Godfrey Kneller": "For Time shall with his ready Pencil stand; / Retouch your Figures, with his ripening Hand; / Mellow your Colours, and imbrown the Teint; / Add every Grace, which Time alone can grant: / To future Ages shall your Fame convey; / And give more Beauties, than he takes away" (lines 176–81).

34. Jack Durant has written two good essays on the picture-auction scene: "Prudence," on Sheridan's moral principles, and "Sheridan's Picture-Auction Scene," on false surfaces and Reynolds' principles of true taste.

35. On revolutionary comic energies in Sheridan generally (the speeches as well as the plays), see Paulson, *Representations of Revolution* 141–50.

36. The classical norm is, of course, to reassemble all actors on stage at the end. One character is driven offstage at the end of Farquhar's *Sir Harry Wildair*, but then he returns to speak the Epilogue.

37. Hasbog, in the best essay I have read on the play, "Zur Reduktion des Sentimentalen," draws sustained attention to the centrifugal tendency of the conclusion, in contrast to Cumberland's *West Indian*. I think, however, that something more is at stake than the playful or comic treatment of sentimentality that Hasbog attributes to Sheridan.

38. Elizabeth Inchbald's play, *Wives as They Were, and Maids as They Are* (1797), provides an instructive contrast. Its situations—a guardian in disguise newly returned from India to test his daughter's love, a profligate

ward, a seizure for debt, an old-fashioned husband—are more extreme versions of Sheridan's. Yet its language of raillery is tamer, its interest in inventing stories and in language is far more limited, and its conclusion is a reassertion of conventional morality encouraging wives to triumph in virtue through total submission to their husbands. What we see by way of situations in Sheridan is less explosive (Inchbald includes a scene parodied from Wycherley in which the doting Lord Priory encourages the rake Bronzely to make advances to Lady Priory), yet what we hear and what we learn by way of outcome gives Sheridan's play an incomparably more radical effect.

39. Loftis (*Sheridan* 92–93) has a good survey of the Wycherley-Sheridan connection. He claims to "know no reason, except the thematic similarity between the two plays, to assume that Sheridan planned *The School for Scandal* with *The Plain Dealer* in mind" (92), and he notes that "Thomas Moore reports that Sheridan denied having read Wycherley" (151). The succession of names in the drafts surely seems purposeful, however, and Moore presents the denial as one of several obviously absurd denials attributed to Sheridan by rumor.

40. Maskwell, in Sheridan's other source, is, if possible, even more explicit about his negations: "Now will I, in my old way, discover the whole and real truth of the Matter to him, that he may not suspect one Word on't. No Mask like open Truth to cover Lies, / As to go Naked is the best Disguise" (*Double-Dealer* 5.4, in *Comedies* 195). A certain infantile quality to the logic and the imagery ("naked") of this self-serving soliloquy is not irrelevant to the subsequent discussion.

41. Act 2, scene 3, of George Colman's *The Jealous Wife* contains an actual, though abortive, sword fight. The overall tone of the play is oppressively moralistic, both in the comic title motif and in the sentimental filial devotion of the young heroine; and by literalizing the swordplay Colman could be understood to be repressing its latent sexual symbolism.

42. On Richardson's Lovelace and his abhorrence of sex see Stevenson, "Alien Spirits."

43. *False Delicacy* explicitly sounds the note of thanatos twice, once in 2.1, when Cecil soliloquizes about himself ("Zounds, I wonder how the grey-headed dotards have the impudence to ask a blooming girl of twenty to throw herself away upon a moving mummy, or a walking skeleton"), and once in 4.2, when Miss Rivers, in obedience to her father's injunctions, dismisses her lover with the words "This parting is a kind of death." "What a wretch must the woman be," she has just protested, "who can dream of happiness, while she wounds the bosom of a father." Kelly, *False Delicacy* 25, 68, 69.

44. The economic issue becomes surrealistically explicit in Kelly's second comedy, *A Word to the Wise* (1770). Here Miss Dormer and Villars cannot acknowledge their mutual love because he is a poor orphan. In due course Villars's heroic rescue of Miss Willoughby from the wiles of young Captain Dormer induces the virtuous father (Sir John Dormer) to agree to a love match. But then it turns out that Villars is the long-lost—and wealthy—

brother of Miss Willoughby. Kelly's crass payoff to the couple, in which the fortune provisionally enjoyed by Sir George Hastings is redistributed to the last child, is in such obvious conflict with his sentimental morality of the heart, and the play is so embarrassed about the whole thing (the text only indirectly alludes to the engagement, which takes place offstage between acts 4 and 5) that it seems inevitable to read the transparent fairy-tale device allegorically. The identification turns on an inscribed picture, not of Villars's mother (the expected motif, as for instance in Clara Reeve's *The Old English Baron*), but of Lady Dormer. There is thus an element of true iconic signs, conveniently contrasting with Sheridan, combined with a hint of predestination (Villars perhaps loves Miss Dormer because she resembles the treasured picture of her mother) that undermines the expressed doctrines of spontaneous free choice. The future seems distinctly less open when the right to marry whomever your heart dictates proves only to be a license to marry your first cousin!

45. In connection with the relation of siblings to one another and to their parents in such plays it is suggestive to read Freud's essay, "'A Child Is Being Beaten,'" although the essay concerns the aggressive fantasies of older children against younger siblings.

46. In the "Ode to Scandal," which was published as Sheridan's in 1819 (most readily available in Sichel's *Sheridan* 618–22), scandal murders Colvilia as well as a nameless and silent maiden (621: "Her pureness had leave in her actions to speak, / The spirit of youth gave the blush to her cheek; / And her looks uninstructed her thoughts would impart, / For her eyes only flashed from the warmth of her heart"). The maiden's story is told in a prosopopeia of Candour; with Candour gone over to the enemy, *The School for Scandal* leaves no one to *speak* for virtue. Whether or not the ode is Sheridan's (I am unable to understand which opinion Rhodes espouses in Sheridan's *Plays and Poems* 3: 359–60), it perfectly captures the issues.

47. The latter contradiction is in 4.3; p. 411—an aside followed by an address. The former contradiction occurs in successive speeches to Lady Sneerwell in 1.1; p. 364—"to smile at the jest which plants a Thorn in another's Breast is to become a principal in the Mischief," yet "that conversation where the Spirit of Raillery is suppress'd will ever appear tedious and insipid."

48. The Teazles' cheerful concord in their quarrel sounds as if it were digesting a running motif in Murphy's *Three Weeks After Marriage*, which had been successfully revived the previous season.

49. Cf. Major Rackett in Samuel Foote's *The Maid of Bath* (1771), 1.1; p. 13: "Pshaw! who talks now of the drudgery of domestic duties, of nuptial chains, and of bonds? mere obsolete words! they did well enough in the dull days of queen Bess; but a modern lass puts on fetters to enjoy the more freedom, and pledges her faith to one, that she may be at liberty to bestow her favours on all." Foote's heroine, Katherine Linnet, eventually rejects marriage altogether, though her real-life model, Elizabeth Linley, was actually to elope with Sheridan the following year. A number of the plays of Foote—

whose self-proclaimed marriage to his washerwoman was never verified— are similarly equivocal about passion and marriage. In *The Devil upon Two Sticks* (1768), for instance, the devil Cupid magically aids a young couple to escape to London from a tyrannical father in Spain; the result, however (quite different from that of the source, Le Sage's *Le Diable boîteux*), is a theatrical career. Foote's comedies appear to be the limit case, or even the exception, to Auburn's already qualified conclusion that Georgian comedies "view marriage as a generally desirable institution to be entered with emotional as well as financial stability" (*Sheridan's Comedies* 30).

50. A crudely articulated antitype for Sheridan's conclusion may be found in Foote's *The Nabob* (1772). Here an unscrupulous India merchant, spouting doctrines of economic free enterprise, schemes to buy Sophy Oldham as his wife by forgiving her father a loan. When she refuses, the debt is miraculously paid off, and her firm will is rewarded with the fiancé whom she always loved. Nevertheless, the desiring-machine here remains regressive—or "old"—in a number of respects that reflect Foote's ambivalence toward marriage: first, the rejection of economics (answered by Sheridan's virtuous India-merchant, Uncle Oliver); second, the endogamous, hence restrictive first-cousin marriage that Sophy eventually obtains; and third, her silence at the conclusion when she is rewarded with her cousin. In view of his elopement to France the same year, Sheridan, if he heard it, must have found the curtain speech by Sophy's uncle chilling: "However praiseworthy the spirit of adventure may be, whoever keeps his post, and does his duty at home, will be found to render his country best service at last" (act 2; p. 59).

51. I put orthodox in quotes because, as Deleuze and Guattari rightly protest, Freud's own writings on the question cannot by any means all be reduced to the schematic oedipal pattern. In particular, *Beyond the Pleasure Principle* and other writings of its period waver between the "orthodox" oedipal view of thanatos as death or destruction and the alternative view of thanatos as entropy.

Chapter Ten

1. This anonymous translation is customarily attributed to Elizabeth Griffith. Susan Staves, who is currently editing Griffith's works, has told me that attribution is a mistake.

2. *Barbier* 2.7; p. 310 (square brackets in passages quoted from Beaumarchais and Diderot mark suspension points found in the original text). Unlike the anonymous literal version, George Colman's truncated adaptation of *Le Barbier*, which premiered (at the Haymarket) some three and a half months after *The School for Scandal*, renders "calomnie" with "scandal": "Yes, Sir, Scandal. A good neat convenient Lie now! Let me be alone to Contrive it. I'll compose it as easily as a new Piece of Music. First of all, the gentle Air of a Report, skimming the Surface, like a Swallow before a Storm, murmur, murmur, pianissimo!—Then raising the Voice a little, it goes from Ear to

Ear piano—soon after Andante, and Spirituoso—and presently from Mouth to Mouth, forte, forte, fortissimo—till it ends in a general Chorus." *The Spanish Barber; or, The Fruitless Precaution*, in Colman's *Plays* 4: 15–16. This is the first publication of this play, which, however, unlike the anonymous version, was successfully produced.

3. "I have seen the devil" is Bazile's exclamation upon learning Figaro's identity, and the real father, Bartholo, echoes him a little later: "He has the devil in him" (*Mariage* 4.10; p. 462; and 5.2; p. 468).

4. On Beaumarchais's names see Scherer, *Dramaturgie* 119–29. Scherer's book remains the best-informed study of Beaumarchais as dramatist, and I will refer to it repeatedly to indicate both the contributions and the limitations of a classically oriented study of a preromantic author.

5. The power of silent spectacle is the concluding topic (863–70) of Undank's rich though congested essay, "Beaumarchais' Transformations." Undank associates silence with the feminine, a topic that I take up in the next chapter.

6. Scherer, *Dramaturgie* 68: "all [the monologues], apart from one celebrated exception, are short or even very short. It is rare, *unless for a particular reason*, for their length to exceed about ten lines." I have emphasized the phrase by which the critic permits himself to evade the general issue.

7. In comparison, Voltaire's *Enfant prodigue*, with many fewer characters jockeying for the audience's attention, has only one five-line soliloquy proper, by a servant (3.4), along with one nineteen-line monologue by the father, spoken without knowing that the servant is also onstage. Diderot's monologues are considerably more extensive than Beaumarchais's, but more conventionally analytical.

8. Whose son is Figaro really? The name has been repeatedly etymologized as Fils-Caron, that is, Beaumarchais; for Figaro, the quick-witted intriguer and master of all trades, has much in common with his creator. But the rebellious Beaumarchais was his father's son only long enough to use the invention of a better mechanism as his passport out of the clock business. Then he became, among other things, a music-master, like Figaro's stepfather. Fils-Caron, then, could also mean son of the playwright Caron de Beaumarchais. Figaro's dubious quadruple or quintuple paternity exceeds even the double paternity that liberates the children in *La Mère coupable* (see just below). The only way to be a dutiful son is to be able to elect your father.

9. For a good summary of Diderot's position see Joly, *Deux études* 26–36.

10. *Le Barbier de Séville* premiered on Feb. 28, 1775. The original plan for Diderot's play is known from a copy in Grimm's *Correspondence littéraire* of Nov. 1775. A completed play by Diderot entitled *La Pièce et le prologue* appeared in the *Correspondence littéraire* in July and August 1777, but the last version, called *Est-il bon? est-il méchant?*, was not finished until 1779 at the earliest, and perhaps as late as 1784. That Beaumarchais inspired Diderot's obviously labored return to the theater can only be conjectured.

11. Scherer, *Dramaturgie* 46–50. Scherer copes with the plot better than Lemonnier-Delpy, who writes cagily in her manual (*Nouvelle étude* 94–95): "Contrary to appearances, the plot of *Le Mariage de Figaro*, however swarming with incidents, thus presents a unity. We have uncovered this unity in the recapitulations of themes (marriage, adultery), in the imbrication of the two plots, but also in the foundations of the action: law (cf. p. 180), chance, the play of feelings. In short, the plot explodes, but in an organized fashion. Finally, the key word of the whole is: dynamism and movement, since the action never stops ricocheting [. . .]." Pomeau, *Beaumarchais* 155, gives up, saying frankly, "The plot is not very well constructed."

12. Ubersfeld, "Un Balcon sur la terreur," is a fine account of fragmentation in the play. For Conesa, the discontinuities are a "ludic" element that reflect a deficiency in "emotional unity" (*La Trilogie de Beaumarchais* 144). That the ludic can be expressive—a portrait of psychic regressions, powerfully intuited—is the burden of Rex's little gem, "*Figaro*'s Games."

13. My discussion of genre develops further the argument of Rougemont, "Beaumarchais dramaturge: Le Substrat romanesque du drame." Conesa, who recognizes more clearly than Scherer does how Beaumarchais departs from Molière's principles of unity and continuity and who repeatedly denigrates Beaumarchais for it and for his lack of psychological depths, finally sees him as moving in the direction of Brecht's epic theater (*La Trilogie de Beaumarchais* 172). Though a primitive and often crude analysis, it cannot prevent itself—because it lacks Scherer's command—from stumbling into some truths or, as in this case, half-truths.

14. Sheridan was moving at the same time in the direction of an omniscient audience; see Auburn, *Sheridan's Comedies* 58–59.

15. Depending on the production, there may be a moment of confusion for the audience when Chérubin appears in disguise in 4.4, but the disguise is lifted almost immediately. The grand mystery, on the other hand, is not really one, for the Preface to *Le Barbier de Séville* had already related the secret of Figaro's parentage.

16. Beaumarchais's pragmatist skittishness about values explains how good essays can have been written in support of such divergent theses as that the play is revolutionary (Ubersfeld, "Un Balcon sur la terreur"), not revolutionary but twitting of the upper classes within accepted bounds (Stachelberg, "Figaros Hochzeit"), and concerned with eternal problems, not class-determined ones (Undank, "Beaumarchais' Transformations" 856–63).

17. On the increasing emphasis on and rising status of acting in the eighteenth century see Goodden, *"Actio" and Persuasion*. The paradoxes I have been describing are implicit in Goodden's profusion of information about the theory of acting in relation to oratory, dance, and popular pantomime, as well as to expressive painting. Dramaturgy as such, however, is not discussed, and the book consequently misses what I take to be the crucial role of Beaumarchais (who is barely mentioned).

18. Interesting essays on particular objects in the play include Mi-

chaud, *L'Oeuvre et ses techniques* 245–59; Adam, *Linguistique et discours littéraire* 23–27; Mervaud, "Le 'Ruban de nuit'"; and, best of all, Bérubé, "A la recherche de la malade dans le *Mariage*." On materialism in Beaumarchais there are evocative essays by Fenaux ("Les Noces") and by Jean-Pierre de Beaumarchais ("Oeil pour oeil").

19. Figaro signs "Figaro," with no family name, and designates his condition as "gentleman," in accordance with his imagined family romance. Marceline signs "Barbe-Azar-Raab-Magdelaine-Nicole-Marceline de Verte-Allure," which seems to cover the territory pretty well. But her designation, "spinster" [*fille majeure*], obfuscates precisely the crucial point.

20. Conesa, *La Trilogie de Beaumarchais* 160, 164. It has recently been argued, with some plausibility, that even Kant's writing is the product not of ideas, but of a language-machine fueled by the body of words: see the conclusion of de Man, "Phenomenality and Materiality in Kant."

21. The original classical urbanity is treated in Ramage, *Urbanitas*, without, however, acknowledging what seems to me its distinctive feature, the waggish association of *comis et urbanus* (as in Horace, *Epistles* 1.4.90 and 1.10.65).

Chapter Eleven

1. For a suggestive discussion of "monstrosity" in *Tristram Shandy* that goes beyond the usual commonplaces about the novel's uniqueness see Flores, *Rhetoric* 116–44. On the general issue see Sperber, "Pourquoi."

2. Uncle Toby is one of the heroes of Tave's broadly normalizing *Amiable Humorist*. And see, in a similar spirit, the discussions of Sterne by Welsh in *Reflections on the Hero as Quixote*, where the prevailing spirit, as the title of the first chapter has it, is "Foolishness, Not Satire." (Consult Welsh's index for page references, but 13–35 should read 13–15.) To be sure, studies of Sterne's innovations must also be aware of the ways he follows tradition or convention. See, in particular, Park's fine essay on the contemporaneity of Sterne's work, "'Tristram Shandy' and the New 'Novel of Sensibility.'" After good comparisons and contrasts of Sterne with Rabelais, Cervantes, and Swift (20–46), Byrd's *Tristram Shandy* contains many shrewd observations tending to link Sterne's themes, motifs, and forms with writings of his contemporaries.

3. The most persuasive historical perspective is that of Reed, who argues in *An Exemplary History of the Novel* (137–61) for a tradition of uniqueness in which *Tristram Shandy* plays a crucial role. Alter's provocative discussion in *Partial Magic* (30–56) reads the novel in the light of negative categories that remain dialectically beholden to the traditions they would resist, making it an antihistory rather than a new and better one. Excellent on Sterne and Diderot is Warning, *Illusion und Wirklichkeit*; on Sterne and Goethe see Jane K. Brown, *Goethe's Cyclical Narratives* 119–20.

4. Sterne, *Sentimental Journey* 132: "Just heaven! for what wise reasons hast thou order'd it, that beggary and urbanity, which are at such vari-

ance in other counties, should find a way to be at unity in this?" *Tristram Shandy* 7.17; p. 599: "Ha!—and no one gives the wall! —but in the SCHOOL of URBANITY herself, if the walls are besh-t —how can you do otherwise?" *Sentimental Journey* 230: "do you find all the urbanity in the French which the world give us the honour of? . . . To an excess, replied I."

5. Noting that Tristram begins by saying that he will trace his story— not merely retrace it (1.4)—and that nevertheless almost all interpreters confuse the narrator who is creating his world "ab Ovo" with the real Sterne, Chahut's lively though abruptly concluded deconstructive reading ("*Tristram Shandy*, ou l'histoire de l'écriture") says aptly that "we pass thus, with *Tristram Shandy*, from a realism of history to the (very coherent) realism of narration" (402). Farrell, "Nature Versus Art," describes the destructive impact of "fidelity to subject matter (assumed or genuine)" (373), though he stops short of analyzing (as I undertake below) the "skill and timing" of Sterne's "crumpled structure" (372–73).

6. New, *Laurence Sterne as Satirist*, argues that Sterne is a rational satirist in the line of Swift and other Anglican divines, and not a sentimental emotionalist in the tradition that branched off from Shaftesbury (see esp. chap. 2). In my view, both the sermons and the novels attempt a passage or bridge between the two camps. My argument, however, depends on New's insight that Sterne's roots lie in a rational faith. It should also be stressed that Sterne remains a psychologist in the eighteenth-century sense, directed towards an understanding and right use of the emotions and other faculties of the soul, and not toward a full development of emotional potential or an indulgence in the life of feelings.

7. I am, of course, not arguing that philosophy is irrelevant to the novel, as Maskill does in "Locke and Sterne, or Can Philosophy Influence Literature?" On the contrary, the philosophy is the novel's central problem and its point of departure.

8. Lanham, "*Tristram Shandy*"; Rothstein, *Systems* 62–108; Burckhardt, "*Tristram Shandy*'s Law of Gravity." There are additional good observations concerning Tristram's belatedness in the chapter "Gravity's Inheritable Line," in Seidel, *Satiric Inheritance*. Also of note, and almost completely ignored by English-language scholarship, is Lukács's brilliant dialogue of 1911, "Reichtum, Chaos und Form: Ein Zwiegespräch über Laurence Sterne." Lukács's male disputants give, respectively, extreme enlightenment and romantic accounts of the novel, thus highlighting the historical tensions within it, while the woman's one intervention defines the resolution as "infinite melody" (206). At the end the woman kisses the "romantic" man; this Schlegelian conclusion seems to be Lukács's one error— unless it is an intentionally ironic presentation of the "male" misreading of the novel.

9. Harries, "Sterne's Novels: Gathering Up the Fragments"; Homer Obed Brown, "Tristram to the Hebrews." Similar in spirit is Weinstein, *Fictions of the Self* 214–32.

10. See John Preston, *The Created Self* 133–95. Also relevant is Kavanagh, "*Jacques le fataliste.*"

11. Briggs, "Locke's *Essay* and the Tentativeness of *Tristram Shandy*," says, "A well-formed work does not offer 'conclusions' but coherent *options* for interpretation" (518). His ending point is my starting point.

12. See also sermon 45 (2: 379): suppose a believer were told "that it was idle to bring in the Deity to untie the knot, when it can be resolved easily into natural causes.— Vain unthinking mortals!—As if natural causes were anything else in the hands of GOD,—but instruments which he can turn to work the purposes of his will."

13. In "Narrative Middles" Miller sketches a deconstructive reading of the way Sterne's curves undermine his lines. One can redress the balance by deconstructing Miller's tacit and linear assumption that the lines come first. Not always so in Shandy circles. The lines are well discussed in the first section ("Does *Tristram Shandy* Have a Beginning?") of Iser's *Laurence Sterne* (1–10).

14. Cf. Mayoux, "Variations on the Time-Sense in *Tristram Shandy.*"

15. Rosenblum, "The Sermon," is a good discussion of interruption as cognition and hence as world-making in Sterne. Schulze, "Do You Know the Meaning of * * * * *?" inventories Sterne's asterisks to demonstrate that we know what they stand for (except when we aren't supposed to), and concludes (428) that they are not (I translate literally) "products of a mentally uncontrolled manner of association," but instead manifest "a creativity of high intelligence and of a decided sense of order," producing a "to this very day never exceeded stringency of 'true-to-life' presentation of scenes achieved by marked ellipses."

16. Stevick, *The Chapter in Fiction*, provides a context for the present discussion.

17. Toby echoes Tristram when he later says that the reader of a merry story should bring "one half of the entertainment along with him" (8.16; p. 682).

18. Drawing on medieval and modern examples, Agamben discusses the horse as a topos for poetry and stopping as the progenitor of thought in the chapter "Idea della cesura" of his book *Idea della prosa* (25–26). One locus he does not mention that is relevant to my subsequent discussion is Boccaccio's story of madonna Oretta in the *Decameron* (6.1).

19. An important line of Sterne criticism, culminating in Swearingen's *Reflexivity*, has explored this dimension of the book—in which the materiality of both events and emotions recovers significance only in relation to the inescapable realities of lack and of death as the ultimate condition of life.

20. On the mind-body equation, in addition to Burckhardt's essay, see Peterfreund, "Sterne" (which says that the clarification must come as a cock-and-bull story, but then locates the accomplishment in Herder and the romantic spiral, rather than in Sterne's own novel); McGilchrist, *Against Criticism* 140–42; Berthoud, "Shandeism and Sexuality."

21. In *Confinement and Flight* 53–59 and 119–27, Carnochan writes eloquently about isolation and solitude, circles and lines, and the psychology of conception. Focusing on the characters, he projects a bleak view of the novel. The discussion of narrative organization in the following passages is offered as a corrective.

22. Rolle, *Fielding und Sterne*, itemizes similarities and differences between the authors, but unfortunately only in the narrators, not in the story forms. Other aspects of the relationship of *Tristram Shandy* to *Tom Jones* (and also to Smollett) are well presented by Borinski in *Der englische Roman des 18. Jahrhunderts* 251–52. The remainder of Borinski's chapter (249–69) is a remarkable attack on Sterne's immorality, enough to make a Leavisite blush.

23. My generalization in this paragraph derives from Lanham's finely observed hint that the chestnut incident is told sequentially: *"Tristram Shandy"* 106. See also good comments about vol. 7 and about the tale of the king of Bohemia in Holtz, *Image and Immortality* 130–34, 142–43.

24. Booth, "Did Sterne Complete *Tristram Shandy*?" Other good discussions of the end of the novel are Swearingen, *Reflexivity* 203–10 (on coalescence), and Loveridge, "Liberty" (on the emergence of authentic feelings).

25. Deleuze, *Proust and Signs* 144. Deleuze traces the problem here resolved to Leibniz, so there is no anachronism in borrowing his formulation.

26. On the tripartite organization of *Rasselas* see Emrys Jones, "The Artistic Form of *Rasselas*," which contains a good comparison of Johnson and Sterne on 392–96.

27. Wasserman, "Johnson's *Rasselas*" 22–25; see also 17–18 on the Johnson-Fielding analogy.

28. Wimsatt, "In Praise of *Rasselas*" 143, points out that the characters were never said to have left home. He sees this as a structural weakness, but it can also be considered another fragmentary image of wholeness, namely, an ending without its antecedent story, and hence, in Johnson's phrase, a conclusion in which nothing is concluded.

29. In one passage in Sterne's first volume Walter Shandy actually sounds like a parodic literalization of the narrator of *Rasselas*, as he inveighs against the "stoppage of circulation"—individual and social death—that results from an influx to the cities. He prefers an eternal pastoral spring ("I should provide, That the meadows and corn-fields, of my dominions, should laugh and sing") in a patriarchal monarchy like those "in the eastern parts of the world" (1.18; pp. 53–55).

30. See the suggestive discussion of Sterne's competition with the painters in Holtz, *Image and Immortality* 21–38.

31. Battestin, *The Providence of Wit* 263. As the remainder of my analysis shows, however, I do not think that the techniques finally worked out by Sterne are "crude," as Battestin here says.

32. Warning, in *Illusion und Wirklichkeit* 15–66, gives an excellent account of the novel as an aesthetic construct. He sees art as play, but too casually acknowledges its difference from Schiller's "fulfilled infinity"

(46–47); in my view, limitation, negation, and sentimental nostalgia are essential aspects of the aesthetic in its origins here and in Goldsmith.

33. My recourse to models in the *Decameron* for the cock-and-bull story and for the story of the Abbess of Andoüillets is hypothetical. The only possible allusion to Boccaccio that I can discern in *Tristram Shandy* is the division of Slawkenbergius's tales (which were, to be sure, Walter's favorite reading) into "ten decads, each decad containing ten tales" (3.42; p. 286). Two Italian copies of the *Decameron* are listed in Whibley's *Catalogue of Laurence Sterne's Library*, items 2198 and 2199, but no conclusions can be drawn from this because most of the books listed actually derive from other collections than Sterne's.

34. In connection with the following discussion, cf. Getto, *Vita di forme* 20–33.

35. One might pursue a suggestive network of structural affinities between *Tristram Shandy* and the *Decameron*. The introduction to the fourth volume of *Tristram Shandy* is "Slawkenbergius's Tale," which also concerns the progress of an unknown youth through town and the consequent arousal of desire, though in the women who watch him and not, as Boccaccio has it, in the youth. The Ninth Day of the *Decameron* ends with the last of Dioneo's series of obscene stories, which, like Sterne's cock-and-bull tale, concerns bestial love and the dubious maintenance of conjugal fidelity. Boccaccio's Tenth Day consists of serious moral tales, and at the end Dioneo atones for his transgressions with the story of Griselda's abject submission to her husband. Not surprisingly the women of the company like Dioneo's ninth story much better than his tenth. By apocopating the tenth volume and delivering an incomplete final installment, Sterne thus confirms the general movement of his book toward the feminine, in contrast to the *Decameron*. On the "feminization of discourse" in the eighteenth century see Eagleton, *The Rape of Clarissa*.

36. Cf. Boccaccio's introduction to the Filippo Balducci story: "I wish in my favor to relate not a complete story, lest I appear to desire to mingle my stories with those of so praiseworthy a company, as I have demonstrated that one to be; but part of one, in order that its very defect show itself not to be one of those" (*Opere* 256). The cock-and-bull story is "one of the best *of its kind*": it is a good instance not of stories in general, but of stories about stories.

37. Rothstein (*Systems of Order and Inquiry* 84) and New ("At the Backside" 19–20) point out that the abbess's "white swelling" (7.21; p. 609) is a pregnancy.

38. After the story Tristram indicates its function as follows: "What a tract of country have I run!—how many degrees nearer to the warm sun am I advanced, and how many fair and goodly cities have I seen, during the time you have been reading, and reflecting, Madam, upon this story!" (7.26; p. 615). The interpolated tale is a virtuoso distraction that forms part of the feminization of discourse. Rosen, *The Classical Style* 71, contains a suggestive paragraph on the role of filler in formal structures of the time. The

new technique became a mainstay of the realist novel, most famously in Balzac, who fills brief pauses in the action with luxuriant description. The more germane the filler becomes, the less usefully it can provide articulated long-range dramatic contrast. Good on the eventual recuperation of description as part of the action is Price, "The Irrelevant Detail," and, on the musical side (the reconciliation of virtuoso display with symphonic progress), Dahlhaus, *Die Musik des 19. Jahrhunderts* 110–17.

39. My account of Sterne's noises and their relation to obscure beginnings and endings is inspired by Michel Serres's analysis of scandal and of *noise* (an archaic French word), chiefly in Beaumarchais, Balzac, and Hugo; see his *Genèse*.

40. Freedman, *Sterne and the Origins of the Musical Novel*. The topic is better than the treatment, which fails to recognize that Sterne travesties musical form just as he does philosophical argument and narrative genre.

41. "My uncle Toby gave a long whistle—but in a note which could scarce be heard across the table." Sterne's reminder of entropy comes two sentences later: "My uncle *Toby* laid down his pipe as gently upon the fender, as if it had been spun from the unravellings of a spider's web" (9.31; p. 803). In 3.11 (pp. 211 and 212), in another medieval context, though not one related to Boccaccio (Ernulphus's curse), Toby's whistle is rendered "Whew—w—w" and "Whu—u—u."

42. On the role of compromise in Boccaccio see my essay "In the Valley of the Ladies." Sterne's commentators point out the derivation of the name Andoüillets from Rabelais's *Quart livre*, chaps. 35–42. In this typical episode Rabelais contrasts two chaoses, the protean chaos of matter, as in the boundless proliferation of sausage types (or, presumably, of virtually indistinguishable religious sects), and a martian chaos of ideas, the inevitable clash of arbitrarily consolidated opposing armies (or, presumably, of Catholicism and Protestantism). Stability is found in the (gigantic) human organism, though only a relative stability in any episode, and not without its cost, such as the needless death of countless sausages for lack of mustard. Rabelais's story thus also provides a foil for understanding Sterne's. But Boccaccio's is much closer thematically, and his world of well-defined forces offers a more plausible object for Sterne's yearning.

43. See Iser's fine account of play-functions in the last chapter of his book (*Laurence Sterne* 91–119); the account concludes that "subjectivity is performative, for it emerges as a continual self-fashioning" in which "the impossibility of failure . . . is accompanied by the equal impossibility of success" (114–15).

44. Fielding's narrative temporality is finely analyzed in Braudy, *Narrative Form* 91–212. For more general contexts see Meinecke, *Historism*.

45. Fluchère, *Laurence Sterne* 318–31. Fluchère quotes (329) the relevant passage from an important fragment attributed to Sterne and generally known as "The Dream, to Mr. Cook": "I can conceive not only an Iliad, but a kind of universe included within ye sphere of a nutshell; as great a number and variety of beings, events as numerous and varying, nay as great and im-

portant within ye space of a *natural day*, as fall within ye reach of sense in the whole solar system, during ye revolution of the great *platonic* year." Fluchère's discussion, however, concerns *la durée* (Bergsonian "lived time") in contrast to clock time, rather than *les durées*. Mayoux likewise suppresses the novel's complexity in favor of an oversimplified binary scheme when he writes, "Whatever the ingenious and proliferating detail of the forms of time in Sterne, one can say that time has two opposite aspects, reversible and irreversible" ("Laurence Sterne" 122).

46. The subtle and closely reasoned argument of New's *Laurence Sterne as Satirist* presents *Tristram Shandy* as a satiric portrait of sentimentality, with the sentimentalist Tristram growing ever more incoherent in the later volumes. Despite New's acknowledgments of the multiplicity of satiric personae, his reading is increasingly predicated on a rational coherence of character and on the homogeneity of temporal experience: "Time and the world proceed in orderly fashion; the confusion and chaos of *Tristram Shandy* come from the mind of its putative author" (123). While remaining greatly indebted to New's shrewd discussion of polarization and chaos in numerous passages in the novel, I have reread many of them as part of Sterne's articulation of a breakthrough to the energized and multilayered temporality exemplified by the cock-and-bull story, which New does not treat. For general considerations, see the last chapter of Lévi-Strauss, *The Savage Mind* 245–69.

47. Loveridge, in *Laurence Sterne and the Argument About Design*, argues that the fear, rather than truly Tristram's, really "is Walter's gloom" and that in the opening chapters "Tristram is borrowing not just Walter's tone of voice, but his entire outlook on life" (41). In general, Loveridge's readings are predicated on a confidence I do not share that the psychological essence of character can be disengaged from rhetorical inconsistencies; he argues that the inconsistencies arise externally and reflect a "plot against Tristram-as-foetus" (165). I find him more generally persuasive on *Sentimental Journey* (167–209); in this section he identifies rhetoric and character: Yorick is defined as a misreader of his own life.

48. Macksey begins his "Alas Poor Yorick"—which is nominally Lacanian, but really contains suggestive Derridean ruminations—by claiming to be the first to have commented in print on the discrepancy concerning Tristram's gestation. Hay, who reports that it was first noted in print in 1895, carefully marshals the evidence in "Rhetoric and Historiography" and concludes that Tristram was premature, which would have comforted him. New, *Laurence Sterne as Satirist* 86, notes the aberration without dwelling on it. But Stedmond, in *The Comic Art of Laurence Sterne* 7, says that Sterne parodies the ab-ovo convention "by pushing it nine months back to the very time of conception."

49. Walter Shandy says early on, without Tristram's equivocation, "*My Tristram's misfortunes began nine months before ever he came into the world,*" and the impotent Toby "understood him very well" (1.3; p. 4). Walter also says in the same chapter, "That I should neither think nor act like any other man's child" (ibid.). But he can draw little reassurance from that,

for he might have read in one of his favorite obstetrical treatises that "though a woman [lie] in unlawful copulation, yet if she fix her mind upon her husband, the child will resemble him, though he never got it," *Aristotle's Master Piece Completed* 16. (See Porter's informative essay "The Secrets of Generation Display'd" on the variant texts of this popular treatise and on its ideology.) And John Burton (Dr. Slop) would have further unsettled him with the discussion of uncertain paternity in his *Essay* 84.

50. I have not been able to confirm the existence of a folk belief that full-term babies are hairy, on which this inquiry appears to be based. Some corroboration appears in the fact that the babies illustrated in Burton's numerous plates have hair, often a lot of it. Parish writes about the hair in "The Shandy Bull Vindicated"; he argues that since the cow hasn't given birth and the bull hasn't lost face, the bull must have sired another offspring, namely, Obadiah's child. To this the notes in the News' edition of *Tristram Shandy* object that lanugo appears on premature babies, so that hair wouldn't necessarily indicate maturity. Is there an expert in eighteenth-century midwifery who can adjudicate the quarrel?

51. The best discussion of male impotence (and female gusto) in the novel is that of Spacks, *Imagining a Self* 129–34. See also Towers, "Sterne's Cock and Bull Story," and Hagstrum, *Sex and Sensibility* 254–59. On cuckoldry see the important discussion by Sedgwick, *Between Men* 67–82.

52. Moss discusses the black and marbled pages as noise in "Sterne's Punctuation" 191–94; Moss's whole, fine discussion of Sterne's "stops" is germane to my account of his ends.

53. Poovey, *Proper Lady* 15–30. Warren, "The Constant Speaker," says that Sterne's women "cannot be reached by conversation because they demand the concrete thing itself or nothing at all rather than the words that partly reveal and partly hide" (57) and that "Mrs. Shandy doesn't need words" (63). Why then does he use the masculines when he writes as follows? "The man who is above conversation is a kind of hero; he is beyond our capabilities. But like most heroes he is doomed by the act that makes him heroic" (58). Surely his syllogism leads straight to hero*ines*. And why does Uhlig mention only enfeebled masculine examples (Trim's reaction to Bobby's death, Toby's to the fly and to Le Fever) when he writes "that in a work like the one under discussion which takes a skeptical posture toward the possibility of 'true philosophy,' . . . wordless action and plain feeling constitute the actual center" ("Wissen und Meinen" 396)? And why does Mullan neglect the societies of the kitchen and the birthing room when he writes, "Fellow-feeling is largely a male prerogative in this novel" (*Sentiment and Sociability* 170)?

54. Sterne's irony is evident when the Sorbonne disputation of 1.20 ironically exalts the reasoning powers of male readers over the enthusiasm of female readers at the very moment when the women are hastening to aid Mrs. Shandy in her labor. For a contrasting reading of the sex roles see the discussion of "remasculinization" in Kay, *Political Constructions* 204–46. Kay demonstrates Sterne's attachment to military themes, especially in her

fine discussion of the Le Fever episode, where "a sequence of male nurses and comforters replaces the traditional female figures" (233). She also persuasively links the frequent exclusion of women to historical and biographical contexts, but she omits or slights the instances of female strength I have highlighted, especially toward the end of the novel. The prevalence of sentimental virtues like "civilized polish and tender feeling" and "solidarity in tenderness" (232, 235) can be considered a feminization of the men as readily as a masculinization of the virtues. (This is also the opinion of Armstrong, *Desire and Domestic Fiction* 4.) Kay trusts the narrator and the author who lies behind him; my argument is that the book has a tendency that transvalues such explicit intentions. The biographical record concerning Sterne's relations with women is in any case too incomplete and ambiguous to be used for guidance.

55. The most interesting start on a psychocritical reading of *Tristram Shandy* is Weber's critique of Lanham, "The Critics' Choice," which draws on Freud's book on jokes to point to the defensiveness that may lurk within the ludic elements of the novel. The focus is on the chestnut episode.

56. In *The Philosophical Irony of Laurence Sterne*, Moglen discusses *Tristram Shandy* as a portrait of failures, "Sisyphus' absurd world" dignified by the "noble persistence of its small heroes" (128), "a silly and perverse work" that ends with a story of "failure," "thematic confusion," and "lack of understanding" (143). She fails to see that, to be successful, a mimetic representation of failure must redefine what is meant by success and failure, and that only a very old-fashioned modernism could be conveyed by the coherent characters, thematic unity, and well-rounded formal closure that she takes as her standards of success.

57. On the novel's gestures at documentation see Zimmerman, "*Tristram Shandy* and Narrative Representation."

58. Nuttall's discussion (*A Common Sky* 45–91) sensibly aligns Sterne with Lockean rationalism to the extent that a satiric perspective presupposes the norms it attacks. The book, he says, is "not a stream of consciousness" but a "stream of ratiocination" (60). Still, to imply an ideal that is never projected even in imagination—think how absurd it would be to award Mrs. Shandy an exemplary role comparable to that of Pope's mother—is to have a crisis or even a revolution lurking in the shadows. Nuttall calls Sterne's tough nut "a sort of embryonic Wittgenstein inside Sterne" (87); it does not seem to me that situational pragmatics (Nuttall's formula for Wittgenstein) responds to the novel's particular problem of conception and temporal ordering.

59. Burney, *Evelina*, letter 73, p. 313. For sincerity as a theme in Sterne see Lamb, "The Comic Sublime."

60. For plentiful information on the topos, without a clear synthesis, see Havens, "Simplicity." Davie compares Cowper's ideal of simplicity with Wordsworth's in "The Critical Principles of William Cowper." On the concept of simplicity in and around Wordsworth see Jordan's excellent presenta-

tion, *Why the "Lyrical Ballads"?* 84–102. Valuable critical discussions of romantic simplicity may also be found in McGann, *"Don Juan"* 68–99, and in the Pushkin chapter of Cook, *Thresholds* 125–38.

Chapter Twelve

1. The verb is "shone in" (metrically an iambic unit), and the subject is "the early light." There is, however, a natural tendency to read this line, like the preceding one, with a trochee at the beginning. "In" then becomes a preposition (like "with," just above it), making "light" its object and depriving "shone" of a subject. I have discussed Bowles's final text, which supposedly reconstitutes the original state of the poem. The first printing (1789) has "Stream'd the blue light" (clearer grammar, but a puzzling image), omits "As," and has "Would wish to linger" in line 13 (but already has the negative in line 14).

2. Wind-reclined is, of course, one of the imperfect rhymes; see *OED*, s.v. "wind." Again I have discussed the final version. The first 1789 printing, entitled "To the River Wenbeck," lacks many of the features I discuss, but most appear in the second 1789 printing, "To the River Wensbeck." This version differs from the late text most significantly in lacking the word "recreated," but the important associations mostly are captured in its line 13, "His heart some long-lost image would renew."

3. Levinson finely describes the pathos of hope in *Wordsworth's Great Period Poems* 116–17: "'Not without hope . . .'—is, to my mind, ["Peele Castle"'s] worst despair, the measure of its hopelessness. The line explicitly installs the old Immanence—the original cleavage and desired reunion of 'the world' and 'the heart's desire.' Hope is always *of*, *for* something outside, other, unowned. To gain that otherness is, of course, to lose it. Hope always constitutes means and ends, and creates the alternating subservience of one to the other. Hope will always create 'from its own wreck the thing it contemplates.' There is no arresting its constructive annihilations." Only the "always" is dubious in this dialectical analysis, in view of the possibilities of a transcendental hope imagined by Marcel ("Sketch"), as also, differently, by Ernst Bloch. Levinson retraces the transcendence as she moves through the "lapidary quality" (128) of "Peele Castle" to the late poems, where she acknowledges—by allusion to "Hart-Leap Well," line 176, but with even greater relevance to *The Excursion*—that "this ultimate 'overgrowing' or erasure should be read not as a negation but as the conscious *product* of that act, an affirmation" (134, her emphasis).

4. Marcel, "Sketch of a Phenomenology and a Metaphysic of Hope."

5. For a related interpretation of Wordsworth, though with different philosophical underpinnings, see Bialostosky, *Making Tales*.

6. On this kind of internal rhyme, chiefly in moderns but also in romantics, see numerous fine analyses in Wesling, *The Chances of Rhyme*.

7. Steveson's "Wordsworth and the Stone of Night" discusses the stone as archetype; Davis's "Stone as Metaphor" evokes the covenantal associations of stones in Wordsworth and the sculptor Henry Moore.

8. On the political resonances of Wordsworth's poetry see the brilliant work of Alan Liu, *Wordsworth* 23–31 (on the apostrophe to imagination in the crossing of the Alps passage), 190–201 (on political allegory in *Salisbury Plain*), and 426–49 (on "Wordsworth's unremitting song of warfare" [445] in the political sonnets of 1802–4 and the late sections of *The Prelude*). Whether "the first and last word still belong [sic] to history" (449)—whether (as Levinson says in *Wordsworth's Great Period Poems* 125, with acknowledgment to Liu) "the first term . . . is, in fact, neither Mind nor Nature, but History"—is not an issue on which the last word will ever be spoken. It is, indeed, a historicist presumption that there are first or last words, as is the other presumption that "history" means political and social history in opposition to history of mind. It is worth balancing what Liu says against the conclusions of another student of Wordsworth's politics: "Wordsworth despaired of . . . all political answers"; "the theorists of the Revolution in France give no answer to his problem"; he is "a poet" as "distinguishe[d] . . . from a political theorist"; in his late verse "the excellent and the political did not coincide"—so we read at various points in Woodring's *Politics in English Romantic Poetry* (89, 93, 122, 144), always in specific contexts from which I have torn the quotes, but to clear cumulative effect. For arguments that a general time-consciousness subtends specific historical and political developments see further Koselleck's theory of historiography (*Futures Past*) and also Fry's critique of the "fallacy of misplaced concreteness" ("History" 217).

9. On Matthew's craziness, see "Matthew," line 22 ("one tired out with . . . madness"), "The Fountain," lines 69–72 ("And, ere we came to Leonard's rock, / He sang those witty rhymes / About the crazy old church-clock, / And the bewildered chimes"), and perhaps a pun on "wilding" in "The Two April Mornings," line 60.

10. These motifs are strewn throughout the *Rêveries*, particularly the First, Fifth (which is echoed in *The Prelude*), Seventh, and Eighth. With respect to the last motif and the proximity of Wordsworth's "conversing" to "communing," cf., in the First Reverie, the sentence "Despite mankind I shall still know how to enjoy the charm of society, and I shall live enfeebled with myself in another age, as I should live with a less old friend," *Oeuvres* 1: 1001.

11. Though unsystematic, Danby's *Simple Wordsworth* often illuminates the wordless feelings that energize Wordsworth's poetry, producing an active ("wise") passiveness (89–127, the chapter "Wordsworth and 'Nature'") that is fulfilled in the unifying accomplishments of the later poetry (128–45, on *The White Doe of Rylestone*).

12. *The Vale of Esthwaite*, lines 25–26: "At noon I hied to gloomy glades, / Religious woods and midnight shades"; "Il Penseroso," lines 131–

34: "And when the Sun begins to fling / His flaring beams, me Goddes bring / To arched walks of twilight groves, / And shadows brown."

13. See Averill's nice discussion (*Wordsworth* 45–51) of the way that "feeling in search of an object" (46) in *The Vale of Esthwaite* leads through objectless feeling toward either feeling as harmony with nature or self-pity.

14. There is a fine appreciation of affinities between Gray and Wordsworth in Kenneth Maclean, "The Distant Way" 143–45.

15. Pottle captures the thrust beautifully in an essay originally published in 1941 and still worth reading: "Wordsworth at times feels an urgency in the objects of nature that goes far beyond anything demanded by the impulse to autobiography, an urgency that the conventional reflective framework of descriptive poetry will not provide sanctions for. He cannot yet define that urgency to himself," though the 1794 revisions show him "trying to get at the deeper thought that underlies his images" in the effort "to moralize his song" ("Emergent Idiom" 131–32). "The moment he had" his religion of nature, Pottle continues eloquently, "everything was clear. He had his subject matter and he had his idiom . . . , a style capable of informing many verse forms with a new meaning and power. It came to him as a muscular skill comes after long and painful practice, not gradually, but all at once" (133). In *Wordsworth's Revisionary Aesthetics* Kelley reads Wordsworth's development in the other direction, as a sustained effort to use the beautiful in order to contain the sublime. The book merits more detailed consideration than I can give it in a note. Basically, I believe that for Wordsworth containing the sublime means also finding a way to capture and communicate meanings—filling out the sublime, rather than dismissing it. Otherwise the "longing for the beautiful as a refuge from the sublime" (61, on "Tintern Abbey") would risk leaving behind the emotion that is supposed to be recollected in tranquility. Kelley's conclusion seems to swing around to Pottle's (and my) view, at least with regard to one text, the 1815 Preface: "This preoccupation with 'the business of poetry,' its representational task, is beauty's contribution to Wordsworth's poetics. Elsewhere it suppresses the sublime; here it authorizes the poet's regard for figures that convey sublime ideas" (205). To see what a poetry would look like that truly needs to suppress the sublime, look at the sonnets from *Paul and Virginia*, by Wordsworth's earliest poetic model, Helen Maria Williams. Here is a relevant sestet: "Let me, where yon tall cliffs are rudely pil'd, / Where towers the palm amidst the mountain trees, / Where pendent from the steep, with graces wild, / The blue liana floats upon the breeze, / Still haunt those bold recesses, nature's child, / Where thy majestic charms my spirit seize!" Who would guess, reading this outburst of studied majesty, that the octave is framed by the apostrophe "Nymph of the desert! . . . / Ah, not for me your studied grandeur pour," let alone that the addressee is "Simplicity" ("To Simplicity," in *Poems, Moral, Elegant and Pathetic*)?

16. An isolated line (96) tells of a single bright daytime sound, that of the "desert [1836 text: restless] stone-chat." I take this counterpointed im-

age, appearing in close proximity to mention of stones covered with gray lichen (lines 93–94) to be a remarkable, if inchoate, foreshadowing of the mature Wordsworthian colloquy, his—as one might say—stone chat.

17. Ramsey, "Seeing and Perceiving," contrasts the pantheist sensibility of the 1794 lines to the manifold disjunctions of the earlier text (isolated scenes, subject against object, laboring humans dwarfed by sublime nature).

18. See Empson's chapter "'Sense' in *The Prelude*," 289–305 in his *Structure*.

19. Presumably Wordsworth is thinking here of Thomson's line "And where the mixing Passions endless shift" ("Autumn," line 1364). For Wordsworth the passions are one dimension of the cosmic spectacle; for Thomson they belong to the dark sensual realm that needs clarification by the light of the mind.

20. An adequate reckoning with Liu's magnificent *Wordsworth*—just published as I revise my notes—will take years. Let me focus a tentative account of differences in approach on the conclusion to *An Evening Walk*, omitting many qualifications that would necessarily complicate a fuller critique. Picturesque, according to the remarkable analysis in Liu's chapter on the poem (61–137) is "edgy," uncannily arrested narrative. More generally, form for him is stasis ("the sense of arrest in experience," 65), and differences are resolved into the ultimately static oppositions of structuralism: "Nonidentity is the basic thought of literature," but only in the guise of "reversal and discovery . . . akin to syllogistic sorites" (49). Hence Liu takes the disturbances of repose at the end of *An Evening Walk* to signal "a kind of panic" (131). And, more generally, "beginning and end, white and black, life and death: these are antagonistic binaries sketching the basic structure or synchronic design of narrative. The structure . . . is *agony*, or agonic conflict" (132, Liu's emphasis). Liu misrepresents the spectrum of this poem, as Hartman does that of *The Vale of Esthwaite*: while Wordsworth's palette does include black and white, the poem's valedictory colors are "dark-blue," "silvery," and "azure" (lines 427–28). Liu's textual deformation is not intrinsically serious, but it signals a sensibility whose inclinations are visually schematic (note the self-conscious "sketching" and "design" in the above quotation) rather than aural, that seeks to pinpoint connotations, and that is more alert to patterned contrasts than to developing resonances. More fundamentally, in this immensely complex yet fundamentally two-valued world, time is either a "pointillistic instant" (Liu 133) or else all of eternity. In contrast to what I take to be an exceptionally rich sense of varied pace and duration in the closing vignette of *An Evening Walk*, Liu finds "a primitive 'now' incapable of poising itself against either past or future to organize the progress of the day" (132). (Why must organization be poised *against* time? See further my comments below on verbal aspect in "Mark the Concentred Hazels.") That is why, in Liu's brilliant coinages, Pan must become panic, agon agony, and emergence emergency. While Liu can hardly be called insensitive to intertextual echoes, the effect of his immense chap-

ters with their frequent digressive insets is to subordinate a sense for Wordsworth's development to the explication of successive conceptual crises, all embedded in an impenetrably grand master-structure. "The Sense of History" (Liu's subtitle) remains antagonistic to the Wordsworthian subtitle "The Growth of a Poet's Mind." Liu is eloquently aware of his commitment to such an externalization of history as "absent cause" (39). He nails it to the door of his book in the form of four theses—"*There is no time. There is no affection. There is no self or mind. Therefore, there is no Imagination*" (ibid., Liu's emphasis)—and he unfolds it with these antithetical formulas for historical movement: "This 'is' but neither was nor will be" and "This is your place but was/is/shall be another's" (ibid.). The integrity of this ideology ensures a coherence of the grandest generalities with the minutest details. Nevertheless, as my counterreading of the end of *An Evening Walk* is intended to suggest, it remains an ideological "prejudice" (in Gadamer's sense), whose interpretations are by no means inevitable.

21. The 1836 text of this couplet dismisses hope along with ills, but appears to revive hope alone in the very last lines: "Tonight, my Friend, within this humble cot / Be scorn and fear and hope alike forgot / In timely sleep; and when, at break of day, / On the tall peaks the glistening sunbeams play, / With a light heart our course we may renew, / The first whose footsteps print the mountain dew" (lines 665–70).

22. Cf. Goldstein, *Ruins and Empire* 160: "The stone and the shell are frail synecdoches for the mind, which, as Wordsworth states in the preamble to the dream, has no element in nature more permanent to stamp its image on. In a world where everything, including words, is to be changed, all such images of perpetuity will disappear."

23. Ramond, *Observations* 251. See also Rosen, "Now, Voyager." As Rosen writes (60), "Reverie was acknowledged by the early Romantic generation as a way of sensing the slower processes of nature, the movement of long duration."

24. On natural types and emblems see the last chapter ("Wordsworth and the Book of Nature") of Brantley, *Wordsworth's "Natural Methodism"* 139–70.

25. On disjunctions in *The Borderers* see Jewett's "Action."

26. Storch bases his fine reading of the play as an allegory of the mind on the premise that psychic energies are more fundamental to it than political and social doctrine. He calls Oswald "a man of strong feelings" ("Wordsworth's *The Borderers*" 351), a phrase that should resonate with the Stolberg essay that I discuss above in Chapter 5, "The Economy of Sensibility." He finds Wordsworth's recovery of humanism to be mediated by fallen-woman figures in the lyrics of the next few years; I argue below that the recovery is presaged within the play by the figure of Herbert (who, of course, has much of the aura of female helplessness about him).

27. See Richardson's discussion of repetition compulsion in the play, *A Mental Theater* 20–42.

28. But see Whitaker's essay on Herbert's moods, "Reading the Unreadable, Acting the Unactable" (published after this chapter was drafted), based on the experience of acting the part.

29. On *Caleb Williams* and *The Borderers* see Osborn's introduction, *Borderers* 31–33. On gothic stones see my essay "A Philosophical View of the Gothic Novel" 277–79.

30. David Marshall's brief essay, "The Eye-Witnesses of *The Borderers*," nicely establishes the dilemmas of externalization in the play, but, while treating Herbert only in passing as an object, neglects the insight that he figures forth.

31. For scientific contexts for the remainder of this chapter see Bewell, *Wordsworth and the Enlightenment*, chap. 5, "The History of Death" (187–234, on religious anthropology and universal voice), and chap. 6, "'A Power Like One of Nature's': The Geological History of Revolution" (237–79, on stones, the history of the earth, and the life of things).

32. The ablest, least reductive account of the "ironies" and "discontinuities" of the mature Wordsworth (who should really be called the middle Wordsworth) is the section called "Wordsworth's *Prelude* and the Elided Middle" in Handwerk, *Irony and Ethics* 71–81. Handwerk concludes that "the elided middle absent from Wordsworth's poetry is the other, as subject" (81), which is exactly my argument. But he postulates that such a middle would be a "center . . . of human communication" (ibid.), not realizing how alien the grounding other was to be for the later Wordsworth. Many orthodox deconstructive readings of Wordsworth—often highly illuminating in their sharp focus—are attempts to limit the damage by naming a middle term that crystallizes and thus ultimately stabilizes the disjunctions.

33. In his essay on the sonnet "Composed Upon Westminster Bridge" ("The Unremarkable Poet," in his *Unremarkable Wordsworth* 207–19), Hartman has illuminated the relation between composure and composition in Wordsworth. Other key terms in his most recent essays, published in the volume just named, are the quasi-Hegelian "elation" ("Elation in Hegel and Wordsworth," 182–93) and the quasi-Heideggerian "lightening" (in English on 183–84; the German *Lichtung*, or "clearing," appears on 200, in the essay "Wordsworth Before Heidegger"). Yet in all the proof poems, Wordsworth's curve seems not just to begin with earth, as Hartman points out ("The emphasis, in the Westminster Bridge sonnet, should be on its initial word: 'Earth,'" 215), but equally to return to earth in the end, not in celestial brightness, but in the grayness of effacement. The Westminster Bridge sonnet climaxes in the "bright and glittering . . . smokeless air" of line 8, but then redescends through "steep" (the sunlight submerging the earth, like a greater Thames) and "valley, rock, or hill" (still an uncertain direction), to "deep" and "lying." "Composed by the Side of Grasmere Lake," with its "grey west" (line 2), does not feature a "raising up of the deep," as Hartman states (184), but a downward turn ("low-whispering" in line 12); conceivably it even repudiates the sky gods rather than "recall[ing]" them as Hartman says (185), since the quatrain devoted to them (lines 5–8) dwells

on Mars, who not only represents or causes but even rhymes with "wars." Hartman's comments (202–6) on the Intimations Ode likewise point toward the stars he finds glimmering in stanza 8, rather than to the deep earth of its conclusion. Subject for a different study would be the elation and elevation that do indeed conclude *The Prelude*.

34. See Derrida, *De la grammatologie* 38, 90. Earlier, Derrida had used the term "effacement": see *La Voix et le phénomène* 56–66.

35. De Man's essay "Autobiography as De-Facement" (*Rhetoric* 67–82) concerns the impasse of a "speaking stone counterbalancing the seeing sun" (75). It is insufficiently attentive to the possibilities that lie in what he elsewhere, polemically, calls "the barren, impoverished world of human contingency, the world of gray rocks and stones that is the landscape of Wordsworth's *Prelude*" ("Introduction to the Poetry of John Keats," in *Critical Writings* 194).

36. In *Poetic Form* (37) Curran defines the subject of the romantic sonnet as follows: "The sonnet is by nature a ruminative form, one conducive but not limited to introspection, in which the natural world supplies counters, context, balance to the mind. In the largest sense that balance will be achieved through linking or even merging the individual and universal, the ideal and real, conception and perception, mind and matter." This could be a definition of romantic lyric generally. I propose the thought/feeling formula as a refinement that better captures the generic specificity of the sonnet, at least in the major poets.

37. "Nuns Fret Not at Their Convent's Narrow Room," line 11. An early draft of this sonnet speaks of "the day of doom" (*"Poems, in Two Volumes"* 663), and the religious imagery, the reference to souls, and the rhyme sound all suggest thoughts of the tomb.

38. For a deconstructive account of "thought," specifically in the Intimations Ode, see Ferguson, *Wordsworth* 113–25.

39. The bower is, of course, an unbuilt building as well as the haven of unwritten writing. The linkage between Wordsworth's ambivalence toward writing and toward building is well presented in Geraldine Friedman's "Writing in Stone."

40. Jones devotes the last chapter (154–92) of *The Egotistical Sublime* to arguing that the later Wordsworth developed a religious, transcendent, antinatural view of the human mind. Obviously, I do not agree with this as a generalization, nor with the condemnation that follows from it.

41. On ghostly personification in "Yew-Trees" see Hartman, "The Use and Abuse of Structural Analysis," in *The Unremarkable Wordsworth* 129–51.

42. One lesson of deconstruction is that all marks are remarks, all images afterimages, all thoughts afterthoughts. See especially Derrida, "The *Retrait* of Metaphor." To the extent that the belatedness is a fact, it cannot be a judgment, let alone a curse; if nothing is primary, then there is no onus in being secondary. Both "The River Duddon" and the "Ecclesiastical Sonnets" begin with a frustrated search for origins, but Wordsworth is rightly

not depressed when the thought (the moral) of "The River Duddon" comes to him in the only possible form, as an "After-Thought."

43. I have already cited Hartman's complaint about "static personifications" in *Descriptive Sketches;* they produce, he says, "high poetic gibberish" (*Wordsworth's Poetry* 108). Of revisions in book 6 of *The Prelude* he says, "absence of personification certainly helps to make the last version the best" (205); of *The Excursion,* "the movement of his verse carries us away from . . . sublimely vague personifications" (323). Less qualified yet among good older critics who confront the topic is Sheats, who finds Wordsworth's "mature style" (i.e., the poems written in his late twenties) characterized, in part, by "literal images" "stripped of . . . passionate or decorative personification" and who considers "a personifying pronoun 'she'" to be "a semantic aberration" (*The Making of Wordsworth's Poetry* 91, 165). The topic is better treated in the more recent essays from Hartman's *Unremarkable Wordsworth;* in various parts of Murray's unremarked but meritorious book, *Wordsworth's Style;* in Knapp, *Personification and the Sublime* 98–129, a sensitive account of the trajectory of Wordsworthian personification toward "the display of an abstract, public consciousness" (127), though Knapp seems to regard this movement beyond psychology as an evasion or a defense; and best of all in Liu, *Wordsworth* 292–94, which discusses personification as a kind of uncanny, "ultimate 'friend'" (294). Harris, *Tennyson and Personification* 30–34 and 45–47, gives valuable background on eighteenth-century condemnations of the delusion verging on madness in the kind of personification that projects a voice onto things. Wordsworth's distinction, I shall be arguing (in line with the account of allegory in Kelley's "Proteus"), is to have perfected a different kind of personification that elicits the spirit moving through all things without surreptitiously imposing personhood on objects or on ideas. Heffernan, *Wordsworth's Theory of Poetry,* is a useful overview of the related themes of liquidity, modification, and blending.

44. Cf. the following, in an essay on heroic personifications of the sun and other natural objects in *Ossian* (*Mirror,* no. 13, March 9, 1779; 1: 85): "To seize these images, belongs only to the poet of an early and simple age, where the undivided attention has leisure to brood over the few but sublime objects which surround him. The sea and the heath, the rock and the torrent, the clouds and meteors, the thunder and lightning, the sun and moon, and stars, are, as it were, the companions with which his imagination holds converse. He personifies and addresses them; every aspect they can assume is impressed upon his mind; he contemplates and traces them through all the endless varieties of season; and they are the perpetual subjects of his images and allusions. He has, indeed, only a few objects around him; but, for that very reason, he forms a more intimate acquaintance with their every feature, and shade, and attitude."

45. I discuss manipulation of temporal aspect in an early Coleridge example in "Toward an Archaeology" 328–33.

46. Cf. the related imagery in Thomson's *Liberty* 3.411–25.

47. "Ambition this shall tempt to rise" (line 71) does not really interrupt the downward gradient; it belongs to an imagined future, not to what the speaker claims to see.

48. On what he calls the Wordsworthian "spherical sonnet" see Curran, *Poetic Form* 40 and 48. On p. 40 Curran quotes part of the letter that I cite in the next paragraph, omitting the discussion of overflow.

49. "Tintern Abbey" can profitably be compared with Bowles's sonnet "To a Friend." The sonnet predicts a city-bound friend's recollections of natural beauty and contains several phrases reminiscent of "Tintern Abbey": "'mid the busy scenes and hum of men," "Not . . . / wilt thou . . . forget," "in heaviness / To me the hours shall roll, weary and slow," which may have suggested the prosody of "five summers with the length / Of five long winters." But the sonnet preserves the linear temporality and the didactic I-thou stance that the romantics complicate or avoid entirely.

50. Wlecke's study of internalization in "Tintern Abbey" (*Wordsworth and the Sublime* 20–46) remains valuable.

51. The low perspective is characteristically picturesque; see Hussey, *The Picturesque* 109.

52. "Resolution and Independence," stanzas 9–10: "As a huge stone is sometimes seen to lie / Couched on the bald top of an eminence; . . . / Such seemed this Man."

53. Cf. the parallel phrase in *The Prelude* 1.77–79: "a higher power / Than Fancy gave assurance of some work / Of glory." Brantley, *Wordsworth's "Natural Methodism"* 85, glosses "a higher power" as "spiritual aid."

54. See the excellent account of chaos and order in Milton by Schwartz, "Milton's Hostile Chaos." The essential point is the distinction between chaos (or, as Leibniz would say, inertia), which is a natural characteristic of matter, and evil, which is an unnatural disorder of mind. The distinction continues in full force in Swift and Pope, though their assessments of the mind's ability to govern itself and to subsume chaos grow increasingly pessimistic. For a far more nuanced history than I can attempt here, see Price, *To the Palace of Wisdom*.

55. Here is another example from Wordsworth, simpler than the sonnet, of the imagination's curiously inert alienation from its object and of the correction that ensues: "This Lawn, a carpet all alive / . . . an apt emblem yields / Of Worldlings revelling in the fields / Of strenuous idleness. . . . / Yet, spite of all this eager strife, / This ceaseless play, the genuine life / That serves the stedfast hours, / Is in the grass beneath, that grows / Unheeded" ("This Lawn, a Carpet All Alive").

56. See the excellent stylistic and psychological analyses in Wesling, *Wordsworth and the Adequacy of Landscape*. I agree with the tenor of Wesling's conclusion that "as the greatest of landscape poets, [Wordsworth] is also the most impure" (92). Yet the book has some tendency to regard nature as raw material, in a Lockean spirit. In a poem like "Mark the Concentred Hazels" the problem is not whether nature is adequate to satisfy the

understanding, but whether the understanding is adequate to comprehend the self-sufficient organization of nature.

57. "Framing" is particularly self-conscious in this context: de Selincourt reports (in Wordsworth, *Poetical Works* 3: 428) Hutchinson's observation that Wordsworth systematically eliminated the term from his poems in 1827, yet he let it stand here. Also (as Andrew Parker pointed out to me), "framing" is grammatically a free agent, with no noun to modify. See too Langen's rich study, *Anschauungsformen*.

58. The Chieftain thus embodies a perfect fusion of the two principles—the princely self and the contracted self—that Michael Friedman sees competing for the allegiance of Wordsworth's ego in *The Making of a Tory Humanist.*

59. Here as in many other contexts, I find musical parallels invaluable in identifying formal norms. The multilayered temporality of romantic literature is equally characteristic of music in the period; compare my understanding of teleological form (though not the term) with Dahlhaus's account of Wordsworth's exact contemporary Beethoven, in *Die Musik des 19. Jahrhunderts* 11–13, 67–72.

60. "A Little Onward," composed in 1816, contains a bower that is more vertically stratified than that of "Mark the Concentred Hazels" (it has, for instance, a "high-arched roof"), with a distinctly scriptive character ("beams of light, . . . / Traceably gliding through the dusk, recal / To mind the living presences of nuns"); I associate these characteristics with the poem's dejected mood. A complete treatment of hierarchy and leveling in Wordsworth would also have to take account of the "Address to Kilchurn Castle, Upon Loch Awe," which follows "The Solitary Reaper" in the "Memorials of a Tour in Scotland, 1803"), and which again shares several themes with "Mark the Concentred Hazels." I will note only that this poem, with its distinct stratifications of altitude, duration, and power, was a problem work that took Wordsworth many years to complete. On ideological affinities see Chandler's page on "the ancient English tradition of equality," in contrast to abstract "egalitarianism," *Wordsworth's Second Nature* 51. A contrasting view is presented in Michael Friedman's *Making of a Tory Humanist*, which concludes "that the entire structure of social relations, as described in Wordsworth's poetry and prose, constituted a mythic structure whose function was to disguise social inequity and show, in its stead, a false social symmetry" (297). Perhaps one might respond that the function of poetry is to project a saving myth. Even so, the reciprocity that Friedman calls "symmetry" is weaker than the leveling I have highlighted.

61. A certain number of Wordsworth's critics, including Perkins (*Quest for Permanence*), Beer (*Wordsworth in Time*), and Baker (*Time and Mind*), characterize his fundamental aim as a quest for permanence. Baker, the least guarded of these three, reveals the awkwardness of this claim by his qualified assertions that "a visionary sensation, a seeing time itself in movement," produces "*a kind of* liberation from time" and that London "*may*

have suggested something to Wordsworth concerning permanence" (134, 186, my emphases).

62. McFarland's *Romanticism and the Forms of Ruin* 3–55 treats fragmentation (which he also calls "diasparaction") as a deficient mode opposed to organic wholeness. That makes him the most recent and, currently, the most influential exponent of a view of organic form that I consider fundamentally in error. Organisms multiply, proliferate, and vary.

Chapter Thirteen

1. I am in sympathy here with Bate's critique of the Hegelian type of history of ideas (*The Burden of the Past* 14–15), though Bate's own practice often falls behind his precepts.

2. McGann has recently argued in "Some Forms of Critical Discourse" that a narrative presentation for literary analysis results from an ideologically motivated choice among a range of possibilities. I see no reason to shy away from implicit ideological presuppositions, let alone to disavow them. But in fact McGann acknowledges that the alternative chiefly discussed in his essay, the array (such as a bibliographical entry), is only intelligible to readers who can narrativize it, a circumstance that leaves narrative as the fundamental mode of perception, even if not of presentation. An analysis of McGann's other alternatives—spatial and panoramic presentations (as in the work of Braudel and the *Annales* historians and, before them, of Burckhardt) or dialogic ones (with which McGann has experimented in his study of Swinburne and in his most recent essays)—must await another occasion.

3. In connection with the touchstone line Owen, *Wordsworth as Critic*, asks what distinguishes the language of prose from prosaic language. "The difference lies in the fact recorded," he says at one point (22), but a few pages later he writes, with some inconsistency, "the line is, in its context, as it were figurative" (25). And toward the end he resumes, resolved not to resolve: "The literary effectiveness of the line from *Michael*, 'And never lifted up a single stone,' lies in its literal presentation of action, or rather inaction, which in its factual context has power; and the literary art . . . lies . . . in Wordsworth's recognition that in these cases [*Michael* and the Penrith beacon spot of time], though not necessarily in others, no 'literary' art is required to enhance the event" (212). More helpful is his chapter on the inward tendency of the 1802 additions to the Preface to *Lyrical Ballads*.

4. Cf. the overemphatic symbolism of two passages in the drafts: "Those small flat stones which, rang'd by Travellers' hands / In cyphers on Helvellyn's highest ridge, / Lie loose on the bare turf, some half o'ergrown / By the grey moss," and "There is a shapeless crowd of unhewn stones / That lie together, some in heaps, and some / In lines, that seem to keep themselves alive / In the last dotage of a dying form." The final version reduces this to one phrase, "a straggling heap of unhewn stones!" (line 17).

5. Levinson, "Spiritual Economics: A Reading of *Michael*," in her *Wordsworth's Great Period Poems* 58–89. The essay accuses Wordsworth of complicity in the aestheticizing Christian dispensation, but Wordsworth does not necessarily side with the version of the story that he exposes at the end.

6. Miller, *Linguistic Moment* 390–422. The evidence for the life in Stevens's other rocks is nicely assembled in Riddel, *The Clairvoyant Eye* 220 and 243–45. Playing the comedian for once, I hypothetically correlate Stevens's occultation of the conclusive C and Wordsworth's elimination of "sea" from his 1850 text.

7. Miller, "The Stone and the Shell" 128: "An essay could be written investigating the role of stones in Wordsworth's poetry." In *The Linguistic Moment* (81) Miller has altered this sentence to, "Stones play an important role in Wordsworth's poetry." Apparently, an essay concerning an image appears less congenial to the deconstructionist that Miller now is than to the phenomenologist that he was.

8. Of the nine touchstone passages in "The Study of Poetry," only the first speaks of origination, in the Homeric phrase φυσίζοος αἶα ("life-giving earth"). For this phrase, however, Arnold espouses the translation "in Earth's soft arms" (9: 168), and in "On Translating Homer" he violently objects to a literal translation as "falsify[ing] . . . the whole strain of Homer" (1: 102). One approach attributes Arnold's misreading of Homer here to a psychological reflex, namely his habitual preoccupation with early death (see Eells, *Touchstones* 34–51), but I prefer to relate it as well to the conscious ideological vision that emerges from Arnold's feelings. For a fine treatment of Arnold that expands on many of the motifs of my discussion see Arac, "Matthew Arnold and English Studies: The Power of Prophecy," in his *Critical Genealogies* 117–38.

9. For the historical situation of Homer see Arnold's "On the Modern Element in Literature"; for that of Athenian classicism see "A Speech at Eton" or the end of *The Scholar-Gypsy*.

10. See the fine analysis of this sonnet in Simpson, *Figurings* 28–30.

Works Cited

Abrams, M. H. *The Mirror and the Lamp: Romantic Theory and the Critical Tradition.* New York: Norton, 1958.

Adam, Jean-Michel. *Linguistique et discours littéraire: Théorie et pratique des textes.* Paris: Larousse, 1976.

Adams, Hazard. *William Blake: A Reading of the Shorter Poems.* Seattle: University of Washington Press, 1963.

Adams, Percy G. *Graces of Harmony: Alliteration, Assonance, and Consonance in Eighteenth-Century British Poetry.* Athens: University of Georgia Press, 1977.

Adelstein, Michael E. "Duality of Theme in *The Vicar of Wakefield.*" *College English* 22 (1961): 315–21.

Adorno, Theodor W. *Negative Dialektik.* Frankfurt: Suhrkamp, 1966.

———. "Parataxis." In vol. 3 of *Noten zur Literatur.* By Theodor W. Adorno. Frankfurt am Main: Suhrkamp, 1965. 156–209.

Agamben, Giorgio. *Idea della prosa.* Milan: Feltrinelli, 1985.

Alter, Robert. *Fielding and the Nature of the Novel.* Cambridge, Mass.: Harvard University Press, 1968.

———. *Partial Magic.* Berkeley: University of California Press, 1975.

Arac, Jonathan. *Critical Genealogies.* New York: Columbia University Press, 1987.

Aristotle's Master Piece Completed. New York: United Company of Flying Stationers, 1788.

Armstrong, Nancy. *Desire and Domestic Fiction: A Political History of the Novel.* New York: Oxford University Press, 1987.

Arnold, Matthew. *The Complete Prose Works of Matthew Arnold.* Ed. R. H. Super. 11 vols. Ann Arbor: University of Michigan Press, 1960–77.

Auburn, Mark S. *Sheridan's Comedies: Their Contexts and Achievements.* Lincoln: University of Nebraska Press, 1977.

Averill, James H. *Wordsworth and the Poetry of Human Suffering.* Ithaca, N.Y.: Cornell University Press, 1980.

Bachelard, Gaston. *La Formation de l'esprit scientifique.* Paris: Vrin, 1947.

Bäckmann, Sven. *This Singular Tale: A Study of "The Vicar of Wakefield" and Its Literary Background.* Lund Studies in English 40. Lund, Sweden: Gleerup, 1971.

Baczko, Bronislaw. *Rousseau: Solitude et communauté.* Trans. Claire Brendhel-Lamhout. The Hague: Mouton, 1974.

Bahti, Timothy. "Wordsworth's Rhetorical Theft." In *Romanticism and Language.* Ed. Arden Reed. Ithaca, N.Y.: Cornell University Press, 1984. 86–124.

Baker, Jeffrey. *Time and Mind in Wordsworth's Poetry.* Detroit: Wayne State University Press, 1980.

Barfoot, C. A. "*The Deserted Village*: Goldsmith's Broken Circle." In *Oliver Goldsmith.* Ed. Harold Bloom. Philadelphia: Chelsea, 1987. 109–21.

Barrell, John. *English Literature in History: An Equal, Wide Survey.* New York: St. Martin's, 1983.

———. "The Public Figure and the Private Eye: William Collins' 'Ode to Evening.'" In *Teaching the Text.* Ed. Susanne Kappeler and Norman Bryson. London: Routledge, 1983. 1–17.

Barrell, John, and Harriet Guest. "On the Uses of Contradiction: Economics and Morality in the Eighteenth-Century Long Poem." In *The New 18th Century: Theory, Politics, English Literature.* Ed. Felicity Nussbaum and Laura Brown. New York: Methuen, 1987. 121–43.

Bate, Walter Jackson. *The Burden of the Past and the English Poet.* Cambridge, Mass.: Harvard University Press, 1970.

Bateson, F. W. *English Poetry: A Critical Introduction.* New York: Barnes, 1966.

Battestin, Martin. *The Providence of Wit.* Oxford: Clarendon, 1974.

Batteux, Charles. *Les Beaux Arts réduits à un même principe.* Paris: Durand, 1747.

Beaumarchais, Jean-Pierre de. "Enfant naturel, enfant de la nature." *Europe* 59 (1973): 50–56.

———. "Oeil pour oeil et boules de Siam: Les Manuscrits du *Mariage de Figaro.*" In *Beaumarchais: Le Mariage de Figaro.* Analyses et réflexions sur . . . 27. Paris: Ellipses, 1985. 25–30.

Beaumarchais [Pierre-Augustin Caron de]. *Oeuvres.* Ed. Pierre Larthomas. Paris: Gallimard, 1988.

Beer, John. *Wordsworth in Time.* London: Faber, 1979.

Bender, John. "Prison Reform and the Sentence of Narration in *The Vicar of Wakefield.*" In *The New 18th Century: Theory, Politics, English Literature.* Ed. Felicity Nussbaum and Laura Brown. New York: Methuen, 1987. 168–88.

Benjamin, Walter. *Gesammelte Schriften*. Ed. Rolf Tiedemann and Hermann Schweppenhäuser. 6 vols. Frankfurt am Main: Suhrkamp, 1972–85.

Berthoud, Jacques. "Shandeism and Sexuality." In *Laurence Sterne: Riddles and Mysteries*. London: Vision; Totowa: Barnes, 1984. 24–38.

Bérubé, Georges-L. "A la recherche de la malade dans le *Mariage de Figaro*: Quelle sens faut-il donner à l'objet fauteuil?" In vol. 5 of *Man and Nature / L'Homme et la nature*. Ed. E. T. Annandale and Richard A. Lebrun. Edmonton, Scotland: Academic Printing and Publishing, 1986. 15–28.

Bevis, Richard. *The Laughing Tradition: Stage Comedy in Garrick's Day*. Athens: University of Georgia Press, 1986.

Bewell, Alan. *Wordsworth and the Enlightenment: Nature, Man, and Society in the Experimental Poetry*. New Haven, Conn.: Yale University Press, 1989.

Bialostosky, Don H. *Making Tales: The Poetics of Wordsworth's Narrative Experiments*. Chicago: University of Chicago Press, 1984.

Binni, Francesco. *L'Idolo e il vero: Cowper nella crisi preromantica*. Urbino: Argaglia, 1968.

Black, William. *Oliver Goldsmith*. New York: Harper, 1879.

Blake, William. *The Poetry and Prose of William Blake*. Ed. David Erdman. Garden City, N.Y.: Doubleday, 1965.

Blom, T. E. "Eighteenth-Century Reflexive Process Poetry." *Eighteenth-Century Studies* 10 (1976): 52–72.

Bloom, Harold. *Agon*. Oxford: Oxford University Press, 1982.

———. *Figures of Capable Imagination*. New York: Seabury, 1976.

———. *Kabbalah and Criticism*. New York: Seabury, 1975.

———. *The Visionary Company*. Garden City, N.Y.: Doubleday, 1963.

———. "Wordsworth and the Scene of Instruction." In *Poetry and Repression*. New Haven, Conn.: Yale University Press, 1976. 52–82.

Bloom, Harold, et al. *Deconstruction and Criticism*. New York: Continuum, 1984.

Boccaccio, Giovanni. *Opere*. Ed. Cesare Segre. Milan: Mursia, 1963.

Böckmann, Paul. "Formen der Stimmungslyrik." In *Formensprache*. By Paul Böckmann. Hamburg: Hoffmann und Campe, 1966. 425–52.

Bogel, Fredric V. *Literature and Insubstantiality in Later Eighteenth-Century England*. Princeton, N.J.: Princeton University Press, 1984.

Bohm, Arnd. "Possessive Individualism in Schiller's *Die Räuber*." *Mosaic* 20 (1987): 31–42.

Booth, Wayne. "Did Sterne Complete *Tristram Shandy*?" In *Tristram Shandy*. By Laurence Sterne. Ed. Howard Anderson. New York: Norton, 1980. 532–47.

Borinski, Ludwig. *Der englische Roman des 18. Jahrhunderts*. Frankfurt am Main: Athenäum, 1968.

Boswell, James. *Boswell in Search of a Wife*. Ed. Frank Brady and Frederick A. Pottle. Melbourne: Heinemann, 1957.

———. *Boswell's Column: 1777–1783*. Ed. Margery Bailey. London: Kimber, 1951.

———. *Boswell's Life of Johnson*. Ed. George Birkbeck Hill. Rev. ed. L. F. Powell. 6 vols. Oxford: Clarendon, 1934.

———. *Boswell's London Journal, 1762–1763*. Ed. Frederick A. Pottle. New York: McGraw, 1950.

Bowles, William Lisle. *"Sonnets and Other Poems," and "The Spirit of Discovery."* Ed. Donald H. Reiman. New York: Garland, 1978.

Brantley, Richard E. *Wordsworth's "Natural Methodism."* New Haven, Conn.: Yale University Press, 1975.

Braudy, Leo. "The Form of the Sentimental Novel." *Novel* 7 (1973): 5–13.

———. *Narrative Form in History and Fiction*. Princeton, N.J.: Princeton University Press, 1970.

———. "Recent Studies in the Restoration and Eighteenth Century." *Studies in English Literature, 1500–1900* 17 (1977): 531–69.

Bredvold, Louis. "The Gloom of the Tory Satirists." In *Eighteenth-Century Literature: Modern Essays in Criticism*. Ed. James L. Clifford. London: Oxford University Press, 1959. 3–20.

———. *The Natural History of Sensibility*. Detroit: Wayne State University Press, 1962.

Bridgman, Richard. "Weak Tocks: Coming to a Bad End in English Poetry of the Later Eighteenth Century." *Modern Philology* 80 (1983): 264–79.

Briggs, Peter M. "Locke's *Essay* and the Tentativeness of *Tristram Shandy*." *Studies in Philology* 72 (1985): 493–520.

Brissenden, R. F. *Virtue in Distress*. New York: Barnes, 1974.

Brooks, Cleanth. *The Well Wrought Urn*. New York: Harcourt, n.d.

Brooks, Peter. *Reading for the Plot*. New York: Knopf, 1984.

Brower, Reuben. "Form and Defect of Form in Eighteenth Century Poetry: A Memorandum." *College English* 29 (1969): 535–41.

Brown, Homer Obed. "*Tom Jones*: The 'Bastard' of History." *Boundary 2* 7 (1979): 201–34.

———. "Tristram to the Hebrews: Some Notes on the Institution of a Canonic Text." *MLN* 99 (1984): 727–47.

Brown, Jane K. *Goethe's Cyclical Narratives: "Die Unterhaltungen deutscher Ausgewanderten" and "Wilhelm Meisters Wanderjahre."* Chapel Hill: University of North Carolina Press, 1975.

Brown, Marshall. "The Classic Is the Baroque: On the Principle of Wölfflin's Art History." *Critical Inquiry* 9 (1982): 379–404.

———. "'Errours Endlesse Traine': On Turning Points and the Dialectical Imagination." *PMLA* 99 (1984): 9–25.

———. "Imitation of Action: Toward a Theory of Plot." Paper presented at the MLA convention. 1982.

———. "In the Valley of the Ladies." *Italian Quarterly* 18 (1975): 33–52.

———. "Mozart and After: The Revolution in Musical Consciousness." *Critical Inquiry* 7 (1981): 689–706.

———. "A Philosophical View of the Gothic Novel." *Studies in Romanticism* 26 (1987): 275–301.

———. "Plan Vs. Plot: Chapter Symmetries and the Mission of Form." *Stanford Literature Review* 4 (1987): 103–36.

———. Review of *The New 18th Century: Theory, Politics, English Literature*, ed. Felicity Nussbaum and Laura Brown. *Eighteenth-Century Studies* 27 (1989): 566–70.

———. "Romanticism and Enlightenment." In *A Companion to British Romanticism*. Ed. Stuart Curran. Cambridge, Eng.: Cambridge University Press, forthcoming.

———. *The Shape of German Romanticism.* Ithaca, N.Y.: Cornell University Press, 1979.

———. "Toward an Archaeology of English Romanticism: Coleridge and Sarbiewski." *Comparative Literature* 30 (1978): 313–37.

———. "What's in a Text?" *Review* 11 (1990): 89–106.

Brown, Merle C. "On William Collins' 'Ode to Evening.'" *Essays in Criticism* 11 (1961): 136–53.

Brown, Wallace Cable. *The Triumph of Form.* Chapel Hill: University of North Carolina Press, 1948.

Bruns, Gerald. *Inventions: Writing, Textuality, and Understanding in Literary History.* New Haven, Conn.: Yale University Press, 1982.

Brunschvicq, Léon. *Le Progrès de la conscience.* Paris: Alcan, 1927.

Burckhardt, Sigurd. "*Tristram Shandy'*s Law of Gravity." In *Tristram Shandy.* By Laurence Sterne. Ed. Howard Anderson. New York: Norton, 1980. 595–610.

Burgelin, Pierre. *La Philosophie de l'éxistence de J.-J. Rousseau.* Paris: Vrin, 1973.

Burke, Kenneth. *A Grammar of Motives.* New York: Prentice-Hall, 1945.

Burney, Fanny. *Evelina.* Ed. Ernest Rhys. London: Dent, 1938.

Burton, John. *Essay Towards a Complete New System of Midwifery.* London: James Hodges, 1751.

Burton, Robert. *The Anatomy of Melancholy.* 3 vols. London: Dent; New York: Dutton, 1932.

Bushnell, John P. "'Where Is the Lamb for a Burnt Offering?': Michael's Covenant and Sacrifice." *The Wordsworth Circle* 12 (1981): 246–52.

Butler, Marilyn. *Romantics, Rebels and Revolutionaries.* Oxford: Oxford University Press, 1981.

Bygrave, Stephen. "Gray's 'Elegy': Inscribing the Twilight." In *Post-Structuralist Readings of English Poetry.* Ed. Richard Machin and Christopher Norris. Cambridge, Eng.: Cambridge University Press, 1987. 162–75.

Byrd, Max. *Tristram Shandy.* London: Allen and Unwin, 1985.

Campbell, Thomas. *The Complete Poetical Works.* Boston: Phillips, Sampson, 1855.

Carnochan, W. B. *Confinement and Flight.* Berkeley: University of California Press, 1977.

———. "The Continuity of Eighteenth-Century Poetry: Gray, Cowper, Crabbe, and the Augustans." *Eighteenth-Century Life* ns 12 (1988): 119–27.

———. *Lemuel Gulliver's Mirror for Man.* Berkeley: University of California Press, 1968.

Castle, Terry. *Masquerade and Civilization.* Stanford, Calif.: Stanford University Press, 1986.

Chahut, Marie-Hélène. *"Tristram Shandy,* ou l'histoire de l'écriture." *Dix-huitième siècle* 19 (1987): 391–409.

Chalmers, A., ed. *The British Essayists.* 38 vols. Boston: Little, Brown, 1856–57.

———. *The Works of the English Poets.* 21 vols. London: C. Whittingham, 1810.

Chandler, James K. *Wordsworth's Second Nature: A Study of the Poetry and Politics.* Chicago: University of Chicago Press, 1984.

Chapin, Chester. *Personification in Eighteenth-Century Poetry.* New York: Octagon, 1968.

Chipka, Robert L. "The Stranger Within Young's *Conjectures." ELH* 53 (1986): 541–66.

Christensen, Jerome. *Practicing Enlightenment: Hume and the Formation of a Literary Career.* Madison: University of Wisconsin Press, 1987.

Cohen, Ralph. *The Art of Discrimination: Thomson's "The Seasons" and the Language of Criticism.* Berkeley: University of California Press, 1964.

———. "Association of Ideas and Poetic Unity." *Philological Quarterly* 36 (1957): 465–74.

———. "The Augustan Mode in English Poetry." *Eighteenth-Century Studies* 2 (1967): 3–32.

———. "On the Interrelations of Eighteenth-Century Literary Forms." In *New Approaches to Eighteenth-Century Literature.* Ed. Phillip Harth. New York: Columbia University Press, 1974. 33–78.

———. *The Unfolding of "The Seasons."* Baltimore, Md.: Johns Hopkins University Press, 1970.

Cohn, Dorrit. "Kleist's 'Marquise von O . . .': The Problem of Knowledge." *Monatshefte* 67 (1975): 129–44.

Coleridge, Samuel Taylor. *Samuel Taylor Coleridge.* Ed. H. J. Jackson. Oxford: Oxford University Press, 1985.

Collins, William. *The Works of William Collins.* Ed. Richard Wendorf and Charles Ryskamp. Oxford: Clarendon, 1979.

Colman, George. *The Plays of George Colman the Elder.* 6 vols. Ed. Kalman A. Burnim. New York: Garland, 1983.

Conesa, Gabriel. *La Trilogie de Beaumarchais: Ecriture et dramaturgie.* Paris: PUF, 1985.

Congreve, William. *Comedies.* Ed. Bonamy Dobrée. London: Oxford University Press, 1925.

Cook, Albert. *Thresholds: Studies in the Romantic Experience.* Madison: University of Wisconsin Press, 1985.

Cowper, William. *The Letters and Prose Writings of William Cowper.* Ed. James King and Charles Ryskamp. 5 vols. Oxford: Clarendon, 1979–86.

———. *The Poems of William Cowper.* Vol. 1. Ed. John D. Baird and Charles Ryskamp. 1 vol. to date. Oxford: Clarendon, 1980–.

———. *The Poetical Works of William Cowper.* Ed. H. S. Milford. London: Oxford University Press, 1959.

Cox, Stephen D. *"The Stranger Within Thee": Concepts of the Self in Late-Eighteenth Century Literature.* Pittsburgh: University of Pittsburgh Press, 1980.

Curran, Stuart. *Poetic Form and British Romanticism.* New York: Oxford University Press, 1986.

Dahl, Curtis. "Patterns of Disguise in *The Vicar of Wakefield.*" *ELH* 25 (1958): 90–104.

Dahlhaus, Carl. *Die Musik des 19. Jahrhunderts.* Wiesbaden: Athenaion, 1980.

Damrosch, Leopold, Jr. *Symbol and Truth in Blake's Myth.* Princeton, N.J.: Princeton University Press, 1980.

Danby, John F. *The Simple Wordsworth: Studies in the Poems 1797–1807.* London: Routledge, 1960.

Davie, Donald A. "The Critical Principles of William Cowper." *Cambridge Journal* 7 (1953): 182–88.

———. "An Episode in the History of Candor." In *Dissentient Voice.* By Donald Davie. Notre Dame: University of Notre Dame Press, 1982. 83–93.

———. "Notes on Goldsmith's Politics." In *The Art of Oliver Goldsmith.* Ed. Andrew Swarbrick. London: Vision; Totowa: Barnes, 1984. 79–89.

———. "Personification." *Essays in Criticism* 31 (1981): 91–104.

———. *Purity of Diction in English Verse.* London: Chatto, 1952.

Davis, Norma S. "Stone as Metaphor: Wordsworth and Moore." *The Wordsworth Circle* 14 (1983): 264–68.

Dawson, P. M. S. "Cowper's Equivocations." *Essays in Criticism* 33 (1983): 19–35.

Deleuze, Gilles. *Proust and Signs.* Trans. Richard Howard. New York: Braziller, 1972.

Deleuze, Gilles, and Félix Guattari. *Anti-Oedipus: Capitalism and Schizophrenia.* Trans. Robert Hurley, Mark Seem, and Helen R. Lane. Minneapolis: University of Minnesota Press, 1983.

———. *A Thousand Plateaus: Capitalism and Schizophrenia.* Trans. Brian Massumi. Minneapolis: University of Minnesota Press, 1987.

de Man, Paul. *Allegories of Reading.* New Haven, Conn.: Yale University Press, 1979.

———. *Critical Writings: 1953–1978.* Ed. Lindsay Waters. Theory and History of Literature 66. Minneapolis: University of Minnesota Press, 1989.

———. "Phenomenality and Materiality in Kant." In *Hermeneutics: Ques-*

tions and Prospects. Ed. Gary Shapiro and Alan Sica. Amherst: University of Massachusetts Press, 1984. 121–44.

———. *The Rhetoric of Romanticism.* New York: Columbia University Press, 1984.

Dennis, John. *The Grounds of Criticism in Poetry.* London: Scolar Press, 1971.

Derrida, Jacques. *De la grammatologie.* Paris: Minuit, 1967.

———. "Economimesis." In *Mimesis des articulations.* Ed. Sylvaine Agacinski. Paris: Aubier-Flammarion, 1975. 57–93.

———. "The *Retrait* of Metaphor." *Enclitic* 2 (1978): 4–33.

———. *La Vérité en peinture.* Paris: Flammarion, 1978.

———. *La Voix et le phénomène.* Paris: PUF, 1972.

Diderot, Denis. *Oeuvres complètes.* Ed. Jean Varloot et al. 19 vols. to date. Paris: Hermann, 1975–.

———. *Oeuvres philosophiques.* Ed. Paul Vernière. Paris: Garnier, 1964.

Dixon, B. Lynne. *Diderot, Philosopher of Energy: The Development of His Concept of Physical Energy.* Studies on Voltaire and the Eighteenth Century 255. Oxford: Voltaire Foundation, 1988.

Donaldson, Ian. *The World Upside-Down: Comedy from Jonson to Fielding.* Oxford: Clarendon, 1970.

Dowling, William C. "Boswell and the Problem of Biography." In *Studies in Biography.* Ed. Daniel Aaron. Cambridge, Mass.: Harvard University Press, 1978. 73–93.

———. "Tristram's Phantom Audience." *Novel* 13 (1980): 284–95.

Downie, J. A. "Goldsmith, Swift and Augustan Satirical Verse." In *The Art of Oliver Goldsmith.* Ed. Andrew Swarbrick. London: Vision; Totowa: Barnes, 1984. 126–43.

Dryden, John. *Essays of John Dryden.* Ed. W. P. Ker. 2 vols. Oxford: Clarendon, 1926.

———. *Works of John Dryden.* Ed. Edward Niles Hooker et al. 15 vols. to date. Berkeley: University of California Press, 1956–.

Durant, David. "The Vanity of Elevation in Mid-Eighteenth-Century Poetry." *Texas Studies in Literature and Language* 28 (1986): 388–406.

Durant, Jack D. "Prudence, Providence, and the Direct Road of Wrong: *The School for Scandal* and Sheridan's Westminster Hall Speech." *Studies in Burke and His Time* 15 (1974): 241–51.

———. "Sheridan's Picture-Auction Scene: A Study in Contexts." *Eighteenth-Century Life* ns 11 (1987): 34–47.

Dussinger, John. *The Discourse of the Mind in Eighteenth-Century Fiction.* The Hague: Mouton, 1974.

Eagleton, Terry. *The Rape of Clarissa.* Minneapolis: University of Minnesota Press, 1982.

Edwards, Thomas R. *Imagination and Power.* New York: Oxford University Press, 1971.

Eells, John Shepard, Jr. *The Touchstones of Matthew Arnold.* New Haven, Conn.: College and University Press, 1955.

Ehrmann, Jacques. "The Death of Literature." *New Literary History* 3 (1971): 31–48.

Eliot, George. *Leaves from a Note-Book: Miscellaneous Essays.* Boston: Estes, 1887.

Empson, William. *Some Versions of Pastoral.* Norfolk, Va.: New Directions, 1960.

——. *The Structure of Complex Words.* Ann Arbor: University of Michigan Press, 1967.

Engelberg, Edward. *The Unknown Distance: From Consciousness to Conscience: Goethe to Camus.* Cambridge, Mass.: Harvard University Press, 1972.

Etherege, George. *The Man of Mode.* Ed. W. B. Carnochan. Lincoln, Neb.: University of Nebraska Press, 1966.

Fabian, Bernhard. "Pope und die goldene Kette Homers." *Anglia* 82 (1964): 150–71.

Fabricant, Carole. "The Aesthetics and Politics of Landscape in the Eighteenth Century." In *Studies in Eighteenth-Century British Art and Aesthetics.* Ed. Ralph Cohen. Berkeley: University of California Press, 1985. 49–81.

Farrell, William J. "Nature Versus Art as a Comic Pattern in 'Tristram Shandy.'" In *Laurence Sterne.* Ed. Gerd Rohmann. Wege der Forschung 467. Darmstadt: Wissenschaftliche Buchgesellschaft, 1980. 365–74.

Feingold, Richard. *Moralized Song: The Character of Augustan Lyricism.* New Brunswick, N.J.: Rutgers University Press, 1989.

——. *Nature and Society: Later Eighteenth-Century Uses of the Pastoral and Georgic.* New Brunswick, N.J.: Rutgers University Press, 1978.

Fenaux, Jean-Paul. "Les Noces et les affaires de Figaro-Beaumarchais." In *Beaumarchais: Le Mariage de Figaro.* Analyses et réflexions sur . . . 27. Paris: Ellipses, 1985. 20–24.

Ferguson, Frances. *Wordsworth: Language as Counter-Spirit.* New Haven, Conn.: Yale University Press, 1977.

Fielding, Henry. *The History of Tom Jones, A Foundling.* Ed. Martin Battestin and Fredson Bowers. Middletown, Conn.: Wesleyan University Press, 1975.

Finch, Casey. "Immediacy in the *Odes* of William Collins." *Eighteenth-Century Studies* 20 (1987): 275–95.

Fletcher, Angus. *Allegory: The Theory of a Symbolic Mode.* Ithaca, N.Y.: Cornell University Press, 1964.

Flores, Ralph. *The Rhetoric of Doubtful Authority.* Ithaca, N.Y.: Cornell University Press, 1984.

Fluchère, Henri. *Laurence Sterne: De l'homme à l'oeuvre.* Paris: Nouvelle Revue Française, 1961.

Foote, Samuel. *The Maid of Bath.* London: W. Loundes, and S. Bladon, 1795. Reprinted in vol. 2 of *Dramatic Works.* By Samuel Foote. New York: Blom, 1968.

———. *The Nabob.* London: W. Loundes, and S. Bladon, 1795. Reprinted in vol. 2 of *Dramatic Works.* By Samuel Foote. New York: Blom, 1968.

Forster, E. M. *Aspects of the Novel.* New York: Harcourt, n.d.

Forster, John. *The Life and Adventures of Oliver Goldsmith.* London: Bradbury & Evans, 1848.

Fowler, Alastair. "The Life and Death of Literary Forms." *New Literary History* 2 (1971): 199–216.

Fox, Christopher. *Locke and the Scriblerians: Identity and Consciousness in Early Eighteenth-Century Britain.* Berkeley: University of California Press, 1988.

———. "Locke and the Scriblerians: The Discussion of Identity in Early Eighteenth-Century England." *Eighteenth-Century Studies* 16 (1982): 1–25.

Franci, Giovanna. " 'Sulla soglia dell' attimo': La sublime finzione della letteratura." *Studi di estetica* 12 (1984): 65–76.

Freedman, William. *Laurence Sterne and the Origins of the Musical Novel.* Athens: University of Georgia Press, 1978.

Freud, Sigmund. *Gesammelte Werke.* Ed. Anna Freud et al. 17 vols. London: Imago, 1940–52.

Freydenberg, O. "Proiskhozhdenie literaturnoy intrigi" (Emergence of the Literary Plot). *Trudy po znakovym sistemam* 6 (1973): 497–512.

Fried, Michael. *Absorption and Theatricality: Painting and Beholder in the Age of Diderot.* Berkeley: University of California Press, 1980.

Friedman, Geraldine. "Writing in Stone: Monumentality and Fragmentation in Wordsworth, Baudelaire and Rilke." Ph.D. diss. Yale University, 1985.

Friedman, Michael H. *The Making of a Tory Humanist: William Wordsworth and the Idea of Community.* New York: Columbia University Press, 1979.

Fry, Paul H. "History, Existence, and 'To Autumn.'" *Studies in Romanticism* 25 (1986): 211–19.

———. *The Poet's Calling in the English Ode.* New Haven, Conn.: Yale University Press, 1980.

Frye, Northrop. "Towards Defining an Age of Sensibility." In *Fables of Identity.* By Northrop Frye. New York: Harcourt, 1963. 130–37.

Garrick, David. *The Plays of David Garrick.* Ed. Henry William Pedicord and Fredrick Louis Bergmann. 7 vols. Carbondale: Southern Illinois University Press, 1980–82.

Genette, Gérard. *Figures III.* Paris: Seuil, 1972.

Getto, Giovanni. *Vita di forme e forme di vita nel "Decameron."* Torino: Patrini, 1958.

Giddings, Robert. *The Tradition of Smollett.* London: Methuen, 1967.

Goethe, Johann Wolfgang. *Werke* (Hamburger Ausgabe). Ed. Erich Trunz et al. 14 vols. Hamburg: Wegner, 1962–65.

Golden, Morris. "Image Frequency and the Split in *The Vicar of Wakefield.*" *Bulletin of the New York Public Library* 63 (1959): 473–77.

Goldsmith, Oliver. *Collected Letters*. Ed. Katharine C. Balderston. Folcroft, Pa.: Folcroft, 1969.

——. *Collected Works of Oliver Goldsmith*. Ed. Arthur Friedman. 5 vols. Oxford: Clarendon, 1966.

——. *The Grecian History from the Earliest State to the Death of Alexander the Great*. Ithaca, N.Y.: Mack, Andrus & Woodruff, n.d.

——. *The Grumbler*. Ed. Alice I. Perry Wood. Cambridge, Mass.: Harvard University Press, 1931.

——. *The Works of Oliver Goldsmith*. Ed. Peter Cunningham. 4 vols. New York: Harper, 1881.

Goldstein, Laurence. *Ruins and Empire*. Pittsburgh: University of Pittsburgh Press, 1977.

Goodden, Angelica. *"Actio" and Persuasion: Dramatic Performance in Eighteenth-Century France*. Oxford: Clarendon, 1986.

Gossman, Lionel. "Literary Scholarship and Popular History." *Eighteenth-Century Studies* 7 (1973–74): 133–42.

Granger, Gilles-Gaston. *Essai d'une philosophie du style*. Paris: A. Colin, 1968.

Gray, Thomas. *The Complete Poems of Thomas Gray*. Ed. H. W. Starr and J. R. Hendrickson. Oxford: Clarendon, 1966.

——. *Correspondence*. Ed. Paget Toynbee and Leonard Whibley. 3 vols. Oxford: Clarendon, 1935.

Greene, D[onald] J. "'Logical Structure' in Eighteenth-Century Poetry." *Philological Quarterly* 31 (1952): 315–36.

——. "'Tis a Pretty Book, Mr. Boswell, But—.'" *Georgia Review* 32 (1978): 17–43.

——. "What Indeed Was Neo-Classicism." *Journal of British Studies* 10 (1970): 69–79.

Grene, Marjorie. *The Knower and the Known*. Berkeley: University of California Press, 1974.

Griffin, Dustin. "Gray's Audiences." *Essays in Criticism* 28 (1978): 208–15.

Gruender, K. "Langage et histoire: Perspectives de la 'Métacritique sur le Purisme de la Raison' de J. G. Hamann." *Archives de philosophie* 24 (1961): 414–25.

Guillaume, Gustave. *Langage et science du langage*. Paris: Nizet, 1969.

Hagstrum, Jean H. *Sex and Sensibility: Ideal and Erotic Love from Milton to Mozart*. Chicago: University of Chicago Press, 1980.

——. "Towards a Profile of the Word 'Conscious' in Eighteenth-Century Literature." In *Psychology and Literature in the Eighteenth Century*. Ed. Christopher Fox. New York: AMS, 1987. 23–50.

Hamann, Johann Georg. *Sämtliche Werke*. Ed. Josef Nadler. 6 vols. Vienna: Herder, 1949–57.

Hamburger, Käte. "My Uncle Toby." In *Herkommen und Erneuerung: Essays für Oskar Seidlin*. Ed. Gerald Gillespie and Edgar Lohner. Tübingen: Niemeyer, 1976. 78–92.

Hamilton, William. *Lectures on Metaphysics.* Boston: Gould and Lincoln, 1869.

Handwerk, Gary J. *Irony and Ethics in Narrative: From Schlegel to Lacan.* New Haven, Conn.: Yale University Press, 1985.

Hannaford, Stephen. "The Shape of 18th Century English Drama." *Theatre Survey* 21 (1980): 93–103.

Hardy, Barbara. *A Reading of Jane Austen.* London: Owen, 1975.

Harries, Elizabeth. "Sterne's Novels: Gathering Up the Fragments." *ELH* 49 (1982): 35–49.

Harris, Daniel A. *Tennyson and Personification: The Rhetoric of "Tithonus."* Ann Arbor, Mich.: University Microfilms, 1986.

Hartman, Geoffrey H. "Evening Star and Evening Land." In *The Fate of Reading.* By Geoffrey H. Hartman. Chicago: University of Chicago Press, 1975. 147–78.

———. "Romanticism and Anti-Self-Consciousness." In *Beyond Formalism.* By Geoffrey H. Hartman. New Haven, Conn.: Yale University Press, 1970. 298–310.

———. *The Unremarkable Wordsworth.* Theory and History of Literature 34. Minneapolis: University of Minnesota Press, 1987.

———. *Wordsworth's Poetry 1787–1814.* New Haven, Conn.: Yale University Press, 1964.

Harvey, W. J. *Character and the Novel.* London: Chatto, 1965.

Hasbog, Josef. "Zur Reduktion des Sentimentalen in Sheridans *The School for Scandal.*" *Anglia* 85 (1967): 321–49.

Havens, Raymond D. "Simplicity, a Changing Concept." *Journal of the History of Ideas* 14 (1953): 3–32.

Hay, John A. "Rhetoric and Historiography: Tristram Shandy's First Nine Kalendar Months." In vol. 2 of *Studies in the Eighteenth Century.* Ed. R. F. Brissenden. Toronto: University of Toronto Press, 1973. 73–91.

Heffernan, James A. W. *Wordsworth's Theory of Poetry: The Transforming Imagination.* Ithaca, N.Y.: Cornell University Press, 1969.

Hegel, Georg Wilhelm Friedrich. *Phänomenologie des Geistes.* Ed. Johannes Hoffmeister. Hamburg: Meiner, 1952.

Heidegger, Martin. *Poetry, Language, Thought.* Trans. Albert Hofstadter. New York: Harper, 1971.

Heinzelman, Kurt. *The Economy of the Imagination.* Amherst: University of Massachusetts Press, 1980.

Herder, Johann Gottfried. *Herders Briefe.* Ed. Wilhelm Dobbek. Weimar: Volksverlag Weimar, 1959.

Hervey, James. *Meditations and Contemplations.* Coventry, Eng.: M. Luckmann, 1792.

Hilliard, Raymond F. "The Redemption of Fatherhood in *The Vicar of Wakefield.*" *Studies in English Literature, 1500–1900* 23 (1983): 465–80.

Hinderer, Walter. "Freiheit und Gesellschaft beim jungen Schiller." In *Sturm und Drang: Ein literaturwissenschaftliches Studienbuch.* Ed. Walter Hinck. Kronberg: Athenäum, 1978. 230–56.

Hogan, Robert. "Plot, Character, and Comic Language in Sheridan." In *Comedy from Shakespeare to Sheridan: Change and Continuity in the English and European Dramatic Tradition. Essays in Honor of Eugene M. Waith.* Ed. A. R. Braunmuller and J. C. Bulman. Newark, Del.: University of Delaware Press; London: Associated University Presses, 1986. 274–85.

Hölderlin, Friedrich. *Sämtliche Werke.* Ed. Friedrich Beissner et al. 8 vols. Stuttgart: Cotta and Kohlhammer, 1946–85.

Holloway, John. "The Rivals." *Spectator* July 29, 1966: 149–50.

Holtz, William V. *Image and Immortality: A Study of "Tristram Shandy."* Providence, R.I.: Brown University Press, 1970.

Hopkins, Robert H. *The True Genius of Oliver Goldsmith.* Baltimore, Md.: Johns Hopkins University Press, 1969.

Horkheimer, Max, and Theodor W. Adorno. *Dialektik der Aufklärung.* Frankfurt am Main: Fischer, 1971.

House, Humphry. *Coleridge.* London: Hart-Davis, 1953.

Hughes, Peter. "Language, History and Vision: An Approach to 18th Century Literature." In *The Varied Pattern: Studies in the 18th Century.* Ed. Peter Hughes and David Williams. Toronto: Hakkert, 1971. 77–96.

———. "Restructuring Literary History: Implications for the Eighteenth Century." *New Literary History* 8 (1977): 257–78.

Hume, David. *Essays Moral, Political, and Literary.* Ed. Eugene F. Miller. Indianapolis, Ind.: Liberty, 1985.

———. *A Treatise of Human Nature.* Ed. L. A. Selby-Bigge. Rev. P. H. Nidditch. Oxford: Clarendon, 1978.

Hume, Robert D. "Goldsmith and Sheridan and the Supposed Revolution of 'Laughing' Against 'Sentimental' Comedy." In *The Rakish Stage.* Carbondale: Southern Illinois University Press, 1983. 312–55.

Hunt, John Dixon. *The Figure in the Landscape.* Baltimore, Md.: Johns Hopkins University Press, 1976.

Hunting, Robert. "The Poems in *The Vicar of Wakefield.*" *Criticism* 15 (1973): 234–41.

Hurd, Richard. *Letters on Chivalry and Romance.* Ed. Hoyt Trowbridge. Augustan Reprint Society 101–2. Los Angeles: Clark Library, 1963.

Hussey, Christopher. *The Picturesque: Studies in a Point of View.* London: Putnam, 1927.

Hutchings, W. "Syntax of Death: Instability in Gray's 'Elegy Written in a Country Churchyard.'" *Studies in Philology* 81 (1984): 496–514.

Inchbald, Elizabeth. *A Simple Story.* Ed. J. M. S. Tompkins. London: Oxford University Press, 1967.

Iser, Wolfgang. *Laurence Sterne: "Tristram Shandy."* Cambridge, Eng.: Cambridge University Press, 1988.

Jaarsma, Richard J. "Satiric Intent in *The Vicar of Wakefield.*" *Studies in Short Fiction* 5 (1968): 331–41.

Jackson, Wallace. *The Probable and the Marvelous.* Athens: University of Georgia Press, 1978.

———. "Thomas Gray and the Dedicatory Muse." *ELH* 54 (1987): 277–98.
———. "Thomas Gray: Drowning in Human Voices." *Criticism* 28 (1986): 361–77.
———. *Vision and Re-Vision in Alexander Pope*. Detroit: Wayne State University Press, 1983.
Jakobson, Roman. "Closing Statement: Linguistics and Poetics." In *Style in Language*. Ed. Thomas A. Sebeok. Cambridge, Mass.: Technology Press; New York: Wiley, 1960. 350–77.
Jameson, Fredric. *Marxism and Form*. Princeton, N.J.: Princeton University Press, 1971.
Jefferson, D. W. "*The Vicar of Wakefield* and Other Prose Writings: A Reconsideration." In *The Art of Oliver Goldsmith*. Ed. Andrew Swarbrick. London: Vision; Totowa: Barnes, 1984. 17–32.
Jewett, William. "Action in *The Borderers*." *Studies in Romanticism* 27 (1988): 399–410.
Johnson, Barbara. *The Critical Difference: Essays in the Contemporary Rhetoric of Reading*. Baltimore, Md.: Johns Hopkins University Press, 1980.
Johnson, James William. "What Was Neo-Classicism?" *Journal of British Studies* 9 (1969): 49–70.
Johnson, Samuel. *The History of Rasselas, Prince of Abyssinia*. Ed. Geoffrey Tillotson and Brian Jenkins. London: Oxford University Press, 1971.
———. *The Yale Edition of the Works of Samuel Johnson*. Ed. E. L. McAdam et al. 12 vols. to date. New Haven, Conn.: Yale University Press, 1958–.
Johnston, Arthur. *The Poetry of William Collins*. London: Oxford University Press, 1974.
Joly, Raymond. *Deux études sur la préhistoire du réalisme*. Québec: Presses de l'université Laval, 1969.
Jonard, Norbert. "Una nozione che non esiste: 'Preromanticismo.'" *Problemi* 5 (1971): 1053–60.
Jones, Emrys. "The Artistic Form of *Rasselas*." *Review of English Studies* ns 18 (1967): 387–401.
Jones, John. *The Egotistical Sublime: A History of Wordsworth's Imagination*. London: Chatto, 1954.
Jonson, Ben. *The Alchemist*. Ed. Douglas Brown. New York: Hill and Wang, 1966.
Jordan, John E. *Why the "Lyrical Ballads"? The Background, Writing, and Character of Wordsworth's 1798 "Lyrical Ballads."* Berkeley: University of California Press, 1976.
Joyce, James. *Ulysses*. New York: Random House, 1961.
Kant, Immanuel. *Werke*. Ed. Wilhelm Weischedel. 6 vols. Frankfurt: Insel, 1956–64.
Kavanagh, Thomas M. "*Jacques le fataliste*: An Encyclopedia of the Novel." In *Diderot: Digression and Dispersion*. Ed. Jack Undank and Herbert Josephs. Lexington, Ky.: French Forum, 1984. 150–65.

Kay, Carol. *Political Constructions*. Ithaca, N.Y.: Cornell University Press, 1988.

Kelley, Theresa M. "Proteus and Romantic Allegory." *ELH* 49 (1982): 632–52.

———. "Spirit and Geometric Form: The Stone and the Shell in Wordsworth's Arab Dream." *Studies in English Literature, 1500–1900* 22 (1982): 563–82.

———. *Wordsworth's Revisionary Aesthetics*. Cambridge, Eng.: Cambridge University Press, 1988.

Kelly, Hugh. *False Delicacy: A Comedy*. London: R. Baldwin, 1768. Reprinted in *The Plays of Hugh Kelly*. Ed. Larry Carver. New York: Garland, 1980.

Kermode, Frank. *The Genesis of Secrecy: On the Interpretation of Narrative*. Cambridge, Mass.: Harvard University Press, 1979.

Ketcham, Carl H. "That 'Stone of Rowe': *Prelude* (1805) II: 33–47." *The Wordsworth Circle* 13 (1982): 174–75.

Klancher, Jon. *The Making of English Reading Audiences, 1790–1832*. Madison: University of Wisconsin Press, 1987.

Klein, Jürgen. *Anfänge der englischen Romantik 1740–1780*. Anglistische Forschungen 191. Heidelberg: Winter, 1986.

Knapp, Steven. *Personification and the Sublime*. Cambridge, Mass.: Harvard University Press, 1985.

Kneale, J. Douglas. *Monumental Writing: Aspects of Rhetoric in Wordsworth's Poetry*. Lincoln: University of Nebraska Press, 1988.

Knoblauch, Cyril. "Coherence Betrayed: Samuel Johnson and the 'Prose of the World.'" *Boundary 2* 7 (1979): 235–60.

Koc, Richard. "Fathers and Sons: Ambivalence Doubled in Schiller's *Räuber*." *Germanic Review* 61 (1986): 91–104.

Koselleck, Reinhart. *Futures Past: On the Semantics of Historical Time*. Trans. Keith Tribe. Cambridge, Mass.: MIT Press, 1985.

Krieger, Murray. "Samuel Johnson: The Extensive View of Mankind and the Cost of Acceptance." In *The Classic Vision*. By Murray Krieger. Baltimore, Md.: Johns Hopkins University Press, 1971. 125–45.

Lamb, Jonathan. "The Comic Sublime and Sterne's Fiction." *ELH* 48 (1981): 110–43.

Langbaum, Robert. *The Mysteries of Identity*. New York: Oxford University Press, 1977. ·

Langen, August. *Anschauungsformen in der deutschen Dichtung des 18. Jahrhunderts: Rahmenschau und Rationalismus*. Darmstadt: Wissenschaftliche Buchgesellschaft, 1965.

Lanham, Richard. *"Tristram Shandy": The Games of Pleasure*. Berkeley: University of California Press, 1973.

Lapp, John C. *Aspects of Racinian Tragedy*. University of Toronto Romance Series 2. Toronto: University of Toronto Press, 1955.

Lehmann, Elmar. *"Not Merely Sentimental": Studien zu Goldsmiths Komödien*. Beihefte zu *Poetica* 11. Munich: Fink, 1974.

Lehmann, James H. "*The Vicar of Wakefield*: Goldsmith's Sublime, Oriental Job." *ELH* 46 (1979): 97–121.

Lemonnier-Delpy, Marie-Françoise. *Nouvelle étude thématique sur "Le Mariage de Figaro" de Beaumarchais*. Paris: Sedes, 1987.

Levinson, Marjorie. *Wordsworth's Great Period Poems*. Cambridge, Eng.: Cambridge University Press, 1986.

Lévi-Strauss, Claude. *From Honey to Ashes*. Trans. John and Doreen Weightman. New York: Harper, 1973.

———. *The Savage Mind*. Chicago: University of Chicago Press, 1966.

———. *The Way of the Masks*. Trans. Sylvia Modelski. Seattle: University of Washington Press, 1982.

Lewis, C. S. *Studies in Words*. Cambridge, Eng.: Cambridge University Press, 1960.

Lipking, Lawrence. "Quick Poetic Eyes: Another Look at Literary Pictorialism." In *Articulate Images*. Ed. Richard Wendorf. Minneapolis: University of Minnesota Press, 1983. 3–25.

Liu, Alan. *Wordsworth: The Sense of History*. Stanford, Calif.: Stanford University Press, 1989.

Locke, John. *An Essay Concerning Human Understanding*. Ed. Peter H. Nidditch. Oxford: Clarendon, 1975.

Lockwood, Thomas. *Post-Augustan Satire*. Seattle: University of Washington Press, 1979.

Loftis, John. *Sheridan and the Drama of Georgian England*. Cambridge, Mass.: Harvard University Press, 1977.

Lonsdale, Roger. "'A Garden, and a Grave': The Poetry of Oliver Goldsmith." In *The Author in His Work*. Ed. Louis L. Martz and Aubrey Williams. New Haven, Conn.: Yale University Press, 1978. 3–30.

———, ed. *The Poems of Gray, Collins, and Goldsmith*. London: Longmans, 1969.

The Looker-On. 3 vols. Vols. 35–37 of Chalmers, *British Essayists*.

Lotman, Jurij. "The Origin of Plot in the Light of Modern Typology." Trans. Julian Graffy. *Poetics Today* 1 (1979): 162–84.

The Lounger. 2 vols. Vols. 30–31 of Chalmers, *British Essayists*.

Love, H. W. "Goldsmith's Deserted Village: or Paradise Mislaid." *AUMLA* 67 (1987): 43–59.

Loveridge, Mark. *Laurence Sterne and the Argument About Design*. Totowa, N.J.: Barnes, 1982.

———. "Liberty in *Tristram Shandy*." In *Laurence Sterne: Riddles and Mysteries*. Ed. Valerie Grosvenor Myer. London: Vision; Totowa, N.J.: Barnes, 1984. 126–41.

Lowth, Robert. *Lectures on the Sacred Poetry of the Hebrews*. Trans. D. Gregory. 2 vols. London: n.p., 1816.

Lukács, Georg. "Reichtum, Chaos und Form: Ein Zwiegespräch über Laurence Sterne." In *Die Seele und die Formen*. By Georg Lukács. Neuwied: Luchterhand, 1971. 179–217.

MacCannell, Juliet Flower. "Nature and Self-Love: A Reinterpretation of Rousseau's 'Passion primitive.'" *PMLA* 92 (1977): 890–902.

Mack, Maynard. "Wit and Poetry and Pope: Some Observations on his Imagery." In *Eighteenth-Century Literature: Modern Essays in Criticism.* Ed. James L. Clifford. London: Oxford University Press, 1959.

Macksey, Richard. "'Alas, Poor Yorick': Sterne Thoughts." *MLN* 98 (1983): 1006–20.

Maclean, Kenneth. "The Distant Way: Imagination and Imagery in Gray's Poetry." In *Fearful Joy.* Ed. James Downey and Ben Jones. Montreal: McGill-Queen's University Press, 1974. 136–45.

Maclean, Norman. "Personification but Not Poetry." *ELH* 23 (1956): 163–70.

Macpherson, James, trans. *The Poems of Ossian.* 2 vols. London: Lackington, 1803.

Madelin, Hervé. "*The Vicar of Wakefield* et l'apologétique des augustéens." *Etudes anglaises* 39 (1986): 257–67.

Mahony, Robert. "Lyrical Antithesis: The Moral Style of 'The Deserted Village.'" *Ariel* 8.2 (1977): 33–47.

Mann, Michael. *Sturm- und Drang-Drama: Studien und Vorstudien zu Schillers "Räubern."* Bern: Francke, 1974.

Marcel, Gabriel. "Sketch of a Phenomenology and a Metaphysic of Hope." In *Homo Viator.* By Gabriel Marcel. Trans. Emma Crawford. New York: Harper, 1962. 29–67.

Marin, Louis. *Food for Thought.* Trans. Mette Hjort. Baltimore, Md.: Johns Hopkins University Press, 1989.

Marmontel, Jean-François. *Oeuvres complètes.* 19 vols. Paris: Verdière, 1818–20.

Marshall, David. "The Eye-Witnesses of *The Borderers.*" *Studies in Romanticism* 27 (1988): 391–98.

Marshall, Donald G. "The Development of Blank-Verse Poetry from Milton to Wordsworth." Ph.D. diss. Yale University, 1971.

Marshall, W. Gerald. "The Presence of 'the Word' in Cowper's *The Task.*" *Studies in English Literature* 27 (1987): 475–87.

Maskill, Duke. "Locke and Sterne, or Can Philosophy Influence Literature?" *Essays in Criticism* 23 (1973): 22–40.

Matheson, Ann. "The Influence of Cowper's *The Task* on Coleridge's Conversation Poems." In *New Approaches to Coleridge: Biographical and Critical Essays.* Ed. Donald Sultana. London: Vision; Totowa: Barnes, 1981. 137–50.

Mattenklott, Gert. *Melancholie in der Dramatik des Sturm und Drang.* Königstein: Athenäum, 1985.

Mayoux, Jean-Jacques. "Laurence Sterne." In *Laurence Sterne: A Collection of Critical Essays.* Ed. John Traugott. Englewood Cliffs, N.J.: Prentice, 1968. 108–25.

———. "Variations on the Time-Sense in *Tristram Shandy.*" *Tristram Shandy.* By Laurence Sterne. Ed. Howard Anderson. New York: Norton, 1980. 571–83.

McFarland, Thomas. *Romanticism and the Forms of Ruin: Wordsworth,*

Coleridge, and Modalities of Fragmentation. Princeton, N.J.: Princeton University Press, 1981.

McGann, Jerome. *"Don Juan" in Context.* Chicago: University of Chicago Press, 1976.

———. *The Romantic Ideology.* Chicago: University of Chicago Press, 1983.

———. "Some Forms of Critical Discourse." *Critical Inquiry* 11 (1985): 399–417.

McGilchrist, Iain. *Against Criticism.* London: Faber, 1982.

McIntosh, Carey. *The Choice of Life: Samuel Johnson and the World of Fiction.* New Haven, Conn.: Yale University Press, 1973.

McKillop, Alan Dugald. *The Background of Thomson's "Seasons."* Minneapolis: University of Minnesota Press, 1942.

———. "Collins' *Ode to Evening*—Background and Structure." *Tennessee Studies in Literature* 5 (1960): 73–83.

Mehlman, Jeffrey. *Repetition and Revolution.* Berkeley: University of California Press, 1977.

Meinecke, Friedrich. *Historism: The Rise of a New Historical Outlook.* Trans. H. J. E. Anderson. London: Routledge, 1972.

Mervaud, Christine. "Le 'Ruban de nuit' de la comtesse." *Revue d'histoire littéraire de la France* 84 (1984): 722–33.

Michaud, Guy. *L'Oeuvre et ses techniques.* Paris: Nizet, 1957.

Micklus, Robert. "Voices in the Wind: The Eton Ode's Ambivalent Prospect of Maturity." *English Language Notes* 18 (1981): 181–86.

Miller, J. Hillis. "Deconstructing the Deconstructors." *Diacritics* 5 (1975): 24–31.

———. *The Linguistic Moment.* Princeton, N.J.: Princeton University Press, 1985.

———. "Narrative Middles: A Preliminary Outline." *Genre* 11 (1978): 375–84.

———. "The Stone and the Shell: The Problem of Poetic Form in Wordsworth's Dream of the Arab." In *Mouvements premiers: Etudes critiques offertes à Georges Poulet.* Paris: Corti, 1972. 125–47.

Miner, Earl. *Dryden's Poetry.* Bloomington: Indiana University Press, 1967.

———. "The Making of *The Deserted Village.*" *Huntington Library Quarterly* 22 (1959): 125–41.

The Mirror. 2 vols. Vols. 28–29 of Chalmers, *British Essayists.*

Modiano, Raimonda. "Coleridge's Views on Touch and Other Senses." *Bulletin of Research in the Humanities* 81 (1978): 28–41.

Moglen, Helene. *The Philosophical Irony of Laurence Sterne.* Gainesville: University Presses of Florida, 1975.

Molière. *Théâtre complet.* Ed. Robert Jouanny. 2 vols. Paris: Garnier, 1962.

Moore, Thomas. *Memoirs of the Life of Richard Brinsley Sheridan.* 2 vols. Chicago: Belford, 1882.

Morgan, Susan. *In the Meantime.* Chicago: University of Chicago Press, 1980.

Moritz, Karl Philipp. *Schriften zur Ästhetik und Poetik*. Ed. Hans Joachim Schrimpf. Tübingen: Niemeyer, 1962.

Moss, Roger B. "Sterne's Punctuation." *Eighteenth-Century Studies* 15 (1981–82): 179–200.

Mullan, John. *Sentiment and Sociability: The Language of Feeling in the Eighteenth Century*. Oxford: Clarendon, 1988.

Murphy, Arthur. *"The Way to Keep Him" and Five Other Plays*. Ed. John Pike Emery. New York: New York University Press, 1956.

Murray, Roger N. *Wordsworth's Style: Figures and Themes in the "Lyrical Ballads" of 1800*. Lincoln: University of Nebraska Press, 1967.

Nancy, Jean-Luc. *Logodaedalus*. Vol. 1 of *Le Discours de la syncope*. Paris: Flammarion, 1976.

———. "Logodaedalus (Kant écrivain)." *Poétique* 21 (1975): 24–52.

Nemoianu, Virgil. *Micro-Harmony: The Growth and Uses of the Idyllic Model in Literature*. Bern: Lang, 1977.

———. "Societal Models as Substitute Reality in Literature." *Poetics Today* 5 (1984): 275–97.

———. *The Taming of Romanticism*. Cambridge, Mass.: Harvard University Press, 1984.

———. *A Theory of the Secondary*. Baltimore, Md.: Johns Hopkins University Press, 1989.

Neubauer, John. "The Freedom of the Machine: On Mechanism, Materialism, and the Young Schiller." *Eighteenth-Century Studies* 15 (1982): 275–90.

New, Melvyn. "'At the Backside of the Door of Purgatory': A Note on Annotating *Tristram Shandy*." In *Laurence Sterne: Riddles and Mysteries*. Ed. Valerie Grosvenor Myer. London: Vision; Totowa: Barnes, 1984. 15–23.

———. *Laurence Sterne as Satirist*. Gainesville: University Presses of Florida, 1969.

———. "Sterne, Warburton, and the Burden of Exuberant Wit." *Eighteenth-Century Studies* 15 (1982): 245–74.

Nietzsche, Friedrich. *Werke in drei Bänden*. Ed. Karl Schlechta. Munich: Carl Hanser, 1966.

Norrman, Ralf, and Jon Haarberg. *Nature and Language: A Semiotic Study of Cucurbits in Literature*. London: Routledge, 1980.

Nuttall, A. D. *A Common Sky: Philosophy and the Literary Imagination*. London: Chatto, 1974.

Owen, W. J. B. *Wordsworth as Critic*. Toronto: University of Toronto Press, 1971.

Parish, Charles. "The Shandy Bull Vindicated." *Modern Language Quarterly* 31 (1970): 48–52.

Park, William. "'Tristram Shandy' and the New 'Novel of Sensibility.'" *Studies in the Novel* 6 (1974): 268–79.

Parker, Reeve. "'In Some Sort Seeing with My Proper Eyes'": Wordsworth and the Spectacles of Paris." *Studies in Romanticism* 27 (1988): 369–90.

Parnell, Thomas. *Collected Poems of Thomas Parnell*. Ed. Claude Rawson and F. P. Lock. Newark, Del.: University of Delaware Press; London: Associated University Presses, 1989.

Pater, Walter. *Marius the Epicurean*. London: Dent; New York: Dutton, 1934.

Patey, Douglas Lane. "Art and Integrity: Concepts of Self in Alexander Pope and Edward Young." *Modern Philology* 83 (1986): 364–78.

Paulson, Ronald. *Representations of Revolution*. New Haven, Conn.: Yale University Press, 1983.

———. *Satire and the Novel in Eighteenth-Century England*. New Haven, Conn.: Yale University Press, 1967.

Pearch, George, ed. *A Collection of Poems*. 3rd ed. London: G. Pearch, 1775.

Perkins, David. *The Quest for Permanence: The Symbolism of Wordsworth, Shelley, and Keats*. Cambridge, Mass.: Harvard University Press, 1965.

Peterfreund, Stuart. "Sterne and Late Eighteenth-Century Ideas of History." *Eighteenth-Century Life* ns 7 (1981): 25–53.

Piper, William Bowman. "The Musical Quality of Goldsmith's *The Deserted Village*." In vol. 14 of *Studies in Eighteenth-Century Culture*. Ed. O. M. Brack, Jr. Madison: University of Wisconsin Press, 1985. 259–74.

Plessner, Helmuth. *Philosophische Anthropologie*. Ed. Günter Dux. Frankfurt am Main: Fischer, 1970.

Poems, Moral, Elegant and Pathetic. London: E. Newberry, 1796.

Pomeau, René. *Beaumarchais, ou la bizarre destinée*. Paris: PUF, 1987.

Poovey, Mary. *The Proper Lady and the Woman Writer*. Chicago: University of Chicago Press, 1984.

Pope, Alexander. *Correspondence*. Ed. George Sherburn. 5 vols. Oxford: Clarendon, 1956.

———. *The Twickenham Edition of the Poems of Alexander Pope*. Ed. John Butt et al. 11 vols. London: Methuen; New Haven, Conn.: Yale University Press, 1961–69.

Porter, Roy. "'The Secrets of Generation Display'd': *Aristotle's Master-Piece* in Eighteenth-Century England." *Eighteenth-Century Life* ns 9 (1985): 1–21.

Pottle, Frederick A. "Emergent Idiom." In *The Idiom of Poetry*. By Frederick A. Pottle. Bloomington: Indiana University Press, 1963. 109–34.

Poulet, Georges. *Studies in Human Time*. Trans. Elliott Coleman. New York: Harper, 1959.

Préaux, Alain. "Le Motif des frères ennemis chez Friedrich Schiller." *Etudes germaniques* 36 (1981): 25–31.

Preisendanz, Wolfgang. *Humor als dichterische Einbildungskraft*. Munich: Eidos, 1963.

Preston, John. *The Created Self: The Reader's Role in Eighteenth-Century Fiction*. New York: Barnes, 1970.

Preston, Thomas R. "The Uses of Adversity: Worldly Detachment and

Heavenly Treasure in *The Vicar of Wakefield.*" *Studies in Philology* 81 (1984): 229–51.

Price, Martin. "The Irrelevant Detail and the Emergence of Form." In *Literary Criticism: Idea and Act.* Ed. W. K. Wimsatt. Berkeley: University of California Press, 1974. 521–36.

——. "The Sublime Poem: Pictures and Powers." *Yale Review* 58 (1968): 194–213.

——. *To the Palace of Wisdom: Studies in Order and Energy from Dryden to Blake.* Garden City, N.Y.: Doubleday, 1964.

Priestman, Martin. *Cowper's "Task": Structure and Influence.* Cambridge, Eng.: Cambridge University Press, 1983.

Privateer, Paul. "Goldsmith's *Vicar of Wakefield:* The Reunion of the Alienated Artist." *Enlightenment Essays* 6 (1975): 27–36.

Puder, Martin. *Kant: Stringenz und Ausdruck.* Freiburg: Rombach, 1974.

Quintana, Ricardo. *Oliver Goldsmith.* New York: Macmillan, 1967.

——. "The Scheme of Collins's *Odes on Several . . . Subjects.*" In *Restoration and Eighteenth-Century Literature: Essays in Honor of Alan Dugald McKillop.* Ed. Carroll Camden. Chicago: University of Chicago Press, 1963. 371–80.

Ramage, Edwin. *Urbanitas.* Norman: University of Oklahoma Press, 1973.

Ramond de Carbonnières, Louis François Elisabeth. *Observations faites dans les Pyrénées.* Paris: Belin, 1789.

Ramsey, Jonathan. "Seeing and Perceiving in Wordsworth's *An Evening Walk.*" *Modern Language Quarterly* 36 (1975): 376–89.

Randolph, Mary Claire. "'Candour' in XVIIIth-Century Satire." *Review of English Studies* 20 (1944): 45–62.

Raymond, Marcel. *Jean-Jacques Rousseau: La Quête de soi et la rêverie.* Paris: Corti, 1966.

Reed, Walter. *An Exemplary History of the Novel.* Chicago: University of Chicago Press, 1981.

Reid, Thomas. *Works.* Ed. William Hamilton. Edinburgh: Maclachlan and Stewart, 1849.

Reiss, T. J. *Toward Dramatic Illusion: Theatrical Technique and Meaning from Hardy to Horace.* Yale Romantic Studies second ser. 22. New Haven, Conn.: Yale University Press, 1971.

Relyea, Suzanne. *Signs, Systems, and Meanings: A Contemporary Semiotic Reading of Four Molière Plays.* Middletown, Conn.: Wesleyan University Press, 1976.

Rex, Walter E. "*Figaro's* Games." *PMLA* 89 (1974): 524–29.

Richards, I. A. *Practical Criticism.* New York: Harcourt, 1950.

Richardson, Alan. *A Mental Theater: Poetic Drama and Consciousness in the Romantic Age.* University Park: Pennsylvania State University Press, 1988.

Riddel, Joseph N. *The Clairvoyant Eye.* Baton Rouge: Louisiana State University Press, 1965.

Rogers, Pat. "The Dialectic of 'The Traveller.'" In *The Art of Oliver Gold-*

smith. Ed. Andrew Swarbrick. London: Vision; Totowa: Barnes, 1984. 107–25.

Rolle, Dietrich. *Fielding und Sterne: Untersuchungen über die Funktion des Erzählers.* Münster: Aschendorff, 1963.

Rosen, Charles. *The Classical Style.* New York: Norton, 1972.

———. "Now, Voyager." *New York Review of Books* Nov. 6, 1986: 55–60.

Rosenblum, Michael. "The Sermon, the King of Bohemia, and the Art of Interpolation in *Tristram Shandy.*" *Studies in Philology* 75 (1978): 472–91.

Rothstein, Eric. *Restoration and Eighteenth-Century Poetry, 1660–1780.* Boston: Routledge, 1981.

———. *Systems of Order and Inquiry in Later Eighteenth-Century Fiction.* Berkeley: University of California Press, 1975.

Rougemont, Martine de. "Beaumarchais dramaturge: Le Substrat romanesque du drame." *Revue d'histoire littéraire de la France* 84 (1984): 710–21.

Rousseau, G. S., ed. *Goldsmith: The Critical Heritage.* London: Routledge, 1974.

Rousseau, Jean-Jacques. *Oeuvres complètes.* Ed. Bernard Gagnebin et al. 4 vols. to date. Paris: Gallimard, 1959–.

Rousset, Jean. *L'Intérieur et l'extérieur: Essais sur la poésie et sur le théâtre au XVIIe siècle.* Paris: Corti, 1976.

Rzepka, Charles J. *The Self as Mind.* Cambridge, Mass.: Harvard University Press, 1986.

Sabin, Margery. *English Romanticism and the French Tradition.* Cambridge, Mass.: Harvard University Press, 1976.

Sacks, Peter M. *The English Elegy: Studies in the Genre from Spenser to Yeats.* Baltimore, Md.: Johns Hopkins University Press, 1985.

Said, Edward. *Beginnings: Intention and Method.* New York: Basic, 1975.

Scalia, Gianni. Remarks presented at the conference "Il Sublime: Creazione e catastrofe." University of Bologna, May 1984.

Scherer, Jacques. *La Dramaturgie de Beaumarchais.* Paris: Nizet, 1954.

Scherpe, Klaus R. "*Die Räuber.*" In *Schillers Dramen: Neue Interpretationen.* Ed. Walter Hinderer. Stuttgart: Reclam, 1979. 9–36.

Schiller, Andrew. "*The School for Scandal*: The Restoration Unrestored." *PMLA* 71 (1956): 694–704.

Schiller, Friedrich. *Sämtliche Werke.* Ed. Gerhard Fricke and Herbert G. Göpfert. 5 vols. Munich: Hanser, 1960.

Schlüter, Kurt. *Die Englische Ode.* Bonn: H. Bouvier, 1964.

Schulze, Martin. "Do You Know the Meaning of * * * * *? Die markierte Aussparung als Indiz für die planvolle Komposition des *Tristram Shandy.*" In *Laurence Sterne.* Ed. Gerd Rohmann. Wege der Forschung 467. Darmstadt: Wissenschaftliche Buchgesellschaft, 1980. 394–436.

Schwartz, Regina. "Milton's Hostile Chaos: '. . . And the Sea Was No More.'" *ELH* 52 (1985): 337–74.

Scouten, Arthur. "The Warton Forgeries and the Concept of Preromanticism in English Literature." *Etudes anglaises* 40 (1987): 434–47.

Sedgwick, Eve Kosofsky. *Between Men: English Literature and Male Homosocial Desire*. New York: Columbia University Press, 1985.

Seidel, Michael. *Satiric Inheritance: Rabelais to Sterne*. Princeton, N.J.: Princeton University Press, 1979.

Serres, Michel. *Genèse*. Paris: Grasset, 1982.

Shaviro, Steven. "'Striving with Systems': Blake and the Politics of Difference." *Boundary 2* 10 (1982): 229–50.

Sheats, Paul. *The Making of Wordsworth's Poetry, 1789–1798*. Cambridge, Mass.: Harvard University Press, 1973.

Shell, Marc. "The Golden Fleece and the Voice of the Shuttle." *Georgia Review* 30 (1976): 406–29.

Shenstone, William. *Essays on Men and Manners*. Philadelphia: n.p., 1804.

Sherbo, Arthur. *English Poetic Diction from Chaucer to Wordsworth*. East Lansing: Michigan State University Press, 1975.

Sheridan, Richard Brinsley. *The Dramatic Works of Richard Brinsley Sheridan*. Ed. Cecil Price. 2 vols. Oxford: Clarendon, 1973.

———. *The Letters of Richard Brinsley Sheridan*. Ed. Cecil Price. 3 vols. Oxford: Clarendon, 1966.

———. *The Plays and Poems of Richard Brinsley Sheridan*. Ed. R. Crompton Rhodes. 3 vols. New York: Russell & Russell, 1962.

Sheriff, John K. *The Good-Natured Man: The Evolution of a Moral Ideal, 1660–1800*. University: University of Alabama Press, 1982.

Sherwin, Paul. *Precious Bane: Collins and the Miltonic Legacy*. Austin: University of Texas Press, 1977.

Sichel, Walter. *Sheridan*. 2 vols. London: Constable, 1909.

Simpson, David. *Wordsworth and the Figurings of the Real*. Atlantic Highlands, N.J.: Humanities Press, 1982.

———. *Wordsworth's Historical Imagination*. New York: Methuen, 1987.

Siskin, Clifford H. *The Historicity of Romantic Discourse*. New York: Oxford University Press, 1988.

Sitter, John. *Literary Loneliness in Mid-Eighteenth-Century England*. Ithaca, N.Y.: Cornell University Press, 1982.

———. "To *The Vanity of Human Wishes* through the 1740's." *Studies in Philology* 74 (1977): 445–64.

Smith, Adam. *The Wealth of Nations*. Ed. Edwin Cannan. 2 vols. in one. Chicago: University of Chicago Press, 1976.

Spacks, Patricia Meyer. *The Adolescent Idea: Myths of Youth and the Adult Imagination*. New York: Basic, 1981.

———. *An Argument of Images: The Poetry of Alexander Pope*. Cambridge, Mass.: Harvard University Press, 1971.

———. "The Eighteenth-Century Collins." *Modern Language Quarterly* 44 (1983): 3–22.

———. *Imagining a Self: Autobiography and Novel in Eighteenth-Century England*. Cambridge, Mass.: Harvard University Press, 1967.

———. *The Poetry of Vision*. Cambridge, Mass.: Harvard University Press, 1967.

The Spectator. Ed. Donald F. Bond. 5 vols. Oxford: Clarendon, 1965.

Sperber, Dan. "Pourquoi les animaux parfaits, les hybrides et les monstres sont-ils bons à penser symboliquement?" *L'Homme* 15 (1975): 5–34.

Spingarn, J. E., ed. *Critical Essays of the Seventeenth Century.* 3 vols. Bloomington: Indiana University Press, 1968.

Squarotti, Giorgio Bàrberi. "La 'Cornice' del 'Decameron.'" In *Da Dante al Novecento.* Milan: Mursia, 1970. 109–58.

Stachelberg, Jürgen von. "Figaros Hochzeit: Zur Frage nach der Gattung und dem sozialkritischen Gehalt von Beaumarchais' *Mariage de Figaro.*" *Französisch Heute* 15 (1984): 293–305.

Staiger, Emil. *Friedrich Schiller.* Zurich: Atlantis, 1967.

———. *Die Kunst der Interpretation.* Munich: Deutscher Taschenbuch Verlag, 1971.

Starobinski, Jean. *Jean-Jacques Rousseau: La Transparence et l'obstacle.* Paris: Gallimard, 1971.

Stedmond, John M. *The Comic Art of Laurence Sterne.* Toronto: University of Toronto Press, 1967.

Steinhagen, Harald. "Der junge Schiller zwischen Marquis de Sade und Kant: Aufklärung und Idealismus." *Deutsche Vierteljahrsschrift* 56 (1982): 135–57.

Sterne, Laurence. *Letters.* Ed. Lewis Perry Curtis. Oxford: Clarendon, 1935.

———. *The Life and Opinions of Tristram Shandy, Gentleman.* Ed. Melvyn New and Joan New. 3 vols., continuously paginated. Gainesville: University Presses of Florida, 1978–84.

———. *A Sentimental Journey.* Ed. Gardner D. Stout, Jr. Berkeley: University of California Press, 1967.

———. *The Sermons of Mr. Yorick.* Ed. Wilbur L. Cross. 2 vols. New York: Taylor, 1904.

Stevens, Wallace. *Collected Poems.* New York: Knopf, 1964.

Stevenson, John Allen. "'Alien Spirits': The Unity of Lovelace and Clarissa." Unpublished essay.

Steveson, Warren. "Wordsworth and the Stone of Night." *The Wordsworth Circle* 13 (1982): 175–78.

Stevick, Philip. *The Chapter in Fiction: Theories of Narrative Division.* Syracuse, N.Y.: Syracuse University Press, 1970.

Stockdale, Percival. *Lectures on the Truly Eminent English Poets.* 2 vols. London: D. N. Shury, 1807.

Stolberg, Christian, and Friedrich Leopold Graf zu Stolberg. *Gesammelte Werke.* 20 vols. Hamburg: Perthes und Besser, 1820–25.

Storch, R. F. "Wordsworth's *The Borderers:* The Poet as Anthropologist." *ELH* 36 (1969): 340–60.

Storm, Leo F. "Literary Convention in Goldsmith's *Deserted Village.*" *Huntington Library Quarterly* 33 (1970): 243–56.

Sturm und Drang: Kritische Schriften. Heidelberg: Lambert Schneider, 1963.

Sutherland, W. O. S., Jr. *The Art of the Satirist: Essays on the Satire of Augustan England.* Austin: University of Texas, 1965.

Suzuki, Mineko. "Chaîne des idées et chaîne des êtres dans *Le Rêve de d'Alembert.*" *Dix-huitième siècle* 19 (1987): 327–38.

Swearingen, James. *Reflexivity in "Tristram Shandy": An Essay in Phenomenological Criticism.* New Haven, Conn.: Yale University Press, 1977.

Swift, Jonathan. *Gulliver's Travels.* Vol. 10 of *Prose Writings of Jonathan Swift.* Ed. Herbert Davis. Oxford: Blackwell, 1959.

Sypher, Wylie. "The *Morceau de Fantaisie* in Verse: A New Approach to Collins." *University of Toronto Quarterly* 15 (1945): 65–69.

Taine, H. A. *History of English Literature.* Trans. Henri Van Laun. 2 vols. New York: Burt, n.d.

Tave, Stuart M. *The Amiable Humorist: A Study in the Comic Theory and Criticism of the Eighteenth and Early Nineteenth Centuries.* Chicago: University of Chicago Press, 1960.

Thompson, Harold William. *A Scottish Man of Feeling: Some Account of Henry Mackenzie, Esq. of Edinburgh and of the Golden Age of Burns and Scott.* London: Oxford University Press, 1931.

Thomson, James. *"Liberty," "The Castle of Indolence" and Other Poems.* Ed. James Sambrook. Oxford: Clarendon, 1986.

———. *The Seasons.* Ed. James Sambrook. Oxford: Clarendon, 1981.

Tillotson, Geoffrey. *Augustan Studies.* London: Athlone, 1961.

———. "The Methods of Description in Eighteenth- and Nineteenth-Century Poetry." In *Restoration and Eighteenth-Century Literature: Essays in Honor of Alan Dugald McKillop.* Ed. Carroll Camden. Chicago: University of Chicago Press, 1963. 235–38.

Todd, Janet. *Sensibility: An Introduction.* London: Methuen, 1986.

Tonelli, Giorgio. "Das Wiederaufleben der deutsch-aristotelischen Terminologie bei Kant während der Entstehung der 'Kritik der reinen Vernunft.'" *Archiv für Begriffsgeschichte* 9 (1964): 233–42.

Towers, A. R. "Sterne's Cock and Bull Story." *ELH* 24 (1957): 12–29.

Trilling, Lionel. *Sincerity and Authenticity.* Cambridge, Mass.: Harvard University Press, 1971.

Tripet, Arnaud. *La Rêverie littéraire: Essai sur Rousseau.* Geneva: Droz, 1979.

Ubersfeld, Annie. "Un Balcon sur la terreur: 'Le Mariage de Figaro.'" *Europe* 59 (1973): 105–15.

Uhlig, Claus. "Wissen und Meinen bei Sterne: Zur literarischen Epistemologie in *Tristram Shandy.*" *Anglia* 104 (1986): 369–96.

Undank, Jack. "Beaumarchais' Transformations." *MLN* 100 (1985): 829–70.

Vanbrugh, Sir John. *The Provoked Wife.* Ed. Curt A. Zimansky. Lincoln: University of Nebraska Press, 1969.

———. *The Relapse.* Ed. Curt A. Zimansky. Lincoln: University of Nebraska Press, 1970.

Van Ghent, Dorothy. *The English Novel: Form and Function.* New York: Harper, 1961.

van Tieghem, Paul. *Le Sentiment de la nature dans le préromantisme européen*. Paris: Nizet, 1960.

Verneaux, Roger. *Le Vocabulaire de Kant*. Paris: Aubier Montaigne, 1973.

Vialleneix, Paul, ed. *Le Préromantisme: Hypothèque ou Hypothèse*. Paris: Klincksieck, 1975.

Voltaire. *Oeuvres complètes*. 75 vols. Paris: Baoudouin, 1825–28.

Walpole, Horace. *The Castle of Otranto*. In *Three Gothic Novels*. Ed. Peter Fairclough. Harmondsworth, Eng.: Penguin, 1968. 37–148.

Warning, Rainer. *Illusion und Wirklichkeit in "Tristram Shandy" und "Jacques le Fataliste."* Munich: Fink, 1965.

Warren, Leland E. "The Constant Speaker: Aspects of Communication in *Tristram Shandy*." *University of Toronto Quarterly* 46 (1976): 51–67.

Wasserman, Earl. "Collins' Ode on the Poetical Character." *ELH* 34 (1967): 92–115.

———. "The Inherent Values of Eighteenth-Century Personification." *PMLA* 65 (1950): 435–63.

———. "Johnson's *Rasselas*: Implicit Contexts." *JEGP* 74 (1975): 1–25.

Weber, Samuel. "The Critics' Choice." In *1789: Reading Writing Revolution*. Ed. Francis Barker et al. Colchester, Eng.: University of Essex, 1982. 147–59.

Weinbrot, Howard. *The Formal Strain*. Chicago: University of Chicago Press, 1969.

Weinbrot, Howard D., and Eric Rothstein. "The Vicar of Wakefield, Mr. Wilmot, and the 'Whistonian Controversy.'" *Philological Quarterly* 55 (1976). 225–40.

Weinrich, Harald. *Sprache in Texten*. Stuttgart: Klett, 1976.

Weinsheimer, Joel. "'Give Me Something to Desire': A Johnsonian Anthropology of Imitation." *Philological Quarterly* 64 (1985): 211–23.

———. "Theory of Character: *Emma*." *Poetics Today* 1 (1979): 185–211.

Weinstein, Arnold. *Fictions of the Self: 1550–1800*. Princeton, N.J.: Princeton University Press, 1981.

Weiskel, Thomas. *The Romantic Sublime*. Baltimore, Md.: Johns Hopkins University Press, 1976.

Weissberg, Liliane. "*Catarcticon* und der schöne Wahn." *Poetica* 18 (1986): 96–116.

Welby, Lady Viola. "Significs." In *Encyclopedia Britannica*. 11th ed. 1911. S.v.

Welsh, Alexander. *Reflections on the Hero as Quixote*. Princeton, N.J.: Princeton University Press, 1981.

Wendorf, Richard. *William Collins and Eighteenth-Century Poetry*. Minneapolis: University of Minnesota Press, 1981.

Wesling, Donald. "Augustan Form: Justification and Breakup of a Period Style." *Texas Studies in Language and Literature* 22 (1980): 394–428.

———. *The Chances of Rhyme: Device and Modernity*. Berkeley: University of California Press, 1980.

———. *Wordsworth and the Adequacy of Landscape*. New York: Barnes, 1970.

Whibley, Charles, ed. *A Facsimile Reproduction of a Unique Catalogue of Laurence Sterne's Library*. London: Tregashis, 1930.

Whitaker, Thomas R. "Reading the Unreadable, Acting the Unactable." *Studies in Romanticism* 27 (1988): 355–67.

Wilde, Oscar. *The Artist as Critic: Critical Writings of Oscar Wilde*. Ed. Richard Ellmann. New York: Random, 1969.

Williams, Anne. *Prophetic Strain: The Greater Lyric in the Eighteenth Century*. Chicago: University of Chicago Press, 1984.

Williams, Raymond. *The Country and the City*. New York: Oxford University Press, 1973.

———. *Marxism and Literature*. Oxford: Oxford University Press, 1977.

Wimsatt, W[illiam] K. *Hateful Contraries*. Lexington: University Press of Kentucky, 1965.

———. "In Praise of *Rasselas*: Four Notes (Converging)." In *Day of the Leopards*. By William K. Wimsatt. New Haven, Conn.: Yale University Press, 1976. 140–61.

———. "The Structure of Romantic Nature Imagery." In *The Verbal Icon*. By William K. Wimsatt. Lexington: University Press of Kentucky, 1954. 103–16.

Wlecke, Albert O. *Wordsworth and the Sublime*. Berkeley: University of California Press, 1973.

Woodring, Carl. *Politics in English Romantic Poetry*. Cambridge, Mass.: Harvard University Press, 1970.

Woods, Samuel H., Jr. "Boswell's Presentation of Goldsmith: A Reconsideration." In *Boswell's "Life of Johnson": New Questions, New Answers*. Ed. John A. Vance. Athens: University of Georgia Press, 1985. 228–47.

Wordsworth, William. *The Borderers*. Ed. Robert Osborn. Ithaca, N.Y.: Cornell University Press, 1982.

———. *Descriptive Sketches*. Ed. Eric Birdsall. Ithaca, N.Y.: Cornell University Press, 1984.

———. *An Evening Walk*. Ed. James Averill. Ithaca, N.Y.: Cornell University Press, 1984.

———. *"Poems, in Two Volumes," and Other Poems*. Ed. Jared Curtis. Ithaca, N.Y.: Cornell University Press, 1983.

———. *The Poetical Works of William Wordsworth*. Ed. E. de Selincourt and Helen Darbishire. 5 vols. Oxford: Clarendon, 1952–59.

———. *The Prelude*. Ed. Ernest de Selincourt. Rev. Helen Darbishire. Oxford: Clarendon, 1959.

———. *The White Doe of Rylestone; or The Fate of the Nortons*. Ed. Kristine Dugas. Ithaca, N.Y.: Cornell University Press, 1988.

Wright, George T. "Stillness and the Argument of Gray's Elegy." *Modern Philology* 74 (1977): 381–89.

Wycherley, William. *The Plays of William Wycherley*. Ed. Arthur Friedman. Oxford: Clarendon, 1972.

Young, Edward. *Night Thoughts.* Ed. Stephen Cornford. Cambridge, Eng.:
   Cambridge University Press, 1989.
[Young, John]. *Criticism on the Elegy Written in a Country Churchyard.*
   London: G. Wilkie, 1783.
Zimmerman, Everett. "*Tristram Shandy* and Narrative Representation."
   Eighteenth Century: Theory and Interpretation 28 (1987): 127–47.

Index

In this index "f" after a number indicates a separate reference on the next page, and "ff" indicates separate references on the next two pages. A continuous discussion over two or more pages is indicated by a span of page numbers. *Passim* is used for a cluster of references in close but not continuous sequence.

Library of Congress Cataloging-in-Publication Data

Brown, Marshall, 1945–
  Preromanticism / Marshall Brown.
    p.   cm.
  Includes bibliographical references and index.
  ISBN 0-8047-1561-0 (acid-free paper) :
    1. English literature—18th century—History and criticism.
  2. Romanticism—Great Britain—History—18th century. I. Title.
  PR447.B75 1991
  820.9'145'09033—dc20   90-21043
                                                              CIP

⊗ This book has been printed on acid-free paper.